I0755766

ADVANCE PRAISE
for

Between Two Millstones, Book 2

Exile in America, 1978–1994

"Aleksandr Solzhenitsyn—perhaps the most significant literary exile since Dante—is a figure of incalculable importance to world history. Yet in these pages, we enter into the life and times not of an austere statue or a respectable oil portrait but of a flesh-and-blood Russian patriot struggling to defend his vision and his humanity amid the loneliness of his American exile and the remorseless grinding of two rival empires. *Between Two Millstones, Book 2* is not only an invaluable addition to Solzhenitsyn studies but also an intimate self-portrait of the great-souled man."

—Rod Dreher, author of *Live Not by Lies*

"In terms of the effect he has had on history, Solzhenitsyn is the dominant writer of this century. Who else compares? Orwell? Koestler? Where Solzhenitsyn's intuition proved keenest was in his prediction when he arrived in the West that his books would surely be published in the Soviet Union and, what was more, that he would himself return to a liberated Russia. It was a firm and intimate belief that even contradicted Solzhenitsyn's dire analysis of Soviet ruthlessness and Western accommodation. Is it too much of an embarrassment in the age of irony to think that his homecoming is somehow Biblical?"

—David Remnick, from "The Exile Returns" in *The New Yorker*

"We know Solzhenitsyn the prisoner of the Gulag and the survivor of cancer. We know Solzhenitsyn the Russian patriot and resolute foe of the tyranny that deformed his country. In the second volume of *Between Two Millstones* we meet Solzhenitsyn the husband and father, Solzhenitsyn the writer. Here we meet a great soul overcoming not crisis but the quotidian, the banal, the small, a Solzhenitsyn for anyone who struggles against the enervating drag of the ordinary in our culture of distraction."

—Will Morrisey, author of *Churchill and de Gaulle*

"The Solzhenitsyn forcibly deported to Germany in 1974 now faces a disconcertingly gaudy array of Western images and effigies of himself. In characteristically vivid and pugnacious vein he tells of twenty years of exile—storm-tossed between the snarling Soviet Scylla and the vertiginous frustrations and perils of this Western Charybdis—nursing the seemingly forlorn hope that he might yet end his days in his homeland. A gripping read!"

—Michael Nicholson, co-editor of *Solzhenitsyn in Exile*

"*Between Two Millstones* provides a unique peek into Solzhenitsyn's life in Cavendish, a small rural Vermont town whose people collectively chose to keep the location of his home a secret from the prying eyes of the press and the curious. This compelling memoir answers some of the locals' own questions about life behind Solzhenitsyn's chain-link fence and provides a glimpse into how it was possible for him to conduct research and to write in such a remote location."

—Margaret Caulfield, director, Cavendish Historical Society

"In these pages, readers meet one of the great men of the twentieth century. Exiled, misunderstood, and often attacked, Solzhenitsyn drew courage from his devotion to truth, his loyalty to his vocation as a writer, and his indomitable belief in the dignity of the Russian people."

—R. R. Reno, editor-in-chief, *First Things*

"This is a happy book. An epic of small spaces, great issues, and large accomplishments, the concluding volume of *Between Two Millstones* covers the years 1978 to 1994, when Solzhenitsyn was living on his beloved Vermont property. At the heart of the memoir lies a touching portrait of his wife Natalia. *Between Two Millstones* is enlivened by the author's impressions of famous figures like Andrei Sakharov, Heinrich Böll, Margaret Thatcher, and Princess Diana."

—Richard Tempest, author of *Overwriting Chaos*

"The Solzhenitsyn who emerges in *Between Two Millstones* is no longer the triumphant and ebullient fighter we saw in *The Oak and the Calf.* Though ready for battle as ever, his assurance in the efficacy of his word is shaken not only by Westerners with their deeply embedded biases but also by his own countrymen who turn a deaf ear to his warnings. A great read!"

—Alexis Klimoff, coauthor of *The Soul and Barbed Wire*

"If Solzhenitsyn did not welcome exile, if he felt torn, as always, between the two millstones of the Soviet 'Dragon' . . . and an uncomprehending and increasingly hostile West, he nonetheless found solitude and happy refuge in his eighteen years in Cavendish, Vermont. It was there that he worked on, and eventually finished, his other great work of historical and literary investigation, *The Red Wheel.* . . . Eventually, Solzhenitsyn would be . . . the enemy of Sovietism *par excellence*, . . . the last major anti-Communist writer to appear in print."

—Daniel J. Mahoney, from the foreword

BETWEEN TWO MILLSTONES

BOOK 2

The Center for Ethics and Culture Solzhenitsyn Series

Under the sponsorship of the de Nicola Center for Ethics and Culture at the University of Notre Dame, this series showcases the contributions and continuing inspiration of Aleksandr Solzhenitsyn (1918–2008), the Nobel Prize–winning novelist and historian. The series makes available works of Solzhenitsyn, including previously untranslated works, and aims to provide the leading platform for exploring the many facets of his enduring legacy. In his novels, essays, memoirs, and speeches, Solzhenitsyn revealed the devastating core of totalitarianism and warned against political, economic, and cultural dangers to the human spirit. In addition to publishing his work, this new series features thoughtful writers and commentators who draw inspiration from Solzhenitsyn's abiding care for Christianity and the West, and for the best of the Russian tradition. Through contributions in politics, literature, philosophy, and the arts, these writers follow Solzhenitsyn's trail in a world filled with new pitfalls and new possibilities for human freedom and human dignity.

Aleksandr Solzhenitsyn

BETWEEN TWO MILLSTONES

BOOK 2

Exile in America
1978–1994

Translated from the Russian by
CLARE KITSON *and* MELANIE MOORE

UNIVERSITY OF NOTRE DAME PRESS
NOTRE DAME, INDIANA

University of Notre Dame Press
Notre Dame, Indiana 46556
undpress.nd.edu

Published in the United States of America

Library of Congress Control Number: 2020940874

The full LC record is available online at https://lccn.loc.gov/2020940874

ISBN 9780268109004 (Hardback)
ISBN 9780268109035 (WebPDF)
ISBN 9780268109028 (Epub)

∞ *This paper meets the requirements of ANSI/NISO Z39.48-1992 (Permanence of Paper).*

CONTENTS

APPENDICES

PUBLISHER'S NOTE

This is the first publication in English of Aleksandr Solzhenitsyn's memoirs of his years in the West, Угодило зёрнышко промеж двух жерновов: Очерки изгнания [*Ugodilo zyornyshko promezh dvukh zhernovov: Ocherki izgnaniya*] (*The Little Grain Fell Between Two Millstones: Sketches of Exile*). They are being published here as two books: The first book—*Between Two Millstones, Book 1: Sketches of Exile, 1978–1994* (Notre Dame, IN: University of Notre Dame Press, 2018)—contains Part One. The present second book contains Parts Two, Three, and Four.

The reader is reminded that the overall sequence of Solzhenitsyn's memoirs, as they appear in English, is therefore as follows:

The Oak and the Calf: Sketches of Literary Life in the Soviet Union
Invisible Allies [=Fifth Supplement to *The Oak and the Calf*]
Between Two Millstones, Book 1: Sketches of Exile, 1974–1978
Between Two Millstones, Book 2: Exile in America, 1978–1994

The original Russian text of chapter 5, Сквозь чад [*Skvoz chad*] (*Through the Fumes*), was published separately by YMCA-Press in 1979. Then the full text of the book appeared over seven installments in the journal *Novy Mir* (chap. 1: no. 9, 1998; chaps. 2–3: no. 11, 1998; chaps. 4–5: no. 2, 1999; chaps. 6–8: no. 9, 2000; chaps. 9–10: no. 12, 2000; chaps. 11–13: no. 4, 2001; and chaps. 14–16: no. 11, 2003). In preparation for eventual book publication, the author twice made revisions to his text, in 2004 and again in 2008. The first complete Russian edition in book form is scheduled to be released by Vremya in late 2020 or early 2021 as volume 29 of their ongoing publication of a thirty-volume collected works of Solzhenitsyn. It is that final, definitive text that is presented here in English translation.

The author wrote *Between Two Millstones* in Vermont during four discrete periods:

Part One—Autumn 1978
Part Two—Spring 1982
Part Three—Spring 1987
Part Four—Spring 1994

Footnotes appearing at the bottom of a page are the author's. By contrast, notes that have been added to this English translation are not the author's, and appear as endnotes at the end of the book.

The text contains numbers in square brackets, for example, [**29**], which refer to the corresponding appendix at the end of the book. The appendices are part of the author's original text. Some notes to the appendices have been added for this edition, and those notes can be found at the end of the book, in the Notes to the English Translation.

Russian names are not Westernized, with the exception of well-known public figures or published authors, who may already be familiar to readers in such a form.

This English translation of *Between Two Millstones* was made possible in part by Drew Guff and the Solzhenitsyn Initiative at the Wilson Center's Kennan Institute. This support is gratefully acknowledged.

The publisher is grateful to Ignat Solzhenitsyn for his assistance in the preparation of this volume.

FOREWORD TO BOOK 2

Aleksandr Solzhenitsyn did not voluntarily depart for the West in February 1974. He was expelled from the Soviet Union for unleashing that great torrent of truth that was *The Gulag Archipelago*. That book, one of unparalleled historical and "literary investigation," did more than any other work in the twentieth century to expose the truth about Communism and to undermine the moral and political legitimacy of one of the most vile regimes in human history. If Solzhenitsyn did not welcome exile, if he felt torn, as always, between the two millstones of the Soviet "Dragon"—as repressive and mendacious as ever—and an uncomprehending and increasingly hostile West, he nonetheless found solitude and happy refuge in his eighteen years in Cavendish, Vermont. It was there that he worked on, and eventually finished, his other great work of historical and literary investigation, *The Red Wheel*, a momentous ten-volume novel and work of dramatized history, an almost superhuman effort to recover the truth about 1917 and Russia's descent into the totalitarian quagmire.

After the speeches and political interventions chronicled in Book 1 of *Between Two Millstones*, culminating in the Harvard Address in June 1978, Solzhenitsyn gradually settled down to the life of a writer-historian, dedicating himself to the peaceful solitude of the literary arts. In Vermont, he found a happiness in free and uninterrupted work—conditions he could only dream of during the years of repression and harassment in the Soviet Union chronicled in *The Oak and the Calf*, perhaps the greatest of his literary memoirs (and all of them are of the highest quality and interest).

Above all, he found a place to work. He was aided by the remarkable resources of the Hoover Institution in Palo Alto, California, which provided him with an ample supply of newspapers from St. Petersburg's revolutionary days, and crucial memoirs and testimonies of old survivors from Russia's "First Wave" of emigration, those who fled the homeland after the October Revolution of 1917 and the Bolshevik victory in the Russian Civil War. With these abundant resources, the crucial centerpiece of *The Red Wheel*, the four books of *Node III: March 1917*, began to take shape. Solzhenitsyn also found a serene and welcome home for his family. His account of his role in the education of his sons, the impressive development of their characters and intellectual talents, their blossoming as young men, is both touching and informative. We see Yermolai's precocious interest in politics, Ignat's striking musical gifts, and Stepan's intense intellectual curiosity. Those traits are evident to this day, together with a deep fidelity to their father's life, thought, and literary legacy.

The Solzhenitsyn home also had some of the character of a veritable publishing house or literary magazine. Natalia Solzhenitsyn ("Alya" throughout the manuscript) was in every sense her husband's intellectual partner—his editor, sounding board, research assistant, and wise confidante—even as she reared a family. She loved Russia with the same passion as did her husband. The Solzhenitsyn boys also helped with typesetting and other literary and publishing tasks. Natalia and the young sons truly lived in Vermont, interacting with the broader community. The boys were as American as they were Russian. Natalia Solzhenitsyn was the author's conduit to the Russian underground, to publishing houses, to the national media, to the political class, and to the local Cavendish and broader Vermont communities. Her strength, energy, talents, and fierce protectiveness were almost preternatural, as described in this and other writings of Solzhenitsyn.

The Solzhenitsyns lived in a community that was both rural and conservative, but increasingly marked by a post-1960s progressivism. Solzhenitsyn amusingly describes educators in New England, like the headmaster Dick (note his ostentatious informality) at East Hill, who was a largely benign figure but totally ignorant of the truth about the Soviet Union (Dick counted Lenin, and even Stalin, among his "progressive" heroes!).

Solzhenitsyn's serenity was marred by his constant appreciation of "Russian Pain" (the title of chapter 6 of *Between Two Millstones*). He worried about those administrators (Alik Ginzburg and Sergei Khodorovich) of the Russian Social Fund (which provided vital help to former *zeks* and their families) who were jailed, harassed, and persecuted by the Soviet authorities. The Solzhenitsyns did everything humanly possible to rally Western governments and public opinion to their defense. Solzhenitsyn also worried about other prisoners of conscience, like Igor Ogurtsov, who languished in prison and exile.

But Solzhenitsyn also saw signs of hope, from the patriotic and Christian historical and spiritual reflections of Dmitri Likhachyov (who'd spent time in the 1920s as a *zek* on the Solovetsky Islands) to the "village prose" writers who had broken through the suffocating fog of wooden language and ideological clichés to reclaim the spirit of a forgotten Russia, one that had been under systematic assault since 1917. Solzhenitsyn also appreciated, at least initially, Vladimir Maximov's editorial efforts with *Kontinent*, an important Russian literary, cultural, and political journal based in Germany that aimed to raise Russian literature—and political and social reflection—from its ailing state. During these more relaxed years of exile, Solzhenitsyn came to reconsider the achievement of Aleksandr Tvardovsky, the editor of *Novy Mir* and the publisher, in the fall of 1962, of *One Day in the Life of Ivan Denisovich*. He had loved Tvardovsky, as every reader of *The Oak and the Calf* knows, but lamented his equivocations and saw him, at the end of the day, as too much of a Soviet man. But with growing lucidity and clarity, Solzhenitsyn was coming to appreciate just how much the great man had done to recover authentic Russian literature. His fundamental stance toward Tvardovsky was now decisively one of gratitude.

In his new situation of comparative leisure, Solzhenitsyn continued to turn down most invitations. Completing *The Red Wheel* was his first priority. But an intelligent and sympathetic journalist at the BBC Russian Service, Janis Sapiets, whom we already met in Book 1 of *Between Two Millstones*, offered the Russian writer an opportunity to speak directly to the Russian people. That interview, broadcast in February 1979, on the fifth anniversary of Solzhenitsyn's expulsion, provides a perfect summary of Solzhenitsyn's principal concerns about the Russian past, present, and future. He was severely critical of newly minted Russian émigrés (from the "Third Wave" of emigration) who never failed to blame Russia, historic Russia, Orthodox Russia, for the terrible crimes of the Bolsheviks (this view would become dominant in the West, too). Solzhenitsyn shared with his Russian listeners his concern for a misconstrued admiration of the reckless "February fever" of February–March 1917, which could destroy, or at least deeply undermine, Russia's path to an ordered and civilized liberty. Émigré intellectuals, such as Andrei Sinyavsky, Efim Etkind, and Aleksandr Yanov, busied themselves with mendacious efforts to link Solzhenitsyn to fascism, anti-Semitism, and new forms of tyranny. Etkind even called Solzhenitsyn a "Russian Ayatollah," fantastically identifying him with the clericalist violence and despotism in revolutionary Iran (this is one of the few calumnies to which Solzhenitsyn responded almost immediately: see "The Persian Ruse," *Jerusalem Post*, 20 December 1979, 8). The author of *The Gulag Archipelago* was said to want new camps, new prisons, and a new despotism. These were lies worthy of the Bolsheviks themselves and, alas, had their effect on elite opinion in the United States.

In the interview with Sapiets, as in chapter 6 of *Between Two Millstones*, Solzhenitsyn would lay out a firm but moderate and manly patriotism that rejected Russian self-hatred and self-abnegation, as well as the fascist, neo-pagan, and neo-Bolshevik temptations. All three of the latter positions falsely identified love of Russia with an immoral accommodation with those who had destroyed her liberty, her intellectual and spiritual life, her property-owning peasantry, and her historic Christian faith. Solzhenitsyn would never make an accommodation with those who systematically tyrannized the bodies and souls of men. As always, Solzhenitsyn's was a principled *via media*, opting for what he suggestively calls "a healing, salutary, moderate patriotism." Alas, he did not find much of it in émigré or homegrown Russian intellectual circles. Facile cosmopolitanism, and hatred of the nation, or an anti-Christian nationalism, were increasingly the order of the day. Many who should have known better confused Solzhenitsyn's proud, principled, moderate, and self-limiting patriotism with fascism and imperialism. Some of these men had come to hate historic Russia: Sinyavsky shamelessly called Russia, still suffering from the ravages of Communism, a "bitch." Many of those who defamed Solzhenitsyn were barely concealed Soviet men who shared Communism's utter disdain for truth, country, and the spiritual dimensions of human existence.

As always, Solzhenitsyn faced the malevolence of two menacing millstones. The expanded edition of *August 1914*, with its praise of the magnanimous and moderate Pyotr Stolypin and his "middle path" of Russian social development, came under bitter attack even before the book appeared in English. One issue was Solzhenitsyn's description of Stolypin's assassin, Dmitri Bogrov, a double agent of the tsarist secret police and leftist armed revolutionaries. Even though Solzhenitsyn drew scrupulously on the account given by Bogrov's brother (in a book published in Berlin in 1930) of Bogrov's motives in assassinating Stolypin (motives linked to the continuing humiliation of Russia's Jewish population), Solzhenitsyn was unfairly and inaccurately accused of demonizing Jews. There was a purge at Munich-based Radio Liberty, where significant excerpts from the book had been read to an audience in the USSR, and the US Senate conducted an ignorant and embarrassing investigation fueled by the calumnies of Solzhenitsyn's cultured despisers in the Third Wave of emigration. By 1985, Solzhenitsyn was under systematic assault of a new wave of ideological lies, this time put forward by self-described "pluralists" and secularists, some nostalgic for the original purity of the October Revolution. But decent men such as Richard Grenier (in the *New York Times*) and Norman Podhoretz (in *Commentary*) came to the defense of Solzhenitsyn and the truth—and the controversy eventually died down. When the augmented edition of *August 1914* was finally published by the New York publishing house Farrar, Straus and Giroux in 1989, there was no discussion of the frenzied and false accusations of just four years before. Two millstones, indeed . . .

Throughout all these accusations and assaults, Solzhenitsyn kept his eye on the prize. He would tell the truth about the Revolutions of 1917, and warn his compatriots about the twin temptations of "February fever" and a turn toward a malevolent, pagan nationalism. And he continued to fight the insinuation that historic Russia, and not Bolshevik ideology, was responsible for the system of violence and lies that characterized the Soviet tragedy. Thus, for Solzhenitsyn, a "no" to the fascists, a "no" to the National Bolsheviks, a "no" to Leninism in all its forms, and a "no" to those who decried Orthodoxy and authentic Russian national consciousness. Following Sergei Bulgakov, Solzhenitsyn knew that a great people could not sustain its life on "the national principle alone." But he refused to conflate Orthodoxy with a soft ecumenism that was "indifferent to their own people's national identity."

As in Book 1 of *Between Two Millstones*, Solzhenitsyn continues his dialogue with the other great opponent of the Soviet regime, the physicist and dissident Andrei Sakharov. Solzhenitsyn continues to admire Sakharov's courage and his increasing lucidity about the evils of the ideological regime in the Soviet Union. Solzhenitsyn never doubts Academician Sakharov's fundamental decency, even though Sakharov had played his own role in spreading misconceptions about Solzhenitsyn's views on patriotism, Orthodoxy, and the Russian future at the time of the controversy over 1974's *Letter to the Soviet Leaders*. Solzhenitsyn could not and did not share Sakharov's unalloyed faith in technology and "technical progress," or his misplaced confidence in "supranational world government," an invitation, in Solzhenitsyn's view, to new forms of despotism and an accompanying erosion of the national and spiritual traditions and principles that inform a truly self-respecting and self-governing people. Sakharov, for all his courage, decency, and contempt for totalitarian tyranny, had little or no concept of Russia as a nation to which one could be dedicated in the moderate, and salutary, ways Solzhenitsyn proposed.

Solzhenitsyn believed human rights, precious as they were, had to be accompanied always by a commensurate respect for perennial human obligations. For his part, Sakharov treated "human rights" as an end in itself, and privileged the "right to emigrate" above all. He loved freedom and human dignity but, in Solzhenitsyn's view, did not truly "feel Russian pain." The two men, Solzhenitsyn writes, were of the same age, fought the same evil system, and were vilified by the same baying propaganda machine. They both preferred peaceful political change to armed revolution. For all their differences—and they were very significant, indeed—they respected, even admired each other. But what divided them, in the end, was Russia itself.

Unfortunately, Solzhenitsyn's principal biographer in the English-speaking world belonged spiritually to Sakharov's sphere: Michael Scammell. He was a liberal anti-Communist who could see no limitations in Enlightenment principles (or the whole edifice of "Progress"). He was hostile to almost every word of Solzhenitsyn's after his arrival in the West in 1974, and approached the beautiful meditations and reflections in *From Under the Rubble*—a noble and deeply thoughtful, Christian, anti-totalitarian set of essays edited by Solzhenitsyn—with suspicion and scorn. Scammell was tone-deaf to nearly everything Solzhenitsyn had to say except for, importantly, their shared opposition to Communist totalitarianism. In his hands, a friend of the West became an uncritical enemy of the West (which Scammell identified rather dogmatically with Western secularist liberalism). To be sure, Scammell's book brought together a great deal of biographical information unavailable to non-Russian readers at the time it was published. For that it remains valuable. But this contentious biographer unfortunately set the tone, for a decade and a half or more, for the American and British reception of Solzhenitsyn's work. And Scammell's biography, not without its merits, was falsely praised by many reviewers for a "balance" that was in fact sorely lacking.

But there are good men to be noted: Harry T. Willetts, the slow but meticulously faithful translator of Solzhenitsyn's books; Ed Ericson, who worked with Solzhenitsyn to abridge the *Archipelago* (his visit to Cavendish in 1983 is charmingly related in this work); Claude Durand and Georges Nivat in France, the first an outstanding publisher of Solzhenitsyn's work, the second a thoughtful and judicious interpreter of his writings; trusted and talented Slavists and interpreters of Solzhenitsyn's work, such as Alexis Klimoff and Michael Nicholson; journalistic admirers of Solzhenitsyn's life and work, such as Bernard Levin and Malcolm Muggeridge, who conducted insightful interviews with Solzhenitsyn when he came to London to receive the Templeton Prize for Progress in Religion. (The lecture on that occasion is Solzhenitsyn's most thoughtful, comprehensive, and measured account of his religious and spiritual convictions, showing that, after his years in prison and the camps, Solzhenitsyn became—and remained—a philosophically minded Christian who freely affirmed Divine Providence, human free will, the age-old drama of good and evil in the human soul, and the powerful workings of the natural moral conscience on everyone who is open to the spiritual resources inherent in the human heart.)

I particularly recommend that readers ponder the superb chapter on "Around Three Islands" where Solzhenitsyn recounts his visits to Japan (which had, admirably, turned from war and tyranny to national self-limitation), and where Solzhenitsyn experiences an old and dignified, if rather alien, culture; and to Taiwan, or Free China, whose courage and resistance to Communist despotism won Solzhenitsyn's approbation. Last but not least, there is an account of his visit to the United Kingdom, where he met Prince Philip (who shared his broad views on the world) and Prince Charles and his young bride Diana (Solzhenitsyn was charmed by both); was interviewed by Levin and Muggeridge (interviews still well worth reading today); and had a cordial and welcome meeting with Prime Minister Margaret Thatcher. This chapter is both a literary *tour de force* and an important chronicle of the *dénouement* of the Cold War.

Eventually, Solzhenitsyn would be published in a Soviet Union undergoing glasnost and perestroika. As the enemy of Sovietism *par excellence*, he was the last major anti-Communist writer to appear in print at home when, finally, *The Gulag Archipelago* and the Nobel Lecture saw the light of day in 1990. This was a famous victory, followed by an even more remarkable one: the tearing down of the statue of Dzerzhinsky, the founder of the Cheka, at Lubyanka Square. Solzhenitsyn waited eagerly for the liberation of his country from Communist lies and tyranny even as a new "Time of Troubles" emerged, marked by an unrepentant Communist oligarchy, mass corruption, the impoverishment of old pensioners, unprecedented levels of bureaucratization, and an intellectual elite that, as a whole, sneered at Orthodoxy and self-limitation and flirted with the worst nihilistic currents of Western culture. In the fall of 1993, Solzhenitsyn bid farewell to friends in Europe, denouncing ideological revolution in the French Vendée; repeating and renewing the themes of the Harvard Address—in a softer, more hopeful tone—at the International Academy of Philosophy in Liechtenstein; and meeting, on 15 October 1993, Pope John Paul II, his great spiritual ally in defending the essential connection between Truth and liberty, and assailing the totalitarian Lie. Solzhenitsyn's account of that visit with the pope is brief and poignant.

In America, Solzhenitsyn had a more troubled farewell. There, he had never truly succeeded in persuading elites that Russia was the first and principal victim of Bolshevism, an anti-human ideology that targeted the whole of humanity. Mike Wallace of *60 Minutes* fame hounded him with the same old, tired, mendacious clichés (are you a fascist? a monarchist? an anti-Semite?). But Paul Klebnikov at *Forbes*, the business journal, conducted an informed, intelligent, and sympathetic interview with Solzhenitsyn that redeemed Wallace's lamentable display. Klebnikov was writing a thesis on the great Stolypin and shared Solzhenitsyn's vision for a strong, free, decent, and self-limiting Russia. In that interview, Solzhenitsyn thus was able to say a proper farewell and to speak his mind openly, without the usual distortions and misunderstandings.

In May 1994, Solzhenitsyn returned to post-Communist Russia. This was a time of new burdens and challenges, to be conveyed in the next set of memoirs: *Another Time, Another Burden*. The story, fraught with significance, continues . . .

Daniel J. Mahoney
Augustine Chair in Distinguished Scholarship
Assumption College
Worcester, MA
2 April 2020

PART TWO

(1978–1982)

CHAPTER 6

Russian Pain

In solitude you're happy—you're a poet![1]

as Pushkin discovered when comparing his creative periods in seclusion with those in the bustle of society.

I too had always felt, since childhood, that this would be the way. And I came to know that happy solitude when exiled to Kok-Terek[2]—and what a wrench it was, honestly, to part from it in the whirl of sudden rehabilitations. It was in June 1956 that I left the exile that had been so good to me, and only twenty years later, almost to the day, in June 1976, that I found my way to the freely chosen solitude I desired, this time in Vermont.[3] And from the very first day I threw myself into the Stolypin volume of *August 1914*[4]—which had now become clear to me—and then into the vast *March 1917*. And for years now I've not torn myself away for so much as a day, except for my Harvard speech.[5]

And I never ceased to be surprised and grateful: the Lord had indeed put me into the best situation a writer could dream of, and the best of the dismal fates that could have arisen, given our blighted history and the oppression of our country for the last sixty years.

Now I was no longer compelled to write in code, hide things, distribute pieces of writing among my friends. I could keep all my materials open to view, all in one place, and all my manuscripts out on capacious tables.

And I could receive from libraries any information source I needed. Actually, even before this, during the first hustle and bustle in Zurich,[6] old Russian émigrés were sending—even without me asking—all the books that were indispensable. I'd put them into my library before I found out what books I did actually need—and it turned out I already had nearly all of them. But the best repository for the history of the Revolution was the Hoover Institution,[7] where both the murder of Stolypin (that enigma had been an obsession since my youth) and the whole enormous edifice of *March*[8] emerged into view from those old newspapers. And the Hoover was always inviting me to come and do some more work there, and sending photocopies of materials by the hundredweight. And thanks to the endeavors of Elena Pashina an invaluable gift was added—microfilm copies of all the Petersburg papers from the time of the Revolution.

But on top of that, how many recollections were sent me by old survivors of the Revolution. . . . Verging on their nineties, strength wasted, vision now poor, they used what were, in some cases, the last words they'd ever write to respond to my appeal. Some told their whole life story, others—singular events of the Revolution that I'd never have been able to find elsewhere, their own recollections or those of relatives now dead, memories otherwise doomed to die with them. There are already over three hundred of them—and they are still arriving. It was Alya[9] who would first take receipt of this avalanche (when ever did she find the time?), and both answer the elderly authors and look through their manuscripts, reading and picking out for me the fragments that might be of immediate use. But my first job would be to select witness accounts of the Gulag for the final edition of *Archipelago*—adding another thirty or so to the Soviet accounts we already had. Finally, starting in autumn 1980, I could sit down to work on the revolutionary memoirs alone. That dying generation of émigrés had breathed out their final words to me, sending me a great surge of help. The link between epochs, ripped apart by bloody Bolshevik hands, had been miraculously, unexpectedly put back together as the last possible moment was ebbing away. (Many of those whom I'd managed to meet personally died only during these last few years. We started calling on Father Andrew[10] to hold a memorial service on Old New Year's Eve[11] in our little chapel at home, for all those who had died the previous year. We told our boys the story of each of them, who he was and what he had been through.)

But the Lord also sustained me in another way, in the fact that, even though living in the West, I did not have to rush from pillar to post to survive, which would have been exhausting and degrading in an alien milieu: I didn't need to look for money to live on. And so I never took an interest in whether my books would be to the taste of a Western readership, whether they'd "sell." In the USSR I'd been accustomed to earning almost nothing, but spending almost nothing as well. Alas, in the West that wasn't possible, especially with a family. I didn't immediately understand how immense was the gift of material well-being bestowed on me: it meant total independence.

I found myself unhindered and alone with the work I'd now found my way to. I was writing books—without having to worry about anything else. Independence! It's broader in scope and more effective than freedom alone. Without it I could not have fulfilled my task. But this way, Western life has flowed past me, to one side, having no effect on the rhythm of my work. And the only irretrievable loss of time has been due to our homeland's irretrievable lapse into exhaustion.

But as for me, I seem to have no sense of the passage of time: I've now already spent over two thousand days following the same regimen, always in profound tranquility—something I'd feverishly dreamed of throughout my Soviet life. There's no telephone in the house where I work, no television, I'm always in fresh air (following the Swiss custom, the bedroom windows are kept open, even in freezing weather), living on healthy American provincial food, never once having been to the doctor for anything serious, plunging headfirst into the icy pond at the age of sixty-three—and still today I feel no older than my fifty-seven years of age when I arrived here—and even a great deal younger. I don't feel the same age as my contemporaries, but rather more akin to people of forty or forty-five such as my wife, as though I were to tread my future path, till its end, alongside them. Though perhaps one element is missing—those days when inspiration descends on you like an *avalanche*[12] and knocks you off your feet and you barely have the time to note down images, phrases, ideas. But even the young man's feeling that I haven't finished *developing* yet, either in my art or my thought, is something I still feel as I approach sixty-four.

For six months I revel in my work in a spacious, high-ceilinged office with "arrow" beams—cold in winter, it's true—with big windows, skylights, and ample tables where I spread out my quantities of little notes. But for the other half of the year, the summer months, I decamp to the little house by the pond and derive a new rush of energy from this change of workplace: something new flows into me, some kind of expanded creative capacity. (Alya has the same feeling: "here we get younger.") Here, nature is so close all around us that it even becomes a curse: chipmunks dart in and out under your feet, several of them at a time, little snakes occasionally slip past you through the grass and a raccoon rustles along, heaving a sigh, beneath our floorboards; at dawn every day, squirrels bombard our metal roof with the pine-cones they've picked, and red flying squirrels (with wings like bats') move into the attic of the big house for the winter, and start romping around there at random times of the day and night. But the ones I dearly love are the coyotes:

in the winter they often roam our land, coming right up to the house and emitting their intricate, inimitable cry. I won't attempt to describe it, but I am very fond of it.

However, all these little noises and cries only intensify the "extraordinary, intoxicating, concentrated silence," as Alya described it one day. She immerses herself in work as passionately as I do: just don't let us get disturbed! She has found her feet and settled, not instantly but quickly and confidently, into an unusual way of life: not the urban one she had always led, but a secluded forest one, with idiosyncrasies and demands, imposing tasks as well as limits on our possibilities.

Alya and I find it easy to talk: to understand each other half a word suffices—or even a slight gesture or facial expression, without wasting words on what's obvious, or what's already been said. But what is said moves things forward, adds something new, or provides food for thought.

One of Alya's main concerns, in our new location, was to find a school for Dimitri. Our Russian émigré acquaintances in America, horrified, chorused their warning against American *public* schools. They were, it seemed, a zone of profound ignorance, with no real knowledge imparted, a total lack of discipline, and no respect for teachers. Thus, we were told, if there was even the slightest chance, we had to send our children to a *private* school. (As it turned out, this horrific picture was true only of the schools in large cities, and then not all of them; and even less true of rural schools.) Now New England happens to have more private schools than anywhere else in the States, and many are indeed top-notch. So, at the beginning of the academic year, off went Dimitri to one such school. Coming from a Moscow school (where he was anything but pampered) he then, at the age of twelve, had to learn German in Switzerland (picking up the local *Schwyzerdütsch* while he was at it) and, having just found his feet there, now at fourteen in America, he suddenly needed to learn English. For a teenager, these displacements were hard—the new languages, on the other hand, he mastered with ease. When he left he was sorely missed, not only by the little ones, who adored their older brother, but by us adults as well; for, being sociable and having his wits about him, Dimitri had been, from our very first days in Vermont, our main link to the community. Thankfully, he was able to spend all his vacations—and there were many in American schools—at home helping his mom and grandma. He very quickly mastered his new environment, too: with his easy-going ways, a much more varied life experience than his peers, and a dynamic personality, Dimitri easily immersed himself in this new world, winning the universal goodwill and even reverence of other youngsters. He stood out, refreshingly different and generous in spirit. No one considered him an outsider.

He had loved all things automotive since childhood, spending all his free time assembling and disassembling engines, and at seventeen years of age he went to Boston University to study mechanical engineering. But at the end of his first semester there, in December 1979, with Dimitri riding shotgun, his friend behind the wheel and another two students in the back, their car was involved in an accident and Dimitri's injuries were the most severe: his ocular and facial nerves and his ear were damaged, and even his life hung in the balance. For ten days and nights Alya sat by his bedside in the hospital in Boston. Six months later the facial nerve was restored and Dimitri's innate health and love of life helped him back to a lifestyle just as active as before. But for a long time after that accident Alya still feared, even expected, some kind of sudden, new catastrophe.

The little ones, meanwhile, had their own life. They grew in size and strength, spending their first years on our plot as if on a Russian nature reserve. Alya read aloud to them every day—both poems and prose—and gave them poems to learn by heart, as well as dictations (differentiated according to age). She was their guide in their independent reading (having brought almost her whole library with her from Moscow), but they were already choosing purposefully for themselves. Naturally, they had Dumas and Jules Verne, but the Russian classics as well, and Akhmatova and Pasternak too. Raised on Russian verse, knowing a good deal of it by heart already, the boys gave "reading recitals" for the Russian and non-Russian guests who came—the Struves (husband and wife) and the Schmemanns; the Klimoffs (father and son); the Shtein family; Gayler from Switzerland; American visitors Thomas Whitney, Harrison Salisbury, Hilton Kramer; from London, Janis Sapiets; and others. It could be called "solitude," but in fact we quite often had this visitor or that, and new acquaintances from around the area, and we would often have longer-term visitors in the summer staying in the "guest" house.

What's more, we had the same old Russian lady from Zurich, Ekaterina Pavlovna,[13] over for several long stays—sometimes of six months—for she could not stand being apart from her favorite three boys who had crossed the pond. Her presence in the house meant the children absorbed the richness of

Russian traditions, such as the whole family making *pelmeni* together, and heard her succulent Siberian speech.

I taught Yermolai and Ignat, together, algebra and geometry and, without my lowering the assessment bar, they would turn in oral answers and written tests deserving only As and Bs. Ignat showed great innate ability and would more than once follow up my explanation with an astute forward-looking question, making the next logical step, as it were—thereby leading to the subject of the next lesson. Later I worked on mathematics with Stepan alone, but at a faster pace, trying to overcome his dreamy absentmindedness. This had alarmed us in his early childhood, but we needn't have worried—in fact it was an early sign of his profound thoughtfulness about the world. —I tried doing physics with all three at once, and that worked well. Then—astronomy too. And so, when the boys were between seven and ten years old, at the end of August, when it was still warm but the stars were already rising early in the sky, I would take them down the hill, past the pond to the only clearing we have, open to the sky, from which we could see the full panoply of stars. They would take a good look, memorize the constellations, and we'd look at the basics of mathematical astronomy and the main lines of the celestial sphere, which, on another day, I would draw on the blackboard. The boys were eager to learn about the constellations. Stepan remembered them—and even each constellation's brightest star—best of the three. (He was also good, indeed outstanding, at geography: outstripping his brothers, even his parents, he already knew all the countries of the world by heart, all their capitals, all their flags. And, even so, he handcrafted his own miniature flags, all hundred and fifty of them, and pinned them up on the wall.) As for Ignat, he was astounded by Algol, the "demon star"[14] (because of its fluctuating brightness)—and told his mother he was scared to go to bed afterwards.

Meanwhile, the boys are becoming ever more avid readers, but each in his own way. Their first acquaintance with Shakespeare was in Russian, and Stepan at eight was enthralled by *Hamlet*, reading it over and over, while Yermolai swallowed up Shakespeare's histories, a passion that would be lifelong, and Ignat the historical dramas of Aleksei K. Tolstoy. By the age of ten Yermolai was engrossed in *War and Peace*, just as I had been. And to Alya's great joy he was rather good at drawing, trying his hand at portraits, landscapes.

Nineteen miles away from us, in Claremont, New Hampshire, there is an Orthodox church, with services on Saturdays and Sundays. Our children always serve as altar boys during the liturgy, and Yermolai has even started doing the Epistle readings. The service is all in English, with perhaps one or two litanies in Church Slavonic (the parishioners being mostly the children and grandchildren of the turn-of-the-century wave of "economic" migrants, job-seekers from the western Russian provinces). Father Andrew Tregubov also sometimes comes to serve in our house chapel, and then it's all in Slavonic. (He has also begun to give the boys weekly lessons in catechism, then Russian history.) Stepan is impressed the deepest by all things religious. He shares his findings with his mother: "Do you know how it gets decided who goes to heaven and who goes to hell? Well, I don't think what you do when you live with Mom and Dad counts. But after that, every day you can take a step up or a step down. But Christ sees us all—it's as if he's at the top of a giant ladder. He sees our footprints light up on the steps beneath, either with a white flame or dark one, and God can easily count where we stand, from these flashes."

Recently we have also been shown an American Orthodox monastery called New Skete. It's rather far from us, on the way to Albany, in New York State. But it has a wonderful, friendly atmosphere, and the abbot, Father Laurence,[15] is both spiritually wise and joyful. They sing magnificently, and to make ends meet they breed and train seeing-eye dogs, which make their way to blind owners all over America.

Leonard DiLisio, an American of Italian origin and a likeable, modest, and chivalrous man living nearby, becomes our children's first English teacher. He is the tenth child, the youngest, of an immigrant family from Abruzzo, was always fond of languages, learned Slavic ones and knows Russian pretty well, and has the qualification to teach Latin as well as, for some reason, geometry. A romantic and gentle soul, considerate to the utmost. Starting in 1979, after Irina Ilovaiskaya left for Paris, he began to work as my secretary, coming twice a week. For the whole day he sorts the endless flow of letters, conducts the inevitable business correspondence, makes all the necessary local phone calls. Leonard is part of our home life, without being any kind of burden.

But it was time to find a school for the boys. Most of the private schools only start at fourteen or fifteen years of age, the last four years of a twelve-year education. As it turned out, there was a private primary school in the area. At seventeen miles away, it was not a short trip to be making four times a day (there and back in the morning, and the same in the evening). What's more, it stands high in the hills and conditions are frequently icy in winter. It's a difficult road. To the rescue came fearless grandmother, a wonderful driver with many years' experience. (Later our new friend and neighbor Sheree[16] helped drive the children, as did Dimitri when he could, having received his driving license at age sixteen.)

This school, in the tiny town of Andover, on the East Hill above the village, turned out to be full of general good will, offered a considerable body of knowledge, and taught through labor and practical skills (it even had its own dairy farm). There were several wonderful young teachers there. But we were surprised by its strident socialist spirit—or was it Mennonite, in keeping with the beliefs of its headmaster. No marks were to be given in this school, so as not to create inequality, nor to traumatize the less-adept students. And no homework assignments whatsoever. It was considered dangerous to love any subject or activity too much, and so students were forcibly made to switch to other topics. The headmaster, *Dick*[17] (all were to address each other by first names only), established and embodied the school's ascetic spirit, considered himself one with the poor, and liked to make ethical and political judgments, such as "Lenin was right to take bread away from the rich," which drew a rebuke from Dimitri that "You'd have been the first target of the requisitions, Dick! Look at your eight hundred acres and three hundred sheep. People were sent to the tundra for having two cows and a tin roof." Dick was taken aback and hardly believed any of it. He defended Stalin too, but ten-year-old Yermolai had the nerve to answer back: "But Stalin was a murderer." When Reagan was elected president, Dick was so distraught that he flew the school flag at half-staff in mourning.[18] The older boys did manage two and a half years there (Stepan joining for the last half year), but the feeling was growing that this was a dead end, something unnatural, and we decided it was time to switch the boys to the local, six-year Cavendish Town Elementary School, which was right near us.

In February 1981 they went through an assessment at the Cavendish school and were placed: ten-year-old Yermolai directly to sixth grade, eight-year-old Ignat to the fifth, Stepan to second grade. After only a semester, Yermolai went on to the next six-year school, a bit farther from us in Chester, Vermont, with a school bus collecting the children "from the hills" and delivering them to the school after an almost hour-long drive. The study there was more intense, but Yermolai made quick work of it, even though two years younger than his classmates. He also started to take karate lessons. A year later Ignat joined him in Chester, while Stepan received the full Cavendish school education. It was hard for him there at first. The academic part was easy as pie and, besides, there wasn't any homework here either. But Stepan, with his good nature, had no defense against the cruelty of pupils' behavior at the school and was incapable of answering foul language in kind. His helplessness only provoked more aggression. And on top of that—he was foreign. During breaks they didn't let him play, and called him "the Russian Negro," made him eat grass, and even stuffed it into his mouth. Little Stepan was crushed, and told his mother there was "no escape from this life." After the explosion at an American base in Beirut that killed two hundred marines, they began to hound Stepan as a "Russian spy." In the school bus they would wrench his arms back, hit him, and keep chanting "Communist! Spy!" (From the organizational point of view, those buses were splendid. But for about an hour the children were without supervision by school staff, and the driver couldn't keep an eye on them all—and it was in the buses that the roughest, the most disgusting behavior occurred.) Later Stepan settled in nicely and had lots of friends in school. But, even so, the children had to pay a price for their father's banishment from his homeland.

I myself didn't keep a close eye on all the details of the children's lives—those had little place in my compressed, densely packed days—which made the responsibility and heartfelt anguish taken on by Alya all the greater. She was constantly reassuring them that our exile had a point and imposed duties on us. And not just in words: the very spirit of our family and the unceasing, impassioned work Alya and I were doing together also had its effect on our sons. And they grew up friends, with a sense of family unity and teamwork. Take Yermolai. From about ten years of age he started typesetting, on our IBM machine, the first book of our All-Russian Memoir Library series, the recollections of Volkov-Muromtsev. How glad we were—not only of the help but also that the courage and noble disposition of such Russian boys[19] might be communicated to him—and that hope was not in vain. Soon after that, he set about typing up an important stream in my correspondence—that with Lidia Korneevna Chukovskaya. Her handwriting was barely legible—but he mastered it eagerly, learning about the problems of life under Soviet rule, questioning us on it. In a spirit of competition, the eight-year-old Ignat immediately rushed to start typing; it was competition, but not jealousy. The alien environment bound them together. In the late evenings Ignat would look from his dark bedroom window across to my lit office window, and would tell his mother that "I think about Papa every evening." A consciousness of our unusual burden communicated itself to all three of them. In all the free days of their childhood, in the school holidays or when an ice- or snowstorm halted the school buses, Alya worked with the children again and again on Russian subjects, and I on mathematics and physics.

Ignat's musicality had already made itself known by the age of two, when he would argue with Yermolai over what records to listen to, Ignat always preferring music and singing to fairy tales. But we hardly gave it a second thought. Then, when we moved to Vermont, the house had a small, old piano, and from age four Ignat was always around it, running his fingers over the keyboard; but still we didn't take it seriously. But once, when he was seven, Rostropovich came visiting, tested him, and announced to us: "Perfect pitch! You must have him taught immediately!" But just you try to teach a child music in our woods. Leonard tried, but very quickly recognized his inadequacy. We found a music teacher near Cavendish—hopeless. Time was ticking away. But Vermont also came to the rescue. At the far south of the state, about a seventy-mile drive from our house, is the international Marlboro chamber-music festival, under the leadership of the famed pianist Rudolf Serkin, who also lives surrounded by woods, just as we do. He agreed to give Ignat an audition. After listening to a short piece Ignat composed he said, "He is Russian, you can hear that right away!" and overall found him to be highly gifted and in need of serious musical tuition. Then Serkin's wife Irene leapt in to help find a teacher and set up regular lessons. The first teacher to take on Ignat was a refined and talented Korean lady, Chonghyo Shin. She soon found in him "both a brilliant talent and a thirst for learning," qualities that don't always go together. Under her tutelage Ignat advanced enough to give his first public concerts: a solo recital aged ten, and a piano concerto (Beethoven's Second) with an orchestra at eleven. He studied music with great passion. His lessons with Mrs. Shin were to the south in Massachusetts, a ninety-minute drive each way, and his grandmother, ever the stalwart, would drive him there. And not only there but also north to Hanover, New Hampshire, to study counterpoint with a Dartmouth College professor. Ignat sacrificed at the altar of music his other great passion—chess, which had also excited him to fever pitch. Painful as it was, he abandoned chess entirely, setting aside the chessboard and its tantalizing figures. But he allowed himself a full diet of reading, both Russian and English classics. (His first experience in comparing languages came after he read the Russian translation of Rostand's *Cyrano de Bergerac* and saw it adapted in an American film. Can there be any comparison between "О нет, благодарю!" and the English version, "No, thank you"?[20]) Later, Ignat would be taught by Serkin's assistant, the Uruguayan Luis Batlle.

Thus, in many ways, the family and children paid the price for my choice to live in wooded solitude. But for my work, for the whole meaning of my life, this solitude was an absolute necessity—especially in America, and for many years to come. Once the conditions are good, the work gets done: over these past years I have written the entire Stolypin volume of *August 1914*[21] and the basis of the four volumes of *March 1917.*

When I look back, I cannot fail to recognize that the past six years, at Five Brooks,[22] have been the happiest of my life. Some disagreeable Western problems descended on us—and passed by, an insignificant froth. It was just then, in those years, that the invective increased—but it didn't spoil a single working day for me; I didn't even notice it, following the advice of the proverb, "hear no evil, see no evil." Sometimes it's better not to know what people are saying about you. Alya, whenever she entered my office, always found me in a joyful, even radiant mood—so well was my work coming along. I've been piling that abuse, those magazines, on a shelf and haven't read it for all these years—until now. For the first time I am now, for *Millstones*, thinking of reading and simultaneously contesting it, to save time.

When you are immersed in a once-in-a-lifetime piece of work, you don't notice, aren't aware of any other tasks. At various times in that period my plays were produced, in Germany, Denmark, England, and the States, and I was invited to the premieres—but I never went. And as for the various gatherings, meetings, these are madness to me, just fruitless reeling in a New York or Paris whirlwind—while to them it's my eccentricity that's mad, retreating from the world to dig my grave. Some American literary critics, judging me by their own standards, decided that it was "well-organized publicity." (Critics! Do they not understand what the writer's work consists of? Every one of us who has something to say dreams of going into seclusion to work. I've been told that's exactly what the intelligent ones do, here in Vermont and environs—Robert Penn Warren, Salinger. At one time Kipling lived right here for four years. Now, if I accepted all the invitations and spoke at the events—that would certainly be advertising myself.)

One day Alya called to mind our catchphrase from before we were exiled, and repeated it now: how to decode the heavenly cipher[23] for these years? How to recognize the right course of action, especially now we're in the West? But, for as long as necessary, the whole message was unmistakable: sit there, write, fill in the Russian history that's been lost. I have a prayer: "Lord, guide me!" And when necessary, He will. I am at peace.

Of course, it's a sorry state of affairs, working your whole life to stock up reserves, reserves, and more reserves. But that is the lot of our ravaged Russia. If the truth about the past were to rise from the ashes in our homeland today, and minds were honed on that truth, then strong characters would emerge, whole ranks of doers, people taking an active part—and my books would come in useful too. But as it is, the old émigrés are nearly all dead and their grandchildren grow up rooted in Western life—my books are more or less foreign to them—and they themselves are by now no force, no nation. And the new arrivals, the Third Wave,[24] mostly read Russian materials, but, while they are quick to pick up my books at a little New York shop where they're free, they don't pay any attention to them and don't follow their ideas. (One little band of swindlers was even discovered taking my lightweight *malyshki*,[25] ostensibly to send them off altruistically to the USSR—but in fact they were selling them in Israel via a book wholesaler there.) As for the Western public these days, it seems to have totally lost the habit of reflecting on books—though perhaps not on journalistic articles—and Western writers themselves, for the most part, do not lay claim to the power of persuasion. Current literature in the West titillates either an intellectual or a popular readership: it is degraded to the level of entertainment and paradox, no longer of a standard to mold minds and characters.

And so—more reserves to lay in, more reserves . . .

The first step, then, was to collect my works together, in their definitive form. My years in the Soviet Union were so full of turmoil, with such fluctuations, that not a single text was ever fully polished or completed, and they were even consciously deformed, the tactic being to stay undercover until the time was right. If I did not complete them, clean them up, finish them off now—when would I? This was not the simple desire of a writer to see that row of volumes as soon as possible—it was the pain I suffered inside, from knowing that nothing was as it should be, nothing in place, and that I might run out of time to put it right.

Contemporary technology, an electronic typesetting machine, made it possible for Alya to set text every day and to do it in our backwater without having to go anywhere else, and proofread it immediately. (I cannot manage without the letter *ё*! With difficulty we found and ordered typeballs with *ё*—they hadn't been available from IBM—in the main font we use and in petit font. But what about the others? It was my dextrous mother-in-law who undertook to place all the missing dots on the *ё* and all the stress marks, for those were also missing from the typeballs. She rescued us.)

Although our first typesetting machine only had enough memory for three pages—which meant we had to finalize them immediately, without turning the machine off—by the end of 1980 Alya had already been able to typeset and proofread the texts, and we could do the final edit of the first eight volumes of my collected works. She also assembled detailed bibliographic information for each work and provided an overview of all the original editions. For all those years Alya packed in an astonishing amount, skillfully combining tasks, at a time when it was a pity to lose even an hour or two out of a day that was full to bursting. She and I, fused together, were led by the unchanging task set for us. Alya led a stressful life—but how vast its range, as well: and all our dealings with the outside world on top of that, answering the phone, running the Fund[26] and plotting with its Moscow staff—another separate communication flow. When there was a rush on, she worked from 7 a.m. to 1 a.m., sleeping five hours a night, till she was in a state of extreme exhaustion. Her sense of duty was always her master—superior to the preservation of her strength.

In spring '81 we acquired the same kind of IBM machine, but with a memory on magnetic cards, which enabled us to work on whole chapters at a time—now things started rolling with new vigor! (But how painful for us were the disruptions when the machine broke down and the technician didn't come, or, if he did come, he couldn't fix it and parts had to be ordered—an extremely annoying holdup in our work, momentum, and schedule!)

The circumstances of our life meant that *October*[27] had had a particular, complicated destiny. I had worked intensely on it in 1971–72, while still living at Rostropovich's home. Then life in the Soviet Union heated up and tore me away from it, and I turned my back on it for a long time. And now, ten years later, I sat down to finish it. Over that period more and more new chapters were being added to the framework of *October*—and were not always finding the best, the correct place within the earlier construction. Then Alya gave me a great deal of good advice, not only on the details—which she always did—but also on the structure. And I took her advice. Alya had dealt with *August* (volumes 11 and 12), finished the *publitsistika*[28] (volume 10), and now took *October* (volumes 13 and 14) over from me, while I went on to the second draft of all four volumes of *March*.

No, neither the electronic typesetting machine with its large memory nor my own zeal and perseverance would have achieved my goal without a wife equal to the task. I doubt whether any other Russian writer ever had at his side such a co-worker and such an astute and sensitive critic and adviser.

As for me, I have never in my life met anyone with such an acute lexical feel for the specific word needed, for the hidden rhythm of a prose sentence, with such taste in matters of design, as my wife, sent to me—and now irreplaceable—in my insular seclusion, where the brain of one author with his unvarying perceptions is not enough. Close attention to the text was needed, a keen eye, a sensitivity to the slightest break in the phonetic or rhythmic form and to the falseness or truthfulness of a tone, a touch, an item of syntax, a sensitivity to everything in a work of literature—from the large structural elements and the believability of characters down to the nuances of images and expressions, their ordering, to interjections and punctuation. Alya helped me, as no one else could, with her criticism, her advice, her challenges, and did a lot to help me improve the clarity of my texts as well. When, in my work of many volumes, there were places where I had grown weary and become careless—and at my advanced age and with greater renown it was a real threat, that I would tire of polishing up my work as meticulously as before—she was demanding, insistent that I must improve those parts (she always sensed where they were) and suggested excellent alternatives. She replaced, for me, a whole audience of trusted readers, which it would have been hard to assemble as an émigré and quite unthinkable in this remote corner. As a one-man band, living in isolation, it would have been impossible to manage such a massive job adequately. Alya didn't allow me to lose my faculty of self-criticism. She subjected every phrase to scrutiny, as I did myself, and her eagle eye contributed to a last reworking of some phrases during the final typesetting. And, on top of all that, she had a brilliant memory. Despite the overwhelming proportions of the *Wheel*, she remembered the repetitions I had forgotten or failed to notice: she would not allow me to repeat myself. With Alya's brain and energy, she could have deployed her talents in social-development projects: she could grasp matters instantly, immediately get to the essence of a problem and its consequences, debate skillfully in public—but, for the time being, all that remained unnoticed, for the sake of my never-ending work, drawn in from the world.

In such a collaboration, assembling and typesetting my collected works was a pleasure—another important step in finishing, giving me a sense of total (or no, not yet total!) completion of the hurried labor of the last few years. Usually, collected works are typeset by distant compositors, and by that time the text is already set in stone. But, for us, page after page was born before our very eyes. Alya would bring them to me, or send them over with the children, in daily portions for my final read-through. As well as everything else, she has a strong graphic sense for the right fonts and their placing. A book would leave us in finished form—in France they'd just reshoot it to print.*

But Alya was not only helping me produce each book in the series and make it better—she put her heart and soul into each volume, and sometimes real passion, as in the interrogations of Bogrov,[29] the fates of leading, but doomed, figures, or the revolutionary writhing of *March*; and in the tense moments of my screenplay, *The Tanks Know the Truth*[30]—the uprising of the Kengir prisoners stoked a fire in her heart, as it did mine. (And would do all the more, with the choir heard above the heads of the tank crews crushing the insurgents, singing the menacing wartime song[31] that had pervaded her early years: "Arise, o vast and boundless land! / To mortal strife arise!" That was the war in which her father had perished. And then it turned out that, by the year she would be going into the eighth grade at school, that tune would find a new and twofold application—addressing both the *zeks*[32] and those crushing them: "Against the evil fascist band / Whom all the earth reviles!" And she was fiercely, selflessly devoted to *those* insurgents—she would never betray or forget them. And would it be possible to bring up our sons with that same loyalty through and through . . . ?)

In 1959, when I wrote the *Tanks* screenplay, I did not expect to see the film on screen in my lifetime. But later I did feel hopeful, very hopeful: how stunned the Western audience would be by our camp uprising, I thought. When still in the Soviet Union, I'd been anxious to start negotiating with Western directors. Now that I was in the West, I was desperately keen to get *Tanks* produced. But nothing came of it.

The first to set about it, with great enthusiasm, was that Czech émigré Vojtěch Jasný,[33] but he didn't have the resources for it. Then I received proposals from American companies and some individual filmmakers. I was not very good at all this, and at one point took the bait and concluded an agreement with a new Los Angeles company, Aurora, which turned out to have neither the experience nor the means to make the film—they just thought they could find funding on the basis of my name. Bruce Herschensohn started writing a shooting script. He had worked in the White House and was very accurate on the politics but not at all creative. He over-emphasized the political aspect, which would have tipped the film over into propaganda.

* And when the time came to be published in the USSR, the Soviet state publishers were only too happy to take our texts, already typeset: thus it was that they traveled the whole breadth of the country, which Alya had never expected beforehand. (Author's note, 1990.)

The company terminated his contract and engaged some Hollywood evaluation teams (madness: they grade screenplays using a points system to calculate how much American audiences will enjoy them), who demanded that, in my epic film without main characters, I single out two main heroes, lovers, add extra elements to the screenplay, and change the order of scenes. Since I was already bound by contract, would I really have to give in on this? It was Vladimir Telnikov that I engaged to do the work—a man with both literary taste and experience of life as a *zek*.

By that time I'd identified the dangers that could distort and destroy the film. The main one was not actually that specifically American cause of damage, the need to make the film entertaining, and neither was it even the danger of a political slant—but rather the fact that that slant would be anti-Russian. They wouldn't show it as it actually happened, as an initiative of many nationalities but with Russians playing the key role (the Ukrainians at Ekibastuz even turned their back on the uprising[34]). Instead, they'd show it as the uprising of various nationalities against the age-old Russian tyranny.

And I could not extricate myself now, fettered as I was by the contract. But the company went bust—they hadn't found the money. And the contract was annulled.

How I loved that film, and for years. How I hoped it would thunder onto the screen! But the screenplay was twenty years old now—and I had lost hope of seeing it produced in a foreign land. Indeed, in the American context there was no one who could have pulled it off, and the atmosphere would have been lost.

(When I was all the rage in the West, films were made of two of my works: a *First Circle* in Denmark [by Ford and Forbert], a total failure, and an honest, but far from perfect, Norwegian-British *Ivan Denisovich* with Tom Courtenay. Now an experimental short film has been added, *One Word of Truth*, set to the text of my Nobel Lecture.)[35]

By now I had thoroughly sobered up, detached myself, given up the idea of having the film made in the West, which was all the more reason to refuse several subsequent proposals to film *Archipelago*. Such a task was much harder still, and it couldn't have been accomplished without my sitting down to write the screenplay myself: it would, after all, have to be a fusion of documentary and art, documentary images and the interplay of actors. I would have to select episodes and put them in the right order, finding the right position for them all, reflecting the relative importance of each. But the main thing was not to lose its general tonality, not reduce it to pamphleteering, to make sure the overall spirit of *Archipelago*, cleansing, cathartic, was not lost.

Such a film must not be made here without my having authorial control over every stage. And that was quite impossible without sabotaging my most important work. I had to say no.

I also turned down a proposal with a better balance, from the artistic point of view, from Herbert Brodkin, producer of the celebrated television film *Holocaust*: he wanted to film "The White Kitten," the tale of Georgi Tenno's escape,[36] incorporating something of camp life as well. It was an intelligent idea. But here too I could not believe that they would render it all faithfully through an American prism. In Russia perhaps, some day.

But for all these years I felt a greater load on my shoulders than just that of my own books. I had been put in such a position, and so many threads were converging on me, that I felt I should—and it seemed it wouldn't be difficult, and would have been wrong not to—marshal at least a small group, whoever was available, to raise our scuttled Russian history up from the depths. I started to plan how we might begin to issue a series of works of history, inviting authors to contribute, and call it, for example, Studies in Modern Russian History[37]—it had to be the modern, because that had been the most neglected, and it was urgent. (This didn't mean that nineteenth-century Russia had been so perfectly researched either—that had also been impeded by the fervor of political division in its time.)

In the early years of emigration, immediately after the Revolution, it was, rather, memoirs and passionate political commentaries that were written, and if there were also attempts at research, at systematization, their goal was still self-justification (which is how even Pavel Milyukov ruined his works). Then World War II came along and caused massive confusion. The books of Vasili Maklakov and Sergei Melgunov stood out as rare successes (though in Melgunov's case, due to the straitened circumstances of his life, they were far from transparent—he'd not been able to leave them to sit for a while until things became clearer). But the Second Wave of émigrés remained silent for the most part, seeking to escape being handed over to the Bolsheviks by our treacherous Allies. Meanwhile, the decades were rolling on—when would all this be brought out of obscurity, have some light shed on it—and by whom? The time had long since come—and was long past!

But distorted, partisan yarns about Russia had been spun by critics as far back as the nineteenth-century *raznochintsy*,[38] then by all the political commentaries of the Liberation movement,[39] and before and after the Revolution by the socialist émigrés. Then they were taken up by Western scholars (it being a very easy stereotype), and now they'd been given a fresh look and stirred up by the rabid political commentators of the Third Wave. And I, finding myself hemmed about by all these lies, was dreaming of collecting together the remains (or the first fruits?) of an honest wing of Russian scholarship—and launching them into public view, supported by my name and by financing from our Fund. And publishing that series (from the very start I was thinking big) in several major languages.

But whom could we include? Those of the old émigrés who were fighting their way out of penury and holding their ground in the world of academia had all, immediately, started writing in foreign languages and were not lining up duplicates in Russian, for Russia's future. Now our lot would be bitter: we must translate their labors into Russian and, what's more, take pains as we did so to hunt down the original Russian quotes the authors used, not back-translating them into Russian from a foreign language. But when we looked round for deserving books of this kind, at first we could only find two: *A History of Liberalism in Russia*, by Viktor Leontovich, and *The February Revolution*, by Georgi Katkov. We received permissions to publish them in Russian.[40] (But the publishers weren't happy about granting those rights, in case they lost a chance of profits on the Russian editions—which were bound to be loss-making anyway—and this alone meant we had to give up the idea of adding in any foreign-language versions of the series.) Irina Ilovaiskaya, who had lived with us until 1979, translated the Leontovich from German, and part of the Katkov from English. (Finishing the Katkov translation and readying it for publication would require further work by several people over several years.) For the moment we could only start with these works of the earlier émigrés, having managed to acquire them. Professor Nikolai Andreev of Cambridge promised to write a book for us—but produced nothing. Ivan Kurganov, soon to breathe his last, and Sergei Pushkaryov, hale and hearty at ninety years of age, sent me extracts from their old, unpublished manuscripts, and some from new ones. But it was bloodless, weak—at best, we could compile from these fragments a volume of assorted pieces by several authors, and even then it would not glitter with scholarly revelations. And by the end of the '70s this was still all the historical scholarship that our Russian emigration had to show for itself. We could also, it's true, reprint yet again some articles from the Association of Russian-American Scholars anthologies, but those too were just odds and ends.

So even here, in freedom, did Russia still not have the capacity to reflect upon itself . . . ?

All we could do now was look for authors among the brand-new émigrés and give them "grants" for two or three years. From the very beginning Alya said she doubted (and she was right) that we'd manage to find, assemble, and persuade such a group of researchers. As for me, I felt this was my undoubted duty: to try and help Russian history as it lay in ruins—it was our obligation, plain and simple.

The first person we came across was Mikhail Bernshtam, a newly arrived dissident with a vigorous, agile brain. After some unpleasantness in the university milieu in Chicago—he had affronted them with his total rejection of all Soviet-Marxist discourse—Bernshtam was delighted to move to Vermont, into our neighborhood, for the lengthy project I proposed. The breadth of ideas and possibilities he revealed was staggering: he was ready to write works on economics, demographics, on the history of Lenin's party, the history of the Civil War anywhere in Russia, and on the genocide of the Don Cossacks. We encouraged him to stick to historical projects. He was an active user of the Dartmouth College university library—Dartmouth was a neighbor—and of its interlibrary loan service (of which I too was a frequent user, grateful and full of admiration for American libraries' precision and their riches). But when Bernshtam moved on to actually writing his works, despite his unmistakable talent and his wealth of local knowledge in various different areas, he perplexed us with the lack of clarity in his writing. Yet he passionately defended every passage we queried. And if you add to the list his inclination, at the beginning, to introduce trenchant political comments into his research—all of this together made the unavoidable, copious editing work with him extremely difficult. And who bore the brunt of it? Alya, of course: I did not have the patience for such work, nor could I divert my attention from the *Wheel* for that long. —After two years of this tumultuous collaboration, Bernshtam had compiled, in finished form, two very useful volumes of documents for the Studies in Modern Russian History series, about popular resistance to Communism in Russia: *The Independent Workers' Movement in 1918* (about how the Bolsheviks, once in power, immediately started oppressing the workers) and, also on a 1918 subject, *The Urals and the Prikamye.*[41] —And then we had to see about helping Bernshtam avoid getting stuck in a little Vermont town, which would be a dead end, and instead pursue his scholarly career. First we managed to secure a grant for him at the Kennan Institute in Washington. (There he would lean more and more towards demographics and economics and, by the way, it was there that he acquainted himself with the most recent demographic statistics for the USSR, which were *classified* for the time being by the US State Department, so as not to undermine *détente.* Already then he passed on to us the painful news that the biological degeneration of the three Slavic peoples might, by the end of the '80s, already be irreversible.) And later my status as an honorary fellow of the Hoover Institution helped us to procure, not without a struggle, a position for Bernshtam there, where—luckily—he was valued on his merits and was an immediate success.

Via the émigré network, through the person of our priest Father Andrew, a request reached us from the recently arrived, flat-broke, forty-year-old émigré Boris Paramonov—he needed setting up with some means of earning a living. His past, the fact that he'd spent his whole life working in a university Marxism-Leninism department, didn't do him any favors with us. When he came to see us and we talked, he seemed to me to be rather wishy-washy, without much substance to him, but certainly knowledgeable: he was prepared to write about anything at all, whatever we proposed, but what he felt most drawn to was a psychoanalytic study of writers' personalities. Among several themes that would have been possible for our Studies in Modern Russian History series, he proposed a *History of Conservative Thought in Russia.* We found that an enticing idea—to parallel Leontovich's already-published *A History of Liberalism in Russia.* All right—let him try. And we gave him a grant (to continue for about two years) from our Fund. But nothing came of it. His talent was for writing short articles, or rather essays, constructed around someone's stated premise, preferably paradoxical. But he could not stretch to constructing a book. He began with Nikolai I and then went on to the Slavophiles—and the chapters turned out to be labored, a disordered agglomeration, where the author's opinions went off in such different directions that they were sometimes even mutually exclusive. At first nothing could dent his self-confidence: he considered that any weaknesses were redeemed by his authorial *pen,* the animation of his phrasing, even when the view expressed was incoherent (and his view was always through a dense Freudian prism). But then he foundered on Chicherin and Mikhail Katkov—and gave up: he could not master the writing of that book.

Vladimir Telnikov, an ex-*zek* of the postwar period who had worked at the BBC since the early '70s, had written a good deal of his planned work on Russian nineteenth-century history. But because of the hardships of his émigré life, the book was not finished and did not get published.

There is also, living in New Jersey, an author close to us in his thinking, Aleksandr Serebrennikov. He has been engrossed in the secret history of Bolshevism for many years and has been excavating most thoroughly, mastering his sources with incomparable skill and finding new ones all the time, and writing detailed drafts of individual episodes—but he too, despite a great deal of persuasion and the help we've given him, has not turned his work into a single, finished book. (But his collaboration did turn out to be exceptionally helpful for *The Red Wheel*: he would unearth rare editions and even rarer, quite inaccessible pieces of information. Thus, for example, he enthusiastically "untangled" the story of Lenin in Poronino in 1914, establishing that Lenin did not serve time in any "prison"—there had not even been a prison there. Serebrennikov was sure it was in Poronino that Lenin had pledged to collaborate with the Austrian authorities, following which he had no trouble getting permission to travel to Switzerland. When the Soviet government came to power, Ganetsky went to Poronino to destroy some compromising documents that would have undermined the whole of Lenin's version of events. Serebrennikov brought us this discovery before we published our final version of the new *August 1914*, in 1983, and although I did not change it to follow his materials and didn't draw on his version, I did tweak my original text so as not to contradict it.[42] And Serebrennikov made even more sensational discoveries relating to the subversive activities of the Bolshevik "insurance workers," Anna Elizarova and others, in 1914–16.)

Never mind. We'd do as much as we could to continue our Studies in Modern Russian History series—though I had not foreseen what a very heavy editing load it would be and what a massive amount of time would be lost. It turned out to be very hard indeed to create a "study group" for Russian history. To do that we would need to be absolutely free of obligations and commit ourselves to it totally.

Another thing I had been thirsting to create ever since my arrival in the West was a Chronicle of Russian Emigration. The First Russian Emigration, brilliantly intellectual, had lived in the West for fifty years, fizzing with activity—debates, clubs, opposition groups, programs, books—and to me, from the depths of our Soviet existence, the idea of getting to know all about it had always seemed so exciting, so enticing! But now I'd arrived—everything had disappeared, half-effaced or fragmented, and there had been no conscientious, capable chronicler of that period. A hefty chunk of Russian culture had gone by and been extinguished—but the whole population of the Soviet Union, and especially today's young people, full of curiosity, have for all the decades of their lives been deprived by their Communist masters of any knowledge of the talented Russian émigrés—and, when the ventilation shafts do open, they will not receive, even from the émigrés themselves, any full, clear summary overview. And people will start putting one together at a stage when new events in Russia will be moving so fast that there won't be any time for it. Someone among the current thirty-year-olds will have to immerse himself, belatedly, in the old publications—and then the chronicle won't, in any case, be written by the time it's desperately needed. We Russians are astonishingly unconcerned, helpless, clumsy, shortsighted . . .

And yet the form of that chronicle was so clear in my mind: there would be several installments, 1917–20, 1921–24 (and so on, everything falling into meaningful four-year blocks, chronologically). Each would have information about the group of Russian émigrés in each country in the period it covered; an overview of organizations, cultural initiatives, newspapers, and journals; the main political and social steps taken in the period, with the main arguments of the different sides. . . . But nothing came of it. I had proposed my project to *Posev* and to YMCA-Press[43] and was trying to rope in Professor Nikolai Poltoratsky in Pittsburgh and Professor Alexis Klimoff (and he worked in our home in Vermont for two winter months, but other tasks of various kinds took him off on a different track).

There were no Russians to take on this work! Well, not enough, anyway.

We did manage to set something up, though—the All-Russian Memoir Library, which had already started to come together back in autumn 1977, after my appeal to émigrés,[44] though the response had not been as enthusiastic as I'd hoped: the Second Wave are apprehensive, frightened of writing memoirs, and the First Wave are fading away. But even so, many are sending them in. Some had already committed their recollections to paper, but not known whom to leave them to; some had not thought their memories worth writing down and lodging in archives, but now they wrote them for us.

To manage this archive and correspond with the authors, taking the place of Father Andrew Tregubov, whom did we find? A UN translator for many years, now retired and losing her sight, the émigré Nina Viktorovna Yatsenko, who lived not too far away, in New Hampshire, and came to us once a week.

Such is the dearth of Russian staff . . .

Our attempt to assemble an archive of recollections by the efforts of Russians alone was the third since emigration had begun, after the Prague archive, snatched by the Bolsheviks in 1945, and the Bakhmeteff Archive in New York, which Columbia University had grabbed in 1977.[45] (The Paris émigrés had not collected their own archive.)

I was constantly hearing reports about the Foreign Archive of the Okhrana,[46] which Vasili Maklakov had sent from Paris to the Hoover, and, more importantly, the Smolensk GPU[47] archive, which the Germans had removed from Smolensk and the Americans later took over (it included, for example, the affair of General Kutepov's abduction from Paris by the GPU). There had, it seemed, been a shortsighted decision to sell them off to the highest bidder. The blood of Russian history was draining into the sand.

I was on the point of rushing to the defense of these archives, but not only would it have been intolerable to abandon my work, my writing—it would also have entailed establishing all the true details of these misappropriations. And also: what Americans would have any interest in a story of lost Russian archives?

Something we could try, which was within our capacity, was to take as a basis our All-Russian Memoir Library and the recollections of people alive at the time of the Revolution that had been sent to us before, and start to publish a Memoir series[48] of the most powerful of these. Financing the loss-making publication of the series (with the émigré book market collapsing under the weight of unsold books) was not the hardest part for us. The main thing was this: how were we to tighten up, slim down these messy, absentminded, repetitive recollections, written by old people losing their strength, approaching their end? Who would do it? Alya again—her incisive editorial skills would save the day. She retailored, with firmer seams, the disjointed and highly repetitive recollections of Nikolai Volkov-Muromtsev, with their constant returns to what had already been said and frequent additions (though not contradicting each other in a single detail). And she did not lose any of the gems in his account of a childhood on the Griboyedov family's Khmelita estate. —And then there were several volumes of the memoirs of Vasili Klementiev—I had urged him to write down these unique recollections, about the anti-Bolshevik underground in Moscow in 1918 and the Taganka and Butyrka prisons in 1918–20—but he'd got carried away, wanting to turn his account into high literature. So again it needed editing down to the plain facts. But there was no time—we'd put it off till later.

Time . . . time . . . Where could we find it? Alya was torn: she had four sons being brought up in a foreign land—and she must give them a rich, unscathed language and keep them Russian. And all the worries with the Fund and the plotting to transfer so many thousands of Soviet rubles to the USSR. As well as that, there was the clandestine correspondence with Moscow and, therefore, with every single link in the chain of go-betweens; she was a fountain of burning compassion for our people there, gratitude to our caring helpers, and vigilance over every detail—she must provide for every eventuality and be circumspect about the way she phrased her letters, so that even if a letter came to grief no one would come to grief with it. Alya would lose sleep from the tension over a packet of these letters, for they always had to be put together rapidly, so suddenly did the opportunities to send them present themselves. But for that same Fund there were also annual accounts and activity reports to be done for the Swiss authorities, itemizing how many of the people we helped were under investigation, how many convicted, how many exiled, what help we had given the families, including help for journeys to meet family members now far away and give them parcels, and how much went to the children. And apart from the figures we also needed documents justifying the expenses, to the extent that this was possible—and these were the most difficult of all for our administrators to produce, preserve, and hold on to until the next chance to pass them on to us.

And as well as that she had to mount, in the West, a public defense of the administrators of our Fund in the USSR. Our constant Achilles' heel was the Fund administrators over there. Now Alya (with the indispensable help of Irina Ilovaiskaya) had, for two whole years, been running a vigorous campaign in the States and beyond, in Europe, for the defense of Alik Ginzburg, who had been arrested. And with no way of influencing the Soviet leaders and great difficulty in touching Western hearts, by an incredible miracle Ginzburg was successfully freed. But would the KGB leave our Fund in peace? There were sinister rumors emanating from the USSR about the Fund: after Ginzburg's arrest there had been a rapid succession of administrators, and then his wife Arina had taken over his post. But she'd been very shaken by threats from KGB plants, by people passing on advice from dissident circles, or by those acting out of plain envy, others for mercenary ends, and some simply suspicious about what was going on in that Fund. And it was indeed unheard-of for an organization of this kind to have been operating for eight years now in the Soviet Union without being throttled! No surprise, then, that there was so much disarray. But Alya and I came up with the idea that I should step in now: I would, from here, write an open letter to those wishing harm to our Fund and send it into the Soviet Union by a clandestine route and distribute it there as a piece of new-style samizdat.[49] So that's what we did. **[25]*** And for some time this appeal got passed around, and to some extent it helped.

Then they started harassing the next administrator, Sergei Khodorovich. He was doing the right thing, not repeating the earlier mistake of getting directly involved in dissident matters. He steered clear of politics, only doing

* Bold number signifies the corresponding appendix at the end of this volume. (Editor's note.)

his work for the Fund. But he too was being intimidated by thugs with knives (KGB hired hands); and sometimes the militia would beat him up, sometimes search his flat, and sometimes detain him in solitary confinement and hypnotize him, trying to find out the routes used to deliver the money. The KGB had been snapping at our heels for the last eight years, but never caught us out. Now, we thought, that was it—they'd arrested Khodorovich. But no, two weeks later he was released, for the time being. (In January 1981, during that most worrying period when he was detained, we had to make an urgent statement. I wrote it[50] and Alya hurried to circulate it—but a Third Wave émigré in the New York office of the BBC, one Kozlovsky, *refused* to take the statement: you just want to *distract attention* from the anniversary of Sakharov's exile![51] What a warped way of thinking.) Khodorovich has behaved with remarkable self-control and diplomacy. But God forbid that he should be snatched again and Alya have to start another desperate campaign to defend him. Where would she go? How would she do it? (And in general, how long would we be able to stand our ground in the USSR against the KGB? . . .) At the end of 1981 I made another statement[52] about Khodorovich, to warn the Lubyanka[53] that I was keeping a close eye on him.

And then, suddenly: somewhere in the Tver region, under the heavy Soviet paw, an intrepid geophysicist, Iosif Dyadkin, popped up with his calculations of the many millions of people exterminated in the USSR—and the figures were very convincing. He was, of course, immediately arrested. It was our duty to defend him, and in May 1980 I appealed to Western sociologists and demographers to intercede on behalf of their colleague.[54] But Dyadkin also managed to get a request through to us to find an independent Western expert to evaluate his statistics. And how were we to find (without leaving Vermont) such an expert in New York or Washington? And, so that the expert could appraise Dyadkin's work, ensure that it was translated into English by a qualified translator? And, at some juncture, find a publisher for it? So it was translated by Tatiana Deryugina (the widow of émigré writer Vladimir Varshavsky), who had stepped in with us for Irina Ilovaiskaya following the latter's departure to Paris. And here again Ludmilla Thorne helped enormously:[55] engaging an expert from Harvard University, finding a publisher, generating a campaign in American newspapers, editing the book, then herself proofing the galleys and writing her own foreword. In 1983 the book came out.[56] —And on top of that, Alya is responding to the many afflictions of people totally unknown to her—and that has drained more and more energy from the thrust of our main work. And there are her parish obligations and her domestic load. . . . She's lost a lot of her physical strength and she's lost heart, I see her hair greying prematurely.

In the Soviet Union we were indigent, but we lived differently: altruistic, fearless individuals (and there was something to fear—prison!) just came running from all sides to help. But over here we're jinxed: all Alya and I would have needed was a third person—but someone as capable and tireless as we are—to collaborate in our literary endeavor, and it would have taken off with a whole new élan. But for all these years there's been no such third person. No third pair of eyes, on Alya's level, to notice and decide, to correct and print. (Will any of the children grow into that person? And when might that be?)

No workers! No collaborators! No allies! This is the state of Russian emigration now—soft, no resilience. Could it be the same with other nationalities? Or is it just the Russians who've petered out like this and grown so improverished?

All the more steadfast, then, proudly holding out for so many years, are the tiny White Guard journals, Orekhov's *Chasovoi* (*Sentinel*); *Nashi Vesti* (*Our News*), the journal of the old Russian Corps in Yugoslavia; and *Cadetskaya Pereklichka* (*Cadet Roll-Call*)—yes, those same cadets,[57] youngsters during the Civil War. And even the *Vestnik Obshchestva Veteranov Velikoi Voiny* (*Bulletin of the Society of Veterans of the Great War*)—that's the 1914–17 war—isn't giving up! The unalloyed monarchists of *Nasha Strana* (*Our Country*) in Argentina are holding on, naïvely waiting for the return of the Romanov dynasty after the Bolsheviks go. Their voice is weak—they know their readership is small, just a few kindred spirits—and as for muscle, they have none. In actual fact, none of these publications has a front to defend, because no "cultural" journals bother to oppose them. They are unread and unnoticed.

Some tried (it was the old Solovki *zek* Khomyakov) to set up a journal for Russians everywhere, *Russkoye Vozrozhdenie* (*Russian Renaissance*)—and I helped as much as I could—but the synod of the Russian Orthodox Church Abroad itself emasculated it—through synodical censorship directing it towards diocesan preaching and away from burning social issues.

Veche (*Assembly*), a Munich-based Russian nationalist journal, started work with great gusto but, in its enthusiasm, saddled itself with the legacy of Osipov's earlier *Veche* (which was sullied by its attempts to find a common language with the Soviet government). And after three issues they discovered that they had neither authors nor secure transmission channels from the homeland. It was just the journal of yet another émigré group.

Vera Pirozhkova's *Golos Zarubezhiya* (*Voice of the Abroad*) is fighting to survive, very staunch, even fossilized in its anti-Communism—to the extent of total disbelief that any kind of beneficial development could ever occur within the confines of the USSR, and a belief that if there were to be a dissident or a trades union movement it would have to be a KGB ploy. From those under Soviet rule they were expecting—and demanding—just one thing: a revolution. —And if that didn't happen? What would be left?

From issue to issue it's subjected to ferocious criticism from the *Svobodnoye Slovo Karpatskoi Rusi* (*Free Word of Carpathian Rus'*), the journal of the Russians in Carpathia (all ardent Russian patriots), which has now been seized by a few shady émigrés of "nationalist orientation" from the USSR. Diametrically opposed to Pirozhkova, they're confidently proclaiming that it's actually the Bolsheviks who speak for today's Russia, and that Russia, even under the Bolsheviks, even if they don't get overturned, is entering a joyful renaissance. To people like that, I am always a nuisance, and their ferocity towards me—now with the opposite accusation, that I'm selling Russia out to the Jews, that I'm the main traitor—can be surprisingly impassioned. My defense of the term "Russian" as opposed to "Soviet" is "a sledgehammer to crack a nut," they say; and "*The Gulag Archipelago*—that's yesterday's Russian history"; "Live Not by Lies"—that was "a con, swindling a brutish breed"; it meant I was setting myself up "in opposition to the current government, and as a result honest, decent people will be left out in the cold and our children will not go to university." "The Elders of Zion are guiding Solzhenitsyn for their own destructive, anti-Christian ends." (This is how a united front against me was formed, from left to right, from Sinyavsky to Sinyavin.)

And from a few issues of all these journals you quickly notice how few of them have even ten writers—sometimes only four or five, who fill up issue after issue with their lackluster efforts. In actual fact, the whole of that émigré workforce would, together, barely furnish the copy for a single substantial journal, rich in content.

But *Posev* (*Sowing*), the political organ of the People's Labor Alliance, stands apart. (When it first saw the light of day, in the '20s, its title was "National Labor Alliance," giving prominence to the Russian theme—but then, embarrassed, it changed its name. They were also, of course, seeking financial support.) The NTS[58] has managed to develop a kind of intelligence network, even under the heavy hand of the KGB, and has limited but active connections in the mother country—which is why *Posev* today gives us the most "Russian" reading experience in the West, offering authentic, lively reporting of news from the homeland, laying bare its problems. The journal is now less occupied with the task of engineering a revolutionary coup, and has transferred its attention to the building of a Russian future with high moral standards. (Generally speaking, the NTS, created fifty years ago and at one time modelling its battle tactics on Leninism, has in recent years begun to wobble in its policy of inciting revolution in the USSR and "taking over power from the weakening hands of the CPSU,"[59] which they used to proclaim. They've understood that a revolution would totally destroy the country and now they are using different tactics to seek out "constructive forces" in the ruling levels of the USSR—are there any?—and they consider themselves, quite rightly, as only a part of such constructive forces.) —Another NTS journal, *Grani* (*Facets*), not having its own circle of literary contributors, is an eclectic mix, a large proportion filled by Third Wave émigrés, some seeking answers, others just looking to be published.

Vestnik RSKhD (*Messenger of the Russian Student Christian Movement*) has, overall, a far higher spiritual level than all the rest of today's émigré journalism: until the channels for sending it were closed down, it had been eagerly read in free-thinking circles in Moscow, and it has retained, from that period, a few routes for getting manuscripts out of the USSR, which gives the journal a marked vitality. It has a very strong religious (reformist) content as well as general culture. But any sense of Russian consciousness is barely discernible. The content of the journal (predominantly theology and the literary archive of the Silver Age[60] and the First Wave émigrés) made it hard for it to be at the center of exchanges on current social issues—only in the '70s did Nikita Struve resolutely surmount this barrier. But in getting involved in these kinds of disputes, he had several times thrown caution to the winds and strayed from his chosen path. (I sent him my objections. But all the same, in emigration there is no journal which accords more closely with my ideas.)

And what about *Kontinent* (*Continent*)? I myself suggested that idea to them, of bringing together the intellectual forces of Eastern Europe. And it has been largely successful. But I've found in it barely a single one of the traditional subjects of Russian interest, such as the current tribulations of the provinces, the countryside, the elimination of the peasantry, the Orthodox faith, the prisoners taken in the Soviet-German war and their repatriation, and a subject that's even more deeply rooted: that of Russian history and tradition. I told Maximov, the editor, that his venture had not, as far as the Russian theme was concerned, been successful. *Kontinent* could have done without publishing Aleksandr Yanov's ham-fisted exercises in Russian history or, without being tempted by parody and gags, could have resisted the urge to eulogize worthless books in reviews or to disfigure its back covers with pseudo-artistic works; it could, in general, have retained a more stringent profile. But, come to think of it, with such a massive expanse of print in his journal, how was Maximov to choose his authors? He had, unwittingly, drifted into a kind of whirlpool, into the hurry-scurry and sickly ferment of the Third Wave émigrés, crazed by their new freedom of speech. (They write things like: "The Third Emigration has a providential purpose.") They have no obligation to say anything profound or responsible to anyone—and what else could a journal (also offering attractive fees) do, in the midst of this seething political cauldron? *Kontinent*'s prose has, over its seven years, delivered very few successes, and is sometimes staggering in its absurdity, eccentricity, and its efforts somehow to make an unusual impression. And then you sense that it's leaving the main path of literature. Yet we should thank Maximov for his impeccable perseverance, holding the line against the Bolsheviks (though, incidentally, sometimes publishing not particularly penitent Soviet authors), against shortsighted Western radicals and against the trashiness of Russian-language radio broadcasts in the West. (And despite *Kontinent*'s overall sentiments, it can also find room for a telegram to a long-term prisoner, Igor Ogurtsov.)

During the First Wave of emigration, up to the Second World War, the living centers of social dialogue were the newspapers—in Europe alone, and only counting the main ones, there were three: the Kadets' *Poslednie Novosti* (*Latest News*), *Rul* (*Helm*), and the more right-wing *Vozrozhdenie* (*Renaissance*), as well as the only thick, literary journal of the time, *Sovremenniye Zapiski* (*Contemporary Annals*)—with strong Socialist Revolutionary leanings. With the war (and in some cases even earlier) they all came to an end. *Vozrozhdenie* was then reactivated in Paris, as a journal—but was not at all influential, or even read. There were also other attempts at various times, but that would be the subject of the Chronicle of Emigration.

Across the ocean, following *Sovremenniye Zapiski*, *Novy Zhurnal* (*New Review*) began publication—and it was still, in the '50s, full of life, with occasional issues finding their way into the USSR, where we read them with great interest. Since then, however, the ageing and dying of its authors (and readers) has begun to tell on *Novy Zhurnal*, and it has been brushed aside totally by the Third Wave émigrés. Miraculously, Roman Gul still brings it out regularly, and it maintains a decent standard—but it is being undermined by inertia, and finds itself at some distance from the burning issues of people's lives.

In the States, thanks to the efforts of immigrants from Russia, the *Novoye Russkoye Slovo* (*New Russian Word*) had already sprung up before the Revolution. Even today it's still holding its own commercially and, being practically the only one for the large number of Russian émigrés here, it has for many years also been the natural, common anti-Communist platform and source of news, even—since there was no other choice—for those who did not agree with the newspaper's other peculiarities. After the war the paper was reinforced by opening up its pages to the ranks of the Second Wave. But in recent times it has opened up even more to the Third—and, to compete with the Third Wave newspapers now appearing, adopted the vulgar style of newspaper ads, and even their sleaziness—and, in its reporting of the news, from the very first page the negligence and the brazenness jump out at you.

In Europe after the Second World War the émigrés could no longer find the manpower to publish their own newspaper. *Russkaya Mysl* (*Russian Thought*) then appeared—but it was supported by the American government, which for the editor, Sergei Vodov and later Zinaida Shakhovskaya, made the policy clearer during the Cold War years and more problematic with "détente." In 1979 Irina Ilovaiskaya took the paper over. But it was not possible—for her or for anyone else—to keep it up to a standard appropriate to its name. Several times she had dared publish large photos of old Russian churches that had been demolished or disfigured, and she'd made a great deal of the centenary of Aleksandr II's murder—whereupon the freedom-loving "pluralists" Etkind, Sinyavsky, and Lyubarsky immediately produced a typical political denunciation and sent it to some American body, saying the newspaper was showing dangerous leanings towards nationalism and monarchy. I gave the paper an extract from my writing on Stolypin for the seventieth anniversary of his murder. This time Irina Alekseevna did not venture to accompany it with a portrait of Stolypin, as I had asked—for he had been cursed in every possible way. (And how! On Radio Liberty they removed my already-recorded broadcast on Stolypin entirely; on the Voice of America—was it a slip-up?—they read seven minutes of my Stolypin chapter and cut out the rest.) And it goes without saying that the ambitious Third Wave types are pushing, forcing their way into *Russkaya Mysl* as well, with all sorts of printed rubbish, at times penned in the most mediocre style. You only get a sense of the ranks of earlier émigrés on the obituary page and in the occasional reprints of émigré publications a half century old. No one is surprised any more that in *Russkaya Mysl*, whose overview of journals now includes new Third Wave magazines such as *Vremya i My* (*Time and Us*) and *22*, there is never the slightest whisper, not even in passing, of the Russian émigré press surviving since the '20s.

What kind of nation are we, if our brilliant diaspora—a million and a half strong, maybe two—is dying, appearing to have borne no fruit? Even our Church is split into three.[61] Clearly, we are not able to hold out when dispersed—and it's a defect in the Russian spirit: we become weak when not close together, in serried masses (and being told what to do).

After sixty years we have no real strength: Russians abroad are being absorbed into alien soil, bringing up an alien generation. (How could I have failed to see that or divine it in my first summer in Switzerland, when I got carried away with dreams of a "Russian University"?[62])

Two million Russians, but there might as well be none. . . . And we cannot hope that "in time our creative forces will grow"—our creative forces can only grow weaker and be snuffed out. Let's just give thanks that they have preserved, for a few decades at least, the citadel of Russian culture.

No, Russia's salvation will not come from émigrés (it never does come from émigrés). It can only come from whatever Russia itself does within its borders.

And what is it doing? This is a characteristic of ours, acquired after the Petersburg and the Soviet periods: we are not united, we lack independent initiative, and we wait for a powerful hand to bring us together. We're the same at home as in diaspora, aren't we . . .

It has been eight years since I was banished. Through the Communist carapace nothing can be seen, heard, or guessed at. But even so, our friends, my co-authors on *From Under the Rubble*, found a way to speak out again, publicly. In issue 125 of *Vestnik RKhD*, they continued the polemic, countering all the attacks against us. But they did not have the strength to do more: who could withstand the decades of being ground down in the Soviet Union? —Could Igor Ogurtsov, most likely on his last legs, who stoically served his fifteen years and was then thrown into deepest exile in the Ust-Vym taiga, withstand it? (And even then, *Russkaya Mysl* would mark the end of his massive term in a footnote.) Or similarly Vladimir Osipov, who was surviving, still standing, through his second eight-year term? Leonid Borodin has returned unbroken from the camps, with his healthy, constructive patriotism and undoubted literary talent. (And his novellas and novels, too, are going into samizdat—where else could they go . . . ?)

Out from under that same carapace, packets of long-awaited clandestine letters from close friends arrive—and the wind of our homeland blows from each little, compactly written page. Once in a while, someone breaks out to the West—Mikhail Polivanov for a mathematics congress. When he writes, it's like balm to my heart. There appears to be no one there, in Russia, nothing happening, yet the water ripples along under the ice—oh, how it ripples! Suddenly, Dmitri Likhachyov's pamphlet *Reflections on the Russian Soul* broke through. Suddenly last autumn they let literary critic Igor Zolotussky go to Milan for a Blok symposium, where he spoke articulately on Gogol's *Correspondence*, which had turned Blok's life in his last months. More ripples—things are coming, unseen, to fruition. And it is only by the guidance of our soul that we can divine and maintain our link with that process.

And with each snippet, Alya feels ever more pain from our living "nowhere." She says it's torture to her when a local train station in the Moscow suburbs comes to mind so clearly, with the little path she knows by heart leading away from it, plowed up by vein-like pine roots. But we also receive potent greetings from our homeland with the abundant snow in Vermont—there's even more of it than in Central Russia. Alya loves the snow—it bewitches and comforts her. The winters here in Vermont are enveloped in it. (But although there's forest all around us, we can't ski: the slopes are too steep, with tangles of undergrowth.)

The main, the decisive processes are, of course, taking place in our homeland, no matter how much they are suppressed or frozen out. And I am losing the opportunity to have some influence today on the direction the next generations will take. But how very many young people are misguidedly striving to pick up the overfed West's leftovers—how alluring that seems to them. What will they grow into? We'll pay dearly for that as well.

And as if this wasn't enough, the villages of Central Russia are being devastated, dying—but how can I intervene, from here? And now those crazed Bolsheviks have had the idea of turning our northern rivers around to flow southwards, drowning our age-old, our archetypal Russian North in the vain hope of saving the harvest in the South—which was destroyed by their own collectivization. It makes me livid. How can we rein that gang in? What force can we rely on, and where is it? There's no such force in the world.

Due to inherent aversion, I do not read the Soviet press. But sometimes people send me clippings and I read them—and begin to ache with melancholy. The decades do not pass for the Communist authorities—they don't change an iota of their phraseology, of their deadened spirit. No, until they're broken, they won't change.

But the definite hope that's visible on the surface of Soviet life—despite everything, it's the "village prose" writers, who are a continuation now, under the Soviet yoke, of our traditional Russian literature. The brilliant Shukshin is dead, but there are still Astafiev, Belov, Mozhaev, and Evgeni Nosov. They're holding their ground, not giving up. And suddenly we see the rapid, confident development of Valentin Rasputin, with such compassion, and such penetration into the essence of things. (And Soloukhin, who'd grown limp in the upper literary echelons, is slowly getting bolder.) It is now over a decade, and the village prose writers are holding on and still writing. And despite occasional officially required inserts or omissions, the authentic tongue, the current debased life of the people, and moral standards that are not those of the authorities all course through their books.

Once, in *Kontinent*, the émigré critic Yuri Maltsev, partially in response to my praise of the village prose writers, came down on them like a ton of bricks. They lie, he said, do not reveal the true situation in that society, and this is not, therefore, real literature. When I read this, I recognized that I too had once thought that way, that without the full social truth it was not literature. Yes, of course the village prose writers do not give us the full truth, and in that respect they are betraying the nineteenth-century tradition. But they are also striking a blow against sixty-five years when all Russian feeling has been trampled underfoot in our homeland. What other branch of literature has better followed that tradition? And if one were to guide a book into a purely moral course, what would that be? would it not be literature?

There is also the one-of-a-kind, promising Georgi Vladimov, who has a good writing style, polished. And the brilliantly talented playwright Mikhail Roshchin. And there are poets' names that traverse the Soviet mire, shining out intermittently: Chichibabin, Chukhontsev, Kublanovsky. (And there are considerable achievements in the "urban" and "intelligentsia" literature as well, some names worth attention.)

When I was serving my time in the camps, still under Stalin, how did I picture the Russian literature of the future, after Communism? Luminous, skillful, powerful, dealing with the ills of the people and all the suffering since the Revolution! And I could only dream of being worthy of that literature and becoming a part of it.

And now celebrated Russian men of letters have come pouring out, emigrated, finally freed themselves of hateful censorship, and society here does not ignore but supports them—with plenty of publishers and editions, with vivid covers and novel designs, with advertising and with translations. So now they'll roll out a top-notch literature for us!

But what's this? Even those (and there aren't many of them) who have now started denouncing the regime from outside, in safety, even they are not letting out a squeak about the adjustments *they themselves* had made to cozy up and be helpful to the regime—the lies in books, plays, film scripts, and volumes of the Ardent Revolutionaries series that they'd written over there, in exchange for favors from the Literary Fund of the Union of Soviet Writers. There is no repentance—a sure sign that their literature is shallow.

No, those emancipated men of letters—with some launching into smut and even into literally obscene language, obscenities in abundance—are like mischievous little boys using their first taste of freedom to pick up swear words in the gutter. (As the émigré Avtorkhanov said, *there* it was written on lavatory walls, *here*—in books.) From that, if nothing else, we can judge of their creative impotence. Others—there are more of these—have gone for no-holds-barred sex. A third group has opted for *self-expression*, a buzzword and the supreme vindication of their literary activity. What a pathetic principle. "Self-expression" does not presuppose self-restraint, either in society or before God. And is there in fact anything to "express"? (That word has already become fashionable even in the USSR.)

And the fourth sign, to add to all that, is a florid, extravagant, and empty avant-gardism, intellectualism, modernism, postmodernism, and who knows what other -isms. It's aimed at the most fastidious "elite." (And for some reason it's the most vocal disciples of democracy who surrender to these "elitist" impulses; but as for widely accessible art, the thought of it is repugnant to them. Yet Gustave Courbet, back in 1855, was already saying that "realism is the democratic art.")

So was it *this* unruly creativity that Soviet censorship had been holding back? In which case the censorship steamroller had hardly been worth the trouble for the Communists, who'd actually been expecting a spirit of antagonism, hostile to them.

And why had that kind of tripe not done the rounds in samizdat? Because samizdat is strict on artistic quality—it simply would not make the effort to disseminate lightweight rubbish.

And what about the language? What language is it all written in? Although this literature has termed itself "Russian-language," it is not Russian language proper, but jargon—it sounds revolting. It is, more than anything, the Russian *language* that they have betrayed (though some of them even swear allegiance to exactly that, the Russian language).

They've been granted free speech—but have nothing substantial to say. They've freed themselves of their external restraints but as for inner inhibitions—they've turned out to have none. Instead of a literature rising from the dead, it's an obscene verbiage that's been disgorged. The men of letters are disporting themselves. (But the estimable Vladimir Maximov stands dignified, apart, in the émigré literature of the late '70s.) It's a different kind of decadence from that under the cover of Bolshevism—but it is decadence. What responsibility do they bear before Russia's future, before its young people? This "free" literature is shameful; it cannot be compared to Russia's former literature. It has no backbone: it is sickly, stillborn, deprived of *simplicity*—an element as natural as the air we breathe and without which there is no great literature.

But it wasn't enough for them—going off into their different corners, writing, and then being freely published. Now they hanker after literary conferences ("a red-letter day for Russian literature," as a New York newspaper had it), to expatiate more loudly about themselves and measure their own growing shadows against the lackluster background of traditional Russian literature, too bogged down in moral endeavors and with, alas, an underdeveloped aestheticism—an asset which, as it happens, the current generation possesses in abundance. Is it from the Union of Soviet Writers that they've inherited the idea that the more often they gather at literary conferences for some empty gossip, the more their literature will blossom? Last spring they assembled in Los Angeles, close to Hollywood, and this spring it's in Boston. And all their pronouncements say that authentic culture now exists only in emigration, and that the "second literature" of the Third Wave is a life-giving force. (The second cul-de-sac off 5th Street, more like . . .) But even here Sinyavsky cannot hold back from promoting his political stance. Again he's talking about the "frightening danger of Russian nationalism," his faithful hobbyhorse of many years, almost his specialty; and, what's more, this top aesthete travels the world giving lectures on that "frightening danger."

But now a terrifying thought: might that not also be the model for a future "free Russian literature" in the mother country? . . .

It is only now, with Russian literature so depopulated and the Third Wave enjoying its saturnalia, that I see, with growing understanding, how much we have lost with Tvardovsky, how much we are missing him now, what a great figure he would have been for us today! At a time when I was embittered from my struggle with the Soviet regime and blind to everything except the barriers of censorship, Tvardovsky already saw that the future dangers that might corrupt our literature did not come down to censorship alone. Tvardovsky had a calm immunity to "avant-gardism," to fake innovation, to spiritual decay. Now, when pretentious émigré literature has begun to slide into narcissism, capriciousness, and licentiousness, we can appreciate all the more Tvardovsky's delicacy at *Novy Mir*, his taste, his sense of responsibility and moderation. Already at that time—but I hadn't understood this—yet another conflict was taking shape: Tvardovsky was fighting off a rising tide of irresponsibility towards both our art and our nation. I could only see that the people surrounding him were all true Communist believers; I didn't see that he was holding back a flood of alien trends (although he was not totally successful in this). With the breakthrough of *Ivan Denisovich*, Tvardovsky prevented the literary thaw from flowing into works with a Revolutionary Democracy orientation or dealing exclusively with the prison torments of educated, urban types. I was so fired up by my battle with the regime that I was losing sight of a national vision and could not understand back then how much Tvardovsky, a Russian of peasant stock and an enemy of "modernist" tricks—which at that time were still keeping a low profile—had done, and how far he'd gone. He could sense in advance the right way for literature: he was alert before I was to the current cacophony. And it is only now, after so many years of solitude—away from my homeland and away from the émigré circle—that I've seen Tvardovsky in yet another new light. He was a warrior hero, like those of folk legend, one of the few to have borne a Russian national consciousness through the Communist wilderness—but I had not fully recognized his attributes or my own future task. I had already then been sent the best ally, the one who would go furthest, but I didn't have the time to help him free his spirit and clear his path. Our sick literature is just getting back on its feet—how much more help, what a leg up his strong hands could give us now!

But he was disoriented and ground down by forty cruel, cursed Soviet years—the entire span of his literary life; all his force was lost to them.

* * *

Given my fruitful writing in these recent years, I had absolutely no inclination to intervene in anything—really! I used to say, quite sincerely, that I was not a political figure. And that's even when I would have been speaking in my own country, in my native language, to fellow-countrymen who'd have understood me, addressing fundamental needs, feeling I was part of the process taking place. But when you announce something to foreign news agencies or write an article for a weekly magazine, your first thought is: what question of using rich Russian style can there be, and to what end?—for it will all, instantly, be wiped out in the translation (and you're lucky if that doesn't go for the meaning as well). So you deplete your language automatically, in advance, and your writing is drab.

And this too: as soon as something happens somewhere, it's like a bump swelling up, and the agencies rush to get my point of view—but it will only last five minutes, and after that there's another bump somewhere else, and the first one is totally forgotten. The media go all out for news value, not profundity. But for me to write even the tiniest public statement I must find a solid chunk, a fusion of thought and feeling, great concentration, commitment, and the upending of my entire being. It's impossible for me to tear myself away all the time from my massive work project and keep expending superhuman efforts on something else.

And, on top of that, every foray into political commentary immediately provokes a string of reactions and letters, greatly exceeding my own lines in volume—and what am I to do? answer them? (I'm surprised it hasn't yet occurred to the Americans to pass a law saying everyone *has the right* to an answer—to go along with the personal right to "know everything." With a law like that I'd be sweating over answers to thousands of letters and there'd be no getting back to literature.)

And another thing: even though I'm "out of fashion" in the West, an avalanche of invitations has been descending on me for all these years—in countless numbers. Invitations to speak, to come and accept a prize or an honorary degree, to send a message of greetings to a conference, to a gathering (and even if you answer in a simple letter a little more clearly, they're immediately publicizing it as a greeting). There are hundreds of invitations, never fewer than twenty in a month, most of them from within the States (and, on top of that, appeals on someone's behalf, supported by a senator), but also from South America, Asia, Europe, and circles with links to the Vatican. In Europe they also like to have discussions, but in the States they're especially keen: it's their life, gathering round tables with a motley array of foodstuffs, giving speeches. I rarely write the refusals myself—usually Leonard DiLisio does it on my behalf. If I answered myself it would dry the writing juices out of my hand, for each answer is exactly the same: I am busy, I cannot interrupt my work, I do not go to any events. But people have never tired of sending them, and sending them again, telegrams and express letters, new ones from all over the place. It goes on and on. And there are, of course, some very worthwhile invitations—to become an honorary member of the Scottish Academy of Sciences, for instance, or the Bavarian Academy of Fine Arts—but I'd have to be, on the exact appointed day, in Edinburgh or in Munich. Am I to tear myself away and go? Quite impossible, just as it would have been to travel from Zurich to Oxford[63]—devastating for my work. —Or I'm invited by an old organization (dating from 1913), the Knights of Lithuania, to their congress in America, to receive the Friend of Lithuania medal. I am indeed a friend of Lithuania, and have been fond of Lithuanians since the camps—but if I didn't say no in this case, neither could I in a dozen others—and it would take eight hours by car to get there. So no, I refuse. And on top of that, people send me manuscripts and books in all sorts of languages (even Polish and Serbian) for me to write forewords for the former and offer opinions on the latter.

Many of the invitations are interview proposals—for newspapers, radio, and television. (Or else they're requests for me to give a magazine, or even just a particular reporter, some kind of clarification on an incidental matter—and for this he would be "ready and willing" to come and visit me. . . .) If you're nice to them—they'll descend and tear you to pieces. . . . For an interview I have to turn my attention away from the history of the Revolution towards contemporary political matters and destroy the whole rhythm of my literary work; it's too painful.

But there can also be some really explosive moments. In August 1980 the Polish workers' strikes flared up—and how plucky they were: the authorities were already making concessions on the bread-and-butter issues, but the strikers didn't stop there! they made political demands! That little patch of earth, so easily crushed—but they were standing proud! (If only we could do the same!) People who'd seen it on European television told us that the workers were holding themselves as upright and dignified as if at a church service. One time Alya and I were listening to the latest radio broadcast about them and she said, eyes aglow, "Cable them a greeting!" And I immediately agreed. We could at least call out to the Poles our Russian fellow-feeling. And within an hour Alya was phoning it through to the news agencies and the Voice of America.[64]

But by December that same year, 1980, there was more: it looked as if Soviet troops were about to enter Poland at any minute. And how could I stay silent *then*? Not that I was hoping to stop them—that wasn't in our power—but it was our duty to cry out, to tell them we were different, that it was the Communists, not the Russians, not us, bearing the shame of this outrage. When the tanks moved in, no one was going to listen to a Russian voice, there'd be no clearing our name then. I hurried to make a new statement.[65]

(But the Voice of America—this was still the Carter era—lost its nerve and toned it down. They could not utter such audacious sentiments into the ear of the Soviet Communists: instead of "the murderous heirs of Lenin," they broadcast "the Soviet Union"; and instead of "how many peoples, their own and others, will be ground up or besmirched in that bloodbath," it was "how many people will die if there is an invasion." They supplanted my words entirely, those seasoned diplomats. Incidentally, with Reagan's arrival, the station became markedly more confident.)

And for another year after that, with a sinking heart we awaited that outrage and that new, irreconcilable breakdown in Russian-Polish relations. But the fervor of the Polish Communists saved the Russian people from a new stain on our character and new execrations. When Jaruzelski brought in martial law, the *Daily News* tried insistently to reach me, demanding that I confirm it was brought in *specially* to spoil Christmas in the West!—well, keep your profound insights to yourselves. . . . But a month later they were again demanding something from me along the lines of "It's unacceptable—I strongly protest!" I sat down and wrote, for the French magazine *L'Express*, an article entitled "The Crucial Lesson":[66] it said that Communism is international and *every* nation has *its own* executioners' lackeys—they are not necessarily occupiers from outside.

And to think that after my Harvard address I'd hoped not to make another speech for the next three years, to keep to the side. But as early as the end of that same year, 1978, Janis Sapiets came to me with a tempting offer: he proposed, on behalf of the Russian Service of the BBC, an interview on the fifth anniversary of my expulsion. (At that same period, incidentally, another member of the BBC Russian Service, Sylva Rubashova, wished me a happy sixtieth birthday on air—and nearly lost her job over it.)

This proposal immediately appealed to me. The less inclined I felt to speak my mind to the West, the more I yearned to address my own people. And it was true—I'd been away from them for five years, unable to talk to them, and not a single Russian-language station had been reading my books to my fellow-countrymen for a long time now.

In early February 1979, just in time for the anniversary, Sapiets came to our home.[67] And we sat down to make a recording in the library, where books deadened the echo and the large windows framed the serene, snow-covered forest.

And in this setting I spoke—slowly, calmly, over the Lethe[68] as it flowed away soundlessly and irreversibly. (I also felt this when working on *The Red Wheel*.)

Sapiets had told me in advance the subjects he would cover in the conversation and except, perhaps, for that of the pope, they were almost all concerned with Russia—which was what induced me to do the interview. And I had before me abundant time to talk about my work as well. And, having already verified sufficiently my conclusions about the February Revolution (and these rootlets were not visible, on the surface, to Soviet eyes—it had taken forty years for them to reveal themselves to me, even though it was the principal quest of my whole life), I decided—perhaps mistakenly—to tell listeners in the Soviet Union, directly, my conclusions on this. To tell them in the form I'd already prepared, and do so seven years or so before *March* would appear. To warn them, years in advance, of the danger that now seemed to me most likely to blight our future: irresponsible, chaotic "February fever."[69] And to defend Russia's name against the malevolence of the American pseudo-intellectuals (and the term "pseudo-intellectual" is absolutely appropriate for today's American liberal-arts intellectuals) and of our new émigré gaggle. And, even more audacious than that, availing myself of that exceptional opportunity, the first in five years, I would try to actually reach the ears—directly, over the radio waves—of those who, when the inescapable convulsion comes, might prevent the country from disintegrating in a new revolutionary anarchy.

Why, in spite of everything, did I never call for revolution in the USSR, even though that would seem to be the only correct thing for anyone who's a doer—and all the more so if he has a pugnacious past? Firstly, it's due to the extreme revulsion I feel towards any revolution (I've already learned more than enough about it from our history). But since 1973 and my *Letter to the Soviet Leaders*, it has become crucial: Communism must be overthrown in such a way that the nation is not destroyed, and, for that, it must be not a revolution but a coup. Over my years in the West, seeing all the malice toward Russia, I've become even more sure of it.

I could not be too explicit, for fear the BBC might refuse to broadcast my interview—but hoped to be clear enough to anyone with some understanding. (And six months later the USSR started jamming all foreign broadcasts again.)

I was grateful to the BBC for allowing me this conversation with my fellow-countrymen. Cocksure, I supposed I had earned such a conversation. I'd totally forgotten the Anglo-Saxon fifty-fifty rule—equal time to both sides. Where ideas are concerned, this means someone plowing straight across everything that's just been said or done, and trying to destroy it. Following my interview, the BBC allowed an equal forty-five minutes, firstly to three British *experts*, who explained with aplomb why a Russian writer didn't understand Russian history while the three of them did. And then the next forty-five minutes to three "dissidents" who again testily insisted that they were the ones who understood Russia, not me. Sinyavsky repeated the Bolshevik agitprop, that by February Russia had already lost the 1914 war, and Plyushch said that February had come too late, otherwise it would have saved Russia—it was laughable. Sinyavsky said I had Soviet convictions and a Soviet upbringing, and that the "messianic pretensions" of Tolstoy and Dostoevsky had not been dangerous because, he claimed, they had few followers, whereas the figure of Solzhenitsyn was extremely dangerous because he was becoming a "leader." (Where? Who are my followers? What nonsense.) I was, he said, acting like the Soviet government towards the Third Wave, because . . . *I cannot abide competition.* (Here it was, the cry of anguish—it was the *pecking order* that kept them awake at night.)

In that interview I did indeed speak quite trenchantly about the Third Wave, and even in too much detail, which surprised friends in my homeland: surely I didn't need to spend precious time on this? surely the émigré issue wasn't important? I had said that the Third Wave émigrés, having left their homeland of their own free will and subject to no great danger, had lost the right to claim influence on the future of Russia and, moreover, to call on Western countries to solve Russian problems. The worst group was even defaming Russia, again with the aplomb of new-minted witnesses and specialists, forcing a way through to seats as Western experts on Russia's future.

Yes, in our homeland, under the Bolshevik boot, those moves by the émigrés were bound to seem trivial. But here—it didn't look that way. By that time, early 1979, I recognized that it was extremely dangerous: they were sticking all the Soviet abominations onto the face of Russia. When the October victory was celebrated,[70] Russia was cursed for opposing it. Now that October has fallen into the garbage pit, Russia is cursed because Russia *is* October. And the label has now stuck: in the eyes of the whole world the Communist plague is none other than a Russian plague.

For a long time I attached no importance to what might develop out of the Third Wave émigrés' influence on public opinion in the West. I didn't think it worthwhile or significant enough to tear myself away from my work for a polemic within the émigré body: it could have no bearing on Russia's future. I hadn't stopped to think that those hundreds of pseudo-intellectuals among the new wave of émigrés would be in a hurry to penetrate the very tissue of Western society's brain—the universities and the press. And that they would undoubtedly succeed, thanks to their spiritual and political affinity with that of the West, and especially America. It was only in 1978 that I noticed the bumptious articles of recently arrived Soviet journalists such as Solovyov and Klepikova, who had suddenly and with incredible ease done a disappearing trick on their Communist past; and then I was sent two of Yanov's books in English, now deeply, aggressively anti-Russian. It was these that decided me to have my say about the Third Wave on the BBC.

Yet it would never have occurred to me to start a fight with them over the Western way of thinking—they'd already won that one. Meanwhile, in public appearances, they were turning their cutting criticism more and more against Russia, against a Russian consciousness and, notably, against me. In June 1979, Efim Etkind, in the left-wing Paris paper *Le Monde*, swore loyalty to the West on behalf of all émigrés. The term "Eastern Europe," he wrote, sounds too good both for the old samovar Russia and for Stalin's Russia—it would be truer to call it "Western Asia." Russians' perceptions have not changed since the time of General Dourakine[71] (who was, he said, a good exemplar of a Russian). Those who have recently found their Russianness (that's me) dream of reestablishing the tsars' throne and the Byzantinism of the Third Rome. (Well, I'd have proposed an essay competition on the subject, "The Third Rome and the Third Wave." Shame Berdyaev's no longer with us![72]) The Russian ayatollahs (that's me) are more archaic than the Iranian ones: they don't even want an Islamic republic, but an Orthodox monarchy (which is, obviously, more reactionary). And, overall, religions only divide humanity—it's secular cultures that unite them.

Immediately after that, at the beginning of July (clearly they'd agreed on the schedule—Maximov had warned me about this), Sinyavsky also gave *Le Monde* an interview. He was, it seemed, very worried by the discord between émigrés (which he himself was fanning) because, he revealed, the Civil War in Russia had been stirred up by—what do you think?—quarrels and disputes (and not the Bolsheviks' coup). With his disapproval of the émigrés Solzhenitsyn is, according to Sinyavsky, raising a barrier that stops people escaping the thrice-cursed Russia of today.

Two summer months later, however, he figured out that it was discord that kept him relevant. Without it he would go unheard: there'd been no new books for years. And now, in an interview for the Swiss magazine *Die Weltwoche*, he declared the opposite point of view: quarrels were the sign of a healthy émigré group, the escape of Russian thinking from the autocratic period into pluralist times. Without this, for the sake of unity we would be forced to march in a solid front, under the pretext that "Solzhenitsyn is a prophet, Russia's and the whole world's Messiah."

Not restricting himself to press vehicles, Sinyavsky verbally, and as loudly as he could, splattered all his interlocutors and audiences with the information that Solzhenitsyn is a monarchist, a totalitarian, an anti-Semite, an heir to Stalin's way of thinking, and a theocrat. (He was parroting the KGB, which mostly used those exact same accusations, trying to frustrate any active political role I might have in the West. But they were wasting their time—I had no such ambitions.)

Kopelev too had never tired of that same old refrain when trying to dupe foreign correspondents in Moscow: Solzhenitsyn, with his dictatorial ways, is Lenin's double, an ally of the Kremlin and a terrible danger; and, as a writer, his talents are extremely limited. And via journalists all this flowed over readily to the West.

Meanwhile, Olga Carlisle, not yet satisfied with just her book attacking me,[73] and her sudden tilt at my Harvard speech, made a feeble attempt with an expansive article for the *New York Times Magazine* entitled "Reviving Myths of Holy Russia," with abundant photographs (of icons, Ilya Glazunov, Vladimir Osipov, and me).[74] Defending her inherited understanding of Russia—as the granddaughter of Leonid Andreev and adopted granddaughter of the Socialist Revolutionary Chernov—she warned readers that "increasing numbers of Russians are romanticizing prerevolutionary days and urging a return to the Orthodox beliefs and chauvinistic traditions of the past," and an obvious element of that trend was anti-Semitism (and she reduced *Lenin in Zurich*[75] to this), and this should ring alarm bells in the West. (In the United States the word "anti-Semitism" is even more charged than "bourgeois hireling" is in the USSR—get that label and they'll be baying for your blood.) Her vast article, pulled together from random oddments, was a model of hotchpotch-style defamation, scraped out of every nook and cranny and pasted in one after the other: "Russians have long considered themselves a chosen people," Moscow is the Third Rome, the Slavophiles, Lyubimov's theatre, *Letter to the Soviet Leaders*, the proliferation of Muslims, Suslov is the main Russophile in the Politburo, the anti-Semitic rebirth of Orthodoxy, and it wasn't worth defending the imprisoned Osipov. She'd found all this confirmed in quotes from Sakharov, Chalidze, Turchin, Yanov, Shragin's wife, and George Kennan. . . . And she ended with an iconic portrayal of the revered Sinyavsky.

Which was how, starting as early as 1978, even the top papers of the American press, all cut from the same cloth, were fully decked out in that same "Russia = anti-Semitism" equation. Articles were constantly appearing in the *New York Times* and its supplements, and in other major papers, saying that the Russian national consciousness now being reborn consisted above all of anti-Semitism—which meant it was worse than any Communism.[76] And when the major papers trumpet something in unison (which is how it usually happens) it tends to bamboozle America's reading public (though it doesn't affect average Americans at all). In a few months all the trumpeting had given rise to the idea that it was not Communism that menaced America but Russian nationalism. (And Ogurtsov and Osipov too—threatening from behind bars.) The tone had been set and it has lasted for years. Just recently the *Washington Post* had no qualms about publishing a cartoon: the Virgin of Vladimir, with a hammer and sickle on her forehead, Soviet medals on her chest, and in her arms, instead of a baby, a little Brezhnev. The caption: "Mother Russia."[77] In the States racism is not permissible, but even respectable people will allow themselves mudslinging at Russia as a whole and at Russians as a nation.

That autumn, 1979, invoking the Ayatollah Khomeini as a curse-name was also fashionable in the West (the Islamic Revolution was unfolding in Iran) and voices were now heard saying that Orthodoxy in Russia was the same as Khomeini in Iran (in the quantity of bloody killings? the callousness of the clerical dictatorship?). What an opportune moment! What indelible stigma shall we slap on that Orthodoxy, so it'll never get back on its feet? And the poetry expert and aesthete Etkind had no scruples, in a 28 September 1979 interview in *Die Zeit*, about putting Orthodoxy on a par with Leninism and branding me as one who wanted his own country to have an ayatollah. The technique of shallow minds is to hook a subject up from the surface, and there you have it—"Khomeinism" (and they thought the term up themselves). But how vicious it is, too, their deviousness. And with such people alongside us, can we really build the future Russia?

That whole rapid anti-Russian U-turn seen around the world showed me that I'd clearly been sitting around for too long—I should have come out sooner to counter this attack. My response was ready in an instant: we must at least free Russians of that stigma. *The Persian Ruse*—Persian powder thrown in the Russian man's eyes when he's barely up from his prostrate position.[78]

I had it published in several countries in Europe. It seemed to do the trick: the overseas press stopped branding us "Khomeinists."

Only the morose, haughty Chalidze, who didn't yet know of my response, brought the tenacious epithet into the United States and unfurled it in big letters over the two pages of his enormous article in *Novoye Russkoye*

Slovo: "Khomeinism or National Communism" (the only two solutions left to those concerned for Russia's future).

I would not have mentioned this article, even in small type, if Sakharov had not, soon afterwards and in print, pronounced it to be of prime importance. Chalidze had developed a bit from his previous stance. He no longer put juridical considerations before ethics, as he had in his first lectures in the West. But he rejected the "inseparability of rights and duties": "I must confess to having but a vague notion of 'moral obligations.' . . . What is a moral obligation?" (And was there no one to prompt him?—why, the voice of conscience, of course!) But what he did know for sure was "the idea of human rights as formulated by civilization" (and what a warped state it's got into now). The earlier human-rights movement had, it turns out, defended the rights of *the whole people* (we hadn't noticed)—but this defense was only available to specific cases, those "who themselves spoke up about their own situations and gave us the information" (urban dissidents, Jewish refuseniks, Baptists—and he'd also known about homosexuals since 1972 and raised the matter at his, Sakharov's, and Shafarevich's Human Rights Committee)—but how to defend the rights of the rest of the people, who have not "spoken up about their own situation" and are not giving any information? How to get information on workers who are being cheated? on the pillaged countryside, on demolished villages, on ground-down collective farm workers? Chalidze was here and there revealing his Soviet roots: the "moral consolidation" of the Soviet government after the Twentieth Congress; and it was "continuing to change and could become more humane"; and even "references to the practice of current Communism and its brutality cannot refute Marxist theory" (so, in Marxism, is practice no longer a criterion for the truth of a theory?); and the unrealizable "aim of Solzhenitsyn is to show that Marxism without fail will lead [hasn't it already led?] to concentration camps."

But at the same time, Chalidze, circumspect, looks round at Sakharov and, in exactly the same spirit and even his exact words, warns about the perils inherent in that Solzhenitsyn: "the situation could get dangerous." And then—what nonsense he's talking about me!—there's the fascist dictatorship in Spain (supposedly, I was there when Franco was in power and gave him encouragement); and apparently I'm demanding from the West vigorous physical support for anti-Communist forces in the USSR; and, the complete opposite, "all the passion of his speeches in the West is directed towards people in Russia," not towards the West (so try and work out who I'm actually trying to convince); and the Third Rome; and what Kurganov wrote in 1957, Orekhov in 1976, and a certain Udodov, of whom no one's even heard—all of that is my fault; and, of course, the anti-Semitism; and there was the unconscionable distortion of what I'd said about the Crimean Tatars, to make it seem that I was their enemy. People were now accustomed to my silence, and concluded that they could spout any drivel about me and I wouldn't respond. (And with the same ingrained arrogance Chalidze would keep republishing this, his star article, for another three years—in *Kontinent* and various other organs, and publishing it as a separate pamphlet, sometimes in Russian, sometimes in English, in some places touching up its content, elsewhere adding a detail or two.)

But even then our dissidents didn't calm down. A month later, in November 1979, in the *New York Review of Books*—the stronghold of American radicalism—printed right across the front cover in bold, black lettering against a dramatic red background was: "The Dangers of Solzhenitsyn's Nationalism." This was a wide-ranging interview[79] between a couple who had finally found each other: still the same Carlisle, who'd now come up in the world, and still the same Sinyavsky. The Russians' opinion of themselves, he said, was taking on a chauvinistic cast. And his main concern: anti-Semitism is being reborn at all levels. He is alarmed by the yearning for Russian isolationism and visions of a theocratic state. He is also alarmed that the émigrés, although many were disappointed by the ideas in *The Oak and the Calf*, *From Under the Rubble*, and the Harvard speech, are going easy on Solzhenitsyn, scared to criticize him. —Carlisle: "In Europe before the war, people closed their eyes to the rise of fascism because of their fear of communism."—Sinyavsky corroborates this: Thanks to Solzhenitsyn, there are many dangers ahead. In his autocratic society there will be no place for either a free press or an intelligentsia. —Carlisle, just as keen, optimistically: Do you think Solzhenitsyn is an anti-Semite? —Sinyavsky: Not psychologically speaking. But a new Russian nationalist movement with neo-fascist overtones is taking shape, with Solzhenitsyn's participation.

"Neo-fascist"! What next? To help the Soviet reader understand: an interview like this in America is exactly the same as an article in *Pravda* (*Truth*): death to the saboteur, the sworn enemy of the people! In this way Sinyavsky was doing everything he could to cut me off from the country where I'd settled. And, furthermore, after my Harvard speech I could be vilified, absolutely unchallenged, in the American press.

Etkind also adopted Sinyavsky's new position: yes, our disputes demonstrate our wholesome pluralism. And he immediately went on to prove it with a few lies and distortions about me regarding *Lenin in Zurich*.

If they didn't make up my philosophy for me, their position in our disputes would be weak. I was calling for concessions between nations, even mutual repentance and generosity (in *From Under the Rubble*)—but they are shamelessly depicting me axe in hand.

Even so I would have carried on working, not reacting, if it had only been about me: for me everything will, in time, get back into kilter. But both to the new democrats from the USSR and the entire radical warrior-host of the American press I'm not the one who is so very repugnant—it is, rather, Russian memory, the reviving Russian consciousness that I personify.

This was revealed to me now; it was bitterly unexpected, very painful, and unjustified. When you live in the USSR you never tire of being outraged at every turn by the lies and violence of the Communists. And that pushes the world's other problems and future possibilities into the background. And then in the West you suddenly hear, from supposedly faithful *allies*, sweeping condemnation not of the USSR but of historical Russia. . . . So even if you lay down your life to warn the West against sinking into Communism, and are successful to boot, the opinion that gains a foothold in the West is all the more ungrateful: what brutes, they say, those Russians, not able to resist Communism while we managed to hold out. So will they just be laying into Russia all the more?

After all, I'm certain that Bolshevism is doomed. I've done enough work to unmask it, but now there are a good many historical forces focused on the same thing. I'd rather not waste any more energy on Bolshevism—but how can I help Russia be reborn in the future, and reborn in a pure form?

New historical configurations are formed long before they become active. And it takes people a long time after that to recognize and understand them.

Nevertheless I could feel something of this instinctively. When, in *The Oak and the Calf* in 1971, I devoted a disproportionate amount of space to the dispute between *Novy Mir* and *Molodaya Gvardiya* (*Young Guard*), even I was surprised—why did I feel this was so essential? But I sensed that it was, and chose my side, not realizing how long that schism would last.

Russian land is not only occupied by the Bolsheviks, but also has a thick dusting of ash from the burned-out Liberation, Revolutionary Democracy, and socialist movements of previous decades. And when you're working your way out from under the occupier's boot you're still breathing that ash in for a good while, without noticing. I too, thinking Communism was the absolute and even the sole enemy, was for a long time tilting toward Kadet[80] ideas, and they were scattered throughout *First Circle*, for example, and the first edition of *Archipelago*.

I had foreseen no disintegration of the anti-Bolshevik front. And it was good that I had not: it gave solidity, invincibility to my attack on the Soviets' concrete citadel—and the Soviet and Western pseudo-intellectuals were all the more confident in supporting me. Without that, the struggle against the

Communists would not have been victorious. Thanks to my incomplete understanding of the situation, the best tactical combination for the battle against the Kremlin and the KGB came together of its own accord. But, unseen by me, a chasm already lay between those who loved Russia and wanted to save her, and those who cursed and blamed her for everything that had happened. That situation, which I hadn't yet understood, was suddenly illuminated for the first time by *August 1914*, which was published in 1971. Although this was a patriotic Russian novel (without socialism), both the yapping mutts of the Communist press and the journal of the National Bolsheviks, *Veche*, lambasted it furiously and the whole pseudo-intellectual readership turned up their noses and shrugged. *August* had broken through—and was polarizing the public's political awareness. And it revealed something to me, too.

Alone one day in Rozhdestvo-on-the-Istya another two years later, I intuitively, feeling my way and under no one else's influence, had sobered up enough to see that I must write my *Letter to the Soviet Leaders*. When I was in the camps all we did was dream of revolution in our country and, through inertia, I continued to feel the same way for many long years. But now I had my revelation: our salvation would only come through evolution of the regime. Otherwise Russia would be totally, irretrievably destroyed.

And what enmity greeted that letter in the West and among our own liberals—as it greeted any concern for Russia, mine or anyone else's. That opened my eyes even further. The Russia-haters are already sinking their teeth into Russia's good name. And what would happen later, when we crawled out, weak, infirm, from under the ruins of the hateful Bolshevik empire? They wouldn't even let us start getting back on our feet.

From a note I've kept, dated 28 June 1979, I can see I had already understood the problem by then. I'd written: "Gradually, over the years, by 1978–79 the true meaning of my new situation and my new task have become clearer. This is my task: to uphold the history of Russia in undistorted form and to protect Russia's future paths. The age-old Bolshevik enemies are now joined by the hostile pseudo-intellectuals of both East and West and, it appears, even more powerful circles. Which is why it turns out that here, in America, I am not genuinely free, but again caged. My freedom is in the fact that my home is not being searched and I can write anything I want for future use—but when it comes to publishing even my Nodes, there's resistance."

Another three years have passed—and I could repeat almost exactly what I wrote before.

How ferocious was their combined attack on the first, feeble little shoots of the rebirth of Russian thought. They've left us with no choice.

So that's how it was? I'd stirred up a battle on the Main Front—but some New Front had opened up behind my back? The insane difficulty of the situation is that I can't ally myself with the Communists, our country's butchers—but I can't ally myself with our country's enemies either. And all this time I have no home ground to support me. The world is big, but there's nowhere to go.

Two millstones.

In actual warfare, it sometimes goes like this: where it was impossible yesterday even to crawl, where everything has been hidden, dug in, and lethal gunfire alone has swept the locality of all life, there—after some preliminary heavy-artillery fire and a breakthrough—suddenly, through breaches effected in the barbed wire, skirting craters, deserted enemy gun turrets and dugouts, along this strip of land that was yesterday so terrifying and inaccessible, the second echelon with support staff in the rear throngs in, heads held high, just as they might throng a boulevard, as if there had never been a strip of deadly fire here.

And for me it's the same now, as I'm beginning to see. For decades I'd felt myself to be a voice shouting on behalf of the millions who had died—and against our main common Enemy. I'd hidden away, got prepared, then done battle, and given all my strength, and almost laid down my life, and broken that Fastness with scheming and plotting, with *Ivan Denisovich, Circle, Cancer Ward, Archipelago*—and what was the result? that I'd only beaten a path for the pseudo-intellectuals. They'd streamed through that breach and immediately made themselves at home, as if no breach had been made, and it hadn't been needed anyway, and there hadn't even been a Main Front. It was all over, forgotten, done and dusted.

And here they are, wandering free in the expanse now opened up, and there are such masses of them already, of visitors and new arrivals—and how quickly they've settled in. And there are just as many, of exactly the same kind, in the West. And the main thing that irritates and repels them all is the eternal, incorrigible, and loathsome Russia that's ruining the life of everyone on Earth.

How could it have happened?

It started long ago, from many causes. One was that Russia was a towering, inconceivably vast state, seemingly menacing by its sheer size, and so richly endowed by nature. Another was the scary tales told by the initially infrequent foreign visitors. Later there were Russia's excessive, senseless military actions in Europe—under Elizabeth, Catherine, Paul, Aleksandr I, Nikolai. More often than not these actions were not expansionist, but silly pieces of bravado or even heavy lifting to please other thrones, other republics. And there was the stunning victory over Napoleon, conqueror of the whole world, even though it was not followed by any self-interested seizures of territory. (And what intense hatred of Russia we saw when Europe replied with the Crimean War.) And because Russia was, and had always kept itself, *different* in terms of faith, traditions, and way of life. And a major factor was that, for the whole century preceding the Revolution, tsarist power had had its head in the clouds, learning none of the lessons of *openness* that had developed in the civilized world—either not understanding it, or not deigning to make use of it to defend itself before society and to explain its actions: what, do we have to justify ourselves? to whom? And whatever accusations were made against Russia for all that century, and whatever cock-and-bull stories told (and on the threshold of the twentieth century the malevolence heated up further)—absolutely everything stuck, accumulating layer by layer and drying on. The hounds did bay, the crows did caw, as the old saying goes. (But then the Bolsheviks leapt in with a single bound, totally paralyzing the Western public and debilitating their leading lights.)

And on top of all that came—especially in the early twentieth century—an increased coarseness and ineptitude of Russian political commentators with right-wing, nationalist leanings. They didn't take the trouble to discuss things patiently, with all the nuances, no—they'd resort to crudeness and even abuse. Due perhaps to their despair at seeing all Russia drifting off "in the wrong direction" and not having the power or the skill to put it right, they only became more and more sure how right their unlistening, insular group was: think *exactly* as we do! Shout loudly—*as we do!*—and if you do otherwise, even slightly—you're not one of us, you've sold out, you're Russia's enemy! Their contemporary, Vasili Shulgin, also a nationalist but with intelligence and subtlety, wrote of them once that "it makes no difference to them who they get their teeth into or why, as long as they have some meat to chew on." So improbable, but how typical too, is the strength of the right-wing Russian nationalists' hatred of their country's saviour, Stolypin. (And how many Russian writers they have rejected in the same way, calling down curses on them.)

Then the Bolshevik steamroller started work on all the nationalists, both extreme and moderate. Most were totally crushed, others condemned to a long, long silence. When new shoots were allowed to sprout they were kept in a greenhouse, under the vigilant eye of the gardener, and must turn only towards the crimson-red sun.

And many did just that. The weakness of the weak: they must find a strong shoulder to lean on. The very first Russian nationalist journal in samizdat, Osipov's *Veche*, was replete with good will towards the power of those who would destroy it, wrote "god" without an initial capital and "Government" with. It revealed to us that "Communism, however, has created a Great Power," that "Russian Communism is Russia's own special path," and that collective farms are our traditional "Russian community brotherhood." And that actually, for this government, "ideology does not now play any role." (A striking and *exact* match with Sakharov's formulation![81] Extremes are doomed to meet up.) This was how Russian nationalism became so weak that it slipped across into National Bolshevism. And now we hear from the notorious Gennadi Shimanov (with whom all the Sinyavskys and Yanovs do as much as they can to put me in the same basket) that the current Soviet system is a ready-made "Orthodox theocracy." All these kinds of malign distortions came into being as a reaction to half a century of anti-Russian persecution.

But no! Russian patriotism was, right from 1918, *anti*-Soviet (just as, before that, the Leninists had insistently declared themselves *anti*-patriots). But it was thanks to ugly voices such as these that the word "Russian" became all the more distorted—and thanks to them that any genuine expression of Russian pain became anathema and was no longer allowed.

In addition, Russian nationalists emerged, of the kind who rushed to renounce Christianity as well: "Christianity blunts the combative spirit"; "Christianity is Judaism's Trojan horse." (But Sergei Bulgakov had answered that long before: "A great nation cannot become established on the basis of national principle alone.") These nationalists call on us to renounce our historical memory, to adopt a new paganism, or else be ready to adopt any faith you like from Asia.

And on top of that, the Central Committee and the KGB had not been asleep on the job either, and were continuing to harass us. They were encouraging these surges of rampant nationalism, stirring them up into anti-Jewish flare-ups—and, before the whole world, striking a magnanimous pose and spreading their hands, perplexed: see for yourself! who else could cope with this unbridled nationalist anti-Semitism? You can see it: the whole world will be better off if Communist power perseveres.

Yes, we've been through (and the older cohort have it burned into their memory) decades of cruel anti-Orthodox and anti-Russian persecution. And you need a noble heart not to succumb to hatred or the urge to seek revenge, not to throw yourself into bombastic trumpeting or mean-spirited derision. (Or into that kind of heedless Orthodox belief where, with ecumenism, believers simply become indifferent to their own people's national identity.)

A constructive nationalism understood in *that* way has not yet, alas, appeared in Russia in any tangible form.

But it's done now: all over the world an unjustified aversion to Russia has found a way in, germinated, and become entrenched. (Yet how they loved us for those four years of the war against Hitler . . .)

A foreign land is a dense forest.

We heard from Russia that some of our friends were surprised: why had I set about defending Russia's good name before foreigners? Feliks Svetov advised me publicly that I should not try to vindicate Russia but, rather, repent on Russia's behalf. And indeed I myself had always thought and done so, had proposed "Repentance and Self-Limitation."[82] . . . (And I personally would have liked to carry on that way, even though my mob of scandalmongers keeps pointing malicious fingers at me and jeering at every one of my admissions.) But you need to get jostled a bit in the Western press bear garden to understand: no, it's *right now* that we have to stand up for Russia—otherwise they'll move in for the kill. It turns out that Russia has been slandered for centuries; our instinct for self-defense must not let us down. Repent? we certainly have things to repent of—we've committed enough sins!—but it's not to biased American journalism that we must repent. (The early émigrés grasped this long ago.)

Well, perhaps it's understandable that Europe harbored such animosity towards imperial, monarchic Russia, it being hostile to all the European revolutions. But why were they so hard on everything *Russian*—now, when the leftist idea loved by the West has been victorious in Russia and our nation is extremely weak, even perhaps nearing its end? Do they not even acknowledge our deaths, our suffering over these last sixty-five years? Is it because the empire is still holding on, even though it's Communist now?—but it is this very empire that is destroying us and sucking out our lifeblood.

And our fellow-countrymen are adding fuel to the fire. The heirs of those glib talkers who already brought Russia to ruin once, at the beginning of the century, are now, at the end of the century, raising their hands again for the coup de grâce. They have indeed been long used to the Russian patriots always being the weaker side in their dispute, with no sense of proportion, rash, and utterly incapable of maintaining a high level of discussion.

I have already fought once for Russia in the war—but it turned out to entrench the Bolsheviks. I do not want to fight a second time, in an effort to entrench new masters of a different stripe. They're just waiting to pounce on the country that's been liberated for them, and to run it: using the newspapers, using their ideas, using a parliament—whose members do not represent their own regions—and using capital, of course.

And now Axel Springer, who has invited me umpteen times (and has been over to see us), says he's surprised at my sudden political inaction after such a fine struggle—and why don't I go over and make some rousing speeches in West Berlin? And there's no way to make him understand that to me, now, that's suddenly in the past. So I'm writing a novel—a historical novel.

Fortunately, fate has decreed that, while following my basic inclination, I also *have to* remain silent; to take *The Red Wheel* on further. These many years of silence, of inaction, of less action—even if I'd tried I couldn't have planned it better. It's also the best position tactically, given the current distribution of forces: for I am almost alone, but my adversaries are legion.

I've plunged into *The Red Wheel* and I'm up to my ears in it: all my time is filled with it, except when I sleep (and even at night I'm woken by ideas, which I note down). I stay up late reading the old men's memoirs and am already nearing the end of a complete read-through of what they've sent. Over their many pages, the writing sometimes shaky, scratchy now, my heart gives a lurch: what spirit, in someone approaching eighty—some of them ninety—years of age, unbroken by sixty years of humiliation and poverty in emigration—and that after their excruciating defeat in the Civil War. Real warrior heroes! And how much priceless material is preserved in their memories, how many episodes they've given me, bits and pieces for the "fragments" chapters—without them, where would I have found this? It would all have vanished without trace.

When I had, in the first draft, assembled the material and made sure I had what was needed for the vast mass of the four-volume *March*—that is, of the February Revolution itself—I went backwards, to *August* and *October*, to fine-tune them into their definitive form. This was also no minor task, for over the last four or so years of rummaging through archives and memoirs, how many new depths I'd encountered in the weave of events, and many places demanded more and more work—changing and rewriting. And yes, I do understand that I am overloading the *Wheel* with detailed historical material—but it is that very material that's needed for categorical proof; and I'd never taken a vow of fidelity to the novel form.

The terrifying thing is: what if there's a fire at home? Would more than ten years' work on my manuscripts—my whole life and soul—go up in flames? And when, starting in spring 1981, Alya set about typesetting *August*, efficiently saw it through to the end, and it was sent off to the printer; and in spring this year she began on *October* as well—what relief! Saving it from being burned was even more important than getting it published—though it was high time to publish, and had been for a good while.

All the unity, the consistency of our life, Alya's and mine, is in that unchanging rhythm of our work. And how good it would be not to be pulled away by any kerfuffle, never pulled away!

Fat chance of that, though. Have the Bolsheviks' teeth got blunter? Are they letting their Front be weakened? It was at this exact time, the end of 1979, that the persecution of Orthodox believers hardened in the USSR (at the very same time that the West was sullying their reputation!): in November they arrested Father Gleb Yakunin, Ogorodnikov's commune, and the Christian Committee for the Defense of Believers' Rights—and, in January 1980, Father Dmitri Dudko as well.

Father Gleb's arrest settled it: it was time for me to do something. Punch that same old Ugly Mug, the one we all know.

But I had never yet experienced anything so complex: I had to start, there and then, in the same piece of writing but alternating, my attack on another enemy too, which was advancing on Russia from all sides with its lies. If only to shield some space around the axis of Russian history from those lies.

And this was how I came to the idea of a large article. As I always do for complex situations, I gave myself "scales" to weigh up the pros and cons—should I write it or not?

Cons. We're not on the brink yet, we can wait, there's still time for fundamental explanations. And it would not enlighten readers in our homeland—for them it would be an incomprehensible squabble. And I'd have to tear myself away from *March* again, and again devote effort to a genre that is not my own. And I must not take this kind of step too frequently—I'd only just handed in *The Persian Ruse*. And was I to appeal, again, to people whose fear of the return of Russian consciousness was clearly not going to be assuaged, who would not be convinced?

Pros. I cannot shirk my duty to exonerate historical Russia, intelligibly, of slander—and who would do that now in the West if I didn't? And we have to clear ourselves of the "Nazism" tag they're hanging on us. And I personally have to explain my position more accurately, explain everything else they've accused me of since the Harvard speech. And defend myself against the "theocracy" accusation they're still saddling me with. And at the same time I must put those fashionable "informants" in their place, those slanderers of Russia, abusing the West's attention unchallenged. And those puffed-up American "Sovietologist" professors. Sovietologists!—a monstrous category of Western science. How many they are, who've never been through the experience—not comparable with any other—of Soviet oppression, and are turning out piles of dissertations and expert appraisals that are just a joke.

I made my decision: I'd write "Misconceptions about Russia Are a Threat to America." But political articles were now the hardest thing of all for me: a waste of energy on a thankless task. And again—my language is lifeless (tailored for translation, for addressing Americans). An alien audience.

Many tasks to fulfill—but it seemed to fall into place and work well. Only I really did not want it in the *New York Times*. Tom Whitney and Harrison Salisbury came to see us and recommended *Foreign Affairs*, a thick quarterly journal devoted to foreign politics. It seemed to be good advice, and I never regretted it.

But when I was in the middle of writing that article a proposal turned up unexpectedly from *Time* magazine: to write fifteen hundred words for them. Tempting! A print run of six million? And read by anyone in the whole world who can read English. I couldn't say no. But I didn't want my attention diverted, either. And how ever could I now cut this one out of the *Foreign Affairs* article? (Two articles could not sprout in my brain at the same time.) But this was just the right dynamic step: to defend Russia to a vast audience all at once. And thus be more sure of influencing the Americans. And show how shortsighted their alliance with Red China was—a new, spirited call for opposition to all Communism everywhere. In other words, the same old Main Front over and over again.

Somehow, it worked. Even balancing out my different goals. And publishing exactly the same material at the same time on two different levels, different heights: for the masses ("Communism: In Plain Sight—and Misunderstood"[83]) and for the governing elite.

How I'd tried to carve out some quiet years of work! How I'd hoped to keep a low profile for three or four years!—it proved impossible. *Time* published my article in February 1980, *Foreign Affairs* at the beginning of April.[84]

And while I was about it I decided to respond to the old Paris Comintern member, Boris Souvarine. Hostile to *Lenin in Zurich*, he had at the time immediately sounded the war horn in defense of his old leader: despite the documents now made public, he denied that Lenin had received money from the Germans and rejected even more vehemently the psychological type I'd attributed to him, saying Lenin had never been involved in anything shady. (You'll never eradicate the old Comintern worldview.) But to the French reader, Souvarine was now a patriarch of socialism, who used to "correspond personally with Lenin" and wrote a book on Stalin, he surely knows a thing or two that young people today simply cannot know! And he attacked my book, misquoting my text, distorting the facts, but what got him really hot under the collar was the matter of Lenin's nationality: he felt that to run Russia's affairs you really didn't need Russian blood. (Yes, of course. But what you did need was Russian spirit! And that Lenin did not have.)

That spiteful and expansive article of Souvarine's had, it turned out, been published in Paris in his own little journal back in spring 1976.[85] But I was in California at the time, up to my neck in preparatory work on *March*, and then ensconced at Five Brooks, writing the Stolypin volume to the hammering of builders, and then the family arrived and we settled in. And that year none of us paid any attention to that article, to how harmful it was. I became aware of it in the form of translated (and one-sided) extracts in the journal *Vremya i My*,[86] and got angry enough to reply. Irina Ilovaiskaya translated the whole of Souvarine's article for me in early 1978. But by then, two years later, it looked rather foolish to respond. I set it aside. But—it had got under my skin: he'd been over-enthusiastic in the way he'd taken up the Russian questions. And although it was disgracefully late—four years late—I was now at full speed, and answered Souvarine.[87]

The *Time* article did not embroil me in any further disputes, though there were reactions. (And, in the case of the old Russian émigrés, reactions such as: how can you say "Communism is misunderstood," when those big shots in the West understood it just fine from the start, and for a long time it even suited their purpose?)

But I wouldn't be able to extricate myself so easily from *Foreign Affairs*. Offended American professors, along with American total nitwits, strewed their responses over the following two quarterly issues.[88] They were happy to remember Ivan the Terrible; but when it came to the early twentieth century, to the ingenious international revolutionary terror: let's forget all that and chalk it up to nasty Russian traditions. And now the editors were inviting the author to respond—and how could I get out of it? How tiresome to expend effort on a dispute at their superficial level, to flounder about in that radical froth of the three-centuries-long degeneration since the Enlightenment, to force a way through the forest of cold incomprehension (for they weren't capable of imagining the Soviet situation—it could have been underwater to them, while they were judging from dry land)—just so as to warn those same wise men of the true danger.

And in summer 1980 I had to abandon *March* again and engage intensively with the polemic imposed on me.[89]

The elderly émigrés were certainly right—Western specialists cannot be so totally deluded that they don't see the evil, the menace of Communism. And it was obvious to me, and to my opponents, that the dispute was not about elucidating the truth of Communism: every line they wrote screamed "we're fed up with that Russia of yours, it's getting in our way!"

Both my *Foreign Affairs* articles, brought together in a separate book,[90] were published in the States, then in Britain and France as well.

As for Souvarine, he also waded in, of course.[91] I answered (in the journal *Histoire*),[92] and towards autumn he issued a new response, his third article now—for he had more time than I did and could come back ten times with a riposte if he wanted to. (But that front, the anti-Communist front, did have pens wielded on its behalf, and in *Russkaya Mysl* others were already finishing off the tussle for me.)

And I didn't manage to get through those two years without public appearances either.

My heart wept for Igor Ogurtsov, now serving with fortitude his thirteenth year of incarceration. In recent times no one else had had to endure such a sentence, but his fate, as a "Russian nationalist," was of little interest to anyone in the West. The dissident émigrés were telling everyone that "under Soviet law his imprisonment is deserved"—so there's no point going to any trouble on his behalf. I had no desire to appeal to an American administration (and I'd never done so up to that point), but I did decide to send a letter to President Carter. **[26]** It bore no fruit, of course, except a form letter from his office.

At the same time I sent letters[93] to two prominent Democratic senators, Henry Jackson and Daniel Moynihan, opponents of the president. But no help was forthcoming from them either. Moynihan was sympathetic, though, and even came to see us—but it all came to nothing.

In September 1979 the third session of the Sakharov Hearings[94] was held in Washington. I wrote an address on the subject of Ogurtsov, and Alya went to read it out.[95] That, needless to say, also produced no responses. (Except hostile ones.)

And each time, of course, one has to find new words, powerful and fresh. They don't come easily.

And then—there was my ninety-year-old aunt Irina,[96] who'd had a great influence on my upbringing. When my family was preparing to follow me, Alya had invited her to leave Georgievsk and come over with them. At that moment there'd been no obstacle to her leaving the country, but she'd refused, apprehensive of the move. But, all alone, she went into a decline, losing her sight and hearing in terrible living conditions—and she asked us to bring her over now.

The task would be difficult, agonizing: was I to appeal, from here, to the Soviet authorities? I'd have to. We began the process through the US Department of State: they would send an invitation on my behalf to the USSR, to Aunt Irina. Forms and more forms. They were sent off. I thought, despite everything, that they'd let her come. I was wrong: they refused. Probably due to nothing but an angry shudder at the sight of my name—they just had to thwart me! The ninety-year-old was left there, to die in her hovel.

But I would have been embarrassed to raise a hullabaloo on TV and in newspapers around the world on account of my family story, as others aren't shy of doing; embarrassed to shout that they'd taken her *hostage*—when the whole world was also sick, and in my homeland countless martyrs were suffering in the camps. I couldn't allow my personal problems to eclipse great, universal matters. But even so I did, via Nicholas Daniloff—a Russian-American journalist of my acquaintance—send a short article to the *Washington Post*, "The Empire and the Old Woman": another tiny but stark example of how the great men of empire take their revenge—keeping an old woman in a hovel with no lavatory, no running water, no electricity, no care, and no pension, and not allowing me to buy her an apartment in the USSR, or her to come over to me, and even blocking our correspondence. The government of a great power was not squeamish about wreaking vengeance on a ninety-year-old woman because her nephew was not brought up in the Marxist spirit.

Adapted and abridged, the article[97] appeared in the *Washington Post*. But, naturally, it made no impression in either the West or the East.

In the meantime, our friends moved my aunt to Moscow, into Dima Borisov's home. (And after that, in Georgievsk, the militia turned up, late, asking questions: who took her? where to? did they use force?) Dima applied, on her behalf, to the Presidium of the Supreme Soviet for her to be allowed to join her nephew, but it was all to no avail. Then, in December 1979, I decided to bow my head and send a telegram to a new rising star:

"USSR, Moscow, Staraya Square, Politburo Central Committee Member Konstantin Chernenko.—Soviet embassy Washington categorically refused my only relative Irina Ivanovna Shcherbak exit visa join me in United States Stop Surely enough public shame without adding outrages against nonagenarian blind deaf hunchbacked homeless woman Question-mark Give order let her leave do not force me make public."

And—what else was there to make public? . . .

Needless to say—silence. How could those petty tyrants concede anything when they had an opportunity to harm Solzhenitsyn?

My aunt's fate weighed heavy on me: for seventeen years, because of my work, my plotting, my struggle, I'd not managed to persuade her to leave the home she knew in Georgievsk and move nearer to us, so as to improve her living conditions. In the summer of 1971 I was going to see her—but on the way I suffered a burn injury* and turned back.

I'd spent my whole life paying my dues to society—was it not, now, finally time to repay my personal debt? So I resorted to telephoning, something I rarely do; and where did I call?—the consul in the Soviet Embassy! I tried to persuade him, pointing out that we'd all be winners if they quietly let the old woman leave: what use is she to you?

It was, of course, all in vain. They didn't let her come.

A few days later they expelled Sakharov from Moscow. The authorities had managed to put up with him, though seething with anger for a long time now—but the scientist's latest supremely audacious statement condemning the sending of troops into Afghanistan got caught up in the enormity of that event. There would, anyway, be an explosion of anger around the world, so why not deal with Sakharov at the same time?

Shortly afterwards, Sakharov's declaration of 18 January 1980 reached us, published all over the place.[99] It was his last before being exiled, a kind of testament up to that moment. And what was it about? Chalidze's article—that craftily constructed piece with doctored facts and a Soviet accent. Was it only because it was against a Russian national consciousness, and against me, that Sakharov had found "its publication helpful," that it was "in the style of

---

* Twenty years later it was shown to be an attempt on my life by the KGB at Novocherkassk. See *The Oak and the Calf*, Appendix 46.[98] (Author's note, 1993.)

a serious and well-argued polemic," and "a discussion demonstrating talent, very important for everyone"? . . .

What about Sakharov, then?

Could his miraculous apparition in Russia have been foreseen? I think it could. It accords with an age-old Russian way of thinking—that people are *bound* to feel the pangs of repentance and conscience. And no matter how self-interested the leading collar that's pulled tight round Russia's neck, no matter how much crueler, how spoiled, how lost to themselves everyone there has become, from time to time some hearts, waking up aghast, repentant, must break out. Given the low quality of that level of society, it would not be as many as had burst forth from the prosperous life of the old nobility, but all the same! And I, for example, with my optimism, was always expecting them to appear! Expecting people to emerge (I thought there'd be more of them), who would spurn creature comforts, eulogies, riches—and set off to join the people in their sufferings. And what possibilities might lurk in conversions like that, if such people were to dedicate their life to the sufferings of the majority of their people! The new situation of a milder time, together with Sakharov's scientific stature and the services he'd rendered his homeland in the atomic area, gave him the chance to effect his heroic conversion.

It was harder to foresee the elements of such an individual's sense of the world—though only because of our limited vision. In retrospect you could easily describe it. In what soil would he grow? It was a soil not only crushed flat for a half century by the Bolsheviks' murderous steamroller, but also sprinkled for another half century before that—as weed-killer might be—with the Liberation movement's disdain for Russia's history. And it was from that very milieu, the Moscow intelligentsia, that Andrei Dmitrievich sprang. Given his origins and the culture of his family, he grew up in an atmosphere of generous, educated "pan-humanism" and was, without fail, true to that ethos, both when elevated to the rank of Nobel laureate and now, when relegated to exile. Given the actual experience of his youth, meanwhile, he grew up on "Soviet internationalism" and imbibed it (indeed the humanist roots were one and the same) and, despite all his later disappointments in the Soviet system, he has not been able to tear himself away from this side of his ideology either. Indeed, he writes quite unequivocally that he considers even the idea of nationhood, any appeal to the nation rather than the individual, a philosophical error.

After that, Sakharov's own life in technical service to the State hardly left him any scope for historical or social reflections ("the ultra-secrecy and high tension" in which he lived for twenty years, "over twenty years in that unimaginable, terrifying world"—his words). All that was combined with the whole Soviet population's enforced ignorance of Russian history as well. In nothing that he'd ever said or written was there any whiff of a recollection that our history was over a thousand years old. Sakharov does not breathe that air.

His natural sphere of activity, the concepts of physics, had not, when he made the transition into the social arena, managed to endow him with his own, original idea of society, but inclined him to exaggerate greatly the role of technical progress. His worldview consisted of the inherited humanistic (anthropocentric) ideas with which society worldwide had stepped, so vulnerable, into the twentieth century. No wonder Sakharov also signed (in 1973, together with three hundred little-known figures) the sweeping Humanist Manifesto II, which reduced ethics to human *interests* and was especially severe in its opposition to all religions (although he did voice a rather feeble reservation here). Apart from that, the manifesto contained Sakharov's favorite ideas yet again: infinite scientific progress; universal (in other words not national) education for all; the need to overstep the bounds of national sovereignty, a single world legislation; a supranational world government; and economic development that mustn't remain within the purview of the nation. (In other words, the nation must not, generally speaking, be in charge of its own way of life.)

So even up to the present day (1981) we are still getting from Sakharov the same idealization of technical progress, still the same ideal future: "scientifically regulated, all-round progress." And there is one more science-based temptation—whether or not to set about the "all-round scientific regulation" of both art (Sakharov's 1968 idea) and all spiritual life (but the latter is exactly where the main possible contribution to progress in human existence lies)—that would be terrifying. Without it, material progress is hollow, and it's no progress at all. Yet Sakharov persists in his belief that it is scientists, specifically, who ought to evaluate progress overall.

At the time of Sakharov's "Reflections on Progress, Peaceful Coexistence, and Intellectual Freedom" in 1968, I took his indulgence towards Communism and socialism ("the views of the present author are deeply socialist," "Lenin had already indicated the solution" . . .) to be only a tactical maneuver on the part of an oppressed author. But it later turned out, to my surprise, to be sincerely felt. It was also a continuation of the old radical sin of the Russian intelligentsia: violence *from the left* is praised and forgiven. Since then we often find, in Sakharov, such ideas as "the source of our difficulties is not in the socialist system"; or he idealizes the 1920s in the USSR for the "great hopes, the spirit of enthusiasm" of the period; or the term "Stalinism," presupposing that Communism had, overall, been better, but was botched. —And he even allows the possibility (in his letter to Brezhnev, 1980, published in *Kontinent*, no. 25) that one of the motives for the occupation of Afghanistan might have been to furnish "generous help towards its land reform and other social transformations."

Yes, Sakharov himself always displays personal moral strength—and perhaps it's for that reason that he invests ambitious hopes in it, never allowing a religious element to adulterate it, not even as a slip of the tongue. (And he won't question whether moral ideas ever existed *in earlier times*, *before* any religions, even pagan ones, appeared.) Religion is to him alien and eccentric, often dangerous and bloody. But in atheism he is secure—there he is the true heir of the prerevolutionary intelligentsia. Even when he calls on man to "recognize his guilt and help his neighbor," he does it under the aegis not of Christ but of Albert Schweitzer . . .

And what must such a worldview inevitably come down to? Nothing but "human rights," of course—a "*human-rights ideology*," as Sakharov himself says more boldly now. "The defense of human rights has become a worldwide ideology."

But how are we to understand "human-rights ideology"? "Rights" elevated to the rank of an *ideology*—what's that? Well, it's our old friend anarchism! And is that the hoped-for Russian future? Yet even back in his time Vasili Maklakov, wise fellow that he was, would correct his furious Kadets: you have to be concerned not just with the rights of man but the rights of the state as well! While aspiring to secure rights for each individual, we must also bear in mind his *obligations*—be concerned for the whole system! Our century-long Liberation movement had striven only for that, rights for everyone—nothing but rights. And it brought Russia to its knees. In 1917 we received just that—unheard-of, matchless rights—and the country immediately crumbled. Did all our events of 1917 really start with the suppression of rights? Was it not, rather, when rights were freed of all restraints? The workers seized the right to punch their engineers and managers on the nose, the soldiers the right to leave the front, the peasants the right to fell forests that were not theirs, to take apart mills and timber works and take land for themselves, and the city-dwellers to demand unlimited pay increases. And the democratic Russian government easily conceded all that.

But when the full panoply of "rights" comes rolling along, there's already no distinction between a word and a threat, freedom and impunity, ownership and thievery. And especially in the twentieth century, when base instincts have been unleashed everywhere on Earth—how ever is it possible to put "human rights" in the first and *only* place? Medically speaking, the importunate dinning in of "human rights" is the trajectory of a single-celled, autonomous organism—in other words, of a cancerous development of society. Sakharov does not seem to grasp what Russian liberals and radicals, all four State Dumas,[100] have never understood and what Stolypin was trying, in vain, to make them see: that civil society cannot be created before citizens are, and it is not the freeing up of rights that can cure an organism comprising a sick state and a sick people but, before that, medical treatment of the whole organism.

But in what way, how seriously, to what extent we are sick—that Sakharov does know. He learned it, in particular, in his years as a dissident, in the gutter, already persecuted, roaming the courtrooms and encountering ordinary life. In that same *My Country and the World*[101] he gives a sizable overview of our maladies: shamefully low wages, poor, cramped housing, tiny pensions, impoverished hospitals, poor medical services, low-quality food, general drunkenness, the impossibility of a normal family upbringing for children, residency permits, inferior education, and the poverty of teachers and doctors.

Yes, today's Sakharov sees enough of Soviet life—he's not closeted away with his work now. So what, then, is the grievous ill, the desperately urgent need that he elevates as the first and greatest of all ills and needs of an oppressed country that is bled dry, robbed of its memory, and in its death throes? The right to breathe? The right to eat? The right to drink clean water, not from nineteenth-century wells or poisoned rivers? The right to good health? To bear healthy children? Or perhaps the right to move freely around the country, together with the right to take a job and leave it freely—in other words, freedom from servitude?

No! The right he proclaims as of prime importance is—*the right to emigrate*! That is staggering, shocking. You could have thought it some silly slip of the tongue—if he had not uttered and written it repeatedly. In *My Country and the World*, after a description of Soviet life comes a second section, even before the disarmament issue, about Sakharov's favorite problem, most worthy of discussion, before universal disarmament: "On the freedom to choose one's country of residence." That was 1975. And since then he has frequently declared that the right to emigrate is the "key issue," the "first and most important" of all human rights—turning on their head all sensible ideas about the preconditions of national life. And there we were, thinking the key problem of collective farm workers was their exploitation from dawn to dusk, working unpaid, owning no land, utterly exhausted, in poverty, lacking clothing and shoes—but no! The key problem of collective farm workers was the fact that they weren't allowed out to America! During that period, thousands of villages in Russia judged to be "without prospects" were being forcibly "closed down," people forcibly removed from their places of birth—Middle Russia was being totally annihilated. Sakharov said nothing about that, didn't notice it. Instead: the right to emigrate!!

The same thing, year after year; so dogged. Instead of all the possible theories for a reorganization of society, what a bizarre ideology of flight. What country has a native population capable of demanding a "first right" of this kind? The explanation that Sakharov concocted ran like this: what is unique about the right to emigrate is that it guarantees the rights of those staying behind. In other words, if people are free to emigrate, then under the relentless threat of the whole population leaving for America, full civil rights will be established in the USSR. It's mind-boggling: how can a learned physicist invent and actually believe in such a fanciful fabrication? It's because not only logic was at work here, but also an emotional coloring of his perceptions: I want it to be that way!*

Not to mention the fact that the very substantial Jewish emigration that had been flooding out of the country for several years had weakened the pressure for civil rights in the USSR—and had largely brought down the dissident movement: for many dissidents an enticing, easy way out had opened up, and the more persistent the dissident was, the wider it opened. As a result, the dissident movement lost its strength and did not effect a social breakthrough.

But it was only words, of course—this "universal right to emigrate." It was all very well for Sakharov to write (in *My Country and the World*) that emigration was a tragic necessity for the Ukrainians, Russians, Lithuanians, Latvians, and Estonians—but those millions or hundreds of thousands of all these who had left during earlier wars are, on the contrary, tragically pining for their homeland, the only place where they would value gaining freedom and bread—which in a foreign land they do not. Sakharov had a convincing example of this, the Germans' impulse to leave—though this was not actually emigration but rather re-emigration, to their age-old home. And so, despite all the additional arguments, it was clear to both supporters and opponents, near and far, that he was talking about Jewish emigration—and this was the reason for the whole theoretical construct. In this lay Sakharov's pain. As he wrote, "I understand and respect the national feelings of Jews

* Now that a time has come when Russia has unlimited free emigration—has it brought us great prosperity? (Author's note, 1996.)

leaving to build up their newfound homeland"—and so do we, many others of us, also understand and respect them. But in Sakharov this is a rare example of national feelings in a positive context. He didn't shrink from getting involved in an equally resolute manner in the internal wrangles of the United States and passionately defending the Jackson amendment[102] against attacks by American critics (it was blamed for damaging US trade). He appealed once to the Supreme Soviet of the USSR, four times to the American Congress, and then to the British, French, West German, and Japanese parliaments, asking them to introduce their own Jackson amendments and, by halting trade and credits, force the USSR to let Jews leave. And he tried to convince them that in this way a complete and honest détente with the USSR would be established.

So much effort, so much fuss and bother (and so much personal risk)—so that a small proportion of the population could secure a privilege which, in the current conditions, will not be seen by the rest.

Involuntarily, even Sakharov was carried away by that surge of emotion, which touched his heart. At various periods he has tried, openly, to get permission for himself to travel abroad (and in those circumstances there'd be no coming back), though adding, soberly, "I cannot count on a journey abroad or emigration as a solution for me."

But, doomed to remain bodily in the country for which he did top-secret work for twenty years and which he has armed with the most terrifying weapon of the modern age, Sakharov is looking ever more intently at the West (not, however, intently enough to discern its vices and dangers), addressing it publicly, turning towards it, and being transported there in outpourings of emotion. He also sees the "leftist fashion that is all-powerful in the West, the fear of being behind the times." But he reassures himself, and the West, that "in the long run the Western intellectual will not let us down—he does not share the demagogues' and politicians' views"; Sakharov views the Western intelligentsia "with respect that verges on envy" and "does not doubt the altruism and humanity of most of them" and simply finds it quite extraordinary that the leading American newspapers censor and misrepresent him, omit the names of *zeks*, and tone down the expressions he uses. He persists in his attempts (mostly fruitless, just like mine) to convince Westerners that the struggle for human rights in the East bolsters the positions of the West itself. Sakharov takes great pains to understand the West's worries, naïvely advising a "worldwide political amnesty." (For the Red Brigades[103] too? and all terrorists?—what a muddle.) And he's an admirer of Amnesty International, with its left-facing bias. And he urges the West "not to fight local [that means internal political] battles"—for these "weaken the Western world." (But that is exactly what it is, their much-envied multi-party parliamentary democracy!) And he is naïvely trying to persuade Europe not to allow anti-Americanism. . . .

Sakharov is a great utopian; and in inspiring the West with his ideas he sometimes addresses the "parliaments of all countries," sometimes the governments; he writes to President Carter in a somewhat schoolmarmish tone about "our duty and yours . . . It is important for the president of the United States to continue his efforts." . . .

Yes, Sakharov's boundless success in the Western press and among Western politicians reflects the closeness of their views and standpoints. They are even paying him the debt of honor that they neglected to pay Raoul Wallenberg for thirty years (Sakharov has now been proclaimed a Prisoner of Zion in Israel, an exceptional decision taken by the Knesset in January 1980).

He had, of course, been aware throughout the '70s of the danger of his already extreme political and strategic opposition to the Soviet state; and yet not totally aware, having lost all sense of political limits, and being, in his mind, at one with the allied West. He has been scattering his fearless (from within the USSR!) and unsparing judgments of the Soviet regime across the worldwide media: a meretricious, ineffective social structure; a fast-changing foreign policy that is unprincipled and uncontrolled, supported by free access to finance; cruelty; secret, subversive activities; an untalented, predatory bureaucracy; the violation of agreements; arms supplied in order to escalate bloody conflicts; and the truth about what's going on in Vietnam. Sakharov has been fearlessly (and with knowledge of the subject) revealing all possible secret calculations by the Soviet government at the nuclear disarmament talks as it seeks to enable the USSR to make the first strike. He has also indicated plausible (but impracticable) ways to disarm: with openness and verification.

Despite this, in December 1976 he had to listen to an indecorous question from a Western correspondent: one gets the impression that Sakharov was more active in the social sphere before the Nobel prize was awarded (1975) than afterwards?

And this referred to the year when Sakharov, outside the trial of Mustafa Dzhemilev in Omsk, struck KGB men and a policeman in the face—and it was asked the day after he had, while demonstrating his respect for the mythical Soviet constitution on Pushkin Square, bared his thin strands of silver grey to the freezing cold and some KGB men, laughing, had tipped paper bags of mud and snow out onto his head.

And was an American correspondent really going to understand that our Russia is so benighted that when people way out in the sticks hear that an academician, a defender of justice, has appeared in Moscow, they send him clumsy petitions, more and more of them, without an address: father, take up our cause! And between solving world problems Sakharov has to read through almost every letter and cudgel his brains to think how, in a situation of general lawlessness, he is to move a perfectly legitimate request forward.

But that correspondent seemed to have invited trouble with his question: in the first days of 1977 Sakharov was forced into a confrontation of unprecedented acrimony with State Security—and I consider those months the peak moments of his struggle, the pinnacle of his courage. It was triggered by the explosion of 8 January in the Moscow metro and Victor Louis's shabby little article suggesting to Western readers that the bomb was the work of dissidents. Sakharov felt responsible for the whole dissident movement—which had been marked out to be crushed—and on 12 January he published his appeal to the international public saying that the repressive organs of government (read KGB) were resorting ever more frequently to criminal methods (there had already been several notorious assaults, on Academician Likhachyov among others), anonymous killings, and now he "cannot dismiss the feeling that the metro bombing was a provocation by the organs of repression or by specific circles within them."

Only Westerners can fail to appreciate what it means to throw such an accusation in the KGB's face and in sight of the whole world—it was putting his head on the block!

But the KGB got cold feet and backed down, as it always did in the face of a courageous move.

In the weeks immediately afterwards, this duel unsettled Sakharov for a while. A menacing summons to the public prosecutor's office also arrived—once there, he might never have come back out—and he conducted himself with dignity there, and did not weaken and give them the retraction they demanded. And yet again, the following day, he repeated his accusation in an interview. And during those fateful weeks he was sustained by a State Department declaration, followed by a personal letter from the newly inaugurated President Carter. The KGB took fright and pushed the public prosecutor to justify himself in the *New York Times*—what a come-down for the Dragon! Sakharov wrote an appropriate reply, also in the *New York Times*. (But President Carter immediately backed off and said that he "should not, publicly," have supported Sakharov. But that he . . . would receive him unofficially, *if* he came to the United States. . . . You didn't know whether to laugh or cry.)

Sakharov held his ground. And he continued to respond to many cases of the persecution of individuals. And the fact that dozens of his appeals were fruitless did not cause him to despair. However, both at that time and earlier, and indeed later, he never hid his fear: not so much of arrest as of the mafia, of "underground, criminal, mafia-style action" (and there again, it was true that the KGB's possibilities in that area were boundless)—especially regarding his wife and her children: "any persecution of them would be incomparably more tragic than anything else for me."

And the KGB knew that very well. And they made use of it. Sakharov and Elena Bonner's whole life was filled with threatening and mocking letters: opening any envelope in their mail, they did not know what filth or derision they would find there, substituted for the original contents. But the threats were absolutely real, for dissidents were now, one after the other, being either beaten up or killed by mysterious, strapping lads, impossible to catch. And so the threats (the KGB acknowledged that Sakharov himself was unshakeable) were now aimed at his Achilles' heel—Bonner's children. This was coupled with three years of apartment-related victimization—a totally original Soviet invention. At one time they would refuse to register Sakharov as a resident of his wife's apartment, another time they would deprive him of Moscow residence registration entirely, or obstruct an apartment swap. Or else they'd create unpleasant work situations for Bonner's children.

Then Sakharov's nerve failed him. Having done so much for other people to emigrate, to make emigration the supreme human right, it would have been irrational for him to hold back from claiming that right for his nearest and dearest too. Now he made specific demands regarding the fate of his wife's children, referring to them as hostages. And quite unexpectedly these insistent requests met with success: within a year of the metro bombing and this bitter conflict, his stepdaughter and her husband were allowed to leave for America, as well as his stepson, whose departure, it was later revealed, was even premature.

Sakharov himself was genuinely prepared to be sacrificed. But when he was suddenly exiled to Nizhni Novgorod in January 1980 it became apparent that he was, even so, not ready for that blow. After two months of exile (in March 1980) Sakharov was still apparently not understanding the irrevocability of what had happened, applying to leave the country "if I am not to be allowed back to my Moscow apartment." But the authorities had really tightened the screws and the conditions were harsher than the normal exile, a stage on the way to arrest: a sentry on the door, an escort when in town, a ban on talking to anyone he met in the street.

The pain of the blow inflicted on Sakharov must be gauged by the eminence he'd lost. Whereas I'd set off on my insurrection from a life lived constantly, since childhood, in the *lowest levels* of society, he had left a life that was permanently, since his youth, lived in the *upper echelons*. That is incomparably harder.

And if, in earlier times, Sakharov had always insisted that no one must ever be asked for sacrifices or firm resistance, now he started blaming all the academicians: "my colleagues' silence is tantamount to complicity." But I always felt that *appealing* was acceptable, while *reproaching* was not, and was the last thing one would expect, given Sakharov's gentle nature. Had some of the other academicians, at times engaged in work that was exceedingly useful for the country, really been guilty of not trampling on it out of solidarity with Sakharov? Each of us must determine what level of sacrifice he can take.

At this point, in his darkest period, Sakharov was doomed to get involved in a prolonged, humiliating situation, in all the ado over an exit visa to America for his stepson's fiancée; the stepson, in his own haste to emigrate, had not actually married her. Sakharov was probably moved by a sense of guilt towards his wife's children, or he could not bear to see her torment as a mother, but the extent and tone of that campaign quickly became grotesque. And now his articles and interviews, dispatched from Nizhni and with content of worldwide importance, started looking like no more than preambles, annexes to the grand finale: scientists of the world, demand that your statesmen procure permission for Liza Alekseeva to leave for America! —Even without any efforts on Sakharov's part, his exile to Nizhni had from the start given rise to loud reverberations internationally—which had gone as far as government declarations and a resolution in the US Congress. However, many in the West who had put Sakharov on a pedestal and been persistent in their efforts to help him, now, with the Liza affair, nevertheless felt a certain embarrassment.

But even those appeals did not immediately rock the planet. And Sakharov sacrificially decided on a hunger strike. The fate of Liza Alekseeva eclipsed the whole world's problems in the whole world's press for several weeks, including those very days in December 1981 when the fate of Poland was being decided before Jaruzelski.[104] Eight years before that, Sakharov had announced his first hunger strike during Nixon's visit to Moscow, in support of the eighty-four *zeks*—and even then, at the age of fifty-two, he had cut it short on the fourth day because of the threat to his health. Now, aged sixty, he made the focus of his greatest concern, and the greatest risk to his life, the emigration of a girl who had never yet been imprisoned or distinguished herself in any struggle, and he went without food for sixteen days and could even have starved to death.

Elena Bonner declared, when she arrived back in Moscow, that: "The triumph of our hunger strike is the triumph of universal human rights!" Alas. The Vashchenko family,[105] Pentecostalists, naïvely believed that the world would support them as well, with equal fervor: the family held out in a long hunger strike, having already forced their way into the American embassy demanding to emigrate—and they were disappointed.

Of course, Sakharov's whole years-long descent, from the top to the lower strata of society ("right down to Nizhni"),[106] at first voluntary, then not, involved a complex spiritual adjustment for him—and his whole personal development probably seems to him to be all of a piece and entirely inevitable. Especially as in 1975 he was still suffering the torments of a Soviet consciousness: "That chapter turned out after all to be rather 'uncharitable,' judged by our usual standards. In my moments of torment I sometimes feel embarrassed despite myself, almost ashamed. The work I do now—is it worthy of the name?"—a question still absolutely consonant with Soviet patriotism. And he replies: "But I am betraying no one, casting no shadow over their honest labor." And: "If my heart is honest, then I have no reason to reproach myself."

His final absolution was just as hasty as his first doubts had been excessive. It is possible to be completely honest and straightforward inside, as Sakharov certainly is, but to be so wide of the mark on the basis of a superficial view and feel for things, on the basis of ignorance and a lack of understanding of your homeland's history—and so to veer off from its course.

Looking at the way Sakharov has dealt with Soviet oppression, the way he protested against the invasion of Afghanistan, we can only, of course, admire him. However, in his progress through life, while developing spiritually and setting up projects on behalf of all humanity, Sakharov has fulfilled his duty to the democratic movement, to "human rights," to Jewish emigration, to the West—but not to Russia, which is mortally ill. There are many real Russian problems that he has not raised, against which he has not campaigned as selflessly, as fervently. When thinking of Russia's future, we dare not remain indifferent to what Sakharov has contributed and what he is promising. He has shown us, on a high plane, the possibilities of the Russian conscience—but he outlines for us a future without nationhood, with filial instincts atrophied. A remarkable, luminous man has been born of our body, but he has invested the whole impetus of his sacrifice and his heroism in the service of something that is not, strictly speaking, Russia. To Sakharov, as to all Februarists,[107] freedom would be enough—and Russia, only vaguely in the picture, has lost its shine.

Is it simply that he does not feel Russian pain? . . .

Although—I have no right to level that accusation: many, many of us were poisoned by the Liberation and Februarist atmosphere in Russia. I felt it myself and only just managed to resist it, so obscure has the truth become. Through Sakharov the nineteenth-century Liberation doctrine strikes at us again in the twentieth.

In that Liberation tradition, fear reigned: fear that you might express some embarrassing sympathy towards the odious concept "Russian," that the word might stick to the speaker or writer. And it's the same with Sakharov: if he ever mentions the issue of Russia it is more often than not in a hostile manner. It is only on that one issue that he manifests an acute enmity that is most unlike him. If he is talking about the *Soviet* occupation of Afghanistan, he is bound to finish with: "the geopolitics of the *Russian* empire." (Russia never tried to seize Afghanistan, whereas the Communists did, from the very start. England clings even today to the Falkland Islands, on the other side of the world—that's *geo*politics for you, but we don't pay attention to that.)

As far as the Orthodox Church is concerned, Sakharov, that scion of a priest, in the spirit of inherited, radical thinking, seems to fear it above all else. If he ever mentions Orthodoxy, it is through gritted teeth, tangentially, coming somewhere behind the Pentecostalists. Yet he has said that "in Poland the influence of the church is traditionally great and benign." That's true, that's how it is!—but why not just once, parenthetically, acknowledge that Orthodoxy too has not been without its benefits in Russia?

He repeats the Moscow pseudo-intellectuals' fable, of which he was not the author: "The people and the Party are as one—these are not totally empty words." Well yes, and the rape victim and the rapist—they're as one, of course, at a certain moment.

But the critical turning point was marked by the hunger strike—he did a lot of thinking over those days. And after his victory, just what did Sakharov write in his first short letter to the West? That he agrees with the "fine words of Mihajlo Mihajlov": "The concept of homeland is not geographical, not national—homeland is freedom." But if homeland is nothing more than freedom, why the different word? What else is included in it? The "fine words of Mihajlo Mihajlov" are a self-seeking slogan, already well-known in Ancient Rome: *ubi bene, ibi patria.*[108]

In 1975 Sakharov shied away from a discussion with me on matters of principle—given the yoke he was under, this was quite understandable. But all this had clearly accumulated in him to such an extent over the years that no sooner had Chalidze's dishonest article "Khomeinism or National Communism" reached him, from a New York newspaper, than Sakharov rushed to offer his own shoulder to move this cart-load of lies along. And he sent the West an "Open Letter"[109] (that was what he called it, repeating the nervous haste of his response[110] to my *Letter to the Soviet Leaders*—for there is, of course, no greater danger to Russia than that of a national consciousness!), hurrying to associate himself with the article: for it was, you see, "a discussion of the views of Solzhenitsyn and his supporters." And just what were my ("our") views? "Nationalism" (to which I do not subscribe) and "the politicization of religion."

Andrei Dmitrievich! Wherever in my writing did you encounter any "politicization of religion"? There's nothing even close to it. *You're* the one who's doing that, with your continual warnings against the "political dangers" of Orthodoxy. Was it not you who wrote that "Orthodoxy makes me uneasy," that it must, to your mind (and to the Communist mind), not be allowed out of the human breast, out of the house, out of the church? Would banning Christians from applying their faith in public life be the only way to stop "politicization"?

Why, Andrei Dmitrievich, does your usual sense of proportion always desert you in disputes about Russia? The label "Great-Russian[111] nationalist"—whoever nailed that one on me, if not Sakharov? And all my current hounding by the émigrés—who, if not Sakharov, gave that a fillip back in spring 1974? Whoever grafted "well-paid young Orthodox believers" onto my *Letter*? Whose idea about the "mild ideologues" and their ruthless followers has now become an epigraph for Chalidze, so as to egg on the harassment of Solzhenitsyn?

It would appear that so much unites Sakharov and me: we were the same age, in the same country; we both rose up at the same time, uncompromising, against the prevailing system, fought our battles at the same time and were vilified at the same time by a baying press; and we both called not for revolution but for reforms.

What divided us was—Russia.

CHAPTER 7

A Creeping Host

By 1979 I had been nursing the concept of *The Red Wheel* for forty-two years and working on it constantly for ten. And throughout all those long years I had been collecting—sometimes on paper, sometimes solely in memory—episodes, incidents, facts, key dates, available material, reflections, assessments, and ideas. I don't think I would have been able to complete this work without my innate and systematically methodical approach or my mathematical mental training. (Indeed, who could?) I had now been writing the first draft of *March 1917* for more than two years, meaning I had embarked upon the Revolution proper and on all the difficulties and peculiarities linked to the material of that period. (It was all the more vexing and distracting, therefore, to be forced to spend three months on *Millstones* instead, prompted by the KGB cacography of Tomáš Řezáč.[1] The return from the present day to 1917 was not achieved without effort.)

Is there any limit, any end to the work of collecting material for a historical epic? It takes decades, at the very least. What about compiling popular archetypes of soldiers, peasants, factory workers, officers, the civilian intelligentsia, and the clergy through photographs, drawings, or verbal descriptions of their external appearances, clothes, bearing, and ways of speaking? Lengthy searches and random scraps build them up bit by bit by bit—in order to provide a single depiction of, for example, a loud and lively gathering of a great many soldiers. The volume of material prepared and studied may sometimes be a hundred times more than that of the author's final text, and twenty times more is perfectly common.

It is very important, though sometimes difficult, to determine when to interrupt the influx of a particular type of material because it is threatening to stretch the overall structure to the point of collapse—after all, theoretically speaking, the material is infinite. A reliable indication is increasing hesitation as to whether or not something should be included. When the border between the essential and the non-essential flickers more frequently into view—there's the sign.

In my case, enormous help has come from *old people*, the elderly émigrés of the revolutionary years. They have gifted me both with anecdotes and with the spirit of the time itself, which can only be conveyed by "non-historical," ordinary people. How very many evenings I have spent warming myself with their recollections in my spacious study that is always poorly heated in winter. For me, each of those evenings was a refreshing encounter with contemporaries of the events—with "my" contemporaries in spirit, the living characters of my tale. In the evenings they strengthened me for the next day's work. A table lamp shone down onto the pages while all the dark expanse of the high-ceilinged study was as if filled with a living, sympathetic, amiable throng of these "White Guards." I certainly wasn't lonely for even a minute.

I felt I was a bridge stretching from prerevolutionary Russia to the *post-*Soviet Russia of the future, a bridge over which the heavily laden wagon train of History is lugged over, across the entire abyss of the Soviet years, so that its priceless load would not be lost to the future.

What doesn't work, however, is first selecting, perusing, and studying *all* possible materials, and only later on sitting down and writing the epic straight off. No, both tasks must alternate, each exactingly clearing space for itself. Which is why mistakes occur too: fresh material, only just read, makes it into the writing perhaps less deservedly than another piece that has long lain unused. But there is also that happy state of affairs of fitting perfectly into the essence and synthetic scope of the subject matter, when the required anecdotes, facts, and excerpts—like burning letters etched in the brain—slide into place of their own accord without needing to be picked through or searched. Lucky breaks begin to ride to the rescue, emerging out of the work in hand. Yet on a different day, the work seems hopelessly stuck, only to be followed by a restless night with bouts of wakefulness and brief jottings by flashlight to avoid waking up altogether—and it is then that thoughts you cannot access by day rise to the surface of the subconscious, and what you most need breaks through. In the morning, you analyze your unfinished scrawls—and hello! it's all there!

Then there are dreams involving my characters—so vivid they're deeply affecting. On three separate occasions, I dreamed about Nikolai II. He was visible, substantial. I had just committed to writing about him at the end of 1976. It was as if we were sitting next to one another in the seats of an empty theater—no performance under way, curtain down—having a conversation. I could see his face, close up, clearly defined—and in color too. —Later, with *March* well in hand, we talked about Russian foreign policy one minute (he spoke gently and with interest in the subject), the next about the succession, and he shook his head sadly that no, Aleksei[2] could not rule as tsar. Likewise, I dreamed about Aleksandr II once, when I was studying the liberals. —On separate occasions, I dreamed of General Alekseev, Aleksandr Guchkov, and even Trotsky in various situations. And surely this was bound to happen when I was spending hours looking at pictures of them, pondering them, thinking myself into the characters. For me, they had become the most contemporary of contemporaries and I lived with them day in, day out for weeks and months at a time, and many I quite simply loved as I wrote their chapters. How could it be otherwise? You can usher one, two, or three main characters through a story or novel effortlessly, drawing only superficially on your own experience, but how can the same be true of a hundred and fifty people when you are equally responsible for Palchinsky, Shlyapnikov, Kozma Gvozdev, NCO Kirpichnikov, the grand dukes Nikolai Nikolaevich and Mikhail Aleksandrovich, generals Kornilov and Krymov, and Mikhail Rodzyanko? (How much I learned about the Duma's much-loved "Samovar" from the manner of his death! It was the only way he could die—his heart ruptured by *joy*: in Serbia, he had been wrongly informed that the Soviet government had fallen. . . .)

And notably, throngs of historical rather than fictional characters came increasingly to dominate the book: some in decidedly tragic tones, others courting a tongue-in-cheek style, but through all of them sounded and resounded the beating pulse of the Revolution.

And alongside these historical figures, absorbed wholeheartedly and experienced as close acquaintances, neither the reader nor I had so much need any more of a plethora of fictional characters. Real-life veracity was well established even without them, through the real people who figured among the ordinary rank-and-file members of the crowd.

A small work of literature arises naturally from an integral and comprehensive plot design. A major historical epic can begin only by reconstituting the framework of events. Only its completeness can subsequently ensure that the narrative is *convincing*, the proffered historical explication persuasive—even though this completeness poses a threat to the narrative in terms of sheer volume and overload. But if an author sets himself no such objective, all he can do is surrender to an irresponsible play of the imagination. (In the early years of my work, I had cast around for material for all twenty

Nodes, right up to 1922—but later realized that this effort would prove of no use to me.)

But even as a writer clarifies and probes this historical basis, it begets further attempts to interpret all the fragments and the connections between them. (There can be no making up for these attempts "later on.") This is the first draft. After that, it seems, the narrative already lies before you—even though it doesn't exist yet. At this point, the second draft of the Node begins (I worked on each of the Nodes separately), in which *elasticity* is achieved and hundreds of internal links in the narrative emerge, which had been utterly unnoticed and inaccessible when the primary material was being gathered and brought to light.

It can be difficult to progress from the first to the second draft, given the vastness of the material. It calls for a kind of inner reinvention, an ascent into a state of flight. So, in spring 1979, working on the vast four-volume *March*, I underwent an inner crisis, a shutdown. There was no need to force myself, however: my feelings bounced back of their own accord all of a sudden, out of the blue—and they drew me on and on. In the course of this crucial draft, dozens more vital chapters would arise, flare up, be written, and themselves find where they fit best. And at this point, the less planning there is, the easier it is to surrender to the unhindered course of instinct.

After the second draft, the book already exists, even if death stops you in your tracks. In actual fact, however, a great deal of work remains to be done and of the most delicate kind. You must still reveal the harmony inherent in these events, and sometimes their magnificence and symbolic nature as well, and help them become visible. And what a lot of other detailed and subtle tasks arise to ensure specially reinforced *borders* (of a volume or Node)—a criterion so familiar to any builder. This occupies the third and fourth drafts, as does putting the finishing touches on many chapters.

An essential role in creating a large-scale work of literature belongs to the properly imagined relationship between its parts, both *horizontally* (how a specific character, specific small community, specific topic continues throughout the Node) and *vertically* (how chapters succeed one another and fit together over the course of hours and days). Both are important and rightly demand attention—but they are not immediately apparent even to the author's eye; they require a patient attentiveness. Each of the narrative links in the horizontal chain must be located and worked out by the author, and somehow signposted or flagged so that it is more easily detected and remembered by the reader despite the vast size of the work. Fusing the horizontal and the vertical is among the tougher nuts to crack. (Just as it is when laying the bricks of different stories.) In the second draft, the horizontal predominates, exerts the pull, so as not to have to part from a character once you have entered into his world.

Plotting the horizontal for social units (the Provisional Government, the GHQ,[3] the headquarters of the various fronts, the Executive Committee of the Soviet of Deputies, the Bolshevik higher-ups) was harder still as their mutual influences were closely intermeshed (a "horizontal cluster," as it's called in mathematics) and not one could be charted on its own. The slightest stirrings of that less-than-brilliant Rodzyanko, for example, had an immense impact on other people's actions until he lost all traction and receded into non-influence. There is a constant need to verify horizontal progress against the vertical: you write one chapter and check another dozen to ensure they don't clash. By contrast, the staccato episodes of February in Petrograd are barely horizontal at all. Rather, they are immediately written into the vertical of their day.

Meanwhile, the *juxtapositions* of chapters along the vertical, that is, their order of succession, provide an extra way of creating an impression. A juxtaposition is like an additional, unwritten piece of text without a single line of its own, which deepens the meaning through contrasting tones or the sequence flow. The juxtaposition can also provide something that cannot be expressed by any text. (Juxtapositions operate particularly starkly in conveying a tumultuous revolutionary situation. As calm returns, the role of juxtapositions diminishes, and you even set the chapters out in such a way that it takes the reader less of a leap to continue.)

It is exceptionally effective, impressive, and conclusive to use extracts from the *newspapers* of a particular day or week. They are an indelible, incontrovertible stamp of the public mood, rich in factual information to boot. (And when the information contains a deliberate error or a calculated lie, it becomes all the more typical of the atmosphere of the times. Newspapers differ from memoir writers in this being of the moment: they do not know what will happen tomorrow.) Linked to a precise date, newspaper columns hammer the indelible details of events into us. For the reader, some will be mere repetition, reinforcement, or the first report of a fact—although always colored by the newspaper's distinctive features and very frequently piquing the reader's sense of humor, heartily in places: the hurried journalists themselves cannot tell how amusing what they are writing is. It remains for the author to group newspaper reports together, to put them in order. This, particularly through juxtapositions, provides yet another bundle of sentiments, arranges an entire newspaper symphony.

Newspaper overviews entail another plus: that the reader is induced actively to work through the primary material on his own.

This activity by the reader is also ensured by the *fragment* chapters—collections of real-life episodes on a theme (the capital, small towns, the railway, the army, the villages). They relate the shards of the period very vividly and intensely, and once again the grouping of the fragments creates a fourth dimension of joins and juxtapositions.

Contradictory ideas are vividly conveyed in faceless group or mass dialogues and discussions. And some public scenes of the post-February weeks themselves invite humor.

The *proverbs* quoted separately in large print between chapters are called upon to express the people's judgment of what has just been heard (read) in the chapter. When successful, these too disclose an extra dimension to be grasped. Sometimes they also shed light on the next chapter.

And finally: difficult to encompass, the scope of the epic insistently requires that a *brief summary of chapter contents* be drawn up at the end of each volume (this device also pays homage to old-fashioned tradition). To help the person who has already read the book find the place he's looking for, and the person who has not—to form something greater than a cursory impression. This task effectively demanded the creation of another subgenre. While singling out the main names and facts, this list should not be a dull enumeration. Signposts, as mnemonics for the reader, may contain emotive phrases, or show an event in a light or from an angle that was not clearly expressed in the main body of the text, enhancing it through some new association.

What wondrous cohesion stems from many months, many years of working on this colossus. There are never enough hours in the day. I move from desk to desk, from manuscript to source material, and the joyful feeling that I am doing the most important work of my life never leaves me. (No matter when Alya comes in, she always finds me enraptured, happy.)

No matter how demanding the normal working day, I am always calm and composed at its end.

And so you live this full life for weeks and months and years—how you long to distance yourself from any external encounters, just so that no one bothers you! But that's precisely the time that they do come piling and swarming in, masses of them. Alas, all this work of mine has proceeded year after year to the growing and intrusive clamor of an external accompaniment. My detractors did not subside; on the contrary, they decided that their ideal time had come.

The English-language edition of *The Oak and the Calf* came out in the US in the spring of 1980, four years later than in every other language but, on the plus side, in Harry Willetts's excellent translation. I have been in the West for eight years now and have not found another English-language translator to equal him. He works slowly at the best of times (as he must, indeed, for quality's sake), and in addition he and his family have been dogged by ill health in recent years. And so my books come out latest in the world's most widely spoken language.

Those who were interested, however, those who were keeping tabs on me, had bided their time—they had long since read the book in Russian—and were now lying in wait for its publication in English. And that's when they were presented with a marvelous opportunity—to crawl all over me at some speed, biting here, stinging there, befouling me, and loudly drawing attention to themselves every time.

First and foremost to rush to put in an appearance, even ahead of publication, was my one-time self-appointed biographer, George Feifer, whom I had thrown from the saddle back then. Feifer now disgorged an article[4] in the literary journal *Harper's Magazine*, which spoke for the whole affronted Burg, Bethell, Zilberberg group and for left-liberal enthusiasm in general, following neatly in its wake. Already aware that any slander or verbal abuse of me whatsoever could be published in America, Feifer gave it fresh impetus with his article, devising clichés for the newspapers: a reactionary and fanatic, Solzhenitsyn makes calculated use of lies and deceit, along with messianic moralizing. I had allegedly gone back to *Novy Mir* and the authorities' new protégés only in order to get published. (And what a tall tale that was; it stemmed from a spurious insinuation by Vladimir Lakshin. How had I "gone back" if I never crossed the threshold of *Novy Mir* after Tvardovsky?[5] How and where could I have been published in the USSR at all after 1970, when I was ostracized by the Soviet authorities as a whole? But American readers had no way to verify this or to find it out—write it down and it will stick. What came next was even harder to swallow: Solzhenitsyn has retained the mindset of a committed Communist, is close to Lenin on fundamental political and social issues. The hypocrisy of the Harvard speech. He has taken on features of the tyranny he is fighting. Qualities like these will generate a new dictatorship. In the future, this threat will be greater than the military threat of the USSR today!! (And where do they find this nonsense about my future tyranny? I sit here, writing books—not going around setting up alliances, or blocks, or conferences.)

Reading Feifer's article, I realized that I had already been completely "educated" by left-wing US journalists, was already used to being dragged through the mud—I have already stopped even noticing. "Criticism" has gone so far beyond all limits that it is not worth objecting, or even reading it. In a foreign country, for which you feel no tenderness and whose "elite's" opinion you do not rate highly, all these aspersions become immaterial. I am not going to fight for my reputation in America: fight here, too, and you will lose both literature and Russia.

What's more, Feifer, who once exalted the Soviet collective farm system, was now swiftly turning his sights on Russia. Russian life is an animal farm. It would be paradise for the peasants if only they had selfless integrity. (The Russian proverb "A pig will scratch itself wherever it goes" refers to judgments of this kind.)

Feifer's article also sought to publicize one by Lakshin, which was soon to come out in book form[6] in the United States and was also timed to coincide with the publication of *The Oak and the Calf.* (It was already several years since it had come out in France, and it should have appeared in England a long time ago but the publishers—Cambridge University, I think—had shied away from publication, wary of the many terms of abuse Lakshin used about me, lest I take them to court.) Lakshin was truly feeding from two troughs. US newspapers now wrote that he was "respected in both the West and the East," "out of favor with the authorities" (not a single day without a prominent post and a sizeable official salary), "lacking the opportunity to respond freely to Solzhenitsyn." Well, he's publishing freely in the US press (unerringly aware that it was laudable for a Soviet critic to challenge the *literary Vlasovite and renegade,*[7] Solzhenitsyn).

Feifer's article gave clear expression to (and helped propagate) a view that was already fully formed among émigré pseudo-intellectuals and eagerly swallowed by their US equivalents: that "Solzhenitsyn is worse than Brezhnev, worse than Stalin, worse than Hitler," and most certainly worse than the sacrosanct Lenin. It set the tone in their press for years. With its irascible hostility, the US press seemed to be in a hurry to convince me again and again that it was impossible for us to form a staunch alliance with them against Communism.

Her eye always on the ball, Olga Carlisle naturally popped up with a shrill clarion call to coincide with the publication of *The Oak and the Calf*—keeping one step ahead of a book no one had yet read. This time she examined historical roots in an interview,[8] talking about her adoptive grandfather, Viktor Chernov, the leader of the Socialist Revolutionaries, and about Lenin, who was "not a murderer in the sense of Stalin or Hitler," but her main disagreement with me was, of course, about my notorious anti-Semitism. The reliable testimony of someone who "has known [me] personally for many years" was the best match to light the haystack of US pseudo-erudition.

The next advance look at my book was Professor Stephen Cohen's lead opinion-forming piece[9] in the *New York Times Book Review*. It contained several erroneous quotations; and several, not necessarily deliberate but nonetheless ignorant, distortions. But Cohen was not the first to pick out the main set of charges. They had already been selected earlier. He was simply summarizing Lakshin: Solzhenitsyn is embittered by his experience of the Gulag. Undemocratic, unkind, intolerant, untruthful, unreasonable. Authoritarian views, contempt for liberal democracy. "A man who by his own admission lies to his friends" (that was when I kept my underground secrets from Tvardovsky). Prepared to sacrifice his own children "to save another manuscript" (that was—not renouncing *Archipelago*, spurning the blackmail of the KGB, but Cohen doesn't explain). "Russian critics who knew them both" (Lakshin) are indignant that Tvardovsky is maligned in the book. While Lakshin was said to be persuasive in his contesting of Solzhenitsyn's memoirs.

Cohen's depiction of me was not as disrespectful as Feifer's and yet, since penned by him and in the most modish publication, would now become the preferred slur. Presenting me as a monster—in this, the efforts of American pseudo-intellectuals decisively coincided with those of their Soviet counterparts.

The task was made easier by the fact that, in the States, the four-year delay in translation meant that *The Oak and the Calf* appeared not amid the glory of my clamorous confrontation with the Dragon but once the heat had gone out of it, and in front of people who had been irritated by the Harvard speech.

Cohen even formulates for the reader a supposedly current saying: "Tell me what you think about Solzhenitsyn, and I'll tell you who you are." And, after all, he's not wrong! Since the publication of *Ivan Denisovich*, I have involuntarily acted as a polarizing ray. First, I split people into Stalinists and those who longed for freedom. Then (over *August 1914* and the *Lenten Letter to the Patriarch*) into internationalist-inclined liberals and patriots. Essentially, I am now dividing people in America too.

However. . . . Although the radical mouthpiece set the tone *for its own* criticism, in America as a whole, it became as polarized as ever. Judging by the bundles of responses to *The Oak and the Calf* that I was regularly sent by the publisher, the positive and neutral nevertheless outnumbered the negative—but not by much, and any acute hostility was more vocal and more resolute. (The tone of British newspapers, meanwhile, was both more seemly and more frequently well disposed.)

Some simply block-copied Cohen into a single lead paragraph: "We now know Solzhenitsyn as someone who lied to his friends, who declined to mourn the death of an old lady, who ignores the fate of Soviet dissidents, and resolved to sacrifice the lives of his children for the sake of a single manuscript." In this way, they cobbled together in a single sentence—"mendacious, cunning, hypocritical, cruel, vengeful . . . this book is an exposé of his personality."

Today's journalism and politics have completely forgotten, have no concept of what it means to talk about one's own mistakes and blunders, much less defects—it is lacking even in their literature—they never feature anyone who does so. Which is why they were so taken aback by my confessions in *Archipelago* and *The Oak and the Calf*—and their sole delighted conclusion was as follows: There, he's shown us his defects (and it turns out we are so much better than him)! And the newspapers at the forefront of any persecution, like the *New York Times* and *Christian Science Monitor*, lashed out in a frenzy.

Arrogant, ruthless. Treachery, boasting. Backbiting, sanctimony. Megalomania, the carping of a fanatic. Neurotic delusions of a confused mind. His psyche has been profoundly affected. Schizophrenia. Paranoia.

Cast into free America with, as I thought, its flourishing diversity of opinions, I never could have expected that it was precisely there that I would be swamped by dull and crass slander, no less potent than the Soviet version! But at least no one believes the Soviet press, whereas many believe America's, and not one Western journalist and practically no "Slavist" has undertaken an honest day's labor to look and see where I wrote or said these things, or whether there is even a grain of truth in them.

More from the reviews. —Now, with the publication of *The Oak and the Calf*, it is hard to love him (Solzhenitsyn). It is impossible to love him. He is constantly wrapped up in his own concerns (the fate of *Archipelago*). He displays a sanctimonious contempt for dissidents. He has endless reserves of contempt ("smearing" the Medvedev brothers and Chalidze). He has proved an ungrateful guest in exile: he criticizes the countries that gave him the chance to speak. (Whereas no, they should only be flattered.) He attacks the country that has given him sanctuary and the leaders of his former country. (They are particularly upset about those baa-lambs, the Brezhnev gerontocrats!) A reactionary force. Following Lenin's example. The great Russian ayatollah. —And from the very-left-wing *New Leader*:[10] "Part of the blame lies with our government for embracing Solzhenitsyn so uncritically." —But it was perhaps Max Geltman, in the Jewish magazine *Midstream*, who outdid them all: Solzhenitsyn "devotes pages to his complete pedigree . . . peasants all, with the cow-dung almost bespattering the pages."[11] . . .

As far back as 1964, Tvardovsky had told me (I noted it down): "Vast hatred is primed against you." It was only the first year that I'd been heard of at all! But there you go. Only now have I felt it in my flesh, and more extensively than Tvardovsky imagined at the time.

When slander offers them an advantage, do these two world forces, Communism and democracy, differ from one another all that much? In their attacks on me, the Americans are catching up to the Soviet authorities. Or going even further. The Soviet press hounded me with dead, dogmatic formulas, which didn't touch me personally at all; they had a mechanical quality but no personal animosity towards me. And the discussion of *Cancer Ward* at the Moscow writers' organization, for instance, was quite simply a model of forbearance, even from the hostile speakers. Yes, even at the height of the battle at the Secretariat of the Writers' Union, I was not inveighed against with such bile, such personal, passionate hate, as I was now by America's pseudo-educated elite.

In German, misfortune, misery, a sorry state—and a strange land—are encapsulated in one word—*das Elend.*

Well, the Western press once raised me up—and is entitled to sweep me from the throne as well. To adapt the Russian proverb: in a foreign land you will be known as a devil for three years. It wasn't quite like that for me: I was transported to them first as if I were an angel, but the scales fell quickly from their eyes, and now I shall be a devil to the bitter end, let alone a mere three years: Solzhenitsyn—the bogeyman, Solzhenitsyn—leader of the right wing. Indeed, that same *Midstream* warns in all seriousness: "A leader with the desiccated fanaticism of a secular ayatollah, albeit more talented and so more dangerous, will require [of us] a sustained and lengthy struggle." (A struggle! Tuck that away to remember.)

(For myself, in 1973, I'd wrapped up the Third Supplement to *The Oak and the Calf*, fiery with the conviction that my death "would be hard to digest" for the Soviet authorities—"you wouldn't envy them."[12] But it wouldn't have, not at all: the West would have soon forgotten me and forgiven my demise.)

And even as a writer, have I ever been understood in the major US cities? Well, so far the translations of my books have been poor, but here was a most excellent translation! They didn't see anything, not a single judgment worthy of the subject.

But alongside the torrent of inveterate "columnists" (spawning hundreds of identical articles at once across the whole of the US press), letters from readers also made it through—and they saw something different in *The Oak and the Calf.* So, Thomas Walters of the University of North Carolina wrote: "If ever a writer has had to seek his homeland within himself, it is Solzhenitsyn."

Of course, we have to allow for the fact that columnists cannot conceive of the real situation in the Soviet Union, nor how heated the battle there is. After all, they have never experienced such a struggle. They can't imagine that it can be fiercer and swifter than a military clash. They aren't to know that it takes at least this much determination to smash through a concrete wall.

But even those of them who had been to the Soviet Union and might have taken something on board hadn't done so. Our acquaintance Robert Kaiser added his review[13] to the slander. Furthermore, he managed to appear as an "eyewitness," saying not only that my book was one-sided but also that "in important ways the book is simply *dishonest,* as I can attest first hand." What are these "important ways"? There's this. *The Oak and the Calf* states: "Two American correspondents [Kaiser and Smith] came to see me without the conventional agreement by telephone" (in other words, as is clear from the text, so that the KGB would not learn about the interview in advance from the bugged telephone, much less the day and time).[14] And this man who had, incidentally, lived under surveillance in Moscow, now puts on an act for those who don't understand, saying: "It appears that we simply dropped in on him, when in fact we arrived after complicated preparations. He had been planning the interview for at least two months, something he, apparently, wishes to conceal in his memoirs." (But which is apparent to anyone who has read this passage in *The Oak and the Calf* with open eyes.) Given one such falsification, "I am afraid that many episodes in the book have been distorted to suit Solzhenitsyn's polemical purposes."

At this, I couldn't stop myself (although not until a year later, when I'd read it) and wrote Kaiser a letter: Why such personal unscrupulousness? *Was* there a phone call, in actual fact?—no, there was not. Was it really not clear to Kaiser that all I was talking about was *protection from the KGB*? If it wasn't deliberate bad faith, I said, please amend it publicly and in the same newspapers. (I didn't even bother reproaching him for one other thing: in the *Washington Post* in 1977, he had arbitrarily attributed to me, and in direct quotation marks too, a reverence for President Carter that I had never expressed. The ethics of a US journalist? . . . Doing the new Democratic president a favor? . . .

But do they even know how to make amends or apologize? Kaiser replied: "I agree that not a single fact in your account is untrue. What I wrote in the review, however, is what I believe. I must remain true to my convictions and see no reason to apologize."

So then, readers, there you have this "living testimony," that "in many ways the book is dishonest." . . . And it is observers like these, dropping into Moscow, who hold in their hands the fates of those who rise up against an omnipotent power!

One might almost say: why did *The Oak and the Calf* have to be published in the States? They'd have managed without it, and we without them.

And yet, however many distortions there might have been in this malicious attack, surely it wasn't entirely untrue? They did see things from aside—and if there's a drop of truth there, why not learn from it?

I read on: "He describes Tvardovsky with cynical ingratitude." —And comes the chorus: he's cruel to Tvardovsky!

I begin reflecting: can this verbiage perhaps be instructive in some way? Cruel? Yes, there were moments of cruelty: I hid myself away from Tvardovsky on occasion; the blows I intended to deal the Soviets, I almost always concealed. It was cruel—but how else to do battle? A let-up in one thing, even the slightest, and the flank is exposed, the battle lost. However, my depiction of Tvardovsky in *The Oak and the Calf* came from a pure and well-disposed heart, and it is impossible to draw from it a nefarious impression about him.*

Or they write: "The thirst for revenge [for victims of the Gulag] that has always dwelled in Solzhenitsyn has obscured any distinction between politics

---

* A LATE AWAKENING: When Tvardovsky and other members of the editorial board *summoned* me urgently to their offices, or required that I report to them my exact whereabouts, that I not conceal my movements, I never acquiesced to their demands, confident that I had no such *obligation*: I was not, after all, a member of the editorial board! I was not in their "service"! After many years of moving around underground, I had a confident sense of myself as of a fully autonomous battle unit, a tank. —And for a long time I could neither digest nor understand what immense pressure the *Novy Mir* editors were under, month after month and year after year, as punishment for having published *Ivan Denisovich*. They were suffering now for having engaged with me courageously in 1962. So, while I was not in their "service," I was morally obliged to help them as the need arose. Tvardovsky was now paying the price on my behalf.

But what exactly was I *obligated* to do? When I prepared my bombshell statement to the Secretariat of the Writers' Union in November 1969, was I to come to Tvardovsky and show it to him first? Precisely so. And inevitably to submit to his angry prohibition. . . . (And so—to lose, to break apart the whole vector of my independence?) Or, before that, was I to have given him the address of my Hiding Place, where I took refuge to finish writing *Archipelago*? . . . (And, indeed, was I to have *told* him about *Archipelago* itself?)

Therein lay the incompatibility of our *strategic* vectors. (Author's note, 2008.)

and literature in his works." Not "any distinction," no; partly obscured, fine. This excessive amount of politics in literature is something to be jettisoned as old age approaches.

Or this: he is "ungrateful to his friends." They don't know I've written *Invisible Allies*,[15] and don't know who my real friends are: they assign Chalidze and those Medvedev boys to me as friends. But to spell it out: whatever madness of battle there was, whatever haste to rush out underground writing, I should have, even so, found the strength of mind and the time to alleviate our harsh circumstances for my friends and covert collaborators. I could have been more solicitous of them. Yes, I am so committed to the fight that I forget to alleviate things even when I should. (I was too late to see Aleksandr Yashin[16] in hospital, after all. . . .) How I would like to become gentler as life draws to a close, and to counterbalance certain things in the past, and everything in the future.

But American critics were probably most united in their surprise and indignation as to how I could be so certain I was right. After all, it is well-known that for any point of view about anything there can only be balance, a fluid pluralism, "fifty-fifty"—that no one is in possession of the truth, indeed the truth cannot exist in nature, all ideas have equal rights! And since I do have that certainty, I must imagine myself a messiah.

Here is the cavernous rift between the Western Enlightenment's sense of the world and the Christian one. As we—as I—see it, a person's conviction that he has found the truth is a normal human condition. Without it, indeed, how on earth can he act? On the contrary, it is a disease of this world, to lose your bearings as to what is being done and why.

But American criticism of *The Oak and the Calf* was not manifested solely in personal demonization; it still sometimes remembered that it was considered "literary" criticism. So now: the book itself was incoherent. A political diary. Not much new. It would seem he has nothing else to say, and we are not interested in hearing any more of his sagas. An atavistic vocabulary. Hybrid prose.

See yourself in a puddle and you won't look like yourself.

It is from this direction that the main efforts of the émigré and American pseudo-intellectuals may henceforth be expected: to prove that I am a minor writer, that it was a delusion to take me for a major one. The pseudo-intellectuals cannot bear a major writer emerging who is not from their ranks and does not have their mindset. And how they raced to go through the list to find me a "polar opposite," how many times they saluted: one minute, it was

"Zinoviev, Solzhenitsyn's polar opposite," the next, his "polar opposite Grossman," his "polar opposite Sinyavsky," his "polar opposite Brodsky," and then even Lev Kopelev became my "polar opposite," and that's still not all.

After all, the Kremlin, too, cast around to find me a "polar opposite" in Soviet literature—but never did find one.

I do not smart under US press hostility towards me, however, because I do not need to be published in it or to communicate through it. Furthermore, it cannot be said that I had no influence whatsoever on America during those years. In 1975 and 1978 my words still sounded an audacious challenge and were censored by the Voice of America. Then Reagan came to power and sometimes quoted me himself; government officials followed suit (even some journalists did, after an utterly shameless about-turn), repeating me, as I was then, almost word for word.

So, should I be speaking out today as well? —No, today, as they make amends for their shameful acquiescence in the face of Communism, today the need for my speeches has fallen away.

Thank God that, given the accumulation of life material, there is no need to become immersed in an environment into which you have been randomly cast. And a writer does not live in the information stream from the newspapers, but at quite different depths; he does not need to ingest this surplus of empty husks. I follow world events solely on the radio. After all, if a newspaper extract is particularly required, it is usually sent to me.

Even so, sometimes you fly off the handle. In July 1980, I was sent a short article from the *Christian Science Monitor*—a venomous left-liberal newspaper, among the most influential in the States. Published in Boston, just around the corner, it once requested an in-depth interview: I declined. Now, one Harlow Robinson writes,[17] under the headline "Solzhenitsyn: Shrill" (or "piercing"—shouty, essentially): "Solzhenitsyn said in a recent interview that he would go back 'at once' to Russia, *preferably as a national political leader* [my italics—A.S.]." What kind of scoundrels are they? They can bark at me however they like—go on, damn you. But "Solzhenitsyn said"—the cheek of it! I didn't say it, and have never thought it. So, what do I do? Get sidetracked, write a rebuttal: "Your highly intellectual newspaper is fully entitled not to know Russian history and not to understand the conditions of Soviet life [this refers to the rest of their article], but it has no right to print deliberate falsehoods. . . . I ask you to publish my letter, and I await a public apology from the author."

And if they don't publish? I'm not going to take them to court—that's not for a normal person to do, much less a writer. And so it will stick.

Three weeks went by—not a word. I couldn't rest, and wrote again: "Must I conclude that you are refusing to print my rebuttal, and I am free to write about this falsification openly in other publications?" An answer from the editor-in-chief!—ah, unfortunately, I was on vacation when your first letter arrived. . . . We have tried unsuccessfully to contact Mr. Robinson for the desired comments. (They themselves are unable to check that I said no such thing, nor anything like it, in my *New York Times* interview. . . .)[18] Eventually, after another month, my letter was published in the "Readers Write" section, as was Robinson's response: "'*preferably as a national political leader*' was [Robinson's] own interpretive addition," and he was sorry.[19]

And the whole episode wasn't worth a fig—and I'd had to waste time and focus on it. But are you really going to keep up with the vastness of all the world's media? issuing rebuttals? —The hydra heads of newspaper lies.

But it's all a matter of scale. This petty nonsense ended on 8 September; on the afternoon of the 11th, I was sitting as usual at my little desk beneath the birches, near the pond, on our plot fenced off by wire netting about two meters high. No one from the outside ever came there, and my family were at least a hundred meters away, up the hill. But here—only chipmunks dashing around. I wrote in this solitude during summer after summer, my soul unbound. A steady breeze is blowing, concealing any rustling. My eyes are on the paper. I can hear nothing and see nothing in my peripheral vision. Only when I happen to look up do I see a magnificent powerful copper-colored creature passing by on a raised path a meter and a half from my head. Could a dog be that size? whose dog? and so noiseless? I turn my head as it goes by, and behind the trunks of the birch trees I see the first wolf, which has already gone past. Now it has turned to look at the one behind, and is baring its teeth in its long snout, as if asking why it's lagging behind. Now I can see the second one in full. It's gone by to catch up with the first. They're gone.

I didn't have time to gather my wits or to prepare myself. There wasn't so much as a stick to hand in any case. The wolves passed by calmly and utterly soundlessly along our usual well-trodden path through the property. My desk, though, was in a hollow, so that they had passed within less than two meters, level with my shoulders, and nothing would have prevented either of them from leaping at my throat. Had God delivered me? were they not hungry? (My neighbor says they don't live around here: they come in from Canada following the starving moose; it had even been on local radio.)

I sit and collect myself: that would have been a fine way to go (and on exactly the same day as the loss of my archive on 11 September 1965[20])—eaten by wolves! At my writing desk on my own property. No Russian writer had yet come to such a pathetic end. Rejoicing and laughter from my enemies. *March* incomplete, my life chewed up while I was still in my prime.

And what dangers I had lived through! . . . Yet you can't tell what awaits you or where. Who can reckon death's quick beckon?

For the first few days, I began to take a hunting rifle with me and to lean it up against my writing desk. And whichever of the children was bringing me pages from his mother[21] had to shout from the mountainside: "Papa, I'm coming!!" and I would go and meet him.

But the wolves never came back.

And how I loved that spot! At my dugout desk, densely surrounded by the trunks of five birches, it was like sitting in an arbor. To one side, a little higher up, was the terrace outside the cottage, evenly laid with flat stones of varying shapes (when they were playing, the children used to say that one was Australia, another Greenland), and you could get a quick bit of exercise there next to the pond, racing up and down these flagstones. On hot days, I would take several plunges into the pond. To the other side, where those wolves had gone, was the only meadow on our entire property, a hundred and fifty paces of it, and the only view open to the sky, where I took the boys to study the constellations. And on moonlit summer nights when I couldn't sleep, I would sometimes wander slowly from the cottage by the pond through that meadow, knee-deep in grass, gazing in wonder at the towering poplars, and, through a chain-link gate that was never used, at the empty byway; and beyond lay the same distinctly defined and silent moonlit world, with only the sound of the three brooks playing as they came together—right there, near a dark dip in the ground. This exile world is still our familiar terrestrial one, but at the same time somehow extraterrestrial. And—why am I here? and—is it for long? . . . I always feel that: no, I am here temporarily; and, because of that, everything feels even more ephemeral than for others on Earth.

How could these copper-colored wolves not make me think of the red ones? Now, those really could have clambered in and devoured me even earlier. So what were they up to?

On the surface, of course, it was still the same old depressingly stultifying Soviet propaganda, too repulsive even to read. The red front still stood firm. But I, being at a distance, had ceased to impact them, and had effectively had no inkling of them in all these years since Řezáč's book. I had vaguely heard at one point of some libelous two-volume "novel" about me being published in the GDR, at another of some paltry little book by the Central Committee–linked professor Nikolai Yakovlev. I had so little need to keep an eye on them that it was only this spring, 1982, as I raked through the archives for this continuation of my *Sketches* that I discovered a BBC report from way back in March 1976, when I'd been traveling in Spain and then gone straight to California. The paperwork built up in my absence, and I never revisited it. So now, six years later, I learned that in March 1976 *Literaturnaya Gazeta* (*Literary Gazette*) had published "Harebrained,"[22] a lengthy and hostile article about me. The whole fabrication had appeared in it even then: that my grandfather, the peasant Semyon Solzhenitsyn, had been some great feudal lord, renowned in the area for his cruelty, and with property of a dizzying 15,000 hectares. Nevertheless, one of his sons, armed with rope, knuckle-dusters, and gags, turned to highway robbery, while another, my father (a man of the most liberal views), couldn't cope with the fall of the monarchy and committed suicide. And two years later I had been furious with Řezáč—when all he'd done was to snaffle the whole thing from *Literaturnaya Gazeta.*

It's only now that I've turned the pages of Yakovlev's commissioned carping, although it dates from 1979.[23] (He turned out to have published yet another book attacking me, this one in English—*Living in Lie.*[24]) It obtusely reiterated over and over again, until it was suffocatingly oppressive, that I was a puppet and loyal servant of the CIA (and had been since Soviet times) but turned out to be not up to snuff, and so was transferred to the reserve and discharged by the CIA into rural isolation in the state of Vermont. That *The Gulag Archipelago* was "the combined efforts of United States government departments." Of me, of course, it said: "The lackey Smerdyakov[25] . . . blinded by the glinting boots of German generals. . . . His 'moral revolution' conceals a call for armed conflict with the Soviet state." But also, "a man with a delinquent, criminal psychology" (what a touching closeness to Lakshin's and Feifer's diagnosis, that I had been blighted by the camps). "He professes totalitarianism. . . . A smug fascist. . . ." (literally the indoctrination given at the US State Department too, as I've already mentioned[26]).

No, deny it all you like, but our humanitarian intelligentsia has the same roots, the very same roots as the Bolsheviks.

I easily resisted the temptation in the West to become a mere exhibit, a tub-thumper. I buried myself in my work, I didn't bother anyone, but would the irrepressible gutter press lay off now? It's their job to niggle away at things. In April 1981 we suddenly noticed photos being taken outside our gate. Some young men were keeping watch and photographing who went in and out. Journalists? Alya went outside. They turned out to be photographers for *Paris Match*, wanting to "film [my] way of life." —Alya tries to persuade them it isn't possible: if someone doesn't want to be filmed, it cannot be done against his will. —But they had a job to do: it was a very long time since there had been pictures of Solzhenitsyn in Vermont. —"Well, we do have some pictures," we said. "We'll send them to Claude Durand, our literary representative in Paris. You can pick them up from him." —They seemed to agree, and off they went. Four months went by, and *Paris Match* dispatched another, pushier expedition. Again we learned that someone was wandering around, asking questions, but we attached no significance to it. Driving past, my mother-in-law, Katya, saw someone's car constantly parked nearby—again, she paid no attention. (It later turned out that photographers had already been all over our property in secret—we don't have dogs, after all—and took photos, but hadn't managed to get any of me.) Nikita Struve was staying with us at the time, and he and I played tennis every evening on the very edge of the property; we'd be casually dressed, just in shorts. As we took a break between sets, my youngest son Stepan, acting as ball boy, came over and said, "There's a bald head bobbing up and down—over there, behind the bank." How on earth? This was a first. I yelled in that direction. Then I spotted someone in grey-black running away across a dark incline behind the trees on our plot. I yelled again, and immediately heard the loud sound of branches snapping. We made our way through the undergrowth barefoot. They'd gone. But we discovered that they'd bent the fencing over the brook: they could squeeze in easily that way, and it was how they left, too, dropping a camera case in their haste. No doubt, they'd already driven off. Only then did we make the association that two days earlier a small plane had been circling over our plot for ages, low and persistent, wings steeply tilted—had it been filming?

It had. About two weeks later, photos appeared in *Paris Match*, pictures taken on the tennis court and from the plane, as well as the snapshots we'd naïvely sent them in good faith. And the accompanying story was full of gossip and nonsense.

Heinrich Böll also wrote to me that year, asking me to grant a literary interview. To whom?—to *Stern* correspondent Jürgen Serke. I don't know what had fooled Böll, or maybe he actually approved of *Stern* magazine? I had the most painful memories of it myself, of how they had distorted my genealogy at the toughest moments of my battle with the KGB, rushed *Prussian Nights* into print *in my name*, and tried to delay *The Oak and the*

Calf through litigation.[27] Naturally enough, I turned Serke down. No worries: after regrouping, he comes to Cavendish with a photographer, and he, too, wanders around the environs, asking questions and collecting gossip. And this at the very same time as *Paris Match* (and I didn't even know). *Stern,* too, hired a plane that flew just as long, low, and brazenly over the property on a different day. And so *Stern* had an aerial photo of its own. But there was no sight of me, so for its "literary interview" *Stern* bought a stolen picture from *Paris Match.* And then Serke had to bluff his way through, pretending the interview had taken place and not letting on that he'd been denied access. And that's what he did: "Solzhenitsyn says . . ." (for which, read "says to him, Serke") something approximate to something I had said that had already appeared all over the place. What about the age-old Russian slavery? "Solzhenitsyn declined to talk to me *about that.*" (By implication, he talked about everything else.) "His biography, which displays hubris. . . . He pronounces an anathema on East and West. . . . It is rare for someone to take this Solzhenitsyn seriously. . . . Just like Lenin—an advocate of an authoritarian system. . . . There is immorality among moralists, misanthropy among Christians. Dostoevsky depicted them in the figure of the *Grand Inquisitor.*" —The whole Creeping Host[28] maintains this, it is the shared image they have of me. They have closed ranks once again, and borrow from one another.

Such petty scurrying, such tiny sorties on so many little legs.

Incidentally, on a closer look, there was nothing accidental about the whole series into which this hostile sketch was inserted; the whole series was designed to show noble artists and exiles—the "humble Christian" Sinyavsky, the deep thinker Zinoviev, the sublime lyricist Brodsky, the martyr Voinovich—in contrast to the savage, filthy inquisitor. And particularly heartfelt regarding Sinyavsky, who "thirsts for the Kingdom of God," and is apparently among "the latest inheritors of Christ's expiatory feat." (What a shapeshifter, to present himself like this. . . .) As Dickens wrote in such cases: "Hear, hear!"

But what this journalist did get right was that I was driving myself out of the Western world.

And it's true: how am I to live here?

A foreign land will burn and brand.

That autumn, some devil got into *France-Soir,* and out came: he has six armed bodyguards, a pack of fierce dogs, an electric barbed-wire fence, but Solzhenitsyn is free of financial worries, he is funded by an American billionaire, unnamed.

In any corner of the Earth, any degenerate reporter can write any lies whatsoever about me—this is what their sacred freedom consists of! their sacred democracy!

How am I to live here? . . .

* * *

What else could they use to harass me? Why, the courts, of course! The free, democratic courts. What was our old acquaintance, Olga Carlisle, meant to do now that she had butchered translations, delayed publications, and doused me with venom in her book and in subsequent untruthful articles, accusing me both of anti-Semitism and of having merged with new Russian fascists—while my only response to all her calumny was a footnote in the US edition of *The Oak and the Calf* [27]; what was she meant to do now? why, take me to court, of course! *She* would take *me* to court! And no matter how dispassionately had the lawyers for the publisher, Harper, pondered and amended this footnote—it had been so thoroughly reworked that I had kept to myself all the invective Carlisle deserved—but no, the Carlisles were going to court!

Oh, the individual's sublime right to legal redress! Throughout his life of freedom, the free Western individual is denied the pleasure of telling a scoundrel to his face that he is in fact a scoundrel.

In October 1980 the Carlisles held a sensational news conference in San Francisco: they were going to court! Solzhenitsyn needed to realize that "he lives in a different world."[29] Ultimately, Solzhenitsyn had to pay for invading the Carlisles' "privacy" (and this after she'd written a book about herself) and for libeling them. And they were initially seeking damages of two million dollars (later to be revised upwards)!! And that figure was all the US press needed. It flitted across the newspapers that the Carlisles were suing Solzhenitsyn for two million dollars! (Utter ruin! even if the house was sold, and everything in it, it wouldn't be enough to pay the bill!) Another flurry in the press: she had run risks bringing *Archipelago* out of the USSR (it wasn't her at all)—and was now being shown such ingratitude. (An immediate howl went up from Third Wave émigrés too: "Solzhenitsyn has sunk so low that his close friends have to sue him for libel!"—and this at a Los Angeles *literary* conference.)

A few months earlier, my blissful, uninterrupted, untroubled work on *March* had just reached the most difficult chapters of completing the first draft—Grand Duke Mikhail's farewell to the Winter Palace, his renunciation of the throne—and now I had to drop everything! To sit myself down and go through the jumbled archive—thank goodness, at least we still had it—to restore the chronology of "events," facts, details, and any documents or potential witnesses there might be—oh, it was utterly draining! And all the documents had to be presented in a notary-certified translation into English. . . . I had been put on trial *there*—I was being put on trial *here* too. Appearing as the accused in the free world.

The case being brought in San Francisco also meant the lawyers, and possibly I too, had to go dashing across the continent. Under US law, lawyers may ask to question the opposing side under oath, even before a trial. And so I would have to drag myself off for questioning. And then the trial. Witnesses had to be assembled for the trial. Betta, at least, would testify to what really happened. Nikita Struve knew bits and pieces. But everything that had gone through Heeb was lost[30]—he would beg off the whole thing. And, God, did it hurt, raking up all that torment again, the one line of our fight that failed back then, going through forgotten papers once more, restoring one little link after another—and what would be left of my work? My heart sank as I thought on this several times each day.

The news of the legal action weighed me down all the more since in that very autumn of 1980 I had been feeling particularly, unbelievably at ease. I was sleeping soundly, in good health, quick on my feet. The work was going very well. I was free of all foolish concerns, such as the Swiss scandal over the Fund,[31] and I was through with the polemic discussions, had emerged from them fairly well, and now all I had to do was work! And what a paltry matter a trial appears when no execution or prison camp looms, and there are no pangs of conscience, no emotional distress, no loss of honor. Can it really be compared to the once-constant KGB pressure, the loss of my archive in 1965, or the painful divorce from my first wife? or to a fire breaking out right now and destroying the manuscripts—my whole life, in other words? Why, even the wolves' passing a mere stone's throw away was more serious. Wouldn't far graver dangers threaten me in future? And in any case, what was this compared to the fact that others of my fellow-countrymen were being oppressed every day? was such rubbish really going to cost me, battle-hardened as I was, my balance, my focus on my work? The insignificance of the conflict compared to the work in hand was the killer.

Indeed, that's what they mean by *it's not the sea that drowns you but the puddle*. It was a Western puddle now. In my final February days in the USSR I had said: all your hounding in the newspapers will not ruin one working day for me! And so it proved! But, over here, I now started to feel regret: had it really been worth adding that footnote about the Carlisles? why ever did I get involved? had I lacked the humility to endure? After all, I had stepped into the puddle of my own accord.

But no, I couldn't have kept silent about all her lies. It would have been humiliating, a failure of character. And, after all, she had played on our shared oppression back in the USSR.

What was to be done? Worry is a normal earthly condition. Such instances are inevitable in the Western world, and my fate must be to experience everything for the sake of a full picture. There was nothing to be done—I abandoned my work and began to put together a plan for our defense, our objections, and our grievances. The extremely long complaint arrived from the Carlisles' lawyer, thirty long "legal" sheets of paper, the lines numbered—a venomous concoction of Western legalism, but firing off emotional accusations instead of legal rhetoric—the two million had to be squeezed out of it, after all. The complaint targeted not just me but publishers Harper & Row as well, although obviously I would be paying. What lawyer could I summon to my aid? It was handy that I knew the famous Edward Bennett Williams, who had already defiantly and nobly defended Aleksandr Ginzburg when he was entombed in the Gulag, and he had certainly influenced Ginzburg's release. Williams was immensely well versed in the law and had won a great many trials in the States. He sent to us in Vermont his promising young assistant, Gregory Craig, himself a native of the state. By straining my memory for several hours and with recourse to my restored notes, I told him the whole vexing history with Olga Carlisle since 1967, our errors, her mischief-making. We could file a countersuit regarding her latest articles attacking me. Drawn into the matter, I was by now out of temper and prepared to fight her to the death, what else? My footnote had been a feeble shadow of what I ought to have said about her. I was prepared for a lengthy trial, to call witnesses, to spare no expense, and to have justice in the end. If I had not bowed to the KGB, why should I now bow to such petty shabbiness?

But we talked and talked and reminisced for seven hours in succession; then, during the eighth, Craig explained that it would be very drawn-out and exhausting, was likely to become a sensational trial, would all be rehashed by the press and TV, and the best we could hope for would be to prove Carlisle had wronged me, and was that really such a big deal? was it worth it? was it worth the money? This is how inflammatory the courts' inhuman grip is: Craig had to try to prove *to me* that it wasn't worth tearing myself away from my work. He had another plan. In publishing her book, Carlisle had made herself a so-called "public figure" and, in America, you can say what you like about them. Therefore, it had to be shown that my footnote gave insufficient grounds for her lawsuit. It had been merely the expression of my personal opinion about a public figure.

That's the system!—anything is easier than simply proving the truth.

It was sound advice. For the umpteenth time, I would have to accept that it was impossible to have it out with Olga Carlisle in the way she deserved. Freedom, where everyone's lips are sealed and everyone is wallowing in compromises. . . .

We adopted Craig's plan, but even that called for a vast amount of work by the law firm. Thirty similarly long "legal" sheets of paper, their lines numbered, were used to compile an equally tiresome legal document, packed with precedents (US jurisprudence is based not so much on laws as on precedents): when, by whom, and where charges of libel had been refuted and the right to freedom of speech claimed. (Nowadays, computers retrieve these precedents from the country's legal history.) A forceful document was produced, apparently. It was delivered to the opposing side prior to the court hearing in July 1981 and was meant to make an impression.

But what did Carlisle do? You would think that, knowing her character already, I could have guessed. Yet I wasn't expecting the next step. Three or four days before the hearing, her lawyer proposed via ours that we surrender!! The Carlisles would deign to withdraw the lawsuit if I made a public statement of the kind they put to me: "I was not familiar with the conventions and nature of the publishing industry in the West. In view of the concerns of Mr. and Mrs. Carlisle at my statements in *The Oak and the Calf,* I should like to clarify that I did not mean to imply that Olga Carlisle used my royalties for personal gain, or to imply that they deliberately misled me about the publication timeline for *Archipelago*. If such interpretations did arise, I am very sorry and distressed at the damage to the Carlisles that might have ensued."

In other words, I was being asked to put my signature to the precise opposite of what had happened and which I was ready to expose. At the same time, it was suicide as a writer: disavowing one paragraph in a book like *The Oak and the Calf* meant casting doubt on the whole of it—and then what about all the other books as well? It was all I needed at a time when I was already immured by a wall of slander.

I was indignant not just with the Carlisles, but with my highly likable lawyer as well: why had he undertaken to pass along such a humiliating request? he had created a sense of weakness that we didn't have! Craig responded that this was just the way things were: he was obligated to pass it along.

His reply to the Carlisles was a curt refusal over the phone.

On 23 July, the court case opened in San Francisco. The wise and diligent judge, William Schwarzer (relying, of course, on Craig's superlative presentation of the case), sternly informed the Carlisles that their lawsuit was completely unfounded.[32]

And yet it could have been completely different—going on and on, taking up time, inflicting shame and financial ruin to universal applause.

The "judge dismisses Carlisle lawsuit" telegram we received was a great joy, a huge weight being lifted after nine months.

But the court-free respite did not last long.

The indefatigable Zhores Medvedev, after his failed attempt to take me to court on behalf of Mikhail Yakubovich, tried again in October 1981—also because of a footnote in the English-language US edition of *The Oak and the Calf.* When it was first published, Zhores had put up with everything I'd written: both the fact that, for years in the West, he had voiced manifold support for Soviet policy, and even that he had come up with justifications for punitive psychiatry (though a victim of it himself). He left all that unchallenged now, too, but what he latched on to was my comment that he had included a hand-drawn map in his book of how to get to my Moscow apartment (unprotected from acts of provocation, and with small children inside).[33] —So now he wrote a letter to the publisher, Collins, to say that the map *had not been* in his book, and he might now take me to court (for the moment, he was still contemplating whether to do it). Collins caved in right away, immediately hastening to apologize that it wasn't responsible for the remark and offering not to reprint it further. The correspondence reached me only belatedly. —What devilry was this? We had actually seen the book and the map, and had been outraged, and had written clandestinely from Moscow to Zhores in London—and all of a sudden the map didn't exist? Zhores now explained to the publisher that the invitation to the Moscow Nobel Prize ceremony had only been photographed for the first edition of his book, with its small print run, but not the side with the map on it: so that the map hadn't been there at all.

You never know when you might need something: why would we have brought his book over from Moscow? It had been forgotten about somewhere back there. Now where could we lay our hands on one? We looked.

There was no invitation in the later editions at all. We commissioned an earlier edition to be found, "the very first" in fact, and Zhores was right: there was the invitation, but not showing the side with the map. What was going on?—had our eyes betrayed us? But we'd seen it, Alya and I! we'd written to him to object.

Fortunately, however, our friend and well-wisher, Alexis Klimoff, who took an interest in everything to do with me, had once bought a copy of the very firstest edition, and then given it to Michael Nicholson in England. He now rang Nicholson to ask him to take a look. Phew! Of course, it was all there, map included.

Basically, when we protested in 1973, Zhores withdrew the print run quick as a flash—and now, certain that the early edition hadn't been preserved, he was playing us for fools. But since he wasn't certain absolutely, he hadn't gone straight to court; for the moment, it was just a threat, testing the water.

Nicholson sent a photocopy of the map to the frightened Collins publisher to show to the trickster.

For the moment, Zhores is saying nothing. (And, in any case, he is now suing Vladimir Bukovksy.) At the same time, I can't be certain that he has given up altogether. He might pull some other trick.

Nor was that the end of our judicial tribulations. Rumor had reached us from Paris as far back as the end of 1978 that Alec Flegon had become a frequent visitor to YMCA-Press, which had once attempted, unsuccessfully, to sue him.[34] He was questioning staff and not even bothering to conceal the fact that he wanted to write a blistering book about Solzhenitsyn and YMCA-Press. In the fall of 1979 Flegon had even written me an insolent letter to that effect. He wanted to know whether I was a YMCA-Press owner or shareholder, whether I was suffering from paranoia and being treated for it, and called me a professional liar. With that letter alone, he was asking for a lawsuit—in Western terms, it was sufficient for a trial. I paid it no attention.

In the spring of 1981, various Russian libraries and shops in various parts of the world, even Brazil and Australia, began forwarding a small advertisement to me, which Flegon had put out in English and Russian for his book *Around Solzhenitsyn*,[35] "a literary bombshell." Flegon also included banned poems from Russia's past, just like his publishing house had already brought out Ivan Barkov's "Luka Mudishchev."[36] Before long, the bombshell would "become a bibliographical rarity and sell at a steep price." Nikita Struve then sent me Flegon's two-volume opus itself from Paris.

Was I to *read* the book? It was evident from skimming through it for the very first time that Flegon had gone completely berserk, even in the photographs and drawings. On several occasions I was depicted as an Orthodox icon—as Christ the Savior, or a saint with wings, or Saint George—and there were crosses everywhere as a jibe, an abundance of crosses and the traditional frames of Orthodox icons. Flegon's hatred of Orthodoxy was diabolically out of control. As was his hatred of historical Russia in general—there were dozens upon dozens of caricatures or illustrations of that repellent country, but as it was in centuries past, before the Bolsheviks. And again, there I was in a general's uniform, wearing a royal crown. And interspersed with these were montages of me with naked women, me giving birth, here in the guise of a prostitute, there several more instances of my photographs in various pornographic settings—pornography was evidently Flegon's main passion and weakness, in which, to his own detriment, he knew no bounds whatsoever. Dozens and dozens of his pages, no matter where you looked, were strewn with obscenities, outright invective, and ribald doggerel. Even without reading the book, it was obvious that it was so licentious that Flegon could be taken to court over any one of its layouts.

The book was so far below any requirements of simple decency, however, that it would, itself, repel readers other than my most inveterate enemies. It would be unseemly to enter into a dispute with it. Such filth was the best evidence of the boundless licentiousness of the "free" press. It was bound to result in such pigswill in the end.* (Incidentally, Flegon's book, contrary to all the rules of publishing, contained no publishing data, and a fake address.)

What was Flegon counting on? Surely he couldn't have thought it would stand up in court. Which meant he wanted a trial to advertise his book. An injunction on the book?—then it would start to really circulate. Financial losses?—they didn't scare Flegon; evidently, he had a lot of money backing him.

Anyway, he wouldn't get a trial out of me.

And in any case he didn't just want a trial—he longed for it with a passion. He only came alive in a courtroom atmosphere. He had already been in

* The Israeli Russian-language magazine *Krug* (*Circle*) responded with "Flegon does battle with Russia"; "no Russian, much less a Jew from Russia, could have overstepped his spiritual boundaries with such heedlessness"; Flegon has, allegedly, *proven* that "all the traditions of censorship, punishments, and prisons were worse in tsarist Russia than in the USSR." (Author's note, 1986.)

court many times, several of them over my books alone—for piracy.[37] He sued Max Hayward from Oxford and the late Lev Rahr of *Posev* over allegations of pirate publications. He took the magazine *Private Eye* to court to prove he had no connection with Victor Louis, when he undoubtedly did: it was Louis who brought him Svetlana Alliluyeva's KGB-sanitized manuscript for advance publication, to drive down demand for the original; that's what led to Flegon's lawsuit with her. And he took other publishers to court as well. And quite often won. And if he lost, he would declare himself bankrupt and for some reason, under the English system, he always got off lightly. Flegon was the archetypal litigator and shyster.

Then, immediately after the publication of Flegon's latest book, in the spring of 1981, Russian émigré Oleg Lenchevsky walks into a respectable British bookshop, browses through the book and, on a naïve impulse, writes a private letter to the shop's owner, Christina Foyle, asking how she could deal in such pseudo-literature and pornography. And what does this lady do (even without knowing Russian she might well have been persuaded and repelled by the illustrations alone)?—she sends Flegon a copy of Lenchevsky's letter. And what does Flegon do? Immediately files a lawsuit against Lenchevsky: after all, he was libelously stating that the book was pornographic! (Which was evident from the very first glance.) And legal procedures commenced! And are still going on.

Two or even three trials at once, it evidently doesn't trouble Flegon one bit—this is the fetid air he breathes. And he waited and waited to see if I would take him to court. Waited for six months—to no avail. And then, in November 1981, he brought a case *against me*! (The *Jewish Chronicle*: "Writer takes Writer to Court"; the *Sunday Telegraph*: "Writer Sues Solzhenitsyn."[38]) He brought his case once again against *The Oak and the Calf*, the 1975 Russian-language edition, and the English court accepted it without batting an eye.

Mind you, it doesn't come as such a surprise after Carlisle.

So we haven't gone six months without a trial—it's only about three since the resolution of the Carlisle suit. With Anglo-Saxon gravitas, Vermont's local judicial administrator came to our home and delivered the complaint Flegon had filed with the High Court in London. (There is apparently an agreement between England and the States whereby lawsuits are valid in each other's territory. Perhaps we could have refused the summons?—Alya didn't think of it in time. No doubt, they'd have found some way to deliver it.)

But what could he, of all people, have against me?

I'd completely forgotten that in my interview with Hedrick Smith and Robert Kaiser in Moscow in 1972, I had said: "The *Stern* article is managed from the same center as the pirate editions of Flegon and Langen Müller."[39] As already mentioned (in the "Predators and Dupes" chapter),[40] Langen Müller had been misled by KGB agents and trustingly brought out *August* in German, assuming there was authorial consent, while Flegon published it in Russian and English, for which Bodley Head had already taken him to court. This whole scenario—of undermining my publishing independently in the West and undermining the rights of my lawyer—was patently obvious at the time and it seemed clear that it was masterminded by the KGB, while my unusual position in the USSR allowed me (and I never even thought about the legal consequences at the time) to level accusations safely in both East and West. And so things moved on. Smith and Kaiser omitted that part of the interview, and so it didn't appear in English.[41] At the beginning of 1975, however, when *The Oak and the Calf* came out in Russian in Paris, the interview with the Americans was included as an appendix.[42] Could it be prosecuted in an English court now, at the end of 1981? What about the statute of limitations?

England's statute of limitations for libel turned out to be astonishing! In France, it's three months from publication—any later and time has run out. (The French are witty and manage to savage one another with insults.) In the United States the period is usually a year. In England it's six. Wasn't that already up in any case, hadn't it already been six and a half years? Nothing of the kind. The libel was considered to *have begun* once the *last copy* of the book was sold in England. In other words, if a single copy was still gathering dust somewhere in just one bookshop, the countdown on the statute of limitations for libel hadn't even begun. And under agreements with other countries (God preserve the Russia of the future from these fastidious agreements!), this same statute of limitations applies to lawsuits there, too.

Oh, the English courts!—the bulwark of all Europe's legal understanding!

So this is what Flegon's suit came down to: my sentence implied that he was a KGB agent. And he claimed—he wasn't!

A mere scrap of paper, and you're off to court.

It would have been easy to quash the case by immediately filing a countersuit to say that his libel of me in his book had been worse. And it would all have been over, and his book banned. But that is exactly what he wanted, an even worse trial, lengthy and sensational, and that's when his book would become forbidden but coveted fruit.

I didn't lift a finger.

(It wasn't long before Flegon cracked, volunteering in a letter to the lawyer I had already hired in England: Solzhenitsyn knows he can prevent publication of my book within twenty-four hours, but he isn't lifting a finger. If he doesn't agree with my description, why doesn't he stop the book? It is his duty, if he is an honorable man, to meet me in court. And your duty, as his representative, is to stop the book through the courts! —We had divined his scheme correctly.)

It was a ludicrous situation: having just been dragged through the mud once too often by his stinking hands, I was now supposed to acquiesce in fighting off his charges that I had libeled him nine years before.

My first instinct was simply to ignore Flegon's lawsuit. After all, what sort of trial could be pursued in the States from England, especially given the time that had elapsed (that was what struck me most of all)? Plus the vagueness of what I'd said. Surely Flegon couldn't seriously base a lawsuit on that—what kind of a ridiculous case would it be? Of course, this was Flegon simply provoking me into a countersuit—but for once he wouldn't get his way. Let them have their trial in my absence and, whatever the ruling, I wouldn't recognize it.

I had to consult Williams and Craig, however, who had recently and spectacularly saved me from Olga Carlisle. Williams's first thought was also to ignore it, but Craig convinced me it was necessary to mount a defense.

So did I need to find a lawyer again, and this time in London? Williams recommended Richard Sykes, a lawyer he knew over there. But did I now have to engage in correspondence in English legalese again?—oh, God! And each new trial meant tracking down lost scraps of papers, long since assumed to be unnecessary. The only relief was that an English court could not summon me for questioning. It would all bubble away somewhere over there, and all I'd have to do was pay, more or less. It would be difficult to defend my 1972 remark in court; today, given my experience of the West, I would be rather more circumspect. Of course, I had only a chain of inferences about Flegon's actions regarding myself and other people. And yet even so, this alleged "Romanian" had easily left for the West, settled in England, and actively engaged in shoddy publications of opposition books from the USSR. And in league with Victor Louis to boot. Irina Ilovaiskaya passed on the story of Bulat Okudzhava, whereby Flegon went to see him once in Munich (he was bringing out Okudzhava's record) and confessed, in drunken candor, that his father, *Flegontov,* had collaborated with the GPU, doing clandestine work in Romania (where the son had grown up and, seemingly, inherited pop's career). Ilovaiskaya recounted that, once back in Moscow, Okudzhava told this to the KGB man Viktor Ilyin, "secretary of the Union of Writers," who cursed Flegon, saying, "He's let the cat out of the bag, the idiot!" (The story may not be completely accurate in the retelling.)*

And, as it happens, Okudzhava is back in Paris at the moment but it's awkward to ask him to testify: a Soviet man can't just decide to give this sort of evidence in a Western court.

So the case will go on. Right now, as I'm coming to the end of this chapter, the case is only beginning to heat up, and perhaps we'll lose.

The West, then, wore me down with these trials as well. With everything it could: superficial and base judgments, libel, trials. The KGB and prison in the East, methods of their own over here. Flegon was a new kind of ordeal, where you feel like lashing out in response to slander, but you mustn't. You must not.

A good deal has been done during these years to drown me in trivia and filth. But I still have a great deal of strength. And it appears that, rather than drowning, I have floated clear.

Such were my quiet years for working, trouble-free, in Vermont.

One by one during this time, dozens of well-known and hundreds of once-silent individuals slipped or crept out of Soviet clutches, and it could never have been imagined previously that in the West they would all prove to have pretentious pens, ambitions, programs, and schemes. It was as if, in moving to the West, which had far fewer émigrés than there had been educated persons in the USSR, they became more important and more noticeable, particularly given the naïve gullibility of the Western public. And their first thought, their first gesture, was to heap insults not on Communism but on Russia and on Russian patriotism and therefore, by association, on me. And this turning on me, and the fashion for such jibes were quickly adopted and propagated in the West even during my years in Europe, whereas I turned a deaf ear, didn't listen properly, didn't pay attention, and then plunged into work at Five Brooks with relish, and was even less aware of the vast number turning against me in America. Only gradually was the full depth and

* And now I see that Okudzhava himself has described and published an artistic reworking of the whole episode in his short story Выписка из давно минувшего дела ("An Extract from a Long-Ago Incident"). (Author's note, 1994.)

expanse of the invective revealed, and the fact that, unlike before, I was almost totally without allies—but had whole swarms of detractors. Once upon a time there had been a single, immense enemy, whereas here there was an innumerable throng of petty adversaries, a creeping host. Not a single dragon's maw, but a petty throng—and what was I to do against them? Surely not tilt my lance at each of them separately? surely not call them each out by name, and dissect their every stunted little step?

And yet, the cumulative pullulation of this Host achieved something the entire Soviet machine had been unable to do: to present me to the world as the acting standard-bearer of chimerical regiments, a vitriolic fanatic, and a ruthless tyrant. And no doubt the impression will long remain.

My work itself suggested the best natural tactics: by sequestering myself away from them all, I could calmly survive four such manhunts, even if they were four times worse. At work, I could glide along for years, an unspeaking iceberg, ignoring hundreds of their preemptive jibes. (After all, they hounded Bulgakov more fiercely and more dangerously—back then it was from Chekist[43] corners—so that after a newspaper article it was: just you wait for the knock on the door, Mikhail Afanasyevich.)

Now they'll come many a time leaping out, wheedling, and trying to draw out a response. In my solitude, the neurotic self-flagellation and irritation that keeps them alive seem astonishing. But I just glide along silently. And I'd never even read three-quarters of what they'd written until just recently, when it came in useful for writing this Part Two. And, I see, ha!—nimble, mendacious, grasping, reactive, they are together deluging not just me but the whole of Russia with waves of calumny, setting the all-too-ready West against her. And, numerically, there is such a surfeit of them!

Am I to shoulder all of this too?

Yes, despite everything, they need to be given a warning at least once.

And so, easily and quickly, I dashed off "Our Pluralists."[44]

CHAPTER 8

More Headaches

It seemed as if nothing happened in our isolated, hermit-like existence during these past four years. But when I look through my hasty notes, sometimes scribbled while working, to remind me of something—oh, what a lot there was! oh, how it had mounted up! We'd been quiet—but our accusers had not been so quiet.

For I had, when I plunged into history, forsworn competition with the present day. Convincing the West that Russia and Communism had the same relationship as a sick man and his disease[1] was clearly not in my power. After my 1980 articles in *Foreign Affairs* it was especially clear what a thankless task it was, explaining things to America. As for what their policy-makers need to know—they actually understand it very well; they just won't say it out loud.

And, on top of that, strangely enough, democracies are barely less susceptible to flattery than totalitarianism is. American democracy laps it up and takes it for granted. Something else the American public is accustomed to is constant repetition of exactly how things stand, incessant repetition of one and the same very simple idea over and over again. But is that proper work for a writer, constantly trotting out the same old argument?

But however much I've been slandered in America, I still have a fair bit of influence, or I arouse some curiosity, and invitations to speak are forever flowing in from various places, various countries. And I'm healthy, I can travel wherever I want and speak at any kind of event.

But there'd be no point. They wouldn't want to understand. It's not what they need.

The only efforts it's sensible to make are very moderate: to create, in whatever way possible, a more benign attitude to the real Russia.

In April 1981, I received from the Ukrainian Institute at Harvard an invitation to a "Russian-Ukrainian" conference in Toronto. It was evident from the letter that what they had in mind was a comprehensive thrashing of the two Russians invited, Dmitri Obolensky from Oxford and me. I must say that it was, unexpectedly, the Ukrainian separatists whose reaction to my *Foreign Affairs* articles was, for some reason, the most savage of all American responses. I could not understand it, but in those articles they had seen some kind of suppression of their national dream—and they even said I was insane. I was trying to wash Russia clean of radical and vengeful calumnies—why ever did they lash out at me? Well, what they said, almost openly, was that they were willing to wait a bit longer for the emancipation of their homeland from Communism—as long as the *moskals*[2] were cleared off the face of the Earth; they were thirsting after acknowledgment that the whole world is suffering not from Communism but from the Russians—and even Mao Tse-tung's China and Tibet are Russian colonies. (It was, of course, Ukrainian separatists in particular who had forced through the US Congress that Public Law 86-90,[3] which said it was not Communism that was enslaving the world, but the Russians.)

You just wanted to throw in the towel. My God, what another gaping gulf lay between us! Just when did it open that wide? Poland was involved in it for centuries, early this century the Austrians stirred up passions a bit, then Russian brotherly inattention was added to the mix and made more toxic by the spectacle of a Soviet "nationalities policy" (in Kiev in 1938 I did not see a single Russian sign, or even any sign with a Russian version). Who will have the burden of dissipating this fervor—and when? In Winnipeg I had talked to the heads of the Ukrainian Congress[4] in such a peaceable manner, it seemed, with no tension. But now? They're inflating their concerns to an agonizing and explosive state.

I'll do it some time—there's no hurry, is there? But there is. I absolutely have to reply, and not just with empty words, but something clear-cut. Write an open letter.[5] And I wrote to them immediately, at the institute. The conference itself would be in October, but I'd decided to get it published in July, before all the regular song and dance of Captive [held captive by Russia] Nations Week started up.[6]

And although I wrote of my feelings about that question in the mildest of tones—for I do, in my heart, also appreciate the Ukrainian side, I love their land, their way of life, their language, their songs—and although I reminded them of my own Ukrainian-ness and swore that neither I nor my sons would ever fight in a Russian-Ukrainian war, even so this letter of mine was met in the Ukrainian émigré papers with the same abuse yet again.

Oh, we'll be shedding a lot more tears over this "Ukrainian question"! . . . (And we still need to study all the details of long-ago and recent history, and that will also take time. . . .)

Meanwhile I was receiving a flood of letters from our Russians working at Radio Liberty,[7] complaining about the increasingly anti-Russian stranglehold there, and saying how alien to Russian audiences the station's voice has become. Radio Liberty consists of fifteen units broadcasting in the languages of the main nations of the USSR—and they work within the compass of interests of *those* particular nations, from *their* point of view. That's fair. But the sixteenth nation, which is called "Russian," is denied this: there can be no "specifically Russian" interests, needs, or views—Washington has put a taboo on them. The sixteenth unit is "pan-Soviet," and the Third Wave émigrés working there, and the American inspectors supervising them, carefully delete from the radio scripts all events of Russian history they deem "unsuitable," and its public figures and thinkers, or emasculate their observations, progressively snuffing out Russian consciousness.

And it's easy to explain: Americans, so very foreign, spending their own, American money—why should they seek what is important and useful to Russia instead of disseminating what is, in the very short term, in the interests of the United States? Yet—how could I not try to put at least something right, the most intolerable thing? That I had to do, that was—for Russia.

By autumn 1981 I had somehow accumulated an especially large number of these Russian complaints and striking examples of censored scripts—and just then the young, energetic, conservative congressman John LeBoutillier proposed a television interview with me, specifically about American radio broadcasting in the Russian language. Our interview did not fit into the allocated half hour (partly because of the abundance of my material, partly because of his provocative political questions), and NBC television promised him they'd free up a whole hour-long slot for our interview to air on an educational channel—but they themselves slashed it irreparably for their program. And thus the TV interview was almost totally ruined: it was badly edited, important material was lost, and they broadcast it after one o'clock in the morning.[8] The only thing all the newspapers picked up—but it was very important—was my cautioning the United States against a military alliance with China.[9] Six months late, the English text of my answers was published[10] in the right-wing fortnightly *National Review*—from which it was reprinted in Canada and Australia.

The newly elected President Reagan had evidently not forgotten our remote exchanges of 1976.[11] The day before his inauguration on 20 January 1981, his people phoned us in Cavendish, from Washington: the president would like to call me that day from the White House; would I be by the phone? That kind of call was a demonstration of intent. Alya asked them to give us fifteen minutes' notice (in the building where I work there is no telephone; I'm not accustomed to using one, and haven't lifted a receiver for years—it's an important condition for a steady pace of work). I did some notes for a rough plan of what I would tell him:

"Mr. President, today even without me you are rich in all kinds of good wishes. But I too wish you a glorious and stable term of office. And I am wishing in particular, not just as a Russian, but also as a member of our threatened humanity, that you will always make a clear distinction between the Soviet Union and Russia; between Communism and the Russian people."

But the president did not phone. It must have been difficult for him to interrupt those ceremonial matters. Or, more probably, it was decided that such a telling gesture would be too extreme for his first days.

Not two months later a young miscreant shot at him. And how to explain, if not as a divine miracle, the bullet missing his heart by a centimeter, and the seventy-year-old recovering so rapidly? Our sympathy for him became even stronger.

In his first speech after the attempt on his life, that spring at the University of Notre Dame, he quoted my Harvard speech a good deal: on the failing courage of the West; and how the American intelligentsia had lost its nerve after Vietnam; what a mistake it had been to seek an agreement with Cuba; on the catastrophe of a humanist areligious consciousness, which has lost sight of a Higher Power. Turning his gaze to God was Reagan's own, personal way, coming from his heart.

During the next few months proposals came—not direct from Reagan, but via influential Washington figures—to discuss a possible meeting with him. Even the American ambassador in Rome sent the same inquiry to his acquaintance, the lawyer Erich Gayler,[12] who had defended our Fund: under what conditions would I accept the new president's invitation to visit the White House? I responded to all the intermediaries in the same, totally forthright way: if there was to be, at the meeting, the possibility of a meaningful conversation, I would be ready to come; if the plan was for a symbolic ceremony—no.

In early winter 1981–82, rumors began to reach us, via Congressman Jack Kemp and Senator Henry Jackson, that an official invitation to me was being organized at the White House, and in fact it was already "signed and sealed." At the start of winter! That's the time when I submerge myself most deeply in work and don't come out of it. I don't venture beyond the gate, not even to the barber—my wife cuts my hair. I tell Alya I'd try to put it off till the spring. She says: "Is that really your prerogative? How can you dictate the president's schedule?"

But I started thinking. Could Reagan do anything concrete to change, drastically, the United States' attitude to historical Russia, as distinct from the USSR? (For in fact no American administration is really free—it is heavily influenced by various circles, some known publicly, others not.) He could do no more than express friendly feelings towards Russia—and he was doing that already. The best I could hope of Reagan was that he would just assimilate some small understanding of the Russian point of view, so that this might be reflected in at least some of the radio broadcasts. Should I offer support for his anti-Communism? Luckily, he was not in need of that. Reagan was already accomplishing a great deal, even if it was just salvaging the economy. That winter for the first time I started watching the TV news as well (before, I'd only listened to radio), which confirmed my view of Reagan's humanity, sincerity, his sense of humor, and I would have been very willing to help, if he'd felt the need of it. But the route to these discussions was long, and the route to real action by him would be even longer. For me, a trip to Washington would mean—it couldn't be avoided—meetings with other people too, participation in various events, press conferences. I'd lose a week at the very least, and it would disrupt my work. Was anything useful likely to come of it? Would it be worth it? All in all, I'd have liked the meeting, if it was unavoidable, to be later.

And that winter was indeed kind to me. Then the palaver over the meeting blew up in early April. The first thing was calls from Washington with rumors picked up in roundabout ways: it seemed that, instead of the proposed face-to-face meeting with the president (and afterward a dinner with many participants), a lunch was planned, in which I would be among a dozen guests—retired dissidents, apparently.

We couldn't believe it—that wasn't right: I'd earlier replied clearly to all the "intelligencers" that I would not travel to Washington for any *ceremony*—still less for the symbolism of a chummy lunch. Then we were told that Richard Pipes,[13] now a senior adviser on Soviet affairs at the White House, could not find our telephone number (it's not in the directories), and was asking us to call him. It was strange, because the White House did have our number. Alya called him; that was 7 April. Pipes hurriedly explained that

Solzhenitsyn was invited to a presidential lunch on 11 May with seven or eight "representatives of different nationalities," and the formal invitation would arrive in a week. He explained no more than that, and asked no questions—and Alya, of course, didn't drag the conversation out any longer than necessary.

Well, now it was quite clear: I wouldn't go. The promised invitation would arrive—and we'd say no.

Fat chance of that! The following day there was an article in the *Washington Post*—and instant tittle-tattle everywhere: the president had been planning to meet Solzhenitsyn but had been persuaded not to, and there would only be a lunch with a group of dissidents.

Like that, was it?—*persuaded not to*?

This was a peculiarity of all the top American institutions: in them, no secrets were kept long. In fact, it even seemed that you couldn't refuse if a member of the press turned up: whatever he asked about, you had to answer. And our acquaintance, the veteran journalist Robert Kaiser, was delighted to demonstrate how well informed he was, and publish an account of how a reactionary meeting between the president and Solzhenitsyn had been aborted:

"But some officials in the Reagan administration advised the White House not to hold a private meeting with Solzhenitsyn now, since he has become a symbol of an extreme Russian nationalist position that many other Soviet human rights activists abhor."[14]

(So these were the "representatives of the nationalities," were they?—they'd made it sound as if nations of some kind had elected them. But turns out these were run-of-the-mill dissidents—now become émigré politicians.)

They're fantastic, the press! Kaiser had given away how my meeting with the president had been replaced by something different, and the real reason why. Of course, Pipes hated me personally and showed it consistently—and all over the place. He could not forgive my criticizing his distorted history of Russia,[15] and took it as a personal insult (in *Foreign Affairs*, it's true, it was not very gallant of me to compare him to "a wolf playing the cello"[16]). Still, Pipes himself was not acting individually, but expressing the mood of the American "elite"—or its most populous stream—and I was just the physical symbol of the Russia they found repugnant, the Russia that was trampled underfoot in 1917, seemingly for good, and had not dared be reborn in any form, even spiritual, not even the idea of the historical Russia; but in my books it *was* being reborn, and appeared to be full of life. With the altered format of the presidential lunch, they were not only belittling me—they were welcome to do that—but also showing what kind of place they would allocate the Russia we were longing for, the Russia of the future. How low had Russia's name sunk in the West, if clownish tricks like this were being played on us here?

But thanks for letting the cat out of the bag, anyway. Without your tittle-tattle, we might not have caught you.

And so it was that, already a month before the meeting, it was not only clear to us that I wouldn't be going, but a letter declining the invitation was also taking shape. Alya, who was far more bothered by this whole business than I was—and also kept on edge all the time by phone calls—would from time to time bring me versions of phrases we might use to say no, many of which found their way into the letter that we composed together. The job of this letter was to present the whole situation in a condensed form, but on its true scale, not as a personal matter. And, in doing so, not offend the president—I was sorry that he'd been dragged into this game against his will and contrary to the way he saw things. And to draw a contrast between Reagan and his advisers. And make it understandable for our fellow-countrymen.

It was the White House's fear of Moscow that had scuttled a first meeting with me, in Ford's time. Now it was the White House's subservience to anti-Russian influences. But Kaiser's formulation gave me the possibility, and even obliged me, to give a broader answer, not on the changed format of the meeting alone.

Because of that, the letter I was forced to write became an important, even provoking step.

Like every battle, this one, too, forced us to advance and expose our flanks prematurely. But even though the rivers of history flow slowly, at some stage the fateful moments must come.

Over the following weeks there were frequent phone calls, with recent changes, information picked up by chance, suppositions, questions constantly reaching us. And now we were learning that the guest list was being chosen as if to be especially hostile and humiliating to me: Chalidze was on it, and Mark Azbel, who had insulted me, and Sinyavsky . . . (writer!—aesthete!—from Paris!—scurrying pathetically to the table, the moment Washington beckoned). But from the White House, surprisingly, the promised letter had still not arrived (Alya shrugged: "how unseemly").

But as long as there was no invitation—there was nothing to decline.

Meanwhile, well-wishers on Capitol Hill had got wind of what was happening (for they were in fact being deceived by the White House secretariat), and demanded that an individual meeting with me—even if extremely short—be added to the program, before lunch. (Yet what good was that to me? No use at all.) But all that effort, for a measly little 15-minute audience

(7½ minutes with translation . . .), was also agonized over in the White House, so frightened were they of even the shortest individual meeting. And that added proviso was so hard to extract from the depths of the administration bureaucracy that it would flutter in late, in the form of a telegram, on the very day of the lunch, 11 May.

As for the invitation itself, that would finally arrive . . . in the form of a little card, an admission ticket, without a single word of explanation.

But what route could I take to get into the president's hands my letter of refusal? [**28**] I wanted him to be the first to receive and read it, not be handed it by his officials. We availed ourselves of the kind mediation of Edward Bennett Williams, who had access to the White House—and he managed both to hand my letter to the president and to explain how basely Pipes had tricked him. And on 7 May Williams phoned us: the president had "understood everything" and "not been offended." Thank God for that.

For us at Five Brooks, it was a great relief.

But not in the White House.

If they themselves had not leaked the news that Solzhenitsyn was to be received by the president, it would have been quietly swept under the carpet by now, and that would have been the end of it. But now—they'd have to explain my absence somehow, wouldn't they? And within a very few days.

We received feverish phone calls, seeking our agreement. First of all the White House proposed as its wording for the press: "Solzhenitsyn's schedule prevented his attendance."

We rejected it.

Then, at the crack of dawn on the 10th—the day before the lunch—Williams passed on an insistent message from the president's chief adviser and friend: think again!—do come!

No, impossible.

Around midday, a call with a new formulation: "He was unable to accept the invitation right now, but the president is expecting to meet Solzhenitsyn later."

Agreed.

But I doubted that Pipes would allow that through to the press.

And indeed, that afternoon of the 10th, already aware of my refusal, they were still prevaricating in the State Department, that Solzhenitsyn would be attending the following day. But then they probably decided not to release any official explanation at all from the White House, just to allow a "leak."

And, just as before, the "leak" went to Kaiser, and from him into the *Washington Post*, which offered this pathetic twist: Solzhenitsyn "was displeased that news of the invitation appeared in the press before he received it." It was not enough—not strong enough. So they offered another little scrap: he felt it inappropriate to count him among the dissidents.[17]

That was instead of any of the substance of my arguments.

That was *forcing* us to make public the essence of the matter, that is, my whole letter.

We decided it would be fitting to publish it only in a modest Vermont newspaper,[18] and after that—whether people noticed it or not—not to offer anything to the hungry press and news agencies.

And—what do you think? A good number of the major American newspapers took the story from the Vermont paper. (Kaiser's, in the capital, in its weekday edition censored and mangled the text, of course—but the *Washington Post*'s Sunday edition, independent of Kaiser, found room for the whole letter.[19])

This was the end of that peripheral, but trying, experience, which had been imposed on us and lasted more than a month. Its organizers did not gain a great deal: Reagan couldn't now cancel the lunch, but he reduced its status to the lowest category—he arrived without his chief adviser, did not give his prepared address, the guests made no speeches, and the event was not filmed for television, as was so longed-for, nor followed by a press conference.

Those who had staged it and taken part were simmering with rage—my absence had spoiled everything for them—oh, how they simmered. But this was strange: if, as they asserted, they were for "human rights" and against the imposition of anyone's will on other people, why were they so angry when I exercised the most modest of human rights—the right to decline a lunch invitation? Why this collective diktat—"you should have gone!" And the dissident Kronid Lyubarsky wrote a rebuke[20] that seemed to choke for breath in its anger (and, again, lack of self-confidence was reflected in length—it was three times longer than my letter to the president): I was "slandering the country that had offered refuge," had forgotten the Gulag Archipelago (I, of all people!), my attitude to my fellow-countrymen was base, and I had no right to determine what was and what wasn't Russian—so was Lyubarsky going to determine it? Were they already reaching for the reins of Gogol's Troika?[21]

General Grigorenko, who'd been with them at that lunch, also rather spoiled things for them: he wrote to the president, saying he felt a profound guilt, was shocked by the "crafty, underhand actions" of the organizers in changing the format of the president's meeting with me, and thought I'd been right not to attend.

(But what the Soviets picked up was: "Solzhenitsyn is a welcome guest at the White House"—and there would be no correction, of course. Who would get to the bottom of that, and when? the lie would likely stick for decades. —I had reproached Reagan over the American generals who were aiming, in the event of an atomic war, to destroy Russians selectively[22]—and at that very moment, on the page of *Sovetskaya Rossiya* (*Soviet Russia*) that celebrated May Day, at the top, across the whole width, were all the leaders on the Mausoleum reviewing stand, and on the lower half of the page an article[23] by some servile poet, one Vitali Korotich, of the *defamation with falsification* type: "Mr. Solzhenitsyn, expelled from the Soviet Union . . . has published the words, addressing *you and me*, 'Just wait, you vermin! A Truman will see you off! They'll drop the atom bomb on your heads!' " —And how were my fellow-countrymen to know that this was a scene from *Archipelago*, part V, chapter 2: it's autumn 1950, in the Omsk transit prison, and the *zeks* shout out to the prison guards as they're being "crammed and screwed into a prison van, like lumps of sweating, steaming meat," and their life is "not worth living . . . [they] should not have minded if [they and their] tormentors were incinerated by the same bomb."[24] —And in the Soviet Union that poison was inundating millions of brains: Solzhenitsyn was calling on America to drop an atom bomb on our country! And when ever would I be able to forge a way through those new clods of lies?)

But overall Pipes had got what he wanted: he'd disrupted my meeting with Reagan, and counted it a feather in his cap.

We were on foreign territory again. Again in foreign hands.

Last year marked the fifth anniversary of our arrival in the States, which gave us the right to take American citizenship—and we had no citizenship of anywhere, of course; no passports. But Alya and I decided not to take it. We stay here in a foreign land on account of misfortune, but only until the time comes to move on.

But on the other hand, if we didn't take it, we'd remain citizens of *nowhere*—would that mean we ended up retaining our allegiance to the Soviet Union? For we'd never had *Russian* citizenship. And in the current, unstable situation around the world, living without any citizenship at all feels defenseless.

But no: even so, we decided not to take it for the time being.

The French magazine *L'Express* suggested I might write some articles for them on subjects of current interest—and I agreed, for my voice was listened to in France. Those articles were then republished in other European countries—but the States didn't lift a finger: they acknowledge only themselves as the center of the world, and the only words articulated must be for them and from them. For instance, my *Tanks* has just been published. Where?—in France. (And the French reviews say it's written in such a way that you can already see it, even if it doesn't get filmed.) *In the First Circle*, the ninety-six chapter version, came out in France and even in Germany, but in the States—on whose behalf Innokenti was exerting himself and ruined his own life—it did not.[25]

When you feel you are in alien territory, you cannot rid yourself of disturbing thoughts about your will: if I died suddenly—and I am sixty-three years old—who would make the arrangements for all my completed and uncompleted works? who would inherit my archives?

I probably have nothing to worry about: Alya would, of course. She's twenty years younger than I am, and no one understands my literary work better. But now—just now, in March—I noticed a dark spot at her temple, which looked suspicious, and it was getting bigger. And since my time with cancer, I have a practiced eye: it was the color of melanoma. She could have been dead in just a few months. I tried to persuade her (but without mentioning melanoma) to go to the doctor but—"no, it's nothing!"; she wouldn't hear of it. Even so, I insisted and she went. Naturally, they took a biopsy immediately. Then some days' wait. It was benign, thank God. And they cut it out.

Ah well—we'll just carry on and hope for the best. And what about the boys? They're still small. If anything like that happened, they'd have their grandmother of course, and we have good Russian friends. But how many years of legal incapacity do our sons have before them, and what about my literary estate then? According to the laws of Vermont, it would be placed under the trusteeship of the Vermont state authorities. . . . A fine mess they'd make of it. . . .

A foreign land will burn and brand. . . .

This spring, the BBC reminded me that the autumn would mark twenty years since the publication of *One Day in the Life of Ivan Denisovich*, and proposed to record me reading the whole text for broadcast into Russia. Excellent! I was happy to agree. And now, in early June, the head of the Russian Service, Barry Holland, came and we recorded the complete text and an interview.[26]

And in the text of *Ivan Denisovich*, as I read it out to Russia, I felt something timeless, which had begun before me, supported me throughout the route I'd traveled, and stretched far into the future, beyond the confines of my life. I felt more certain now that I was a link in Russia's indestructible and enduring progress.

In the interview, I said of Tvardovsky what I have just now put on record in these chapters.

Now I'm sizing up whether this is the moment for a trip to Asia. It's a journey I thought of two or so years ago, for the anticipated break between Nodes. Because it will be the first time I've traveled anywhere in the last six years, I have also decided to write this addition to *Millstones* now—who knows if I survive the trip—and explain myself, just in case. Before each new step I like to draw a line under the previous one.

At first that journey was conceived simply as a way to limber up: all this sitting and writing, sitting and writing—when I am actually free to move around the whole of planet Earth! So I should at least, once I've finished *March*, take a trip somewhere. Although I feel no monotony in our Vermont life and am quite prepared to live here until our hoped-for return to Russia—even so, a break from work does incline you to introduce something unexpected, something unknown into your life, opening up a new field of vision. But where? Not around America or Europe—I've already done those trips. And here the eternal Russian interest in the lands of the Far East comes in.

But I began to understand that this would be no holiday jaunt, no. In Japan, Korea, and Taiwan I am known, read, and translated. Over there—I couldn't avoid the burning issues. The South Korean Cultural Association has been urging me to go over for some public appearances. (And the newshounds there won't set about contradicting everything I say, using the "fifty-fifty" system.)

I've mulled this over for a good while: what about the four Kuril Islands? I probably wouldn't be able to avoid speaking about them. I began to study the history of the issue. Giving them back would be absolutely the just decision. The old Russia never laid claim to them—Captain Golovnin didn't, in the early 1800s, and neither did Admiral Putyatin in the mid-1800s. And now the Japanese are insisting on nothing but those four little islands—and want to make friends. That way we could help them forget about South Sakhalin.[27] The response should be: this shows you the difference between the old Russia and the new Soviet Union—the islands too are part of the Communist problem.

As for Taiwan, that would offer impressions of a purely Chinese nature, like being in China itself—and mentally adding a layer of Communism would be easy for me. Taiwan is the reference point for a great passion of mine—it's what Wrangel's Crimea could have been for us[28] but never was.

Vermont
Spring 1982

PART THREE

(1982–1987)

CHAPTER 9

Around Three Islands

And then the Asian trip materialized all by itself. In the summer of 1981, my first Japanese translator, Hiroshi Kimura, wrote to say that he was going to be in the States and would like to come and see me. When we met in Vermont, I was impressed by his familiarity with life in the Soviet Union today. He had been there many times and knew a great many writers. Whether this seemingly un-Japanese characteristic was inborn or whether it had rubbed off on him from mixing with Russians, I always found him to have a Russian open-heartedness, and this included all the weeks we later spent in Japan. I told him in confidence that I planned to spend some time traveling in Japan after going to South Korea. I asked him to help by accompanying me to Honshu Island. But I still had no firm schedule for my public appearances in Japan. Around six months later, Kimura suddenly sent an invitation from *Yomiuri Shimbun*, a leading Japanese newspaper (supposedly, he hadn't engineered it himself, but they'd come to him with the request). They wanted me to speak three times—on Nippon TV, which they owned, on Nippon Radio, which they also owned, and in an article in *Yomiuri Shimbun* about the situation in the USSR. They also requested that I commit not to deal with other media companies. And in return for all this—hassle-free arrangements, a chauffeur-driven car for my travels around the country, and a not-insignificant fee. I had never received an invitation of this kind before but, after all, it was certainly how everyone else traveled. I gladly accepted. And for all their kindness, I agreed to their request to relegate Korea to second place so as to still be fresh when I spoke in Japan. Later they asked for a roundtable discussion at *Yomiuri* to be added to the conditions. I agreed. Then, to swap the radio appearance for an address "to a select circle of the leading figures of Japan." And why not? It was precisely the leading figures that I needed to win over. Was the address to be considered open or closed? (Different degrees of candor and bluntness of expression.) —Consider it open, and there will be five hundred people. —Brilliant, I agree, couldn't be better. I envisaged public appearances as inevitable—and sensible—measures in order to make the journey I had contrived. (Although, having already quaffed a full measure of miscomprehension in the "white man's" continents, what hope of being understood could I still entertain?)

I began to make preparations. I finished the second part of *Millstones,* and sat down to read myself into Japan and Asia in general. I had to read a great deal for the journey itself, to get my bearings, and all of it in English, as well as making notes. The Japanese were particularly insistent that I should write my article about the USSR before I arrived in Japan, so that they had time to translate it and needn't delay publication. And the "address to the leading circles" was so crucial that of course I ought not merely to think it through in advance, but to write it out word for word as well, only tweaking it later on to include impressions from my trip. I spent a month and a half on these preparations; never before had I taken myself so thoroughly away from my main work.

What sort of article about the USSR could it be? "How Communism cripples nations" (all nations, in general, but using the example of the USSR)? I knew only too much about that, but I had also talked too much about it in various places. I didn't want to repeat myself, although perhaps the Japanese hadn't read any of it. Instead, I ought to provide a highly condensed, compact, and specific overview of Soviet life today. The article was shaping up to be not particularly my own, but a composite, of a kind I'd never written before. I wasn't attempting to argue a specific position, but compressing a great whole into a small space—that was something I could do. (My books have grown already to thousands of pages over the years, yet I consider myself concise, given the volume of what I've crammed in.) *Yomiuri* had nine million readers. The subject matter had to be accessible to the masses, highly specific, and adapted to Japan's practical mind, as well as conveying how unbearable the Soviet Union was, most importantly in terms of the economy and day-to-day living.

And what about the address to the leading figures? Even the modest study of Japan I had pitched into had revealed three key moments of their modern history: the beginning of the Meiji period (in the 1860s)—the catastrophe of 1945—and what may or may not happen in the next few years, but is already coming to a head. It wasn't difficult to come up with this structure. What was difficult for a Russian to settle upon was giving advice to Japan; did I even dare?

On top of everything else, I had set about reading both Pilnyak and Goncharov—*The Frigate "Pallada"*[1]—so as to keep abreast of what Russians had written about Japan and the region. I read a book about Taiwan as well. I barely started on Korea—there wasn't enough time left till my departure.

But what was more important for me than anything was to travel altogether privately around Japan, without any fuss, without being surrounded by journalists. Hiroshi flew with me from the States to Japan. On leaving the plane, we were greeted by people from Nippon Radio and plainclothes police officers. Away from the public, we were ushered through immigration and through customs—and the next thing I knew, there I was in a Mercedes with the head of Nippon Radio, Kagehisa Toyama, sitting next to me. He turned out to be approximately my age. Among the first things he said was that he didn't look Japanese, and it was true: he was tall, did not have black hair, and his eyes had an almost European set; rather than composed, he was extremely energetic, with quick, theatrical gestures. It turned out that before Khrushchev's speech to the Twentieth Party Congress he had been . . . a Communist, but was now prepared to die in the fight against Communism. Before long, we were sitting in his country house, being served green tea (his wife waiting on us but not joining us, as is traditional in Japan). Some intimates from the company knelt around a low table in the Japanese style (it seemed servile to my unfamiliar eyes), and Toyama, who had no children, declared: "These are my children, I am bequeathing all my wealth to them." And, apparently, it was true.

Here we touch upon the specifics of relationships in Japan, where office and family connections are not clearly divided. There is something family-like about a company head's concern for his employees, and about the employees' heartfelt sense of duty towards him, and so towards the work that they do.

Even before I arrived, Toyama had drawn up a daily timetable for the whole of my month's stay in Japan. More than that, his friend and driver, Matsuo (himself incidentally a wealthy businessman—I couldn't understand why he was working as a driver for Toyama, probably that semi-family thing again), had traveled the whole of my future route in advance—the height of Japanese solicitude!—locating and booking hotels. But I immediately discovered one bit of silliness: I was supposed to spend nearly three days "resting" at Toyama's house, and only then to go with him to the home of Japan's elderly former prime minister, Kishi. I began to object: I didn't want to rest; I was meant to be going north from Tokyo early the very next morning, heading for less formal places, off the tourist trail. At this point, I had my first excruciating argument with Toyama, which went on for an hour and a half: he attempted to prove that the schedule couldn't be altered, that it was too late to book hotels, and, most importantly, that we mustn't let the police down like that—they had been given the precise schedule of my movements. What???—the police were going to accompany me everywhere?—that's not a trip, then; I refuse, I won't see a thing! The quarrel broke out again; it was already late, nearly midnight. (I immediately remembered Goncharov describing how the Japanese engage in draining arguments about ceremonies for hours on end.)

Nevertheless, I got my way: the following day we traveled north, completely unaccompanied, looped around via Nikko (I didn't know at the time that Admiral Kolchak and his beloved had paid a visit there before he went off to be slaughtered in Siberia), Fukushima, and back for our meeting with Kishi.

Toyama attached great significance to this meeting, stressing that his friendship with the old man, who was now nearly eighty-six, was based on shared ideas. As I later found out, Kishi had been one of the main founders of the puppet state of Manchukuo.[2] After the war, under MacArthur, he spent more than three years in jail as a "war criminal," but MacArthur released him at the beginning of the Korean War. He was prime minister from 1957 to 1960, and was now on the right wing of his Liberal Democratic Party and a prominent champion of Taiwan. I awaited the meeting with interest.

We went to see Kishi with an interpreter, Nishida. Short, impassive, and unemotional, he had previously been a Ministry of Foreign Affairs interpreter (and Kishi knew him—he had interpreted when he met Khrushchev). There we also came across the charming, grey-haired professor Kichitaro Katsuda. He was constrained in speaking Russian, but could understand everything. (He gave me his book on the history of Russian political thought, graciously inscribed in Russian, "This is a memorial to the ardor of my youth," and containing portraits ranging from Chaadayev to Dostoyevsky.)

There were five of us at dinner, all men, seated at a very large table (an ordinary table of European height) and on ordinary chairs. The women (including Toyama's wife) didn't set foot out of the kitchen, and we were served by waiters in black suits and bow ties, from Balalaika, a nearby "Russian" restaurant, as it turned out. We were given a very authentic-seeming "borsch," but Japanese-cut vegetables completely altered the main course. Kishi was a dignified old man, although apparently no longer active. I tried to jolly him along by asking how Japan's lack of defense was being overcome, but also about Taiwan being betrayed; he said nothing substantial about it. Katsuda gave a vivid account of how he himself was being hounded for his "conservative" thinking: students at Kyoto University would stand outside with placards calling for him to apologize for a particular bit of a lecture. (So, this sort of thing was already happening in Japan, too! . . .)

That same morning in Fukushima, I had witnessed an impressive demonstration. A number of dark, covered trucks with loudspeakers had been broadcasting in the square outside the station, playing Japanese military music from the last war. (Seeing me, a light-haired foreigner, they cranked the volume up threefold as I approached.) Then, they set off across the city, waving purple flags, loudly urging everyone to join their patriotic organization and seek the return of the "northern territories," those same four small Kuril Islands. It was a really sore point for them! Now, visiting Kishi, I was ready to field questions about the islands—but nobody asked (out of tact?).

We arrived back at Toyama's at half past midnight. I was already desperate to go to bed, but Toyama came up with another request: that I give a public press conference on my return. I declined: they hadn't asked for it before, and I don't generally acknowledge the press conference as a format. It's not for a writer—I don't want to stumble along in the wake of reporters who might lead me in all sorts of directions. (What's more, I didn't want to jump the gun and dissect the talking points of the speeches I had already written.) And once again we argued until one in the morning. (Furthermore, he dug in his heels over my desire to sit in on school lessons, insisting that I go to see high-tech industry firms.) The next morning, Kimura, Matsuo, and I continued our travels.

They lasted twelve days. The kind and perceptive Hiroshi Kimura did a lot of translating for me, and he was good at guessing what to tell me unprompted.

Meanwhile, a country of hills and mountains with no particularly expressive features was unfolding before me. There was little flat land for housing (although more of it towards the south of Honshu Island), and it was entirely packed with modern industrial buildings and housing estates, with not a curved "Japanese" roof in sight, so that, had the characters on the signs been replaced with English, it would have been impossible to tell which country it was. And I found the whole of modern Tokyo just as anonymous: a city built with a disconcerting lack of feeling for architectural integrity, harmony, or style. The move from the previous tiny houses to mass construction had unveiled no major indigenous architectural forms. (Tokyo's lighting is unconventional, however. There was one astounding building: every now and then in just a few spots—and this was what constituted its charm—individual silver points flared up and subsided while others appeared elsewhere. It wasn't an advertisement and what it was intended to express, I don't know. But I liked it.) —Outside the small town of Kurashiki, we saw a leaning house (that's how it had been built)—leaning far more than the tower of Pisa. And rows of windows tilted toward the ground and parallel to one another. How did people live there? . . .

Japan usually has good weather in September, but there were hardly any sunny days during our trip, just mist, smog, cloudy skies, and stuffy air. "The uncommon Japanese blue" (Pilnyak) or "clear weather such as is never seen in Russia" (Goncharov) I didn't see once during the month. And I heard no birds except repulsive crows (a local kind, not like our own). —In Nara Park, I, along with everyone else, stroked the tame young deer (they wander around in their hundreds). Cyclists don't struggle to breathe in Japanese cities; they are allowed to ride even on narrow sidewalks—and pedestrians aren't in the least bit bothered about it. Dozens upon dozens of bicycles stand outside the shops, all fitted with small baskets—no one minds. And the shops, as they are all over the Western world, are filled to bursting with a multitude of both essential and superfluous goods.

On the other hand, near a typhoon that never made landfall, we were caught up, on our way up to Hakone, in a water blizzard. I don't know what else to call it, I'd never seen one in my life. Just as we have snow blizzards that whirl around and you can't see a thing, so this water blizzard descended with the heat and started spinning around. Profuse drops of water went whirling sideways rather than coming down like rain, and did so together with waves of surging fog. I can only marvel that Matsuo-san was able to get us to our destination along the winding mountain road—the headlights of oncoming vehicles couldn't be seen (and driving on the left-hand side, which is unnerving when not used to it)—and suddenly, with only two hundred meters to go to the hotel, it all cleared up as abruptly as it had started.

In Japanese hotels, there is much to wonder at when it comes to preserving traditions. Even outside the door, there is one man, or maybe two, who makes a low bow. And through the door, on a raised floor reached via a low step, three, five, or even seven women (it's impossible to imagine how the abundance of female servants in hotels is justified) are already kneeling in workaday kimonos, waiting for us. We are barely at the door when they place their hands on the carpet and bow silently to the ground: in gratitude that we have deigned to visit their hotel? (Likewise, all the servants line up to bow when each guest takes leave of the hotel.) Before crossing the threshold, we routinely remove our shoes (each person's shoes are remembered, you're never given the wrong ones when you go out) and put on a pair of the slide-on slippers that have been lined up. Everything the guests are carrying, even if those guests are men, and even the heaviest items, are taken and carried by the female servants. (I kept trying to decline and not let them.) We went along the hotel corridors (if we had to cross a courtyard, we were to swap our slippers for outdoor ones this time and then swap back to indoor ones). At the new elevation of the room itself, at a sliding partition, the slippers had to be removed altogether, leaving you on clean matting in just your socks. (And no matter how many times you returned to a particular spot, someone's unseen hand had already managed to turn your slippers toe-first—so that they were easier to put on.) Inside the room, there were more fresh slippers at the entrance to the bathroom, and again at the entrance to the toilet. (And it goes without saying that it was immaculately clean everywhere.) A clean robe with wide sleeves is laid out for each new guest; it's the custom to change immediately, as it is to walk around the hotel and into the dining room in these robes. Guests are instantly served green tea (with strange Japanese sweets), then a dinner of many dishes is served on a low table. Nothing is brought in by the waitress standing at her full height; she always sits back on her heels by the screen, slides it away, and moves on her knees, even as she switches the food around. Only in the other room may she stand up. Sometimes, one woman just serves, while another (an elderly woman in a severe black kimono) pours the wine and engages in conversation. After dinner, the table is moved aside, a bed is made up in the middle of the room, and shown to the guest—is it all properly made? You must bow in gratitude. A night light is placed near the bed, again on the floor. The Japanese take a bath before going to bed and, what's more, an unbearably hot one, to our way of thinking, and on top of that it's deep, you're almost standing (in the past, it was a wooden tub, nowadays it's made of contemporary materials). The bath is drawn, prepared, in advance.

There is a mystery to these age-old unchanging rituals, unshaken even by the twentieth century (and Hiroshima); how could there not be? The mystery lies in the rituals themselves, but even more in the Japanese character. And it is not for a passing traveler to penetrate them.

Sound travels through the hotel's paper walls as it does in any Japanese home—conversation and movement can be heard far into the evening.

Moreover, every Japanese house endeavors to hear the constant sound of running water—even where there's no stream, water should at least trickle from a pipe into a stone recess—it still splashes, after all.

A great deal of thoughtful beauty goes into the rooms and lobbies; it is dispensed in details and may even be excessive or go unappreciated. It's impossible to take in everything in our busy lives: what design is on the wall or what flowers are in a vase (and how they are arranged!—this is a complex art in Japan, *ikebana*, which is studied for many years), sometimes in a niche, illuminated by its own light, sometimes a single chrysanthemum in an individual vase. Here, a lily adorns the frosted glass of a bathroom. High-relief carving decorates a black lacquered closet. There, pictures—or, rather, posters of characters—hang on two walls of a bedroom. One is gold: "The eight happinesses are imminent" (the Japanese regard the number eight as very lucky). Another, blue and vertical with tassels, has the inscription: "If people know their age, they know no sadness" (from a Chinese classic; for the Japanese, the supreme literary classics are Chinese). Each guest room has a dedicated alcove—a *tokonoma*, always with a decoration of some kind—and the most important guest sits at the table on that same side. (And the music in all public places is either classical or very pleasant and light, and always soft, nothing like the horrors of America. And Japanese books are snuffboxes compared to America's bricks.)

One hotel deep in the forest near Hakone—the Kansuiro ("Amid the Greenery")—has very much stayed with me, as has the separate pavilion we were put in. Legend has it that the emperor once stayed with a former owner of the house—and all this beauty was built for him just for that one night. Utter stillness—and the eternal sound of water: a brook flows beneath the building. The pavilion is surrounded by a Japanese garden—myrtle bushes and azaleas and, between them, winding stone paths going up and down and across the brook, sometimes over a small bridge, sometimes over steppingstones. Underfoot are either large stone flags, crazy paving, or simply scattered gravel. Great carp come and go freely in both flowing and still water. Lights on small stone columns shaped like pagodas are dotted about.

The art of the small garden is a specifically Japanese one—minuscule waterfalls, dwarf trees, little gardens of moss and grass, as well as pure "rock gardens": rocks of various shapes, singly or in groups, stand tall in a field of gravel—that's all there is to it, and yet it is a feast for the eyes and lasting food for thought. These kinds of rock gardens, even if only two meters square, are also created in the cities, where houses have no plots of land (and land is expensive)—even so, there's a place to ease the soul. And where running water cannot be arranged, a stream is depicted in gravel as it is in the small "Admire the Moon" garden at the great statue of the Buddha in Kamakura. But where there is real water, there is always a proliferation of large variegated fish and even ducks. There are big fish in all the (short) rivers, and the pond outside the Imperial Park in the middle of Tokyo, and even in small urban canals, as is the case in Tsuwano (latticed partitions keep the fish on their owner's property). A new four-story Nippon TV building has gone up on a small footprint in Tokyo, but even so the little Japanese garden beside it has been preserved, with a pond, a separate tea house for the tea ceremony—and they have even contrived, despite the cramped space, to place a water-purification facility in the ground beneath the garden for the water from the main building, so that it may be drunk from the tap. (This is a frequent convenience in Japan.)

What I couldn't get used to in the whole of my month in Japan was their food. Not just using chopsticks (both held in one hand, the lower one still and only the upper one moving, like the jaws of a crocodile), but the food itself: not even the rice (completely dry and tasteless), not even the noodles (olive-colored, made from buckwheat flour), not one of their sauces, not one of their dressings, not to mention all the seafood—lobsters, prawns, and shellfish—and even if there was fish, it was raw. Of course, it was unfair of me, I could probably have picked out something, but I could barely consider as familiar even simple pieces of chicken, deep-fried in some special manner. The smell of raw fish haunted me everywhere, perhaps even when it wasn't there; even when meat was on the menu, it seemed to smell of fish, and so did all the buildings; during a festival at Kegon Falls, there was such a dense, nauseating smell from the food stands that it was barely possible to walk past them. Near Chūzenji Lake, the girls sitting next to us offered us homemade pies—I barely touched them, they seemed as if they'd been fried in cod-liver oil. They say that "the Japanese eat with their eyes," and it's true: every dish is served primarily for its appearance. A vast amount of food in small portions is displayed either on flat porcelain plates of a sophisticated asymmetrical design or in opulent, earthenware pots or bowls (plates like our own don't exist) like still lifes, perhaps three or five items. An open shell stands on three small black pebbles, ready for its contents to be consumed; on a sheet of foil is something that looks like lobster claws and a lobster skull. Even putting a single sour plum, and nothing else, in a bowl of green tea in the morning made no sense to me. In Japan, I discovered that you cannot fall in love with a country if its food is incompatible with you. (When

I was staying in a hotel in Tokyo, I cravenly ordered simple European fried eggs.) And on top of that, you have to sit on numb bent legs; crossing your legs, Muslim-style (so much more familiar to us!), is already unduly bold, while stretching them sidewise on the floor or forward under the low table is utterly indecent (although I was constantly obliged to do just that). Meanwhile, I had been predisposed towards the tea ceremony in advance: it is the art of transforming the most mundane of tasks into *joie de vivre*, spiritual peace, and a symbol of friendship!—yet when, at a temple, I was first served the peculiar, bitter, unbearably thick green tea, with its impenetrable froth, whisked up with a brush, I managed only that first bowl as a mark of respect and never touched a drop again when it was offered.

Somehow, inadvertently, our trip came to revolve around visits to temples, temples, and more temples, Shintoist and Buddhist: these sanctuaries are where Japanese antiquity is embedded in its most concentrated form, undisturbed by modernity, where Japan cannot be confused with another country. (Can there really be more than two thousand temples in Kyoto alone, as they say? more than the number of churches in old Moscow?) To tell the truth, all these temples—their names and the details of their structures—were soon jumbled up in my memory and, even as the trip was coming to an end, I had to use my diary to tell them apart, where and what they were: Hakone-jingū, Ise Jingū, Heian-jingū (a *jingū* is a Shintoist shrine), Daitoku-ji, Hōryū-ji, Tōshōdai-ji, Yakushi-ji, Tenryū-ji, Ninna-ji, Ryōan-ji (a *ji* is a Buddhist temple), Tōshō-gū, Kasuga, Daibutsu. Some temples are named after individuals but, as a rule, their names have a meaning: Temple of Many Lanterns, Great Eastern Temple, Heavenly Dragon Temple, Temple of Dragons, Temple of Sacred Pure Water.

What remained was an overall impression and the main difference: Shintoist shrines were more aesthetic, more graceful, lighter, and Buddhist temples—heavier, and less sophisticated with their statues, although Shintoist shrines have statues too: terrifying giant guardians with orange bodies at the gates. Somehow neither the excessive carvings nor the mixture of bright colors (red and green, or red and gold) spoils the Shintoist shrines, Japan's unfailing good taste coming to the rescue. On approaching a shrine, you must wash your hands using a ladle. Then you usually proceed via long, straight, graded ascents, past some sacred cedar planted in the ninth century and now encircled by a thick supporting rope, past the *omikuji*, the divine lottery—a stall on which lists of wishes, written on scrunched-up bits of paper resembling papillotes or on little boards, are hung up and sold right there and then. The space around Shintoist shrines is usually sprinkled with loose gravel that takes some effort to wade through—you are deliberately being slowed down. The main part of the shrine (the altar faces north) is always entered in slippers; you either take your shoes with you in a plastic bag or leave them lying outside. Sometimes, you get the impression that these are no longer sacred places, that a shrine has been converted into a mere tourist attraction, which only tour groups shuffle through. But no, there's a glimpse of the orange-and-white robes of the *miko*, maidens who serve as priests' assistants at the shrines, and there's the priest as well, in a white kimono and lilac skirt-like trousers. A muffled drumming accompanies a prayer for those who have given money. Then comes a general prayer: people sit back on their heels as it is read out and then, as if to order, they bow and clap their hands twice—another means of attracting the attention of the deities. But there is no one God, nor even deities as such: ancestors and nature itself, the spirits of objects, are deified. It is strange to hear even laughter in a place of worship—but, for the Japanese, laughter is one of their modes of speech.

So this religion comes across as a collection of superstitions, omens, and invocations of good fortune. . . .

The great Shintoist shrine in Ise has links to the imperial family and is considered so central that at one time every Japanese was obliged to visit it once in his lifetime. Before the Second World War, every new prime minister and his whole cabinet came to present themselves here, but the postwar constitution prohibited any mixing of politics and religion, and the custom was discontinued. It is a long way (constantly sinking into the gravel) through the park to the shrine—passing a most peculiar platform for sacred dances, a palace of sacred music. Meanwhile, the shrine itself is simply an old veranda with a straw roof on a stone foundation. It turns out, however, that this main shrine (and maybe others too, I didn't understand) cannot remain in the same place for more than sixty years; after sixty years it has to be moved somewhere else, even if only alongside. So right now another is being built beside it. Meanwhile, the logs from the old structure will go to be used in one of the main shrine's 120 subsidiaries (across the whole of Japan). This very much expresses the Japanese awareness of universal transience—in a country rocked by earthquakes and typhoons, where, in an hour, a sudden storm may sweep away the much-loved beauty of the cherry blossom.

In Kyoto I saw a small shrine where young women go to pray for a good husband. They also hang up their wishes on bits of paper, and later display their thanks for a successful marriage. One kind of fortune-telling takes place in the area outside the shrine: a girl screws her eyes tight shut and walks cautiously along, trying to stick to a straight line for about fifteen meters (while, behind her, friends call something out)—unless she misses and keeps going, she will bump into a narrow standing stone and be granted the love she desires.

In Nara, at a Shintoist shrine, I happened to see the dedication ceremony of a week-old baby. The parents, both grandmothers, both grandfathers, and the baby's little brothers and sisters are all in attendance. Some kind of red plaster in the shape of a slanting cross is stuck on the baby's forehead, and he is enveloped in a special white shawl—from then on, only his maternal grandmother may hold him. All the relatives sit back on their heels, legs bent, on the covered veranda, facing what seems to be an altar. To the side are two priests in gold robes and black hats. To the front is something like a drum—sometimes they beat it, sometimes they blow on a wind instrument (similar to a *zurna*), or clap their hands twice. The main person, however, is the *miko*, dressed all in white and, as it happens, graceful and pretty (they aren't all), so that what she does is particularly affecting. At one point, she kneels to face the altar and raises her thin, bare arms heavenward, with a mute plea for the fate of this infant (expressive, artistic gestures). At another, she stands up and turns slowly towards those who are seated—it is all a form of austere dance, each movement meaningful, the gaze detached. Then she takes from somewhere a golden rattle in the shape of a human head—and, holding it in her right hand, she turns in a semicircle, her outstretched arms as if conferring upon the child a heavenly benediction she has already received. From time to time, she is supported by the *zurna* and clapping from the sides. The parents bow. The *miko* enters the sanctuary. Then the priest does the same and comes back with gifts, little caskets one on top of the other, a cup. The parents are given something. While the grandmother holding the baby (which doesn't cry) is solemn and motionless throughout.

Thus do the Japanese use Shintoism for all their happy occasions—but Buddhism for anything sad, and for funerals. (All Japan's cemeteries are Buddhist; there is no other kind.) This is astonishing: one and the same nation, one and the same people, profess two different religions on different occasions in their lives. Is this an encouraging sign for the future of humanity, or a recognition that both religions are inadequate?

In terms of its contents, the Buddhist religion is incomparably more profound, but seems colder in practice, than Shintoism. Bulky statues loom in the semi-darkness of Buddhist sanctuaries, sometimes beneath ornate hipped roofs. They are mostly of the Buddha himself and his disciples, creating an oppressive sensation, particularly with their excessive size and quantity (eighteen arms, thirty arms). Buddhist teaching is much more than its temples. Some of them do, it's true, have a sense of grandeur, such as Tōdai-ji in Nara, the biggest wooden building in Japan. As is almost always the case, there is an incense burner outside, a great bowl of hot ash. People buy thin sticks, thinner than our slender candles, light them from those that are still smoldering, and plant them in the ash. But the smell is not fragrant, a far cry from incense in church. (At some temples, young children hold their hats over the incense burner: wearing a smoked hat makes you cleverer.) Proper candles burn inside the temple. The black-marble altar rises in stages towards the great central, black-bronze figure of an immense, seated Buddha. At various levels, there are more large candles burning, as well as piles of fresh fruit and bouquets of flowers. A gong hangs in the temple and visitors strike it once or twice with a hammer to rouse the Buddha and remind him of their wishes. Coins are tossed through the slatted lid of a large box. (When Buddhists pray, they stand up straight, though not for long, before the figure of the Buddha, palms placed tightly together before their chests.) —In that same temple, a square hole has been made in a pillar: children aged six and under can just about squeeze through (their parents bring them specially) to bring them good fortune in life. Separate pagodas often stand next to a temple, with three, four, or five layers of curves on their Japano-Chinese roofs. There are no bells in these pagodas, but their many levels bring our own bell towers to mind: they are visible from a distance to remind people of their faith. A great bell sometimes hangs in the temple courtyard, with its own roof, like the ones over wells in Russia. It is struck 108 times at New Year—so that the 108 human torments known to Buddhism may depart from the world. A swastika sign may sometimes be glimpsed—on a drum or a wall: in Southeast Asia, it is a symbol of luck, prosperity, and fertility. We never got to visit Kyoto's Saihō-ji temple, famous for the moss garden that surrounds it, because tourists' feet are ruining the moss. The only option, and even then not straightaway, is to join a two-hour-long procession of worshippers. This is a prohibition I respect!—all the temples have by now been turned into thoroughfares.

Elsewhere, one might see a Daibutsu (Great Buddha)—a broad-shouldered, twenty-meter-tall statue of green copper, free-standing, without a temple, hands placed calmly on his lap. For some reason, there is an entrance into the figure from behind—via a small underground tunnel and then a spiral staircase. Visitors wander in a cavalier manner around the interior of the sacred statue, testing the sun-warmed bronze with their hands, and laugh. Or, in Kamakura, there is a temple—Tōkei-ji (Joy of the East Temple)—where wives sought refuge from their husbands if things became intolerable, their husbands unable to take them back from here. (Some later became nuns, others returned to secular life, and so—to other husbands too.)

But there are also temples (Ninna-ji), which have no statues of the Buddha at all but, out of the blue, you come across rooms of Japanese art—it is impossible to convey how delicately and rhythmically, even in their faded condition, they depict tree trunks, branches, birds, and animals!

Outside many Shintoist shrines and Buddhist temples stands a string of booths selling souvenirs and sacred objects, protective amulets for a good career, souvenirs for tourists. They are impossible even to look at, let alone enumerate (there is, for example, a fan inscribed with Buddhist truths). And as for what happens to these rows of stalls when the temple has a festival!—many more stalls selling toys, sweets, and treats to guzzle on are added to them. —There, a solemn procession of thirty priests goes by—while indefatigable toy hares beat their drums, and the vendor does nothing to stop them.

I happened to see one such festival in Kamakura quite by chance. It was 850 years since the birth of a famous priest from some branch of Buddhism. First, still in the city, we saw the initial procession of monks in black habits and wide straw hats. Then, near the temple of Kōmyō-ji itself (the Temple of Shining Light), we came across a parade of monks in purple robes, with white collars and gold coverings on their shoulders. At the head of the procession were several small boys, whose hats were also purple. The priest at the front rang a small bell he was carrying in one hand. Then, with each step they took, two young monks in black struck the road's paving stones with tall staffs of black metal. Next came a priest carrying a small black smoking incense burner. Another carried a white broom that looked rather like a mane. Almost all the rest held glass-like prayer beads or fans. By this point the interior of the main temple had been lavishly decorated for the occasion with gold hangings, a gold canopy, and a whole lot of incomprehensible objects. On three sides of the central platform, worshippers sat back on their heels, most of them elderly, men and women. They did not move for a couple of hours, nor did they chant with the priests. The huge incense burner by the main entrance filled the whole temple with thick smoke. The thirty priests also settled on the platform, legs tucked beneath them, and they too did not move, pretty much for hours on end. The senior priest, who wore a white tubular headdress (like a piece of paper rolled up horizontally), first used a stick to tap the objects, brought up by two of the boys at a time, as if dismissing them. Then, for a long time, all movement ceased, and only the priests' mournful chanting lingered, plus an occasional tapping sound of some kind.

And so, it is undoubtedly divine worship. And yet from all these visits to Shintoist shrines and, particularly, Buddhist temples, there was a pervasive sense of extreme otherness, an abyss, between us, which I hadn't expected when I went to Asia; I had assumed that, for all that, they were closer to us. What is the point of the races? What is God's intent? We have to live on the same planet, and we need to understand one another. We will never truly come together—dare we seek to convert them to our faith? I think not.

But then I attended liturgy at Tokyo's mighty Orthodox Cathedral of the Resurrection—and I wanted to answer that perhaps we can. There, also Japanese, were three priests, two deacons (one with a fine voice, introducing himself: "I'm Ivan"), and several dozen parishioners. The entire service and the singing were in Japanese—but you could feel the warmth, unlike everywhere else until then. It was touching to see Japanese people in an Orthodox church and to hear our hymns in Japanese. It was a very heartfelt service. (Christianity, in the form of Catholicism, reached Japan in the mid-sixteenth century, but several years later, in 1558, a terrifying ban was imposed, with the death penalty introduced for Christians, while all missionaries were expelled. When Hieromonk Nikolai, the future "Apostle of Japan," arrived in the country from Russia three centuries later, in 1861, the mortal ban on Christianity remained in force, and the Japanese were afraid even to teach the missionary their language, while the first secret converts faced brutal persecution. However, in keeping with the new Meiji era, freedom of religion arrived in the 1870s, Nikolai became a bishop, this cathedral was erected in the 1880s, and, during the Russo-Japanese War, Orthodox Japanese actively provided assistance to Russian prisoners of war, who were astonished by the very fact of their existence.)

I traveled to Japan hoping to make sense of the Japanese character: its self-restraint, industriousness, and capacity for small-scale but intensive work. But, oddly, I experienced there an insurmountable alienation. Just you try and understand them. You don't exactly dissolve in their warmth. Nor does the abundant Japanese politeness melt the heart. (Although it is often startling:

caught in the rain in a park, we sat on the railings of a covered bridge. Suddenly, we see our taxi driver approaching, holding three umbrellas in an attempt to rescue us.) There is also that odd mode of speech—of laughing a great deal at inappropriate points in a conversation: you expect the Japanese to be serenely equable. In mass groups of Japanese tourists, you notice that coarse faces predominate (particularly, for some reason, among boys of secondary-school age). And their daily television films are full of cruelty, not to mention martial arts combat. On the other hand, no one is mugged on the street, and it is safe for a woman to go out alone at night. Magazine covers display pleasant girlish faces, but no naked or semi-clothed women: there's censorship. And even today, two-thirds of marriages are concluded at the behest of the parents. And a Japanese taxi driver returns two million yen (eight thousand dollars) left in the taxi to its owner. Is it one of the most moral countries?

It is marvelous how steadfastly Japan's spiritual world continues to be preserved, rather than scattered by the winds of modernity.

But also I feel sorry for them in their current defenselessness. On a rainy day, a throng of fragile colorful umbrellas sways across Kyoto's pedestrian crossings. Oh, honestly! Communism hasn't even reached you—then you'd have more to think about than your umbrellas! What's more, even graduates of their (free) military academy suddenly decide that they don't want to be officers—and off they go to Civvy Street. . . .

Most sympathetic, as in all peoples, are the peasants. There aren't many of them left, most of them elderly, while the young people work in the towns, and if they do come to help in the patchwork of rice paddies, then it's on Sundays. In the villages in the north of the island, you still come across the old thatched roofs (albeit with TV aerials), although metal ones are more frequent. Even the most remote villages have asphalt roads. Village houses are fairly like barns and, as with us, they are the repository for all the out-of-date equipment the owners are reluctant to throw away. But alongside the new television might be fine antiques: lacquered boxes, statuettes.

Nor did we let pass the beauties of nature and architecture. We saw Kegon Falls, a jet of white foam among the cliffs, ninety-seven meters high, with ten tonnes of water falling every second. (A quarter of a century ago, a young student threw himself off the top. The Japanese regarded this suicide as "philosophical"; it found a good many imitators—and nowadays a statuette of the Buddha stands in a niche in the passageway leading to the fountain, in memory of all who took their lives.)

What could I have learned or grasped of all this without Hiroshi's constant explanations, which were very wisely considered, and discriminated expertly between what was generally incomprehensible to a foreigner and what might be of particular interest to me?

Amid the overall fragility of Japanese structures, one is astonished to see a real castle (Hakurojo, White Heron Castle), built in 1333. On a hill in the middle of a plain, the castle's foundations reach as far as the upper courtyard, and the first floors have exceedingly strong stone walls and scarps (held together by an oil-based compound of some kind)—not even artillery could take it. Higher up are several stories of wooden superstructures with curved Japanese roofs, these a silvery white. Inside are oak floors, oak wall panels, and displays of knights' armor and helmets with horns. (Not something you expect in Japan, somehow. Later on, at home, Hiroshi, "Kimura-san," donned his great-grandfather's samurai suit of armor for me—it made a menacing impression.) Every floor of the castle has a far-reaching panorama and a wild wind blows in through the windows. (And all the visitors carry their shoes in plastic bags—you have to scramble up to each floor in slippers.) There is a miniature shrine (a domestic altar) on the sixth floor, with gifts offered by believers. Those who wish to do so may have their notebook stamped with a red picture of the castle. (I did, of course.) Among the structures at the castle is a separate little courtyard and a small edifice—the Hara-kiri Maru (for committing hara-kiri). —In Kyoto, we also saw the Golden Pavilion—one of Japan's loveliest buildings, if not its very symbol—magnificent proportions. True, you expect the colors to be beyond compare as well, whereas they are much faded. In fact, this pavilion is a restoration—the original was burned down by an ambitious young priest, a Japanese Herostratus.[3] It also has another name—*shariden*, "a sacred place housing bones" of the Buddha (these exist in many Asian countries and, what's more, there are several in each one).

One of the strongest impressions of beauty was the pearl-diving in Toba. The divers are girls wearing white—(it's six meters deep here, and even deeper in places)—they dive for a long time in glass masks so that they can keep their eyes open underwater, but without aqualungs, for some reason. The diving is artistic: already in the water, they lift the lower part of their bodies and their legs into the air in a straight line and disappear vertically beneath the surface. Holding their breath so long is exhausting; it takes training, and even afterwards, they can't breathe in straightaway. When they resurface, they use a rope tied to their waists to haul over a large floating basket, and place in it the shell they have found. (When you look now at pearl jewelry, you remember them holding their breaths.)

From the "pearl road" that runs along the coastline, you can see the small, humpbacked "pearl islands," and there are floating pearl plantations in every bay. (The baskets are suspended underneath in the water, where the pearls grow, and somehow they remain intact even in typhoon season.)

The small town of Kurashiki was also striking, with its abundant museums and folk-craft stalls. It is four hundred years old and all thoughtfully set out, like the interior of a single house owned by people of good taste. The sinuous river is set about with willow trees and framed by spruce little stone embankments. All the museums and stalls are in this area, and fortune-tellers sit here and there at low tables (on the basis of a date of birth and a name, they write out their calculations in slender columns of characters). Here is simple homemade ice cream for sale, while over there a young rickshaw driver waits to take tourist ladies for a ride. The small houses still have tiny plots of land at the front, each one fifty centimeters wide—containing either a plant or a stone garden. The stalls sell pottery, crystalware, items made of cast and wrought iron, lockets, lacquered and wicker knick-knacks, wicker furniture, decorated trays, key rings, lockable jewelry boxes—artwork of every kind, too much to examine closely. Plates are decorated with pictures and put in the kiln right there and then. Suddenly, via a side lane, you come upon houses and walls completely covered in ivy. —As if you weren't in Japan, there are piazzas, shopping arcades, and a sixty-by-sixty-meter brick-paved square in the middle of a brick-building quarter, with round aluminium tables and wicker chairs like Venice—and as you look you realize that, just as in Venice, the square is edged by a canal. Then again, through a small gate, you unexpectedly encounter the secluded courtyard of a little Buddhist temple with a mass of stone standing lanterns (without lights)—and looking up the hill slopes, during the evening's utter absence of people, you see a great accumulation of stone grave-lights. And if you take the steps up the hillside to above a small pagoda with a curved roof, you still have time to see, from the cemetery heights, the deep red of the sky after sunset.

I was immediately recognized here by the daughter of our hotel owner, a Tokyo student—and the owner herself arrived towards suppertime, an astonishingly cultured, slim, intelligent older lady wearing spectacles. After making the traditional bow to the ground on her knees, she talked about the town's bygone days, the river twice as wide in her childhood but the embankment really narrow, and in winter the children would wait for boatloads of oranges to float along the river, and the rowers would toss them from the boat to the children on the bank. (And around that same year, we for some reason went to war with that country . . .) But now she was afraid that there were too many tour groups, that too many souvenirs were for sale—they would ruin the town.

We also experienced a dinner with geishas in Kyoto; it was Matsuo-san's treat and was, I think, very expensive and hard to come by—through friends. Geishas are rare nowadays and booked up well in advance. The quiet restaurant ("a tea house") was tucked away in a quiet spot. As usual, the waitress bowed to the ground as we swapped our shoes for slippers. I was expecting a great hall, a vast number of tables, and a platform somewhere—nothing of the kind. We were taken into a three-by-three-meter room, with mats on the floor and a low square table in the middle (we'd left our slippers outside and were in our socks), and sat down on the cushions offered. But once again, where were we meant to put our legs? I attempted to stick just one out indecently under the table, and to keep the other folded under me. A waitress in a casual dark-blue kimono entered on her knees every time, placed something behind the screen partition, and then from there, rising slightly from her knees and bowing to each person, she served the thick green tea, whisked and impossibly bitter, with a miniature sweet in a separate saucer—and it turned out that, during the whole of the tea ceremony, the drinkers must rotate their cup three times in their hand before drinking (to express enjoyment) and, when they've finished, they must continue to hold the cup, as if admiring it. (I knew the taste already, and didn't drink, nor did I have the energy to turn the cup.) Next (as is always the case when any Japanese food is served), rolled-up napkins, hot and moist for wiping your hands, were brought in on individual trays (and replaced several times during the meal). Then (still kneeling behind the screen each time and bowing low to each diner) she ceremoniously presented trays holding aesthetically pleasing crockery—miniature dishes, miniature condiment sets with lids, carved boards: the same array for each person. First came a mysterious seafood starter of some sort, which I was frightened to touch, then some kind of first course (the smell was so bad it made my head spin but, thankfully, it wasn't long before they opened the window onto the garden).

Suddenly and all at the same time (not kneeling but just bowing slightly), in come three geishas (the same number as there are visitors), all three in light-colored kimonos (white and cream). As a matter of fact, kimonos are ugly garments: they are spoiled by a very broad sash (around forty centimeters wide, covering the whole torso from the chest down), which turns into a ludicrous bump at the back. But the main thing is that two of the three geishas are unacceptably old (nearly sixty?), the third well past forty, and none of them is pretty. They occupy the empty places on the floor, which don't have cushions, each one close to a visitor whom she begins to regale, pouring hot sake vodka (it isn't strong, 16 percent) into his glass from a tiny carafe and giving an exaggerated smile. What was most wounding of all was how they were under strict instruction to be talkative (intelligent conversation spices up men's food), attentively and incessantly animated, and to nod hasty assent, smile their consent, flutter their eyelashes—while, at the same time, not eating or drinking anything; they didn't even have any crockery. Only later did the client, the table's host (Matsuo-san), order that they be given beer, and that was all. (Drinking beer is taken very seriously in Japan, and used for toasts.)

And they keep on and on bringing in dishes. I am horrified: when ever will they stop? And the smell is more and more revolting. I drink the sake, but there are no snacks; somehow, with the chopsticks, I manage to raise two mangled pieces of cucumber to my mouth. The third time, it's a heap of slightly rancid horseradish. Something with an outlandishly unpleasant smell is brought in, in covered ceramic bowls. I hope to signal to them not to lift the lid in front of me but no, off it comes: crayfish of some kind, shrimp, scallop shells, mutilated vegetables, suspect mushrooms—all of it red-hot and steamed, with a black pebble placed inside the bowl to keep it hot. I can see how it's going to go: I've eaten nothing since early this morning and there will be nothing until tomorrow morning, it all turns my stomach. About me (I am "Professor Hjorth, from Sweden"), there is only a general feeling of regret that I'm not eating—and one geisha begins to pour me beer. But everything would have been fine if I'd been able to write my observations down in my diary during the ceremony—but it's not the done thing, and additional effort is required to remember all the details and the order in which they occurred. The small talk is in Japanese, and I no longer bother asking Kimura to interpret. It has nothing to do with my unfamiliarity or the age of the geishas but nothing erotic is envisaged, not even the touching of hands, let alone embraces—only strained but "clever" verbal encouragement, so that the chitchat doesn't dry up (and quotations from classical Chinese poetry, if the guest is able to appreciate it).

Next a special porcelain bowl of hot water appeared on the table, and this was its purpose: if a gentleman wishes to treat a geisha to sake (and she isn't allowed a glass of her own), he rinses his glass in this shared bowl and pours some for her. (No one at a Japanese table ever pours anything for themselves.) I thought this was the end—it wasn't. Once again, olive-colored noodles, with an extra something, were served in exquisitely lacquered black bowls. The noodles were safe, you could eat them with chopsticks, but they didn't go with all the combined smells. Next came ceramic teapots—not with a slice of lemon on top but a similar sort of Japanese fruit. Surely, it must be ordinary tea now? Nothing of the kind: it was hot salty soup. And now something that I could eat!—a bowl of rice, but so dry and so lacking in seasoning, it was impossible to get down. And finally a slice of melon and even a spoon to go with it.

During the second half of the meal, however, a young *maiko* floated into the room—like a character from a Japanese painting come to life—how long it must take to do all that makeup! It was as if her whole face had been covered in plaster—an impermeable layer of white paste, not a scrap of living skin to be seen. Her lower lip was painted red, her upper lip lilac. All the geishas wore their hair smoothly, but not too elaborately, pulled back. The *maiko*, however, wore a complicated headpiece with a round canopy, like a Japanese roof, like a wing, as well as *two* posies of flowers on the crown of her head and *two* different pendants—one on the left-hand side (half a dozen little dangly things) and one halfway down. She wore a light-blue kimono but, rather than an unsightly bulge at the back, she had orange-gold wings. She was shapely and fairly tall but the kimono was even longer, getting under her feet, and she walked cautiously in her white socks. She held herself just like a painting—adopting set postures, barely speaking. As a mark of honor, she sat next to me first, with perfect posture, but soon moved over to Matsuo-san, beginning to talk a little, and lighting matches for his cigarettes. But even beneath all the plaster, she was evidently pretty. Here Hiroshi interpreted for me, telling me that she was sixteen, that the role of *maiko* only lasts until twenty, and that they then either go on to become geishas or leave altogether. And that there were currently only thirty *maikos* in the whole of Kyoto, with its population of two million; it is a dying profession.

There was an announcement at the end of the meal that the *maiko* was now going to dance. How could she possibly?—there was no space in the room, and she would get her feet tangled up in the overlong kimono, she couldn't even walk in it. By then another hideous creature with a coarse, unwomanly face, had come in (a little earlier, and had already sat by the table). She'd brought in a samisen—a simple three-stringed instrument. Now she sat in the corner (the screen partition had been moved and the door into the corridor slid away) and began to play a primitive, dismal, monotonous tune. One geisha sat beside her and began to sing, just as primitively and monotonously. The *maiko* meanwhile, after bowing to the ground before us, began to dance (the "Bridge of Maples") with unflappable dignity in a space two meters square. She was holding two red fans and used these, her arms, and her face in the performance, while her feet hardly moved. One minute she folded the fans to form a complete circle of red by her sash. (She too wore a very broad sash, gripping her chest, and pulled tight.) Then the fans disappeared (I didn't see where—into pockets?) and she began to perform without them, using only her hands, now examining her outstretched palm as if in surprise, then arching it through the air. She even used individual fingers, with great significance. And her wide, trailing blue sleeves—separately, stretching them out. As if admiring her outstretched hands one minute, her sleeves the next. (At this point, I discovered that the dance had something in common with the *miko*'s ritual dance at the infant's dedication at the Shintoist shrine: the hands and the face were more important than the torso and the body, and there was meaning to the individual fixed postures, familiar from Japanese painting. Later, when I became acquainted with seventh-century Noh theatre, I could see it all came from the same root.)

We applauded, the *maiko* bowed to the ground once again, and performed a second dance, a "Song of Kyoto," although it wasn't much different from the first. Then she sat down at the table again, but was no longer such an exaggerated, aloof, and self-absorbed beauty, talking instead in the voice of an ordinary young girl. She dabbed her perspiring forehead with a handkerchief, but didn't drink anything even so. Meanwhile, the perfect fright began playing, tapping the samisen in some kind of solo, and the geisha beside her started singing. It turned out to be the highly popular "Song of Sakura" (the cherry tree). Then Matsuo-san placed the money for the geisha he knew right there on the matting below the table; she rolled it up and put it in an opening of her kimono. And almost immediately, without any sort of ceremony, the waitress took my rain jacket out of the closet and everyone stood up. It was no longer raining—and all the geishas came out of the house to say goodbye (the Japanese change their shoes at speed, in an instant). There were the usual reciprocal bows, and we got in the car. Suddenly, they gestured that I should roll down the window. The *maiko* came over and extended a hand. I don't know whether etiquette required it, but I kissed her hand. She did not offer it to the others.

I had also planned to go by boat around the "inland" sea (between the three main islands), Japan's ancient thoroughfare, a multitude of little islands and half-abandoned tranquility. The approach of the latest typhoon put paid to that. I never did experience the direct onset of a typhoon, however. A typhoon is the more fearful and strong, the slower it moves. And one was advancing, right across our path. Suddenly, it sped up without warning, changed direction—which weakened it considerably—and fell, impotent, on Hiroshima. Which was exactly where we were going.

You experience a burning sensation even as you enter Hiroshima. (Increased by the fact that one green and one yellow sphere hang right there for some reason, looking like some sort of advertisement—like suspended, unexploded bombs.) The atomic-bomb museum has a circular model of the city that was left: few buildings, and none in the center—and there, hanging over it, is a red sphere of just the same kind, marking the blast. There is a stand showing how the order came down from President Truman via several generals—from 23 July to 6 August. Hiroshima was picked because it was a major naval base with a dense concentration of service personnel and military installations, and because the surrounding mountains meant the radiation would settle there (was this the purity of an experiment? or the protection of other people?). To this day, the Americans believe there were 120,000 victims, the Japanese 200,000. Of the three planes that flew in on that bright, windless morning, one dropped the bomb—and fled at such speed that it was already sixteen kilometers away by the time of the blast. The bomb fell in a column of red flame, and exploded at a height of 580 meters after forty-three seconds. An unimaginable white-and-yellow ball of fire, the column of smoke rose as high as nine kilometers and became a mushroom cloud (it still hadn't dispersed when it was photographed an hour later). There were a great many fires, and the whole area was reduced to ash; people hoped to save themselves by leaping into the river to escape the heat. Someone managed to take photographs of the wounded and bewildered inhabitants, huddled together. Now, before the figures of the victims behind glass—melted fingertips dripping, skin peeled away, eyes crazed—an elderly Japanese man folded his hands in the Buddhist gesture of prayer, while the usual inappropriate standardized laughter came from a group of schoolchildren, laughing not at the victims but at their own humor. Remnants of half-burned clothing. A tram thrown from the rails. A horse, its muzzle ripped away (it lived until

1958). The shapes made when coins, nails, watches, a bottle melted together. Excavated skulls.

And next to me was Matsuo-san: he was stationed here at the Hiroshima garrison in the summer of 1945. But on 1 August he was dispatched to Yamaguchi, came back on the 15th, and could still see bodies in the water. At the time people thought vegetation would never again grow in that place. But it did. As did a new city.

The living destiny beside me—of a man who just happened to miss the bomb, and such a fine, well-disposed man at that—allowed us to walk the city with one foot in *that* day, the other in the present.

It was chilly in Hiroshima. Even walking, visiting, staying the night.

I managed a visit to a school in Yamaguchi—two lessons of maths and one of physics—all as the "Swedish Professor Hjorth," who was interested in the education system in various countries of the world. That was how I was introduced to the students; then the teachers had their photographs taken with me (after all, when will another foreign guest drop into Yamaguchi?). During a discussion of the lessons in the head's office, one of the maths teachers suddenly asked Kimura-san why it was that the Swedish professor spoke Russian. Kimura didn't miss a beat: I (Kimura) don't know Swedish, he said, so we decided to speak Russian. It was shameful to pull the wool over their eyes, and I wrote the head an apologetic thank-you letter from Tokyo as soon as my presence was made public. I was happy with the lessons: given the mass of subject matter, the students were attentive, engaged in the lesson. It was serious teaching.

And I could have continued traveling around Honshu, turning along the western coastline—but I was already full of impressions and time was running out—and I had to go to Tokyo to prepare for my public appearances. Also, I presumed I would soon come back to Shimonoseki on the same high-speed train, and cross the ill-omened Tsushima Strait[4]—the route I would take to Korea.

In the evenings, I became lost in contemplation of the view of Tokyo's lights from my room's spacious balcony. It made a deep impression after the night-time solitude of the forest from the veranda in Vermont.

Toyama now went ahead and himself gave that promised press conference about my arrival in Japan and, given his right-wing slant, needlessly slipped in the remark that Solzhenitsyn was considered a potential terrorism target, and so the security services had been alerted well in advance. And it found its way into the papers that this was why I'd been traveling incognito! Toyama then wanted to announce, when actually introducing my speech, that I might be assassinated, like Leon Trotsky—it was all I could do to prevent him both from making the vile comparison and from the idea as a whole.

But the police, who began to provide me with protection in Tokyo (at the insistence of the authorities rather than of Toyama), did a really first-class job: they were quick, courteous, and resourceful. It was impossible to enter my section of the corridor on the twelfth floor without being seen and questioned. No matter where we drew up, the senior police officer, who always escorted us out of the hotel, was already there, as if transported through the air, and showing us where to park. The police car always had a radio link to the people traveling in ours, and gave us orders as to which route to take and how to avoid reporters, or went ahead itself, with a rotating red light on the roof and a siren, and guided us between the streams of braking vehicles. I had never been driven like this. (*O tempora*! It's not a great way to live. Some years later, these precautions will be incomprehensible, but our time is the heyday of a terrorism intensively managed by the Soviet KGB.)

At the last moment, *Yomiuri Shimbun*, the "right-wing" newspaper that had invited me, shied away from being publicly named (so as not to ruin relations with the Soviet authorities, and its correspondent not be expelled from Moscow?)—and charged the rampantly right-wing Toyama and Nippon Radio to take responsibility for the invitation. So much for being "right-wing" brave-hearts.

Everything important, all the key points I'd wanted and was able to talk about in Japan were in that address ("to the leading circles"), drafted while I was still in the States, and almost nothing needed changing after my travels; everything was fine. Two other promised appearances lay ahead first, however: the interview with Nippon TV[5] and the roundtable at *Yomiuri Shimbun*. I was afraid questions might be asked that would reveal the key subject matter even before the address was made—what would the address become then? And on television I did indeed have to argue about the "peacefulness" of Red China; the rest was secondary. Subsequently it turned out to have been a good thing that I had spoken there: otherwise, the issue would have vanished altogether—I wasn't asked about China anywhere else. On television, it was former Vice-Minister for Foreign Affairs Shinsaku Hōgen who crossed swords with me, saying that China was a kindred country to Japan, and Communism there was not at all dangerous: "The Chinese are a very intelligent people, and they are now moving in the direction of progress." I sought passionately to prove that it was just the same kind of Communism as in the Soviet Union, that Communism was the same the world over; after all, this was the main purpose of my trip. (But why should the Japanese believe me? Don't Asians, and neighbors too in this case, have greater knowledge of one another? . . .)

As agreed, I'd prepared my speech[6] to be open to the press—the press were not admitted, however. There were two ministers, the minister of education and Ichiro Nakagawa representing science and technology. There were a certain number of intellectuals, a certain number of socialists (they wrote down the bits about socialism)—otherwise, they were all businessmen. I was touched that, in the modern auditorium of the Chamber of Commerce, at the end of the single central aisle was a window right opposite the speaker: it might well have been the only window, but it looked out onto a garden! The green of a cloudy day. Such skill! —The audience applauded in unison at the beginning and at the end. Unfortunately, my interpreter, Nisida, read timidly, without taking the text to heart or attempting to convey emotion. (I heard from several people and the newspaper later wrote: "What a fluent, vigorous, and resonant language Russian turns out to be." They hadn't really had the chance to hear Russian spoken.)

There was only the most restrained reporting the following day, summaries in a few right-wing newspapers. Toyama's company, meanwhile, sold the address to *Shinchō* magazine, which tinkered with the whole thing, deleted the bits about topical politics, probably a third of it—and published it like that. (Without even pointing out that the text had been cut. . . .)

And so Japan did not hear my speech at all and didn't read it: I'd put it together for nothing. And my interview for Nippon TV—although well produced—went out at midnight, for some reason. Normal people couldn't watch it. To be fair, the discussion at *Yomiuri* was interesting. I can't remember one as interesting in eight years in the West; it's impossible to imagine one like it appearing in an American newspaper. The extent to which the Japanese are devoid of superficiality and look into things profoundly, seeking out their depths, is striking. (The discussion also touched on the riddle of what underpins Japanese morality: a sense of beauty! a sense of dignity! There's "beauty will save the world"[7] for you.) But was it for a mass readership? The discussion was published after I left[8] and I don't know what impact it had, if any.

All those interviews, and no one asked me the question I was most expecting—the one about the Kuril Islands. Was this Japanese tact? or my collocutors' professorial loftiness?

The Nobel Committee in Norway was due to award the Nobel Peace Prize on the day of the *Yomiuri* discussion. I was very much expecting it to go to Lech Wałęsa, and was planning to say something. However, Norway is considerably behind Japan in terms of time, and nothing was yet broadcast as of our late evening. Should I wait until tomorrow? Hiroshi convinced me to draft a statement that evening: he would translate it and keep an eye on the news, so that when the announcement came late at night, he would immediately pass the statement on to the press office. Well, so I wrote a statement in advance: "The Committee's decision to award the Nobel Peace Prize to Lech Wałęsa is a highly worthy one. Sadly, there have been instances, in the Committee's past activities, of capitulation to an aggressor being seen as working for peace. Today, this prize has been bestowed upon an unarmed man of generous spirit, the most outstanding fighter not just for the rights of the masses but for the future of the whole world, in the very thick of the fight and during Poland's darkest months, the days of the crackdown on Solidarity." But in the morning, I learned that the prize had gone to the extremely left-wing Mrs. Myrdal and to some Mexican for their fight against nuclear weapons (had they defused even a single bomb?). And I began to toy with another statement: "The Nobel Committee's cowardly decision reflects the moral decline of the whole of Europe . . ."—but it wasn't quite right for Japan. And how had Wałęsa and all the Poles been looking forward to it! How it would have bolstered them up! Wałęsa's wife couldn't hold back, and made a statement. (A year later, Wałęsa was given the prize, after all. And the Poles asked me to say something. By then I wasn't saying anything at all—but in honor of Wałęsa, I adjusted my aborted statement slightly—and delivered it.[9])

Later on, in the States, I offered my Japanese speech to *Foreign Affairs* and received a rejection from the editor, William Bundy, on the following reasonable grounds: they were prepared to tolerate my remarks about American impotence; they agreed with my advice to Japan to arm itself better in order to defend itself and the surrounding maritime space. But I was suggesting that Japan actively defend other nations in East Asia as well, and even liberate China, Vietnam, Laos, and Cambodia from Communism (that wasn't in my address, was it?)—the free nations of Asia would be alarmed at and repelled by such assistance from Japan. In this way my advice could prove a danger to Asia, create dangerous complications, and even destroy the current security system—and do so even before Japan had armed itself properly.

It was all very interesting. After all, my advice had not been politically but purely ethically aimed: since Japan has military forces, surely (when it is so much at fault regarding East Asia) it should offer those forces to expiate its guilt? But no: apparently, in international relations, it takes more than a declaration of atonement to wipe out guilt. Will no one trust Japan now, and will it find all roads closed?

In which case, is ethical advice in contemporary politics simply unrealistic? This is something I have come up against time and again.

Six months later, my Japanese address was published in Taiwan as well—but also in abridged form, and also taken from *Shinchō*. And so, an address judiciously aimed at the Japanese was never read by anyone other than in Russian and then only by émigrés—though also in the States, a year later, in *National Review*, which was friendly towards me, although with characteristic cuts: anything that didn't flatter the Americans was removed! they really can't stand criticism in America.

And yet the *Yomiuri Shimbun* article[10] did make a splash: it was quoted in part and then carried in full by *National Review* in the States, *L'Express* in France, and went out on radio in Russian to the USSR on a number of occasions.

Even while still in Tokyo, I'd begun to feel tired.

I went to Kabuki and Noh theater shows. I saw several famous Japanese films. The theater shows were astonishingly distinctive but hard to understand. The films were outstanding. And I saw far too many temples. Did I now have to go to Korea—to another restricted-access hotel in Seoul with a police guard? And then do the rounds of countless Buddhas, just like the ones in Japan? Then again, I'd done so much preparation for Japan, I'd said so much—and all of it virtually for nothing. I'd written earlier to Kim Kyu Taek, the chairman of the South Korean Cultural Association that had invited me, to say that I wanted my trip to be a cultural mission. He'd had no objections. But now, when he happened to be in Tokyo, he informed me that he would take me to see how the North Koreans had dug what was already their third tunnel under the demilitarized zone. This was like when I'd been asked to speak at the Berlin Wall!—was I going to be turned into a politician once and for all? I understood, of course: I would have to try and persuade South Korea's rioting students that they did not know the value of the freedom they had, that they were striving to reach not freedom but a concentration camp. Did this mean calling on the students not to revolt but to submit to a military government? appearing as a "reactionary" once again? But something didn't feel right in Korea: corruption had recently been exposed in its ruling circles—so on whose behalf would I be exerting myself? I remembered how a year ago they had stifled Russian radio broadcasts (by Aleksei Retivov) from Seoul. It was the same old blind South Korean line: their only enemy was North Korea, while the USSR and Red China were not entirely enemies, or even enemies at all. (A few days later a Chinese air-force pilot crossed into South Korea—they started to draw in their horns, as if they might not even hand the pilot over to Taiwan so as not to infuriate Beijing, while the aircraft, of course, was sent back there. Later they returned a civilian aircraft and its passengers as well, even though refugees from Communism are put on trial in China.) I would be sorry not to see Korea—I had loved Koreans since Kazakhstan but, after all, you'd see nothing of their life with a police escort. And Korea isn't decisive for the fate of Russia, their conflict doesn't affect the Russia of the future. It's all about China (and, therefore, Taiwan) and Japan. And South Korea, unlike Taiwan, has not been abandoned by the States.

And so I had a change of heart: I wouldn't go to Korea. I suggested they send a television crew to Tokyo for an interview. No way!!—it turned out that Korean hostility towards Japan because of colonization was so great that the Koreans couldn't possibly interview me on Japanese soil; they'd rather go to Vermont! (Even the act of going to Korea *after* Japan would taint the visit. The Koreans had also become more sensitive after Japan's recent reform of its history books, which didn't acknowledge Japan as at fault in World War II.)

My broader plans were now also up in the air. Should I go to Singapore, Thailand, Indonesia? As if the equator and the heat, which I would find unbearable, weren't enough, you'd never see or find anything without a guide and a good interpreter. And I couldn't even travel privately for my own enjoyment—that chance had gone, I was bound by circumstance.

No, evidently, on this trip, I had only enough enthusiasm to see me through Taiwan.

* * *

I flew to Taipei on the upper deck of a Taiwan Airlines plane. There were plenty of empty seats—and till the end of the flight I did not know or even suspect that the people traveling on the upper deck with me and my companion, Wu Kai-min (the son of the person who had invited me), were plainclothes police officers. And the Chinese stewardesses (as a type they seemed gentler and pleasanter than the Japanese) recognized me immediately, asking for autographs and to take photos. I went on to discover that a group of

Taiwanese reporters from Tokyo had been on the lower deck and also for some reason knew that I was on the plane—and they snapped away with their flashbulbs when I disembarked. Only after a few days was it explained to me that the Wu San-lien Arts Awards Foundation, which had invited me, had overplayed its hand: *in order to* keep things under wraps, they had told the reporters about my arrival themselves—in return for their word of honor that they would keep it secret. And amazingly, out of thirty newspapers, they *all* kept their word (the Chinese—such self-restraint!) bar one: the English-language *China Times*, which did publish. (And a newspaper mêlée flared up for a few days: everyone was indignant at the traitor, which, of course, cried "freedom of the press" and "everyone has the right to know everything": crumbs from the West's table.)

The press tracked me till I went to the country villa of the founder of the Wu San-lien Foundation—then they calmed down. It turned out, however, that I had been taken there only for a tea ceremony, after which I went to the nearby Yangmingshan Hotel. And—nobody noticed the move. In this way, I would have gained two peaceful days in which to compose my speech, had I not been taken for breakfast at the villa the following morning—whereupon reporters suddenly descended from somewhere, and I was forced to stay at Wu San-lien's home for several hours to avoid leaving a trail to my hotel. I went outside and sauntered about so that they could take their pictures and leave. And the foundation's secretary Wu Feng-shan declared, in a bid to lure all the correspondents with him, that he was going to the foundation to hold a press conference. Once there, however, in order to plunge the knife of reproach even more painfully into the treacherous *China Times*, he concocted and announced the idea that I was enraged about the exposure, wanted to leave, and that those several hours had been spent attempting to persuade me not to do so. He did me a disservice: UPI's (evidently venomous) Taiwan correspondent hastened to inform the whole of America, and in great detail, how I was in high dudgeon about the exposure and how I was demanding to be put on the first plane out—a complete nutter, in other words—and how they had been pleading with me not to go, since it would discourage the anti-Communist nation of Taiwan, and how I believed I was the prime target for Communist terrorists, and how I had finally agreed to stay on temporarily but was set on departing the island at the very first opportunity. This extensive hostile report[11] was published all over America—and remained the only evidence the country had of my entire stay in Taiwan. And once I had made my speech in Taipei, and it could not be kept completely quiet any longer, the highly competent *New York Times* barely mentioned the speech itself but did add the explanation that I was a "defector from the USSR, 1974."[12] How am I to be friends with this world and this press? (People who left with the consent of the Soviet authorities and on an Israeli visa—they're the ones the US press calls "exiles." . . .)

At first I *thought* that I'd managed to slip away to the hotel unseen. And I continued to think so until the evening. The hotel was shabby but quaint. Wicker furniture made from bamboo and straw, all of it old-fashioned. A door from my room opened onto the building's spacious roof; it had a flower bed, and you could take a stroll in the mountain breeze (fortunately, there was one "cool" day of a mere 23 degrees Celsius). I sat down to work on my speech. (In the morning, I'd met my future interpreter—Professor Wang Chao-hui from Harbin, who spoke barely any Russian and declined to translate from my handwriting, instead sending me a Russian typewriter so that I could type it out. Yet he was the person who had translated *The Oak and the Calf* into Chinese, and imposed arbitrary cuts. I can just imagine! While *Archipelago* had been translated from English—and that was all there was in Chinese . . .)

I had not, however, spotted the danger from the outside steps up to the roof, a kind of fire escape. And suddenly that evening, through the window, I see a woman, hear bits of English. I attempt to wave her away—but she comes in through the door from the roof and there she is in my room. She hands me her press card and demands an interview. It was all I could do to escort her out.[13] At that point, I learned that there was a whole swarm of reporters downstairs (she was the only one who contrived to get onto the roof). They were waiting for me. I would have preferred to work quietly on my speech: there were guards on the fire escape as well now but no, the foundation insisted I go outside again, into the Chinese garden (with its plaster animals) along with the elderly Wu San-lien, and saunter about for the photographers and television crews. From that day on, I was seen daily on all three television channels. I had hoped they would take sufficient photos, make themselves scarce, and not accompany me on my journey, that I would travel around Taiwan as unimpeded as I'd been in Japan—but fat chance. . . .

And so off we went on a four-day trip, tailed by a couple dozen press cars. It was impossible even to think about distracting my translator from the speech, and anyway he really wasn't up for oral translation at all. So I had to travel using just English, but my inseparable Wu Kai-min and I understood each other just fine—his English was very precise.

We traveled first through west Taiwan. The flatland here is more sprawling than anywhere in Japan, and pleasanter to a Russian eye. The rivers, meanwhile (short, on account of the island's relief and dimensions), are completely dry and waterless in the rainless summer season. We began our trip out of Taipei at the twenty-fifth latitude, and the next day we were to cross the Tropic of Cancer. The vegetation was immediately striking: avenues of palm trees and roadside plantings, banana groves—there were banana trees even along the highway in the towns, and out beyond the green rice paddies (with their second harvest) stood entire palm forests. The trunks of the *baihua* trees were white like those of poplars. For our afternoon snack we were served fruits I'd never seen before: the ribbed starfruit, papaya, shangua, mango, and one old friend, the pineapple. We climb up into the mountains—and it's all the same lush tropical vegetation that gladdens the heart. Lotuses. A flash of the narrow-gauge railway for hauling out sugar cane. Bananas are carried in two large baskets on the shoulders, and the tiny roadside stalls are packed full of them. And it's nice that nothing is kept especially neat or dolled up like the tourist areas. This is humdrum hard work; it takes no thought for beauty. The workers wear the conical Taiwanese straw hats (everywhere work in the fields goes on late into the evening). But you rarely encounter a curved Chinese roof—everything's industrial nowadays. But the modest mountain settlements are so quaint: the provincial flavor of the formerly neglected island has been preserved. The little houses have been cobbled together any old how, just to make them livable—this climate allows it.

We went up to a height of 750 meters to the mountainside "Sun Moon Lake"—Ri Yue Tan. (It's difficult to transcribe Chinese place and personal names accurately into Russian. You have to ask them to be repeated several times and to pay close attention. All the sounds are intermediate, they don't coincide with our own. On the Russian map, for example, the island's second city is written Gaosiun but it is far closer to Kao-Shyon.[14] Likewise, all the "ng" endings written in English are an awkward attempt to put the Chinese sound on paper. You don't hear Chinese people saying "ng," and the foundation's secretary, Feng-shan, suggested that I write his name as Fonsan. Conversely, the Chinese find it hard to reproduce Russian sounds accurately, and no one who tried to learn how to say my name correctly had it right even after a handful of attempts.)

Chiang Kai-shek, having lost China, ended his days at Sun Moon Lake. It was his favorite place for relaxation, privacy, and work. Opposite his house, and visible from its windows, a pagoda in memory of his mother rises up on the other side of the lake. Up on a hill, the pagoda is tall and slender. Chiang Kai-shek himself, however, turns out to have been a Christian, and a Protestant church was built here on a slope, for him and his wife. His house is now a hotel, and that is where we stayed.

We arrived before sunset. The water of the lake was a bluey-green, and the tops of the encircling mountains, amid which the lake had originally emerged, were covered in haze and ragged cloud. Adding to the lake's beauty was a little island in the middle—a knot of trees behind a white picket fence, slopes paved with stone.

A reception had been arranged for me as if I were Chiang Kai-shek himself. A covered passage to the jetty, built especially for him, was opened. There a motorboat was provided (while the reporters had already hired another and were on our trail). We drove around the little island, moored on the opposite shore, and clambered up a flight of steps to a Buddhist temple. The light was already fading when we angled back across the lake, which was vast even for a motorboat. And then I was up at half past five in the morning—a wealth of rapidly changing colors playing fluidly upon the clean-scoured sky, to the left above the mountain, before the sun came up! how smooth the lake was, and what peace. And marvelously positioned on the near horizon opposite was the mother's pagoda.

The poor Taiwanese, spurned by the world[15] and not spoiled by the attention of foreign visitors, welcomed me triumphantly everywhere. We stopped in Taichung for brunch (I had no need of these meals, they simply wasted the best time of day, but Wu Feng-shan couldn't live without them). We were allocated a positively presidential room in the hotel in terms of size and appointments, and the mayor of Taichung immediately appeared—to give me the keys to the city. For this we went down to the lobby, where he presented them in front of three dozen reporters and two hundred assembled residents. They applauded, waved, and a charming Chinese girl dashed out to shake my hand.* Later I was also given the keys to big, industrial Kaohsiung, and to small but historic Lukang, and then quite simply to the Ambassador Hotel. Officials in various places kept on introducing themselves—I would mix up their appearances and their positions. From the second day onwards, the president of the republic, Chiang Ching-kuo (son of Chiang Kai-shek), issued instructions to beef up my security, and police escorts were

* And so many people in Taichung have now been caught up in a devastating earthquake. . . . (Author's note, 1999.)

added front and back (and all of them required long-drawn-out lunches; the afternoon breaks grew longer). And, needless to say, local reporters joined us, we already had up to forty cars on our tail—and I would turn up in busy places with this whole motorcade to the constant clicking of cameras. It drew the local residents, they beamed, waved, offered greetings, clapped. I shook hands here and there, had my photograph taken with old men and little boys (Chinese children have hair as stiff as wire). Just such a motorcade followed us onto the hilly campus of Chi-To-u University, where we were expected for lunch at a rest home that had an amazing smell for a wooden construction—but it wasn't ordinary wood, and in addition it was enhanced by Taiwanese orchids, their accumulated scent across the premises as a whole sweeter than it was close up. To go for a walk in the park on my own, I had to slip away along a forest path.

At a spinning factory a *pu ti shu* (lime tree) was planted in my honor, and I was photographed with the workers. The factory—with Japanese and German machinery, it must be said—was astonishingly automated. From the African cotton to the reels of thread for export—there was almost no one in the huge production shops: the cotton was driven through tubes, turned by machines, stretched, and turned again. Spools were automatically replaced, and containers of thread moved along the shop floors via cleverly contrived cogs in the floor.

In Kaohsiung we entered an auditorium during a break in a concert—the people nearest us noticed immediately and began to applaud. Then, all 1,500 or so got to their feet. A bouquet was presented from somewhere. (The poor, poor Taiwanese!—practically doomed, abandoned by everyone.)

I also visited the docks in Kaohsiung—fantastic shipbuilding, enormous tankers for export, and the dry dock is said to be the second biggest in the world—I don't know if it's so. The impressions were so great and came so thick and fast that I didn't bother trying to take notes. Giant hulls of ships that were already seaworthy. The smells of the sea and the continuous noise of work, which sounded like sandblasting. Fabricated blocks were being welded in the dry docks. Computers quality-controlled every detail of the parts and blocks. I wanted to stay longer to try to gain a proper understanding—but I was embarrassed to take up the attention of the engineers and workers.

The island is still not prosperous everywhere, however. At one and the same time, Taiwan is both flourishing and dragging itself out of the destitution of Japanese colonial rule. (Incidentally, its level of development can only be wished upon the rest of China.) We also visited many impoverished places, particularly on the coast. They have their labor-intensive industries too. Drying salt from sea water: the water arrives via ditches, is poured into first-concentration, then second-concentration basins, and then into square drying beds. The salt is skimmed off these and carried away in piles, the workers barefoot all the time. —A shallow pond, into which small *sabahi* fish are released from the ocean and fattened (although they die when it's too hot). Two fishermen in nothing but skirts emerge from a poor hut alongside, sail out on a raft, leap down, and haul in the net (usually at night, so that in the morning the fish are fresh for market). There is no shortage of dingy hovels, the bricks seemingly without cement, loose and jutting out, but then winter is unknown here.

And Lukang has its narrow, fairly malodorous alleyways and backyards with their squalid existence. How do people live and breathe there? It's a cramped and public two-story existence. All of a sudden, at second-floor level, there's a bridge over a dirty alleyway, and even a memorial plaque about it. It was built by Chen Chi. Poets and writers used to meet on it to exchange ideas about calligraphy, painting, the art of gardening, poetry, chess, and music, and to greet the moon.

You will even come across an ox-drawn cart in the city of Tainan (the island's one-time capital). But there, and even more so in Kaohsiung and indeed everywhere, motorcycles abound (like bicycles in Communist China). There are hundreds and hundreds of them on the roads at the end of the working day, thronging the streets. They are the main mode of transport, although there are plenty of cars as well. (Even an enormous live pig is transported in a motorcycle trailer.) Traffic lights exist only in the big cities. There are traffic controllers everywhere—they're cheaper. (And there is an abundance of staff in the hotels, as there was in Japan.) People, even children, cross the roads wherever they like. Although it may be a long time before proper housing is built for everyone, new ten-story blocks are going up, with lifts—I visited one to see a primary-school teacher's small four-roomed flat.

The shopping street is rendered completely blue by the sunshades of the shops on either side. But business is slow in the afternoons, when people don't eat much either. Commercial life begins from five in the afternoon, and goes on until midnight. We encountered it in full flow at around nine in the evening on a street for shopping (and eating) in Kaohsiung. A multitude of stalls pack the sidewalks, an abundance of provisions and preparations: frying, steaming, and shouting—although the majority is seafood and, for me, the smells are unbearable. People eat right there, leaving their motorcycles in the dark (no one locks them up or puts them away safely; just under a million people live in town yet it is perfectly safe all night long). The Chinese eat often, and in copious amounts. Nor do they have any qualms about drinking—their vodka is about 70 percent. Although I avoided a lot of Chinese cooking, I also ate far more than I had when faced with Japan's "food for the eyes." Chinese food is far tastier. Just as the language in Taiwan was softer than Japanese, to my ear, and the Chinese themselves warmer.

Naturally, I didn't skip the temples either. Taiwan has a good many Buddhist temples (40 percent of the Taiwanese practice Buddhism, which became firmly established after World War II). I was already familiar with this kind of temple after Japan. I shall single out only the Fo Guang Shan (Buddha's Light Mountain) Buddhist center near Kaohsiung. An enormous gilded statue of the Buddha sits *on top of* a building—more than a hundred meters above ground level. The temple has a very simple rectangular structure. There are three huge figures close together, seated, legs bent—the Amitabha Buddha, the Shakyamuni Buddha, and the Buddha of Medicine. And niches contain 14,800 little buddhas, with small lights above them. Then there is the "world of treasures"—a multicolored revolving cone made up of many small glass windows, a little Buddha with a light bulb in each one: the light is switched on by the person praying for health or good fortune, and his name put on a piece of paper on the outside. Music plays as the cone revolves. The Buddhists' pursuit of immensity and quantity is hard for us to understand—I cannot grasp how it is connected to the transience of existence, which they preach. Even the approaches to the main statue are furnished with hundreds of utterly identical gilded buddhas. The biggest statue's lowered left hand symbolizes wisdom and greetings from paradise, the raised right hand signifies mercy. There are 250 resident monks (dressed in black, but some have cameras and they too are snapping away).

Next in the cards were visits to Confucian temples and outright pagan ones. Sometimes the two are combined. One such huge combined temple[16] stands on the slopes of the aforementioned Sun Moon Lake. Three temples, almost touching as they stand three deep, and several more consisting of three buildings in a row, all with Chinese curved roofs and liberally adorned with carved figures and molding. Two great red-faced guardian lions, paws supported on white balls, are located in front of the nearest, and on either side is a Chinese arbor. The first central temple is encircled by a gallery of red molded pillars, and the gallery itself dedicated to the mother goddess, Mazu, protector of the island (may she at least protect it from the Communists!).

Legend has it that the "Holy Mother in Heaven" was born on a small island off Taiwan, taken alive up to heaven, and now saves people and, especially, sailors. An incense burner gives off smoke outside the temple. Those who pray here do not remove their shoes. Before the sanctuary niche is a table for offerings, where paper money has been tossed "for good luck." It's impossible to describe all the carving and molding. Decorative lanterns hang in every aisle. Deep in the sanctuary, other deities—Yue Fei and Kaiji—sit beside one another in chairs, like two jointly ruling kings, both with black beards and gilded raiment, Yue Fei's face closer to a normal color, Kaiji's a bright red. There are figures of other deities in the side chapels.

Advancing deeper and higher, you cross into the Confucian Ta-tsenti Temple. There, deep in the sanctuary, sits Confucius himself, dark, unpainted, in a layered hat. He shields his mouth with some kind of rod or scroll; his face is depicted as wise, even rather sly. And before him, as before any deity, is a table for offerings. There are bananas on it. Above the altar recess is the inscription: "Great Teacher for Ten Thousand Generations." To the sides are red-gold tabernacles and, in two side chapels, figures of Confucius's disciples, Yan Hui and Mencius. Plus various shields, axes, horse heads on poles.

By contrast, the Confucian temple in Tainan (which is three hundred years old) has little decoration. The interior is very plain, just two symmetrical orange and purple lanterns, and there is no statue of Confucius in the altar recess. (Being constantly seen in statues may erode Confucius's authority; instead, there is a shield with one of his sayings, and along the top his words: "Everyone may be taught." It's like something out of Tolstoy . . .) Next to the temple are the students' study rooms. (And next to those is a baseball field for ordinary schoolkids. The game has traveled even this far.)

The great pagan temple near Tainan has a good hundred red pillars, over a dozen curved, tiled roofs, with dragons, horsemen, eagles, swans, boats—an extravagant profusion of figures—on the eaves. My entrance was hailed by the ring of a bell and a noisy tambourine of some kind. The tables for offerings here are rather more impressive and roofed by sheets of metal, since pigs and calves are being slaughtered. Incense was burning thickly in my honor and the main sanctuary had been opened. There in the altar niche were five deities: Wu-Fu, Jin, Shui . . . The moldings on the side walls were tigers and something like sea scorpions, unspeakable monsters: heads with long, curled mustaches and streaming rivulets of hair. Further on, outside the temple, was a vast flower garden containing a curved pool, fanciful piles of stones (in profuse amounts, unlike the Japanese style) and a mass of stone figures—a zebra, a giraffe, a roe deer, a crane, a lion, an eagle, a camel. Brick paths, a cement bridge (made to look like bamboo) over the pool, and then a stone maze, walls chest-high—and you go up into a two-storied gallery, which has Chinese ink-drawings on the walls, and offers a sweeping view of the low-lying coastal area.

The temple of Mazu in Lukang was similar. There too I was greeted by a bell being struck. It had the same abundance of colorful curved dragons on colorful curved roofs. There were incense burners in the courtyard and inside the temple itself, giving off a strong burning smell. A great many offerings of foodstuffs had been placed on the altar table. There were cones with lots of lightbulbs, derived from Buddhist temples, but each tiny recess contained Mazu rather than the Buddha. The altar was densely carved, and there were more statues of gods behind glass. Behind the altar itself was a small courtyard with a dragon fountain and a second temple, two stories high, with towers of a delightful architecture added on. This temple is dedicated to the Chinese deity Yu Huang Dadi. Bearded old men sit beneath glass domes in groups of three. Yet amid all the commotion and the flashbulbs of swarming reporters, a woman kneels before the altar and, as if oblivious to it all, is deep in prayer.

Furthermore, scattered about the whole island, even close to the roads, are small, sometimes really tiny shrines and altars, lit up inside, their size depending on the locality's funds. Each little place has its own individual protector and builds him one of these small temples. The soul is drawn to Heaven. Cheng Huang Ye, a deity that protects humans and confers health and happiness, is worshipped. Here is the Fuan Shrine, the roof over the table for offerings supported by four red columns. Behind a small iron door is a tiny altar resembling a stove. It contains a few items—and a tiny seated figure with a black beard, who wears a golden crown.

Taiwan has no enervating daytime television. But in Kaohsiung in the evenings, masses of young people spontaneously take to the floor in the half-lit area in front of the "cultural center." And, my goodness—there is no clasping, no vulgar swaying. Instead it's demurely innocent: either circle dancing hand in hand, as in the old-time Russian dances, or hands on shoulders, or else splitting into pairs and dancing around one another in small circles, or clapping and stamping. And nowhere do you see couples embracing. We went into the center itself for a concert: a student quartet performed pieces from the classics, then the sweet voices of a girls' choir, some forty strong, sang two songs by a local composer—very pure, like our liturgical singing.

I also went to see a fort in Taiwan—Chikanlou, built 320 years ago by Koxinga of the Ming dynasty. When the dynasty was overthrown by the Qing, he fled the mainland. (Like a forerunner of Chiang Kai-shek . . .) The sculptures also depict the Dutch envoys to Koxinga. (The island was "discovered" by the Portuguese, but then captured and pillaged by the Dutch.)

The trip was also a trial by heat. I had been wearing cheesecloth shirts since we crossed the Tropic of Cancer. None of the showers anywhere had cold water; it was always warm. Even so, I was still fit at the age of sixty-three—I'd spent six weeks traveling around in the heat and I could have done more, had there been a reason. But I didn't go to the tropical Kenting National Park and the coral reefs, or to Taiwan's mountainous east, as I'd planned.

We returned to Taipei the day before my speech. I worked with the translator—he seemed to understand more than I'd expected. I was persuaded to don a black suit even though it was the middle of a hot day, but I took the planned presentation of bouquets of flowers off the agenda. The subject matter was too tragic, and I'm not a showman.

The speech lasted fifty minutes, including the translation. It was rewarding to address such an uncommonly understanding audience (more than two thousand people in an auditorium with tiered seating). They responded sympathetically and sensitively whenever something hit home. At the end, the audience rose and applauded. Among those who came up to me afterwards were the young, no-nonsense information minister, the speaker of parliament, and the head of the non-Kuomintang Young China party (himself a little old man). The information minister asked for permission to disseminate the speech worldwide in English. "Only if you have a good translator," I said. Apparently they did. Really?

After the speech, various invitations, offers, and interminable wearisome gifts were brought to me in my room to sort through. It was only at the very end that I was given a letter from a Russian, which had been waiting for four days: it was from Georgi Aleksandrovich Alekseev, once a figure in the Vlasov movement.[17] In Taiwan!—that really was a surprise. I rang him. He came along—seventy-four years old, self-possessed, intelligent, strong-willed. (It turned out that he had both done the English translation of the speech and been the person the Chinese translator went to for an explanation of every other sentence—hence the "astuteness" of the translation, which had surprised me.) I immediately began to interview him about Vlasov and the Prague meeting of November 1944—but he shifted the conversation to the future of Russia. Disillusioned by the petty squabbling of our émigrés in Australia and the extent to which they had been undermined by Soviet agents, he had moved to Taiwan to work in the Radio Liberty studio[18]—but Kissinger closed it down as part of his "détente" with China. Now, Alekseev wanted to use my visit to ask the island's leaders to set aside a special hour of broadcasting in Russian from Taiwan to go out to Siberia.

I would have attempted to do this via President Chiang, who was forever planning to issue me an invitation, but somehow never did. The meeting wasn't, in fact, appropriate for me after I'd turned down Reagan's, but an hour of Russian-language radio was a good cause and worthy of a meeting. (It never did take place, and it was later explained to me that, after my speech and its harsh words regarding America, Chiang Ching-kuo could not show open solidarity with me—it would have put him in an awkward position. The Taiwan government would like to achieve success without taking any risks. And they would never dare quarrel with the Soviet Union either, say by launching Russian radio broadcasts. Later on I also learned that in his youth, when he was living in Moscow, Chiang Junior was such a fervent Communist that he was at loggerheads with his father for a long time, and they were reconciled only after he fled the USSR, anticipating arrest. But the leaven of his youth had left its mark. . . .)

My speech was simultaneously broadcast that evening on all three channels, but each filmed it differently. My speaking Russian was heard straight through, overlaid by subtitles in Chinese characters.

The speech[19] contained an unmistakable hint, unacceptable to the United States, that it had turned its back on Taiwan. Furthermore, I mentioned Mikhail Gruzenberg, who had imposed Mao Tse-tung on China, and compared the fate of the Taiwanese people to that of the Jewish people—the comparison suggested by the fact that these peoples were equal in number and by the similarities and differences of their fates at the United Nations. This new angle was spotted straightaway in the States. My Taiwan speech gained the support of only the right-wing newspapers; the liberal press didn't even mention it.[20] Voice of America "gagged" the speech for several days, equivocating over whether or not to broadcast it to the USSR in Russian. In the meantime, Third Wave émigré Boris Shragin hastily put together a roundtable for Radio Liberty's Russian-language (Soviet) section in order to tarnish my speech. "How do you explain this praise for Taiwan from Solzhenitsyn?" he asked an American Slavist, Alfred Friendly Jr. And the latter bounced back with, "They probably fed him well over there." And this program, on such a level, was slotted to broadcast to Russia right away. Radio Liberty Director George Bailey managed to prevent it going out, but when he was fired later on, he was reminded of this as one of his main transgressions. —(The text of the 18 November broadcast to China by Moscow's Radio Peace and Progress reached me later on. Everyone in the Soviet Union and in every part of the world knows who Solzhenitsyn is: a fanatical anti-Communist and advocate of autocratic monarchy, a traitor to his homeland. The statement he made in Taiwan shows without a shadow of a doubt that the traitor's visit is part of Washington's hostile policy towards China. Acting as an agent of Washington, Solzhenitsyn applied the greatest efforts of his eloquent rhetoric to heightening the ambitions of the Taiwanese tyrants.) —Between two millstones—as always.

I spent three more days in Taiwan after my speech. I was already eager to conclude the trip and keen to leave earlier, but the flight schedule didn't allow it.

I was invited to see the film *Portrait of a Fanatic*, based on Bai Hua's book *Bitter Love* and banned in mainland China. I found it very moving, so poignant were even the sketchy scenes of real life in Red China. This is what it means to preserve a piece of your territory—if only in order to speak the truth. I told them, "Films like this can only be made by people who have suffered. America could never have made a film like that. Nowhere can China be expressed like that except from the territory of free China. I envy you: we Russians have no such territory and we cannot make anything like this."

We toured a museum of Chinese artifacts. There was no longer any time to take a railway trip along the east coast (something like our Circum-Baikal Railway). I didn't even see Taipei properly: it was the time of their festival on the anniversary of liberation from Japanese colonial rule, a rally, a parade—it was awkward for me to be always hanging around. Meanwhile, my stay for one extra day meant more invitations. I had not gone to receive doctorates at the university or at the academy—and now I had an invitation from a general at the Pescadores Islands garrison—I'm sorry, but no. You should always know the precise time for your exit.

I drafted a farewell statement for the press. We went down into the hotel lobby to read it out. Around thirty reporters shone lights, snapped photos, and thrust whole sheaves of microphones at me.

Still ahead of me was a farewell dinner organized by the elderly Wu San-lien and his foundation. We went to yet another hotel. There I spotted the heads of all three Taiwanese political parties—the Kuomintang, the Young

China party once again, and the Democratic Socialist Party. I asked the latter whether he shared the tenets of my speech—and learned with surprise that yes, he did. (I was told, however, that some in liberal intellectual circles were not happy: why had I not demanded unlimited democracy in Taiwan? They even managed to put together some kind of roundtable of professors to respond on television.) Having all assembled, we waited another forty minutes until the information minister brought me a gift from President Chiang, his father Chiang Kai-shek's book *Three Principles of the People* in Russian. They didn't dare start beforehand. . . .

Next, fifteen Chinese took their seats at a round table—and a two-hour dinner began, which I found grueling. In the middle of the round table was a revolving concentric disc. Each newly served dish was placed upon it and then just one waitress, spinning the disc, used chopsticks to fill each plate in strict order: myself, then the two people on my right, then the two on my left, then again right and left (turning the disc in different directions and constantly running around the big table), then the host opposite me and only after that the three less important guests sitting near him. And this procedure was repeated about sixteen times over, as many times as there were dishes. Then I noticed that no one started to eat until I did. And some dishes I was afraid even to put in my mouth, complicating the overall sequence. But then something that was undoubtedly pork and something that was undoubtedly beef were served—at this point, it was explained to me that the Chinese custom is not to eat everything, but always to leave something on the plate. By contrast, I noticed, it was better not to touch your glass at all—no matter how much you drank, it was topped up right away. The Chinese do not drink like the Japanese: they do not err on the side of caution. They even have a punishing system of inviting individuals to drink: all it takes is for one person to raise a glass in your direction—and you must drink with that one person separately, and then with the next, and the next (and they drink wine that's been warmed up). There was lobster as well, of course, a whole one in its shell with artificial red eyes and pieces of meat removed and steamed separately; the smell was unbearable. There was bird's nest soup. There were four types of pork: first came a single large piece, but only a tiny bit of the roasted skin was served up; then there were slices, followed by well-roasted ribs, and then, separately, fried fatty lumps. I didn't think the meal would ever end. And it was impossible to hold a serious conversation: my interpreter was useless, and only two people had decent English—but then my own was limited. Apart from a couple of dozen compliments on my speech, and my visit being described as epoch-making for Taiwan (indeed, a parliamentary resolution later had my speech included in school anthologies), plus my remarks to them about Russian-Chinese relations, there was no conversation to be had. They talked to one another in Chinese, and I was bored. Finally, dessert arrived, but that wasn't the end either: now there was fruit, presented in several stages (the waitress served it up artistically). Eventually, everyone began to bow slightly, so that I would bow even more deeply. This I did, and the company dispersed.

After my farewell statement reporters remained on watch at both the airport and the hotel. But my departure had been cleverly arranged: we left through the hotel's tradesman's entrance and drove to the airport behind schedule, when the highway was clear. At the airport we were taken to wait in a completely separate area and put on the plane via a separate gangway, ahead of everyone else. And only three men traveled with me on the empty upper deck of the China Airlines plane—by now I was aware that they were security guards. (It was reminiscent somehow of my expulsion from the USSR . . .) We flew over the Pacific Ocean for eleven hours nonstop; it was tiring.

On our midnight approach, from a great height, New York astounded me: no individual lights or even highways could be made out; rather, it was as if this crocodile-shaped expanse was lit by some hellish sun which had wrested it from the darkness. The source of light seemed external to the object illuminated, its origin incomprehensible.

Could I at least presume that the Taiwan speech had spread, had an impact, perhaps even pricked someone's conscience? I don't know. Several months went by—I understood less and less.

No, this whole Far East trip, and with all its special preparations, had been time lost, too luxurious an expenditure of it in relation to my tasks as a writer. I should probably have kept out of it all, and simply stayed put to plow on with my work.

* * *

I had headed off on my trip to the Far East in good spirits but oh, how thrilled I was to be home: here it was, my real place. I wouldn't budge again for years! I would get to grips with *The Red Wheel* once again! Now that is happiness: work! It seemed so certain that I would not be going anywhere now, but, after a mere two weeks, a letter arrived from John Train of America's right-wing circles (a financier and conservative journalist), asking whether, if awarded it, I would accept the Templeton Prize (a religious prize I'd never heard of). Would I go to London to receive it from the hands of the Queen's husband, the Duke of Edinburgh?

A brochure was included, with a spiral nebula on the cover; it contained an explanation of this strange prize: "established to call attention to a variety of persons who have found new ways to increase man's love of God or man's understanding of God . . . new and effective methods of communicating God's wisdom." Did it smack slightly of Freemasonry? Rosicrucianism? It was reassuring that they were not intent on replacing all religions with one that was higher than them all; rather, the prize sought "to encourage understanding of the benefits of diversity." It is bestowed on people "with a substantial record of achievement" in strengthening "the spirit in the face of the world's spiritual crisis." Mother Teresa had received it, as had Brother Roger Schütz. It had been awarded ten times, and not once as yet to anyone Orthodox: how could I not seize the moment to speak to the whole world about my own people? It was annoying, however, that the tenth person to receive it, the one immediately before me, was Billy Graham, who, at the very time he received his prize, made the deplorable statement that he had *not noticed* any religious persecution in the USSR (he'd just been there for the first time, and had been given a lavish reception).

They wrote that the prize would be announced on 2 March, and received in London on 10 May. So that left another six months before racing off again, and the winter at home. I said yes.

(We didn't know anything about Templeton himself except that he was a millionaire. Only in the spring did Train send a slim volume that said Templeton had come by his wealth through the ingenious method of buying shares which most people had turned their backs on, or which were utterly worthless, in a moment of crisis when a boom was expected to follow. Surely ingenuity was a more acceptable source than the Nobel brothers' capital, brought almost untaxed out of Russia thanks to the Russian government's misplaced naïveté. What's more, Templeton "occasionally abandoned profitable enterprises if they were too time-consuming: one should never be so busy that one does not have enough time to think—to ponder one's investments, the wider world, and the religious aspects." Such was this American Protestant, a Presbyterian, in a colonnaded white house in the Bahamas.)

I agreed: they might or might not actually give it to me but, meanwhile, it was the start of a six-month interlude that could be used for work. Almost all of it went on the third draft of *March*. It was a pleasure after my Far-Eastern break. Essentially, this was the first time I had read *March* all the way through, in order. The four volumes were such a behemoth that, working on different parts of it at different times and more often than not tracing the horizontal development of characters and actions, I'd retained only a mental image of how it played out along the vertical axis of days: now I was perusing those vertical progressions for the first time. And they didn't let me down. In the chapters themselves, however, in the details and the repetitions, a considerable amount of work remained to be done. And after the third draft, the only conclusion I could reach was that a fourth would be needed—although not right away, after a bit of a break. A lot needed to be finished off that winter, which Alya and I had not succeeded in doing earlier on: printing the end of *October*, the second volume, which meant more editing.

Then again, I very much wanted to publish "Our Pluralists" in *Vestnik*[21] (it had initially been a fragment of the *Millstones* chapter "A Creeping Host"). It was something I'd been planning as much as a year earlier, but Alya was against it. I had put it on the "scales," more than once, in fact. *Pros*: that one ought not meekly relinquish for so many years the Russian-language audience, both in emigration and in Russia, and that it would help clarify my confederates' minds; it would draw attention to the dangerous influx of future new Februarists; it was the natural continuation of my "Smatterers,"[22] so why not develop it further, and issue a response once in seven years? It was wrong to let the calumny stick. It's already written anyway; and if not published now, in ten years' time it would be irrelevant: no one would need it, not even in *Millstones*. *Cons*: that it was not in fact urgently needed, and that my main task had nothing to do with this debate. And, Alya maintained, they were fading away, going under in any case (oh, ill-judged prediction), there was no need to stoop to their level, and such a petty, extraneous discussion was of no interest to our people back home; I would only cut myself off from Russia. (And that wasn't true either.)

Nevertheless, I decided to publish. First of all, Alya, as was her wont, threw herself into rigorously checking quotations by the "pluralists." I hadn't identified all the pages accurately so she went through those hundreds of odious pages again. When I was reading their opuses myself last May, I had found it excruciating to be doing such pointless, needless work—and it's impossible to work when you feel such contempt. Alya now discovered that I'd been in too much of a rush and had made an awful lot of mistakes in copying out the quotations—innocuously for the most part but inopportunely nonetheless, since they would be gone through with a fine-tooth comb. She found everything, she checked and rechecked everything—it was unassailable. Next she argued that I had no experience of debating with such a horde of small-minded types, and that I'd adopted a passionate tone that was appropriate when confronting the Monster but not the creeping host. And she hacked away at my exasperation about many controversies, fashioning it into restraint. (I am myself aware that the greater the restraint, the greater the impact, but it is hard to hold back.) As for her main suggestion: I'd been pointing out the danger that "they want to go back and be in charge of Russian culture at the very least," but she sought to convince me that *some* were already quite nicely set up in the West and would not all relish returning to a barren land, while the real danger was that *others*, and an ever increasing majority to boot, had come of age in the USSR beneath the cast-iron shell of the regime—and *they* were the ones who would stir themselves on Day X. And it's true, she was right—very perceptive. I accepted this; wasn't it the case that just such a skittish brood had now grown up, over there, under the Soviet carapace, if not a multitude of them? Alya also convinced me to make several substantial changes to the structure of the article—she has an unerring sense of structure too.

After all that, the announcement was made in Washington that I'd won the prize. Three weeks earlier, I'd been congratulated by Templeton, and Train, and even . . . former US President Gerald Ford, who turned out (this had not been announced earlier) to have been one of the international judges of the prize. And now, in addition to the set program, the Templeton Foundation was summoning me to Washington to be there for the announcement and even to hold a press conference. (Would Ford also turn up and attest to our "reconciliation"?) Oh, for goodness' sake! You never set that condition, and I would never have accepted it. Not to mention disrupting my work, but going to receive the same prize twice?—honestly, they're making me into a laughingstock. This was my answer: no, I can't come, I will only go to London. For the time being, I got myself out of it with just a little telegram. (As I understand it, the Templeton Foundation took umbrage.)

However, the documents for awarding the prize, which were made public in Washington and sent on to me, were more in-depth than I had expected. Most astonishing was the formulation: "the continuing vitality of the Orthodox tradition of spirituality" in Russia has been demonstrated, the very thing our most heated debate with Russia's enemies was about. Researchers for the Templeton Foundation—or for the panel of judges, perhaps—had gone to some trouble, done their homework, and gathered from my books what to submit for the award. They were right to pick out both my poem in *Archipelago* and the separate "A Prayer."[23]

I was flabbergasted by these unforeseen pathways. "A Prayer," after all, had been printed, been referred to, and had left its mark many times over; and yet I wasn't the one who had had it published—that was Elizaveta Voronyanskaya, acting of her own volition, and what a tongue-lashing I gave her for it! Similarly of her own volition she protected *Archipelago* until the KGB turned up[24] and ensured it saw the light of day. And for both these acts of willfulness I now owe her posthumously nothing but gratitude. She was an instrument of God.

So I had to prepare a speech in response to the prize. Something else to do. All these years I had avoided speaking directly about faith: it was both immodest and it offended the sensitive ear. Faith was not to be proclaimed, but allowed to flow soundlessly and irrefutably. But now the moment had come—a speech was required precisely about religion. Given this novelty, however, the speech would still be a big step, even for myself. Especially in understanding earthly life as a stage in the development of eternal life. I'd already long since come to realize, and had written, that the aim of earthly life is to end it on a morally higher level than that dictated by one's innate qualities. And yet, does the aim of spiritual growth not extend beyond the earthly plane as well?

At this point, rolling back the decades, a fellow countryman came to my aid. This was Igor Sikorsky, the distinguished aircraft designer, who also happened to be interested in the philosophy of creation. Out of the blue, his son sent me one of his speeches on the subject,[25] which had been given in 1949 to indifferently comprehending Americans—and this prompted me to consider further whether life after death could access speeds greater than the speed of light—only under these circumstances might the Universe be inhabited. (And only then did I truly grasp why suicide is such a great sin: it is the voluntary interruption of growth, the pushing away of God's hand.) For me, everything was falling more firmly into place.

As always, of course, this speech too had an overly political thrust, but I was unable to speak otherwise in the West, there was always a mass of things to tell them. Both about the West in general and about how they had immorally introduced the atom bomb to the world—when they were already victorious!—and dropped it on a civilian population. The global picture is not so simple. I couldn't miss the chance to take a swipe at the World Council of Churches as well, which was suspected of being under Soviet influence. Nor could I fail to mention Billy Graham's scheming remarks the previous year. If I couldn't digress from politics even in a speech of this kind, however, it would be better for me not to speak at all. I should call it a day.

Furthermore, the foundation informed me that I needed to deliver a four-to-five-minute speech at Buckingham Palace, thanking Prince Philip. What was I to do? As it was, my main speech was ballooning beyond the required length. I decided to split the material and make the short speech, in a way, part of the whole.

The speeches were already written, but there was still a month to go until London. Various preparations had built up—for a meeting with the publishers, for a meeting with the translators: my favorite, Harry Willetts, who translated my books so slowly but so well, and the likable Michael Nicolson, who tended not to translate as a rule, but would evaluate translations and was compiling a detailed bibliography about me—he was a great help to Alya regarding the notes for the social and political commentary volumes of my Collected Works. Just then my *Feast of the Victors* and *Prisoners* were unexpectedly published in English, introducing two new translators—so I had to see them, perhaps they were a find? But then their translations needed to be analyzed beforehand? (This can sometimes be more easily done by the author than even by someone who knows both languages.) I set about it, spent a good bit of time, and found no shortage of mistakes, although I felt that the tone and the mood had been conveyed pretty well, despite the verse dialogue being translated as prose. (To some extent, this is evidence that there is a seed of something in *Feast* that can never be lost. I remain tenderly disposed toward the play.)

And now there was also some reading about England proper to be done—after all, I hadn't been planning to go there.

But right then in March (1983), Sergei Khodorovich was threatened with arrest. He managed to release a statement, and we were able to support him with one of our own, but to no avail: he was arrested at the beginning of April. Nor had our correspondence had time to reach Moscow to say that, given the about-turn under Andropov, it would be better if the next administrator did not announce his appointment and thereby sacrifice himself, before Andrei Kistyakovsky (his nomination had been agreed with us previously) went public. And within the next few days, the news came in that he'd been immediately carted off to the KGB and warned of his imminent arrest. And so, against all odds, when the ears and attention of the West were focused on something else (and understandably so), Alya launched a campaign in their defense. After all, and typically for Andropov, they had contrived to accuse Khodorovich and Kistyakovsky of *high treason.*

It is not always possible to predict the secret movements within Soviet power circles. I said nothing for several months, biding my time, until Andropov showed his mettle more clearly. By accelerating the Northern river reversal project[26] and arresting Khodorovich, he'd now revealed himself to me in all his true colors: his new ideas amounted to just turning the screws, Stalin-style.

And it was then that a request arrived from Templeton: to hold a press conference in England. It was the most useless format, but I couldn't turn him down. I set just one condition—that there should be a small number of reporters rather than a whole crowd.

Oh well, those months were already bent out of shape for work: they might as well go to rack and ruin altogether! I was still managing to spend about three hours a day dipping into the newspapers for *April 1917*, but it just added to my frustration. As I had before Japan, I set about putting my journalistic card-index (my raw material) in order—the European one this time. And why not? It wasn't without benefit, and even seemed right to create some kind of balance with the trip to the Far East.

Dealing with Western journalists isn't much more difficult than dealing with Soviet mandarins: generally, you always know what preoccupies them most, what's on the tip of their tongues. In pride of place at that time, of course, was my attitude towards Europe's nuclear disarmament movement. It was simplest to say that the movement was being fueled by the Soviets. That's just how it was. However, my visit to Hiroshima and Professor Guertner's scientific proposals for the selective annihilation of ethnic Russians[27] had given me good reason to reflect more upon US nuclear achievements, and, in my Templeton speech, I came out against them and, indeed, against the whole idea of a nuclear umbrella. It became so clear to me that, the moment it reached for the diabolical gift of the nuclear bomb, the West went out of its mind. It was clinging on to that lethal shield as its own defense mechanism, but a fatal temptation lurked within: in its wake, the fine men of the West—Bertrand Russell, George Kennan, Averell Harriman, and dozens of others—began urging their compatriots to make more, more, and still more concessions to Communism, anything to ensure there was no nuclear war. (Incidentally, I never believed there would be: it would obliterate the Creator's plan for humanity.)* I drew up a detailed and precise, if lengthy, overview of the problem for the press conference. (Once again I forgot the

* Throughout the '70s and into the '80s I unequivocally expected new victories for Communism. But while our ageing leaders were still enjoying the carefree life, Reagan had strengthened America—and, faced with a new arms race, the Soviet economy (though not Soviet science!) threw in the towel. Thus did Lenin's onslaught on the planet end even before Andropov. (Author's note, 1990.)

main defect of press conferences: that no answer comes across coherently and intact; instead, each reporter plucks out shreds and tatters.)

There were other questions and answers too, Alya and I taking turns to respond. About Khodorovich, about the fate of our Fund in the USSR. The press tore it all into little pieces, each journalist pecking up something and carrying it away.[28]

Meanwhile, necessary, even essential meetings in England were constantly being cobbled together, and they were all being crammed into London, as if it had been booked ages ago and all we had to do was get there. Above all else, however, that scorpion, Flegon,[29] was still over there. And I'd now been corresponding for about a year with Oleg Lenchevsky, who'd also got into a legal tangle with Flegon because of me. It was simple, really: the very first meeting I needed to arrange in London was with Lenchevsky. Meaning that before I got to London I also had to read through a parcel of legal papers about the case, which he'd sent me earlier—a delightful task!

Oleg Stanislavovich Lenchevsky, sixty-seven, tall, wiry, and energetic, proved unflinching about the truth and unbending on matters of principle—such people are rarely encountered nowadays. In 1961, he was a successful research scientist and, moreover, a Party (CPSU) member, when he was sent to a conference at UNESCO and defected, leaving his defenseless family behind in Moscow—so that he could address Khrushchev publicly about mistakes in Soviet domestic and foreign policy, the growth of a ruling class, and thought control. He didn't want always to agree dutifully to everything, or always to vote "for." In addition to the Russian desire to pour one's heart out, Lenchevsky also had the (forlorn) hope of finding sympathy in the West for the tribulations of our people.

His family in the USSR were subject to relentless harassment, and he himself found emigration hard; he'd even had cancer (although he beat it). He kept his footing in his new and difficult life, at one time working for the BBC, then making a living from technical translations. Twenty years later, in 1981, he got into horrendous trouble when he stepped in to protect me from Flegon's filth. From that moment on, he was engulfed by the all-consuming machinery of the immutable English courts—to my mind, the putrefying sore of contemporary England.

And this sore requires that I recount what follows.

Flegon immediately took steps to intimidate Lenchevsky and, once he'd received a fitting response, took him to court. (I don't know why, but in England this means the "high" court right from the start.) A month later the *Guardian* carried a tasteless article, saying "Russian writers brew up storm in samovar. . . . Every Russian émigré worth his salt is booking tickets to get to London for the trial."[30] And none other than David Burg[31] is quoted as commenting favorably on Flegon's book. Lenchevsky responded forthwith, writing to the *Guardian* to say, "How many readers of *The Gulag Archipelago* or *Cancer Ward* would be prepared to believe that their author is said to be—I quote—a compulsive liar, an informer, a traitor, a coward, a hypocrite, a slanderer, a fornicator, a perjurer, a megalomaniac, a paranoiac, a gossipmonger, a dishonest demagogue," who has, moreover, "concealed his Jewish descent [yet] is alleged to be an anti-Semite. An admixed plethora of dirty Russian words . . . makes the whole thing look like a bait [by Flegon's reckoning] for many an unsuspecting buyer."[32] —Lenchevsky went on to abandon his own income and devote himself to challenging Flegon with increasing passion. Although Flegon knew Lenchevsky from the BBC, he had underestimated his doggedness and commitment to his principles; litigious as he was, Flegon touched him at his peril.

Lenchevsky had hoped that, given the loathsome quality of almost every page of Flegon's book, it would be easy to gather fifteen to twenty witnesses of good standing and flood the judge's bench with them, leaving no doubt about the standard of Flegon's book, which, apart from its brazen illustrations, was inaccessible to the English reader. —Nothing of the sort, however: he had not reckoned with the ethos of the Russian émigrés, which was, incidentally, entirely natural. The émigrés in Paris whom he asked had responded with, "There's really no point getting involved with Flegon; it simply gives him extra publicity." And the only person to swear the requested affidavit (a statement under oath) was Oleg Kerensky (with whom I'd only very recently been arguing about his father's role in the Revolution): "I have never read in any language a more offensive, obscene, pornographic, defamatory, and racist book. . . . The text is written in foul language and offensive terms, which normal Russian literature does not use."

Lenchevsky, however, in his passion for justice, his honesty and daring, was already in fighting mood: to tighten the screws once and for all on this "unique printing-press terrorist," who had escaped sentencing in all his previous trials. Months and months of the usual legal proceedings dragged by—while Lenchevsky classified his issues with Flegon into ever new categories: the reasons why the book was substandard as a literary work; a compilation of the pornographic bits; comparative lists of quotations in which Flegon spoke benevolently about the KGB and malignantly about the CIA; and a selection of anti-Semitic passages (anti-Russian ones would have no effect on an English court). All this obliged my champion to produce, himself, more than seventy pages of translation from Flegon's thousand-page book to be admitted as evidence, an immense task, and then to have the accuracy of the translations certified by authoritative bilingual Englishmen: Peter Norman and—names I wasn't expecting to see—Gerald Brooke and Michael Glenny. Leonid Finkelstein-Vladimirov, who sympathized with me and was also at the BBC, managed to obtain a letter from the chief executive of the Board of Deputies of British Jews to Foyles bookshop: "The book is hostile to Jews: I wouldn't want to give it undeserved publicity." (In actual fact, Flegon's book is acutely anti-Russian rather than anti-Jewish, but he did discharge several dubious remarks and stories in that direction too.)

Flegon faltered at these measures taken by Lenchevsky—he hadn't expected such persistence. In his previous legal escapades, he'd instead encountered a fear-driven longing for settlement. He kept his head down, refrained from answering summonses, declined to appear before the "Master" (a lower-level judge for interim procedural decisions). Incidentally, his latest advertisement for his book found yet another way to twist what Lenchevsky had said, and a new protest from Lenchevsky followed: ban that advert too! He was a wily one, Flegon; you couldn't let him out of your sight!

In the lengthy phases of what are always protracted proceedings, England's illustrious Lady Justice inches her victims through pure technicalities, the emphasis on extremely rigorous procedure, without venturing into the crux of the matter at all. Lenchevsky appealed, to no avail, for someone to have at least leafed through the case materials, to learn Flegon's own highly litigious history and what kind of person he was. He also came across an article in English law, 3390, about restraining vexatious litigants: but how could it be applied? Flegon, meanwhile, was in his element in this legal murk, and the legal authorities were very favorably disposed towards him as an offended, defenseless, and impecunious character. Here too, he successfully sought to defer a trial that was not to his advantage. A rumor emerged that he was preparing the English edition of his book during this time, and would probably reduce the unacceptable content so that proof would have to be presented in court that this version was "not that one."

As early as the summer of 1981, Lenchevsky had sent me a letter, not by mail but via Janis Sapiets—only the latter decided not to distract me and didn't pass it on. He had little hope that Lenchevsky would achieve anything. Everyone around Lenchevsky was trying to talk him out of it: drop the case, abandon it, settle out of court even. I learned of his case in a roundabout way, with a delay of several months, and it was I who first wrote to him, already in the summer of 1982. And he replied then that he hoped the Flegon case was close to completion: "It's no longer he but I who am insisting that the case be referred for trial, the criminal plaintiff has become the defendant in my lawsuit. . . . English legislation simply does not provide for such a slippery litigant." (Alas, alas! It is precisely England's legendary law system that looks kindly upon litigants!—we read about it already in Dickens.) I was stunned by his firm and confident tone. By contrast, Flegon weakened and wrote a letter to Lenchevsky that November, artificially puffing himself up into fighting form, and saying that he *agreed* to halt his lawsuit if Lenchevsky paid his legal costs and his loss of income resulting from the letter to the bookshop, and withdrew his accusations against the book.

To pay—this was suggested in the form of a question, and nine out of ten people in Lenchevsky's position would have accepted an out-of-court settlement simply to have done with the matter. But Lenchevsky was made of different stuff. He felt he was defending not so much me as *Archipelago*: "To the eternal memory of my relatives who did not survive, and out of duty to them: the ashes of Claes beat upon my heart too."[33]

The date for the trial had already been set—for June 1983. But Flegon took the following extraordinary step: he asked the court for permission to reformulate his initial lawsuit against Lenchevsky, which was already eighteen months old, and to expand it to cover both Solzhenitsyn and YMCA-Press—a twist in the litigation undreamt of even by Dickens: for *his* book libeling me, he was going to take *me* (who'd done nothing at all) to court for *libel*! (Ultimately, he desperately needed the trial to be between him and me and about the book.) And for a jury not a judge to decide. (Lenchevsky: that way there's more likelihood of hitting upon idiots.)

And what was the Master's decision? That he should have thought of that earlier? that it was inappropriate to change an ongoing lawsuit? Not at all—he let Flegon do just that.

In short order, Lenchevsky managed to obtain (by dint of how much more effort?) a fleeting, split-second audience with the Master, and hastened to drum into him that Flegon was a professional litigant and that English justice should not be put to shame in this way. In reply, the Master asked whether Lenchevsky would agree to close the case with Flegon paying him damages. It would have been sensible to agree, but Lenchevsky was already too worked up: "No, I insist that it be extensively examined in court, in order to shed instructive light on the whole story in public!" —And to me he wrote: "My friends have the impression that I am beginning to out-Flegon Flegon by an order of magnitude. However, I am aware of my prolonged powerlessness, my mouth plugged with a legal gag, and aware too that this filth will slither into blinded Russia." What fighting spirit! "He must be kept under relentless pressure! He has always won because of the other side's defensiveness and passivity. He must be crushed, utterly and as soon as possible, like any harmful creeping thing so that he cannot set about doing it all again!" And he collected ever more new files of arguments and proofs, ever more new translations of bits of the book. He had already translated more than three hundred pages. There were already nine case files—"but in the event of trial by jury, twelve copies of these will have to be made. It's so disheartening." (My overall impression of the courts, and not just English ones, is of a massive reworking of nothing at all. A minor technicality swells into mountains of paperwork.) Lenchevsky was hoping that now, after a trial of two years, "the game is entering the final stretch . . . the defeat of the enemy is at hand." He was constantly cheerful but "battle fatigue is beginning to make itself felt"; he fell ill before I arrived. He was waiting for me to put up some resistance at last and to take action!—he was puzzled to see passivity in someone as energetic as myself.

And Lenchevsky was quite right! And I did feel ashamed! But at the same time, I couldn't step away from my life's task. . . .

Just look how much of my time a grasping rat like Flegon was costing me, how much strength he was forcing me to expend! Did I even have that strength? Alya and I did everything, everywhere ourselves, and we were barely managing. Here was a rare case of lucking into the assistance of a noble person. Dear Lord! How could I get by now, never having dealt with lawyers before? I did it in the Soviet Union for fifty-five years, after all. But in the free West, whatever step I took, it was—hire a lawyer. Indeed, by that time I'd already engaged, remotely, a lawyer in England, Richard Sykes, who'd been recommended by Edward Bennett Williams. And now here he was, the man himself, in a London hotel—tall, burly, extremely self-assured, barely able to squeeze himself into the armchair, eyeing the raging homegrown truth-lover that was Lenchevsky and my own inexperienced ignorance. He merely grimaced with contempt at our conviction that Flegon was really a KGB agent—"Oh, they wouldn't take someone like that," a nonentity, in other words. Did Sykes know the KGB? . . . He knew the whole collection of English laws, the full set of legal maneuvers, and yet he was already giving Lenchevsky advice, and all of it was wrong. How on earth was he going to handle my case, in which I had specifically called Flegon an agent?

The whole Western world is riddled with reciprocal international treaties regarding legal investigation—but of civil not criminal cases. A lawsuit for slander can creep up on you from any distant corner of the planet for any freely and directly spoken word. (May the Russia of the future at least keep well away from such treaties!)

Having seen for myself how hopeless, how undiscerning the burly Sykes really was, there was only one thing I wanted to know: how to be rid of both him and the lawsuit. My life did not allow time for these pettifogging courts and innumerable legal documents in English.

A wise man never goes to court; a fool never leaves it.

And it was simply impossible for me to *win* a trial against Flegon: no matter what, he would declare himself bankrupt, and I would end up liable for all the costs. I had to admit also that the sentence in *The Oak and the Calf* was hard to defend[34] since it seemed clear, from the comparison with *Stern*, just which "Center" was running them.

But here was the vortex: Lenchevsky was wearing himself out, devoting all his energy to the case. His eyes shone with the thrill of the fight: was I really not going to hold the flank? It turned out that I would have to. We had to fight our way through. Ah, whoever wants to fight must gather all his might.

That Sykes was going to be no use to me, Lenchevsky saw even before I did. His advice, however, was to engage a really combative lawyer; he would help me find one.

Perhaps that really was what I ought to do? I charged him with looking into it. Meanwhile, once back in Vermont, I wrote to Sykes with categorical instructions to suspend all activities and not take a single step without me. There was some consolation in the estimate that the trial wouldn't be held for eighteen months at least—and eighteen months was an excellent delay: such a respite for writing, so much work I could still get done!

That same year, 1983, Lenchevsky found me three potential lawyers in London, and I began to correspond with them. One of them, Lionel Bloch, I quite liked. Energetic, with a keen political sensibility, he understood the KGB's game and was familiar with Flegon's previous legal adventures. I would have signed a contract with him but he began to paint a picture that entailed the longest possible trial, involved experts on Communism, and required me to go to England in person for the trial. Well, there was no way I could take on all that, I'd rather lose three times over.

Once again, I was dependent on Sykes. How stupid. After all, you should put your heart and soul into everything you do, or else not bother. If I wasn't prepared to go there and fight, then I shouldn't have agreed to any halfway measures.

A trial is like mud—you don't come up smelling of roses.

The year 1984 was passing and nothing was being done, but the trial was drawing closer nonetheless. I wrote to Williams in alarm: Sykes would ruin me, could I not back out altogether, not mount a defense at all? Williams and Sykes, however, turned out to have graduated from the same school at one point, and the latter listened to his friend who was now a star lawyer. And Williams undertook to guide Sykes from America, while I didn't need to worry about anything. He wrote: "I accept complete responsibility for everything that happens from here on." And I gave in: well, what was wrong with Williams's version? It was precisely what I needed—not to have to read legal documents or to rack my brains about them. I asked Williams to set to work, while I put it out of my mind for two years. (And yet again—yet again—I was forgetting the complex English system. Your lawyer, that is, the *solicitor*, does not appear in court but merely prepares the paperwork. It is another lawyer, a *barrister*, who conducts the case in court, someone you haven't retained and have never met. Is it so that people have to pay for lawyers twice? And what kind of barrister could Sykes have? Someone just like himself, another Sykes, no doubt.) And no matter how much correspondence Sykes and I exchanged—and even met each other in London—he never once warned me that my personal testimony would be required in court, even if only in writing. In the spring of 1986, however, with the trial imminent, precisely such a document was required as a matter of urgency, and once again it fell to Edward Bennett Williams in the States. Oh, that Sykes! How come I always end up with people like that? . . .

But what about Lenchevsky's trial in June 1983? Flegon wriggled out of it, didn't put in an appearance—and only belatedly did Lenchevsky learn (his nerves in tatters, he'd done so much preparation) just what decision the Master had taken in December. While Flegon redrafted his initial lawsuit, the whole legal process was suspended *indefinitely*!—it could be delayed by as much as ten years if the plaintiff wasn't ready to go to trial. Such is the English court's unfailing bias towards the plaintiff. During that time, however, I invited Lenchevsky to approach several legal experts, and they convinced him to seek to have the case dismissed on the grounds that there was no case to answer. And eventually the court dismissed the case. But cue another objection from Flegon. And the case was reinstated! The legal marathon was set to drag on for years to come.

We arrived in London unnoticed (the Templeton Foundation flew us over on the supersonic Concorde), but the name "Solzhenitsyn" appeared on the front pages of the day's newspapers even so. It wasn't mine this time, but twelve-year-old Yermolai's. Just before we left home, he'd managed to distinguish himself at school. They'd had a visit from a pompous Soviet delegation (the deputy editor-in-chief of *Izvestia* [*News*]), and Yermolai, already immersed in political issues, asked them a cheeky question about disarmament, and in excellent Russian to boot, something they hadn't been expecting there. It was immediately picked up by all the US reporters,[35] they found it entertaining, and lo, the story even reached England. Was Yermolai, bursting with political passion taking after me? The poor lad doesn't yet know what a rocky road that is, nor how much strength, supreme awareness, and inner steadfastness are required.

The prize-giving timetable meant we had to go to London just before Orthodox Easter. The Russian Orthodox Church Abroad[36] knew from Templeton Foundation circles that we would be attending the midnight service at their cathedral. Already during the afternoon, I'd been given the message—and I now encountered a postulant at the door—asking us not to stand in the body of the church like everyone else, but to slip into the choir gallery behind the great icon. I declined—Alya and I took our place with everyone else. Several minutes went by, the postulant returned: Bishop Constantine was inviting me into the sanctuary. I calmly declined—I wanted to stand with everyone else. Alya was already becoming very stressed: for all her cultural refinement, in the presence of clergy she was as tremulously humble as a simple peasant woman. People were already gathering for the Procession of the Cross when they sent for me again: the bishop wanted me to carry an icon in the procession. I didn't bat an eyelid: I am here to pray with everyone else, please don't pay any attention to me. But Alya, almost desperate, was saying, "Oh, please, please!" in a tense whisper. Here rational thinking failed me too, and I agreed. (My ingenuous thought was: I've never taken part in the Procession of the Cross in my life.) I went into the sanctuary, an icon of the Descent into Hell was handed me from the altar table, and I was put into the procession right behind the bishop. And that was all he needed: a pre-arranged photographer immediately appeared with a flashbulb and, as we strode between parked cars (that was our whole route—there was no room to walk around the church itself), he took a couple of dozen snaps. And there's no waving a photographer away in that position. (I thought wistfully that this was what the Church Abroad was like—where was the simplicity of Holy Russia? It was the second time photographers had caught me unawares at a church service, and in each case it had been at the Church Abroad. I attended all the Holy Week services at the Orthodox Church in America cathedral in Montreal: they weren't even tempted.) And that was that. The following day, in pride of place on the front page of the *Times*, there I was looking slightly dimwitted, holding the icon and a cloth[37]—this was how my arrival in London was announced. For modern-day Europe, it was almost a caricature—to the jubilation of the left.

A pity. Not only did it undermine the strict balance of my Guildhall speech in two days' time, but it also damaged the special correlation I'd achieved so naturally until then of linking a Christian's faith with a tone acceptable to the modern day, never overdoing things—striking the truthful, natural note that is the only one permissible for non-clergy when encouraging, drawing back to faith a society that's gone astray.

Alya and I packed the whole of Easter Sunday with preparations for business meetings planned for London. There had been such a surge of them—it was as if everyone in London had been expressly waiting for me.

It is also my eternal fate to discuss corrections and more corrections to the translations of my texts, this time for the upcoming speech. The entire speech had been meticulously translated back in the States by Alexis Klimoff, conferring across the pond with Michael Nicholson; then I myself reviewed it at home and asked Klimoff, here and there, for changes. Now it was

Laurence Kelly, son of the former British ambassador to the USSR (and himself the author of a book on Lermontov), blond-haired, with a supremely lively face, and a very open manner for an Englishman, who was to read out the translation at the main ceremony—and the elegant, grey-haired John Train alongside him—who presented me with a new list of corrections (here the differences between US and UK expressions played a role, too). And I had to delve in, and at times agree without any longer notifying the first translator—and it would be sent for urgent retyping. A forgotten joy of youth: to write in Russian and give no thought to any translations.

Also I had to map out, with Kelly, where to place pauses—so that he would translate no more and no less than I'd spoken, sometimes just one clause at a time; I consider this method to be optimal for comprehension of a translated speech, and even the sound of the Russian profits thereby. And then—the same work with Train on my brief "Response" to Prince Philip, but complicated by Train not knowing a word of Russian.

A "reception at the House of Lords" was on the agenda for Easter Monday evening, Alya and I read in great astonishment. It turned out not to be with the lords at all, but merely to be held in their building, in a lobby hired by Sir John Templeton for his numerous relatives and friends who'd gathered from various parts of the world. It was only the eleventh time the prize had been conferred, and the ceremony retained its family character. It was, typically, an unbearably vacuous reception: standing around with a glass in your left hand, while shaking hands and performing one instantly forgotten introduction after another with your right. (And where . . . where on earth had this unlooked-for trip to England taken us? . . .) Given its proximity, Alya and I were taken into the public gallery of the chamber itself. The evening sitting was still going on, attended—honestly—by just ten lords. The rest of the chamber was unoccupied (it must have been a committee rather than a plenary meeting), and in the empty depths of the great hall a speaker was portentously analyzing the issue of red-salmon fishing.

Fortunately, the whole reception lasted only an hour and a half, and from there we went straight for dinner with Michael Ramsey, the Archbishop of Canterbury.

The archbishop lives in what is almost a castle, the courtyard, the buildings, and their interiors in a restrained English style, and all the décor in the same spirit. Hospitality entailed a pleasant dinner, neither the preparation nor the serving of the meal cooled by any standoffishness. The archbishop was extremely kind to me—and I was quick to ask for his public intervention on behalf of the arrested Khodorovich. He promised. (From what I knew of Church of England diplomacy, I wasn't confident.) I gave the amiable archbishop a potted version of what I had to say—but without hope: the armor of prosperity is the stoutest armor of all. (A few days later I read in the *Times* that England's churches had been losing worshippers in recent decades. It's the same the world over.) Margaret Thatcher was also keen to attend the dinner but was unable to do so and, in any case, it would not have been a proper meeting then—it would have been chaotic. A pleasant elderly gentleman was in attendance, however. This was Laurens van der Post, confidant both to Thatcher and to Prince Charles.

We went to Buckingham Palace on the sunny morning of our Easter Tuesday, passing the curious public who always keep watch outside the gates. Then came an unmemorable series of steps, lobbies, and servants (but it was far removed from our Winter Palace, no comparison even!) and there we were, in a small hall of some kind with not too many mirrors, wainscot paneling, chandeliers, and antique armchairs and sofas. There were no more than a dozen people altogether. An usher marshaled us into a single curving file.

Prince Philip—tall, a little over fifty, slim, with a military bearing (a naval officer), in a regular suit—entered through one of the doors, in no way haughty or ceremonious, with unfeigned simplicity and, what's more, in a quick and businesslike manner. He did the rounds of us all, shook hands, and told me he also belonged to the Orthodox Church, by birth (I knew he was a Greek prince). Then he was handed a certificate rolled up in a tube, a medal in a small box, and a check in an envelope. With simple gestures, he uttered a few words of welcome to the lineup, handed the things to me (all of it captured by the palace photographer), I passed them on to Alya, and then John Train and I read out my response,[38] which was probably overly solemn for this little auditorium and ceremony, but, Alya observed, both the prince and the others present were moved. John Templeton's modest, beaming smile is visible in all the photographs (he would later listen in the same way to my speech at the Guildhall). He had a natural, kindly modesty, and was clearly delighted that his prizes had become a fixture, his future memorial on Earth.

In the lunch break between the ceremonies, we also managed to meet in person the worthy Nikolai Vladimirovich Volkov-Muromtsev, one of our outstanding elderly memoirists, whose book begins our memoir series. Unfortunately, his book had still not been published at that point (and he was already so old). It turned out he'd also written a history of the Russian navy. We shall see. He had been an émigré for sixty years, and all of them in England, cut off from Russia and speaking no Russian for years. He'd offered his English-language memoirs to publishers; no one had ever shown interest.*

It was still early evening when we set off for the Guildhall. This is effectively the venue for receptions held by the City of London. It was built in 1411 (although there was something similar on the same spot even before that). It was damaged in the Great Fire of 1666 but had been fully restored, as were the nine-foot-tall statues of Gog and Magog, which guarded the entrance to the Musicians' Gallery. In 1940, however, the roof of the Great Hall was destroyed once again, this time in a German air raid, and the steel-and-glass windows exploded. It was restored again, but now without the mysterious Gog and Magog, who would have been highly appropriate for today's speech. Even without them, however, the Gothic arches of this medieval hall and the opening and closing prayers (by the queen's chaplain) were very well suited to what I was going to say. I delivered the speech without gesticulating at all, or modulating my voice too much. Despite this, reporters later wrote that the translation, in Kelly's reading, had sounded much more conciliatory.

It was printed in the *Times* the next day[39] but with substantial arbitrary cuts, which always grates on me. What is this flippancy on the part of newspapers? Ideas that an author has laboriously brought into existence and shaped at length, slashed to pieces by fifteen minutes' worth of cocksure pen strokes. (The speech did go out in full on Russian-language stations.)

And then, the next day, 12 May, the *Times* carried a leading article entitled "Ultimate Things."[40] Some unknown idealist (later it turned out to be the chief editor of the *Times*, Charles Douglas-Home himself, soon to meet an untimely end), inspired that it was possible to talk about faith so unashamedly

* His book of memoirs in our series later made an impression on the Soviet authorities, and they sent restorers working on Griboyedov's Khmelita Estate in Smolensk oblast to Nikolai Vladimirovich for advice about the details of how life was lived and of furniture. Nikolai Volkov-Muromtsev, Юность: От Вязьмы до Феодосии, 1902–1920 (*Youth: From Vyazma to Feodosia, 1902–1920*), All-Russian Memoir Library 1 (Paris: YMCA-Press, 1983). (Author's note, 1990.) Later it was published back home, too (Moscow: Русский путь, 1997). (Author's note, 2003.)

in our day and age, wrote—in the country that had first given birth to an entrenched materialism!—that faith, and not reason, is the basis of freedom; faith, and not reason, provide us with an altogether independent standpoint from which to assess the circumstances of our life; whereas political types are fully in thrall to material and rationalistic criteria when assessing social conditions. —After this, a debate arose from one edition of the paper to the next, as happens in England, trenchant and extreme views both for and against being dashingly expressed. That the West had always understood its faith to be rational, that religion in the West grew from rational roots (alas, if that's the case); that the early Christian Church had allegedly been communist, whereas what was irrational was a state founded on terror and lies; and that all discord and persecution stemmed from religion and not atheism; "we protest against Aleksandr Solzhenitsyn's Templeton Address [and] deny that the evils of this or any age derive from the loss of faith in God, or that godlessness leads to . . . oppression; for centuries, all kinds of suffering and persecution have been accepted and justified by religion in general and by Christianity in particular." The opposite point of view was that Solzhenitsyn's opponents, with their letters and "humanist psalms," were themselves proof of the premise that "men have forgotten God," and that it was all the more imperative, therefore, to speak of religious truths in all the influential organs of the press; that divine righteousness flowed from individual faith rather than a majority social consensus; that economic solutions were irrelevant, and human reason could, of itself, bring about the self-destruction we all fear; and even that, in their families' quest for a second television and exotic vacations, women should not go to work while leaving a child under lock and key, staring at the TV.[41]

I think the meeting with Margaret Thatcher took place the day before.[42] She'd already received Alya several years earlier, when the latter was traveling around to plead on behalf of the arrested Aleksandr Ginzburg.[43] Thatcher had received her warmly at the time, provided a degree of help, said that she'd read my books, and that she liked *First Circle*. —Now we were off to Downing Street, and not just two of us but three: Irina Alekseevna Ilovaiskaya had flown in specially from Paris to provide the vital interpreting.

The press had previously been asking Thatcher's office whether I would agree to joint photographs being taken. I couldn't see why not, and she had no fear that she might ruin her reputation merely a day after announcing the start of an election campaign. The photographers, who are presumably always at their posts, were outside Number 10, Downing Street, and then inside one of the rooms.

Far from standing on ceremony, I kissed Thatcher's hand. Rarely has a woman's hand been more deserving, and I felt both deep admiration and liking for this stateswoman. Unfortunately, she had a terrible cold, and her voice in her tight throat was muffled and strained. Nevertheless, she retained her composure, as she probably did always. And both the course and power of her thinking process were those of a man.

For exactly an hour we sat on sofas around a low table, an hour of the most substantive conversation, while Irina Alekseevna translated accurately and effortlessly. There were no patches of empty courtesy, and no distraction at all—just world and British politics today.

I think it began with her asking what I could tell her about Andropov. (How Western leaders longed to see a leader of intelligence and feeling in the Kremlin!) I said that it had become clear to me, already after six months, that his was a predictable personality without any lofty or original ideas, merely a repetition of Stalin's turning of the screws. (However—was it merely a state formality?—this did not stop her sending a telegram to Moscow a year later when Andropov died, saying: we share "*the grief of your entire people*.") I could see that the state of affairs for the West was a dismal one (this was before Reagan had managed to reverse it), and I said so: there were formidable trials in store for Britain. Thatcher countered by saying that things weren't so bad—the number of missiles would be equalized, a balance created. (And, with Reagan's help, she turned out to be right.)

At such a rare meeting and with such a pivotal leader as Thatcher, I wanted to rise above politics to a fully fledged ethical point of view. How many appeals I'd made by then for self-restraint, for the rejection of superfluous acquisitions and victories. Were all the lessons of world history really pointless, futile—for *all* the world's politicians?

After all, there had been a recent and dramatic example: the Falklands War. Right on the other side of the planet! A remnant of the overseas empire, and such an insignificant bit of land. And the navy was sent in for that, shedding blood on both sides? How fine and noble it would have been to relinquish, to renounce these islands! But Thatcher had such an awful cold and such a hoarse voice that I couldn't launch that debate, I couldn't bring myself to say it. After all, the Falklands War was a matter of her personal pride, a success for her party—and now, with elections coming up . . .

No, I must surely abandon all hope of ever urging any politician to make ethical decisions.

I didn't manage afterward to jot down any notes about the conversation. I do also remember advising her to rid herself of the awkward British Commonwealth of Nations: it did not strengthen Great Britain in any way, merely distorted its policies, its international persona, and the ethnic composition of the motherland. Thatcher smiled sadly and waved it away, "Oh, it barely exists any more." (And it's true—that is the way things are heading.)

I left feeling a bitter sympathy for her.

As we flitted around London, which was sunny during our days there, the city seemed very appealing, but we were barely able to visit any of it: Alya and I devoted every break to some impending meeting or other.

Claude Durand and Nikita Struve had come over from Paris to attend the ceremony at the Guildhall. With them we met British publishers from Collins and Bodley Head. Among ourselves we discussed French and meager Russian émigré publishing affairs. YMCA-Press had brought out my collected works in a large-format print run of five hundred copies, as well as a couple of thousand *malyshki*, which found their way to Russia—the crowning achievement of Alya's inimitable work in Vermont.[44] (If you read Bunin's letters, you discover that he didn't live long enough for even this much to happen, so poor were his affairs.)

Our one and only Harry Willetts came from Oxford to meet us, likable and sad. He had lost his wife the previous year. ("And it gets worse as time passes.") He was ill himself too. Over the years, Willetts had become so steeped in Russian culture that we felt he was almost a fellow-countryman. And he approached all of my texts attentively, delicately, and lovingly. Which was why he worked slowly. We were very close, but distance kept us apart. As for letters, he was not, by nature, inclined to them, or wrote them only with great effort.

Time was approaching for us to leave for America. Even before we'd left Vermont, however, I had received a letter from Buckingham Palace to say that Prince Charles was inviting me to lunch on 17 May; before that, he would be traveling, shackled to his schedule. Meeting him could be interesting: Prince Charles had publicly voiced his support for my views on more than one occasion. But ought we to hang around for another four days with nothing to do?

In the autumn of 1982, Alya, who'd gone to New York to defend Zoya Krakhmalnikova (and successfully too: she'd managed to persuade the US delegation to the United Nations to raise the issue, and that may have had an impact on the Soviets),[45] encountered a group (Anglo-Nordic Productions) who'd made a film based on my Nobel Lecture. They were touring various countries, attempting to show the film and spread its ideas. They were a group of enthusiasts who'd raised the money from donors; they all worked for free, out of sheer conviction. They had handled the audacious challenge of the film pretty well, communicating the lunatic atmosphere of our modern times.[46] Of the group, Alya got to know Patrick Colquhoun—a tall, thin, well-born half Scot, descended from an ancient clan on his father's side, with a suitably ancient surname that was almost impossible to spell. Patrick's father had been one of Eton's most celebrated teachers, and that was where Patrick grew up—on the playing fields of Eton. He finished school and went to Oxford and all of Britain's best career paths to success were open to him. But he turned his back on it all, and selflessly embarked on a life of unpaid altruism, in the course of which he married Frances, who was exactly the same, much to the distress of his aristocratic mother.

Now, in London, Patrick endeavored to persuade us to wait until Prince Charles returned from his travels and, at the same time, he offered us a private house right in the center of London and, if we liked, several days traveling anonymously around Scotland. Scotland decided it.

The house, into which we immediately moved from the hotel, belonged to Malcolm Pearson, also a Scot, a financier, whom Patrick had got to know when Malcolm donated money for the film. Malcolm also made the arrangements for the trip to Scotland. He proved to have a wide range of keen interests, and to be exceedingly well-meaning. He created a friendly atmosphere for us right away. It emerged that he too had Eton connections (he was a former pupil and his second marriage was to the daughter of the Eton provost—the rector, in other words). This also decided the meeting with Prince Charles, and we informed his entourage. And I was starting to succumb to the idea of giving an unscheduled speech at Eton.

To avoid wasting daylight hours on the journey, we took the night train to Scotland that same evening. (It was lovely—the train and the layout of the compartments far more comfortable than any we had seen in Europe, or Canada's "roomettes." It was good to relax to the gentle rocking of the train after our packed days in London.)

We'd already passed Glasgow when we woke up in the morning. It was a distinctive and somber landscape, thinly populated. On the sparse highlands and the treeless hillsides with their patches of red-brown heather was the slow-moving straggle of placid sheep, left untended. Occasional thin copses. Hundreds of foaming white torrents. We left the train at Rannoch station, in the very heart of Scotland, and set off by car to Pearson's estate, which happened to have a deer farm attached. Those servants who lived there full-time raised the deer.

We also visited more cultural places, like the small town of Pitlochry and Scotland's picturesque Blair Castle with all its trappings—museum exhibits inside and, outside, pheasants, crossing the road at a leisurely stroll, plus, at set times, a piper playing at the entrance to the castle. I was impressed most of all, however, by an off-road journey we took, just the men, near Loch Rannoch. We towed there a squat, multi-wheeled all-terrain vehicle, and then drove it up into the mountains over a kind of rock-strewn tundra, scrambling noisily over gullies, sinking sideways into hollows—I hadn't experienced anything like it even at the front. Somehow we didn't overturn, and we made our way up to the top. A very cold wind was clearing the mist away. From there, we went down to the lake on foot over tussocks of moss, leaping across gullies and hollows, while the pointer with long droopy ears, which accompanied us, trembled from time to time, one paw raised, as it pointed towards prey it could sense somewhere nearby. With its owner's permission, it would hurtle away to find it. Black-and-white, red-billed oystercatchers and whistling grey curlews flew and darted here and there.

An austere and sparse world, beneath overclouded skies for days on end, but it is what shapes the Scottish character and our picture of it. (Then again, you rarely encounter such warmheartedness as our host's.)

After the chilly outings came the traditional sitting by the fireside, with hot drinks.

During two days at Malcolm's estate, I'd pondered and thrown together a rough draft of my forthcoming speech at Eton.

On the third day we went to Edinburgh by car via Aberfeldy and Perth. In the wilder areas by the roads, you would sometimes see solitary standing stones, their ancient significance lost. Then came an ever more farmed and cultivated area, with abundant crops. I was particularly rewarded by the sight of the fateful Birnam Wood: a strip of forest that really does follow the curving ridge of a hill so closely that it's like a line of troops ready for action.[47]

Edinburgh's deep sea gulf, the Firth of Forth, is traversed by a bridge of the kind that now crosses the Bosphorus. We spent a whole day roaming the wide streets of the later Edinburgh (the tops and gables of its residential buildings seemingly the model for many streets in St. Petersburg), and in the center of the city was a tall, broad cliff, on which a strikingly picturesque castle still stood, all one color, all one style, the tower shaped like a crown, and the medieval city clinging to its feet. A stately building within the castle contains a list of all the battles Scots have fought, some of them as part of Great Britain, and a list of all who died. The royal Holyrood Palace expands the Old Town a step further. It is very Scottish. Holyrood Abbey, meanwhile, was burned down by the ruthless Cromwell (a sorrowful Polish Catholic recognized me in the ruins and came over to us; Scots who recognized me held back—that's what they're like). Princes Street Gardens are in a drained lake at the foot of Castle Rock, and blackbirds sing tunefully there. On one of the hills are a burial ground and the grave of David Hume: a patch of ancient grassy land encircled by a stone rotunda with bars. A tower on Princes Street remembers the Scotsman Walter Scott. —All of a sudden, with mounting clatter, a foolish, yelling crowd of Sunday soccer fans races past us in the rain, taking no thought for bygone days. —There beneath us, under the bridge, is the station we will depart from for London, taking the night train once again.

It's a shorter distance, and a high-speed train. It arrives in London well before dawn—but then comes a very English convenience: the passengers aren't forced off the train. They may sleep their fill, and need leave only at seven in the morning.

Refreshed by our trip, I was ready to resume my former packed schedule—and that was how I spent the next two days in London. I was delighted to be able to sustain the load—I might yet have great need of stamina in the Russia of the future.

Times journalist Bernard Levin came to see us at Pearson's house that first morning. He was unlike the usual type of reporter: piercingly intelligent and deliberate (and, it appeared, a perceptive music critic). With him was an excellent interpreter, the Russian émigré Irina Arsenievna Kirillova, with whom I'd first worked seven years earlier in my BBC *Panorama* interview with Michael Charlton.[48] I was aware of the range of Levin's questions in advance but, depending on my answers, he would immediately alter their phrasing and inter-connection, while I sought to respond without repeating my three previous interviews (it was impossible to avoid repetition altogether since the interviewers' questions were doggedly reiterated). It was very intense work for us both, but, seemingly, a success.[49]

Levin and I had been well disposed toward each other since our meeting back in 1976. Now, there was also the substantial support he'd given Khodorovich in the *Times* (it had been published[50] while we were in Scotland, and we didn't even know).

Next, Alya and I went to some other private English home (a luxurious one too, with period furnishings) and I was interviewed there for television by the thoroughly decent Malcolm Muggeridge,[51] a radiant, grey-haired old man. He was eighty that year. He'd attempted to arrange interviews with me before, I had declined, and he'd written to me sadly, "In that case, we shall not now meet in this world." And yet we did. He had been a socialist in his youth, and had taken those views with him when he arrived as a correspondent in 1930s Moscow. But his own spiritual values allowed him to see through the deceit and begin to turn away from Soviet socialism when no one else was yet doing so. He then published a book about his impressions of Moscow, but the West did not want to understand or accept it: a different way of thinking was the fashion at the time. (Muggeridge recently decided to republish it, and asked me to write the foreword, but this is the most burdensome of the things requested of me. I'm wary of speaking on matters that don't originate with me, aren't essential to me; I don't consider it possible to write a foreword without reading the book in detail and mulling it over: but if it's also in English, where on earth can I find the time? I said no, and Muggeridge joked in response that Samuel Johnson used to say, "It is easier for me to praise a book than to read it.") In recent decades, Muggeridge has become a notable Christian and moral thinker in England.

On the morning of the 17th, Patrick drove us to Eton. The main outlines of my short speech were clear to me, whether I delivered the text as I'd jotted it down or otherwise. I'd been warned that Eton's senior pupils were not children, they were fifteen to seventeen years old, and more mature still in terms of their education. This age group was in fact the most approachable for me—it was exactly the age I'd always taught, and I found it very easy to strike the right note with them. After an initial exchange of greetings with the provost, Baron Charteris, and Head Master Eric Anderson (effectively the president and prime minister of Eton—it was they who drew the comparison), we were taken straight to the chapel where the speech was to be given. It too had Gothic arches and, built in 1440, was the same age as the Guildhall. The central aisle from the door to the pulpit was empty and we walked over the ancient flagstones between two rows of pews, alongside which around five hundred older pupils in black tailcoats, waistcoats, and white shirts (apparently no one ever repealed the mourning once declared for George III, so that it has continued down the centuries) stood in several rows, facing the aisle. As far as I was able, I examined their faces as I walked slowly by. They were all well-groomed, many even sleek, although I wouldn't say that I spotted many keen intellects; some even seemed pretty average. But be that as it may, it was the hothouse of Britain's future elite, and perhaps my speech would not fall on deaf ears. Irina Kirillova interpreted once again, standing next to me. The requisite number of loudspeakers were dotted somewhere about the hall, but I couldn't hear them and inadvertently spoke so loudly that my voice reached the full height and length of the chapel, at the far end of which sat invited guests. Then, pupils approached a microphone in the middle of the hall and asked questions which could be heard by the public but were barely audible to Kirillova and me—though she somehow did manage to make them out. One boy, who was studying Russian, even asked his question in Russian. My answers unwittingly repeated things I'd said in my series of interviews; it was inevitable: appearances on a single trip to a single country always form something of a whole. Loud and lengthy applause then followed, which, from what has been written, isn't the usual practice in that chapel. Again I walked between the two lines of boys and studied their faces with mixed feelings. Press photographers appeared outside (by tradition, the press are not allowed inside Eton's buildings). A heightened significance of some kind was imparted to these photos with the pupils: they later appeared in newspapers, and not just English ones, perhaps to condemn me (for hobnobbing with "aristocrats"). My Eton appearance itself was widely reported (although the text remained unpublished).[52]

Patrick then took us to lunch at Kensington Palace. It was built in 1689 as an out-of-town residence by William III (William of Orange), who hoped the country air would alleviate his asthma. Since then several kings have died and Queen Victoria was born there, while the palace itself has long found itself within city limits. It is now the home of the heir to the throne and his young wife. Irina Ilovaiskaya was with us again. She'd once again made the journey from Paris, especially and selflessly, in order to interpret this conversation, which was being kept under wraps. The proceedings, approaches, and the number of servants were far more modest than at Buckingham Palace. We were taken into an empty drawing room. Our escort departed, but immediately, via a small, snug service door so narrow they could barely fit through it, came the even slimmer Prince Charles and Princess Diana—both of them tall, modest, even shy, particularly Diana. The five of us sat around the low drawing-room table and, after a few sentences, the conversation took a turn that saw Diana leave the room: immediately outside, she was handed her first child, the heir to Britain's royal line, one-year-old William, all ready to go. She brought him in to be introduced to us, and he behaved excellently, in a friendly manner, causing no trouble at all. Diana was radiant (she was pretty as a picture) and Charles was too—in a more measured, manly fashion. And somehow all of it—the loneliness of the parents in the dormant, half-empty palace, their hounding by the vulgar press, Charles's well-known and steadfast interest in the depths of things, greater than required for today's pared-down British throne, and the hazy future of that throne itself, created in me (and in Alya too: we compared notes later) a bittersweet sympathy for these young people.

The dignified and elderly Laurens van der Post, whom we already knew, arrived. We went into a neighboring dining room and spent about an hour over lunch, the six of us. And that hour too was as packed with conversation as had been the case with Thatcher; I couldn't remember a thing that appeared on the table, although I certainly ate and drank my share. Irina Ilovaiskaya translated my conversation with Charles while, along the other side of the table, Alya (she'd given her English a real workout on this trip) talked to everyone else, and then they listened to what we had to say.

Basically, the conversation should have been almost a repeat of the one with Thatcher, plus introductory provisos—that I was aware that the British crown has virtually no constitutional rights of state, although it has great moral authority, and that, as a result, the prince might be able, in his own country, to command a strong spiritual movement, even if not a political one. Then, as with Thatcher: there was no need to fight or be ill-disposed towards *Russians* as such (it was unbearable to see during those days that all the English newspapers were using "Russia" whenever they meant the USSR). The fact that Russians had been handed over to Stalin in 1945[53] should be loudly and definitively condemned. Prince Charles listened, absorbing what was said and throwing in the occasional question.

I'm no confirmed monarchist, to sympathize wholeheartedly with each and every crown, and, in addition, I gravely reproach the British throne: frightened of public opinion, George V refused to offer basic shelter to his deposed cousin, Nikolai II. None of the past was forgotten, yet there prevailed in me that bittersweet sympathy for this amiable young couple in the stifling calm before the storm. (I wrote Prince Charles a letter of thanks from Vermont but with an undertone of a recurring sentiment Alya and I had shared since our visit: "My wife and I took a very warm feeling away from our meeting with you, and we are genuinely moved by your fate. I would like to hope that the darkest of my predictions when talking to you do not come true." —Out of the blue, Prince Philip sent me a copy of his book *A Question of Balance*;[54] a lecture to an engineering symposium on modern technologies; and a letter: he'd been deeply impressed and had taken to heart what I'd said at Buckingham Palace and the Guildhall. "You still have allies in the West." Now that certainly went beyond the duty he had undertaken to present the prizes! We were touched. I wrote to Prince Philip: "I have deep respect for the difficult task your family performs: to preserve and bear aloft the commendable ideas and qualities necessary to your people—as they are to all mankind—but which, in its blindness, mankind is increasingly losing.")

From Prince Charles, Patrick immediately drove us across the whole of London to see Georgi Mikhailovich Katkov (the great-nephew of the famous writer on current affairs, Mikhail Nikiforovich Katkov), who was living with his married daughter who spoke no Russian. Another precious life that hadn't served Russia to the full and was fading away in emigration. A charming and sincere man, and such a warm voice. He had a multitude of illnesses, and his right hand was no longer strong enough to write, but, outwardly, he was holding on. There he was, sitting in a chair, and with all his marbles. He presented me with a copy of his book in English about the Kornilov affair[55]—he had found time to write that too. And how accurate were his words about 1917. (He and I almost completely coincided in our views, including when it came to Kerensky and his prevarications: incapable of giving clear answers to Katkov's questions about the Kornilov affair, he'd flinched still more from providing a precise record of the events.) And here were the memoirs Katkov had begun, again in English, but had no energy to complete. We agreed to find him a Russian typist, and he would dictate the Russian version to her. An original version, not a translation! Perhaps he might also manage to produce a Russian version of the Kornilov book? Meanwhile, we're thinking of publishing his *February Revolution* in our Studies in Modern Russian History series in reverse translation from English, if he doesn't delay the editing. (It must be so upsetting to see your own book translated into your mother tongue by somebody else.)*

And so our trip to England came to an end. We had fit everything on the advance schedule into eleven days. On the morning of the 18th, the devoted Patrick took us to the airport, and the press cameras clicked away out-

* We did publish *The February Revolution* in the Studies in Modern Russian History series at YMCA-Press in 1984, and *The Kornilov Affair* in 1987. Февральская революция (*The February Revolution*) was subsequently republished in Russia (Moscow: Русский путь, 1997). (Author's note, 1999.) Дело Корнилова (*The Kornilov Affair*) followed (Moscow: Русский путь, 2002). (Author's note, 2003.)

side the Concorde (and we were bound to be upbraided for the luxury of the trip—as if we were the ones who'd organized it, rather than the Templeton Fund). The Concorde was certainly fast, but it was cramped and stuffy, and breaking the sound barrier wasn't necessarily pleasant. We flew into New York in the morning even "earlier" than the time at which we left London, and, after a few more hours by car to Cavendish—a long, long day—we were able to cast off the strain of London. Ah, all trips are just a distraction. Now it's back to work, as soon as possible.

And yet you don't return in a flash. You have to seek out a new stillness; it takes a while to break free of the pace of all that dashing about.

And here in America, the only thing the thoughtful press took from my Guildhall speech was that I'd launched "a scathing attack" on Billy Graham and the World Council of Churches—this was the one thing they picked up on.[56] To be fair, *Time* offered more in-depth quotations,[57] and an unexpectedly favorable response subsequently appeared in the upmarket *New Yorker*.[58] Meanwhile, the only thing the American press extracted from my detailed and considered response to a question at the press conference about the antinuclear movement was about Bertrand Russell's "better red than dead" and lobsters in boiling water.[59] Of the West's blame for nuclear weapons, of the naturalness of all antinuclear protests, there wasn't a word, of course. It was a lesson, for the umpteenth time, never to hold press conferences.

In England, my interview with Bernard Levin covered a full page in the *Times*. Evidently, however, someone at the *Times* then realized that they'd published too much that was favorable to me, and they came up with a crass caricature of my alleged drinking session with Evgeni Evtushenko and some British spy who'd died in Moscow.[60] The *Daily Telegraph*, for its part, carried the affectations of some clowning veteran journalist, one Jack Moron: "Keep your trap shut, you Moaning Old Misery Tangle-Whiskers. Get back to your personal concentration camp in the backwoods of America. Stick to your 'goulash' and write your so-called books!"[61]

And that is all they took from the Templeton speech about how we are losing, have already lost, a higher faith.

The mass nature of today's culture is destructive, and the artist will inevitably be among the first to suffer from it. Yet it is that same artist who will have the fortitude to stand firm.

We want the same thing: the press is irritated by every speech I make, they want me to be quiet—but that's exactly what I want too. Fine, no more! Not another word to anyone, anywhere, about anything!

CHAPTER 10

Drawing Inward

Not a word to anyone—anywhere—about anything. . . .

On the way back from England, Alya and I came to a firm agreement: now, finally, I would draw inward to work. I'd never managed it yet but I must do, now at least. Now I won't talk to anyone, on any account, for any reason. Not a peep! No matter who asks, no matter how high their standing. *March* was at the third draft in some parts, in others still at the second, but the whole thing needed four, and then some editing while being typeset. But my thoughts were running ahead: what next?? *April 1917* would be the start of Act Two—"Rule of the People"—for all of 1917 up to the autumn. And in those short months, what a telling image of the whole twentieth-century world! Could I manage all that? I mustn't get distracted—I wouldn't go anywhere, for any reason!

But just you try falling silent in an "open society." . . . As if to taunt me, an irritation the moment we arrived back: I started getting grateful letters from readers in the state of Maine: how well, how kindly I'd written of American democracy! What on earth?? . . . And here were the press clippings: I had allegedly dictated to one Anita Berlind a letter to the editor of a York County newspaper, and the paper had proudly announced that I'd passed through that area not long before and been struck by the number of bookshops (full of airport novels and crime thrillers)—and that had shown me the high standard of the local education. And, it said, then I recalled my youth in Russia (where all we did was read serious books): ah, if only everyone there could have held a book in his hands! Oh, how I too would have loved to live in their Maine: with the cultivation of young minds comes freedom. "*This is how we meet the challenge of democracy.*" (And that was the headline.)[1] Some idiotic girl had made it up, hoping it would make her famous and assuming their local newspaper would never reach me; and as she saw it, she was even doing me a favor by uniting me more closely with their ideal democratic world—I couldn't possibly think differently, could I, when comparing America and Russia? And it would have been music to the ears of that duffer of an editor as well—and he printed it without checking. . . .

And what was I to do—ignore it? I wrote to the editorial office: how ever could you print without checking? When did I "pass through"? When and where did I "dictate"? I do not know your correspondent, I have never set eyes on her, and I would like you to print a retraction. (The editor printed one, belatedly,[2] in a position where it was barely visible and with scant explanation—you couldn't tell whether it was really a retraction at all. The *free* press is free of all restraints.)

But now there was something of greater import. The *New York Times* suddenly realized it had not made enough of my non-attendance at the presidential lunch—they could have got in a dig at Reagan! First (at the end of 1982) Harrison Salisbury passed on an invitation from the paper for me to have my say. I didn't respond. Then the editor of their famous, prestigious "opinion page" (*Op-Ed*) herself, Charlotte Curtis, also wrote proposing it. I replied that the lunch incident was now water under the bridge. (But no. Even in 1986, the *New York Times* would publish another article to stir things up: why ever will Reagan still not receive Solzhenitsyn? —They needed a bit of scandal associated with the president. But for me there was absolutely no point, no need to "replay" the meeting.)

Or another episode, typical of the States. At the end of 1982 I had a letter from someone I didn't know, one Henry Delfiner (and, since he didn't introduce himself, he must have been an important figure), telling me that some Boston World Affairs Council would like to establish communication and hear my views, during the forthcoming Christmas vacation. (Strange that I'd never heard of it; and who could tackle world affairs in Boston?—and why? it was, it turned out, a "group of leading Americans.") Enclosed was a list of people expected at the meeting. They felt that seeing this list would make it easier for me to accept the whole idea. For further explanations, Delfiner was proposing to visit me in Cavendish on a Sunday in the near future. There were twenty-seven names on the list. Five were from the State Department, two having been assistant secretaries of state—Lawrence Eagleburger (for European affairs), and Kissinger's right-hand man Helmut Sonnenfeldt—and Malcolm Toon, who, as ambassador to Moscow, had understood nothing; and another, Perle, who was unknown to me; and, to be fair, the sensible Jeane Kirkpatrick as well. Then there were two senators. And someone from the financial world, but what do I know about all that?

And Lane Kirkland, who had taken over leadership of the unions after George Meany: the only thing I agreed on with them was anti-Communism. Then there were seven professors, some of them well-known Russia-haters. And another five, these representing the press—and among them, it's true, right-wingers William Buckley and Norman Podhoretz. And one general—Goodpaster. And other members of their council. And the list ended with "others," that is, people who did not, now, occupy clearly defined posts: Kissinger himself and my publisher Roger Straus. Kissinger was all I needed for a confidential meeting!

What a strange "council" and what a strange invitation. They were trying to drag me into something serious. Why such a wide range of people, from different areas, with different occupations—and undercover like this? No, I was not at all inclined to attend this council.

I wrote in clear terms declining Delfiner's invitation, and hastened to mail the letter so that he wouldn't get a chance to turn up the following Sunday as he'd proposed. I said that conferences were not the right discussion format for me; that in cases where I felt it had become essential to speak out on current problems I, as a writer, preferred to write the text myself. So it would make no sense for us to have a meeting now.

I desperately wanted to fall *absolutely* silent now. Absolutely silent! And straightaway. Enough is enough!

But if you've spent as many years as I have tramping the boggy path of a life in the public eye, you can't pull your feet free immediately. Now John Train was intending to publish in *Reader's Digest*, with its seven million readers, an account of what I'd said in London.[3] —Now *National Review* intended to publish the full text of my Templeton address[4]—and it would be good to have at least one published English version, given that there hadn't been a proper one. (It's only in France that things always go right for us.) —Now, suddenly, NBC television proposed a one-hour interview for the tenth anniversary of my expulsion from the USSR (it was the same producer—Gordon Manning, then working for CBS—who had set up that major interview in Zurich[5] during the early months of my exile). That sounded worthwhile. Should I accept? I hesitated. And I don't know how that would have ended up had they not begun to propose an entirely unreasonable measure to save themselves some time: in September 1983 their long, fourteen-month (!) period of "work" around the forthcoming (1984) presidential election campaign would begin, so it would be convenient for them to come to me in August 1983 and plan the interview, which would be aired in February 1984. —But what can you know, six months in advance? What use would that conversation be? I turned them down, they took offense, and at that the negotiations came to a halt.

It was at that same time, July 1983, that my full text of *August*, composited by Alya, was published for the first time in Russian. But so what? Who was going to read it? The Third Wave émigrés would hardly be able to assimilate it. They wrote weak, superficial reviews, not up to the historical dimension of the Node—and there were precious few of them anyway. All the volumes of my Collected Works, of which there were now twelve, had barely made an impact. They were pining for Russia, but there was no way into the USSR for them.

But the French had *August* translated very well and rapidly, and in December 1983 it was already out. Claude Durand proposed that I should give an interview to French television, to the extremely popular Bernard Pivot (for his weekly literature program). His whole team would come to me in Vermont. What should I do? This wasn't politics, after all, it was my own books, a conversation with my readers. I'd thought Taiwan was the end—but no; I'd thought England would be—no; we'll receive Pivot.

The leaves were autumn gold when for two days, the last of October and first of November, we had with us a noisy French crew, sixteen strong. These were the first camera lenses I'd allowed into my "workshop," under my "arrow" roof, with windows on three sides and even in the steeply sloping ceiling.

This wide-ranging interview was about *The Red Wheel* proper, from my original idea as a young man and through the next fifty years; about the comparative tasks of the historian and the novelist; about the development of revolutionary terror, which has spread so wide this century, worldwide already; about the whole downward trajectory traveled from the nineteenth to the twentieth century; about laws common to all revolutions. (That interview was very successful in France, was rebroadcast, and then shown in other European countries as well.)[6]

But of course we couldn't do the whole interview with no mention of the present. My "Our Pluralists"[7] had only just come out in France, so we talked about it as well. Then Pivot jumped in with: will the Communist regime be defeated from within? what fate awaits Poland? the island of Grenada has just been freed from the Communists—what now? I got fired up, launching into a passionate response. And only later, looking back on it: try as I might to fall silent, I just couldn't stop myself.

But how could we fall silent when, Sergei Khodorovich having been arrested in the spring, the Soviets were still trying to destroy our Fund that autumn? In that same October 1983, we received news that Khodorovich was being beaten during investigation in his cell, his replacement at the Fund was being dragged in for interrogation, and he too would be imprisoned any moment now. Alya had only recently, just before Pivot's group arrived, been to Washington (taking Yermolai to help her, and to familiarize him with our concerns), met there with senators and congressmen, gained their support, and held a well-attended press conference—were we to fall silent now? How could we??

But even so, I had to plunge into my work. Right into it, otherwise I'd never see it through. After every public statement I returned to my writing table in the agonizing hope that now might be the moment that I wouldn't have to voice my opinions any time soon, that nothing would happen that might oblige me to speak out. And that I wouldn't get dragged into any verbal sparring! If you fight for every cause, you'll never unclench your fists.

And oh my goodness—it was only in the summer of 1983 that I got round to unsealing the boxes brought from California in 1976. And there were books I'd not looked at, letters of that year not opened, invitations, information—some of it left too long to be retrievable. (And there are things brought from Zurich at the same time that have still not been opened.) Seven years at Five Brooks, and there's not been time to look through the books of my library in a systematic way and arrange them properly!—we're sweating over our work the whole time.

I'd thought that, once I'd shaken off the dust after my Far East trip, I could forget about it. But no! Elena Bonner's son-in-law Efrem Yankelevich sent a letter[8] to *Vestnik RKhD*, peeved at my *incorrect* representation of Sakharov's views at the Yomiuri roundtable.[9] What was I to do? I had to reply (that same autumn of 1983), yet again pulling out and rereading Sakharov's articles so as to demonstrate, yet again, that I had represented him correctly. And the situation was, of course, so delicate: Sakharov was in exile and couldn't be criticized. Everything in my response was repetitions—I couldn't do anything else. Only on the subject of the economy did I advance, just a small step, when I said: God forbid that our economy should ever have to be managed from outside.[10]

As it happened, in the summer of 1983 Sakharov had expressed an opinion (in *Foreign Affairs*) with a letter addressing Stanford physicist Sidney Drell,[11] which was unusually on the mark (and his point of view was surprisingly similar to what I had recently, in spring 1983, said in London about nuclear armaments): that the West's fatal mistake was in pinning their hopes on a "nuclear umbrella," whereas the solution lay in conventional armaments. And, contradicting Drell (and very much favoring the West), that armaments should not even be frozen at the current level—the States must deploy new, massive MX missiles. After that, Sakharov was immediately attacked by four Soviet academicians in *Izvestia*: "hatred of his own country and people . . . he is calling for war against his own country." But at the same time the *Washington Post* also expressed its disappointment:[12] we thought Sakharov was in favor of stopping the arms race, but his position is actually coming closer to Solzhenitsyn's. . . .*

How brave, from within the USSR—indeed, from internal exile! And what a slap in the face he got, from both sides.

Now, with some hindsight, I felt that the whole of my Far East trip had been a mistake. So much preparation, so much study of unfamiliar material—and what did I achieve? The friendship between Japan and China was becoming ever more obvious, and in April 1984 Reagan went to Beijing, and Red China drew closer to the States, while the deranged Soviet leaders had managed to turn the whole world against our country. No, I should plunge into an even deeper silence. Sowing another man's field is a waste of seed. And changing their minds would, anyway, be beyond me: my only task was to work in seclusion, putting pen to paper. And would it have been better not to give the Templeton speech, either? talking about faith too directly doesn't work—and now even Pivot seemed to be reproaching me indirectly: "you talk about God a lot." A lot?—when, where? So had even that speech been unneeded? . . .

Falling silent was also right for another reason: who was I to judge the West? I'd neither devoted my full attention to studying it nor observed it much at first hand. This is, of course, why my judgments on the West at times meet with serious objections. And in fact there's no need for me to convince today's West at all costs. My motto should be: know how to talk—and how to keep silent.

But leaving the job of "public speaker" was not at all easy: everyone expected some kind of regular pronouncements from me, and sent questions

---

* And it was true: in our misconceptions about the nature of the West, Sakharov and I were similar, trotting out the same error. How concerned I'd been about the fate of America when I was writing *In the First Circle* with its real-life "atomic" plot[13]—the version which, due to an irony of translation circumstances, has still not been published in America. For so many years I'd been sure I was right: the atom bomb must remain with them, and not on any account get into Communist hands. But I gradually saw the light: no good would come of their having it, given their criminal use of it in Japan. (Author's note, 1994.)

and invitations. And, on top of that, 1984—the "Orwell year"—was approaching, and everyone in the West was eager to discuss whether or not his predictions had come true. And when I refused, what reason could I give? Only how busy I was with my primary work. And when that year had come to an end, in London they thought up a conference entitled "Beyond 1984," an impressive one, invitations issued by Lord Chalfont. In my letter of refusal to him I said openly—for the first time—that I'd stopped speaking publicly about politics, precisely because my previous appearances hadn't achieved their goal. And since then I'd answered several others that way as well.

But although I had finally, abruptly, fallen silent—this was not immediately noticeable, and invitations continued to flow in for another three years: to Yale, to give a Terry Lecture, whatever that was, and take part in a symposium; to Downing College, Cambridge (UK), to give a "speech as you did at Eton"; to the University of Miami; to the University of Arizona; to the University of Waterloo in Canada (to be given a doctorate there, as everywhere else); to give the Jefferson Lecture for the National Endowment for the Humanities; and the Erasmus Lecture in New York; and to New College, University of New South Wales, Australia; and to a seminar at National Defense University; and to accept honorary doctorates at regional colleges; and to St. John's College, Annapolis, as commencement speaker; and to the Greek Orthodox church's Hellenic College in a similar role; and to Seoul, to address the International Council of Christian Churches; and to our neighbor, Dartmouth College, as a "guest professor" for discussions with students; and the irrepressible Senator Helms, on the strength of being an "old friend" of mine, was always passing on invitations from someone or other and insisting he'd send his plane to pick me up; and more, and more—no way to remember them all now. And then, of course, there was television, with several people inviting me two or three times, like Ted Koppel, well known in the States; Boston's Channel Seven; a Canadian channel; the American ABC. The *Times* of London suddenly wanted to take some pictures of our life in Vermont (we refused); *Der Spiegel* asked me for my general opinion on Heinrich Böll, who had just died; the *Daily Telegraph* wanted my comments on literary events in Moscow. Another time I was invited to join the jury conferring the Albert Schweitzer awards. And in 1985 the fortieth anniversary of the end of World War II came hurtling along—and a new flood of invitations.

All these were, of course, now of a secondary rank (or less)—but invitations of the first rank did not stop. Just now, in March 1987, an invitation has arrived to speak at a world media conference to be held in Seoul in September.

They want me to give a "keynote speech—an up-to-date appraisal of the ideological and political battle between East and West, including [my] thoughts on the moral responsibility of the world's media towards its democratic institutions"—so that this address "might stand as an equal alongside the Harvard speech." Seoul was chosen, meanwhile, as the front line between Communism and democracy. (And, to be more sure of convincing me, there was a fee of $150,000 for that hour-long appearance—how about that!)

Yes, it is a location of great resonance. Even too much resonance. It's even the exact opposite of what I was intending: it would mean meddling in politics again—and severing myself, irrevocably this time, from my homeland for the rest of my life. I've refused.

Or another recent one: President Mitterand and Elie Wiesel invited me to a Nobel laureates' conference in Paris—about saving civilization. —And the Shah of Iran's widow wanted to meet me. —And the Dalai Lama was visiting the United States, and expressing a wish to see me. . . . —Or the *Times* again, now proposing that I write them a substantial article for the seventieth anniversary of the Russian Revolution. —But I couldn't do any of this now. If I accepted just one single invitation, it would attract more, and disrupt the whole series on which I'd held firm.

And what a long, very long time it will still take to extricate myself from that constant stream. Not for the first time in my life must I sacrifice public actions for the sake of a long-term goal. (But if I'd in fact had the misfortune to be elected an "honorary citizen of the United States,"[14] I wouldn't have such freedom to refuse all public activities in this country, would I? I wouldn't have been such a private person, then. In this, too, God has protected me.)

But now, here was my long-standing debt to Edward Bennett Williams, the benefactor who helped me both to save Alik Ginzburg and win the case against the Carlisles.[15] All he asked was that I accept an honorary doctorate at his *alma mater*, Holy Cross College in Massachusetts. I'd been putting it off for two years or so, but in 1984, when I'd fallen completely silent, it became clear that I could not now refuse—I'd refused everyone, but for this I had to attend. However, I managed so well not to open my mouth there that it did not even become the one time in a hundred where I infringed my rule.

And now the most recent, this spring of 1987. It was a letter from Nikolai Tolstoy-Miloslavsky, who had published two books in English exposing Britain's betrayal of the Russian Cossacks in Austria in the spring of 1945:[16] first it was a combat array of two thousand officers who were tricked into laying down their arms (some among them had been Britain's allies in the First World War and had still not been sufficiently betrayed), and later as many as forty thousand Cossacks from the lower ranks. It was a cunning and cruel story, so typical of British policy. But then came something even more staggering: a wagon train of thirty-five thousand Cossacks, old men, women, and children—who, during the war, had escaped their Soviet paradise and fled the Don, the Kuban, their home soil—was now returned by British rifle-butts and truncheons to the Soviets for reprisals. (I portrayed the funeral service they held for themselves in anticipation of their death,[17] those harrowing reprisals, and their suicides, in *Archipelago*, pt. I, chap. 6.) The senior commander of that repatriation was Brigadier Toby Low—created Baron Aldington after the war (thanks to Harold Macmillan, who'd himself been involved in this cruel operation at the highest level).

Anyway, his lordship the baron had had to put up with the book by Nikolai Tolstoy. But now one Nigel Watts had distributed around Winchester College, of which Aldington held the role of Warden,[18] ten thousand leaflets with quotes from Tolstoy's book and his own conclusion from it: that Aldington must, because of his past, be dismissed from his wardenship. The baron, who was immensely rich, promptly filed a case against Watts, which promised to cost the latter £500,000 to defend, and £1 million if he lost. And Nikolai Tolstoy, with his aristocratic background and noble character, considered it his duty to become, voluntarily, a co-defendant. The prospect chills me: how will the trial turn out? I cannot think of the English legal system without a sense of loathing: it will of course leap to the defense of an "Englishman's honor" and cover up for the war criminals; as to the Russians' feelings—in England they won't spare a thought for them.

So must I again fight, rouse the English social conscience? And will I inevitably have to read more English legal documents, sink into their mire? No, I'm capable of seeking the truth even in the strongest winds of history, but not in law courts. An agonizing decision to make. I limited myself to financial support when a collection for Tolstoy was announced.*

* Then the trial dragged on and on, in the English style. And they ruled that Nikolai Tolstoy (they'd forgotten about Watts by now) must pay Lord Aldington £1.5 million sterling!!—in other words, be put in a debtors' prison. And this was not just about the Cossacks in Lienz—for how many defenseless Cossacks were later handed over across all of Europe![19] (I wrote about this, too, in *Archipelago*.) I could not restrain myself, and wrote a letter to the queen of England. **[29]** I asked the queen to find a way of righting that monstrous judgment, even if it were only a symbolic gesture. But no, I received a note from a Buckingham Palace official fobbing me off, saying the queen had "been interested to acquaint herself" with my opinions. . . . (Author's note, 1991.)

How hard, how very hard it was, and how long it took me to withdraw into silence.

And then there's another event that's particularly Russian—the commemorative celebration! Russian émigrés love building memorials on foreign soil (the St. Vladimir Cathedral[20] is a "memorial church"—and what future will it have in the States?) and gathering for solemn ceremonies (I've been invited several times to be "inducted into the Hall of Fame" of the Congress of Russian Americans). And now a truly great date was approaching: the Millennium of Orthodoxy in Russia. But at a time when our homeland is devastated, downtrodden—is such a sumptuous celebration appropriate? Wouldn't a long fast and humble prayer be better? But no, every "jurisdiction" of Russian Orthodoxy overseas was setting up a committee, preparing a celebration with a speaker attending, and that speaker would, they assumed, be me. In autumn 1985 I received an invitation from the Paris archbishopric and, in spring 1986, from the Church Abroad. I responded with refusals, but giving as the reason only my unworthiness and unreadiness to make such a speech.

And, on the subject of that same Millennium, the BBC asked me for an interview; and so did the international Catholic magazine *Communio*, in twelve language versions—but surely I'm no teacher to them?

Of course, it will be strange for me to live through that period without any public gesture. But I'll have to.

To preserve the continuous line of my life, these refusals were unavoidable and salutary.

Long books take long years to write—this has many reasons and many advantages. When you are writing for such a long time, various moods, various opinions develop and form layers within you, and that whole multiplicity spills over organically into your work and makes it more profound. You speed through the first, or second, draft of a volume, and you can't stop. But later it's good to set it aside and work on other parts and, after a break, come back again to the part you set aside. In that time a maturing will have taken place inside you, even in your major ideas and, all the more so, an accumulation of small details and items of characterization. (Perhaps you'll also have given some thought to routes that weren't taken, an alternative course of events; this enriches your thought. And not only that: no matter what depths of evil the narrative has plumbed, this must not be allowed to warp the soul of either author or reader—you must arrive at a harmonious contemplation.) —And when it comes to publishing the book, it must feel like a slow and even solemn exhalation.

It is as if the *Wheel* allows me to live yet another, additional, full life—from the end of the nineteenth century and up to my age of reason.

Yes, of course a leviathan has emerged. But the reason I was obliged to cover this mass of material was to provide *proof*, rather than impressionistic daubs, which convince no one. A historical epic is not some diversion for the pen—it only has substance if it is truthful all the way through. And when the historical material is so abundant, surely a fictional treatment is no temptation? For it is the material that leads, and I must be precise, even scientific. But, at the same time, the atmospheric layer in which I breathe is above science. Spengler said, very aptly, that the work of a historian demands a special facility, a special concentration of feeling and imagination, allowing him to experience each moment of history from the viewpoint of eternity, in harmony with both the past and the future.

And you can only wonder at the way the epic propels itself along.

The move from *March 1917* to *April* confronted me with more new challenges, which almost sent the Nodes method reeling. It might seem that from 31 March (end of Node III) to 25 April (beginning of Node IV) was just a short hop—but how many events and nuances were lost. Where had they gone? And the "Internode" idea emerged. The Node method didn't allow me to describe it, but the chain of events demanded that I offer at least something of it, if only the tiniest bit. Just as you can draw any curve smoothly with the help of a template, so it was here: I had to draw in some of the connecting material.

But, first of all, it was time to introduce a new form: the Calendar of the Revolution—dispassionately beating out the main events in this interim period. Secondly, for matters of the utmost necessity—I had to know how to put a flashback to good use, to weave it into the chapters of the following Node.

April itself, on which I started work in autumn 1983, opened up many areas that were a novelty after the revolutionary storms of *March*. *April* would open the cycle of "Rule of the People" Nodes, which would include *September 1917*,[21] the inglorious, six-month-long story of how the "victorious" democracy (fabricated, in Russia, by the educated types) foundered, helpless, *of its own accord*. As the democratic fan opened up, the socialist movement widened massively and immediately splintered. (For Soviet readers, who had experienced this school of socialism at first hand, it was extremely valuable material.) And the socialist way was gaining ground over the bourgeois as early as the crisis of 3 and 4 May (instigated by the Bolsheviks)—but amidst such a multiplicity of conflicting opinions! It was impossible to separate out the mishmash of discussions on the street—and I mustn't recount any argument only once, for then there'd be no crowd. So it must be repeated, in different forms—fleshed out, in other words. A motley array of opinions—this was the air they breathed in that brief epoch. Speeches, more speeches, and debates between newspapers—April was drowning in speeches (and how many more there were to come! Russia was being lost in the constant talking and chattering at meetings); and the Russian language, with the shift towards the socialists, was becoming more and more colorless, wilting.

And all those little episodes—flowing out from the Petrograd streets across the whole of Russia: provincial towns, railways, villages—all Russia was seething. For weeks on end I sat at the microfilm reader, studying the newspapers of those days.

And there was Lenin again! Only now he was in Russia for the first time, making his first moves on the actual battlefield, not in émigré squabbles—and forcing his way, with razor-sharp asperity, through the motley array of socialists. (With many blunders, however, and with what unspeakable idiocy in some of his slogans—now cloaked in the dense mendacity of the Bolshevik *sources*. It even turned out that, despite the massive amount of Lenin research I'd already done, *April* afforded me a most curious addition: at the two Party conferences in April, prominent Bolsheviks reasonably and convincingly refuted Lenin's far-fetched plans. But when it came to voting, for some reason Lenin always won. Some kind of biological Party instinct.) The work on *that* Lenin was like starting again from scratch.

But during those same weeks Trotsky also came back to Russia—I couldn't leave him, either, without some more development. How different he and Lenin were—and how malignant their rapidly forged complementarity.

It's for a long time that I'm cutting myself off from contemporary life. (Today's United States and I live at opposite ends of the twentieth century and on different continents.)

Once I'd thrown *April* open and begun to tame it, I realized that these first four Nodes of the *Wheel* would already, by the end of April 1917, show the total collapse of "February fever."[22] I could even leave the rest unwritten.

I already had a great deal of material investigated and compiled, enough for all twenty Nodes. Then this idea began to dawn: just as the Nodes themselves had been lifted out of the flow of history in the form of individual samples, I could also use a lattice of samples to pick out the primary events from the unwritten Nodes—and present them as a dense summary. An outline of the remaining Nodes—a Summary volume?

But even to reach that volume I still had a long, long way to go. Meanwhile, by spring 1987 I would have spent eighteen years *without a break* on *The Red Wheel.*

How I'd love to return to short-form work now. Return to the '20s and '30s, which I retain in memories of my own life, not from books or secondhand accounts.

However, renouncing public appearances did not yet mean drawing inward to work on the *Wheel.* I still had burdens and obligations with the Studies in Modern Russian History and the All-Russian Memoir Library series. Some promising young authors came to discuss the next installments: Yuri Felshtinsky (twice), Anna Geifman, and Viktor Sokolov. Nikolai Ross (third generation of a renowned military family of the First Wave of emigration, who was writing about civil and social aspects of the way Wrangel ran the Crimea[23]) came over from Europe. Professor Nikolai Poltoratsky came with his wife—to my delight he was attracted by our Chronicle of Russian Emigration.[24] Alya, taxed to the utmost, tore herself away from her work publishing *October 1916* and her hundreds of obligations, both domestic and parochial (and the parish now also had a regular summer camp for Russian children, and that also needed looking after—even Yermolai, Ignat, and Stepan were "teaching" the younger children there). But she was still contributing to my articles not connected with the *Wheel,* readying the memoirs of General Gerasimov[25] (dealing with 1905–6), and had burdened herself with editing the difficult manuscripts of World War II POWs (we had compiled the first book of this kind in forty years, and Yermolai was enthusiastically typesetting the collection, as he had the Volkov-Muromtsev memoirs—but Alya still had to check everything with an eagle eye).

But the main thing wearing Alya down all these years was the problems of our Fund: safeguarding the secret routes for money to flow into the USSR, and later also setting up consignments of food and clothing to anyone able and brave enough to receive them direct from here (given that Chernenko's law of February 1984 said that availing oneself of resources offered by foreign organizations could mean a "ten plus five"[26] prison term: would that be the end?—would people be too frightened?). And, in response to specific requests from Moscow, organizing urgent deliveries of various medications.

And on top of that, and the most desperately urgent, was—for all these years since 1983 (starting again after Ginzburg) and until this spring of 1987—the defense of Sergei Khodorovich, still under arrest. And for that, many letters, appeals, and calls for help were needed. From our forest Alya would send them to Lyusia Thorne in New York, and Lyusia would then send them to the news agencies and major papers. And, on top of that, there were Alya's trips to Washington, to see senators, congressmen, and political commentators of substance (such as George Will) and American delegates who might be going to Moscow or to top-level international talks (in Geneva), asking them to defend Khodorovich—and not infrequently receiving that help. And there were interviews and articles to send to the Paris and London newspapers. —And in the meantime, after Khodorovich, the running of the Fund in Moscow was again thrown into turmoil, when the new acting administrator Andrei Kistyakovsky was sometimes picked up on the street, sometimes threatened with a spell *inside* (and if senators were going to Moscow it would be: defend Kistyakovsky! visit him—that would itself be a defense); and now he'd been diagnosed with melanoma—a most dangerous cancer. In America a brand-new medication had just been developed but was not yet on the market—we had to get it via the American Academy of Sciences and arrange delivery through the American embassy in Moscow. (And one had to fit all that into terse, densely packed letters and send them to Moscow by clandestine routes, the opportunities for which always appeared unexpectedly; and then letters would arrive back—a sudden avalanche of them—and Alya had to answer them all urgently, and not leave out anything important. But in these letters, as Alya says, are "the radiance, the meaning, and all the seriousness of life.") We didn't save Andrei—he died, too young.

Alya could never totally clear her tables of the piles of files and letters accumulating there, yet she also contrived, whenever opportunities arose, to send parcels of "banned" books to Moscow, each a hundred pounds or so in weight, for our fellow countrymen there to read. (Alya: "I haul along with me—it's like crossing the taiga loaded down—a feeling of not just tiredness, but exhaustion." She looked forward to Great Lent, she said, "as a rock amidst the mud"—to regain her footing.) She is always fully occupied from early morning till late at night, when she falls into bed, dead to the world. Yet what she enjoys most is working on my texts. And she is, in truth, so imbued with them that she hears, divines what word I would naturally, gladly use in a given position.

And friends came to see us, as a matter of course. Apart from the Struves and Bankouls and their sons, now adults, there were Mstislav Rostropovich, sometimes alone, sometimes with Galina Vishnevskaya (at Shrovetide), or our much-loved "invisible ally" Stig Fredrikson. Or our faithful friends Aleksandr and Ella Gorlov, from Boston. Or, from Switzerland, the lawyer Erich Gayler, the benefactor who saved our Fund from those false allegations.[27] Or our Zurich friends, the Widmers. Or, from Buenos Aires, Nikolai Kazantsev, who grew up in emigration but is passionately patriotic, publishes *Nasha Strana* (*Our Country*) there, and is the only Argentinian correspondent to have covered the whole of the Falklands War—a slender young man with a spring in his step. And there were now brand-new acquaintances, picked up in the course of Ignat's musical path, as well as his teachers. The director of the Library of Congress, James Billington, also came, cordially and insistently inviting me to come and do my work there. But now there was no need—I had all the necessary materials at home.

And there was Professor Edward Ericson of Calvin College, Michigan, with whom I'd become acquainted through an exchange of letters after his book *Solzhenitsyn: The Moral Vision*[28] was published. He had been suggesting for a good while that a single-volume version of *Archipelago* should be produced for America—where almost no one was capable of reading three volumes—and that I myself should do this, or entrust someone else with it. If I liked the idea, he said, it could be Ericson himself, and he would willingly take it on. I had taken a look at his proposal and—why not? it could certainly serve a purpose. Without the deeper probings into Russian matters, and with the loss of historical details and some of the atmosphere, it could work well for the incurious or cluttered brains of American youth. And the assiduous Ericson set to work. Then I had to look through all the places he'd bracketed and correct his choices here and there. (To make things easier for me, Yermolai undertook to go through all three volumes of *Archipelago*, transferring Ericson's brackets from the English text to the Russian. To do this he laid the work out on a table in the guest room, facing a large window with a panoramic view over the hills, and he worked there for at least a week. One day, when he'd come down to the kitchen for ten minutes to have breakfast, there was a deafening noise of breaking glass. We ran up—it was a large hawk, which had flown with such force into the double-glazed window as to shatter it. It lay, a dead hulk, on the table—which was, along with all the *Archipelagos* and half the room, covered in fragments of glass. If Yermolai had been sitting there, he'd also have been disfigured.)

At the end of 1983 Ericson came to discuss the progress of his work. I corrected some choices, but to a large extent he'd chosen well, knowing as he did the mentality of young Americans. He turned out to be well built, big, sturdy, his face framed by a close-cut beard—with something of the ship's skipper about him. Measured, very good-hearted—and concerned above all with spiritual matters. He worked absolutely selflessly and, to ease the procedure of negotiating with publishers, he renounced any fee. (Later the publishers, Harper, dragged their feet. And when they did publish, in 1985,[29] the book did not do very well in the States—sales were sluggish: "that's all in the past," and far from readers' concerns.)

But apart from all these natural encounters—with friends, or for necessary business reasons—there were still, hanging over me, requests for meetings with large numbers of people I didn't know or whose names were only vaguely familiar. Just you try drawing inward! Americans especially, but also a good number of émigrés, have a great penchant for face-to-face meetings, considering them absolutely necessary. So they press hard for them: we have to meet!—we do, really!—we must see each other! (Sometimes it's only to get a photo taken together.) For the most part I can see in advance that the meeting isn't needed at all: barren soil, empty words. There are also some—these are rarer—where one can't tell in advance what the point is: could it be something that is necessary? But if during the meeting, in the course of a casual, noncommittal conversation, I've said something to my guest, by tomorrow this opinion of mine will go on a spree, from sitting room to sitting room and, what's more, get garbled—better, then, if I'd just said it myself in print. One phrase, and the distortions will spin off, jingling as they go. No—falling silent means falling silent. "Emigration in emigration."

And on top of that there's a particular characteristic of our life in this out-of-the-way place: people can't come a long way to visit us and stay only two or three hours—the return journey can't be fitted into that day, and they have to spend the night somewhere. The Russian way isn't to throw people out into a hotel—which means: stay with us for the night! And that means at least a day and a half for every meeting and, what's more, you can't then instantly get back into the flow of your work. All my work, 365 days a year, can only flow if I do it continuously—every day, every single day, never breaking off.

There were also insistent requests for "five minutes on the phone" with me. But I am absolutely not telephone-oriented, and I broke myself long ago of allowing the speed of telephone communications into my life. In fact, I don't like taking decisions at that pace either: you can't take everything into account; you can make mistakes. To "telephone people," preferring a letter seems absurd when you can "say it all in one go." But for me the reverse is true: it's absurd that people don't want to recognize any space between them, any separation, any seclusion. Instead it's: listen right now, answer right now. I learned a long time ago, back in the camps, that the best ideas, the right ones, always come after some thought.

On various occasions over the years I've also declined persistent urgings to meet—very, very many of them, some even several times, some from people it was hard to refuse. It could be writers (Evtushenko asked to come, to "explain" to me the correct way to behave in America), or sometimes émigré writers on current affairs, or sometimes dissidents the moment they were allowed abroad.

And on one occasion, at the request of Vladimir Soloukhin (who'd been let out for a short trip to Switzerland), I was sent his latest poems. It wasn't for their form that they were notable—as always with him—but for his well-judged ideas. In one of them he wrote that in the Civil War "I could have died for Russia / But then I was not born," and told how he had escaped dekulakization, and the front, and the camps, and other deaths—and that was precisely what now imposed a debt: "Emerging from the trench, I leave / Behind me boorishness and fear. / No tears are due, no need to grieve, / It's my turn now. It's here." Is he just dreaming? Or will he suddenly do it? A single such act of self-sacrifice by a celebrated figure in the USSR could do more to move things along than a long-established émigré organization. But will he dare? . . .

In autumn 1979 Soloukhin had been in the States and wanted to come and see me—but I declined. Had it been any other "village prose" writer, I would have agreed immediately, but Soloukhin—did he seem to be rather a favorite with the authorities? We exchanged letters, a couple each. I had a look at his recent works of social commentary and wrote to him, saying that any author now publishing in the USSR had lost the habit of expressing his true thoughts, and had been, for many years, involuntarily allowing himself to produce work of a lower standard. It's hard to maintain it at the level demanded by genuine challenges.

However, in 1980 Soloukhin published two stories in *Grani* (*Facets*)—"The Bell" and "The First Mission," set in collectivization times. It was a notable and bold step. And when, in March 1984, Father Viktor Potapov phoned us from Washington to say that Soloukhin was in the States and again asking to see me, I agreed. Our meeting was cordial: we recognized each other as writers of a shared literature (although he'd acquired, in the years since 1963, a fairly "Soviet establishment" look about him). It happened to be 22 March, the spring equinox—Alya baked the traditional "lark" buns. For Alya and me this was the first time (apart from Eva's visit once) that anyone, any Soviet citizen, had come direct from the USSR to our home. It gave us a strange, emotional feeling, but was also a reminder of the extent to which all human borders are purely notional. Soloukhin's secret book, at which he had hinted in his letters, turned out to be some kind of exposé of the Soviet regime, which his patron, Leonid Leonov, was apparently calling an "atom bomb." Oh, I doubt it. Such bombs have to go off at the right time, not wait. And wait for what?[30] —I presented Soloukhin with the *malyshki* of my collected works such as they were at that time, the first twelve volumes, in pocket editions. He took them and got them into the USSR. And no one would have known of our meeting if he himself hadn't wagged his tongue: he told someone, and the Party bosses got wind of it and summoned him (and then, alarmed, he told me about it via Paris; but it came to nothing). —If you let a rumor like that spread, then again it's: they're cobbling together a "Russian party"![31]

By now, Georges Nivat had already asked me several times for an interview, but it had always, for some reason, been inopportune and I'd refused. But he'd been in Pierre Pascal's Russianist group,[32] and had studied for some years at Moscow University. And, now a professor at Geneva University, he retained a ready affection for Russia and followed my work closely. (He sent me, out of the blue, an amazing photo of a fresco in a basilica on one of the Venetian islands: it depicted a *red wheel* by the pedestal of God's throne—what did it mean? It seemed to refer to "Ezekiel's chariot,"[33] symbolizing the heavenly host.) He had published a monograph about me in French, a separate book;[34] everyone said it had come out well. At the end of 1984 he also sent me the Russian edition.

In places, the book did indeed have acute literary vision, a refined spiritual insight with which few critics are endowed, and it came to accurate general conclusions. (Although I don't understand what he meant by my "hallucination of reality" or where he saw my "realism of excess.")

He wrote very articulately on matters of composition, rhythm, the Russian theme, and my organic affinity with the Russian language. Nivat had had to put in a good deal of work to ensure that the biographical facts were precise (because of his remove in time and place, there were inevitable errors, a good few of them), and a good deal more to break through, intuitively, the misrepresentations of me that were going around. (Some of them remained: the legend that I'm writing so single-mindedly because it gives me hope of delaying my death; my alleged admiration of theocracy; the hatred of Plekhanov that I've never had.) But he did understand my position between the émigré coterie and the pseudo-intellectuals of the world: that the animosity had closed round me and was inescapable. He correctly predicted: "Solzhenitsyn has ever fewer chances of being heard."

Yet when the French version of *October* came out in the summer of 1985, I had to refuse Nivat an interview yet again, because I'd already given one on the same subject to Struve. But in autumn 1985 Nivat was working at Harvard—which is thought of as "just nearby"—and said he'd like to visit. He was very pleasant, unassuming, even meek and soft-spoken. He and I spent an agreeable day together, but I don't think our conversation gave Georges the profound insight into my work that he sought: for that we would have needed more time together—with work, and more work, on the texts.

Meanwhile, at the end of 1983 Yuri Petrovich Lyubimov had emigrated to the West. He wrote to me from London, saying that West-German TV wanted to do a production of some of my books, first of all short pieces about Lenin and Stalin (the plot and scope not yet defined). Did I agree? I replied that I'd happily agree to the production, but that to begin with Stalin would be a simplification of our history, while *Lenin in Zurich* had faced powerful adversaries in the West—there'd be obstacles put in the way.

Freshly arrived from oppressed circles in the USSR, Lyubimov didn't yet understand much of how things were set up here in the West.

My relationship with him had begun when we met through Boris Mozhaev. Lyubimov and I responded to each other warmly and unreservedly, and met several times (and we attended Tvardovsky's wake together). For me, what made him remarkable was his consistent openness, sincerity, and receptiveness, which was in no way lessened by his prominent position in the theater world. He was very much at ease, with a radiant smile and heartfelt impulses. I particularly remember him for a brave visit, with Mozhaev, to see me in Peredelkino—just a day before my expulsion, when all the storms were rumbling over my head. They walked so boldly through the cordon of KGB watchers.

Yuri Petrovich wanted to come and see me in Vermont that same summer, in connection with the planned production, and I was already sending him the plane and bus timetables. Then he fell silent for more than a year, offering no explanation. Clearly he had now understood the situation in the

West. And he was right. In the meantime several wide-ranging interviews with him had been published: he was still eaten up with all the pain he and his theater had suffered *over there*—and in my opinion he'd gone too far in his nitpicking criticism of Anatoli Efros. I knew Efros from our unfinished work together on *Candle in the Wind* at the Lenin Komsomol Theatre and, although I didn't develop any kind of friendship with him, neither did I find him at all odious.

Two years later, Yuri Petrovich suddenly called from Boston, saying he was here for that whole month of November (which we'd already read in the papers) and urgently needed to meet me. I'd be pleased to see him, but I knew that, tactically, the meeting wouldn't help him in any way: our life experience was too different; we had different viewpoints. He came, and spent twenty-four hours with us. He was still, as before, deeply wounded by his own situation and that of his theater. And now his plan was this: he, Rostropovich, and I would together make some kind of public statement on the arts situation in the Soviet Union. And he was surprised when I told him that my participation would only scuttle this statement. (As it happened, the hounding I've suffered in the United States was at its peak just then.) He was so wounded and, additionally, a year older than me—I didn't know how he still had the strength for his work, surely intolerable in foreign languages he knew only slightly. But I was amazed at the vigor with which he managed it. (A year later, with Gorbachev's new thinking, a possibility suddenly appeared for him to go back to Moscow, and he called to sound us out—we strongly recommended that he should go.)

In the autumn of 1986 Yuri Kublanovsky also turned up in our neighborhood, at Dartmouth College, and he too came to see us. From the moment he emigrated, in 1982, he had openly expressed, out loud, his support for my books and agreement with my way of thinking, and for that he'd been subjected to the most humiliating mockery from Third Wave émigrés. But on the day of his visit we both happened to be unwell, and we gained little from the meeting. But, in his absence, reading his poems and exchanging good letters with him seem to me to be no lesser meetings. I consider Kublanovsky to be very talented, among the best of today's Russian poets, and with a very true social and patriotic sense—although his elaborate use of metaphor, often eluding the reader's grasp with its play of colors, vexes me. I do not believe it's impossible, today, to write "simply."

And aside from the meetings, how many unguarded phrases leak out, incautiously, via my letters. The most honest people, as it seems, write to me with the most honest of intentions—how can I clench my teeth and keep silent? how can I not stretch out a supporting hand? Now it was Mikhail Grigorievich Trubetskoy, of the generation following the celebrated Trubetskoys,[35] who sent me his father's memoirs, which I read and gave my response—but he used extracts from my letters (for one having asked my permission, the other not) as "forewords" to his publications. —Igor Glagolev, who had defected in 1976, was wearing himself out in his battle with the Soviets and I answered him with a sympathetic letter, only to learn shortly afterwards that, in my absence and without my knowledge, I'd been elected "honorary president" of his political coalition. —Oleg Krasovsky was traveling round the States and Europe and, as validation of his newly re-created journal *Veche*, reading out loud my absolutely private letter to him. —The artist Nikolai Dronnikov published a little book of statistics about old Russia, of a reliable and useful orientation, and sent me a copy—how could I be unfeeling and stay silent? I sent him a letter of just two or three sentences—and in the next edition they'd been printed as a blurb on the cover! —A young man, Oreshkin by name, sent me a scrapbook of his research into the Etruscan language. I wasn't intending, nor could I manage, to make out its essence, but he was so desperate for support—everyone had rejected it and was mocking him—that I wrote a sympathetic letter: I couldn't just stand like a cold statue, fixed in its chilly heights. He took from my letter what was favorable, left out anything that wasn't, even reordered my phrases as suited him—and published that fabrication as the foreword to his book!

So what now? Does that mean I shouldn't even write letters to anyone? Draw inward that tightly—not a single letter? Is that the only way I can stand my ground amid this émigré swarm?

Do I regret that, for the ten years starting from *Letter to the Soviet Leaders*, I did not abandon my intensive social and political commentary or my attempts to "save" the West? That activity was perhaps a mistake, but I don't regret it: "my soul demanded it"—I had no choice. My irruption into social commentary and politics did not, by any means, start with my expulsion to the West, for I had already, in the USSR, written the *Letter to the Soviet Leaders* and essays for *From Under the Rubble*, not to mention the battle I'd had with the Union of Soviet Writers. This was what my irrepressible heart cried out for, and treading that path was unavoidable. (And Yermolai has taken after me and his mother. His interest in politics becomes ever keener. He has grappled with the typesetting of my article "Aspects of Two Revolutions." In the morning before leaving for school he listens, without fail, to the news—and when he considers an item to be of extreme importance he runs over to my work building to tell me; I myself don't listen until midday. And so it was that, in a state of high excitement, he brought me the news of Andropov's death. —"But God said unto him, 'Thou fool, this night thy soul shall be required of thee; then whose shall those things be which thou hast stored up?' "[36] And how much power he had indeed stored up. . . .) My social activism was certainly in the tradition of Russian literature: if I saw danger threatening, my duty was to try and open everyone's eyes to it. But in the West it was not the politician-journalist fraternity that I was trying to convince, but ordinary people. And in the East, how else was I to protect my allies, my collaborators, the Fund? how else, if not by waging war on the Soviets through my social and political writing? But then what?—was I to attack only the side where it was no longer dangerous for me? in the West, no matter what I saw—was I to keep silent?

No, I don't regret it. And yet I've fallen silent since 1983—towards both sides. And fended them off. And drew inward.

In actual fact, the problems of the twentieth century cannot all be laid at the door of current politics: they're a legacy of the three preceding centuries. A writer has to reflect on the deeper elements of these problems rather than fiddle around with today's superficial issues. It is the call of time from *above.* From the top.

I have never lived, anywhere, in such astonishing, boundless silence as at Five Brooks, out of reach of the obtrusive loudspeakers that had hammered away at me, tormented me throughout my Soviet life. Here, if you wake up in the night you feel, in your whole body and soul, that you are part of an unbounded, silent World. I lie in its lowest reaches, while in its unattainable, unknowable heights is our Lord, and thanks to this I have a keen sense of being protected, kept perfectly safe. Noises—no, none whatsoever. But if you do hear the distant barking of farm dogs, or the gurgling, snuffling sound, quite unlike any other, of the coyote's call (my favorite! come closer, coyote, over here!), then those sounds only allow us to feel more intensely the incomparable dimensions of our Universe.

And suddenly, when I couldn't sleep one night, an idea lodged itself in my brain, like a taunting jingle, for my first *binary tale*. If only, after the *Wheel,*

I could manage to write several of these, to sketch the contours of this natural subgenre of the short story.

And that wasn't all! Since 1947, since the *sharashka*[37] at Sergiev Posad and through all the camps and my exile, through all thirty-five years of that life, I had been making selections from the succulent words of Dahl's dictionary:[38] I would start by copying out a first, culled list, then selecting from it the most vivid words, forming a second culled version; then a third. All that was written in little notebooks in tiny writing—but what would their fate be thereafter? I didn't have time to work them up in any way.

But I noticed that my youngest son, Stepan, had—in addition to his ardent interest in geography at first, and later in liturgical texts and all their riches, and in both Church Slavonic and English—a definite linguistic sensibility, too. And I don't remember whether I suggested it to him or, more probably, he reached first for those little notebooks of mine, but from August 1983 (he would remember the date as well, any date, for years afterwards) he, at ten years old, and I set to work following this procedure: from my last culling, we would make another, following my notes in the little booklet, and he would immediately type it out on small, half sheets of paper. His output rate was, at first, two half sheets per week, then three, then even up to five, but his working days he chose for himself. For him this was a good exercise for appreciating the amplitude, the meanings, and the colors of the Russian language. And for me it was a real help: no one but Alya would have undertaken the typesetting direct from my handwritten notebooks, but she was fully occupied as far as the eye could see; but, once I had those typewritten sheets, I myself could prepare them, clearly, for a compositor. The year 1987 marks four decades of my ceaseless work to preserve the Russian vocabulary that is being destroyed—and at the end we must complete the job by publishing a dictionary. (At the beginning, Stepan had some moments of weakness: suddenly, while reading out the list, he burst into tears and confessed that he had sometimes skipped words that I'd marked for him, hoping the work would be finished more rapidly that way. . . . But, having repented, he never did it again.) He and I worked at it, exceptionally well, for four years, and now we're at the final stage.

If it hadn't been for Stepan, I'd never have found the time for that work. Now it just remains for me to read it all through again, twice, put in some more selected examples of usage by various writers—and hand it over for the complex work of computer-typesetting (there will be more than a dozen different fonts).

The idea of adding examples from Russian writers will be useful evidence, for skeptical readers, that this whole dictionary is not something I've made up, but words that have been in use for a very long time and offended no one's eyes or ears. —The idea also came from the fact that most of my work on the vast mass of historical material was now, gradually, falling behind me. And now—after seventeen years constantly bent over the *Wheel*, when every evening, every single evening had been devoted to getting the next piece of historical material into shape, so that the following morning's work would not, at any cost, fall behind—for the first time there was some clear space in my evenings, and I could permit myself *simply to read*, simply to read Russian literature! This reduced tempo gave me a strange feeling, and I absorbed my reading with delight. And how much nineteenth-century literature I'd missed. And how little I knew from the twentieth!

Starting that winter—and, indeed, for the first time since my years of reading in prison—I could allow myself to read, not specifically for my work alone, but also "just because," as a matter of choice, for pleasure. The first I chose were Bunin, Goncharov's *The Precipice*, Gleb Uspensky, Ostrovsky. And I could not resist copying out words I found there—they squeezed themselves willingly into my dictionary. After that, and now specifically to select words, I read Melnikov-Pechersky, Mamin-Sibiryak, and then started copying words from Valentin Rasputin, Vasili Belov, Viktor Astafiev, and on and on it went.

But my keenest hunger was to read the Soviet literature of the '20s and '30s—there's much there I don't know, and much left unsaid. (And I felt somehow drawn to return to my youth, to the start of my literary life.)

But it turned out that I couldn't manage "simply to read": my hand was always reaching out to note down my judgment, my appraisal, either of a particular aspect or in general—of the author's techniques, structure, characters, the views expressed. I noted specific quotes, too. But when you've made such a quantity of notes, you don't want to leave them around gathering dust, either: you have to work up your notes and put them into some kind of harmonious form, into a coherent text. And in this way, based on a disparate selection of books, a collection formed—they weren't literary reviews exactly, no, just my impressions. And now, as more are added, I've started calling this my "Literary Collection." Perhaps more will accumulate in the coming years.[39]

What a pleasure it is to be able, finally, to imbibe what I've missed in the constant rush and the constraints of my whole life, to fill in gaps in my knowledge—for I have been running all my life, like a horse driven hell-for-leather, without a moment to take a sideways glance.

Now they're writing, as if it's indisputable, that I'm influenced by the Slavophiles and am perpetuating their ideas—but up to now I've never read a single one of their books, or even seen one. And people are demanding interviews about what I think of the "Goethe-Mann tradition of harmony"—but I have never read so much as a line of Thomas Mann. Or else they detect the "obvious influence" on the *Wheel* of Andrei Bely's *Petersburg*—but I'm only now thinking of reading it. How could any outsider possibly imagine how crammed full my life has been?

But, more importantly: the artist does not in fact require too detailed a study of his predecessors. It was only by fencing myself off, and *not knowing* most of what was written before me, that I've been able to fulfill my great task: otherwise you wear out and dissolve in it, and accomplish nothing. If I'd read *The Magic Mountain* (and I still haven't), it might somehow have impeded my writing of *Cancer Ward.* I was saved by the fact that my self-propelled development didn't get distorted. I have always been hungry for reading, for knowledge—but in my school years in the provinces, when I was freer, I didn't have that sort of guidance or access to that sort of library. And starting from my student years, my life was swallowed up by mathematics. I'd just set up a fragile connection with the Moscow Institute of Philosophy, Literature and History when the war came, then prison, the camps, internal exile, and teaching—still mathematics, but physics too (preparing experiments for demonstration in class, which I found very difficult). And years and years of conspiring under pressure and racing, underground, to complete my books, for the sake of all those who'd died without a chance to speak. In my life I've had to gain a thorough grounding in artillery, oncology, the First World War, and then prerevolutionary Russia too, which by then was so impossible to imagine. Now I walk through our own library, assembled by Alya, and look enviously along the spines: so much I haven't read! so much I've missed! But now that I've written the most important parts, the pressure I feel inside is lessening and the weight is lifting from my shoulders—and a space for reading and knowledge is opening up. It's now that I must make up for everything I've missed over those frantic decades. European history, for example, starting from the Middle Ages. (At the Moscow Institute, I'd raced through the Marxist textbook, but have forgotten it all.) And especially

European thought, from the Renaissance on. And the Bible, which I'd never reread since my childhood. And the Church Fathers—I'd never read them. Shouldn't I now, at the end of my life, catch up with all that?

The younger the brain, the more you'll retain, they say. But here I am—getting old. I've begun rereading the philosophy summaries I put together in prison, which were saved from the Marfino *sharashka* by Anna Isaeva.[40] I've started reading the history of the French Revolution. And the great Russian poets of the twentieth century. (Alya knows them, almost all, by heart.)

I still have my full strength—it must have been given me for a reason. And I'm young at heart. I'll study in old age, at least—and what a shame so few years are left. All the strands I began at some time—I must not let them go to waste, but guide them to completion. In my constant haste, burrowing forward via tunnels of intuition, how many, many mountains I've left behind me, never conquered! But, of course: *tantum possumus, quantum scimus.* (The more we know, the more we can do.) I'd like to climb up to an observation platform with a view of the centuries behind us and a half century ahead.

A hundred years you'll score, and still be learning more.

So my motto from now on is: not a single superfluous movement outwards. I'll draw inwards, to myself and to what's most important in life. Don't talk—do.

Good Lord, the working conditions here—could I ever have dreamed of any so wondrous?

"Thou hast set me at large when I was in distress. . . ."[41]

But through everything, events recalled in these pages and others not, Alya, with her uncanny capability, has always stayed by my side and, for my sake, preserved the freshness of her spirit and her attentiveness. In our first years together (disjointed as they were), in our homeland, I did not yet grasp what reserves of spiritual gifts—quite apart from her quick and sharp mind, clear thinking and energy—would be thrown open to me in the person of my wife! But over and above that, there is also the unfailing refinement of her artistic taste, and the way she has *doubled* the possibilities of my life.

And over the Vermont years, which are many now—have I appreciated how carefully Alya has sustained in me a constant joy of creating? Appreciated how weighed down she's been by her constant worries as a mother—about the fates of her sons as they matured, hurled out into a strange land? How many concerns and afflictions she did not burden me with, even in our closest moments. But she has always lived through my quests as one with me, with the totality of her feelings and her memory—and, in *The Red Wheel*, its chapters, its plotlines, its episodes. (And persuaded me to make changes in a good number of them.) And, indeed, how many of the errors I've made in life, too, she's corrected—and in time.

You are my soulmate—and the uplifting Wing of my life! For all of this, for everything—I bow my head before your great heart. . . .

CHAPTER 11

Ordeal by Tawdriness

There have been ordeals in my life—poverty, bullying in childhood, war, prison, a potentially fatal illness, a clandestine existence, fame, persecution across the whole of the USSR, homelessness, expulsion from my homeland. Enough to be going on with, wouldn't you think? And yet, to begin with, tawdriness was missing from this list. Bit by bit by bit, it too crept in.

Tawdriness is the preferred weapon of baseness, when outright violence is unavailable. Or may be an addition to it. A foul reek of wickedness was added to the mix used against many of those condemned by the Soviet authorities, and the first expert in vilification, in "branding" (his word) an opponent, was Lenin. Although no, before him: it was Marx. And in politics in general—how much tawdriness is bandied about in today's election campaigns?

At the beginning of the '70s, in the USSR, when they hesitated to arrest me, I too was smeared in fake foreign articles and by lecturers at closed-door gatherings—with what else but tawdriness? After all, they had nothing to use in a high-minded debate. And when they had to release me from their clutches, they came after me again, wielding—what else?—falsifications, sordid gossip, and, later, books written to order by my vengeful first wife, by Řezáč, by Thürk, and then by that devil, Flegon. Subsequently—and the KGB was right about this—recent émigrés and others in the West would no longer need any guidance to hurl themselves eagerly and of their own volition into this torrent of tawdriness, their passions not at all political but basely human, each as he was able.

This is exactly what happened: there was no shortage of such people, and even today the line remains unbroken. And as for going public, that presented no difficulty: one could always find an unrestrained press outlet, one that has cast off all sense of responsibility, its every utterance nothing but tawdriness, tawdriness, reductiveness, oversimplification.

In the summer of 1978 a print run of Řezáč's book came out in the USSR (but didn't go into circulation for some reason).* Also that year (although it was another seven before I knew of it) Harry Thürk's two-volume novel, *Der Gaukler*—the conjuror, the street clown—was released in East Germany.[1] (Why was East Germany chosen in particular? Was it perhaps because information about me, television programs even, seeped in more easily from West Germany?)

The book is a mishmash, a freakish hodgepodge of stories and imaginings by my ex-wife, Natalia Reshetovskaya, some already in the public domain, some completely made up—all of it vague, the events jumbled up with no resemblance to the truth, so that it was impossible to untangle them or to find even the slightest solid ground. The KGB had been excised altogether: they didn't operate in the USSR at all. By contrast, since 1964, the guiding hand of the CIA had permeated the whole of my life and my literary career: it was the CIA that had decided to make an international star out of a *Novy Mir* author, encouraged me to write *Archipelago*, and provided the blueprint for it. It was the CIA again that advised me to make a speech at the writers' congress and, if that didn't work, to write a letter to the congress covering such-and-such topics.

Descriptions of the hapless writer rained down from the book's author, and from certain noble Soviet persons, as well as from CIA operatives themselves: "Mr. Jaws . . . a post-Stalinist Ostap Bender[2] . . . now a fascist . . . a monster in a socialist society . . . a fascist liar . . . a literary Vlasovite." Only one incontrovertible thing was not denied: his "high intensity of work" and "bee-like diligence." At the same time, he reveled in sex (as did the whole book, by the way—and all the CIA agents). Lifted with grateful thanks from Natalia Reshetovskaya and Kirill Simonyan was: that the writer had been ambitious since childhood, that his scar was from anti-Semitism,[3] while his father, who had not fought for the Whites and "was given a compassionate pardon by the Soviet authorities" (for what, in that case?), nevertheless went off into the forest and shot himself. —The son, meanwhile, once his story had appeared in *Novy Mir*, was forever chomping at the bit to leave for the West where the money was, pleading for some sort of invitation to be arranged. —My poor Alya, who perceived the loss of her homeland as a misfortune more keenly than anyone, was also dragged into this with vindictive fervor: depicted in the book as a gold-digger, intent solely on the money of

* I now learn, in letters from Soviet readers, that it was in fact circulated, in no great numbers. It was read in various parts of the country and readers were taken aback by how nasty I was. In Petrograd, for example, it went not into the Public Library but into the library at the Political Propaganda Palace, in other words, to trustworthy readers. (Author's note, 1993.)

the free West, "her place in the Latin Quarter," and all kinds of similar slurs; she must have really become a thorn in their side.

By contrast, Reshetovskaya, "who had squandered her talent as a pianist" solely because she'd spent her entire life since youth allegedly "helping her husband in his work, looking up material for him," now sat abandoned in the countryside, selflessly retyping and retyping the manuscript of *Archipelago*—which was entrusted to her instead of being safely kept by the author—and, having submitted the work to him, tried to kill herself.

The KGB itself, meanwhile, didn't meddle in the whole affair, not once in all those years.

Flegon's one thousand pages, also in two volumes, while seemingly written in a different way, in another year, and in a Western country, with no claim to be a novel and full of blatant personal hatred, nevertheless concurred in everything that mattered: an inactive and completely innocent KGB (spoken of with the utmost tact and even unconcealed sympathy), ferocious attacks on the CIA, a seething malice towards me—and an ocean of pornography.

And it was now, in February 1987, that, after being put on hold for so long, the time had come for the Flegon court case. Now too, albeit with a delay of six years, I could not avoid reading the whole of that loathsome book for the first time, having previously merely riffled through it in disgust. And it was right during the days of the trial that I read it.

Well, I'd been right not to read it six years earlier: all this fades with the passing of time, and time renders it worthless. I've mellowed in recent years, finding an inner calm by completing my most important works; my blood is no longer up, my shoulders have relaxed—and this hackwork doesn't affect me. (Merely—the audacity of his lawsuit.)

The tone of the book is a vulgar swagger, as if a common flunky were to be ensconced as guest of honor.

And what do we discover? That *Archipelago* consists of interwoven prison fables; but, alas, "the *Gulag* is a good weapon in the ideological struggle against Communism," although, if compared with what was done in old Russia, "the whole Gulag would vanish, along with its puny tortures." And, in general, the only bad thing about the Soviet Union was Stalin, and even then, "the Russian people itself virtually forced Stalin to annihilate people." Nor does Flegon refrain from openly interceding on behalf of KGB operatives—several times to defend Řezáč but, more especially, Victor Louis.

One of the best ways of defending the Soviet regime is to excoriate the old Russia. Disowning detainees and victims "is a national characteristic of the [insincere and cowardly] Russian people, which has been clearly demonstrated throughout Russian history." —"Russia differs from all the countries of Europe in that it is not individuals who tell lies there, but the whole country, en masse. Honest people are the exception."

Meanwhile, when it comes to the malice avidly focused on me—it knows no bounds. —An insolent liar. A consummate illiterate. A crazy despot. A swindler. A turncoat. A traducer. A charlatan and hypocrite. The Stalin of our times. The mongrel spawn of a hyena and a chameleon. A villain. A braggart. An underdeveloped cerebral cortex. "Russian people sighed with relief" when he was exiled. And, by the way, "in actual fact, he was never really interested in fighting Communism." "He devoted whole years of his life to revenge for not receiving a Lenin Prize." "He receives money from intelligence services . . . he receives money from the CIA." And, of course, "he is prepared to sacrifice his children for the sake of a rotten little book" (i.e., to defy KGB blackmail and publish *Archipelago*).

And as I write all this out, I'm finding it all so insignificant—water off a duck's back. Whether the enemies were Soviets, Third Wave émigrés, or New York pseudo-intellectuals, they all lambasted me in practically the same way, word for word, *ad infinitum*.

Nor did Flegon shy away from expressing his opinions about literature itself: Solzhenitsyn "won't last long in literature." Sartakov is a far better writer than Solzhenitsyn. "*The Oak and the Calf* is literary shit." Since nine chapters could be cut from *In the First Circle*, "a lot of it is superfluous." —As if that were not enough, he confidently passed judgment on my use of language as well, quibbling over my grammar in the title of *In the First Circle.* (Oh yes, he actually went ahead and altered my Russian title in his pirate edition, losing the literary flavor and allusion.[4])

Nor was Flegon averse to forgeries of any kind. Where I'd used an ellipsis to represent an obscenity, he wrote it out in full and presented it as a quotation by me. But then, you wouldn't expect scruples of him. Lenin's famous "not the brains of the nation but its shit," he attributed directly to me. And, naturally, he not only failed to mention that I directed all the royalties from *Archipelago* to the Fund[5] for the aid of prisoners, but turned it right on its head: "I accuse him of not sharing the millions he earned with his hapless co-authors, the former prisoners."

But for all his frothing invective, all these unprincipled forgeries and convenient omissions, is Flegon really much different from the procession of vulgarizers already considered in these sketches? Although some of those spear-throwers would shrink from the comparison. Flegon differs from them in one thing only—his pathological and unbridled passion for pornography, which lowered his book beneath acceptable standards, and it didn't sell.

Of Flegon himself, we also learn: "I have devoted my whole life to Russian literature." And that many people supposedly suspected him of having written Solzhenitsyn's books himself.

And, in exactly the spirit of the KGB, Flegon also floats the Jewish theme: "That he is not Solzhenitsker cannot be taken at face value"; "I am inclined to think that he is not Russian."

But here was my comeuppance for not having read Flegon earlier. He wrote, "There was no point pursuing a case against a defendant [D. Pospielovsky] who had gone to Canada." Much less in the States, therefore. I made a serious mistake, then, agreeing to mount a defense in Flegon's lawsuit. As always, driven by my work, I didn't have enough time to go into the details of the case. (Two English lawyers I have asked think the same: that the master of the English court had quite simply been wrong to give Flegon permission to file a lawsuit in America while we, dimwits that we were, accepted it—yet how were we to know the law?)

In the meantime, my case involving Flegon in England was perpetually being delayed—it had been more than five years now, and I was happy with that: all I wanted was to set that concern aside for the next six to twelve months, so that it wouldn't prevent me working uninterrupted. I'd given little thought to how Edward Bennett Williams was going to instruct, from America, the slumbering Richard Sykes, and I had no idea that it was precisely a trial by jury that had been appointed at the plaintiff's request (just as Lenchevsky had warned me).

And now, at the end of February 1987, we discovered that the trial (presided over by Mrs. Justice Kennedy) had been already under way for three days, and that Flegon had been addressing the twelve jurors for *all that time*. (As Lenchevsky described it, he turned up in shabby clothes and, in an appeal to the emotions, removed his dentures—he had no teeth. The jurors, for their part, had been selected by drawing lots—goodness knows who they were, they could have been vagrants who slept under bridges.) Flegon was recounting his defenseless existence since his Bessarabian childhood (according to his own book, incidentally, it is doubtful whether he'd been living in Bessarabia when it was annexed; he seemed to have an excellent knowledge of Soviet life in the '30s and of Odessa), reading out letters from his late lamented mother, and, impoverished and exhausted (a superb actor!), was bewailing with tears in his voice how his entire life had been ruined by that cruel and wealthy man, Solzhenitsyn. Success was immediately ensured, the jury's egalitarian instinct on the side of the downtrodden plaintiff. It was already clear that I had lost, but the trial, occasioned by that half a sentence[6] in several *Russian-language* copies of *The Oak and the Calf* published in Paris twelve years ago, lasted *a full nine days*!—that's England's immortal Lady Justice for you! In fact, this pettifogger (in fact, an amazingly concentrated archetype of the venomous litigator, so well portrayed by Dickens) has held triumphant sway in England's crown courts for a quarter of a century now—and no one can stop him. And against the KGB, the English courts are completely powerless.

And these ill-informed jurors, safe in their jury box, decided that fifteen years ago in the USSR, bone-weary from the unequal battle with the KGB, I ought to have expressed myself with greater caution about the pirate publisher who, during those same years, was debasing my books in the West, and they sentenced me to the greatest possible fine under the circumstances—£10,000. With all the legal costs and the ineffectual lawyers, it would be three times as much. (And who would have paid if Flegon had lost? he's always bankrupt.)

There was a lesson here, after all: not just never go to court myself but also never even mount a defense, they'll sully you anyway. I was affronted by this false ruling from an English court. The saying's true: better a robbery than an unjust trial. I'd never been hurt by all the dirt that had been, or was still being, written about me. But this festered. It was humiliating to suffer personal defeat by a tawdry nonentity who had, moreover, besmeared me unchecked. I had suffered plenty of defeats but, in America too, it had always been when I was acting against a vast anonymous force, and so there was no shame in losing. But here it was in a piddling little place. What cliffs I had scaled, only to slip on a piece of filth, a woodlouse. It might, of course, be thought that this too was payback for failures in my erstwhile fight against the KGB.

Well then, you've proved the more skilled—take your winnings. And to top it all off, by losing I'd strengthened Flegon's position in Lenchevsky's forthcoming trial! My losing might also encourage others to take me to court, it's never too late under England's statute of limitations: George Feifer? Zhores Medvedev? It's a wonder *Stern* magazine hasn't done so. I would be completely worn out.

In any situation, it's easy to console yourself that "things aren't so bad" and could be much, much worse.

. . . But Lenchevsky—won his case against Flegon! Despite all the toll it took on his nerves ("the lion's share of all my energy and time"), and with meager financial resources, albeit supplemented by me, he won his marathon of so many years!

After the summer of 1983, when Flegon had managed to suspend their trial indefinitely, Lenchevsky put together a "press statement" about him and circulated it all over the place (no one published it, not even the émigrés). He wrote me: "Not seeing that scavenger's case through to its logical conclusion is out of the question. Flegon's masters have inexhaustible resources. The fight isn't so much against the scoundrel himself as it is against them. I realized that from the start—and that's what inspires me." And he was quite right too, of course.

And it's true that, in the meantime, Flegon was performing some astonishing maneuvers. Somehow he was able not only to reactivate the lawsuit a court had dismissed, but also to avoid the tight deadline newly set for January 1984, and then, in February, to secure its radical revision: he wasn't able to drag me into it, but he did include Lenchevsky's letter to the *Guardian* in the charges—don't let him mount a defense, slap his wrists! "Lenchevsky's words in their actual or inferred meaning imply that Flegon is the author of pornographic, distasteful, and libelous material, and is incompetent in his profession as a writer" (and for Anglo-Saxons, professional incompetence is the most outrageous accusation). And so Lenchevsky ("the phenomenal, satanic cunning of that lowlife!") had to explain that he wasn't accusing Flegon as an individual, but only his book. Having done the rounds of several lawyers with my assistance, Oleg Stanislavovich was convinced they were "a cursed guild, only there to milk as much money as they can from the client. As before, I am my own best lawyer in all three roles—defendant, solicitor, and barrister." In the summer of 1984 he submitted his fifteenth affidavit, seeking the dismissal of Flegon's amended lawsuit and a trial based on the original, and as soon as possible! Flegon's lawyer, however, insisted on a fresh adjournment. And Master Topley acquiesced. "It is particularly harsh and hurtful to be facing an utterly heartless bureaucrat of the worst possible kind, a court automaton, who doesn't have the slightest interest in knowing anything about the Gulag, and being seen by him as the likely guilty party. He doesn't read any affidavits, doesn't bother with the merits of the case. Despite all the travails of this legal battle, however, my confidence in eventual victory has not diminished even today. But I'm bothered by signs of nervous exhaustion." The wheel of the law caught him up once again, however. He addressed a request to the attorney general, reporting a vexatious litigant with innumerable trials behind him: surely there is a law against this in England. The attorney general's reply was that yes, Flegon had often filed lawsuits, but there was no proof that they had been frivolous, and he'd even won some of them.

While the fate of his lawsuits was being decided, Flegon went so far as to take his book out of shops where it was for sale. The danger past, he took it off to a Slavist conference in New York to market it in person. The trial was postponed until the end of 1985. Meanwhile, Flegon was "clearly preparing a 'softened' English-language version of the book," Lenchevsky reported. "As long as that poisonous filth slithers around the world, I will have no inner peace." And he was so excited at my every impulse—maybe I might become more involved?—whereas I would merely set out to find a new lawyer and would soon pull out again. Indeed, I wrote to him, saying, "There's no need to work yourself up; years of life and strength are more precious. Flegon's book should die a natural death from literary infirmity, rather than from a court ruling that would crown it a legend." No, he replied, you must "shake off the web of litigation in which he has ensnared you and take your defense into your own hands." In 1985, I wrote him: "If only Flegon were my sole problem. But I am besieged by hounding in the press, and if I took it upon myself to respond to it all, it would consume all my strength. In this context, the accusation that I libeled Flegon thirteen years ago is neither here nor there. Only a fusty English court can feed off such rotten stuff. Apart from *The Red Wheel*, all earthly matters are very much on the back burner for me now."

Flegon sent Lenchevsky threatening letters to throw him off course. To no avail. Adjourned for the umpteenth time, their trial was set for July 1986, and so was due to take place after ours. Lenchevsky hinted to Sykes that Flegon was maneuvering to have my simpler case come up first. He hinted that there were grounds for a deferment, but Sykes took no notice. As always, Lenchevsky brought his friendly witnesses to the appointed trial, but once again it was in vain: Flegon, brandishing his book's English-language proofs, secured yet another adjournment—"until November at least." (What about Lenchevsky's nerves?) Lenchevsky objected in vain that investigations had been under way for five years, that in any case it was the *Russian-language* version of the book that was on trial, not the English, and, finally, that files full of his own translations had been ignored time after time—why then was it necessary to wait for Flegon's translation? —No, the master's order was to wait.

Even in November 1986, their trial would have been earlier than ours, which was set for February 1987, but Lenchevsky had guessed right: while Sykes slumbered, Flegon rescheduled their trial to June 1987, after ours, and meanwhile won his case against me. Even so, Lenchevsky won their five-day trial!

A spurious English-language edition of Flegon's book had already been produced, and was submitted as evidence, but it didn't help him. Mr. Justice Phillips had, he said, read it from cover to cover. (So England does have conscientious judges of this kind!) A considerable part of the obscene Russian text had not been included, but Lenchevsky presented translations of the key passages Flegon had omitted—and Flegon could not deny them. The same applied to the illustrations. The judge also dismissed Flegon's revised supplementary lawsuit. Lenchevsky had twenty-two witnesses in court! Many weren't even based in London, but made the effort to turn up nonetheless, and not for the first time either—Michael Nicholson, Harry Willetts, Martin

Dewhirst, Dmitri Pospielovsky, Aleksandr Lieven, Catherine Andreyev, Gennadi Pokrass, and Leonid Finkelstein yet again. People still have such reserves of warmheartedness in this shoddy, overburdened world!

The judge concluded (there was no jury, fortunately) that Flegon's book did indeed libel Solzhenitsyn. It cast a slur on his honesty as a writer, on his literary talent, and on his personal morals. The book ranged from vulgar invective to complete outrage. Collage had been used to insert Solzhenitsyn's face into offensive and obscene settings. "In summary, I find it hard to conceive of a more comprehensive or offensive assault upon a man's character and conduct. . . . A series of gross libels." Furthermore, the book attacked the character of the Russian people as a whole in general terms. No proof had been adduced to confirm his disparaging accusations. Flegon had attributed the words of Solzhenitsyn's characters to the man himself (I "would shoot youngsters") or completely distorted their meaning ("he readied himself to sacrifice the lives of his sons simply to see his book on the shop shelves"). The judge also deemed unsatisfactory Flegon's explanations as to why he splattered his book with obscenities (allegedly it was "to publish for the first time erotic writings of certain great Russian writers, which would be of interest and value to students of Russian literature"). No, the reason was that obscenities would appeal to the black market in books. The judge acknowledged Lenchevsky's description of a "pseudo-literary monstrosity" as "fair comment on this distasteful book."[7]

So there—an English court was capable of this, too. They come in all sorts.

I first heard of Michael Scammell back in Moscow from Lev Kopelev and then Veronika Shtein: here was yet another person insisting that he wanted to write my biography. It was an obsession with them. I'd had enough with George Feifer and David Burg, and simply waved it away.

Meanwhile, either Betta Markstein had discovered Scammell in the West or, more probably, he himself had made contact via Fritz Heeb. By the time I was expelled, they had already taken him into their confidence: it was he who was entrusted with proofreading and correcting Thomas P. Whitney's US translation of the first volume of *Archipelago.* (Scammell's towering reputation as a translator was based on the fact that he had translated Nabokov's

The Gift into English.) While still in Moscow, however, I learned in a letter from Betta (5 January 1974) that "Michael Scammell talks a lot." And, in early January 1974, I heard for myself his BBC interview about *Archipelago*. (Where would the BBC have found out that he was on "our team"? it must have come from him.) He was asked, "What makes the greater impression in the book—the facts or the author's voice?" Scammell replied: The facts. Question: Are there many new facts? Answer: No, there are no new facts; generally, they are already known, but there are a lot of new and specific details.

So what had he actually understood of *Archipelago*? of its dynamic of the soul? He had pored diligently over the translation—but discerned little. It was at that level that Scammell's understanding remained ever after. And I should have drawn the appropriate conclusion, but, in my frenetic life, it faded from sight and was forgotten.

At the end of that January, before I was expelled, Betta managed to get a reply to me in Moscow. "Yes, he's upset me in many ways as well. It's a Western feature to try and exploit everything to boost your own reputation. In the West, the main thing for an intellectual, especially a writer, is to become someone, to be known, to acquire a reputation. And, to a great extent, it isn't those with knowledge who become famous, but those who shout loudest. However, beyond just being a good translator, Scammell is not a bad chap—I'm sure of it. . . . In short, don't be so demanding and intolerant. There are undoubtedly other people in the West, but, reticent and humble, they keep to themselves. How are we to find them, when we're obliged to work in secret ourselves?"

And, really, perhaps one shouldn't be so demanding of well-meaning assistants acquired by chance?

Commissioned by Heeb, Scammell coordinated the translation of my *Letter to the Soviet Leaders* into English (he didn't do the translation himself) and then he attempted to arrange its publication (through an intermediary literary agent) in the *Sunday Times* and the *New York Times*—but in the States it fell through.[8] He explained the failure in his very first letter to me in the West, and with such a gushing outpouring of bonhomie. "Do I have your confidence for further work on the *Gulag* or not?"[9] Well, why wouldn't he? And at my very first request, Scammell tracked down the eagerly longed-for translator of the *Miniatures*—Harry Willetts in Oxford (who, Heeb claimed, had gone to Australia and disappeared). He kept on offering to come and see me in Zurich too. —From the autumn of 1974 onward, Scammell undertook to manage the English translations of the articles in the collection *From Under the Rubble*, to which I attached prime importance at the time. Meanwhile, Reshetovskaya's memoirs[10] were due to be published any day, already in English—Scammell volunteered to write reviews of the distortions in them.

He was so well-intentioned, and so keen to meet; let him come?

And in September he did come to see us in Zurich. A young and determined Anglo-Saxon. He displayed no brilliance in conversation or in company (Alya and I compared notes), but he appeared distinctly decent—and so willing, so well disposed towards us. And didn't all this naturally establish that he was also entitled to write a biography? there was no way to turn him down now. (Ten years later, he publicly admitted in the *Times*: "I had congratulated myself on my cunning."[11])

Before long, in order to hold talks with the publisher about the biography, he wrote: "I *beg* you to write even the tiniest little note as soon as possible. For the moment, it could be your agreement *in principle*—or provisionally. Or, if you like, I'll write you a summary of my views on the planned biography, how I approach the subject matter, and how I envisage our collaboration. . . . It's important to find out your opinion of the project and whether I can get down to work."[12] (There was no room in my life for "collaboration"—and I didn't ask for a summary, which was a big mistake. I gave him permission in writing, and he used it to enter into a contract with the publisher.)

On parting, he left me his opening chapters to read. And immediately asked in a letter: "Well, what do you think?" As if I didn't have enough on my plate. I sat down reluctantly, and found the reading dispiriting.

Here's what I wrote to him about my impression (1 October 1974): Your friendliness and conscientiousness have to be acknowledged, but "on the topics you include here . . . you have picked out and done a good job of shedding light on perhaps 10 percent of the material but, more frequently, even less than that. And the way you have sometimes managed to discern matters that are difficult to assess—for example, the fact that I did not change in accordance with external circumstances—is impressive. However, in the majority of instances, given the severe shortage of material [I thought that was the only reason!], you have not divined the motives or the thrusts of my efforts. At times I closed my eyes and imagined already being in the grave, listening to what had been written about me back on Earth, but no longer able to object or to put it right—and, you know, it was a little creepy: as if someone's face was rippling in the water, but apparently not mine. Perhaps many biographies on Earth are written like this. . . . My advice is not to be in too much of a hurry with your plan . . . at the moment you are still too unprepared." And I suggested that, for the time being, he work on translating *The Oak and the Calf.*[13]

He deviously replied (18 October 1974) as if he perceived my response as approval of his "method and approach." He agreed to translate *The Oak and the Calf,* but only as preparation for the biography, not instead of it; in the main there was pressure and duress: "We can, if you like, put aside for the moment the issue of how much you might *approve* my planned biography, and are prepared *to help me and cooperate* (although it would be more reassuring for me to know your position right away), but I am firmly set on writing it, and have thought of nothing else since we met."[14]

I resisted and kept him at bay, if only to avoid reading his subsequent chapters. "As you will appreciate, I have neither the right nor the intention to dissuade you or to stop you. . . . But assuring you that your biography 'has my approval' is a very delicate matter and may appear unseemly: it would immediately be as though I had commissioned a self-advertisement and was promoting it. It would also make it necessary to hold a great many consultations and to correct your material—none of this is to my taste, nor do I have the time."[15]

Of course, Scammell explained, "It will be a pleasure to begin translating your sketches [*The Oak and the Calf*] if they do not take up too much time. . . . The point is that this really is the right time for a biography, and interest in you is so very great that it would be a shame not to seize the moment."[16]

He was certainly frank! There was the explanation and the full background to his plan: "It would be a shame not to seize the moment." Whereas I, in my whirl of activity, had once again not really grasped this, had not come to.

Moreover, "I am not writing just a 'biography' . . . it contains more about your work than about you and your life." It will be a literary-historical sketch and, even more broadly, a look at the history of the Soviet Union. "To begin with, I had no intention of touching upon your biography in anything other than the most general and rough terms. But then the publisher persuaded me that the reading public wants some sort of outline of your life. . . . We know from Burg and Feifer's book what frivolous and indifferent commentators write. And Reshetovskaya has shown us how an ill-intentioned commentator can write when possessed of incomparably more material than everyone else. . . . The author's literary *persona* is of greater interest to me than his personality. I am in no wise looking to write an 'intimate biography' with reflections on your personal motivations or Freudian impulses, family fulfillment or family strife (with the sole exception that where that strife is already in the public domain—in Reshetovskaya's case, let's say—it is better to set the facts out coldly and concisely). . . . It is impossible to embark upon a work of this kind without mutual trust and agreement as to what is possible, what is doubtful, and what is unacceptable.[17] . . . By *The Gulag Archipelago* you completely subverted the book's primary subject—to re-create the world of the camps, and shed light on Soviet history in the guise of a biography. . . . But no better method than your *Gulag* exists, nor is likely to exist in future. . . . [Now] my camera lens will zoom out, so that I can examine your activities against a Russian backdrop, rather than just a Soviet one."[18]

And I believed him. How wrong I was. Why stand in the way of such sincere intentions, such an unconventional, broad approach? (Nor did the baffled, basic questions about *The Oak and the Calf,* which he soon sent, alert me.)

After Scammell's umpteenth query, I wrote to Veronika in New York (she was Reshetovskaya's cousin but a good friend of Alya's and mine): tell him what you know—less trouble for me.

The translation of *The Oak and the Calf* had still not got off the ground, however. At the same time, Scammell was expected to finish working with Whitney on the translation of the second volume of *Archipelago*, despite their disagreements. As a result, they descended on Zurich in January 1975, along with Winthrop Knowlton, president of Harper publishers. (Scammell's superior tone towards the older, mild-mannered Whitney grated.) Furthermore, it goes without saying that I was awaiting Scammell's help in managing the group translation of *From Under the Rubble.* I was increasingly reliant upon him.

(Scammell later declined to translate *The Oak and the Calf* once and for all, writing that he wasn't happy with the payment offered by the publisher, Collins. Besides, he was simply dying to get to the biography, "to seize the moment." So much the better for me: Willetts would translate *The Oak and the Calf* brilliantly. Of Scammell's translation of *The Gift,* Vera Nabokova had told us in a letter that when he "was working for my husband . . . he could only be praised out of kindness, and even then it was mostly because he was trying so very hard." When I was in London in February 1976, I freed Scammell from his promise regarding *The Oak and the Calf.*)

In the meantime, he'd begun to send me dozens and dozens of questions about my origins and my family, wondering if I could sketch my family tree and if he could come to Zurich for a few days to ask questions (12 July 1976): "My research will be finished by October, and I would like to talk to you before getting down to writing."[19] And he was very keen to help refute the KGB lies forwarded by a Swiss journalist,[20] but I handled it without him. —No sooner had he discovered that we'd moved to Vermont, than he asked to come and visit there.

Then, out of the blue, he sent a copy of an old map he'd made in a London library. It showed the exact position of the Solzhenitsyns' farmstead (where my father was fatally wounded) near Sablya. I was very touched. And again I was led astray by the treacherous thought that if someone was going to write a biography in any case, had already started in fact, and seemed a decent, friendly sort as well, then at least let him get his facts straight. But I didn't have the strength to fill endless screeds with explanations, either. Let him gather all his questions together and come to visit. I could answer them all at once, spend a few days replying verbally rather than months corresponding by mail—the perfect way to save some time.

We agreed that he would come in June 1977. With a firm proviso: we will answer *all* questions freely, as many as you can fit in, but that's *the end* of it, don't come back for any more. —Yes, yes, of course.

He came for three days—but stayed a week. He used a tape recorder to quiz Alya and me, leaving no stone unturned. I even let him in on *The Trail,* which no one knew about at the time.* And he took a good deal from it: my conversations with my grandfather, and how he went off to die in GPU[22] custody, how the GPU took away my parents' engagement rings, my encounters with trainloads of prisoners as a young man and—getting it pretty much all wrong—the mood in which I was transported from Prussia, under arrest. He became absorbed in my trivial juvenile jottings about a bicycle trip around the Caucasus in 1937 and, as is now apparent, copied out whole paragraphs and shoehorned them into the biography without my permission. At the same time, his academic eye did not miss what it saw as a telling

* A verse novella conceived in the camps, composed and memorized without pen or paper. I published it for the first time only in 1999, along with other early works: Протеревши глаза (*Seeing Anew*) (Moscow: Наш дом–L'Age d'Homme, 1999). (Author's note, 2000.)[21]

feature—the cover of one of these meager notebooks of mine, dating back to the Second Five-Year Plan,[23] bore a quotation from Stalin as the printer's mark. He put that in the biography too, calling it a "motto." But a "motto" is a slogan, a watchword, an epigraph—and my adversaries interpreted it as *my* "epigraph quoting Stalin" or even as "a dedication to Stalin." In this way, they hoofed my youth about, like a football, from one person to the next.

He followed up by writing Alya: "I'd like to express to you and A. I. a huge thank-you for your generous hospitality and for the priceless help which you provided me. The information I received has literally transformed my conception and understanding of A. I.'s early life. . . . My stay with you was enriching not only intellectually but personally."

However, "it is already clear, alas, that I omitted several significant points, or perhaps did not 'interrogate' you sufficiently. What should I do? send you my questions . . . or forget about them and be grateful for what I have already received?"[24]

Fine. I replied[25] to his questions.

In the spring of 1978, however, he again asked to visit us! No, I was deep in my work, "I can't tear myself away."

More questions, then, in writing. Surely these had to be the last? I answered them.

At the end of 1978, however, the Rockefeller Foundation gave him a grant to write my biography and "since December [he] had begun working at a faster pace"[26]—and a new cascade of questions followed. This went beyond any agreement. And there was no end in sight. Despair. I wrote (February 1979): "I simply cannot fit the amount of work I envisage having to do with you into the time that I have. . . . I'm at the moment psychologically incapable of tearing myself away to undertake this work. I can find no time at all even for the most current, pressing correspondence. Let us acknowledge that I've given you an absolutely sufficient basis as it is."[27]

No: he immediately asked to visit again "for three–four hours with the tape recorder." And again that spring: "to come in the summer and put all my questions at once."[28] I replied (June 1979): "You are asking the impossible. . . . I have furnished your book with unique information as it is. It has to stop somewhere. It is very difficult for me to be mentally and emotionally distracted just now."[29]

Besides, every time he went to New York, he grilled Veronika over and over again. In Europe he had meetings with Panin, Kopelev, Etkind, Sinyavsky, Zhores Medvedev, Zilberberg, and in the States with Olga Carlisle and

Pavel Litvinov—almost all of them my overt detractors. And all we wanted was for him to leave us in peace.

In the autumn of 1980, he reported that "the whole text will be ready by the end of the year . . . and if it were possible to see you and discuss the book one last time, it would be of immeasurable help to me."[30] Discuss it? He himself accepted with relief that we wouldn't be doing that.

Alya replied (January 1981): "Reading your manuscript is unnecessary. For all our mutual liking, our views differ considerably. . . . We do not want, or consider it possible, to influence you. From a purely factual point of view, we hope you will be sufficiently thorough and tactful."[31]

In reply, he said: but it would be good to come along for a couple of days. . . . "As for [you] reading the book, I'm completely happy with your decision, even relieved. . . . I very much appreciate your tact. . . . What different interpretations could there be of A. I.'s social role? As for his literary role, there is even less room for differences of opinion there."[32]

And then—nothing for three years, silence. The biography did not come out in 1981. It didn't come out in 1982. Or in 1983. But news reached us from Moscow, via Natalia Stolyarova, that Reshetovskaya was corresponding with Scammell and showering him with material. Well, let her, it clearly fulfilled a need for her. (Interestingly, though: who was facilitating their correspondence? These were the very darkest years, everything had been stricter since the start of the Afghan war, all the clandestine channels had dried up. David Shipler of the *New York Times* had taken our urgent letters to Moscow, but over six months wasn't able to deliver them, and returned the whole packet. But the Novosti press agency's channels must have been at Natasha's service. And if the flow was simply by mail, the *Index on Censorship*[33] editor had to be aware that his collaboration with Reshetovskaya had the blessing of the authorities.) Veronika at first couldn't believe it: after all, how many years had he been pumping her for details, and now not a word? She ran into him at a conference of Slavists and said she knew about the correspondence. He was embarrassed. "Why didn't you tell me?" (It turned out that Reshetovskaya had stipulated that he should hide from me that she was supplying materials, right up until the book was published. And he promised. In other words: he'd agreed not to verify them at all.)

And then, in August 1984, after a three-year silence, there was a letter from Scammell: the book is going to press. "I imagine that not everything in my book will please you; it wasn't written to please, but to seek and to illuminate the truth. . . . Posterity will decide [that was aiming a bit high!—

A.S.], but I was guided solely by my conscience . . . I doubt you will write to give me your opinion. [He knew very well what he was doing. . . .—*A.S.*] I would like to thank you for the trust you placed in me, and for the lack of any kind of pressure or attempts to influence my text."[34]

Two weeks later—there's the book itself. The title—*Solzhenitsyn*—in large letters, and a photograph of me, filling the cover. The same gimmick Carlisle used. *One thousand* densely filled pages! I leaf through them. The book contains photos obtained from Reshetovskaya. But what's this? The caption to one in three photos is incorrect: either the name's wrong, or the location's been mixed up, the year's wrong, or the situations aren't the ones indicated. So much for accuracy!

I begin the preface. Straightaway—I couldn't believe my eyes—I was shamefully misrepresented as having apparently considered it *essential* to authorize the biography (instead of having refused to do so, from start to finish)! Whereas he "was unwilling to commit" himself to a certain "degree of supervision" and had managed to talk me into a compromise. And then came a dishonorable complaint, lamenting that I'd "cut short" our collaboration, had first made a promise and then gone back on it, plus "the impossibility . . . of obtaining answers . . . to even the simplest questions" because of "Solzhenitsyn's temperament"! (This after he'd stayed with us for a week and all that I had revealed to him! And no mention of the proviso: you come once and that's it, *we're not doing this again.* So who was it that reneged on his promise? And I gave him so many extra answers too. Well, there you go—he had to ratchet up his value: how very, very hard it had been for him to come by his material, how I had resisted, and yet—he'd done it!) By contrast, there were hundreds of references to Reshetovskaya: to the pages and pages of her "letters to the author," her "unpublished chapters," and, above all, to her reliable book, co-authored by the Novosti press agency.[35] Several hundred pages of Scammell's book are a novel written by an abandoned wife. Of *The Oak and the Calf* (which he had milked to the utmost—what would he have based the biography on without it?), he said that it was a contradictory and boastful memoir, "misleading," disorientating, lacking "objective analysis." And Solzhenitsyn himself was a "controversial" figure (exactly the sort of thing they all say, it's the only way they can write), while Scammell's aim was to "illuminate and explain" this figure.[36]

How his tone towards me had changed from that pleading one in 1974, when my recognition was at its peak, to this one now, when anyone who felt like it could give me a kicking.

In the meantime, Scammell's presentation of the insufferable difficulties of working with me (and therefore all the greater merits of his research) were immediately and widely seized upon. The earliest review, in the *Washington Post,* spoke of Solzhenitsyn's "almost paranoid suspiciousness . . . from start to finish he was a hard man from whom to extract information."[37] Then dozens of American reviews came raining down and barely a single one failed to discuss the travails Scammell had endured with me. . . .

The publication of the book left me with an acute feeling of having been much maligned, a bitter lesson in libel. If *The Oak and the Calf* was not to be believed, then I was quite simply a liar. He was the umpteenth arrogant Western writer to dive in to judge and disparage me in the eyes of uninformed readers who would never have the possibility of verifying anything.

And now what? respond?—it would mean reading and studying those one thousand–plus pages about me, and abandoning *The Red Wheel* in the thick of things. Impossible. For the moment, I would read only the reviews, while several close friends (especially Irina Ilovaiskaya) sat down to read everything, wrote their impressions down in detail, and pointed out the most caustic patches of tawdriness, tactlessness, and ignoble interpretation. But reading it myself would also be unavoidable.

There had already been several occasions when I hadn't responded—to Zilberberg, Feifer, Chalidze, Sinyavsky—and all of it had stuck to me for years like a drying scab.

As Böll advised me on the basis of his own experience: "Let us choose the path of disdain."

So here too, I must put it off for years; perhaps God might send more life. And endure—this too.

But it's a foul thing to carry on living, maligned in every respect.

Still, at least the book has been published in my lifetime, thank God; had it been after my death, it would have been even worse.

I must read it and make notes for the future.

So how was it, this book?

Uniformly lacking in elevated emotional and intellectual understanding throughout, it takes a low view of lofty subjects.

Two constant efforts by the biographer run through the whole book. Firstly, wherever possible, he aims to reduce my actions, movements, feelings, and intentions to the mediocre, to an order understood by philistines;

to work out which motives make most sense to the biographer himself—and ascribe them to me; to select the tawdriest and basest of all possible explanations, and to "set me straight" with greater irritation the further he goes into the thick of the book; he has absolutely no understanding of deep, extreme, impassioned feelings and motivations. None.

Secondly, he suspects me of insincerity, of concealing my real motives at every one of my crisis points, my watershed moments; he strives always to be on the side of my detractors in interpreting these moments, and this is probably not out of malice towards me but because, by his reckoning, it's the best way to secure the balance, the "fifty-fifty," required by "scientific practice." Maximum mistrust of the subject, no *integral* character can exist by nature, and unless he is torn to shreds, his contradictions exposed—where are the Freudian complexes, and where's the objective, self-sufficient researcher and biographer?

How much merrier—and more honest!—are open disagreement, contention, attacks, even invective—than being mired in this ordeal by tawdriness.

So whose is the face rippling in the water? . . .

Not so much for the general reader as for the specialist who will need to delve deeper—here are more details.

Already his overall assessment of *The Oak and the Calf* is that it's not far removed from the self-justifications in Ehrenburg's memoirs.[38] (Had he understood anything? Ehrenburg had to justify thirty years of collaboration with the regime. What did I have to justify?—the front? prison? the underground? explosions right in the face of the authorities?)

What motives could have driven this writer, who for some reason rode out to attack a mighty power? He was impelled by vanity and the desire to get ahead, of course. (Reshetovskaya's and Novosti's explanation and, indeed, the philistines' age-old explanation of anyone at all: they can see nothing in people but vanity—well, and greed.) Of course, he has adverse character traits: innate irritability and pigheadedness. (He didn't get along with the Union of Writers where everyone had always got along.)—He joined the Komsomol as a fervent eighteen-year-old? it was an opportunistic decision; in other words, the young man couldn't possibly have held such convictions. But oddly, later on, in the *sharashka*, with my apprenticeship in prisons and camps behind me, I have views that are "very close" to those of Kopelev. Like him, I'm a "Leninist in a hostile environment," we "identify with the establishment," we both regard our sentences as a "miscarriage of justice." (Well, I didn't, not for a minute. It was Kopelev who always felt that way, and tarred me with the same brush, which Scammell willingly accepted.) As if that isn't enough, even in exile, after eight years in the camps (with

Prisoners and *Feast of the Victors* already written)—Leninism "struck an answering chord." So much for the biographer's understanding, so much for his insights. (Scammell even has "Sacred Baikal" down as a "Soviet song."[39]) —Is it then even worth mentioning his view that "the situation seems to have been less simple than that"[40]—that my not marrying in exile was apparently for the sake of my manuscripts (and, in all honesty, why bother preserving and hiding them if they are lit with a Leninist light?)

And I couldn't possibly have had so much self-possession and inner calm as not to have rushed[41] to lap up Konstantin Simonov's article about *Ivan Denisovich* in *Izvestia* (an article by a Soviet favorite in a dyed-in-the-wool Soviet newspaper, as if my biographer could have grasped the wild notion that, for me at that time, *Ivan Denisovich* was done and dusted, while my concerns clustered thickly around my subsequent works). —I couldn't have turned down the privilege of meeting the great Sartre[42] out of anything other than a combination of pride and timidity: "I should suffer too much." (He doesn't allow that I might have simply despised Sartre.) This refusal "perhaps reflected a certain paranoia on Solzhenitsyn's part." (The word "paranoia" is dotted about the book—it is the master key the biographer finds most convenient for an understanding of his subject.) —Or again, Sakharov's memorandum on coexistence and progress appeared[43] and made a great splash in the West—how must Solzhenitsyn feel? There is a "hint of rivalry" from Solzhenitsyn. (This when I was horrified at Sakharov's naïve arguments and his poorly thought-out characterizations of Soviet socialism: where on earth was he sending the liberation movement, and how distortedly did he view the world?[44]) —Again: the arrest and trial of Sinyavsky and Daniel. Solzhenitsyn gave "the impression that he was frustrated by this sudden switch of the spotlight and jealous of the publicity they attracted." (*Who* was given that impression? Quite the opposite—it came as a relief! that I had not yet been dealt the worst blow, that I had still been spared for *Archipelago*. I was full of *Archipelago*, performing two superhuman workloads a day in my Hiding Place[45] in Estonia, solely in order to finish in time! Was Scammell once again measuring this fabricated envy against himself?) —And when Sinyavsky came to bid me farewell (and to make my acquaintance) before going abroad,[46] I was apparently "posturing" when I appeared to be in the throes of grief at fewer and fewer people being left who were willing to share our Russian lot.[47] I was simply lying, in other words; I couldn't possibly feel like this about Russia, and it was clear that all I did was dream of high-tailing it abroad myself. (Why then didn't I go to collect my prize in 1970? why didn't I accept the ominous nudge of the KGB in 1973, brought to me by Sinyavsky's wife?)

And what about when he comes to the critical moments, the turning points in my life, where fate changes dramatically or implodes? Here I am even more incomprehensible to him, here he has all the more need to apply the plaster of mediocrity.

My letter to the Congress of Soviet Writers. "I shall fulfill my duty as a writer in all circumstances—from the grave even more successfully and incontrovertibly than in my lifetime. No one can bar the road to truth, and to advance its cause I am prepared to accept even death."[48] —Is it really possible to be like this?[49] A philistine cannot get his head around it!

My archive's disaster at the home of Veniamin Teush.[50] A touch of mockery: "Solzhenitsyn's suspiciousness and almost superstitious dread pointed his mind away from chance and in the direction of a premeditated act as the only explanation for the raids."[51] And in actual fact? It was obvious: the KGB must have been blindly feeling their way, with no idea of where to look or what to look for; maybe they would flip a coin to decide whose house to search. —And the whole of this highly detailed exposition has one firm rule: to believe Zilberberg and not to believe me about anything.

The smashing of *Novy Mir.* In the Second Supplement to *The Oak and the Calf* (1971), ***looking back a year later,*** I wrote: having put up no public resistance itself, the editorial top brass should not have demanded sacrifices from the junior editorial staff: leave your jobs, call it a day! or from authors—take your manuscripts back, don't try and get them published![52] —Scammell misrepresents this so that, in the very weeks that *Novy Mir* was being brought down, in talks with other contributors I was apparently criticizing the magazine's regime and Tvardovsky's indifference towards his junior colleagues. Allegedly, I even "offered [my] support to Tvardovsky's replacement, Valeri Kosolapov" and "encouraged other writers to do the same." (Did this come from Feifer? He was the one who dreamed up that I'd gone to offer my services to Kosolapov. Libel's like coal—even if it doesn't burn, it leaves a mark.) —"Solzhenitsyn was beholden to no [Soviet] magazine, loyal to no editor." That's because my path began not during Khrushchev's "thaw," but in the flames of the revolution, and looked likely to finish only around the end of the century. I was saving myself for an immense amount of work, for great battles against this Dragon, but Scammell is unable to get his head around this, and he seeks out mediocrity: was there cooperation with the Soviet authorities? And, indeed, he sees that "cooperation" at every step in my life: after *Ivan Denisovich,* I "joined the Writers' Union" (was I supposed to remain a schoolteacher, then?), "attended meetings at the Kremlin" (whereas I should have said, to hell with the Central Committee's invitation, and thrown it back in their faces), "competed keenly for a Lenin Prize"[53] (how did I "keenly compete"? I didn't move a muscle during that whole episode).

That is how he defamed me.

He takes great pains to place himself above his subject and "above the fight," as it were—but he never misses a chance to adopt every argument of my adversaries, including the KGB. He uses material from my books widely and at length (often without references, as if it was his own discovery), but retains a wary mistrust: what should he find fault with? where should he dig around? what stroke might tarnish his subject best?

Scammell preaches that I shouldn't compromise. But he also preaches that I should not be stubbornly opposed to reality or push the authorities into something impossible (this is straight out of Novosti-Reshetovskaya: we have to spare the authorities!). Some teaching . . .

Having undertaken to set forth my family life as related by my ex-wife, and accepted her scenarios unquestioningly (with all their disparities and cover-ups, the concealment of another six-year marriage while I was in prison, the inflation of her nonexistent role in my work), he transgresses still further by using testimony from her, of all people, to explain my relations with Tvardovsky, my face-to-face meetings with him and what happened at *Novy Mir*, which Reshetovskaya herself didn't witness. And to Scammell, all this is more authoritative than my direct account. And my relations with the authorities, and the whole political interpretation of events are also taken from her. And should her versions seem in any way debatable, then, after self-serving deliberation, Scammell always inclines in her favor.

And this must be why Scammell didn't write a *literary* biography, as he was supposedly planning; because he got carried away—with divorce proceedings. . . .

How ever could I have thought that someone had sent Reshetovskaya to me to negotiate about *Cancer Ward*?[54] (No, I suppose she was proposing *of her own account* to bring it out herself at *her own publishing house*?) And, at the very most, if she had been sent, it was by the Party Central Committee, not by the KGB! (What a joke! And, taking his cue from Reshetovskaya, Scammell tries to differentiate Novosti from the KGB. . . .) How on earth could I ever have imagined that we were being photographed or taped at Kazansky Railway Station in Moscow? This "testified to a highly colored vision of reality, if not symptoms of genuine paranoia." (I wonder whether Scammell still believes it's paranoia, now that Sakharov has been secretly filmed at the Gorki regional hospital? Or since Galina Vishnevskaya's testimony that, after I left them, security operatives dragged a great box of devices out from under the floor of "my" part of the dacha—was that paranoia too?) And could I seriously have believed that the KGB (after anonymous threatening letters, sent through the same mail system that it monitored) might do something to my children? "To what extent had he become the captive of his self-created myth?"[55]

Scammell was bound to wander into this kind of quagmire by constantly and specifically seeking arguments that would benefit his subject's opponents. And how everything from Novosti-Reshetovskaya's book suits him; he draws from it with abandon.

In Scammell's opinion, I exaggerate danger at times and am simply playing at an unnecessary conspiracy game. (Did he understand how that daily conspiracy oppressed my spirit, how it ruined my normal life and writing?) He sees "excessive self-satisfaction" in how I memorized texts and then burned them.[56] (But that's all that saved them. He can't even imagine how many of my predecessors perished, unknown, on that journey.)

Lastly, even my banishment from my homeland must be smeared. In *The Oak and the Calf* I write that when I suddenly jumped up in the plane and went to find the bathroom (this was only the second time in my life that I'd been on a plane), the next section toward the rear was empty—it's not as if I had a chance to look closely, in any case, before a KGB operative placed a hand on my shoulder and turned me around.[57] But on this basis Scammell constructs an exultant detective story: aha! he's lying! We know there were passengers in the rear section—and suddenly there's no one there? (That's right, I saw no one during the whole flight and never suspected anyone was on the plane apart from my KGB guards.) So, might this mean all the rest is a lie as well? Perhaps Solzhenitsyn connived voluntarily at his departure?!—then the astounding conclusion is that this makes my expulsion the same as the departures (via the Visa Department) of Sinyavsky, Brodsky, Maximov, et al.! "Like many other mysteries in his life, this one has still to be resolved," so says the biographer's instinct and the researcher's intelligence. (What are his suspicions based on?—why, on nothing at all, on the biographer's obligation to be suspicious, come what may.) —There's more too, this question even: who chose Germany, anyway? Is it really possible that Solzhenitsyn didn't know where the plane was going until it landed in Frankfurt and he saw the name[58]—surely he's lying here too? were there really no loud-speaker announcements of the destination in his section of the plane? had the Soviets really managed to switch them off?[59] (That's exactly what they'd done.)*

Without understanding them, Scammell has no difficulty glibly explaining my motives in the West as well. I didn't respond to my opponents' attacks?—it means they hit home, it's all true. I did respond (to Carlisle)? But with "well-known irascibility and unpredictability." Why did I get involved in politics in the West? It is "a subconscious

* A compilation was published in Russia in 1994, entitled Кремлёвский самосуд: секретные документы Политбюро о писателе А. Солженицыне (*A Kremlin Lynching: The Politburo's Secret Documents on the Writer A. Solzhenitsyn*) (Moscow: Rodina, 1994). It contains documentary evidence of how the Politburo of the Central Committee planned and executed my expulsion. (And how, since at least 1965, according to KGB reports, my every step had been examined through a magnifying glass.) —Work to translate this book started in the States, and who on earth should jump in, omniscient, to write an introduction and serve as editor? Why, Scammell, of course, undaunted by his track record and seeing no kind of moral impediment in it. (*The Solzhenitsyn Files: Secret Soviet Documents Reveal One Man's Fight Against the Monolith*, ed. Michael Scammell, trans. Catherine A. Fitzpatrick [Carol Stream, IL: edition q, 1995].) (Author's note, 1995.)

escape from some of the problems he was encountering in his historical novels. The flood of information available to him in the West . . . was proving to be very difficult" (in other words, I was given access to the archives, and I reveled in them!—oh, to have worries like yours. . . .). What about the Washington speech in 1975?[60] "One can only speculate about the reasons for this extraordinary outburst." (He had studied *The Oak and the Calf* from every angle, but he didn't get it. Every personal—and base—motivation you like, but none of principle. He couldn't grasp the simple thrill of the fight—so what on earth *had* he understood about me? why had he even set out to write about me? just for the prestige? for the money?) —Scammell also found it "difficult to account for the high-pitched tone of Solzhenitsyn's radio address" in England.[61] (A bit of digging is required, it's true: it was Russian bitterness at Britain over its treachery in the Civil War and in World War II. It's not me he's interested in here, though; he'd felt an upsurge of his unfeigned left-wing outrage towards his homeland: how could Britain take such delight in Solzhenitsyn and even in the insults he delivered? "The low state of British morale and the multiple inferiority complexes engendered by half a century of decline . . . [an] orgy of masochistic euphoria."[62] Indeed, it's the same in France as well—yuck!)

Finally, how is my isolation in Vermont to be explained? it cannot just be that a writer needs secluded peace and quiet!—clearly, this too is a "psychological quirk."[63]

And if, in addition, the subject himself has shown remorse here and there in his various books about previously undisclosed actions in his life, what further opportunities to cut a caper are presented to a base soul! Contrition of a kind you couldn't make up yourself can be introduced to striking effect at the end of your bloated book—but no longer by the subject, of course, but by the conscientious biographer.

Nevertheless, Scammell does sometimes admit that I am difficult to interpret. He produces some juicy quotation from my book, uses it, and then comes the sneaky sting in the tail: of course, it might be true, but only in part. There is a constant dread of adopting a clear and definitive position, an ambiguity of tone just to be on the safe side.

Has the literary and historical sketch he once announced—"more about your work than about you and your life"—slipped feebly into mere politics and mundaneness after all? is there truly nothing specifically about literature in the 1,100 pages of this "biography of a writer"?

Yes, when you lack artistic taste and personal tact, it's hard to plod through a writer's life. There's no point looking for a spiritual dimension, worldview, or outlook on history here, much less for the meaning of my books themselves. Scammell didn't even understand the straightforward articles published in *From Under the Rubble*—he reduced it all to hackneyed politics. He wants to rise above his subject—but slithers ever lower, vulgarizing everything in succession. He hasn't spent a minute in the spiritual world I have inhabited all these years. It is beyond his ken to believe it genuinely possible to have a sense of duty to the dead, of duty to Russia. Being himself a tangle of small-minded features, he has no chance of explaining my life, even if he wanted to.

In fact, Scammell himself writes (in an attempt to make the "authoritarian" Solzhenitsyn see sense) that freedom lies in being "trivial, sensational, irresponsible as well as [in being] serious and objective."[64] Exactly: it was inevitable that a quasi-literary vulgarizer would turn up to write my biography—and one most certainly did.

It goes without saying that the American press showered praise on Scammell. The critics copied their accolades from one other (not all, of course, having plowed through the thousand-plus pages): a well-balanced biography (that's what matters most to Americans) . . . he has pulled off an incredibly difficult task . . . it may well be one of the great books of our time . . . possibly the most significant biography . . . a masterpiece of the biographer's art. . . . It is much more than a survey of one exceptional life—it is a history of Soviet society as well.[65] . . .

Isolated voices were completely lost in the chorus of delight. Some people found no "serious and profound narrative" in the book, others lamented that "there is next to no analysis either of the author's literary craftsmanship or of the tradition in which his political thought has to be placed."[66]

One can imagine just how the unambitious Scammell blossomed beneath the flurry of praise, how he gazed, open-mouthed, at fame. They were comparing him to Shakespeare, after all. The massive biography brought him a doctorate at Columbia, a chair at Cornell, and a national tour of US universities, where he could also inform the students about *how he wrote* Solzhenitsyn's biography, with what difficulties and resourcefulness.

But you cannot tour Britain, your own country, because the critics there have both deeper knowledge and taste, and Scammell's hefty but superficial biography occasioned no transports of delight. At first it was dubbed a considerable achievement . . . a persuasive interpretation . . . but Scammell was promptly put in his place in the leading newspapers: this "industrious biography . . . tends to miss the wood for the trees," the book has "no colour at all . . . no metaphors . . . never a flash of unexpected wit . . . a grey style must diminish a biography's truthfulness . . . deprives us of any feeling for the joy of battle." But if Scammell didn't feel it himself, where was he to get it from? "Much of it already familiar from *The Oak and the Calf*. . . . Scammell lacks literary imagination, literary talent and spiritual insight. . . . Serious doubts about Mr. Scammell's overall conception of his biography begin to multiply. . . . For all its lesser virtues, his book ultimately falls to pieces. . . . His narrative peters out in a series of platitudes—a mark not just of the writer's exhaustion, but of the fact that he has failed to realize his enormous goal."[67] . . .

Shortly after Scammell's book, there was another review in the United States, by Carl Proffer in the *New Republic.* I remembered the name: it must have been the same Proffer whom Lev Kopelev had brought over to see me during my last Russian winter, in January 1974 in Peredelkino, during my darkest days.[68] Lev brought Proffer and his wife along without warning me, but had evidently promised them a meeting. Lev found me in the grounds under the far pines. "The Proffers are here! Come on!"—"Who are they? . . ."—"American publishers. Important ones! Come on!" Oh, God, what for? Leave my poor tormented soul in peace, I'm not coming! I can't even think about holding a conversation right now. Lev got really upset and tried to persuade me: nothing doing. I imagine he explained by telling them that I was capricious and difficult. It would have been natural for them to feel affronted: we've come from America, he's right here, but not coming.

Later, in the West, I think his wife and co-publisher wrote to Alya in Switzerland, but we never managed to meet in person. (And they really were influential publishers: they had set up and were successfully running Ardis Publishers in Michigan.) Apparently, we had really offended the couple. When *Prussian Nights* came out in English, Proffer instantly reviewed it,[69] asking what was the point of writing about the subject without a spark of talent (in 1950), when Kopelev had written talented memoirs of his own observations in East Prussia (toward the '70s)? And now there was this review.

I read it alongside other US reviews—before I'd read Scammell's immense tome itself. Even among them, its harshness made it stand out.[70] And, like all of them, Proffer found Scammell's book "thorough, judicious, balanced." Scammell had him absolutely convinced that Solzhenitsyn "was capable of altering facts." Here "Scammell documents [that Solzhenitsyn] changed details of his exile" (with what *document*?). But gazing from the heights of his own American culture upon the Russian culture he had studied so thoroughly, Proffer allowed himself to make general pronouncements about "the pallid Russian literature that stretched from the Middle Ages to the Pushkin period," about the fact that Russians always write "hagiographies" about their own whereas, by contrast, "the basic books on many Russian institutions, politicians, and literary figures have not been written in Russia—not even, in fact, in Russian." (This is a conceit inherent in many Western Slavists, that they are the ones to have written the main studies of Russia. We read about Proffer himself that, having played basketball at university, he initially contemplated turning professional,[71] then opted for a life working on Russian culture.) From these heights, it was easy for Proffer to mock the notion that suffering (rather than comfort) uplifts the spirit. In that case, he snorted, "the Cambodians must be spiritual giants by now." And he understood me through and through: my speeches were "claptrap . . . prattle"; the Harvard address was "high-school drivel"; my success with *Ivan Denisovich* was simply due to my "getting in with the subject [of the camps] before anyone else did"; any praise for *Circle* was unfounded; but in *Archipelago*, too, "Solzhenitsyn never mastered certain basic rhetorical techniques." (I soon learned that Proffer wrote the review when he was dying of cancer, and knew that he was nearing his end. With a dying hand, he scrawled out *what* the hateful Solzhenitsyn deserved and then—peacefully, we hope—he died. The article was the last thing he wrote.)

Proffer's review stood out to me, however, not for these nasty comments but for the following: it said that Kopelev had described "a different Solzhenitsyn-Nerzhin—a Soviet patriot, an enthusiast who stays up late nights to catch the enemy of the people, this sellout to atomic America."[72]

It made my hair stand on end! Where had this gibberish come from? What Lev, and Lev alone, felt in the *sharashka*—why was it being attributed to me?

I began to search through Scammell's book—there it was! "From conversations with Kopelev": here was how very Leninist my views had been in the *sharashka*, and how Kopelev and I had considered ourselves the victims "of an awful miscarriage of justice"—outrageous! that was how Lev felt, but I certainly did not! And what was this "help with some of the mathematical problems involved" in recognizing the diplomat's voice?[73] Firstly, mathematics could not have been any use to Lev, as his whole method in that group consisted of rough estimates of the "one step forward, one step back" variety.[74] Secondly, not only did I never belong to their top-secret group, but I recoiled from Lev's first telling of this secret case[75] and rejected his generous offer to join the group in future if it turned out to be a success. All I did was desperately try to grasp more and more details from Kopelev about what was going on since, at that very moment (rather than years later), I became tremulously aware of what a splendid plotline it would make! Meanwhile, Scammell, according to his rule of always assuming a negative interpretation of me to be true, accepted Kopelev's version as a matter of course. And hence Proffer's spiteful capering.

So, what was going on, Lev?? Why did you make this up for Scammell? After all, there's nothing of the kind in your published memoirs.[76] (You write the truth about my views—thank you—that I was opposed to Lenin but "a disciple of the skeptic Pyrrho.")

So why? What was it for?

I began to ponder. I don't think Lev did it out of spite. He might have concocted it quite unconsciously: although he had indeed tried to catch the "atomic thief," as he called him, as the years went by—and finding himself in the West to boot—he might well have felt awkward about that activity and the burden of it and, intentionally or not, he had now begun to extend it to me as well.

. . . From my return in 1956 from exile in Kazakhstan until my expulsion in 1974, during all those eighteen years, my relations with Lev remained the warm ties of a friendship forged in prison, despite the radical and multifaceted differences in our views. But . . .

When we were still living in the *sharashka*, Panin and Kopelev, both six or seven years older than me, were in the habit of treating me like a junior, as if I needed guidance. They retained a trace of this even many years later, after we had served our sentences: I wasn't supposed to "stand on my own two feet." I remember Panin berating me angrily in 1961 for risking exposure by passing *Ivan Denisovich* to *Novy Mir* without asking him first. Dmitri considered this the worst fiasco of my life—and of his (since any moment now he too would be found out . . .). Lev, by contrast, helped it along and, at the heart of the Moscow whirlwind, became the person best informed about my plans and actions—and was regarded as such by Moscow society. Indeed, I would often go to see him and Raya when I went to Moscow. But it was precisely because of their openness to everyone that I began to visit less frequently and kept all my work on *Archipelago* from Lev, as well as my absences at various hiding places because of it. This caused Lev a great deal of pain and prevented him being informed about me in the way that everyone expected of him. And since, ideologically, we were drifting further and further apart, I also didn't let him in on my preparations for certain political and social writings and moves (*From Under the Rubble*).

Next, Lev was angered by "Peace and Violence,"[77] whereas my *Letter to the Soviet Leaders* he read only after my expulsion, and wrote a vast, incensed rebuttal, seeing it as a betrayal of noble liberalism. As a result, once I had been expelled, there was no clandestine correspondence between us, and Lev became increasingly disheartened and jealous that he wasn't informed about me anymore, had no news to pass on, and could not guide me about whom to befriend in the West, and whom to steer clear of.

And before long, something about Lev changed drastically. From our many friends in common, and later from random visitors to Moscow, I began to hear in letters and verbal accounts, and with increasing emphasis and bitterness, that he'd started lambasting and disparaging me in Moscow, or simply swearing about me—in anyone's home, in any company, wherever the talk turned to me.

I was at a loss. We'd rubbed along so well in the *sharashka*, spent hours in heartfelt conversation, always been so close despite our differences of opinion even then—and now this, all of a sudden? What's happened to you? I can't keep giving you the benefit of the doubt, and we can't have it out from opposite sides of the Curtain. And yet the invective is rattling around Moscow, out of control.

And it proved extremely poisonous, because Lev mixed constantly with Westerners as a highly authoritative interpreter of Soviet life and, indeed, "the person closest" to me, who knew me inside out—and all his opinions were just as authoritatively communicated to the West, becoming firmly entrenched there among the intelligentsia, in literary studies, and in the press: that my literary ability was limited solely to what I had seen for myself, that I couldn't manage anything else; that my Lenin was an artistic success only because I was describing myself—he had my cruel and terrible character as the leader of a ruthless party; that my party was already being put together in real life—it was extreme Russian nationalism and would be more terrifying than Bolshevism. Kopelev went on to conflate me even with Stalin and the Ayatollah Khomeini, while "member of the Black Hundreds,[78] monarchist, theocrat" were some of his mildest monikers.

Nevertheless, in 1978, the Kopelevs instructed a Western journalist to pass me their congratulations on my sixtieth birthday. In 1979, Kopelev publicly denied having assisted Řezáč in any way (the latter had thanked Lev in his foreword) and said Řezáč's book was grubby. In 1980, when the Kopelevs emigrated, I sent Lev a friendly and conciliatory letter. At the time, still not appreciating all the consequences of his hostile rumor-mongering, I wrote: "In years gone by I was saddened by rumors that reached me, from various people, that you were speaking of me with animosity. I've never spoken ill of you anywhere, either verbally or in writing, and should a copy of *Circle-96*, which has now been published, come your way, you will see that my affection for you has not diminished one iota." Lev replied that there had been no animosity, merely disagreement. A formulaic correspondence now arose between us—on birthdays, at New Year, one time they sent us "Christ is Risen" greetings at Easter. It seemed relations might return to normal altogether. Lev warned that he didn't want any public or private discussions, and I wasn't desperate for them either. I did remark to him on one of his public speeches, though: "You're spot-on about a 'united German nation' but why don't you tell it like it is about the GDR? Who else knows it (and its people) if not you?" —He'd mentored many East German shapeshifters who had converted from National Socialism to Communism. Even today he is a very eminent and respected figure in the FRG. He has publicly stated that he forgives the Germans both as a Jew and a Russian—and the Germans craved forgiveness, as well they might! who isn't hounding them even today? —"If you can find time to vilify an old Russia which doesn't exist, the GDR is right there, and most certainly does." I was pleased, however, that unlike most Third Wave émigrés, he was "well disposed toward a metaphysical Russia." Lev was indignant at this: he was not "well disposed" toward Russia, but loved it passionately, it was his native country—he sent me an edificatory letter, running to twelve long pages. Why he went easy on the GDR, he didn't explain. He did, however, express a "sad and bitter pity" for me and called me a "Soviet-made anti-Communist" living in "isolation," although he contradicted himself by also mentioning a host of "sycophantic admirers" and suggesting that Suslov and I were kindred spirits.[79] He made sure to lash out at Reagan as a "Hollywood cowboy." But what staggered me was his opinion that what I said and wrote was *not what I thought*, that these weren't my true beliefs—I was merely convinced that they must "be instilled in the people and the leaders."

Well, then, how could we engage in further conversation? No matter how I'd been railed against in both East and West for thinking the wrong thing or writing the wrong thing, no one before Kopelev had contrived to level the charge that what I wrote was not what I thought. . . .

Then again, should I be reproaching him? . . . Did Lev really *think* this about me? No, certainly not. It was the suffering of disappointed love that thrummed within him, so to speak: how in the world could I have ceased to be his confidant? have pulled away from him? Outwardly, Lev could be tough when angry, but his heart was vulnerable and soft.

And so again we shifted to the formulaic picture postcards and birthday telegrams. . . .

After the nonsense in Proffer's article, however, since he and Kopelev were such friends, I couldn't resist asking Lev for an explanation: how was I to understand the heinous phrase claiming that I had "stayed up late nights to catch the enemy of the people, this sellout to atomic America"? After all, it referred only to Lev himself. He was the one doing the catching, not me.[80]

A reply from Lev rolled in—sixteen long pages of it.[81] A great many reminiscences, and distorted ones to boot: after *From Under the Rubble* (as I come across in it, in other words), I "had become an ordinary member of the Black Hundreds" and "a Bolshevik turned inside out"—but there was *not one word* to explain that phrase of Proffer's! To be fair, he included four small Xeroxed pages from his own book[82] about the *sharashka*. I read them. There was none of that calumny there.[83] All the same, it was different from what had appeared in the wretched little magazine,[84] it wasn't the same. It was more malicious, and also led him into a ridiculous flight of fancy whereby I'd attempted to curry favor in the *sharashka* in front of the KGB girls. Er, Lev, you're a fine one to talk about "currying favor": in the speech-articulation group, there I was, pronouncing ruthless sentences on high-level covert telephone systems, and for that I was packed off to the camps—but, when I'd gone, you hung on for four years, safe and sound, in your very same role, so you had to have *gotten along*, right? —Lev was also extremely nasty[85] about our pleasant lab chief, Trakhtman ("Roitman" in *In the First Circle*).*

Our friendship in prison had been so harmonious—and now it had collapsed foolishly, enviously, pettily. How painful.

We shall never now reach an understanding on this Earth, I suppose. If *The Red Wheel*, he writes, is a "Black Hundreds fairytale about a Judeo-Masonic conquest"—had he ever peeked inside the book?—what could we write to one another any more?

When Heinrich Böll died, I saw from his posthumously published correspondence with astronomer Dr. Theodor Schmidt-Kaler that, "from the explanations of his Russian-speaking friends" (and who were they, if not Kopelev and Etkind?), Böll went to his grave with the impression that I was hostile to any diversity or freedom of opinion. (This was the interpretation he'd been given of the as-yet-untranslated "Our Pluralists.")

---

* Now, in Moscow, I have met up with Avraam Mendelevich Trakhtman. He had read Lev's book and was most aggrieved by its unfairness. After all, he respected Kopelev very much, and tried in any way he could to make prison life easier for him. And here's a good story: upon his release, Kopelev had asked Trakhtman to provide him . . . a reference for rejoining the CPSU. . . . (Author's note, 1995.)

Oh, Lev, Lev. I have borne my outward success in life with equanimity, whereas you have not. Not mine, nor your own.

Here my friendship with Lev came to an end. How bitter.

Ever since he emigrated to Paris, fifteen years ago now, that soft-spoken grandmaster of vituperation, Sinyavsky, has also used the "oral propaganda" method against me. In the more tightly knit Parisian circles, it was "Solzhenitsyn is a cancer on Russian culture"; in wider circles, in speeches to émigré groups: "what a great writer has perished for want of criticism!," spoken with Tartuffe-like regret. He spoke on the radio, too, of course. And again at the Wilson Center and in other key Washington circles. Again too, and more and more robustly as the years passed, in the foyers of all the literary and Slavist conferences he never tired of attending. Shrewdly taking the measure of his listeners, he would launch against me long-blooming maledictions, with subtle variations according to time, place, and audience. Against the backdrop of this tireless, persistent campaign, Sinyavsky's appearances in print were less frequent and more cautious; however, they too were mind-boggling.

After replying publicly in 1974 to his "Mother Russia, You Bitch" article,[86] I held my tongue for a full eight years until "Our Pluralists" (1983). That essay evidently threw Sinyavsky very much off balance (had he really expected me never to utter the least word in reply?). He was particularly wounded by "Our Pluralists" coming out quickly in French as well.[87] (I hadn't planned its translation into any language—it was an article for Russians—but Claude Durand wanted a translation, believing that there was no shortage of such sentiments in France, either.) The Russian article was already six months old, and no one had responded to me in Russian, but now, on foreign turf, Sinyavsky had to reply right there and then. Within a matter of days, he spoke out in both *Le Monde* and *Le Nouvel Observateur*.[88]

He didn't respond (nor ever thereafter, nor did anyone else) to the main arguments taken as a whole. But at this point, for the French papers, that wasn't what he needed, but rather something quick and incisive to prevent "Our Pluralists" making an impression. He lashed out with "the dispute is about freedom of thought and speech" (it wasn't, not at all, but it was a very convenient hobbyhorse), "we are being forced into unanimity," "is this not a relapse into Marxism?" He was too hasty to lash out, since a patient French reader could easily check that my article contained nothing of the kind. His (fairly correct) calculation, however, was: who would bother flicking through to see that I had actually written, "In the whole universal flux there is one truth—God's truth, and, consciously or not, we all long to draw near to this truth and touch it." Whereas Sinyavsky had the snappy: "There is one truth, and it belongs to Solzhenitsyn." (Etkind was fast on his heels: "The truth is one, God's truth, and it is he, Solzhenitsyn, who knows it.")

Oh, where are those worthy men of centuries past, possessed of sophisticated understanding and the ability to debate with balance and high-mindedness? Why is it that today, even among *aesthetes*, all discussions degenerate into crooked lies? It is astonishing that Sinyavsky, refined as he is said to be, lowers himself to the infamy of blatantly falsifying quotes, and not just once but far too often.

In "Our Pluralists" I write about an elite that has been suborned by the authorities: "they all lived for decades in the capitals, and several of them served . . . as Marxist philosophers, journalists, feature writers, lecturers, cinema directors, or radio producers, even as Central Committee propagandists, Central Committee consultants, or—yes—in the public prosecutor's office, and to us down below, in the camps or the provinces, they looked (as they were) indistinguishable from the Central Committee men and the Cheka[89] men, from the Communist regime. They lived in harmony with it, they were not punished by it, they did not fight against it. *And when I was getting ready, in the pervading hush of the Soviet '50s, to make my first breach in the wall of the Lie—they, and their lies, were what I had to break through, and I could expect no support from any of them.*"[90] —Sinyavsky quotes only the sentence that I have italicized here, and inserts the false claim that I applied it to the "Russian intelligentsia" *as a whole*. Furthermore, he appends his own seedy personal note: *to those* who "marveled at, and warmly supported" *Ivan Denisovich*. (So could there be anyone more ungrateful and unfair than that Solzhenitsyn?! —And right there and then he has the nerve to call me his *kum*,[91] claim *kum*-ship with me for some reason.[92] It's an odd ruse: we've only ever met once, though he and Alya served as godparents to Aleksandr Ginzburg's son at his christening.)

What's more, he sows this fertile little seed (now in the *Observer*, having crossed the Channel):[93] Solzhenitsyn is fanning a new, "very dangerous myth" that the West is allegedly infected with Russophobia. Reiterating that Solzhenitsyn "hates the Russian intelligentsia" and especially "blames Jews, Poles, Latvians," he concludes with a dramatic flourish: does not Solzhenitsyn's "myth" in fact support Soviet propaganda that the imperialist world is striving to annihilate Russia? Meaning, Solzhenitsyn's idea is "pregnant with the idea of war"! (The BBC immediately seized the chance to broadcast the interview to the USSR in Russian.)

He had calculated cleverly: I'd already been stigmatized as a "warmonger" in the West (for demonstrating the hollowness of détente), so this accusation would have legs. As for "anti-Semite," it was not the first time he'd said it—but how he had enlarged upon it.

Having either gathered momentum or screwed up his courage, Sinyavsky now declared that henceforth there would be "open civil war" between him and Solzhenitsyn. (He just forgot to check it against my work schedule.)

Evidently, there was no need to teach our pluralists how to falsify quotations in a debate. Following on from Sinyavsky, the émigré *Tribuna* (*Tribune*) (no. 5, January 1984) in New York took up the baton during those same weeks. And it contained several falsifications at once.

I'd written about the African standards of living in our homeland, about great and terrible goings-on, but "our pluralists fail to notice that Russia is dying"; they have but one concern: "whether unlimited freedom of speech will triumph the very day after the present regime is overthrown . . . and how extensive are the territories over which their free thoughts will flutter tomorrow? They do not even stop to ask themselves how they will build the *house* to do their thinking in. Will they have a roof over their heads? (And will there be real, not ersatz, butter in the shops?)"[94] —Utterly unaware of any irony at their own expense, they tarred me in all earnest as rejecting freedom of speech and worrying about butter instead. In the meantime, they wrote, "is it really not obvious that, where there is freedom and pluralism (even too much, even in excess), there is also meat and bread (also in excess)?"[95] It all comes so easily to you. . . .*

I'd found it comical that pluralists here would openly complain that the mass of ordinary "Jewish émigrés find American freedoms dangerously excessive. It is impossible to read [Shragin's] complaints without smiling"[96]—and I list their wishes *as set out by Shragin himself.*[97] This is misrepresented twice in *Tribuna*: firstly, as if the wishes were *mine,* and then as if they didn't refer to the States but were my "interdictions" for a future Russia.[98]

* The reformers of the 1990s proceeded to demonstrate to a destitute Russia that you can have all the freedom you like, but can many people actually afford butter and meat? (Author's note, 1998.)

Is this any way to conduct a debate? Or is it just that you don't have any objections at heart? (Again in *Tribuna*, they revealed with breathtaking candor, confirming my dismay: "it doesn't matter if that homeland is confined solely to Moscow oblast, and next door lies a friendly or fraternal Ryazan oblast," just so long as you can buy a ticket, they said, as you can from France to Germany . . .[99])

Alya pointed out the main falsifications in a brief, no-nonsense memo in *Vestnik RKhD*.[100] Well? If you have been traduced, then take outraged exception! No, they said nothing. And, if you've been caught stealing, then hands off! Nothing of the sort. Another year went by (making it two since Sinyavsky's first distortion) and now, in his in-house magazine, *Syntaxis,* having already been caught red-handed, Sinyavsky repeated the same fabrications word for word without batting an eyelid[101]—that I'd been attempting to break through the "Russian intelligentsia" rather than breaching the corrupt elite, plus the same old "relapse into Marxism," plus I was no longer merely his *kum* but "very close *kum*." (Can't you just feel what a long-standing and firm friendship we had? how many bottles of vodka we had drained together? so he, more than anyone, knows this man on whom he passes judgment.)

One must assume that his pen had become enfeebled. If you've been exposed as a liar, and if two years have gone by—why not write a completely new article? why drag up all the same sundry falsifications here too? Why was he so loath to part with them? This happens only to the destitute, when eking out an existence on leftovers.

It's true, he had freshened it up a little over the two years. Now he had come up with: "For Solzhenitsyn, Evil and the Lie began with the Renaissance" (another falsification—what I'd said was: that's when the erosion of public morality began), and this so that he could stand, hands on hips, and say, "I personally submit that the Lie and Evil began with the Fall." He *personally*!—without reference to Scripture and the Church, do you grasp the scale here? Solzhenitsyn himself, meanwhile, was an "undereducated patriot."[102] Ah, how all these thinkers preen before me because they graduated from a Soviet, Marxist-ridden humanities faculty. —Roughly another year went by and Israel Shamir, again in *Syntaxis*, reiterated the same, the very same fabrication from *Tribuna*, attributing Shragin's quotation to me. It was the focus of his accusations.[103] Granted, Shamir might have slipped up, but Sinyavsky was well aware that it was a lie, and Alya had shown this too in her "Memo." So maybe restrain the author? correct him? No. (And in the next issue of *Syntaxis* the same fabrication had spread to Vail/Genis as well.[104] It had stuck and could not be removed.)

What is one to think of this man? How could a surpassingly refined aesthete wage war with such weapons?

He explained himself to us as follows: "When I read or write, I am supremely frank. I take off the mask I usually wear in life."[105] Leaving unexplored his reasons for always wearing a mask in life, is it a supreme frankness that these epistolary devices reveal? . . .

Incidentally, he didn't abandon oratorical devices, either. Once again he went on a tour of the States to address Third Wave émigrés: "Why would you listen to Solzhenitsyn? His admirers are Black Hundreds! And his Parvus[106] represents the Yid incarnate!" (That appeal again: Jews, wake up! help! throw a punch!)

So, what does this lover of enmity want from me?

His long-running obsession with "the Solzhenitsyn theme" raises émigré eyebrows: it's as though he is unable to digress, be distracted, take an interest in anything else, as if he has chosen this as his lifelong role, as if he's taken it upon himself as an ineluctable mission. Some juxtapose it with his pardon and early release from camp, with his preferential emigration—without an Israeli visa—straight to France, retaining his Soviet passport into the bargain (as well as a great collection of old icons—unheard of); plus his erstwhile cloak-and-dagger cooperation with the KGB, which he has written about himself (*Spokoinoi Nochi* [*Goodnight*]), as has his childhood friend, Sergei Khmelnitsky, now too.[107] And they conclude that he's been unable to disentangle himself from the "ministry of truth."

Others, on the contrary, regard Sinyavsky's reputation as unimpeachable, his authority incontestable, and see his persistent preoccupation with me as the legitimate intensity of a principled debate.

But *is there* a principled debate? After all, out of falsifications, distortions, and substitutions, Sinyavsky incessantly fashions my ideas and words into straw men and then knocks them down, points a finger at them, daubs them in pitch, and invites anyone who wishes to join in. He himself, given his refinement—aesthetic if not intellectual—and his genuine ability *to read a text*, cannot truly find such aberrations in my work, or even believe they exist.

So, what to make of it all?

No, I don't think the *root* of his attacks has any external motivation, nor is it a clash of views. It is more deeply personal.

Amid the spotlights and thunder of *Archipelago*, my sudden, enforced arrival in the West—where he had only just settled, only just published his camp-based *A Voice from the Chorus*—evidently generated phantom terrors about his *fiefdom*. His darkly fantastical imagination endowed me with attributes and intentions that couldn't have been further from my mind. The Sinyavskys, man and wife, were unable back then, in the early months, to contain these fears that I wanted "to eat, to destroy" him, that I was establishing a "dictatorship," thinking only of "my own crown." It would seem that this painful obsession did not pass and he began to refashion it into a "debate." Simply put, my existence thwarts him to the point of exhaustion, and therein lies my guilt.

It is old hat, fruitless, depressing. . . .

Émigré publications were everywhere, too many to count. And they did not forget me—they most surely did not.

It turned out that even the dissident human-rights activist Lyudmila Alekseeva had—and I'm not joking—published a book containing reflections on the harm wrought by Solzhenitsyn.[108] And with nifty scissors, Aleksandr Yanov also clipped out enough to sound the alarm in a book for, I think, the fourth or fifth time. And anonymous authors seethed away in *Syntaxis*. And, foaming at the mouth, the socialist Leonid Plyushch responded to "Our Pluralists" with fresh imputations, and seriously surpassed himself with a verbal pirouette that went as far as a *Protocols of the Elders of the Soviet Union*.

Using "anti-Semitism" against me was one of the KGB's very first impulses even before I was expelled—and then they doggedly promoted it though new émigrés to the West. From Sinyavsky's interview with Olga Carlisle[109]—and see, thenceforth—what an intense longing to accuse me specifically of anti-Semitism. Not content with their own strength and intelligence, perhaps, they were forever striving to set Jews against me, to get Jews to sort me out once and for all.

And who didn't try their strength against me, who didn't write an incriminatory open letter to Solzhenitsyn? Some atheist Krutikov challenges me to a public debate, to prove to him that God exists, no less—on with a letter to Solzhenitsyn. —Pyotr Egides has reviewed and totted up those who have spoken out yet again in defense of Sakharov and Bonner—how dare Solzhenitsyn say nothing this time?[110] On with the public shaming! —And from the tireless Belotserkovsky comes the definitive verdict: "By your silence, you have placed yourself outside the Russian people, outside the community of people with a conscience and, as far as I understand it, outside Christianity!"[111]

What kind of democracy, what kind of conscience is it that inveighs against someone not for what they said but for what they *didn't* say? that needles a writer because he *didn't* make a public statement that this, that, or the other dissident wanted? How shrill they are. I defended Sakharov when I was under the ax myself, and those in the West said nothing. And when all the presidents, all the prime ministers, all the parliaments, and the pope have spoken out in his defense—then why ever would you want, speaking from a place of utter safety, the voice of that racist, chauvinist Solzhenitsyn, who doesn't understand anything properly and distorts everything?

And now that Sakharov has, thank God, been restored to academe,[112] am I permitted to be numbered again among Christians and the Russian people? or not yet?

The dogs growled, the ravens scowled. Was there any, any creature's snout that passed up a judging shout?

. . . And then there was the satirist, Voinovich, "the Soviet Rabelais." In the past, a brilliant exposé of the flatmate who pilfered half his loo—with one stroke, he wreaked vengeance on the neighbor and became one of Russia's literary greats. Now to wreak vengeance on Solzhenitsyn. (Over and above merely existing—and that was the main issue—I was guilty in his eyes of having once, at the insecure start of his life in the West, given him, through friends, unsought advice: that he shouldn't go to court to resolve his financial claims against an impoverished émigré publisher, but should somehow sort it out without the courts. He absolutely exploded, and responded with invective.) Wreak vengeance—and yet another immortal creation of Russian literature will arise!

It has to be said that, although Voinovich was absolutely livid with me, and this came across even in direct speech, nevertheless he wasn't quite Flegon. His book about the future of the Soviet Union[113] was a faint-hearted replication of Orwell, and its portrayal of the Soviet world wasn't funny, but its nonchalant storytelling, combined with a dynamic plot, wasn't bad. As for me (a key figure in the story), it was entertaining in parts of the introductory descriptive section. It's amusing to see the funny aspects of yourself, even in the most malicious caricature, but what didn't work was that Voinovich made no sparkling discoveries of his own. He just clattered along in the same old rattling charabanc, with me as the frightfully fearsome leader of a Russian nationalism that loomed over the world. Our secluded life in Vermont was derided in biting satirical terms; fine, let's share in the laughter, although his grotesque send-up of me went to extremes. What Voinovich did pull off was planting the illusion in the reader's mind that he'd in fact been to see me in Vermont, that he was *writing from life*—who would be so bold as to invent such a thing from beginning to end? For a long time, he was referred to as "a reliable witness" of my life in Vermont. (Whereas we weren't even acquainted, we had never spoken or exchanged a single word.) But the pity lay in how clumsily and unskillfully Voinovich served up his outlandish lampoon of authentic language—here he was let down by spite; after all, it wasn't the language's fault that the satirist didn't catch its spirit. And the book was particularly weak where the author's claims to a literary caliber of his own showed through in such earnest.

Voinovich went on to lose all sense of balance in his comedy, attributing to his odious hero both the status of a true, but secret, son of Nikolai II, and the sweet and cherished notion of becoming tsar with, of course, the most imperialistic impulses. What tawdriness of imagination, what small-mindedness. —And he strode beyond all these already satirical thresholds into mass reprisals and executions. The book came out with a cover mocking Saint George on his steed, but the face was mine; turning up in Moscow now, it will do a good job of inciting the pseudo-intellectual public into hatred and fear, which are rampant there as it is.

As to myself—gazing round amid the tightening whirling chorus, the words of Aleksei Konstantinovich Tolstoy spring to mind:

I am no great Laocoön,
Bare hands against the sea snakes' coil,
But humbly see I'm set upon
By trifling rainworms from the soil.[114]

They've got it into their heads that I want to take power—and for years now they've been working together on their lilliputian task to ensure I "not come to power"—for nothing could be worse than that.

There are more printed pages whirling around than any one person can absorb. Not everything floating in the water can be taken on board. But I am saved by my fortunate inner disposition: no irritation, however strong and sudden, no petty vexation stays with me for more than a couple of hours: they're automatically quelled within me by the pull of my work, and there I am at my desk.

"Our Pluralists" was my only response during thirteen years in the West. From "Our Pluralists," indeed, I noticed that I bore no ill will toward even my fiercest attackers, and became angry only when they were up to their doctoring and falsifying tricks. I wished them no personal ill at all, and not because of the Christian commandment to "love your enemies," but rather from a sort of benign indifference: if it wasn't them, it would be someone else; they are part of the elements. There's no escape from badmouthing. Was it on account of age?—you become unresponsive to whatever nonsense is said about you.

Don't fight all day—claws wear away.

CHAPTER 12

Alarm in the Senate

Practically all the abuse leveled at me over these years has been political—it's very rarely about actual literature. And it's been this way not only among émigrés but also, generally speaking, the American public. Translations, especially of my major books, are inevitably very late, and at the exact time that *August 1914* and, soon afterwards, *October 1916* came out in Russian, American journalists were insisting that I had long since stopped writing—I'd written myself dry. However, a witty note appeared in the literary magazine, the *New Yorker*, in February 1986: its author had been utterly unable to find *Archipelago*, not one volume of it, in a very well-known New York bookstore, and the surprised salesman had even asked him what the book was about, and sent him away from the World History and Current Events sections to the Fiction department. But it wasn't there either, and there, too, none of the salespeople knew anything about it. The author of the piece looked around: "No Dragon or Minotaur," he said, "would be more daunting than the antagonists Solzhenitsyn would encounter in the US." He had been through the war, the camps, cancer, had buried his notes, tightly rolled up, in a bottle in the earth, had mastered the new craft of concealing manuscripts, shot them onto microfilm, constructed his whole life around secrecy, donned a mask of indifference, then openly fought the state "as an equal"—and, now he has reached our shores, what does he meet here?—"cupidity, boredom, sloppiness, indifference."[1]

Ah, if only it had been indifference! . . . What blissful calm would have prevailed—for my work, for me, for my family.

Is there a law obliging adverse circumstances to bunch together? It's well known that troubles never come singly—they breed. The same summer, 1984, when Scammell's book came out, bringing down on me an avalanche of American invective, that same summer we received from Yuri Kublanovsky a long article, still in typescript form, to read. It was by Lev Loseff, about *August 1914*. (Loseff, coming from the very heart of the Leningrad literary milieu, was now, and had been for several years, a professor at Dartmouth College, just nearby. He lived forty miles from us, but we had never met or, until that moment, corresponded.)

Alya and I read the article with mixed feelings. It was, at last, an attempt at serious literary analysis, pretty well the first, and we marveled at the way this critic had utilized, with equal success, both ends of the "long glass": he proposed that the reader should sometimes observe the past and future prospects through a historical telescope, sometimes try to catch the assonances, spot the alliterations through a phonetic microscope. He sought a genre precedent for *The Red Wheel* (rightly rejecting a comparison with *War and Peace*); he reflected fruitfully on the roots of my prose and on the "quality factor"; he understood correctly that my language is not artificial, not an invention but, simply, that "Solzhenitsyn's pen does not allow the Russian language any slacking." At the same time there were also strange failures of perception: the chapter about Nikolai II was a "satirical tale, pamphleteering" (it was nothing of the kind!); and "the Lenin essay was also satirical" (here I would say, immodestly, that I'd dug rather deeper than that);[2] and he, too, said that it seemed I'd borrowed "a good deal from the experiment of *Petersburg*" by Andrei Bely (which I have still, even now, not opened)—these appeared to be the professional errors of a prejudiced template, of certain generally accepted judgments. Loseff calls himself a disciple of Bakhtin, but he is not without nods to Freud: it seemed to him that the "repressed id" in Bogrov is seeking compensation, "aspires to be the center of attention" (how that Freudism simplifies everything, and all in the same way). Loseff also noted that the two-volume structure of *August* was not all of a piece (and that's true: it was not constructed in one fell swoop).

He analyzed the "Bogrov-Stolypin antithesis" at length, in detail, approaching it from different angles. He acknowledged that my version of Stolypin's assassination had been worked out "thoroughly, and with that almost excessive respect for the historical material that is characteristic [of the author]." And that Bogrov himself "named, as one of his motives, revenge against the government for the anti-Jewish pogroms" ("I fought for the welfare and happiness of the Jewish people"—these were Bogrov's actual words before death). Then Loseff got carried away with his analysis of my representation of Bogrov: although the author never uses the word "snake," Bogrov was, he said, given a snakelike form. But Loseff immediately contests his own view: "So what? The snake is in everyday use as a figurative term of abuse." But no, the sophistication or the passion of this penetrating reader carries him over into structural generalizations: "The mythologem of the conflict between Good and Evil, Light and Darkness, the Cross and the Serpent is clearly outlined"—he'd got carried away! And he sailed on further: "In the image of the snake that has bitten and killed the Slav knight, the anti-Semite will have no trouble seeing a parallel with the *Protocols of the Elders of Zion*." But why on earth was he dragging the *Protocols* in, when there's neither hide nor hair of them here, and Bogrov is definitely not part of any conspiracy? However, "Solzhenitsyn bears no more responsibility for an anti-Semitic reading of his book than Shakespeare does for such an interpretation of *The Merchant of Venice*." And the narrative is on multiple planes: behind the historical, the philosophical is revealed, behind the political, the anthropological. "In essence, we are no longer talking about Bogrov and Stolypin, revolutionaries and reformers, or Russians and Jews, but about an existential conflict built into human nature itself. . . . Here, 'pure reason' gone mad attacks the 'organic principle.'" —And Loseff finishes with a mixture of sad irony and faint hope, which explains the title of the article:[3] "Judging by its powerful opening, *The Red Wheel* is a letter to the whole of the Russian people. If the wheel reaches Moscow, the letter is read and taken to heart—then there can be no doubt that Russia will have a splendid future."

That article could perhaps have invoked some kind of response in the émigré press, but of course would not have constituted a new stage in the course of *events*, if Loseff, away in Europe for the summer holidays, hadn't compressed the article (before it was even published!) into a radio program. And he read all of this out in his own voice on Radio Liberty—including the bit about the *Protocols*—to its listeners under Soviet rule.

And what was the result?—that Radio Liberty had somehow broadcast into the USSR (at the American taxpayer's expense) "sympathy with the *Protocols of the Elders of Zion*"? . . .

At first glance, this latest action, the radio broadcast, was no greater a step than when Loseff, in his enthusiasm, had stepped from the plain, run-of-the-mill snake towards the biblical Serpent and the *Protocols*. But no such luck—it wasn't seen that way—and it would have been more surprising, in fact, had a distorting anger not immediately flared up.

It came pouring out over a few days in two internal reports addressed to James Buckley, president of the joint American radio stations, Radio Liberty and Radio Free Europe. One ("An Openly Anti-Semitic Program") was signed by Lev Roitman of Radio Liberty's Russian Service, the other (much longer) by Vadim Belotserkovsky, also from that Service.

The former wrote that, "Solzhenitsyn's book aside, the presentation of the terrorist and his victim in RL's broadcast goes beyond 'intellectual' anti-Semitism but features [a] brand of racist, biological attitude towards Jews. . . . It is an insult to [the] listeners and employees [of the station]." And the scribbler proposed to send a recording of the program to US senators and congressmen, "to clarify if RFE/RL's public funding is meant for broadcasts of such nature."[4] The way he put this made it serious—he was trying to nail the director via the budget.

All together now! The second whistleblower, in his customary, hysterical style, came out with: "This program amounts to propaganda for extreme anti-Semitism and complements the CPSU's and KGB's anti-Semitic propaganda, which has not yet ventured to quote the *Protocols of the Elders of Zion*, Hitler's favorite book." So there they were, all much of a muchness. And, he continued, Loseff's "reminder that the *Protocols* are a vile anti-Semitic fabrication" is nothing but a "cynical trick," given that the quote "agrees with the main idea of the broadcast, that Bogrov personifies the 'Jewish Serpent.'" And, moreover, Stolypin had "ruined the evolutionary development of the country" (when that was precisely what he was trying to get on track) and, he said, a program so full of praise for Stolypin discredited the station—in whose eyes, do you think?—those of "Russian patriots"! They were the ones the denunciator worried, agonized about most.[5]

And there was a third report as well, from Liberty staffer Leonid Itselev (but I didn't see that one).

And what a volcano erupted! Loseff had really fouled up! He had put that out on air (with the thoughtless cooperation of Yuri Schlippe—who surely, with all his years at Liberty, must have realized what would happen?) and gone home to New England, where he immediately received an official interpellation from Radio Liberty: *how do you explain all this??*

He was in for a good roasting. If you're labeled a dyed-in-the-wool, "biological" anti-Semite, life won't be too comfortable for you in an American university. Loseff wrote a serious note, explaining. In it he demonstrated, correctly, that the furious attack was not, in fact, directed at him but at Solzhenitsyn—but again, in the spirit of his singular thesis, he attributed the "mythological figure of the Serpent," the "ancient creeping thing" to "Solzhenitsyn's system of metaphor." "I can easily imagine how my same analysis of the Bogrov chapters would have raised applause [from Roitman and Belotserkovsky] if I'd written: now, good people, just look what a horrible anti-Semite Solzhenitsyn is, how he hates us Jews! But what am I to do, I am not blinkered by my ethnic origin, and have no intention of simplifying either the complexity of history or the complexity of art." He defended Stolypin, comprehensively and fittingly, and finished by expressing his fear that the critics wanted to "set up jammers between Solzhenitsyn and listeners in the USSR."[6]

When all this was happening, and Loseff sent us copies of the paperwork, Alya and I felt sorry—for him. Why ever should he, with his good intentions, now pay the price? But all this was only the beginning: we'd underestimated what Loseff's interpretation of *August* could develop into. We had still not imagined all of it, all the responsiveness to sensitive issues that would be chorused by the American press, and most acutely and immediately—to "anti-Semitism." But to start with, for the next few months, it was as if nothing had happened, except that the cycle of broadcasts of *August* that had begun on Liberty was suddenly cut short. I was replaced by the repeat of a series with the same number of programs, of Vasili Grossman works—at least no one could object to those. But clearly Roitman and Belotserkovsky had not immediately found the right addresses, had at first pulled the wrong strings—but at last found the right ones. And the result of their efforts made itself known in January 1985—with a loud and well-orchestrated cannonade.

American magazines have a strange practice: they don't bear the actual date on which they're published, but a date two or even three weeks ahead (they're all racing to get "ahead"—whoever gets there first will contrive to outstrip God's time). Because of this, it can be hard to establish the actual date on which magazine articles come out; even so, the prize apparently must go to the magazine *New Republic* which, on 22 January (but dated 4 February), wrote:[7] "Is America broadcasting anti-Semitism to the Soviet Union? Incredibly, the answer may be yes . . . the announcers described Bogrov as a 'cosmopolitan,' with 'nothing Russian either in his blood or his character' . . . they contrasted Bogrov—a 'serpent' with Satanic qualities—to Stolypin, a 'Slavic knight.' They said that Bogrov's act was 'a shot at the Russian nation itself' . . . the implication that Jews are to blame for Bolshevism. . . . Not even official Soviet anti-Semitic propaganda has gone as far as quoting the *Protocols of the Elders of Zion*." But what about us?? The conclusion was that "Radio Liberty has fallen under the influence of Russian émigré zealots . . .

the Reagan administration appointed as Radio Liberty's director an émigré named George Bailey . . . he installed a group of Russian émigré broadcasters who share Solzhenitsyn's particular Russian nationalist views."

And instantly, the next day (23 January), New York's *Daily News*, having lain in wait, clearly prepared in advance, girded its loins and showed itself: "Tax-paid anti-Semitism"! The author of the article, Lars-Erik Nelson, was shouting excitedly into American ears: "Did you know that your tax dollars were being used to transmit anti-Semitic broadcasts into Russia?" It turned out that now even "Senate investigators confirm" that "Radio Liberty is often pro-tsarist . . . has repeatedly transmitted anti-Semitic commentaries to the Russian people, most often under the guise of religious or historical analysis." (And to think, meanwhile, how heatedly Liberty itself criticizes both the old Russia and the Russian consciousness.) "The most glaring example occurred . . . when Mordko Bogrov [was described] as a 'cosmopolitan'—Stalinist jargon for a Jew . . . then quoted from the . . . *Protocols of the Elders of Zion* . . . and blamed Bogrov for setting off a chain of events that led to the Bolshevik Revolution. . . . 'The average Russian is pretty much an anti-Semite', says a senior [unnamed] US diplomat." And now the radio station is saying, hypocritically, that it wants to please that "average Russian." And "Russians mutter that Lenin was Jewish on his mother's side; Leon Trotsky was certainly Jewish." Even so, the newspaper allowed that the station's anti-Semitism was not deliberate, but "the result of loose US control over a crazy-quilt collection of Soviet émigrés": in the First Wave of émigrés there were some monarchists, in the Second—"devout Russian Orthodox" as well. The Third, it's true, consisted mainly of Jews and liberals. But Bailey was also to be blamed for increasing the amount of religious broadcasting.[8]

In the West you have to look sharp! If someone lets fly at you in the press, you have to get your rebuttal into the next issue (as you do in the Soviet Union with your repentance). And James Buckley, previously a Republican senator from New York, now head of the joint radio stations, sent his rebuttal to the *Daily News* immediately: malicious slander! Our station has the strictest possible safeguards; from our five thousand hours of programs, the only one to slip past was this ten-minute piece and it was, anyway, written by a Jew.[9]

But Buckley's answer was too short—he'd probably not yet grasped the full extent and seriousness of the attack.

In the same issue of the *Daily News*, Nelson cited in response a little list that someone had prepared in advance, of where and when in 1984 Liberty had let anti-Jewish language slip through: saying, for example, that the

1919–20 series of pogroms were explained by many Jews having joined the Bolsheviks; or, in a religious program, that Jews "keep trying to debunk the Resurrection," in abiding by the version that the disciples had stolen the body (according to the Gospel of St Matthew). And on one occasion they had extolled General Wrangel—who was *known* to have organized pogroms. (There hadn't been a single pogrom in Wrangel's Crimea!) And how could all that have happened? Apparently, the station had "fallen under the effective control . . . of right-wing Russian émigrés" (who, browbeaten, did not even constitute 3 percent there).[10]

And what about the *New Republic*'s accusations? Here too they'd have to look sharp, get a rebuttal in quickly. Two magazine issues later, both Frank Shakespeare and Ben Wattenberg, the top brass in charge of Liberty, contested them: yes, extracts from *August 1914* were broadcast but it still had to be determined (and they certainly would be working to determine it!) whether or not they were anti-Semitic. And Bailey wasn't an émigré at all, he was American. And many people he'd recently appointed to key positions were Jewish. And "Jewish-oriented broadcasting constitutes a sizable block" of the Russian Service's programming. And, "under our management, stringent controls have been put into effect to prevent any possible anti-Semitic statement . . . we check our broadcasts more carefully than any other station in the world." (An important assertion; take note.) But when did the *New Republic* take up a *pro-censorship* stance? You might or might not agree with Solzhenitsyn's ideas about democracy, but they can't be ignored. We intend to carry on "airing a spectrum of responsible views."[11]

The magazine replied immediately, of course. Censorship or not—if you don't broadcast pro-Communist opinions (but, well . . . some might feel they do sometimes broadcast them . . .), then don't broadcast anti-Semitic views either. In fact, they quoted George Bailey's boss, James Buckley, following Loseff's broadcast, as saying "he was 'appalled' that 'despite meetings . . . in which we underscored in every possible way the need to pay attention to sensibilities where the subject of Jews and Judaism were concerned. . . .' "[12] (And he'd demanded that *every* text where the word "Jew" appeared be submitted to him for checking.)

And they managed to get rid of Bailey within just a month of the press attack starting. No, don't tell me that Western papers are any less powerful than the Soviet ones. In addition to Bailey, they fired another two from responsible posts, and the hapless Yuri Schlippe (as he was known at Liberty—he was "Melnikov" back in the USSR) was subjected to an inquisition-style interrogation. And, despite the "effective control of right-wing émigrés," they stopped my name even being mentioned on Radio Liberty, and did so just as thoroughly as, until then, only the USSR had done.

Between two millstones . . .

But the hullabaloo in the American press was only just beginning. Instantly, on the opposite edge of the continent—across which the Alarm had traveled at lightning speed—the *Los Angeles Times* became very agitated:[13] "The broadcast picked up several phrases that have traditionally been used by Russian anti-Semites—and even quoted a passage from the *Protocols of the Elders of Zion*." And so "closer supervision is needed over Russian and other Soviet Bloc refugees" so that their broadcasts are "consistent . . . with American values and purposes."

But all that was about radio stations in Europe, financed by American money; what about the wretched Solzhenitsyn *himself*? Why this brouhaha about the assassination of some Russian prime minister seventy years ago? And how to pronounce judgment confidently, when the book still hadn't come out in English? But the main thing, they suddenly realized, was that for several months now (in small weekly doses), America's official Voice of America had little by little, in its half-hour literary slot, been broadcasting into the Soviet Union the whole of that very story of the assassination! And, by an extraordinary coincidence—you couldn't make it up—the first broadcast in this Stolypin cycle had gone out on the Voice of America on 16 August—and the Loseff program on Liberty, quite independently, on 19 August. You might have thought it the devil's work, to sabotage the cycle of Stolypin chapters. And they instantly went after the Voice as well, screaming bloody murder: we'll get them for this!

A broadside against me followed immediately, in the *Washington Post*, America's second-most influential newspaper (4 February 1985): "Version of Solzhenitsyn novel, broadcast by VOA, causes flap. Parts of *August 1914* viewed as being subtly anti-Semitic" (in that "subtlety" they'd left themselves, for the time being, some room to maneuver—they could still retract their claws). At the same time they had polled a range of experts: there was Richard Pipes, my opponent on principle (of the shooting by Bogrov: "Solzhenitsyn does not say anything that is explicitly anti-Semitic . . . but to a Russian audience it's very clear in the way he dwells on Bogrov's Jewishness that he is blaming the revolution on the Jews. . . . Stolypin is good for Russia and therefore is bad for the Jews"—??); and Carl Proffer's widow, Ellendea, who would evidently now become one of the leading experts on Russia for many years to come ("Solzhenitsyn would say he's pro-Russian, not anti-Jewish . . . it's this Great-Russian[14] nationalism that—if you push it . . ."); and there were plenty more American historians, self-importantly repeating Lenin's appraisal of Stolypin, and saying that "Bogrov acted . . . as an agent of the czar's police"—and who on earth understands Russian history better than they do? (Since *August* didn't yet exist in English, the paper had commissioned Professor John Glad specifically to translate all the bits suspected of being anti-Semitic—only those bits, of course!—and was obliged to mention that he had "found 'no grounds for accusing [Solzhenitsyn] of anti-Semitism.'") The newspaper added, on its own account, that since, as the novel said, "'these bullets had already killed the dynasty' in 1911"—"Solzhenitsyn is, in effect, pinning the Communist victory on Bogrov."[15]

That would be just the first brand of shame slapped onto me!—already the following day, the *Boston Globe* (and it was not the only one across America, you couldn't keep track of them all) readily picked it up. It reprinted half of that same article, but tweaked the headline: "New 'August 1914' is alleged to have anti-Semitic tone" (but now without the "subtly")—and the Pipes pull quote jumped out at you, in massive type.[16]

At that time, totally absorbed in my work, I only skimmed those articles, half asleep somehow, and the tussle that was starting didn't jolt me awake.

But how was Roger Straus—who would be publishing *August* in the States—feeling about it? He could also face some kind of accusations now—and he'd have nothing to show in his defense, as Harry Willetts was taking such a very long time to finish the translation. Straus immediately, and pluckily, sent off a rebuttal to the *Washington Post*: "The suggestion that . . . *August 1914* contains passages that might be construed as even 'subtly anti-Semitic' is entirely unjustified and misguided. This will be obvious . . . when Harry Willetts's translation is published next year." The newspaper didn't print the response. Straus sent it to Claude Durand for information, and a copy to me.[17] Keep silent now?—how could I not respond to my publisher? I wrote to him:[18]

> Until now it was only in Communist countries that such techniques as these existed: 1) saddling books with public accusations, when no one had read or had the possibility of reading them, and 2) sticking crude political labels onto complex works of literature. Now, with its article of 4 February, the *Washington Post* is bringing this remarkable custom over to the United States; the newspaper is to be congratulated.

> The primitive level on which they construct their accusations is astonishing. The article also contains gross errors demonstrating an ignorance of history—saying, for example, that Stolypin was . . . the minister of *foreign affairs,* and that under him—but why, in that case, "under him"?—there were anti-Jewish pogroms; but in actual fact it was at that very time, under him, that there were none.

I could, of course, have answered this way publicly too—but I was definitely not inclined to enter into an American press discussion.

But you can't isolate yourself completely. John Train, our acquaintance from the Templeton trip, asked us to show him the places in *August* that could help refute the "subtly anti-Semitic" label.[19]

Here, too, it would have been awkward not to respond. Alya set to replying: *August* came out a year ago in French—and in France no one shouted "anti-Semitism." But here, who is to refute it, if the book is not yet accessible to readers? And what kind of reasoning is this?—if Bogrov was a Jew, and the death of Stolypin was a disaster for Russia and made it easier to start a revolution, then *that means* Solzhenitsyn blames the Jews for the 1917 revolution? In effect, they are demanding the censorship of history. Alya's clear-cut conclusion: "A writer cannot humiliate himself and his books to the extent of justifying them to journalists who have not even read those books, and to Soviet émigrés with highly dubious biographies."[20]

At this point Alya and I had a difference of opinion: generally speaking, I didn't want to respond to anyone in America or justify any of my actions. Sticks and stones . . . But Alya was far more susceptible to, and left more edgy by, this attack, and now was even compiling supplementary material for Train: a copy of my answer to Straus, an analysis of Loseff's broadcast and the stir the reports had caused, how Pipes was disregarding sources, and how lies were being told about Stolypin.

It was truly staggering: even seventy-four years after Stolypin's assassination, the truth about him could not be endured by the "free" press!

And this was how, in America, discussion of the book started up before it had been published.

But Alya and I had another shock during these weeks, and it didn't come from the Western press: while 4 February, in the States, saw the start of a long-lasting attack on my "anti-Semitism," on 19 February in the USSR, where for years now, it seemed, my name was never mentioned, they showed on TV (and, leading up to it, on many cinema screens) an agitprop film entitled *The*

Plot against the USSR,[21] containing a vile attack on both me and the Russian Social Fund, saying we were "CIA agents." They'd kept that millstone turning for many years. Two world forces at the same time, flattening me!

And that's what between two millstones is. Grind him to a powder!

But in New York, too, it was clear that the "intellectual boiler" had already been simmering for some weeks and months, before now erupting. As a result of that simmering, the conservative Norman Podhoretz, editor for many years of the right-wing Jewish magazine, *Commentary*, published his long article, "The Terrible Question of Aleksandr Solzhenitsyn"[22] that same February. But it would take the reader a good while to get to that question. Podhoretz had previously been a literary critic (then, however, moved into political commentary). And now, having retold my literary career at length for anyone wanting it, lavishing praise on Scammell's book along the way, he gave his verdict: that *Ivan Denisovich* is not a work of literature and "the impact of the story is weakened" because Ivan Denisovich does not lead an intellectual life (exactly the same idea as the Moscow pseudo-intellectuals had been circulating); well, you could just about understand the enthusiasm of Russian readers, given the meagerness of Soviet literature; but the novels *Circle*, *Cancer Ward*, *August* "are dead on the page, denied the breath of life"; on the other hand, *The Gulag Archipelago* and *The Oak and the Calf* are two of the "very greatest books of the age" (here Podhoretz runs counter to the chorus of American critics who had torn *Calf* to pieces) and "there is so much vitality in the three volumes of *The Gulag Archipelago* that it threatens to overwhelm."

And it is only at the end of the article that he approaches the burning issue of the day—so, am I an anti-Semite or not? He doesn't undertake to form a judgement himself, as the book doesn't exist in English, but—people are saying all sorts of things. However, "my own impression," he says, "based on an acquaintance with . . . everything by Solzhenitsyn that has been translated into English . . . is that the charge of anti-Semitism rests almost entirely on negative evidence. That is, while there is no clear sign of positive hostility toward Jews in Solzhenitsyn's books, neither is there much sympathy." But, all the same, my "anti-Semitic potential" remains an unsettling factor. And is that, then, what "the terrible question of Solzhenitsyn" is about? No, that's still not it. Podhoretz consolidates his place on the right flank: Solzhenitsyn is mounting "attacks on the democratic West [for its] loss of 'civic courage' . . . capitulation to the 'Spirit of Munich,' and 'concessions and smiles to counterpose to . . . bare-fanged barbarism.' . . . It is this, rather than any intimations of anti-Semitism, on which Solzhenitsyn's liberal critics have fastened in trying to write him off." And this is the "terrible question": do we really need his courage in order to escape the fate with which Communism threatens us? "To seize upon [his] anti-democratic Slavophilia . . . as an excuse for continuing to evade the challenge of his life . . . would only confirm the [truth of his] charge that we are cowards," and coming ever closer to the terrible "pit out of which Solzhenitsyn once clawed his way" so that the martyred millions might be remembered, and the living saved. —Consciously or not, Podhoretz had turned the "terrible question" into something quite different from the one that was thumping, pounding in the hearts of American pseudo-intellectuals.

Podhoretz had obviously structured the article wrongly: he'd spent too long getting to his "terrible question," with the result that no room remained for it, and few people grasped what it actually was; it ended up just a distraction. The volume of mail responding to the article was far greater than the portion published in subsequent issues of the magazine. People wrote that Podhoretz was "brushing aside thousands of pages of fiction . . . without giving a shred of specific criticism": he had given no examples, and even those who "always agreed with him" did not agree now, and argued about the novels, about Kostoglotov,[23] and asked whether, "in literary criticism . . . there is no question of right or wrong, truth or falsity? How otherwise can I square my respect for Podhoretz with my profound moral and aesthetic debt to Solzhenitsyn?" —And Scammell too had been dragged into that article quite unnecessarily, so there was something about Scammell too: it was wrong to "respect biographies too much." Instantly, Scammell himself emerged to join the fun: he was glad to have been the cause of Podhoretz's publishing such a magnificent article, but hastened to assure readers that he too, Solzhenitsyn's biographer, did not rate him highly as a novelist—he'd been misunderstood. His appraisal did not much differ from Podhoretz's—the error had been the result of Scammell, weighed down with unique biographical material, not applying himself sufficiently to the literary analysis of Solzhenitsyn that he'd planned. Otherwise, otherwise, he would have expressed everything clearly! But, actually, one cannot fail to acknowledge that, even aside from *Archipelago*, Solzhenitsyn has written some things, some things of value. . . . —And, flooding back from readers: "Solzhenitsyn spurs controversy . . . more severe than most . . . yet he offers almost the only voice . . . that carries sufficient clarity and strength to be heard." "Solzhenitsyn hit where it hurts most: he explored the issues of the costs of ideas, ideologies, and social arrangements of intellectuals to ordinary people." —But some only thanked Podhoretz over and over, saying they'd read nothing better in their lives than that article, and it was a rare writer who could write about Solzhenitsyn with such authority.[24]

And the "terrible question," as Podhoretz had posed it, was almost completely lost; and if anyone did pick up the word "terrible," they understood it as: is Solzhenitsyn an anti-Semite or not? And some remembered the Zionist prisoners in *Archipelago*, and the respect shown for the Israeli experience—no, he's no anti-Semite. Others said that Solzhenitsyn's anti-Semitism was "implicit, rather." A third view said that Jews had been "the most numerous and active perpetrators of Communism in Russia . . . what is to be gained by denying it?"; and it was a fundamental error to come out against "a possible tinge of anti-Semitism that may or may not be in Solzhenitsyn's writings," which told us about the "radical hostility of Communism to mankind as a whole." A fourth angle: Solzhenitsyn's Parvus was already a gross caricature, while Solzhenitsyn's own plan was to establish "an Orthodox totalitarianism . . . and can we be indifferent to his dark goals for Russia, as human beings or as Jews (there are about two million Jews still prisoners there)?" "The ideology of Marxism . . . at least acted as a brake on native anti-Semitism [in Russia]."[25]

And Podhoretz, concluding the exchange: "I cannot remember writing anything that has provoked so wide a range of conflicting responses as [my article] . . . but the issue that has called forth so many letters that are at once passionate and thoughtful (not a common combination in the correspondence columns of any magazine) is Solzhenitsyn and not my essay about him"; and, summarizing the discussion about novels, democracy, and Slavophilia, he himself now loses his way: "Finally, there is the 'terrible question' of anti-Semitism." Nevertheless, "in my opinion, Solzhenitsyn's evident bitterness over the fact—and it is of course a fact—that revolutionaries of Jewish origin played so important a role in bringing Communism to Russia is overridden by his consistently fervent support of Israel."[26]

With all that, Podhoretz had, if anything, restrained passions.

But that discussion would only emerge towards the summer of 1985, while the March events were developing much faster. Again Belotserkovsky's piercing squeal resounded. We don't know how many more denunciatory internal reports he had written over the past months, as they weren't published, but now, tearing himself away even from his seminal work on the threat of a "Russian military party," he helped fan the flames, in alliance with the notorious American (dyed-in-the-wool pro-Soviet) magazine, the *Nation*.

A week ahead of Belotserkovsky's actual article, the *Nation* published a summary of its contents in anticipation—and sent it out to all the American press:

Solzhenitsyn, it said, had taken control of a *network* of radio stations broadcasting in Russian (of which there were only four or five in the whole world—but how would the Americans know that?—anyway, it was clear that he'd taken them all over)!—and a press *network*!—and a network of publishing houses! He'd *monopolized* everything that was communicated to the Russian people by the Western media in the Russian language!! The influence of the Solzhenitsyn camp was growing! (only the camp itself was nonexistent)—while "democratic émigré groups lack financial resources." But the main news was that Democratic Senator Pell had already given the order to *start an investigation*! "Congress is beginning to wonder."[27]

Beginning to wonder . . . Look out!

No matter which camp the *Nation* was in, the Senate wheel had begun to turn!

Belotserkovsky's initiative was immediately taken up by Herbert Aptheker, the top theoretician of the American Communists, in their *Daily World* (which is also sold at Moscow newsstands): "the Solzhenitsyn gang is favored by the Reagan Administration"—and those were the same, the very same Russian ultranationalists, "the fascist scum . . . financed by Hitler" and set up as *gauleiters* in Ukraine and Belorussia.[28] . . .

And the *Washington Post* tried to outdo them with yet another article, "Trouble in the Air":[29] in programs broadcast into the Soviet Union by the American government, it said, there has been "a trace of anti-Semitism," giving rise to *a number of* complaints, both to Radio Liberty and to the Voice of America, which had been broadcasting Solzhenitsyn's novel. (They'd got themselves into a sticky situation with my *August*, you had to pity them, and there'd been just a little bit of the Stolypin cycle left—if only the Voice could hang on! They defended themselves as best they could. . . .)

But the *Boston Globe* rushed in even more precipitately: "The controversy is dominated by the brooding, apocalyptic presence of Alexander Solzhenitsyn. . . . Harvard's Marshall Goldman questions whether broadcasts do not even play into the hands of Soviet authorities" . . . since the Reagan administration is inclined to rely not on the current, pro-democracy Jewish émigrés from the USSR, but (a good opportunity to take a dig at Reagan) on "Great-Russian nationalists, monarchists and World War II refugees, [with] their hard-line anti-Communism." And although an official from Buckley's entourage tried to justify the station, saying that Soviet Jews constituted Liberty's most numerous and "most enthusiastic audience," and "there has been no negative feedback on any Solzhenitsyn broadcast"—no, a Senate investigation was essential![30]

Boom! Turn your guns on the Voices' sons!

And the main thing, the most important: it was necessary to bring back "strong *pre-broadcast control*" of radio programs! And, "it seems clear, from the reaction to the Stolypin broadcast, that it will be a long while before [Solzhenitsyn] is again featured on Radio Liberty." (Now that was right—you could be sure of it.)

And no American voice would be found to offer a response and make them see sense.

That campaign soon generated a reaction in England too: the *Evening Standard* (for which Victor Louis was a correspondent) joined in at the same time, repeating the verdict of the *Boston Globe* and Richard Pipes: "Solzhenitsyn considers himself the uncrowned head of Russia," refused to have lunch with the President, and his books "are implicitly anti-Semitic"; and that of Marshall Goldman: "There is a growing antipathy towards Solzhenitsyn on the part of Americans . . . he may go to live in Europe." (It was this newspaper campaign itself that had given birth to the rumor that I was already fleeing for France.) And it concluded by saying that—right now, in the next few weeks—a Senate committee would "join the anti-Solzhenitsyn artillery," and in the hearings Solzhenitsyn's anti-Semitism "will undoubtedly be raised."[31]

Yes, yes! The Alarm was swirling, the Alarm was billowing—and it could not help but soar towards the marble columns of the Capitol itself. (And it must be said: American senators and congressmen like nothing better than to be entrusted with some kind of *Investigation*, given an opportunity to sit at microphones, on lofty platforms, brows sternly knit, and display their uncommon perceptiveness and superior intellect.)

And so Hearings were convoked on 29 March 1985. Not hearings of some minor commission or subcommittee, no—but of the United States Senate Committee on Foreign Relations! The moving spirit of these Hearings was one of the leading Democrats of the United States, the worthy Claiborne Pell, a gentleman from the State of Rhode Island. That august gathering was to investigate the Enigma of how an approved—and thoroughly, super-vigilantly controlled—American radio station could plunge so recklessly into the abyss of anti-Semitism, and how that impudent Solzhenitsyn had contrived to use American money for propaganda hostile to America. (And now, lying in front of me, is the transcript of the august gathering—a hundred and forty pages of it. And all this was said in just a single day—what could they disgorge in a week?)[32]

In fact, the distrust of Radio Liberty had already begun to accumulate before this, especially after the station asked Congress for an extra subsidy of $77 million. That was when Senator Pell had sent a team of auditors from the United States General Accounting Office to the station and, while they were at it, as an extra job within their sphere of competence, he commissioned the accountants to verify how many "infringements of our policy direction" there had been, and of what nature. Whether by questioning employees in the corridors, or by some other means, the accountants had evidently obtained information that was disappointing, if not outright depressing. And now that result hovered, menacing, over the Hearing—although naturally the vice-chairman of the Board for International Broadcasting (BIB), Ben Wattenberg, now tried to voice a defense in this unsatisfactory way: "When audited and quantified by accountants—not by journalists or academics—games with numbers can be played." As for Solzhenitsyn, how could we keep his views "off the air . . . when his words are featured on page one in the *New York Times* and lead the news on the international service of the BBC?" And what are we to do "when half of the political figures in America [are] making a somewhat similar point—that the Western democracies had lost their nerve?"

Director of the Joint Radio Stations James Buckley assured the senators that the past three years on Radio Liberty had seen an especially "significant increase in attention . . . to items of particular interest to Jewish listeners."

Really? And the fact that Solzhenitsyn was quoted?

Hot on Wattenberg's heels, Frank Shakespeare, chairman of the BIB, also sought to justify the station: yes, "Solzhenitsyn is an extremely controversial figure [but] he is also a figure of awesome dimension." We have been told "that we should not be putting on [Solzhenitsyn's] statements because Solzhenitsyn is . . . unduly critical of the United States or the West. . . . Our feeling is that if you are going to be a credible operation and you take a man of the prominence of Solzhenitsyn you quote him verbatim when he says something." But the guidelines of the Station remained very strict—extremely.

For example, so as not to irritate Soviet listeners, comparing "capitalism and Communism," in the general sense, was banned; and the phrase "Communist satellite countries," as applied to Eastern Europe, was banned; and hence, Shakespeare added rather caustically, "If President Reagan were a commentator on our air . . . he would be in very frequent violation of our guidelines."

But Shakespeare insolently revealed that, in this case, in this specific case that purported to be a dispute on matters of principle, "a lot of it swirls around the emotion that surrounds one man, Aleksandr Solzhenitsyn."

Alas, that seemed to be true. The question got confused, lost focus: where ever, in truth, was democracy? where was the freedom to criticize? And then what about this damned novel that no one had read, about the anti-Semitism of which the worthy senators would have to render judgment?

Senator Pell got little for his trouble: the Hearings were wound up after a single day.

What a blunder. (They'd satisfied themselves that this whole storm had originated with those denunciatory reports.)

From the newspaper articles on the Hearings that came out at the same time, we can see that Wattenberg himself is also Jewish, as are the majority of the Liberty staff and, of course, once again: "Russian Jews are among the most receptive of Radio Liberty's audience." Meanwhile, that same *Washington Post* published a Democratic congressman's view: even assuming the objective of that hapless program was not explicitly anti-Semitic, even assuming it was historically correct, "policy guidelines that are supposed to prevent the airing of inflammatory programs were violated"—"why broadcast to the Soviet Union a program that . . . *can* be perceived as anti-Semitic?" Which meant, don't broadcast anything at all about Bogrov. "Some of these historical programs may be appropriate for US consumption" (given that they're so advanced over here!) but not "for an audience fed since birth with Soviet propaganda" (that crowd mustn't get to hear anything serious). No, no—the programs must be vetted more and more stringently *before* they go out![33]

So it's long live Advance Censorship in the United States! . . .

That's how many unforeseen developments spooled out from Loseff's chance broadcast. Maybe it was good that he threw them that bone: they all rushed in and revealed themselves tellingly. Although this whole pointless hubbub would have arisen anyway, one way or the other.

But the Alarm, the Alarm that had been stirred up, could not now abate so rapidly. It was to dissipate in ever-decreasing circles.

Even the whole Third Wave émigré press, so hostile to me, was now refusing to publish that louse Belotserkovsky—but he summoned the get-up-and-go to find, in Los Angeles, the new, recently-launched *Panorama*—and from then on he'd pour out his thoughts via that organ. Bold-font headline: "Solzhenitsyn: Soviet propaganda's 'fifth column'"! So there we are. It turns out that the body I serve is the Central Committee of the CPSU! (There was nothing new in the article—he was paraphrasing what was in the *Nation*, but formulating it more trenchantly.) Yes! The Soviet authorities have never yet had such a powerful propaganda apparatus as they do now: "Solzhenitsyn and his followers" are at their disposal—and financed by the United States! (What a powerful combination!!) That's why Soviet society has remained so passive for so long in its opposition to totalitarianism. After all, when Soviet people hear their Soviet propagandists tearing the West to shreds, they don't believe it (this is true—I didn't believe it either, when I lived in the USSR), but when they hear criticism of the West from Solzhenitsyn, then they start thinking. (If only! It's true that I don't want our people, sheep-like, unthinking, to follow in the West's footsteps—let them think where to tread.) And, magnanimously, "I shall not be discussing Solzhenitsyn's anti-Semitic propaganda here" (we'll put that off until the very near future) but, in the West, "a real, Stalin-like personality cult has been created around Solzhenitsyn . . . they are dignifying him by using his first name and patronymic![34] . . . and, at the sight of a 'Prophet' of such power, more and more new émigrés from the USSR are joining their ranks." In the end, things had gone so far and so badly that "to remedy the situation, extreme measures are essential." And in another, separate headline: EXTREME MEASURES ESSENTIAL.[35]

Despite that, and in that same, biased *Panorama*, contradicting and sometimes even sarcastic voices were heard ("Sign me up! Sign me up for the fifth column with Solzhenitsyn!"), and many Jews also protested. —Valentin Goldman: "*The Nation* is a pro-Soviet magazine. I am Jewish, and I'm sick of the accusations of anti-Semitism against Solzhenitsyn. From the pages of *Archipelago*, we felt a breath of freedom and hope. . . . And why are our homegrown liberals constantly trying to scare the West, Russia, and the émigrés with 'Russian nationalism'? Why are Russians not allowed nationalism, while Georgians, Lithuanians and Armenians are? Is that not racism—banning a people from having its own aspirations, and at the same time threatening the West with that nationalism, as Belotserkovsky is doing?" —Mikhail Galperin: "There's not a whiff of anti-Semitism in Solzhenitsyn's books." —Lev Dubinsky: the Bolsheviks "were not able to eliminate Solzhenitsyn—they were, inadvertently, too soft on him. So how can he be stopped? By slander, of course! In the USSR, lecturers are telling people about the Yid, landowner, fascist, Zionist, Vlasovite, traitor Solzhenitsyn. In the West, they are telling us that Solzhenitsyn is a KGB agent, a fascist, a Russian

Khomeini, a Kremlin fifth column. May God give Solzhenitsyn a long life and give his homeland freedom!"[36]

All that was to come later, however, in the summer and autumn of 1985—but those zealous spring attacks were not yet quite played out. (You could hear Sinyavsky's old call: come on, Jews!—give him a beating!) Still in reserve was Lev Navrozov, the *literary genius* (who had brought with him to the West several novels he'd already written, but his first, *The Education of Lev Navrozov*, hadn't been acknowledged by the crafty Westerners as the greatest writing of the twentieth century; as for his others, it seems things didn't even get that far). In the USSR he'd stayed hidden, not making a sound or gesture of opposition—he had "lived underground," as he presented himself, coquettishly, in *Kontinent* (although the next-door neighbor at his dacha was Gromyko)—but in the West he immediately became a mainstay of conservatism, the author of intransigent anti-Soviet columns in the *New York City Tribune*. (This was an almost universal law: it was those who had been quietest in the USSR that launched themselves the most boldly in the West.) But, to be fair, Navrozov had not shied away from legal conflicts with Golda Meir or the *New York Times*: if it wasn't principles, then it was rage that gripped him. Just now (1987) he has resolved to attack Sakharov too, for reverting to Soviet allegiance. Meanwhile, he writes of himself, in all seriousness: "I am blazing my own trails," "the general flow of my intellectual activity" . . . —And he has become such a steely anti-Communist that, although I knew him to be a scorpion, I didn't expect him to bite me in the flank.

But it happened. He went for me in his newspaper in February, two weeks after the first signal had been seen in the press. It seemed, from what he said, that he'd spent twenty years restraining himself, not touching me, waiting till I was no longer such a sensation and he could strike a blow—and now, finally, he could. He'd restrained himself—but now he could so clearly smell blood! He'd understood: it was the signal to strike, but, for his aim to be true, he mustn't get distracted, must concentrate on the main thing: "By now, Jews are groaning, finding ever more proof" of Solzhenitsyn's anti-Semitism.[37]

Then Navrozov, an excitable type, was transfixed by two conjectures that needled him: (1) perhaps the Stolypin volume of *August* would never be published in English—was it being deliberately kept under wraps? (2) meanwhile, if Jewish criticism of Solzhenitsyn increased, might he not flee the West for the USSR? (And what would the anti-Communism he flaunts be worth then?)

Those two conjectures had, evidently, piqued Navrozov so much that abundant consequences ensued. He embarked on a surge of activity that was outstanding by any yardstick.

Articles started flooding onto the pages of his conservative *New York City Tribune*, and not just from Navrozov himself, but from the paper's editorial staff. And what's so remarkable about this Solzhenitsyn, anyway? The Gulag?—but everyone knew all about it, even before Solzhenitsyn. And now, with his anti-West position, he's helping the Soviets. And if he's a nationalist, how can he not be an anti-Semite? And again "Solzhenitsyn: Soviet propaganda's 'fifth column'": an enlarged reprint of the headline from the émigré *Panorama*, in bold Cyrillic characters—this in an English-language newspaper.[38] . . .

Right-leaning America was rattled, became alarmed—and began to distance itself from that Solzhenitsyn: no, we'd bet on the wrong horse. (Here, again, the second millstone creaked into action, so as not to be outpaced by the first.)

But the editorials were nothing: it was Lev Navrozov himself who now rose up for the decisive, final attack. These were the headlines, plastered across two newspaper pages: "A 'Prophet' of Freedom or of Anti-Semitism? A Double-Faced Totalitarian of Stalin's Vintage; Does Humankind Need Totalitarianism with Solzhenitsyn's Face?" And the article was massive. Navrozov was refusing absolutely to understand the "phantasmagoria that the press, for twenty years, has been fashioning out of the Solzhenitsyn sensation." Can Solzhenitsyn be called anti-Communist?—that's a joke. Courage?—he hasn't shown any. The *Archipelago*?—what's so good about it? The simple fact is that Solzhenitsyn was lucky that Khrushchev published him, not the others. And in his conservative purity, Navrozov even recoils from me on such unexpected matters as: why am I "vilifying" Nikolai II, who was a "pro-Western constitutionalist"? And why do I "belong to" the Orthodox Church in America, not to the intransigent Orthodox Church Abroad? But, anyway, what was there to worry about? "The media just ignore him, and without them his greatness is gone. . . . [There are] hints that Solzhenitsyn may return to Russia . . . a beloved, if somewhat prodigal . . . son of his beloved Mother Russia." It's possible that the whole "campaign of hatred and slander against Solzhenitsyn in the Soviet media is just a show." But for eleven years he has refused to take citizenship of any Western country—why? how are we to take that? Yet the current Soviet regime has no need of Solzhenitsyn, now he's no longer the sensation he was. No—most probably they won't take him back.[39]

But even that wasn't all! There was a large advertisement in the same paper,[40] announcing Navrozov's forthcoming opus, set to appear in *Midstream* magazine (left-wing and Jewish, as it describes itself) in the June–July 1985 issue: "*August 1914* as a New *Protocols of the Elders of Zion*." Be afraid!

Midstream was one of the magazines that had written about me several times. In fact, it was the one that had published the mind-boggling idea that Mark Perakh had sniffed out (Solzhenitsyn's anti-Semitism is not in his words but in the *absence of words*: why, for example, in *Ivan Denisovich*, is the word "Yid" not used even once??—that was no accident!!).[41] It was none other than *Midstream* that had said my books (given my peasant origins) smelled of manure.[42] Its editor, Joel Carmichael, is "one of the best conservative historians of Russia";[43] and now, in that capacious magazine, Navrozov, hungry for more celebrity, launched attacks on *August*: "inferior Russian language . . . semiliterate provincial. . . . When *I* read *Ivan Denisovich*, *I* said Solzhenitsyn *might* develop into a minor novelist, which was a compliment *on my literary scale*." *August* is no novel, but a myth . . . mythical figures . . . preconceived notions." —Using his free translation from the Russian, because the book did not yet exist in English, Navrozov emphasized—more than anything else, till one's ears rang with it—the Jewish theme, over and over! —And now such a vile, anti-Semitic book "was pumped into Russia via US radio . . . until the public outcry" in America.[44] Our scorpion knew—knew very well—where to sting: the place already charred, already burned.

If I turn and look back, these disputes did, after all, begin way back with *Ivan Denisovich*, with my first appearance: why does Tsezar receive parcels? and why does Ivan Denisovich look after him?[45]

But now, during these months, when things were heating up all over America—it spread like wildfire. And the *Wall Street Journal*, sympathizing with me, naïvely suggested a way for me to *save myself*: I should write a foreword to Shcharansky's forthcoming book, and so prove that I'm no anti-Semite. (But would that actually prove it? And would it even count as commendable behavior?)

Throughout this story, what astounded me most was people's fear of truth about the past. Clearly, it wasn't only NKVD pensioners and CPSU officials who feared it—no. And at what an early stage my attackers here flew into a rage—as early as Stolypin's assassination, and immediately at the top of their voices—even though the whole Revolution, all of it, had yet to unfurl! They won't have enough reserves of anger and argument left in them.

And how fascinating, the way things repeat: I am being hounded again in the country where I live, and again because of books that are not available to read there. And, like my Soviet attackers, those here also drag any problem or idea down to a shamefully low partisan level, to name-calling and labels—so now it's "anti-Semitism"—and seek out the basest of personal accusations. They can't keep their minds out of the gutter.

I wanted to draw inward to work. What—they won't let me? Dragging me into battle, are they? How they provoke me, how they wait for me to "respond to criticism in the press" (exactly as in the USSR!), how they ache for me to adopt the stooped posture of the accused. But I won't budge—let them say what they like. (At the time, Alya made a note that I was quite ready for the hounding to increase up until the day of my death, to blot out the whole sky.)

Curses can't injure you, can't put your eyes out. We'll manage. Our adversaries hadn't taken into account my resilient nature, nor the fact that I'd been battle-hardened. I was calmly waiting out this squall. A period when you're either cursed or not talked about is the most useful one for your work: you get fewer unnecessary disturbances. It was without the slightest feeling of upset that I entered that period of demonization just as, by contrast, when *Ivan Denisovich* was published I'd entered a spell of celebrity.

But Alya suffered from this constant assault on us—suffered acutely. Unlike me, she felt she really lived in this country, where she'd been the one meeting people, communicating with them, working on both social and personal matters, and organizing various kinds of defense for the administrators of our Fund in the USSR. And—even more painful—all that invective could not fail to embarrass and bewilder our children, who lived in this country as if in their own; for the time being, it was their only country—and how many more years did they have before them here? And Alya wanted me now to start actively defending myself. My arguments, that we had to wait it out, weather the storm—wasn't sturdy silence a kind of response?—failed to convince her.

But meanwhile, there was also the *New York Times,* and it was being worn to a frazzle! The whole initiative of launching the "anti-Semitism" campaign had been snatched away by its eternal rival, the *Washington Post*, and then it rolled on and on through other newspapers—while the supreme Oracle hadn't yet managed to open its mouth. Yet it alone had the standing to decide and render definitive judgment.

And now, in mid-July 1985, I received a letter from Richard Grenier, asking whether, given the somewhat "special situation" at the moment, I might be ready to overcome my aversion to interviews and speak out? In connection with the conflict over the anti-Semitism accusations he'd been commissioned by the *New York Times* executive editor, A. M. Rosenthal himself, to write an article about it, and he would do so under the editor's direct supervision. Grenier wrote that he had read both the expanded version of *August 1914* and *October 1916* (in French; at last!—someone who'd *read* them!), and he himself had found no anti-Semitism there. Now he would question about twenty "experts," so that his account would be "balanced." But, he said, I could preempt this process before the others joined in if I decided to speak out myself, and in that way I could "put an end to the whole debate." Of course, he did accept that the time to discuss this would be when the book is published in America, and that giving interviews cannot be a writer's mission—but all the same, the debate had begun, and public opinion could harden before the book even came out. He assured me that I would not find, in all America, a more ardent well-wisher, and that he had taken in even my Harvard address with a thrill of pleasure. He asked me for an interview.[46]

Alya urged me to give it. She felt "we could win that way, going onto the attack ourselves!" I declined flatly: I must endure, stay silent for a considerable length of time, and in that way teach them restraint, wean them off their squealing. She argued: "We can't treat all these attacks like we're holy fools." Later she began to resign herself, recording that: "We've lived in glory—and we'll live in obloquy for a while."

I was absolutely sure: my proper course of action now was to stand my ground in silence for a few years. Winter's nothing new to the bear.

All the same, anything appearing in the *New York Times* would be no needle in a haystack. So, while there'd still be no interview, we decided I'd write him a letter,[47] spelling everything out clearly. The very format of a private letter, to an individual who'll understand, inclines you to explain yourself in greater depth.

17 July 1985

Dear Mr. Grenier,

I really do consider it impossible for a writer to appear in the role of advocate for his own works, especially before they are even published.

I must say I was extremely surprised that, in the United States, discussion of *August* began 1) when no readers had access to the book; 2) by attaching political labels to it. Up to now, such practices have been applied to my books only in the USSR.

As for the "anti-Semitism" label, the word has, like other labels, lost its precise meaning due to thoughtless use, and different social and political commentators over the decades have understood a variety of different things by it. If it is taken to mean a biased and unfair attitude towards the Jewish people as a whole, then I can say with confidence that not only is there no "anti-Semitism" in my works—nor could there ever be—but neither could it be present in any book worth the designation "literary." To approach a work of literature with the yardstick of "anti-Semitic" or "not anti-Semitic" is tawdriness, an underdeveloped understanding of what constitutes a work of literature. With such a yardstick, Shakespeare could be declared an "anti-Semite," and his work struck out.

However, it seems that people are starting, quite arbitrarily, to designate as "anti-Semitism" even a mention that the Jewish question existed, and was a burning issue, in prerevolutionary Russia. But at that time, hundreds of authors, including Jews, wrote about it, and then it was actually *not* mentioning the Jewish question that was considered a manifestation of anti-Semitism—and today it would be unworthy of a historian of that period to pretend that the question had not existed. If we do not want the horrors man has inflicted upon himself in the twentieth century, all the forms of revolutionary and ethnic genocide, to happen again—we have to study history as it was, obeying only the demand of historical truth, with no concern for the possible censorship of today, the "what will people say?" or "how will that be taken?"

I am unfurling *The Red Wheel*—the tragic history of how Russians themselves, in an act of folly, destroyed both their past and their future—but I am having the vile accusation of "anti-Semitism" flung in my face, being bludgeoned with it: my accusers are basely trying to trip me up with a series of false arguments.

All the claims put forward in the press up to now, regarding the historical element of my epic, either rely on incorrect information or are mere assertions. As for Bogrov, not only did I study thoroughly and use *all* the material on him, but in my explanation of his actions I accepted the motives advanced by his own brother, who wrote a book about it (V. Bogrov, *Dm. Bogrov and the Assassination of Stolypin,* Berlin: Strela, 1931).

If you wish, you may use this letter, in any form you see fit, for your article.

I am pleased that you will not judge based on rumors, as most of those now speaking out do. . . .

But no, Grenier was not satisfied with that. Two weeks later he replied, at length: If your criticism of the American press is right, it is better for you to handle it yourself, "rather than let others manipulate it against you. I have the feeling" (and yes, he's right) "that you don't care very much what the American press writes about you. But what the American press gets excited about is generally reflected throughout the world." (That's also true: Europe despises the United States but closely follows life there. Say something in America, and it will resound everywhere. Say it in Europe, and America might not even hear it.) "I will quote bountifully . . . from your letter" but, in accordance with the "news story" concept, I shall also quote the opinions of your enemies. However, "if you consent to receive me in Vermont for an hour or two, it will be a completely different kind of 'news' story. You . . . are a major public figure, and as such you can 'preempt the opposition.'" The president of the United States, for example, does this all the time, and just recently New York Mayor Koch did it successfully (and then Grenier gave an example). Even if you only repeat to me, *viva voce*, what you have already written in your letter, and answer some additional questions, then "your statements in themselves become the story [and] I will not have to go to your enemies for a rebuttal. Aleksandr Solzhenitsyn will have spoken. The story will be *on the front page* of the *New York Times* and will be read everywhere." You may ask, what difference would it make if you replied by letter: it is the "vanity of the newspaper." You may ask, why should we discuss it at all—why not wait until the book is published in English? Because "this is just the way the American press works. When something is in the air, readers want to read about it. . . . Charges of anti-Semitism, as you must realize, are *exceptionally dangerous in this country* . . . there are people in the United States who are doing their utmost to destroy your reputation, and who will not wait until the appearance of your new books in English. . . . [It is] a matter of extreme urgency, to take advantage of your position as a public figure to defend yourself."[48]

And there was another heated argument at home. Alya was urging me: into battle! charge! my silence would, she said, be interpreted as "he's hiding."

But no, I was sure: this was a rare occasion when Alya's gift for making the right decision, and her enduring self-possession, had failed her. For me, appearing like this on the front page of the *New York Times* would mean a kerfuffle, hysterics, a humiliation, a display of fear. And I didn't want to accept the *Times* as my arbiter. Do they want me to swear an oath? Well I won't, not for anything! At the first sign of hounding to assume an attitude of self-justification?—that would be an indelible stain, shameful kowtowing. No way.

I replied:[49]

6 August 1985

Dear Mr. Grenier,

Thank you for your kind intentions.

But I do not feel I am in the same position as politicians: what they need is maximum impact right now, and then to get reelected—but I don't. My task is to write a truthful historical study of the Russian Revolution, and after that it's not so important to me whether my books are accepted in this particular decade and this particular country. Yes, I am perfectly aware of the harm anti-Semitism accusations can do here, and I even assume that my enemies will now have total and rapid success in the American press—but, in the grand scheme of history and literature, this is nothing. I feel that appearing in a newspaper unmediated, to fend off base accusations artificially cobbled together, would be impossible for me.

My letter to you of 17 July is the outermost limit of what I could do. . . .

No! Grenier did not agree, and sent a third letter. No, he hadn't lost hope: even if it's not a full-scale interview—even just a few words, if you say them to me directly—will ensure you "a dominant role in the article." We must be able to demonstrate that you "said such-and-so to our very own reporter"—that is "the nature of competitive journalism in the United States." You might be totally indifferent to it, but the great prominence given your views "will strengthen your position" in this country. You will be vindicated. You did defend yourself in *The Oak and the Calf.* You cannot, "'in the short run' . . . be totally uninterested in what happens in America. . . . You can be, or could be, a great moral force" here.[50]

He wrote with great passion. But this correspondence was already too much for me. I didn't respond any further. But Alya, counter to her own conviction, maintained my defense, endlessly having it out with him by phone—that's how insistent he was.

And thus—I made my choice, and was happy about it, and have no regrets.

But, after all his polling and some delays, Grenier's article[51] didn't appear in the *New York Times* until November (and, according to Maurice Friedberg, suffered heavy cuts in the editing). It was now on a page a long way back, with equal-sized photos of me and my judges, Harvard professors

Pipes (against me) and Ulam (for). The structure of the article was untidy, with repeats, non sequiturs, and the usual borrowings from the press—but in the polling of opinions it turned out that the balance was, all the same, in my favor: what was said about Stolypin's significance and his death was not bad, and the *Letter to the Soviet Leaders* was favorably appraised (in that same newspaper in 1974 it had been anathematized[52]). And the balance was leaning towards the opinion that: although *Archipelago* was less "impartial with respect to Jews and gentiles" than Robert Conquest's *The Great Terror*, and although I had "an unconscious insensitivity . . . to Jewish suffering" (Elie Wiesel), my "anti-Semitism" was "nothing to do with blood," not racist, but "fundamentally religious and cultural," and in that way I am like Dostoevsky, who was, as is well known, "a fervent Christian and . . . a rabid anti-Semite" (Pipes).

But the Oracle is the Oracle. The *New York Times* having expressed itself in moderate terms, the sea of indignation began to calm for a while. Some local newspapers reprinted the article, as did our local Vermont paper, with the headline: "Solzhenitsyn refutes charge of anti-Semitism"[53]—and this was the first our neighbors would read of these accusations; curious classmates asked our sons, "What's anti-Semitism?"

It crossed the pond as well, to the *Daily Telegraph* and *Evening Standard*; and Loseff defended himself in the *Spectator*.[54]

The *New York Times* itself published readers' responses in only one issue, and these, too, were equally balanced.[55]

The alarm sounded in the Senate had fallen silent.

But as for the secondary ripples from the great Alarm—they just wouldn't calm down.

So, how could some Jews—first in America, then wider afield—*not* take this successful slander campaign on board? Responses appeared in the Jewish press, for example in the Los Angeles paper *Israel Today*, in October 1985: "VOA: Voice of anti-Semitism?" —"A true Russian . . . was foully murdered by a bullet fired by a Jewish assassin . . . by a murderer so contemptible that he is a part-time police informer." —The article consisted of a selection of quotes from different places in the book, jumbled up and in high density, the better to demonstrate its anti-Jewish malignance, references to the authority of Lev Navrozov, "a brilliant essayist and scholar"—and nothing else.[56]

But, as ever, there was a diversity of opinion among Jews. And, for example, the *Detroit Jewish News* that same autumn put, next to a photograph of me, also one of Raoul Wallenberg, and—regarding the current debate about my "anti-Semitism"—repeated at some length its commentary from 1975 and my words about Wallenberg at the 1974 Stockholm press conference[57] (it was only after them—and even then not straightaway—that an international campaign to search for him was launched) and concluded: "How interesting, that Solzhenitsyn should suggest Jewish activism in Raoul's behalf."[58] (Suggest?—awaken, more like . . .) The reminder was most opportune.

There were also private individuals who wrote to me. For example, twenty-five-year-old Philip Averbuck from Boston. He had read my books and articles and agreed with my criticism of the West. He was sure that Russians and Jews could "play a great and beneficial role in the not-so-distant future of mankind." But now disputes between Jews, on the subject of my feelings about them, were increasing: some wished "that all Gentiles had such views as you have," others asserted that mine was a "typical traditional Russian anti-Semitism," and both sides were "picking through [my] writings to support their positions." But Averbuck, having read Navrozov in *Midstream*, now came up with this simplest of solutions: he would conduct a direct interview with me, and all doubts would vanish into thin air! And here were the questions: (1) "How much do you know about the religion and history of the Jews, and from where did you obtain this knowledge?" (2) Is it true that you believe "only Russian Orthodoxy can save Russia" and, if so, then how will non-Christians fare in your *ideal* Russia? (3) What do you think of the state of Israel, of Israeli society, of "Israel in relation to other countries of the world? Do you feel that Israel possesses any universal significance and, if so, what does it represent?" (4) Do you recognize the significant contribution of Jewish philosophy to Russian culture in the last two centuries, excluding Marx and Trotsky? (5) "How do you assess the philosophies and actions" of the new Jewish émigrés? (6) Do you have "any advice, criticism or commentary" for the Jewish people in the Free World?[59]

So all I have to do is abandon *The Red Wheel* and work up this whole dissertation, then submit it to him and—it's in the bag, I'm rehabilitated!

Meanwhile, that very autumn 1985 happened to be the time (it was once every five years) for the World Congress for Soviet and East European Studies[60] (Slavists). And since this had become such a hot topic for everyone around, how could the Congress not also busy itself with that same Stolypin cycle and not settle once and for all that confounded question about Solzhenitsyn's anti-Semitism?

But they didn't get very far. Some delegates, having discussed in detail both the Stolypin period and his assassination, slid clean away from "anti-Semitism," as if they'd never heard of such a thing. Others pluckily took the bull by the horns and said that Stolypin was a truly great man; that Bogrov's shot had made Jews no happier, but had turned out tragically for them (which was true); that Bogrov had been portrayed polyphonically, and it was up to readers themselves to interpret this figure; and that there was no anti-Semitism in *August*.

It would be another week before the *New York Times* article appeared, and the international Slavists, like the American pseudo-intellectuals, had not yet received the signal telling them which way they were advised to lean. But even the *New York Times*, alas, was not to give them an absolutely definitive decision.

But neither did it open its pages to our indefatigable Navrozov, for his several thousand words of condemnation. What was he to do? Where should he aim his sting? In desperation, he lunged headlong into a frontal attack: to strangle the American edition of *August* before it was ever published!—(although he had only just complained that it was my evil intention to leave it unpublished in English). A hectoring letter direct to my publisher, Roger Straus! —In the novel, he said, Bogrov was portrayed a dozen times in the image of a snake, *which Solzhenitsyn transforms into the Jewish Serpent*! And now a transfixing conjecture: that there are probably two different versions of *August* in existence—one anti-Semitic, earmarked exclusively for Russian anti-Semites (there was no other kind of Russian reader, anyway), the other for the Western languages, for me to wriggle out of trouble and show the Western public, *and especially Western Jews*, that all the accusations against the book were groundless. —And so, Mr. Straus, if your translation corresponds in detail with the Russian edition, then "you are publishing the most anti-Semitic book since the *Protocols*"! Or your translation excludes or tones down the anti-Semitic passages—in which case you are engaging in political double-dealing! (You can recognize the Soviet terminology). I would like (the public prosecutor would like!) to receive an answer to two questions: *when* did Solzhenitsyn propose this version to you for publication?—and *exactly which* text is it?[61]

Our publisher must, at that, have experienced a moment's vacillation: such resounding, confident pressure from someone *who knows*—while Straus hadn't even read the translation yet, as Willetts was dragging his feet endlessly! Not without some hesitation, he asked me, too: what actually was there in the book about that Jewish Serpent? (Alya sent clarification.) What did he reply to the slanderer? I don't know. But overall he stood firm, waited till Willetts's translation arrived, and relaxed.

But, once awakened, could this alarming subject really settle down so quietly?

Midstream, having waited six months (the statutory time limit in America to sue for slander—which I didn't do), provided Navrozov with space for a dozen pages to carry on fulminating against me: "Solzhenitsyn's 'spiritual development' paralleled that of Stalin"; in Solzhenitsyn's youth he was a *dukhobor*[62] and, for that reason, "he would have tried to . . . become the head of the KGB or Secretary General of the Communist Party"; "it is only in the West that Solzhenitsyn added publicly [his] anti-Semitism" (i.e., in the most suitable environment for it . . .); while those who assure us that Solzhenitsyn is no anti-Semite are either crusaders, or Jews wanting to be nice to conservative Christians, or bootlickers, or else they've been bought off.[63] . . .—And

Carmichael's respectable journal disseminates these ravings; do they think—Americans will believe anything?

Professor Alexis Klimoff answered in *Midstream*, never abandoning an academic tone, saying that Navrozov did not know the facts pertaining to Stolypin, Bogrov, or biblical symbolism.[64] —Navrozov replied with invective, saying that Klimoff's approach was "basic to Stalin's Nazism" and that, on the whole, no one can disagree with Navrozov without "joining the American Nazi Party."[65]

And Navrozov's efforts were not fruitless—they were deftly snapped up by *Alef*, a Russian-language magazine in Israel, widely read in America too, where the polemic carried on. (In Israel it was Mikhail Heifets and Dora Shturman who defended *August*. —The discussion was topped off with responses to them in *Alef*, in tones more like a fishwife: "Look at them, trying to teach us manners?!")[66]

Aleksandr Serebrennikov published, in the States, a collection of *documents* under the title *The Assassination of Stolypin*,[67] so that mendacious debaters would have less material to lie about. He had also provided documentary information on Gruzenberg's role in China (about which, in *Panorama* again, another debate was also in full swing, still on my Taiwan speech).[68]

Needless to say, the fury would wash over America, from one publication to the next, for a long time still. That same nagging Lars-Erik Nelson, this time in the respectable *Foreign Policy*, expounded his menacing indictment of Radio Liberty for its lack of vigilance.[69] And the pertinacious meddler Belotserkovsky talked nonsense about me hating the West while at the same time corrupting Russia and despising the Russian people.

So now, while I was writing my Nodes, that pack was slinging mud at me in unison. (A vivid memory from life in the Swiss mountains: farmers using fire pumps to douse their meadows with liquid manure.) Anyway, you'd need more than that to down an old *zek*. What if Dostoevsky had had to live and get published in America?—he'd have been trampled underfoot here. But dead—he's much loved.

There's just one thing that these spiteful types don't understand: as La Rochefoucauld joked, nothing helps you live quite like knowing your death will please certain people.

When I gave *The Oak and the Calf* the subtitle "Sketches of Literary Life," it was ironic: this was, it said, what a "literary life" comes down to when it's held between Communist fangs—nothing left of it but horns and hooves.

But I'd never have thought that, in the United States too, a literary life could fall within the scope of Hearings and Investigations.

So now, in a break from the *Wheel*, the time has come for me to spend some months revisiting *Millstones*. By now my life has been covered in so much slander, on issues big and small, that I'm obliged here to sort out this whole throng of muddles as well—if only for my sons and future grandchildren.

. . . But my life is no longer kept afloat by lifelines of ringing steel; I haven't the strength to launch into tasks beyond my capacity. Five years ago, when I was approaching sixty-four, on the way upstairs I started gasping for breath for some reason, and my chest felt tight. At first I didn't attach any importance to it, but then it turned out to be angina. And on top of that, my blood pressure has always been high as well. So by then it no longer seemed appropriate to dive headfirst into our pond, and I stopped.

Now the thought would sometimes come to me: what if I don't live to see a return to Russia? It's actually strange that this doubt never occurred to me before: the belief that I would return had always carried me along.

But the way back was not open to me. And, for the enormous mass of the USSR to budge, to change—how long must we wait?

I'd driven myself on and on, rushing to get everything done, to manage it all—but was my life perhaps declining in this way towards its end? . . .

Should I not rather be thinking about what patch of earth to be buried in?

I went over various possibilities: our own wooded plot (Alya didn't want to hear talk of that!), a temporary grave, so that my remains could be taken to Russia later, or the Orthodox "corner" of the American cemetery near us—and we concluded that it would be best for me to repose in the Russian (the "White Guard") cemetery near Paris.*

---

*By then it was almost impossible to acquire a burial plot at the Sainte-Geneviève-des-Bois cemetery. But Nikita Struve bought one through friends of his, anonymously, not saying who it was for. Later it turned out I wouldn't need it—now I will lie in Russia. Meanwhile, Vladimir Maximov died in Paris in 1995 and his family started panicking—there was nowhere to bury him! Struve told me about it, and we gave them my plot. In recent years Maximov had, for some reason, been very annoyed with me and had already attacked me so much in the Soviet press—could he have imagined that he would be laid to rest in "my" grave?

But a year later I would learn (*Nasha Strana*, no. 2358) that the celebrated World War I pilot Evgeni Vladimirovich Rudnev, later head of aviation in the Volunteer Army, had already, in 1945, been buried in that plot. But forty years passed, none of his relatives remained, and the cemetery administration sold the plot again, with no name attached. It's understandable—there were no plots left in the cemetery, and the remaining émigrés were dying: where to put them? But even just the thought of lying there, with a predecessor, is chilling. (Author's note, 1996.)

CHAPTER 13

A Warm Breeze

Throughout all our years in Vermont, eleven now since 1976, I never ceased to feel them to be heaven-sent, a safe haven, despite the succession of external vexations and calumnies. Not only did they set before me the *opportunity* to write *The Red Wheel,* but that work of history was, in turn, my *salvation,* as I engaged tirelessly and with unflagging zeal in, I believe, a productive endeavor for Russia, while at the same time taking a genuine step away from the blind alley of the modern age. I breathed the history of the revolution during all the years of exile—and it led me away far into the depths of time.

However, the epic was by now acquiring such proportions, extending beyond my single lifetime and, more importantly, beyond the reader's potential capacity, that I began to hesitate over just where to call a halt. In August 1918? before the October coup? or even earlier? This was also induced by my age. And, as I went more deeply into *April,* I became convinced that the beginning of May 1917 was an easily demonstrable dividing line in the history of our revolution, when a great deal of what was to come came into clear view. By May 1917, the liberal "February fever"[1] was utterly supine, sickly, doomed—anyone could come along and seize power, and the Bolsheviks did. So I would finish *April* and that would be enough for me, that would be it for now. And, if I had time in the future, I could try to construct a bare-bones Summary volume for all the unwritten Nodes.

The growth of *The Red Wheel* archive meant it was becoming impossible to lug everything I needed to the summer house by the pond and so, since 1984, I'd stopped working on the *Wheel* all year round, and done something else during the two summer months. The wheel of time was slowing down.

I had only to take a look backwards—there were plenty of obligations unmet. An unfinished novella, *Love the Revolution,* about the start of the war, had been left hanging since 1948, since the *sharashka.* I wasn't going to finish it, but perhaps I could work it up a bit? It's not a very productive task, editing your own old work when you're not able, indeed aren't even trying, to start rewriting it as you would today. Let it stay as it is, early and unfinished. I didn't really feel like working flat out on it. What the novella does pull off is that it's funny, constantly lampooning its foolish hero. But as I reread it, the burden of the years was immediately lifted, and I went back to that young man, to the atmosphere of the '30s—and I longed to write about them! I could really *remember*, body and soul, the whole of that blistering atmosphere (now gone—suppressed, in fact). How I'd like to give future readers a wide view of it, especially the mood of that literature, beneath whose filthy covers we were raised. At the same time, I realized just how heavy a burden *The Red Wheel* has been for me, it turns out—although I hadn't felt that during the years of everyday work. How I longed to offer my pen the relief of a short and dynamic form of prose! To write insubstantial stories of barely any length at all, longer than the *Miniatures* but shorter than "Matryona's Home," say from two to five or six pages. But this isn't possible with anything other than contemporary Russian material—and that means, if and when I go back home.

That same year also saw the publication of Scammell's warped biography, and I had the sinking sensation that I too would have to recount my life—the part of it that didn't overlap with *The Oak and the Calf.* In the summer of 1985, I plunged into bygone years—my childhood, youth (and my disgust, now, at its sterility), the front, and imprisonment and the camps too, and exile, and the anxious joy, even if accompanied by mistakes, of returning from exile.[2] By the summer of 1986, one more month and I would have finished, I'd have covered my life until my expulsion. I was almost seventy, after all—would there be any other time to come back to it?

Trying my hand at literary criticism, too, appealed as part of a general pull back towards literature. I felt Sinyavsky's *Strolls with Pushkin* to be a defilement, but, as the years passed, I could see that no one was going to offer a fitting response. It was a thankless task, and took an annoyingly long time. But it was a blessing, while doing it, to reread, to immerse myself once again in Pushkin, to look at him afresh.[3] —Furthermore, ever since the '70s, still in the USSR, I'd also been planning to respond to Andrei Tarkovsky's *Andrei Rublyov*, which had grated at the time with its falsifying misuse of Russian history in a contemporary debate. But I needed to watch it a second time, and there was nowhere to do it. Then, out of the blue, the Russian version of the film was brought to a small neighboring town; we found out quite by chance. It had to be fate. We went and saw it—and I wrote my piece.[4]

(It was published to an explosion of outrage among Third Wave émigrés—Tarkovsky, it turns out, had been deified.)

Shortly afterwards, because of the Don-based chapters of *The Red Wheel,* I set out to reread *Virgin Soil Upturned*, for the language—and again a sketch begged to be put down on paper.[5]

And if I carried on, where would these sketches end up? There was no time. I abandoned them.

Plus, the Studies in Modern Russian History loomed over me. These too had been an overly ambitious undertaking: after all, manuscripts had to be read, evaluated, and edited. We thought we'd found a permanent editor of the series in Nikolai Ross—but no, he couldn't cope; there were unfortunate slips. Mikhail Bernshtam went off into American academe, and lost touch with the series altogether. At this point, an exuberant young émigré turned up in the form of Yuri Felshtinsky, who embarked on the Socialist Revolutionary uprising of 1918. —Basically, there were no Russian writers of history among the surviving émigrés, so that even Russian authors had to be translated from foreign languages, as was the case with Viktor Leontovich's *A History of Liberalism in Russia*, two books by Georgi Katkov—*The February Revolution* and *The Kornilov Affair*—and Nikolai Tolstoy's *Victims of Yalta*.[6] And now Joachim Hoffmann's *A History of the Vlasov Army* had just been published. Thankfully, at least the Germans were writing about the reverse side of the war. We'd be publishing that as well.[7]

By the spring of 1987, six books had been published in the All-Russian Memoir Library series, and a seventh was on the way. Alya was very keen to continue the series and make a success of it. She'd adopted it as her pet project but, what with my never-ending work, she had no time even to go through our own stocks, to select something off our shelves at home. —I had persuaded four of our former POWs to come out of hiding and write their memoirs of German captivity.[8] Alya had edited the volume by Fyodor Cheron and Ivan Lugin, and Yermolai had typeset half of it, but I wailed that my work was at a standstill: this wouldn't fly. So the only hope is that we'll manage it at some future date. (Two of the prisoners were also thinking of writing a research work on the whole system of POW camps in Hitler's Germany.*)

* They spent a long time working and gathering material. We brought the book out only in 1994 (Iosif Dugas and Fyodor Cheron, Вычеркнутые из памяти: Советские военнопленные между Гитлером и Сталиным [*Crossed Out from Memory: Soviet POWs between Hitler and Stalin*], Studies in Modern Russian History 11 [Paris: YMCA-Press, 1994]). —This was the fate of five million! (Author's note, 1998.)

In the summer of 1986, I got down to rereading and retouching the details of *Calf* (who knew when it could be typeset, but it had to be copied and saved in case of, say, a fire). Next up was *Invisible Allies* and then—that is, now—there's *Millstones* and, my, what a lot I've written; too much, perhaps? It was so long since I'd been through *Calf* that I was startled by the daring of the narrative and language, and the light touch of its roguish twists. I found this infectious—but none of it's possible in *Millstones*. That material is from over there—not the same thing at all—and I'm not the same, either. *Calf* still bore the intense heat of the camps, now lost, but, most importantly, it had the fearlessness of truth, the recklessness in speaking out, which the West has been constantly knocking out of me for thirteen years now, training it out of me. Also, over there—there had been one great and dangerous enemy, while here the enemies are sticky small fry, baby foes—you wouldn't bother writing at full strength about them. Working on my biography wore me out, whereas *Calf* rejuvenated me, kindled an inner feeling that there was so much still to finish in Russia (to start, even!), and a conviction: I would go back! I would go back and would still play some part in something!

Thereafter, I launched into finishing *April*. Which I've done, to all intents and purposes. Meanwhile, Alya and I ushered into print the first two volumes of *March* in Russian, finished typesetting volume three, and began typesetting volume four. In the process, Alya kept sending me back to make this or that improvement.

Just a few years earlier it had seemed that the *Wheel* would be supported in the West, and so protected, by French and English translations, at least. But the French managed to produce *August* and *October*, and then began to run out of steam, while the English translation was hopelessly bogged down with Willetts. Not even *August* had been finished; the date kept being put back. (Willetts is so genuinely sensitive to the quality of a translation that he will deliver it to the publisher, then take it back and rework it. He wears himself out doing it, and his health is getting worse and worse.) But if the *Wheel* didn't exist in the major Western languages, it would become a very convenient target for all my opponents among the Third Wave émigrés and Slavists. With the imperiousness of knowledge, they could fabricate whatever they liked in the languages of Europe, and there would be no one to check it or contest it. Indeed, in the States, a frenzied attack on *August* in Russian was already taking place, so were we supposed to hang *March* out as well, to face a fresh onslaught?

We drew up the "scales," as is our wont. In favor of publishing was the book's natural life. And then also the preservation of the text. We were safeguarding two or three edits—what if they perished? Only after publishing it, even only in a pitiful émigré print run of fifteen hundred copies, would we be able to relax about its safety. —*Against* were those preemptive attacks. And also, practically nothing was making it into the USSR in any case: very little was filtering through, and then only with difficulty. So, why publish?

Still, we went right on waiting and waiting for Willetts's *August*. Eventually we gave up, and at the end of 1986 brought out two volumes of *March* in Russian.

There's no point waiting for *March* itself to come out in the various translations. Meanwhile, *August* has the added complication that its single volume had, after all, already been published fifteen years earlier and, for publishing reasons, it cannot be brought out again, even in an expanded edition. For some reason, *October* has to come out first: that was the decision taken by the Swedish, German, and Italian publishers.

Whereas Russians would read them straight through, if only they could. That's what is needed over there, but is not allowed. The book has a torturous path.

In the autumn of 1986, the complete *October* appeared in West Germany. I can read German, which meant I had to take a look. I wrote to the publisher, Klaus Piper, about some of the shortcomings in the translation, while he began sending me newspaper and magazine reviews, a lot of them too, over fifty—and asked me to give an interview on German television. I declined: I'd fallen silent a long time ago, after all, and didn't want to start speaking in public again. I did, however, read the influx of reviews and, among the left-wing mockery and grumbling, and complaints about the size of the book (ah, it wasn't for you that it was written in all that detail!), I encountered no shortage of understanding, or attempts to understand, by accurately applying Russia's prerevolutionary history to Europe's today. After all, the Germans are the only Europeans who shared our history, albeit on the enemy side: the *Wheel* is indirectly about them, too, and they can tell. (Although you'd be amazed at the way some people deduced from *October 1916* that even then, with a year still to go, the October Revolution of 1917 was *inevitable*! . . . Just the opposite, even the February Revolution could still have been avoided at that point.)

After reading several dozen of these reviews, I gave in: I ought to give an interview to further these attempts to understand. If my book was to have such a grotesque fate, unfolding outside Russia for who knew how much longer, I needed to support its life in Europe as well—Europe was not at all foreign to us. Not, of course, to explain "what I wanted to say with this book" or what "its message" was (the usual stupid questions), but perhaps to achieve a serious conversation, sotto voce. Just not on television—it's superficial. Piper was delighted at my consent but explained that not many people read a newspaper like the *Frankfurter Allgemeine*, and all the readers of *Die Welt* supported me in any case, whereas, if it were in *Der Spiegel* magazine—that had a print run of a million and was read by ordinary people. I had unpleasant memories of clashing with *Der Spiegel* in 1974,[9] but so what?—anything was better than *Stern* magazine. I did, however, set Piper an apparently awkward condition: that the interviewer, even if not from the staff of *Der Spiegel,* should be highly knowledgeable about literature and history. And, furthermore, the interview should only be about my books—nothing about politics. Piper replied that the editor-in-chief of *Der Spiegel*, Rudolf Augstein, would come and do the interview himself. We settled on autumn.

Meanwhile, in the spring of 1987, just as the BBC was fizzing with broadcasts of *March* (jamming having been lifted), Deutsche Welle put in an order as well: they wanted to read *March* too, even if only a bit of it. I agreed, of course.

Ultimately, if a book is significant, it makes headway under its own steam.

Only the Voice of America, hounded for my Stolypin cycle, kept silent. Alya joked that *March* now had more chance of being published in Moscow than of going out on Voice of America. But she was wrong: Voice, too, proposed that I draw up a dense but abridged version of *March*, around twenty-five hours in total.

And my hurry to finish what I'd begun earlier was not in vain. In the autumn of 1986, I was assailed by several health problems at once. My angina recurred. Gallstones were discovered, and an operation was apparently required. Most surprising of all, I had multiple skin cancers (as almost never happens, I know). Cancer—it had got me again! wasn't it a lot to ask of one person? what a dire fate! However, I found my way to an experienced doctor, although not immediately, and he explained that people who'd once been exposed to any intense X-rays or chemicals might, approximately twenty-five to thirty years later, be stricken by skin cancer precisely in the places subjected to radiation. (Here in Vermont and New Hampshire, he had observed that, after the war, little boys on farms were tasked with spreading chemical fertilizers; in those days, they scattered them from buckets, without gloves, with their bare hands, and a quarter of a century later many of them went on to develop skin cancer.)

It had been exactly thirty years since my treatment in Tashkent. Payback. But to be granted thirty years of life—it was worth it! for that, I didn't mind having to pay.

The illnesses immediately changed a great deal in me. The immeasurably strong, unfailing drive that had possessed me all these years disappeared. People can live twenty years with these ailments (they included high blood pressure, and arthritis, and others), or it might be less than a year. I must hurry to do not what "I want," but what I still have time to do.

To train myself to look on earthly matters with a meeker, semi-outsider's view: they'll sort themselves out even without me. Humble acceptance.

I remembered from Tashkent that, more often than not, skin cancer is curable, but it takes a long time and a great many bouts of X-rays, with unsightly swelling of the affected areas. But marvelous technology has now emerged in America: cancers are frozen off in one go, and three weeks later it's as if they've never existed. And they don't metastasize. Thank God! The cancer has been staved off—for now.

But we were brought low when Alya fell ill and remained unwell for two whole years. In April 1986, on the very day of the Chernobyl disaster, she had serious surgery. Thank God, it was successful. But it coincided with agonizing worry about the Fund: a crucial bit of its backbone, a key link in the supply chain of our aid sent into the Soviet Union, had been dislodged in the autumn of 1983. In the increasingly terrifying circumstances on the ground, perhaps only Eva could have found a replacement—but, less than a year later, our dear Eva died during a failed operation.

Alya would have to patch up, or even perhaps rebuild, the chain of tightrope walkers—and doing so required meetings with the "starting" links in person, rather than by mail, and that meant trips to Europe. She'd already done this in the autumn of 1983—she'd seen Eva in Switzerland (for the last time, as it turned out) and Vilgelmina ("Mishka") Slavutskaya in Vienna, and the meetings had evidently been noted. Mishka was searched on the train going back, and when they got home there was a noticeable increase in surveillance of them both. Alya was distraught that it was her fault: having no citizenship, she was obliged to request a visa for any trip, and for several weeks the documents would wander around European consulates, from which informers could easily report—and, in that case, all her movements, down to the exact dates, would have been known in advance. For that reason, the already great risk to our selfless volunteers would have increased many times over.

The only solution Alya could see was to take US citizenship, to which we had already been entitled for four years but had never acquired. It would enable rapid, unimpeded travel in the West, without special passports or visas. However, the spotlights were trained on us at the slightest movement, let alone a step like this, and Alya felt that taking citizenship on her own, without me, was unthinkable—it would look like she was making some kind of point. (Just then, at the beginning of 1985, a film attacking the Fund was shown, quite openly now, across the whole of the Soviet Union.) Alya was burning up, insisting the goal was more important than striking a pose, and I could find nothing to contradict her.

And, really, why stand out like a solitary heron in a marsh?

We turned to the Vermont branch of the immigration service. They sent us forms full of little boxes and questions. I couldn't even be bothered to read them closely—after all, they were rather like the ones we filled in for every visa, in duplicate or triplicate; I never read those either. I gave my secretary, Leonard DiLisio, instructions to fill them all in and, if need be, to come back with questions. And he did, asking for some biographical information about both Alya and me, nothing more, everything was fine. We sent them off. I did know that, as part of the procedure, we would also have to raise a hand to swear an oath of some kind—I'd seen pictures, but I thought nothing of it, a mere formality. They swear on the Bible any time they bear witness.

Some weeks went by—Alya and I were summoned to that same immigration branch office. An obligatory interview took place, with each of us separately. We had to answer some very simple questions about the constitution. We'd brushed up. But the clerk asked me more, about myself. From lack of practice (I hadn't conversed in English for years) I listened intently to understand what she was saying. Again, please. —"Are you willing to bear arms on behalf of the United States?" Absolutely not! I hadn't even been expecting the question. I replied: "But I'm sixty-six." —"But, still, in principle?" What is this principle? You've got young men here of an age to be drafted; they burn their draft cards and get away with it, whereas I, at more than sixty years of age, could be called up? I expressed bewilderment. Then she said that, on the form, I'd already confirmed and signed that I was willing. Wha-a-a-t? (DiLisio had filled it in without the slightest hesitation, and hadn't told me.) I felt sick. . . . All I could do was mumble, "Well, in principle, not literally . . ."

I had been shockingly lax to miss this—that's how casually I'd approached the issue of citizenship.

We went home and now I did read the form and, at the same time, the text of the oath—it turned out to have been sent us as well.

". . . I absolutely and entirely renounce . . . allegiance and fidelity to any foreign prince, potentate—(they've kept that since the eighteenth century)—state, or sovereignty, of whom or which I have heretofore been a subject or citizen . . ."

But to *which* state was I renouncing fidelity? The Soviet state? My Soviet citizenship had been taken away eleven years ago. And there's no *Russian* state on the planet.

But all the same, it jarred. I didn't feel right.

". . . I will support and defend the Constitution and laws of the United States against all enemies, foreign and domestic. . . ."

Well now, I've been trying to warn you about your *domestic* enemies, about the loony-left press and crooked politicians for years, but you never picked up on it.

". . . that I will bear arms on behalf of the United States . . ."

There it was. I'd have to fight against my own country. And yet you're not even capable of waging war on the Communists as such, you've already declared it a war on the "Russians."

". . . and I take this obligation freely, without any mental reservation or purpose of evasion . . ."

Ah, there's the rub. Of course I did have a reservation: I wouldn't go fight Russians.

But so what? Hadn't we told plenty of lies at Soviet meetings? Hadn't I once taken an oath of allegiance when I was in the Red Army, without identifying myself with Stalin's top brass? And wasn't it water off a duck's back?

True enough, but it still jarred. An oath is laughter to the foolish and terror to the wise.

I felt very perturbed. Somehow I'd wrong-footed myself into a dark impasse. Hurting my own cause.

Meanwhile, we already knew the exact date and time of the procedure, and in which building of which town it would take place.

No! I refuse! I dig in my heels. I'm not going!

Alya, like a lamb to the slaughter, her face darkened, did go (accompanied by a teenage Yermolai, attenuating my absence); and there, already, was a crowd of reporters, and photo upon photo of her raised hand—and questions about me.

And the news in the American papers was confused: either both Solzhenitsyns had taken citizenship, or only his wife had and he would soon. The American press approved, of course (and even interpreted it as follows:

now he'll throw himself into US politics!). A bureau chief from the *Washington Post* brazenly proposed that he would spend the upcoming Independence Day at our house, for reporting purposes. (While Navrozov did not miss the chance to check in, writing that I'd taken citizenship because *his* articles had frightened me.)[10]

In Europe, though, and especially in France (we hadn't even given this any thought beforehand, nor even imagined it) there was discomfiture and distress at this outcome: what if he really does take it? "Solzhenitsyn—US citizen? . . . This is heart-wrenching news. . . . Is this mighty figure really going to take the practical option? He wants to secure the future of his three sons. . . . He has said that America is not yet a nation. But it can, nevertheless, provide a refuge."[11] By coincidence, moreover, two months earlier, a rumor had arisen in France, and had found its way into the magazines, that "because of the paucity of attention in the United States" towards me—it couldn't have been greater!—I intended to move to France.[12] We'd never even discussed such a thing, but perhaps taking citizenship was seen as a response to the rumor?

And that rumor struck those who remained of the old wave of Russian émigrés as an insult: never, not even in direst straits, had they considered it possible to take foreign citizenship.

What could I do? I'd made a mistake. Shame comes to us all in due course.

Inwardly, though, I felt liberated that I hadn't sworn an oath to America. (And gradually, American writers caught on: no, he hasn't! no, he's in no hurry! then Navrozov said that I'd "given America a slap in the face.")

And really, what sort of a country is America? Naïve (although supposedly so enlightened and democratic): through a clutch of its professional politicians, it blithely betrays itself on a daily basis, yet will fly into a sudden brief fury—but an utterly blind one—and destroy whatever is in its path. The Soviets bring down a Korean Air Lines plane—then, in New Haven, the windows of a Russian Orthodox church are smashed *in revenge* and filth sprayed on the frescoes. —A US army barracks in Beirut is blown up—and a quarrelsome resident of the small town of Pittsfield, Vermont, a people's avenger, arms himself with a revolver, goes off in the morning to a local shop run by an Iranian and his Russian wife, Tanya Zelenskaya (the daughter of First Wave émigrés), and shoots her dead, thereby expressing America's revenge on the Iranians and "the Russians standing behind them."[13]

Shaky. Russian soil may not be accessible to me for a long time to come, perhaps until death, but I cannot sense American soil as my own.

With no solid ground beneath my feet. With no visible allies. Between two World Forces, to be finely ground up.

Dreary.

* * *

We hadn't been able to see at all from where we were that, precisely from the spring of 1985, when I had found myself between two millstones and my situation had seemed so dire, indeed from April 1985 (the date the Soviet press now gives as the start of the changes), something new had begun to dawn in the USSR. We'd seen nothing other than a comment on America's NBC channel, showing the May Day parade in Moscow: "People in the USSR are joyful today." (Just as they have seemed "joyful" to them for the whole sixty years.) Georgia's top KGB man, Eduard Shevardnadze, became Gorbachev's new minister of foreign affairs. In a show of their usual outright lunacy, and in a bid to curry favor, they contrived to give the United States the gift of the Bering Shelf,[14] ceding both a strategic location and its fisheries, and then, in a further, unconnected act of madness, they planned to reverse the northern rivers—and it seemed there was no stopping the Bolsheviks here either, in this ultimate outrage for Russia. It was then that Lev Timofeev was arrested and sentenced to "six plus five,"[15] yet another desperate figure defecting from the ruling caste to join the side of the doomed. Conditions in the camps were becoming still more hellish, if such a thing were even possible. Irina Ratushinskaya was thrown into solitary confinement for six months. Our attempts to rescue Sergei Khodorovich were still fruitless. Alya made speeches and sought to persuade prominent Western journalists and major Christian organizations to speak out. But nothing helped. In 1985, already suffering from tuberculosis, Khodorovich was placed in disciplinary isolation, and then in a cell with criminals. In April 1986, in the Arctic city of Norilsk, he received a second term under the "Andropov article" (extension without a new trial). Alya fired off a furious retort.[16] Shortly before that, Vilgelmina Slavutskaya had been caught as she was being given the thirty thousand Soviet rubles we had sent for the Fund. The threat of arrest hung over her, and her name, along with that of the late Natalia Stolyarova, was bandied about in *Sovetskaya Rossiya*.[17] The Fund was forced to suspend activities in the USSR for the time being, and Khodorovich—and who would have blamed him?—could quite well have given the assurance demanded of him that he "wouldn't do it anymore" but he, with his one lung, left himself to rot in Norilsk. That same spring saw the Chernobyl apocalypse, the leaders' criminal silence, and the gut-wrenching sight (picked up by US television as well) of Ukrainian dancers in the radioactive air of the May Day parade on Kiev's Kreshchatik. Immediately afterwards, as Yuri Orlov was being released from prison, he was shown, in Lefortovo, the investigation file that had been opened against the Russian Social Fund as a whole—whether to intimidate everyone or for real.

Everything seemed hopeless, as it always had since Lenin's day. (Although a shift of some kind seemed under way in China: in summer 1985, compulsory Marxism was abolished in tertiary education and the population were to be polled regarding their opinion of local leaders. Miraculous?!)

Suddenly, as summer 1986 approached, after a year and a half of Gorbachev, a rumor reached us, a triumph: there was to be no reversal of the northern rivers!! Whether it had been rejected for good or only temporarily, it wasn't going to happen yet. Then a couple of congresses flashed by, the writers' and the filmmakers', with some very brave speeches and even some changes of leadership. (Alya said, "My heart's racing! We must hope!") Ah, but I knew too the inescapable morass of the seventy-year-old Soviet lie. Sometimes, I would see new examples of it. I saw a new film on video, *The Tavern on Pyatnitskaya*, a most unconscionable skimming off of cream from features of the old life not yet crushed during the NEP.[18] Then, wiping the cream away, it spewed out the same old nasty, unremitting, unrelenting Soviet ideology (screenplay by Nikolai Leonov); even on their deathbeds, they'll try to prove that they were right. —Or Nikita Mikhalkov's recent accomplishment, *A Slave of Love*. Here the cream was the memory of Vera Kholodnaya and, what's more, the White Guards were denigrated yet again as unparalleled villains, a Red detective story with its noble Bolshevik underground. So what had changed?

My only consolation was the new works coming out of the USSR by Valentin Rasputin, Viktor Astafiev, Georgi Semyonov, Evgeni Nosov: for all that, the flow of authentic and not at all, not in the slightest bit, sycophantic Russian literature had not dried up—it still flowed in the Soviet desert. But was it enough for a general rebirth of consciousness?

All of a sudden, at the end of summer 1986, a quite extraordinary document arrived from the Soviet Union: an abridged *samizdat* record of Gorbachev's meeting with thirty chosen, trusted writers! How on earth did that "escape"? . . . Who would have had the nerve? . . . Did he *himself* order it to be released? . . . Gorbachev was genuinely calling on writers for support in opposing some kind of internal enemy: in other words, he needed the forces to do it. (And the old lackeys, Aleksandr Chakovsky and Georgi Markov, were the first to rush to *reassure* him.) And he gauged correctly how long, how very long, serious reforms would take. From that document, I could sense that Gorbachev's intentions were sincere (but entirely within the confines of Leninism . . .). And that he wasn't planning a foreign war. For the first time, I felt some sympathy for him. And that he could be overthrown if he didn't use some stronger levers. However, he did also say, "If we were to begin dealing with the *past*, we would extinguish all the energy."

Really?? But unless that happens, the future will not open up either. His levers were really pretty short.

So, my train was not yet pulling in. As for understanding, I'd understood: many more of these milestones would have to pass before my return was possible. And yet my heart was about to jump out. . . .

A short time later, another bit of "Kremlin samizdat" arrived: Yeltsin's address to Moscow's propaganda activists had been put into circulation—how about that? And it too contained determination, toughness, significance.

What on earth was going on? . . .

Nothing substantial as yet, of course. But we'd all been so little indulged that even this was a great deal to us.

We felt immensely stirred up.

From autumn 1986 onward, our Boston friends were transfixed by the most excited calls from Moscow: believe us, *something completely new is happening*!

Hidden joy: cup it in your hands, like a fledgling.

We went on living and working as before, but Alya was right to say that the air was *full* of what was taking place *at home.* A new way of life.

But, amid these vacillations of the disobedient heart—wanting to *believe*! to have faith! to trust . . . —and of sober reason we wondered: *what* was actually going on? *what* was Gorbachev preparing? After all, he hadn't announced a clear program, just the strident word *perestroika*—but we had suffered the cruel experience of February 1917: uh-oh! what else was still to come? where else would it lead??

Then suddenly, in December—Sakharov's release from internal exile, and his return to Moscow, with unimpeded access for Western correspondents to film and to ask whatever they liked, as much as they liked! And he, fine fellow, demands the release of political prisoners and a pullout from Afghanistan. And keeps his distance from Gorbachev.

Was it unexpected? To Western minds, it was practically a revolution! Gorbachev's calculation was spot-on: to the West it seemed beyond all reasonable doubt that if Sakharov was being released from exile, it was the Soviet Union with a human face from that point on!

Yes, Sakharov had spent five and a half difficult years in exile in Gorki, his health undermined particularly by hunger strikes. Then suddenly a telephone was installed in his flat and Gorbachev was on the line: "Now then, Andrei Dmitrievich, isn't it time to get back to work?"

(I wasn't aware at the time that Sakharov really had voiced his objections to the US space shield[19] to some doctor in the Gorki hospital, and that this had been captured on tape and passed on to the Kremlin. In this case it was all the more essential for the authorities to bring Sakharov out of exile, and worthwhile to give him back his former freedom to dissent as well. —And what can one say here? Arguing purely from the position of the state, Sakharov was actually right: by the Soviet state's reckoning, however lethal the introduction of the neutron bomb—an outright removal of any threat against Europe; the bomb had been only just halted by a groundswell of European public opinion—Reagan's space shield would have been just as lethal. What would then have become of all the missile stocks? —Question: would the pseudo-intellectuals have forgiven *me*, had I returned *even the slightest bit* to a position of loyalty in this way during Communist rule?)

I was very pleased: immensely relieved about Andrei Dmitrievich, and feeling it would be beneficial for the social situation as a whole. In the early weeks, Sakharov established strict oversight over the release of political prisoners, which had been promised by the authorities and was starting to happen at that time. This was another good thing and the best way of stimulating glasnost.

Meanwhile, American political observers—who more often than not looked only at the surface and were used to the names Sakharov and Solzhenitsyn being linked together—naturally expected, now that Sakharov had been brought out of exile and Lyubimov was also planning his return, that offers had also been made to Solzhenitsyn. Were talks already under way? Reporters had got hold of my secretary DiLisio's home phone number, and rang him to ask.

They (like many in the West) did not understand that Sakharov and Solzhenitsyn were separated by being from different eras. Sakharov was needed by that system, and had already done great things for it, and in any case had never repudiated it altogether. Whereas I was hacking away at their Leninist root itself, so it was either that system or my books. (Only the right-wing *Washington Times* seemed to have understood: in January 1987, it recalled how Sakharov and I had argued over my *Letter to the Soviet Leaders*.)

And, I had specifically recommended, both in that letter and, indeed, always, a *smooth* exit from totalitarianism—God forbid it should be a "leap."

And, thank God, it seems to be moving gradually, evolving. I'm happy that events aren't developing via revolution or total collapse: there won't be the second February I had so feared.

Given that it's an evolution, however, the changes will be somewhat icebound too, a slow, slow shift along the whole political spectrum. Oh, the road is still long, hooking along a far-reaching arc, and our own path isn't even in sight. But if I don't live long enough to go back, at least I will dic in pcacc.

(For the moment, the main plea is for workers to increase labor productivity—now there's a novelty!)

At the end of January 1987, however, jamming of the BBC was lifted (then again, it had been lifted for a while under Brezhnev too). At the beginning of February, everyone in an accursed, long-established camp for political prisoners near Perm was released, forty-two inmates. (Although each one had to sign that they'd accepted a *pardon*. Lev Timofeev spoke out on the dishonesty of "pardoning" the innocent.) Also in February came the release of the long-suffering psychiatrist Anatoli Koryagin, jailed for exposing the practice of punitive psychiatry. (General Grigorenko did not live to see it, however—he died that same month in New York.)

During the meandering process of releasing prisoners that was underway, we worried most of all, of course, about the fate of Sergei Khodorovich. They'd announced as early as the end of January 1987 that he'd be released, but he remained incarcerated in Norilsk, with no movement, for the whole of February. What to do? If nothing changed, he would end up buried alive in Norilsk's frozen wastes. Alya asked senators and congressmen to intervene, to put in a good word. At the end of March, Margaret Thatcher was planning to go to Moscow. I wrote her a letter asking her to remind the Soviets about Khodorovich. To my relief, however, we managed to stop the letter from being passed on when we heard that Khodorovich had finally been released on 17 March, on the undertaking that he would leave for abroad. Well, better like that than not at all. But here's the strange thing: two days before that, *Sovetskaya Rossiya*, always bitterly hostile to our Fund, had delivered another malicious article, "Swindlers' Donors," and it was immediately reprinted for émigré readers in *Sputnik*, a nasty little promotional magazine containing a digest of the Soviet press. (Did one hand of the regime not know what the other was doing?) Again "the CIA." Again the names of our contacts, Slavutskaya and the late Stolyarova, were bandied about. And to us it all sounded like the war was still going on and there would be no cessation of hostilities, forget it![20]

But there were signs of the first stirrings in culture, still lacking in confidence but stealing a march on the granting of any other freedoms: Akhmatova's *Requiem* was brought back from the outer darkness, as were Platonov, Nabokov, Gumilyov, and even (most unexpectedly) Merezhkovsky and Gippius. (And posthumously, albeit with unbearable hypocrisy, they reinstated Pasternak in the Writers' Union.)

How could our heads fail to be in a whirl? . . .

Had Russia roused itself? Really?

Not only our heads—the whole world was in a whirl.

Since developments in the USSR had unfolded with only a small shift of the political spectrum, the Third Wave of emigration was all the more in a tizzy and ferment: it was precisely this first part of the spectrum that they'd coveted—and many of them had been trying it on for size and were eager to visit. Now they're the first in line.

There's to be a Chagall exhibition in Moscow! A Pasternak Year is in the offing! And what ever has become of the menacing prophesy of "Russian party" dominion, brandished before us for years on the grounds that it would be first to race for power? No, it was specifically to the "cultured circle" that the chance was opening up to draw close to the new powers-that-be.

Given the inevitable differences of opinion among émigrés, however, all sorts of things were heard. Aleksandr Zinoviev excitably trumpeted "An Address to the Third Russian Emigration" (and only to the third; he didn't acknowledge any other compatriots): "We have arisen against our social system . . . our mass [?] *uprising* has materialized." (The word "uprising" appears nine times in the "Address"—did anyone notice an actual uprising?) Alas, "we were supported only by an insignificant minority" of the population. But it was these very dissidents who'd forced the Soviet authorities to back off. . . . And now "any collaboration with the authorities is a betrayal of our uprising. . . . Let us bear the fate of insurgents to the bitter end"![21]

In this new situation, Vladimir Maximov was dashing to and fro. Not long before, he and some friends had set up the portentous-sounding Resistance International, competing with the NTS[22] as to whose émigré organization was the more antagonistic towards Communism and the more entitled to subsidies. Had the advent of Gorbachev's glasnost cast, perhaps, a shadow of superfluousness and inefficacy over his International? Maximov clung to his intransigent stance, and when Yuri Lyubimov was wavering over whether to return to the USSR, he put pressure on him not to do so! (And he had an adverse effect on Lyubimov: he, of all people, should have gone back right away.) —In February 1987, Maximov suddenly sent us a printed declaration, a "Statement for the Press," and a list of people who ought to sign it. I was in first place, Alya in second. And in that format, with its cut-and-dried wording, it had been sent out to the rest, creating the impression that I'd already entered into some sort of conspiracy with Maximov about both the text and the signatures. It was an unpleasant tactic. And why did Maximov think that I needed strongly worded collective expressions to condemn the fragile, diffident process in the USSR, which God grant will ultimately succeed? I was angry and wanted to retort harshly. Alya, as she often did, restrained me from an irritable outburst. (Less than twenty-four hours later Maximov was checking by phone via Ilovaiskaya in Paris whether or not we were going to sign, asking apprehensively, "Or what? Are they packing their suitcases?")

Maximov is a serious and a good writer, not a "self-expressionist" at all. Over the years, I'd grown used to thinking of him as a direct and principled person. His convictions, both inside the USSR and subsequently abroad, already passionately announced in public, had always seemed right to me—regarding both the Bolsheviks and Western lefties and pseudo-intellectuals. At one time his invective against the First Emigration and the Whites used to rankle me; later, he abandoned that line and, on the contrary, started singing Kolchak's praises. He behaved amicably and judiciously towards Israel, visiting twice and making speeches full of promises. He defended Israel in *Kontinent* even when the whole of the world press was berating it for the atrocities at Sabra and Shatila[23]—but at the same time he would not allow anyone to tip over into Russophobia, be it the designers of a monument in Israel or Simon Markish.[24] He recoiled, fairly early on, from Sinyavsky's clownish methods, survived a clash with him and his left-wing supporters in Germany, came under vigorous attack in the *Frankfurter Allgemeine,* and, during these clashes, always waited for me, too, to enter the fray. I was unable to drag myself away from work at every external demand, however. Yet he defended me for a long time in *Kontinent*, very much wanted to publish me, and, for that reason, even got hold of a tape of my lost news conference in Madrid.[25] He marked my sixtieth birthday with a good deal of well-disposed attention. Shortly afterwards, he became jealous and took umbrage at my support of the "village prose" writers. He considered them dishonest for not openly rising up against the authorities and enjoying print runs in the hundreds of thousands.

But perhaps on account of running this fee-paying magazine in which everyone wanted to appear, of occupying this seat of power, Maximov's character seemed to have become haughtier, more cruel over the years. His editorials were increasingly acerbic and caustic, his angry letters and outbursts increasingly hard-hitting. Forced to maintain a flexible *editorial policy*, to neutralize those who might become new opponents, and to strengthen links with supporters (for example, Sedykh and *Novoye Russkoye Slovo*), he had left the stance of an independent writer far behind and plunged into diplomacy and calculations.

In 1985 one of these calculations was, apparently, to put some distance between us, and to do so publicly: I had in any case never offered him direct support, and had become a dangerous ally in light of the hounding for anti-Semitism to which I'd been subjected in the States. And he distanced himself, in particular in an interview with Slavist professor John Glad, suggesting that I was at odds with all interests bar those of Russia. I found out about the interview only the following year—it was published in an émigré magazine alongside one with the Sinyavskys and, unexpectedly, it was even nastier about me than theirs was.[26] And he might at least have checked against *The Red Wheel*, rather than repeating the hackneyed cock-and-bull story that I blamed ethnic minorities for the Russian Revolution. Forget what good I've done, just do me no evil. My rejoinder, in a private letter, reminded Maximov that I was the one who'd suggested, back when it was being set up, that *Kontinent* should not focus solely on Soviet ills but "become a mouthpiece for suffering Eastern Europe" (1974),[27] and later (1979) urged an expansion of the concept of the "continent" by including East Asia on the same grounds as Eastern Europe, and extending a permanent hand of sympathy to them too. What kind of "only Russian" interests are these? I now suggested that Maximov himself should issue a public correction saying that his statement was wrong. But, alas, he didn't. I didn't challenge it in print, either. He wasn't the first to lie about me, nor was he the most pernicious. And he could, he really could have taken offense that (sensing no kindred spirit in *Kontinent*, as it developed) I had not sustained a collective front with him over the years.

No, it's not a dissident *uprising*, and not chance, and not Gorbachev's "treachery" that is squeezing out the Bolshevik regime, if such a movement really has begun. It's the internally driven collapse of Communism, which was bound, inevitably, to come about: death from premature decrepitude, because its earthly "religion" has proved short on spiritual endurance; the pool of willing sacrifices for the sake of a "radiant future" has run out and, resting on their laurels, both bosses and foremen have turned swinelike.

Oh, how to divine what is transpiring *over there*? How to sense it? How to interpret it above the beating of our hearts?

If it's approached analytically—logically and soberly compartmentalized, as it is by some—then of course Gorbachev hasn't achieved a substantial shift in two years—in either the economy (which is the key), or the social setup, or the ramshackle conditions of daily life. (The only success has been his cult in the West.) —And all this should already have been acknowledged as defeat or deliberate deception, because two years is not an insubstantial amount of time, especially given such apparently vigorous efforts from the top down. And, of course, there can be no qualitative change in anything in the country without a renunciation of the accursed Communist doctrine. And there will be desperate resistance from the nomenklatura, as well as backtracking, the zigzags of reversal. (And how great the danger of the next steps going off course, and how prescient the required vision.)

Synthetic perception also exists, however. It sees everything as it is, as a whole, without analysis—fresh air! a warm and gentle breeze! To one who had personally endured the walled-in decades of Soviet life, the unquestionably brighter public mood could not fail to seem a wonder and a marvel: this greater warmth and surging hopes, this first chance to speak and write far more widely than the ax had previously fallen, to read with fascination the wretched newspapers (in my day, no one even picked them up, we were forced to subscribe to pre-allocated copies), and even to take independent social steps, to make speeches or gather together without the guiding hand of a party committee! Here's what they write (Mikhail Roshchin): everyone is in the grip of *impatience*—more! further!—and *fear* that everything will suddenly go careering backwards—"after all, nothing's been done yet, it's just words!"; "does our people really not deserve better?"; "we've already got it wrong once by confining ourselves to half measures" (in Khrushchev's early days). But, outside the big cities, there isn't yet even this breath of air. And moral standards are still crumbling, and the land is still without an owner, and industry's output is still vast in quantity but low in quality, and there's still nothing in the shops. —The sudden burst of yearning for our concealed and trampled history was met by a flood of Communist hackwork, produced in millions of copies—Mikhail Shatrov, Anatoli Rybakov—saying that the problems all stemmed not from the radiant Lenin, oh, no, not from the revolution, not from the annihilation of the peasants, but from some malign turning point when Kirov was assassinated.[28] Hurry, hurry to entrench this lie in people's minds! The ideologue Egor Ligachyov issues a call to order: "Against the falsification of our glorious past!" There are exceptional publications of deceased writers, banned for half a century—but the cry goes up: "a whiff of literary necrophilia," don't publish! It's "bringing the contemporary literary process to a halt!" We discover that the new Tretyakov Gallery has been poorly built; it's not at all suitable. The MKhAT (Moscow Art Theater) breaks up into two companies, and classical music is running at a loss. I bet it is! After all, the Iron Curtain prevented anything good crossing over from the West, but it allowed rock 'n' roll and cheap Western fashions to slip underneath, and already Soviet television is pandering to that same nightmare, hastening the banding together of insensate youth into some sort of barbarous hordes.

For us, in emigration, reading Soviet newspapers and magazines is creating the sense of a breakout. Oh, not all of them, a mere 5 percent of the previous government-issue drabness; the avalanche passes me by. Only the best selection reaches me. No matter what, real life is over there, not here! And the émigré press pales, confused, into insignificance—even *Posev*, which has been so interesting in recent years.

When would I ever have read *Literaturnaya Gazeta*, let alone a report of a Writers' Union plenary meeting? Yet now I avidly devour eleven of its full newspaper pages, and it's impossible not to feel old wounds reopen: real live people (and I know a lot of them) are talking about real life—writers turn out to be a highly changeable community. "Why were we blind for decades?," "the servile habit of terror," "we're tired of losing our self-respect"; they dare challenge both the immense arms surplus and the never-ending class warfare, "ideology remains hard of hearing." (Of course, sharp dividing lines are still in place: there is Someone and Something you can't mention.)

And yet. What a perilous reminder of our disoriented February: everyone and everything has burst out talking, a vortex of talking—but there's no sign that anyone is doing anything of use.

The sledges don't come out at the first sprinkle of snow.

Sure, one longs for this indeed to be the start of a great turning. And it's such a weight off my shoulders that they'll now undertake their own breakthroughs and advances in Russia. What had once been the main front for me, on which I'd fought so hard, has become the front line for all of them. Will the turn in the road ever come when I, too, will be needed on the ground?

But now things have started touching upon me directly. In January 1987, rumors began reaching us in one, then another clandestine letter from Moscow that, at some closed lectures, promises were being made to publish *Cancer Ward.* A sign of some importance, it meant that at least something was under discussion *in certain spheres*. Then, on 3 March (the same March when *Sovetskaya Rossiya* was continuing to hound our Fund) a staggering piece of news reached us: *Novy Mir*'s current editor, Sergei Zalygin, had apparently said he was intending to publish *Cancer Ward*! But for some reason he'd said it to a Greek correspondent and, what's more, for a Danish newspaper, and it had been in print in Copenhagen for around a week already, but no one had noticed it. To some extent, this vague combination suggested the KGB's usual methods. Was it a trial balloon?

I didn't think so, no. I immediately deduced that it was true. It will happen! Not right now, not specifically on account of this statement. But the time is near. No matter how winding or long a road Soviet society has traveled, I'm there, somewhere far ahead, like a boulder in the middle of the unavoidable main highway.

And if, for the moment, it *was* a trial balloon, then they were shooting themselves in the foot.

It had seemed like this Solzhenitsyn had already been vilified and marginalized in America. But from a newspaper in faraway Denmark, a snippet of news had emerged that was among the world's leading stories: "Is the Soviet past vanquished?" Some news agencies even got through on our Vermont telephone number, but very few people knew it, so they also rang people they could ask and who were bound to answer: my US publisher Roger Straus, Voice of America, our Vermont congressman, and, in Paris, Claude Durand and Nikita Struve—who, in turn, rang us, asking our reaction. —But what reaction could there be to a *rumor*? Alya and I replied that no one had approached us "officially or unofficially."[29]

No, I didn't believe that the long-awaited hour was finally upon us; no, for the moment that wasn't the case. But my heart was leaping for joy. It was true: right now, *Cancer Ward* was a good fit for the current Soviet era—the very first stirrings of public hopes, as in 1955. And what good timing it would be for me! I'd become so heavily bogged down in the West and, all of a sudden, it appeared as if my hands and movements were becoming freer—I felt as if I had far greater scope. Here it was, the template for my return: first

Cancer Ward, then the short stories would also be reinstated, then one odd thing or another published in Soviet journals—and then you're halfway back! We remembered now that, two years earlier, in April 1985, a rumor arose in New York that Gorbachev would summon me back—and although we put not the slightest faith in it (and the rumor never did come true), transports of joy had swept over us then as well.

A warm breeze from home! . . .

And where else could it come from?

Sensation or not, but it went down poorly, pleased few in the States. Those on the left had no interest in my being once again of significance, and in the USSR to boot. (Pipes in the *Washington Post*, 5 March 1987: of course, at the top of Gorbachev's hierarchy, *they* "found Solzhenitsyn's line acceptable because he does not . . . call for human rights, or democracy, or pluralism." Ellendea Proffer, in the same paper, said it was no surprise, since "a lot of people taking power now are Russian nationalists."[30]) But it didn't suit the American right, either: they were used to me being an anti-Communist, so how could I suddenly "support Gorbachev"?

As for the usual liars with too much time on their hands, they came up with, "Solzhenitsyn has already been in contact with the Russian government more than once!" Well, you couldn't snarl your denial of everything.

Several ordinary Americans wrote to me during those days, saying: Don't trust *them*! Don't return![31]

All the radio stations were broadcasting the news back into the Soviet Union; it would spread there, too. But over here, there was a curious reaction from recent émigrés. Etkind, Lyubarsky, Faibusovich said it came as no surprise: in terms of ideology, Solzhenitsyn was closest of all to the Soviet powers-that-be. —Mihajlo Mihajlov, terrified of what was to come, said it heralded the arrival of an Orthodox monarchy. —Some writers were outraged. —Maximov took it as a personal misfortune. —The French newspaper *Libération* carried out a survey among the émigrés it considered most important. And who might those be? Zinoviev: "The Soviets are creating an alibi that comes cheap. Harmless book . . . *Doctor Zhivago*, *Cancer Ward* enable them to rob readers of works of real interest, capable of affecting their emotions. The authorities are resurrecting the dead in order to be more certain that the living have been buried. My point of view is simple: when they publish *my* books is when I'll take the Soviet authorities' intentions seriously." —And then there was the gallant Limonov: "I wasn't expecting this at all. I don't like Solzhenitsyn, I consider him a mediocre writer, but the publication of his books in the USSR could be a second revolution . . . the second major event since the death of Stalin." —And, of course, Sinyavsky. But how wily he is! "It's marvelous. The ricochet from publishing *Cancer Ward* will rehabilitate *all those in emigration*. . . . The whole *healthy part of the émigrés* is delighted to welcome this turnabout."[32] What? If they publish the books of this racist, fascist, chauvinist, theocrat, tyrant-autocrat—that will be a victory for our pluralist émigrés? . . . But, privately, Sinyavsky knew all that was at stake, and understood the gravity of such a turnabout. (It was during those same days that I lost to Flegon in court, and Maria Sinyavskaya instantly offered my lawyer her testimony that Flegon was a KGB agent. They were prepared to be our allies now, to portray themselves as not being my personal enemies at all, claiming they'd criticized my fallacious views only out of lofty principle. . . .)

The scale of the sensation was so unexpected that the Soviet Foreign Ministry's official chatterbox (General Gerasimov), and then the Writers' Union, had to issue denials just a day later that no, of course, not a single work by Solzhenitsyn was being considered for publication.[33] (Okudzhava, who was in Paris at the time, just before Zalygin got there, explained that it was all a *stunt*, as he put it, and that words were being put into Zalygin's mouth[34]—whereas I think Zalygin did have it in mind, and somehow it came to light.)

I hadn't appeared in public for months. I'd been sitting at home working, but now it happened that on 6 March, the very day we found out that publication wasn't going ahead, Ignat was playing a solo recital in Chester, less than an hour's drive away. The whole family went. The concert was brilliant, the auditorium full, he received an ovation—it would have all been an absolute delight, had journalists not grabbed us as we left and begun grilling us, after all. Alya covered for me: it would be terrific, but no, there's been no confirmation, *Cancer Ward* isn't being published at the moment. The next morning, of course, her remarks appeared in the local newspapers, cheek by jowl with a report of the concert and photos of Ignat at the piano.[35]

The world press stood down, too. The *Washington Post* (6 March 1987, "Moscow: No Solzhenitsyn Publication") forgot what it had written the previous day: that I was harmless to *them,* that I was *one of them,* a Soviet. Solzhenitsyn now turned out to bear the stamp of "extreme anti-Sovietism" and even if there was no prospect of publishing his books, it was an event in itself that Zalygin had made favorable mention of him.[36] —The *Wall Street Journal* (6 March 1987, "Siberian Rainbow") wrote warmly: "This, if true, was by far the most radical example to date of the liberalizing Gorbachev policy of *glasnost*. . . . 'Soviet officials' quickly denied the Danish report. But for a brief moment . . . it was a marvelous fantasy, like a rainbow breaking over a Siberian gulag in mid-winter."[37] —Meanwhile, *Le Matin* (*The Morning*) in Paris came out with, "There was confusion among Russian émigrés. Some émigrés in the West had gone up in estimation, whereas Solzhenitsyn, quite the reverse, had gone down. The denial has at least restored their composure. . . . If Solzhenitsyn's books were to start being published in the USSR, it would confound many notions."[38]

For now, however, the *notions* remain in place. . . . After all, the Central Committee might come to its senses and go into reverse at any stage of perestroika.

It's true that the Third Wave of emigration has been churned up by these reports—Solzhenitsyn is sneakily preparing to hop back home! Strangely, they can't see that the current Soviet situation is far more compatible with them than with me.

However, could the shake-up—coming from below, organically—become irreversible?

Furthermore, as we had predicted in *From Under the Rubble*: with the slightest loosening of state screws, ethnic strife would flare up. And where would that lead?

And what about Russian feelings?

So trampled on, once these began to revive, it would be in a predictably twisted, ailing form.

Which is what happened.

Was it on some massive, unforeseen scale, however? A supremely alarmed *global* press campaign instantly got off the ground: in the USSR, the monumental Pamyat (Memory) society, chauvinistic, fascist, and anti-Semitic, was burgeoning, posing a threat to everyone. And so universal a threat, that a question about it was debated at a sitting of the European Parliament!

And straightaway brisk pens in the West (or was it in Moscow?) composed, lamented, and complained, "There you go! Those are Solzhenitsyn's allies! He'll be the one to take command of them!"

Then the notorious Astafiev-Eidelman debate erupted,[39] and those pens were again at the ready: and *who* had spoken in praise of Astafiev?—Solzhenitsyn! So *those* were his leanings! *That's* whose side he was on! (*Strana i Mir* [*Our Country and The World*], no. 12 [1986].) —"So what was Solzhenitsyn's 'live not by lies' about?"—it "corresponds to Gorbachev's present-day party slogans!," nothing more.

And I can now imagine this incandescent, riven, *ethnicity-based party spirit* in Moscow—not informed by reason and balance from either side.

Meanwhile, the propaganda of my lying adversaries, like a light froth, has reached Russia ahead of my books—and certainly, self-evidently—before *The Red Wheel*, and anxious questions are reaching me from there: so does the author believe that the revolution was merely an infection brought in from outside? a series of contingent events? "a handful of foreign-born civilians versus an armed nation, many millions strong? was our history made by outsiders, monsters?"

You just try and persuade them differently when the books aren't getting through. When ever will the *Wheel* roll up there?

Not trusting entirely in the artistic success of his latest lampoon, Voinovich also set off on the campaign trail: now (in Washington) he was very troubled that Solzhenitsyn wasn't speaking out to condemn the anti-Semitic movement in the USSR. —That I hadn't spoken out about anything at all for four years didn't matter; that a writer might simply not be speaking out didn't matter; what did matter was: why wasn't I speaking out against the anti-Semites. *It must mean . . .* —mix him up with that rabble as much and as quickly as possible. (And Navrozov didn't forget to stick the knife in, either, asking why Solzhenitsyn hadn't spoken out against Soviet power for such a long time.[40] *It must mean . . .*) The impatient *Novoye Russkoye Slovo* also jumped in on behalf of the agitated Third Wave of emigration: "Why do you keep silent, Master?" Why, indeed? There's the threat of the "village prose" writers, there's Pamyat, there are the *lyubers*,[41] so why do you remain silent and aloof?[42]

How they've longed all these years for me to shut up. And I have—but now it's my silence that they can't bear.

Meanwhile, during recent months, my name has been bandied about in the USSR. In rumors—that I've already lodged an application with the Soviet embassy to return. But also in public. Aleksandr Podrabinek suddenly (on 5 March, the day of the Soviet denial about *Cancer Ward*, although this was mere coincidence) wrote a letter to the government saying that now, with the onset of Glasnost, it would be intolerable hypocrisy to continue to hush up Solzhenitsyn, who had called for honest and total *glasnost* eighteen years ago[43]—and he suggested repealing the decree that had stripped me of citizenship, giving me the opportunity to return to Russia; and that I be published in massive print runs. He made the letter public one month later.[44] Then, another month later, he, a man who'd been in internal exile not very long before, was suddenly visited in Kirzhach by the Communist Party district committee secretary for propaganda, bearing the official response that "the Central Committee is looking into Solzhenitsyn's case."

This response was not binding upon them in any way (although they most probably did have discussions of some sort). Was it to give me a pretext to jump first, if I really was pining to return? But my return right now would be a huge propaganda success for the authorities, especially if secured without concessions.

For my part, although I understood all the lack of commitment, the expedience of this gambit, my heart still beat faster. After all, the wall is slowly melting—it's melting, and my exile is coming to an end! And, indeed, given my age, it's one of my last hopes.

And the signals coming from Moscow were ambiguous. In this same March, Vitali Korotich, the new editor of the liberal *Ogonyok* (*Little Flame*) (who had already grossly slandered me over *Archipelago*), declared that I was "not a writer, but a political opponent and a fool."[45] —And in April, the seasoned *Sovetskaya Kultura* (*Soviet Culture*) enlisted my remark from an old BBC interview where I praised the "village prose" writers, saying that Russian literature in recent years had been successful not in the freedom of emigration "but in our Russian homeland . . . *under enormous pressure*."[46] And so they deceitfully scrapped "under enormous pressure," then casually added the name "Solzhenitsyn" without further explanation, as if it might be encountered on any page. —And on 16 May, an extremely peculiar article erupted onto the pages of *Pravda*.[47] Or rather, it was perfectly normal: a justification of why Sholokhov, in the thirty-five years from the end of the war until his death, was simply unable to complete *They Fought For Their Country*—and the only reason turned out to be that he was undermined after thirty years of work by the publication in Paris of *Troubled Waters of the "Quiet Don"*, by D–, which questioned Sholokhov's authorship. Well, it was Solzhenitsyn who wrote the foreword, and Sholokhov's reaction was, "What does that crackpot want?"[48]

This was staggering. After I'd already been branded a traitor, a literary Vlasovite, an enemy of the people, and a CIA agent—that was it, just a *crackpot*? . . . Had someone even at *Pravda* censored it, and so prevented me from being dealt the full force of the blow?

It will be a long time before they figure out internally how to deal with me.

They're not calling me home, and it can't be hurried along from the sidelines; all the more reason for me to keep silent, just as I'd fallen silent four years ago. Now that Khodorovich has, thankfully, been released, not even Alya needs to make public statements; what a relief. Keep silent for now. For *what,* in all conscience, can I say about Gorbachev's perestroika?

That *something* has started—glory be to God. So can it be praised?

But all the innovations have, from the start, been harebrained and have *gone wrong*. So should it be criticized?

As it turns out, neither praise nor criticism is due.

In that case, all that remains is to keep silent.

Just now I was very touched by dear Irina Ratushinskaya: she's sent her complete understanding of my silence, my immobility, and my refusal of meetings.

But are there many like her, who truly understand? What about when speculation about me multiplies, and it all goes off in different directions? what about the Soviet show of "the Central Committee is looking into Solzhenitsyn"?—(I've heard not a whisper from those quarters)—it does get me worked up; and those affecting rumors that I've "already filed an application with the Soviet embassy"—isn't it strange to say nothing about oneself at such a moment?

And in any case, it's not possible to stay dead silent. A request made its way to me: it was the fortieth anniversary of Voice of America's Russian Section—speak out! And how could I refuse them?—after all, they had suffered for the sake of my Stolypin. Alya resourcefully suggested an old quote of mine about Western radio broadcasting. And right away—VOA as a whole had been going for forty-five years, and Reagan's greeting to them quoted me: "The mighty nonmilitary force which resides in the airwaves and whose kindling power in the midst of the Communist darkness cannot even be grasped by the Western imagination."[49]

This coincided with the reading of two volumes of *March 1917* over the un-jammed BBC. (And reports came in that it was being listened to in the Soviet Union.) Of course, the excerpts were selected without me, by Vladimir Chugunov, but he did it with understanding. I listened and was glad. And they suggested that I conclude the series myself, in my own voice—broadcast to Russia! —Well, how could I not agree? We arranged an interview. And just now, at the end of June, Chugunov came along to do it.

How could I not take advantage of this exceptional opportunity to address my compatriots, not through jammed airwaves but with my voice unadulterated—and especially now, during such stormy, troubled months, with contradictory rumors proliferating and the authorities paralyzed and holding their tongues about me? To speak directly, yes, directly to listeners and readers.

And what should I say?

Still, we took stock: were they trying to entice me with *Cancer Ward*? But that had come very, very close to being published—in 1967. So, was that how far things had advanced in twenty years? (Or, indeed, not yet advanced . . .) What about *Archipelago*? It was the reason I was banished. And the whole of *The Red Wheel*? How on earth could I betray them? First of all, I should *name* them, right now, on air! And let the authorities, not me, rack their brains about what to do. . . .

And I concluded the interview by saying I would go back after my books, not before them.[50]

The situation at home in Russia is unpredictable. The country might not accept me for a long time yet. And in terms of strength, work, and age, how many more years must I remain uprooted in exile?

And what about our children? They have to move along. The time has come for our two eldest to leave home to further their studies. Where? Our homeland is not yet calling us.

Yermolai is just now, in June 1987, coming to the end of the twelve-year school system, two years ahead of his peers. And we've resolved to send him to Britain, to Eton, for the two years he has left before university. He's retained his passion for modern history and politics. In recent years, Yermolai and I have been studying Russian history in detail—from the end of the nineteenth century to the revolution, and he has read copiously. And this summer before Eton, he'll take an intensive course in Chinese, at the summer language school in neighboring Middlebury (a year's study in nine weeks).

Ignat is fourteen but he, too, is off this autumn, to London. In recent years he's been studying with Rudolf Serkin's assistant, Uruguayan pianist Luis Batlle, and has spent three summers in a row at music camp, enthusiastically immersing himself in chamber ensembles. Since his debut with orchestra at the age of eleven (Beethoven's Second Concerto), he has played quite a lot in public, and Rostropovich now recommends that he go to Maria Curcio in London, a famous teacher and former student of Artur Schnabel, and finish school there at the same time. It's a bit scary letting him move overseas alone, still just a boy. Although he's more mature than his years and, in general, is growing up quickly, with a wide range of interests, an eager and perceptive reader in three languages.

And they've both found time to help us.

So, following on Dimitri's heels, another two will leave. Only the youngest, Stepan, will stay with us—but for how long?

Our life here in Vermont is changing, but the warm breeze from over there hasn't deceived us, has it?

Will God allow us to return to our homeland, allow us to serve? And will it be at a time of its new collapse, or of a sublime reordering?

Twice already it was sent me to do the impossible, the unpredictable, in my country: ushering a tale of the camps into print under Communist censorship, and publishing *Archipelago* while in the Dragon's maw. When publishing *Denisovich* and when banished to the West, I was raised up by two explosions of the kind where immeasurable forces hoist you up to an unexpected height. (And on both occasions I made plenty of mistakes.) If I have twice pushed my way through a concrete wall, will something similar suddenly be asked of me a third time? (And how not to make mistakes then?) Should the war-horn sound—my hearing is still keen, and I still have strength. Old steed, fresh speed.

Even if it is only to be a living presence at future events, even without playing a direct part in them? and might that presence itself become a form of action? and help transmit to future generations the worldview I have built up. Perhaps the task can be completed not through risk and drive, as before, but simply by living longer: could longevity itself become the key to fruition?

And, not for the first time, I've noted that the length of a person's life depends greatly on the retention of his life task. If a person is much needed for his task, he lives. As the saying goes: die not when old but when your task is done.

Ever since *Ivan Denisovich*, I've served so many times as a sword of division. And the fiercer battles of the last dozen years have constantly divided me from a multitude of forces, whether of Western or of Russian origin—and it was inevitable, all of it. But the heart's desire is neither to be divided nor to divide, but rather to *bring together* everyone it can reach, to act as a hoop binding Russia together.

That, after all, is the real task.

And so on life's journey you climb from plateau to plateau and each time you're tempted to say: now my peak years are upon me. Yet on you go, and it turns out that those too were not yet the summit.

Or else you cease to expect them any more.

Make clear my path before me . . .

Vermont
June–July 1987

PART FOUR

(1987–1994)

CHAPTER 14

Through the Brambles

After that *warm breeze*—what a very long time we still had to wait.

"Liberating changes" unfurled across the Soviet Union, "new thinking" was promoted—something serious was really happening there, wasn't it? Now the rambunctious Yeltsin had been removed—perhaps because of his crusade against the "closed distribution outlets" and other Party privileges?—from the Moscow committee of the CPSU. Gorbachev was giving speeches laden with promises, but clinging on frantically to Party power and the banner of Lenin. And sincerely, it seemed. And he'd entrusted the Ministry of Foreign Affairs to the head torturer of the Georgian KGB.[1] What promising prospects . . .

It was always the same old refrain about the triumph of socialism and "international help" in Afghanistan. And now, for the benefit of the West (in an NBC interview): "We took away the power from the landowners and the Tsar [and gave it] back to the people."[2] And everyone in the West extolled Gorbachev's virtues, the most rapturous of all being Margaret Thatcher. Well, who wouldn't take a shine to him after the eighty-year-old, deaf cripples? And he'd ended the Cold War!

Only it was not done on equal terms—but by hurried, accommodating national concessions.

For such a vast country, his was not the right intellect. (But from what soil could the right one have arisen?)

What he trumpeted first, and wholeheartedly, was "Acceleration" (of all workers' productivity). But that didn't catch on: it was not adopted, and the government very soon withdrew that watchword in embarrassment; it was never heard again.

The second slogan, "Perestroika," was announced from above in ringing tones, but was also taken up by a thousand voices, full of hope, rising up from below. But no one, it seemed, even in the Soviet Union, understood what, exactly, it consisted of. Cooperatives (a reliable and fruitful format, which had, in its own, distinctive way, successfully blossomed in prerevolutionary Russia) were praised to the heavens; but before long they were being dismantled. Small village enterprises were permitted (most vital!—absolutely necessary, truly!) but in practice small, private vegetable nurseries were immediately trampled underfoot and destroyed, as "unearned income." . . . Or they announced the democratic election of factory directors, and some kind of strange "socialist market," clearly designed to destroy the clamps that had held the old system together—but not replacing them with anything likely to survive. We should have seen small-scale enterprises, small workshops, seamstresses, cobblers, bakers, little shops, so that the people could come back to life, have enough to eat, and have some clothes!

How alarming, all this blowing hot and cold.

They were definitely leaving all the old *nomenklatura* in their positions, even allowing them to use the nation's wealth to line their own pockets. There was a constant series of paltry, self-seeking, cautious steps to benefit the Party. But for Gorbachev, everyone's darling, it hardly seemed urgent to seek the paths of fruitful reforms—not when the rapturous West was showering him with an array of credits.

The taste of authentic innovation was more real in the third element—the "Glasnost," openness, that had been announced. (But was Gorbachev himself fit for glasnost when he was, at that moment, trying to cover up the Chernobyl contamination?)

But anyway—glasnost? Really? Glasnost, that we had only dreamed of before—and now it was starting to come true? Really?? People could still not believe their own daring, their own tongues: things which, yesterday, you could only whisper about in the kitchen—could they say them openly now, out loud?

In print, of course, things were still very circumspect, and still within strict, undoubtedly Communist bounds—but was it possible? Really possible? . . . (As before, "liberated" Soviet newspapers were still calling the administrator of our Fund, Sergei Khodorovich, a "common criminal." And Len Karpinsky, having committed the offense of Party dissidence, was compelled to express, in the newspaper, gratitude for being restored to the CPSU, and for the duration of his continuous Party membership being retained despite his expulsion; and he was made to assume full responsibility for it.)

True, the first rehabilitations of the Bolshevik past were coming now, with Bukharin and Rykov. It was a slow move towards the center ground. (Had I been there at that moment, I'd have worn myself out trying, yet again, to prove that the issue was not Stalin alone—because we can't spend our whole life repeating the same thing. But perhaps they were going, full steam ahead, to cross even that boundary?) And there was more: they were talking about rebuilding the Christ the Savior Cathedral! Change really was in the air.

As for publishing, the first ones out were, of course, the "socially friendly"[3] writers; then, carefully on the camps theme, came Vladimov; then bolder writers on the subject; the newspapers became bolder; and at last Vasili Grossman was allowed—and even Shalamov! This was a big step. But, all the same, a firm hold was maintained: there was still nowhere, no one, nothing against Communist power itself.

But now they were even *letting people cross* the border! They started with freely allowed visits; firstly recent, Third Wave, émigrés going to see how things were, back in the USSR; then the first Soviet citizens starting to make visits, to the West.

There were encounters and more encounters, stories, stories, and more stories, a great surge of vivid accounts. They made their way through to us at Five Brooks, in excited phone calls and ever more frequent clandestine letters arriving from Moscow; and something of all this could be gleaned from *Russkaya Mysl* in Paris, and *Posev* in Frankfurt. And in amateur videos and on TV we glimpsed real, live faces, the Russian faces of today, caught sight of bits of streets, houses—it warmed the cockles of your heart, that.

And there was more and more of it: in our homeland (mostly in the capitals, of course) they were feasting on human communication! talking! talking! And how! They'd been hungering for it after the decades of silence—all intoxicated by that new right! And they talked—about everything, absolutely freely!

Yes, they talked, oh how they talked—but was anyone *doing* anything? was anything nailed down *in practice*? Were events just to follow their own course now? And to crown it all, the gracious West was to help us in everything. The sooner everything in our country became just like theirs, like the grown-ups, the better?

Society was bubbling over with good will towards Gorbachev but could only find, apparently, one form of support for him: participation in Glasnost. (Just you try and find them, effective forms of action, after decades of oppression.) And that's how they passed the time—in endless debate.

But some people were hauling themselves out of their enforced asceticism and going into commerce—you have to make hay while the sun shines! And this observation reached us: that the old maxim of the intelligentsia, "it's better to be poor but honest," was already starting to wither on the vine; you didn't hear it now.

And personal letters from our Moscow friends reported this alarming situation: society was ill!—floundering pathetically, even going under, despite Glasnost.

And how very familiar all this was to Alya and me, from February 1917: the boundless enthusiasm of the population; and the drunken fogginess of their hopes; and that recklessness in the way they expressed themselves. So much happy intoxication after such a long wait!—but in that state, all sense of proportion was getting lost, deformed. And there was a negligence towards the historic paths Russia had taken, an indifference to her singularities, a heedlessness of any duty to preserve them.

In the meantime, all over the West, Soviet Perestroika and Glasnost were giving rise to unabated jubilation. But in autumn '87, taking up the émigré chorus, the Western press got anxious (the *Washington Post* began, others followed) and started asking: *why does Solzhenitsyn keep silent?* Such monumental happenings in the USSR—and he's got nothing to say? *what does that signify?* but what could he say, actually, that "monarchist, reactionary and mystic"?[4]

Well yes, it was natural to expect me to be delighted with *Glasnost*, which I myself had called for twenty years ago.[5] But what if I saw that all the *other* changes were being brought in pell-mell, recklessly? It was terrible for me to watch these events bowl along. Everything that was being *done* (apart from Glasnost getting under way) was so insubstantial, shortsighted, or even damaging that it was clear they were beginning to thrash about: they had no idea where to go next. I would have liked to give Gorbachev some advice: "Don't unpick the stitches if you don't know how to sew."

But the major events in Russia, if they'd not already started, were about to; they would explode onto the scene any moment now. I'd been expecting them for a long, long time (as early as our camp mutinies of the '50s), and readying myself with *The Red Wheel.* The more deeply immersed in it I became, the more acutely I understood all the danger that would come from an unbridled "February fever."[6] I was hoping, and ready—though what paths should I take?—to *exhort* my fellow-countrymen, via *March 1917*: in the explosion of joy, just don't repeat the madness of February! just don't lose control in that crazed vortex!

And how ever was I to make my voice heard in my homeland on the most important thing, the thing I'd been so shocked to uncover in the course of my searching: the acute dangers inherent in an irresponsible February? But then came a favorable turn of events. The Voice of America, which in Kissinger's time had not had the nerve to broadcast readings of *Archipelago* to Soviet listeners; which had never dared so much as utter the name of Lenin in a condemnatory tone ("the Soviet nation idolizes him"); and which, in 1985, had been the object of threats from the Senate over the broadcast of the Stolypin chapters of *August 1914*—that same Voice of America, in the summer of 1987, in the dawning of the new Gorbachev policies, suggested that I should read a series of extracts from *March 1917*, missing only by a little the seventieth anniversary of the February Revolution.

How overjoyed I was! A living link would thread its way to Russia! Now that they had stopped jamming broadcasts, it would bring the fiery senselessness of February *viva voce* into today's seething USSR.

Only I did not want to read a "series of extracts," unconnected, but rather to put together for radio broadcast a substantial, concentrated essence of the whole of *March 1917*. A new, till then unthinkable, density of content. A very tempting idea: to transmit through the ether to my homeland the whole essence of the Revolution, downtrodden and forgotten, which had destroyed Russia. To give them an understanding of its stumbling, demoralizing *course*. But to do that, what would I need? I'd have to cut into the flesh of my book, all four volumes. I must put together a text composed not of separate chapters, but of little bits of chapters, of paragraphs even, attaching one snippet to the next, gathering together only what was most essential.

Very hard. It was like writing that same book again—a lot of work. But, unless I did it that way, it wouldn't all fit in.

I set to work. The job turned out to be enormous, laborious, and took almost six months. How could I manage to produce a complete picture in so little space? Poring over the multitude of pages, I had to weigh up what to take out, what to sacrifice. How could I tease out some of the most important threads and the most important actions? But also people's state of mind—without that we'd lose the atmosphere. And each broadcast segment must trace a complete arc of ideas—and fit exactly into twenty-three minutes. (If you read out extra minutes, they might be cut, but I was also loath to relinquish even one precious second.) I timed what I had prepared, reading it out loud. I learned how to turn pages silently at the microphone. And a felicitous signature tune popped into my head quite involuntarily—from Tchaikovsky's

Second Symphony; overall, it is a tranquil work, but *those particular* bars convey the force of revolution amazingly well.[7]

The recording crew came to us from Washington twice: in October 1987 for the first half, and April 1988 for the second. They used the old system, with large reels but superior sound quality, and made copies for me on standard, small cassettes, which were not as good. It was so well prepared and smoothly carried out that not once did they need to record any segment a second time.

And my broadcasts began to flow out towards my homeland, starting in November 1987. I listened to each one and rejoiced—maybe, just maybe, I was managing to get them out in time for the current perils. Because so many people would hear them![8]

. . . However, reactions seemed rather slow to arrive. Voice of America sent the dubious information that my broadcasts had been "heard by 33 million"—but we very soon understood: in the Era of Liberty now unfolding, who in Russia, except those set in their old ways, would be listening to Voice of America? Now people were occupied with something else: *today's* Russian history was being made before their very eyes.

And so—all my efforts had been derailed, pointless. *March 1917* had been too late, in the end, for the *new February*.

In September 1987 Alya took Yermolai and Ignat to London, both to follow their studies. Ignat was almost fifteen, Yermolai nearly seventeen. We were sad: they were leaving, in effect, forever, for an independent life. They would not be with us, under our wing, any more. But letters began to arrive and, although up-and-down in mood, they were always rich in content, Ignat writing the more often; he was acutely receptive and quite often anxious.

We had arranged for him to live for the first year with a British family, which was straitlaced and very strict about their routines. ("You'd even think they weren't a family, or not in our Russian sense of the word," wrote Ignat. "They live together as if under contract—but observing its terms very strictly.") In the second year he asked if he could live alone, in a rented room. But he reveled in his lessons with Maria Curcio; for the first time he abandoned himself to a thirst for, and pleasure in, playing the piano, entirely self-motivated, for hours on end. He also got a place at a London music school,[9] and graduated the following year. At that time Rostropovich was spending quite a bit of time in London, and Ignat sat in frequently on rehearsals that he was conducting, learning a great deal. But Ignat was not finding his solitary life in that unfamiliar country easy: he flew to Vermont for the very first Holy Week, and did not miss a single service in our parish during that week and then Bright Week. And the following winter he came for Christmas as well.

As for Yermolai—previously, in his Vermont school—he'd always felt cowed by the two-year age advantage of his classmates, along with the close-knit self-assurance afforded by their shared mediocrity. Now, at Eton, though sometimes inclined to rebel against the strict rules (and punished accordingly), in that intellectual atmosphere he now stood tall, began to develop by leaps and bounds, and to get top marks—and in history the top marks in his whole year group. And he found time for parachute jumping, and carried on with his karate. —As for Dimitri, having already, literally with his own hands, rebuilt a good number of abandoned cars and motorcycles and successfully developed his own motor shop in New York, he now gave Yermolai a well-used but still perfectly functional Buick for his eighteenth birthday—and took him for a summer trip, crossing the continent to California on his own wheels. The boys really bonded. Yermolai thirstily imbibed strength from his older brother, who was loved by his whole New York circle for the cheerfulness and daring he showed, for his Russian geniality, and for his unfailing friendliness to everyone.

Another year was passing.

Dimitri, now twenty-five, often drove up to us from New York (doing a five-hour drive in four) and started bringing friends, male and female. And only Stepan remained living with us full-time in Vermont. He was always business-like, even-tempered, indifferent to the television, except for major news. With me alongside, he confidently finished off the work on my dictionary. He already found his typewriter laughably inadequate, was the first in the family to have a computer, and threw himself into learning its secrets. The least of his education came from the local school (he had no desire to be "like everyone else" there, and calmly put up with jibes), but with his mother he studied Russian grammar and, alone, took pleasure in learning French. He was also fascinated by Latin. ("What a treat!—to learn, learn, and learn!") In our parish church he arranged the service books, compiling them for all the feast days of the church year. As for the much-bemoaned "awkward age," Stepan seemed to show no sign of it, except when he'd occasionally dig his heels in and refuse to budge.

Yermolai applied to Harvard for the following autumn, and was accepted. At the same time Ignat was eager to come back to America and continue his studies here. So now they would all be close by again, in the States, even though they'd left the family nest.

And all four of them followed the news from their homeland—in a state of ferment and paying close attention, as if to their own true destiny. And they listened to our explanations and additions, answering with their own observations. They were still Russian in spirit. So far, we'd managed to keep it that way.

But, should our stay here drag on much longer? . . . It seemed almost impossible that the children, indeed my whole progeny, would escape paying a heavy price for my exile.

In October 1987 a large team of journalists from *Der Spiegel* arrived, headed by the editor-in-chief, Rudolf Augstein, as had been arranged through the good offices of my kindly German publisher. Our discussion—lasting several hours, rich in content, and well translated—was about the historical paths Russia had chosen, with direct reference to the *Wheel.* Although there remained no antagonism between Augstein and me from our 1974 clash, the conversation was very tense at first: it seemed that, even now, the magazine might not be averse to portraying me as an irredeemable obscurantist. However, as the hours passed the tension lifted, and both sides were left satisfied.

A few weeks after the *Spiegel* piece[10] appeared, it became clear that it had made an impression on the *Washington Post* and *New York Times,* and both suddenly commissioned articles about me, their task being to ascertain whether Solzhenitsyn was still alive, or was he now a figure of the past? (All that talk of his about Russia's historical path, the depths of time—but what about Gorbachev's Perestroika? and something easy to understand about the present day?) The *New York Times* pushed hard for an interview as well, which I didn't give them.

Did they want to bury me in advance, to be on the safe side, before the *Wheel* was published? There was no sating them. But I was, deep down, totally indifferent to what they thought of me, what they said about me, what they wrote. I know that some time—even if it's after my death—*The Red Wheel*'s time will come, and no one will be able to contest its picture of the Revolution.

The *Washington Post* article did, by the way, despite a number of half-truths and snide remarks, turn out to be something of a rehabilitation, after the hounding of 1985: it now seemed I was not anti-democratic, not anti-Semitic. . . . (Another year later, the *New York Times* again proposed an interview—to mark my seventieth birthday—and I refused.)

In the USSR, meanwhile, my name was still banned. The breath of Glasnost was felt by some, and some names and books were finally wrested from the darkness of oblivion—only not mine. To the Soviet authorities I remained a sworn enemy, and a dangerous one; I was still being hounded in the Central Committee organ, *Sovetskaya Kultura*. The millstone of the Central Committee ground out ever the same message: Solzhenitsyn is the most dangerous figure of all!

And had Zalygin's tentative announcement of March 1987—that he was intending to publish Solzhenitsyn—been ditched? Well, we'd already waited longer than that—we could wait a bit more. Such was the level of official Glasnost three years after it had been granted.

But how about the unofficial glasnost, the public's version? We were struck by the pettiness of the various, sometimes contrasting, opinions reaching us. Some said: Solzhenitsyn will arrive and take charge of Pamyat,[11] and that will lead to the dictatorship of Russian chauvinism in the USSR. Others said no—he'll come and sap Pamyat's strength, remove its moderate and healthy elements. They discussed me in terms of a political plaything, not a writer. And even on this level of discourse, they could see only the chilling specter of Pamyat—that of Communism, it seemed, no longer hovered over them.

Meanwhile, the year was ending.

The weather was changing but not yet fair. . . .

Unexpectedly, President Reagan made several attempts to introduce me back into Soviet reality. For the 1988 New Year, it had been agreed that he and Gorbachev would exchange short speeches on video, each addressing the other's televiewers. Reagan had said: in the words of a wise man, "Violence does not live alone and is not capable of living alone: it is necessarily interwoven with falsehood."[12] (The Soviets could not cut it out of the broadcast. But they got round that problem by not announcing in advance what time the program would be aired—and put it out early in the morning of 1 January, when everyone was still asleep.) —After that, in April, in one of his speeches Reagan suggested point-blank to the Soviets that they should "publish Solzhenitsyn."[13] (The Soviet press came down on that speech like a ton of bricks: "banal fantasies," "not conducive to a positive dialogue." That same April, in one of the Harvard debates, Richard Pipes joined in, saying that, were it not for Gorbachev, Solzhenitsyn's reactionary orientation would win the day.) —At the end of May, during his trip to Moscow, Reagan was at the Danilov Monastery on, as it happened, Whit Monday, and there he quoted from my prose poem *Along the Oka.*[14] The Moscow press, despite Glasnost, totally ignored this quote. —Immediately after that, Reagan mentioned my name when speaking at a literary gathering at the Central House of Writers. (The American correspondents there promptly fell on my fellow-writers, wanting their reactions, and heard from Granin and others: his writing's boring, reactionary—it's no loss, not having him here.) And the *New York Times* immediately joined in: "For many Soviet intellectuals, including some who once viewed him [Solzhenitsyn] as a heroic figure and who still heartily defend his right to be published," to them as well "he has become a distasteful character, the spiritual scion of a reactionary Russian nationalist strain that favors a mystical seclusion in a fortified enclave [that was my Five Brooks] from the secular evils of the West."[15]

Again and again! We'll be at loggerheads till kingdom come. When it comes to me, how amicably, how harmoniously those two millstones grind, be it the KGB (and even the pseudo-intellectuals) or the State Department and the *New York Times*.

Despite the turmoil our feelings had been thrown into by the events in our homeland, our work schedule—Alya's and mine—never slowed, not for so much as a day. I had already parted company with *March* and, in '88, moved into *April*—which I found terribly seductive, with its headlong rush of newness and Russia's relentless slide ever further into the abyss. Alya typed each new chapter on her IBM machine, accompanying it with her criticisms and advice, in ample margins, suggesting moving some bits, tightening up others, and, sometimes, throwing things out. These notes of hers were an unflagging quality control, which sometimes irritated me, sometimes delighted me—but always constituted eagle-eyed assistance and tireless support in this work, so vast both in its mission and in size. Then Alya would reprint the text (ah, thank goodness for new technology: given the scale and pace of our work, we'd have been sunk with just a typewriter), sometimes raising more, new objections. I would again come to a decision—and she would produce a fair copy of the chapter. Thanks to the success of this shared process, we were both feeling more youthful. (But Alya also said she felt depressed following, over so many years and in such detail, the unstoppable downfall of Russia in 1917. And not just following—she was living it.)

We were working so hard, so immersed in the job, that our machine's breakdowns and malfunctions, which were not infrequent, were all the more irritating. We had to call in a technician, who came from many miles away and was not available every day of the week; and the road over our hills was often a solid sheet of ice; and we never knew how soon he'd be able to fix it, or whether he'd have all the right parts with him. But work never stopped when our composing machine was out of action: Alya would immediately turn to editing manuscripts from our Memoir Library—for we had also taken on that massive, back-breaking task. Of those, the easiest one had been Krieger-Voinovsky, the last Minister of Railways in tsarist times, a man of high-minded culture and intellect, with experience in the affairs of state and, thanks to that, fine writing skills; our century is favored with ever fewer such people.[16] —The poorly structured manuscript of Sergei Evgenievich Trubetskoy, youngest member of the celebrated family of intellectuals, demanded a good deal more work.[17] —And coping with the Moscow man Okunev's engrossing memoirs of the early Soviet years[18] was a Homeric task. The trouble was that we had come by a typed, samizdat copy with hundreds of errors in the figures, dates (and the ordering of the individual entries was also wrong), and geographical and personal names interspersed throughout the diary. We had to check things in quantities of encyclopaedias, various one-off sources and, most of all, in newspapers of the time, which I had on microfilm. But this editing job was surely worth the effort, for, under the oppression of early Soviet times, almost no such eyewitness accounts had been preserved. They too were not yet fit for today's Glasnost. (And we published another, similar book, with the YMCA-Press, by Ivan Schitz, *Diary of the "Great Turning."*)[19]

But Alya never had a single day without interruptions from outside. Numerous phone calls, from pushy reporters always in a rush to hatch some tasty news item, from émigrés keen to talk, and just from unexpected people (our phone number was somehow getting ever more widely known). And there were many émigrés with requests, with problems, and Alya always helped. —And sometimes, completely unforeseen, people would ring at our gate: twice, women who were clearly mentally ill turned up and complained that they were being tormented by the KGB—it was making zombies of them. They wanted me to defend them, rescue them. The weather was inclement, or even freezing-cold, and one of them seemed to have nowhere to go—which meant she had to be driven to the nearest hotel, installed there, fed, and calmed down. One of them left, but the other stayed to run riot in the environs, and our neighbors blamed us for the kind of visitors we had—"those Russians." —And once, while our gate was wide open, a Third Wave émigré arrived in his car, this one from Toronto and also batty. He had brought with him his "ideological bomb," a plan to save the world with a fusion of Darwin, Marx, and Freud. He arrived—it was -25°C, but hot in his car, and he would not leave unless we read through his plan and gave our approval. —Another time, the wife of a Moscow artist, having seen in *Novoye Russkoye Slovo* directions for reaching us by a forest track, arrived on foot with a suitcase. There, in the suitcase, were samples of her husband's work: he had painted three thousand pictures in all and was giving the whole lot to the United States; but the American embassy in Moscow was taking its time over accepting this inestimable gift, and would I exert some influence on the American government and hurry this along. And she and her suitcase had to be driven back to where she'd come from. —And on top of all this there would, not infrequently, be a passing American, or a whole family, or a tour group, ringing at the gate: "Just a half hour! To shake Solzhenitsyn's hand!"

And the aid furnished by our Fund to the families of *zeks* absolutely had to be got over to Russia. Since Perestroika, communication had become more active—there were letters, money, parcels.

The load was too great—and it all had to be done at the same time, always, continuously. Time was being condensed, so that we never lost a minute. By the evening—where to find more energy? Yet it was still not the end of the day. Work went on beyond midnight. And then a short, inadequate sleep—which wasn't always even deep. And no one could do that work for Alya.

It was grueling. But what could we dare stop doing? what could we leave undone?

The Perestroika thaw also produced greater jolts from outside. When we didn't as yet know anything for sure about the latest event or text, there would already be calls from the press wanting our reaction. And Alya would try to extricate us. (Did they think I owed them a daily opinion column?)

There was one definite lightening of the load: by spring 1988 my forty-year labors on my dictionary were at an end. In New York, Elena Dorman began typesetting it and sending galleys for correction.

Now we had a subscription to *Novy Mir*, which arrived direct from Moscow. As we pored over its pages, still so cautious, so timorous, we felt the wondrous sensation of a *return.* —Books began to flow more freely, and now YMCA risked printing a further five hundred copies of *The Red Wheel* and added some *malyshki*[20] as well: newcomers from Russia would buy them up.

Yes, the unimaginable was actually happening: open communication between people. In Copenhagen they had just convened the first meeting of "culture representatives." Soviet figures arrived, still shy, still greenlit by personnel departments[21]—and those energetic Third Wave émigrés made a beeline for it. Among the first to make his voice heard there was Etkind: Solzhenitsyn "is disseminating hate!"[22] And he was not the only one. A terror of Solzhenitsyn, already inflated by Third Wave émigrés in the West, was now being pumped into the educated circle of Soviet society—and those had no objection: "We don't need prophets!" (Evidently, it was a bit galling that I'd already spoken out openly, fifteen years earlier, about today's new developments, and a lot more besides. Who wants to be outstripped that far in advance? . . .)

Dmitri Panin did not live to see this moment, so full of hope, for he died in Paris in November 1987, at the age of seventy-seven. His cardiac stimulator implants were no longer up to the job.

And so his tragic life came to an end. Having undergone a bruising investigation, and this was in a camp, during the war, in starvation conditions (and his camp term was increased from five to thirteen years), and having worked up, within the constraints of camp and prison life, his philosophical and political principles for running the state and society—he had to keep these secret, even when living in Soviet "freedom" when he was already over fifty. Later he hoped to find wide recognition in the West—but he did not; and neither did he master the skill of conveying his ideas by hooking his listeners in, so as to convince them of the value of his principles and increase his support. So he remained a misunderstood utopian. And his black-and-white way of thinking did not help: *Creators and Destroyers* was the title he gave one of his main works, with the idea that people are divided into two such precisely defined categories, with no stages between the two, no transitions. (He proposed exiling the main destroyers to uninhabited islands, thereby simultaneously saving the human race.) From emigration he used underground channels to send into the USSR calls for strikes and violent opposition to the government. —In emigration, moving from philosophy, he also wrote some works on physics subjects, on which I would not venture a judgment; but they too failed to win recognition.

Becoming desperate, Dmitri asked me, at one time, to arrange for these works to be promoted in the United States and, another time, to find for him in the States some kind of advance payment for his future social and political writing—an impossible challenge. Then, finally, he agreed to accept direct help from us. But all his calls, addressed to the society of both East and West, and to the Holy See, remained fruitless, and could find no practical application.

For me, this friendship—of forty years, since the Marfino *sharashka*—had been enlightening and difficult. The death of Dmitri Panin now brought an era of my personal life to a close.

In accordance with our tradition, on Old New Year's Eve, 13 January, we held a joint memorial service for those who had passed on in 1987. As well as Panin, there were the magnificent poet Ivan Elagin, whose whole life was ruined by the calamities of emigration; Boris Koverda, who had kept the White cause going and was celebrated for shooting the Bolshevik, Voikov, in Warsaw in 1927; and the Red general, Pyotr Grigorenko, who had risked life and limb, fighting his way through to the truth.

* * *

Events in the Soviet Union were starting to move, though with difficulty. In 1988 they were at last preparing to withdraw troops from Afghanistan after a pointless, eight-year war. In June, American television showed a demonstration in Moscow—"Land to the people! Down with the KGB!" (But at the end of June the Communist Party conference decided that Party control must, of course, be retained!)

As we had already predicted in *From Under the Rubble*, the Soviet "friendship of the peoples" turned out a mirage! nationalist explosions awaited us. They took it in turns. But Gorbachev seemed resigned, even nonchalant. Wherever anyone was being expelled, as the Georgian Meskhs were from Kazakhstan, with Georgia refusing to take them back into their mother country, Gorbachev gave way. When it came to the terrible slaughter of Armenians in Azerbaijan, there too Gorbachev kept out of it, punished no one, and assumed an unruffled, liberal mien, to give the impression that nothing special was going on—though by then the clamps holding his State together were cracking up. —Gorbachev was busy with a more important matter: solidifying his majority in the Politburo. He got rid of Demichev and that permanent fixture Gromyko, moved Ligachyov over to Agriculture, gave Ideology to Vadim Medvedev, installed the reliable Kryuchkov at the KGB—and? And—nothing. He continued to enjoy endearments from the West, and to doze while the State collapsed.

But in the capitals the public mood continued to heat up. In speech, glasnost was getting bolder, and now it began to force its way into print, where it touched on today's burning issues. And here and there in the papers, articles would appear remembering the victims of repression—and the horrors of the camps. And Sergei Zalygin, apparently, hadn't given up his efforts. On 11 May 1988, a year after the first trial balloon he'd launched, we received an inquiry by phone from *Novy Mir*, though via a third party: they asked, on Zalygin's part, if I would agree to their publishing *Cancer Ward* and, after that, *Circle*. And would it be possible to announce it right now, and publicly? In June, Zalygin was in Paris and confirmed his intention openly.

But now this request was past its prime, and did not excite Alya and me as just the rumors of it had the year before. We no longer felt that *warm breeze*. Since then, the murky progress of Perestroika—with its showpiece (and often mindless) measures—had become transparent to us, its essence expressed in the self-serving calculations of Party circles. So was there perhaps, in this proposal channeled *through* Zalygin, some political trick? Maybe to announce *Cancer Ward* just before the Gorbachev-Reagan summit?

But *Ivan Denisovich*, "Matryona," and "Krechetovka" had been burned in the Soviet Union[23]—why weren't they proposing to rehabilitate them? Pretend they hadn't been burned? And now, all at once, this "generous step"—let's publish *Cancer Ward*?

What was the difference, basically, between this proposal of 1988 and the KGB proposal of September 1973,[24] which had come via Reshetovskaya, that they would publish *Cancer Ward* if I, in exchange, didn't press forward with *Archipelago*?

Yes, a year earlier, when Zalygin had first talked about it, the publication of *Cancer Ward* would have been a landmark event. But now, left unpublished for twenty years, how much would it mean in the current situation, which was giddy, agitated, verbose, and already publishing endlessly? It would only obscure the fact that, for today's Glasnost, I was still unacceptable (and not only to the authorities—to the leading lights of the cultured circle, too: their fear of my return was clear in the writing of Pomerants, Etkind, and many others).

I knew Zalygin from earlier years, and I trusted him: his proposal had no ulterior motive. But was there not some *game* being played here, of whose scope he himself was unaware?

No, I had to settle this on a grand scale.

Archipelago had been the reason for my expulsion. For reading *Archipelago* in secret, people had been put in prison. *Archipelago* would transpierce

Perestroika with a penetrating light: did they want actual changes—or just a quick touch of paint?

And Alya and I made our decision—right or wrong—and it was: no!! To agree to *Cancer Ward* now would only delay the appearance of *Archipelago*—if it didn't put paid to it altogether.

If I was to make a return into Soviet publishing, it would be brandishing a red-hot iron bar: the *Archipelago*.

And Claude Durand sent similar advice from Paris. (He'd already shown himself more than once to be a true fencer, understanding the value of holding back and enjoying the battle.)

In 1962–63, against Tvardovsky's advice, I'd been champing at the bit: publish as soon as possible! any of my works! take advantage of every opportune moment to widen the bridgehead! And now, twenty-five years later, having published almost nothing in the USSR, now I'm the one slowing things down. . . .

And what if this meant *Archipelago* would be delayed for another fifteen or twenty years? And would it be as necessary then, this long-ago, neglected past . . . ?

This difficult decision had already taken shape by the time the first direct proposal arrived from Zalygin himself. It was a telegram—a "telegram"?—dated 27 July, which reached us from Boston, in an ordinary envelope, five days later. (How many censorial hands, how much suffering had this "telegram" gone through?) The authorities had no desire to allow Zalygin direct contact with us. We read, in Latin characters: "Intend publish Cancer Ward First Circle Awaiting your agreement proposals Novy Mir Sergei Zalygin." (Zalygin, meanwhile, thought his telegram had vanished into thin air—why had I not responded *in any way*? Trusting, naïvely, in the post, he was already thinking that I didn't even want to negotiate with him!)

The following day I replied by registered letter. [**30**] But what hope was there that even a registered letter would arrive? No, we had to sort it out by some speedier, more direct means. But how? Because of the danger in any contact with us, no one from Moscow had phoned us for the past twelve years—and we, likewise, had phoned no one. But perhaps it was not so dangerous by now? And Alya decided to phone Dima Borisov, a close family friend who took part in our underground activities in 1972–73. In those days he'd been fearless in the face of the KGB, and of a like mind with us. And it worked—they did not cut the conversation off, and Alya read our message out to Dima, asking him to pass it on to Zalygin. (Which was lucky, because they didn't let the letter itself through to *Novy Mir* for two weeks. Zalygin had made inquiries at the Ministry of Communications, but to no avail.)

You can imagine the disappointment, the despondency of Sergei Pavlovich, faced with the burden I had dumped on him—and the impregnable barrier set up by the Central Committee. (Weighing it up, Zalygin's task seemed harder, scarier, more dangerous than Tvardovsky's in 1962: back then the issue had been a "story of everyday life" by some provincial schoolteacher, while today it was an explosive missile by a "traitor," exiled from the USSR and stripped of his citizenship. That's the courage Zalygin had to muster up in those weeks!) It was at that very time that he decided to put the question of *Archipelago* up for discussion by the editorial board. (And now, naturally, Dima was also brought in, and he vigorously encouraged Zalygin to stay firm.)

Meanwhile, Zalygin replied to me on 26 August by express mail: "*Cancer Ward* would still have been better! But never mind—we'll try." (We also learned the content of this letter through Dima, by phone—but, as for the actual letter, we only received it a month later, in a very roughly opened and resealed envelope—they were even making a show of the farcical way they executed this procedure.)

As for the Western media, they could not stand Gorbachev marking time any longer and tried to whip up some action with stories they simply fabricated. French radio reported that Gorbachev was proposing to Solzhenitsyn that he should return—and then they would publish *Archipelago*. —Or they whipped up something even more brazen. Bavarian Radio had already, in July, announced that Gorbachev had written me two letters—*handwritten*, what's more—to the effect that, if I came back to the USSR, he would publish all my books. And that it was already agreed: at the end of the year Alya and I would go to Moscow to "sign all the contracts." These reports had come from their New York correspondent, who had *himself talked to Solzhenitsyn's wife over the phone*, and she had confirmed to him that, yes, such letters had been received from Gorbachev.[25] Alya was livid, and called Munich to refute the claim: there had been no letters from Gorbachev! and no conversation with that correspondent! But the Bavarian liar insisted he was right: yes there had! And furthermore, he had, he said, a letter from Mrs. Solzhenitsyn herself, but didn't have the right to show it. (Why shouldn't he show it?—show it!)

But how about this? Now the very reputable London *Economist* joined the fray—why were *they* muscling in? Their verdict was that such letters from Gorbachev certainly existed! Although Solzhenitsyn's wife denied it, such a conversation undoubtedly took place.[26] —Alya was now seriously angry, it couldn't be left like that! It took her three weeks to obtain, through the efforts of a lawyer, a retraction from the *Economist*, which appeared only in the middle of August, along with a small apology.[27] (I personally had thought it was all unnecessary fuss and bother—that we should give up on it and it would die down of its own accord. As for the Bavarian originator of this tittle-tattle, he wasn't even reprimanded by his journalists' union—how would the press survive without tittle-tattle? . . .) —Now the Associated Press joined in: they knew that all the necessary papers for Solzhenitsyn's return to the USSR had already been drawn up in the Soviet Embassy in Washington. (Only no one had thought to tell us. . . .)

At the beginning of August the *Moscow News* thumbed its nose at the authorities by publishing, first in English and then in Russian, an article entitled "Hello, Ivan Denisovich!"[28] (Who's that Ivan Denisovich, then?)

And around the same time Lyusha Chukovskaya—it was her own idea, her own decision—added fuel to the fire with an article in *Knizhnoye Obozrenie* (*Literary Review*) demanding that the authorities start to publish Solzhenitsyn and restore his citizenship![29] (How had Averin, the editor-in-chief, had the nerve? publishing that almost cost him a heart attack on the spot.)

That article caused a sensation: it was taken as a challenge. The nervousness that had held the public back from commenting was swept away. On the same day that the issue came out, excited readers were phoning the editorial office and turning up in person, and the first supporting telegrams arrived. Crowds thronged the paper's display boards on the street, and international news agencies picked up the story.[30]

The next day, the readers' passionate response—in the form of hundreds of letters—descended on the editorial office. And the paper had the courage to print those letters, in two issues, over double-page spreads.[31] Brave voices flooded onto the pages of that brave newspaper. Among them:

"A writer, an artist, anyone has the right to express his thoughts without fear. We, our whole people, have won that right through our sufferings." —"Just think of that leviathan he's taken on! More terrifying than facing a tank, I should think!" —"Solzhenitsyn anticipated much of what is now being wafted, by an invigorating wind, through our Fatherland. . . . He has served it better than all his detractors, who call themselves patriots." —"The time has come to annul that unlawful act, and free the man of the slanderous charge of treason—which he did not commit . . . this is necessary, most of all, for us ourselves. To cleanse our conscience as citizens. To appease our moral sense of justice." —"Our real intelligentsia has never turned its back on Solzhenitsyn's works: they have always been integral to it." —Solzhenitsyn "must be returned to the country whose destiny has always been his own personal destiny as well." —"Forgive us, dear Aleksandr Isayevich, for not speaking out on your behalf at the time and, instead, for accepting as inevitable those disgusting things they wrote about you and their exiling you beyond the bounds of our Fatherland."

But there were some who called Chukovskaya's appeal "an insult to those who went to war." Restore his citizenship?—no!—"don't allow Solzhenitsyn within firing range of the USSR!"

In the editorial office of *Knizhnoye Obozrenie* they were not even counting the letters—they were weighing them. And later they sent us a selection, about three hundred of them.

(That ample packet of readers' responses to Lyusha Chukovskaya's article, those that had not been published in *Knizhnoye Obozrenie*, reached me in early 1989. To me this was the response of the real Russia. What a sudden and voluminous reacquaintance with my fellow-countrymen! But . . . I read them, read them, was really gripped—but it produced a feeling of dejection. Until then, until that very moment, I'd not imagined how much and how methodically Soviet propaganda had, over the decades, sullied my reputation, and how it had been instilled into people's minds, to such an extent that you could hear it even in many of the letters sent me by well-wishers. What amazed were not the standard-template critical letters, but, actually, the heartfelt ones. Only now did I first realize that the long years of propaganda against me by the authorities had been far from fruitless, for it sank its venomous claws, its lies, into so many trusting souls! Almost no one, even now, saw me as I really was, especially in the full context of my works. If the "pro" sentiments were in the majority, it was not by much. And it was hard to believe that all this had been written about *one and the same* man. The threshold separating me from my readers was so high that it could not be surmounted with a single impetus—with just one major publishing event, or the fact of my arrival there. How many such endeavors—and, what's more, how many years—would it take to wash away that lie? —Many of the letters fell between two stools—their authors' ideas were ill-defined, their outlook vague. So perhaps it would be better for ordinary people to be given *Ivan Denisovich* and "Matryona" as soon as possible, and the more educated readers *Cancer Ward* and *Circle*? So perhaps there was no point in digging my heels in over *Archipelago*?—were we letting a most opportune moment slip through our fingers? Or, then again, it might not be too late if we pulled back, if necessary, in a year or two. Who could make this judgment? —But there was this, one of the most recent testimonies to reach me: When, in the '70s, there were anti-Solzhenitsyn rallies going on absolutely everywhere, in Primorye one participant, more wary than most, his grandfather having been shot and his father's life ruined in the camps, and having himself been on the front, innocently asked the speaker, "Why weren't leaflets produced in time, explaining *exactly how* Solzhenitsyn had slandered the Soviet people?" The speaker replied, glib, confident, "The Party has deemed it inadmissible for our populace to take his punishment into their own hands.")

Suddenly, on 8 September, a "letter by phone" from Dima. The editorial board of *Novy Mir* had come to a decision: in issue 12 of 1988 they would publish my Nobel Lecture with a foreword, cushioning the shock, by Zalygin. And in issue 1 of 1989—*Archipelago*!!

We could not believe it—or get a good night's sleep. And we didn't dare rejoice. I was amazed by the boldness of the usually placid Sergei Pavlovich, as I remembered him at long-ago meetings in *Novy Mir*. And to make things easier for him, I allowed them to remove for this publication several chapters, those that would be the most insufferable to a Soviet ear: "The Bluecaps" (about the Chekists), about the Vlasovites . . .

But, according to Dima, "almost no one" of the Moscow intelligentsia understood my obstinacy: just why was I demanding *Archipelago* first? Let the old works be published—that would be good enough.

But from Estonia came a request specifically for *Archipelago*. And the previously unknown *Literaturny Kyrgyzstan* (*Literary Kyrgyzstan*) wanted *Archipelago* first! The journal *Nashe Nasledie* (*Our Heritage*) asked for some chapters from the *Wheel*. And *Knizhnoye Obozrenie* now had all the more right to publish something, after everything they'd been through. *Neva* wanted to publish *Circle*. In Leningrad an actor we hadn't heard of was appearing in clubs with readings of my stories, and someone else was giving lectures about me. The film *Solovki Power*[32] came out—and in it several extracts from *Archipelago* were quoted, but the filmmakers were too timid to name the source. Despite everything, these little streams were cutting a way through. . . .

Now there loomed an anarchic, unauthorized, pell-mell publication of my texts—even, perhaps, in a corrupted form, no one having checked them. Having heard about *Novy Mir*'s decision, others pushed to publish something of mine, some of them wanting stories, others—miniatures, others—old pieces of social and political commentary. And the critic Bondarenko, very determined, was already preparing to publish— with Sovetskaya Rossiya, of all places—a whole collection, the contents chosen by him personally, without *Archipelago* (and the American press was already calling him the "first publisher of Solzhenitsyn"[33]). And someone had taken it upon himself, quite unauthorized, to bring *Ivan Denisovich* to the stage. This way, things could go topsy-turvy, start down the path I'd rejected.

There was still no authorization regarding me personally when the interim head of the Cinematographers' Union, Andrei Smirnov, phoned from New York: we'd like to organize an evening at the House of Cinema in December, for the author's seventieth birthday. What could I say? I'd certainly have no objection, but of course I couldn't go.

We were amazed. It was like a disconcerting vision in the early-morning mist. What other surprises could we expect?

And now another one rolled along. While I'd been procrastinating over *Archipelago* (was I the one procrastinating?), Memorial[34] had been set up in Moscow—and sent a telegram inviting me to join their council. While still in Vermont? (Their first telegram, incidentally, had been returned: "Insufficient address." This story found its way into the *New York Times*[35]—then the second telegram got through.) There were sixteen signatures, headed by Sakharov. —But surely I couldn't, with the charge of "treason" still not lifted, cross the ocean without a care in the world to engage in real work? How should I reply? And behind the leaders of this Council there was perhaps a growing mass, young people with inquiring minds—I must not give offense to them. I sent a telegram.[36] **[31]**

Pressure from the public—so unusual, so unfamiliar to the authorities and to the people themselves—this pressure, woven from their decisiveness, their consciousness, their will, was increasing. And it was in favor of my books—and me as well—returning. Starting in summer 1988 and continuing into the autumn, letters poured into the editorial offices of newspapers and magazines; voices were heard at meetings, rallies, and soirées: "We want to know the truth! And what is Solzhenitsyn actually writing? Publish his books!" (We learned much of this through the Parisian *Russkaya Mysl*, so prompt with its reactions in those days, the rest sometimes reaching us a great deal later.) The newborn Moscow magazine *Express-Khronika* (*Express-Chronicle*) and the Riga samizdat had already, in January 1988, wanted to publish *Archipelago* in a massive print run and "hold a cycle of lectures on Solzhenitsyn to mark his seventieth birthday."

But the Party, steadfast, stood guard. In July, a high-level briefing at the Central Committee stated: "We do not know what Solzhenitsyn is *thinking* now [this was because of my silence on Perestroika]. If he speaks out, he could upset the balance of power." And now, after the decision of the *Novy Mir* editorial board, Zalygin was told, firmly, from the *very top*: don't even think of publishing *Archipelago* now; it is "not the right time."

But Zalygin was already riding the crest of public support. —On behalf of the Cinematographers' Union, Andrei Smirnov wrote to the Chairman of the Presidium of the Supreme Soviet (still Gromyko at that time): the expulsion of Solzhenitsyn was totally unlawful; there has been, for a long time now, no such article in the Criminal Code! We ask you to abrogate the decree stripping him of his citizenship, and reinstate him in the Union of Soviet Writers.[37] —4 October, the Memorial Council to Gorbachev: "We are extremely concerned that the publication in *Novy Mir* of chapters from *The Gulag Archipelago* has been put on hold for an indefinite period. It has been read all over the world, and the nation whose fate is the subject of that book must, at long last, give its verdict. Through its long-suffering history, it has earned that right."[38] —6 October, twenty-seven writers to the secretariat of the Union of Soviet Writers: Solzhenitsyn must be reinstated in the Writers' Union, and the Presidium of the Supreme Soviet petitioned to abrogate the decree stripping him of his citizenship.[39]

And a comment was quoted somewhere, from a KGB boss—the Ukrainian KGB, for some reason—Galushko: "Solzhenitsyn returning is out of the question." (But I was no longer an "enemy of the people"?)

And two weeks later, as if to taunt him, right under his nose in Kiev, the railwaymen's paper, *Rabochee Slovo* (*Workers' Word*), published the full text of "Live Not by Lies"—what a sensation![40] (Other similar little papers, many others, immediately wanted to reprint it from *Rabochee Slovo*.) It was on that day, 18 October, that I took my first real step towards home.

Then someone informed the Central Committee that Zalygin had dared put one line of advance publicity on the cover of the October issue of *Novy Mir*: it said that in 1989 the journal would publish *something* (unnamed) by Solzhenitsyn. Zalygin was called to the CC and sternly informed that his escapades were intolerable and that he was smuggling an "enemy" into print. And they gave the printers a direct order: stop the presses! pull the covers off the copies already finished (and there were now almost five hundred thousand of these)—and shred them. A truly Bolshevik-scale exercise!

But times had changed: the print workers were outraged and refused to tear them off! But where could they go to complain? They made up their mind: to Memorial. (In October we also received our first letter from Dima, which is how we learned the details. Sergei Pavlovich had taken that blow, the order to tear off the covers, hard. Dima, with great determination, and restraint too, was helping Zalygin stay firm. And, the main thing—the public pressure was not letting up.)

Nineteen Soviet writers, on the other hand, "supporters of perestroika" (I hope their names will be preserved for posterity), had obsequiously written to the Central Committee saying the exact opposite: this is not the time to publish Solzhenitsyn, it would destroy Perestroika![41] And a figure well known from the '60s added a heartfelt appeal: not only must *Archipelago* not be published, but neither must Solzhenitsyn himself be brought back to his homeland—he would damage the country, he is a monarchist, dark forces would gather around him. . . .

The covers were, of course, torn off: they don't count costs in the USSR! But it was actually those covers that launched the scandal—on an international level.[42] And photocopies of the cover were making the rounds of Moscow in samizdat form.

The era now dawning in Russia was certainly not one for bootlickers. Protests were coming thick and fast. 21 October, a group of sixteen writers and academicians, to Gorbachev: the publication of Solzhenitsyn has been halted, but his oeuvre "will nevertheless reach Russian readers, with the inevitability of a physical phenomenon. Today the publication of Solzhenitsyn's works in his homeland is awaited not only as a major literary event, but also as an unquestionable testimony to the completeness of our social renewal and the irreversibility of the transformations taking place in our land." —Immediately after that, again to Gorbachev, this time from eighteen scientists, artists, and writers: "We are extremely alarmed. . . . Banning publication could undermine trust in the ideas of perestroika." —24 October, from an evening event at the House of Medical Workers to the Presidium of the Supreme Soviet: the decree stripping Solzhenitsyn of his citizenship must be abrogated. There were 291 signatures (with addresses!)[43]

And, in the final days of October, the pan-Soviet Memorial held a conference in Moscow at the House of Cinema, and a good few former *zeks* gathered, from all over the country. And there was a proposal to vote for Solzhenitsyn's "treason" to be repealed, along with the decree stripping him of his citizenship and expelling him. And it was inevitable that the resolution would of course be immediately adopted.

But the nest of vipers wasn't dozing on the job! From the presidium, Izyumov, Chakovsky's deputy at *Literaturnaya Gazeta*, showed himself at the rostrum. And, so bashfully: "I may be divulging an editorial secret, but I'm going to tell you anyway. We have in our office, already typeset, material about Solzhenitsyn collaborating with the Ministry of State Security for many years—and very soon now *Literaturnaya Gazeta* will be publishing the exposé." Those Communists—how their hearts palpitate with indignation!

So Lyusha ran up to the stage, grabbed a microphone, and began to shout: "Get out of here!" Instant uproar!—the whole hall erupted, they were angry and rowdy: "Get rid of them! Out! Clear off, you bastards!" One of the two microphones got broken. The burly Igor Dobroshtan, a leader of the Vorkuta uprising, yelled in his clarion voice: "Don't believe them! Don't believe their documents—they're all fake! We know that man, and not by any bits of paper but by his deeds!" They wanted to drag the slanderer out of the presidium and throw him out of the hall, but he'd vanished. (Were my enemies actually thinking of publishing that "denunciation" again—that same well-worn fabrication that I myself had made public and unmasked twelve years before, in 1976? **[31a]** —Surprising, how necessary they found that falsification when attacking me. What ever could they cling on to, without my story in *Archipelago*? But those crooks were clearly cowed by the way the wind was blowing in this new epoch.)

There was an immediate vote, with the resolution carried unanimously: to repeal the charge of treason; to reinstate citizenship of the USSR; and to publish *The Gulag Archipelago* as soon as possible! And Sakharov, at the presidium desk, raised his hand, arm straight as a die, towards the ceiling. (But even in January '89, in Memorial's newspaper with the account of this conference, the point about *Archipelago* was not passed for publication, so a blank line was left.)

On 21 October, Agence France Presse reported (and Lev Timofeev also published this in *Referendum*, which at that time he edited) that Gorbachev had, in front of other people, stamped his feet in anger at Zalygin.[44] Lydia Chukovskaya wrote to us that "Zalygin stood his ground magnificently." On 2 November he sent Gorbachev a most determined letter. And on 9 November, at a newspaper editors' meeting at the Central Committee, it was drummed into them for the umpteenth time that everything by Solzhenitsyn was banned. "He is hostile to us. And, in general, we do not need such figures hanging around." (At the end of November, just before his seventy-fifth birthday, Zalygin suffered some heart trouble. He paid a heavy price for that long-drawn-out rigmarole.)

On 12 November in Riga, at an Ideology meeting, the Central Committee's new head of Ideology, Vadim Medvedev, had a lot to say about me—

about how unacceptable Solzhenitsyn was "for us." His words leaked out through the Western wire services, but he did not back down and repeated it once more at a 29 November press conference: "To publish Solzhenitsyn is to undermine the foundations on which our present life rests. His attacks on Lenin are intolerable."[45]

But at least this Medvedev, when talking about me, did not actually slander me or resort to sly insinuations—as had Sinyavsky, Voinovich, Korotich, and countless hundreds of others.

The House of Culture of the Moscow Electric Light Factory organized, 19 to 26 November, a "Conscience Week" and set up a "Memory Wall" in the foyer, with a raised-relief map of the USSR showing the locations of the camps, an exhibition stand with photographs of the victims of repression, and portraits of Shalamov and myself; and they'd put up "Live Not by Lies," from the Kiev *Rabochee Slovo*; and those wanting to express their feelings in writing were invited to do so. In just the first three or four days there were more than a thousand notes—in favor of the immediate publication of Solzhenitsyn and his return to his homeland.[46] And the number kept rising. Reading them was a very emotional experience.

All these obstacles, but also the whole development of this new pressure, reaffirmed over and over that we had been right: it was with *Archipelago* that we had to start! We had to shake things up, rather than wait for Gorbachev's censors to wake up.

During that time of our defeat, I wrote (1 December 1988) to Sergei Pavlovich: "I owe you my heartfelt gratitude for the steadfastness and courage with which you have tried to give the historical truth about our sufferings, and give my books, a path toward publication. I am sure that the history of Russian literature will not forget your efforts. You are not to blame for them now being blocked by such impregnable barriers—but that will only last for a while: there is no way to escape the truth."[47]

Sakharov's participation in the pan-Soviet Memorial Council was one of the most natural steps for him, because of both his heartfelt sympathy with the cause and the general direction in which he was moving: returning to the public life of his country after exile. Although he undoubtedly pined for the scientific work from which he'd been parted by the years spent serving his penalty—he had, it's true, in recent weeks been elected to the presidium of the Academy of Sciences, but this was not yet a real return to scientific work—he also felt keenly the burden of social issues on his shoulders and continued, as before, to intercede on behalf of various groups. These included the last few political *zeks* not yet released; the Crimean Tatars; he had interceded several times, and especially fervently, for the liberation of Karabakh;[48] and also—this was his own original idea—for the period of army service to be halved. But beyond that, liberal public opinion was also drawing him into its own initiatives of the time: into the collective anthology *There Is No Other Way*[49] (and into passionate support for the Gorbachev program—but *what was it*, his "program"?); into that debating club, the Moscow Tribune (where, in fact, a critique of that program had already appeared, in the form of a valid defense of the suppressed cooperatives); against possible restrictions on the press, meetings, and rallies; and against a "dangerous deviation to the right," which people constantly fancied they could see. (And how was it to be understood? For us Russians, the terms "right" and "left" in the party sense had long since become muddied.)

And on foreign issues, in June '88, at a press conference organized for him at the Ministry of Foreign Affairs, Sakharov's answers showed panache, resourcefulness, and a statesman-like quality.[50] His stance there was perhaps what persuaded the authorities to lift the ban on his traveling abroad, starting in November. And in November and December Sakharov made a trip to the United States, where he had important, high-level meetings, and publicly supported the Soviet objections to the Americans' Strategic Defense Initiative (missile defense). Then he enjoyed an even more triumphant visit to Paris, where he had occasion to give a contrary point of view, distancing himself from the Soviet position: the West should not give unconditional support to Gorbachev—it should only be offered as long as the policy of Perestroika is not abandoned or watered down.

During those few weeks Irina Ilovaiskaya met with Sakharov a couple of times and told us that Andrei Dmitrievich would tire rapidly, that he looked far older than his years, and was tormented by a good few doubts. He had asked her for our phone number.

But he wasn't phoning.

Then, on 8 December, he phoned from Boston. Alya spoke to him first (while I was being fetched from the other building). Andrei Dmitrievich was polite to her, but without the least trace of warmth. And when I took the phone he immediately launched into the burdensome task he had set himself. "So that everything is out in the open . . . I found the way you portrayed Elena Georgievna in *Calf* very offensive. She's not that kind of person at all."

This was about those two or three lines. And it was fourteen years ago.

I sighed: "I'd like to believe that."

And he said a bit more—still the same one-sided reprimand.

I also had a few things on my mind, things I'd have liked to say. About how, in March 1974, he had attacked me over the *Letter to the Soviet Leaders*, having clearly not even read it properly—and using turns of phrase rather unlike his normal style. And he'd been in a hurry to communicate it by phone to New York, when Alya and the children had not yet landed in Zurich.[51] Surely that was not like him? Surely there was a powerful influence showing through?

At that time he'd heaped accusations of "dangerous, bellicose nationalism" onto me—he was the first, at the very beginning, with all his authority. And for many years—fifteen, in fact—it had undermined my position in the West: how come? why? To the advantage of State Security and the glee of New York radicals. He had been the main voice, and the loudest, in predisposing Western educated circles not to listen to me, to accept none of my work except *Archipelago*.

But now something stopped me from reproaching him for that. It didn't matter by this stage—I'd missed my chance; and he was not the same person after his exile in Gorki.

Apart from clips on the radio, I hadn't heard his voice for those fifteen years. It sounded feebler to me, and with a hint of sickliness. I asked after his health. He replied: "Given my age, it's satisfactory."

And, as if having fulfilled a painful duty, he hung up.

Three minutes later I was still near the telephone when it rang again: "Oh yes—happy seventieth birthday!" That was what he'd phoned to say, but had forgotten.

I sat by the phone with a heavy heart. We should always, and on every subject, explain ourselves fully. But now—some other time?

As it turned out . . . as it turned out, this conversation would be our last: Andrei Dmitrievich died exactly a year later.

At that time, in December 1988, to mark my seventieth birthday, several unauthorized evening events were held in Moscow. At that time, this took courage. —At the House of Medical Workers they had been forbidden to hold such an event, but somehow, at their own peril, they did. —As for the cinematographers, they were as good as their word and organized one, which was extremely well attended (but they'd made a private commitment "not to go too far"). Among the speakers were Yuri Karyakin, a real live wire, and Igor Vinogradov, full of conviction and persuasion. But running the event, perfectly at ease, was Vladimir Lakshin who, not long before, had been vilifying me.[52] —The House of Architects had been forbidden to hold an event but, just two weeks late, they nevertheless managed to. (And later we were given an amateur videotape of the evening.) Anatoli Strelyany, Igor Zolotussky, Vyacheslav Kondratiev, Dima Borisov, and Vladimir Lazarev spoke; the Chukovskayas, mother and daughter, spoke passionately from the stage, Lidia Korneevna with her recollections and Lyusha—reading from letters that had not found a place in *Knizhnoye Obozrenie*, and naming the writers who had previously hounded me. —And another event: in a club of no great standing, that of the Bauman factory, an event was organized by patriots who were being harassed by *society*—but not the kind of nationalists who'd already pronounced a curse on me.

But a large sector of public opinion had judged that I was wrong: there had been no point in demanding that *Archipelago* be published first; I should have agreed to the old works being republished little by little, eventually getting to *Cancer Ward.*

And so, during those four years of thaw in the USSR, they had managed to publish all the banned authors who'd died, and all the banned ones still living—all except me.*

Well, I wasn't surprised. I just understood that in *that* Glasnost—there was no place for me.

And my books were not only forbidden for publication—they were also still being seized at the border, at customs.

Just before the 1989 New Year I made a note: "I cannot remember a time when the contours of events, and of the decisions to be taken, were so indistinct—except for 1972–73, before I was exiled. I am facing an anxious, tempestuous old age."

* Now there are publications (e.g., *Obshchaya Gazeta* [*Common Gazette*], 10 December 1998, 8) explaining Gorbachev's tactical calculations in retarding the return of my books to Russia. Chernyaev, Gorbachev's deputy at the time, writes that in 1988–89 Gorbachev did not want to restore my citizenship, in order to prevent my becoming the leader of a united opposition—that's what he was scared of. . . . (Author's note, 1999.)

And I told my wife, "Our life hasn't been simple, dear—but its end will be even more complicated."

And in December we wrote, in a clandestine letter to Dima and his wife Tatiana, who'd also been actively helping us: "Although everything has resulted in what appears to be a defeat, in fact it is not, and your contribution and the superhuman efforts of Zalygin will not have been in vain. With the years, and perhaps not many years, it will end up back in your hands."

And in the meantime?—they had simply left me more time to finish my works.

But it was sad.

CHAPTER 15

Ideas Spurned

And at the beginning of 1989 Gorbachev was still repeating, over and over (though now perhaps, in his heart of hearts, less confidently): "The critics are going too far. Our nation has chosen, once and for all, the Communist route and will not deviate from it." Reports were coming in, specifically from Moscow, that within the last year the situation with regard to everyday life, the provision of food and water, had taken a sharp turn for the worse; the epidemiological center was warning people not to buy dairy products since, in Ryazan oblast, the potatoes were contaminated with chemicals, and when you cut into them they were pinkish and had to be thrown away; Muscovites feared famine or major accidents (news from the Southern Urals of two passenger trains colliding head-on, catching fire, and killing six hundred people,[1] had rocked the whole country); and, in Moscow itself, demonstrations and posters threatening strikes were already starting to appear (we'd even seen it on American TV). But despite all that, what most concerned *society* in the capitals, in Moscow and Leningrad, was something else: passions were really aroused by some freak manifestations of Russian-Jewish conflict. (People had even started saying that Pasternak was an "unworthy son of a worthy father," and they would not forgive him the Orthodox themes of his poetry; they were even taunting Academician Likhachyov over his Orthodox faith; and in Moscow the term "village prose writers" was only used as an insult—even Valentin Rasputin was branded a dyed-in-the-wool fascist.) Harassed *patriots*[2] tried to give as good as they got, sometimes in coarse terms. Even among émigrés such a sharp schism had never been known. (But everyday life in the rest of the country seemed to be untouched by this psychosis of the capitals.)

The violence done to the cover of *Novy Mir*, obviously to bar the way for my books, made an unfavorable impression both in the USSR and in the

West—so the Soviet authorities tried to deflect the odium with a well-tried technique: discrediting me. And people happy to take this on, either voluntarily or in response to an appeal, were soon found. Within the first few days of 1989, Sinyavsky jumped at the chance, on the Moscow stage now. Although he had, apparently, come over for the funeral of his co-defendant, Yuli Daniel,[3] the constant leitmotif of his appearances and interviews was still, as for all his years in the West, malign disparagement of me. The least of his new accusations was: Solzhenitsyn is against Perestroika. (At that time I'd not yet said a word about Perestroika, and Sinyavsky and I had never exchanged so much as a line of correspondence or a phone call—but he *knew for a fact.*) The *New York Times* correspondent did not ask Sinyavsky where he'd picked that up from: if the master said it, that meant he knew.[4] It's hard to imagine now, but in those years, not too long ago, of perestroika propaganda such an accusation sounded overwhelmingly harsh: it signified what an incorrigible, evil reactionary that Solzhenitsyn was! —It was the favorite branding by which that whole Host[5] tarnished me. —They were also joined by the diehard Communist paper *Pravda*: "Sinyavsky's *Syntaxis* is a good magazine" (*praise like that will cost him dear . . .*),[6] we must distinguish between émigrés with a positive influence, like Sinyavsky, and the hostile ones, like Solzhenitsyn, who has no place in Soviet society; he wants (?) to bring back autocracy.

America was singing along in unison where I was concerned, be it the *New York Times* or *Boston Globe*.[7] —In the mass-market, widely read *US News & World Report* editor-in chief Roger Rosenblatt was trying to instill into American minds the idea that Solzhenitsyn represented a return of monarchy to Russia.[8] —And in the *New York Times Book Review* a certain Irving Howe wrote an ignorant and vitriolic review of *August 1914*.[9] (And the job's done—these days, of course, it's not literary critics or literary scholars who appraise literature, but popular newspaper reviewers.) In the *Washington Post* he was joined, naturally, by *my biographer*, Michael Scammell, immediately taking up his place in the rear.[10] But the surprising thing was that four years earlier, in 1985, when *August* had not yet been read in the States, it was unanimously branded anti-Semitic. Now, however, the English translation had appeared and—as if someone, somewhere had waved a magic wand—*all* those critics seemed, in an instant, to have lost their memory, lost their tongue, and no one now remembered Bogrov, or the "Serpent," or the *Protocols*—what masterly conducting!

The way those two millstones worked together, year after year, was by that stage nothing new—I was accustomed to it now. And between the

Soviet and the Western millstones, Third Wave émigrés never failed to provide the link, grinding out the image of a "monarchist, theocrat, and cruel fanatic."

But despite all the incantations, the party dam in our homeland nevertheless turned out to be a bit leaky: here and there unauthorized trickles filtered through, even if they sometimes missed the point. Viktor Konetsky was quick off the mark, deftly contriving to be the first to publish my letter to the Congress of the Writers' Union, as part of *his own* memoirs.[11] Suddenly a Moscow journal, a political one, *Vek XX i Mir* (*Twentieth Century and Peace*), published . . . "Live Not by Lies."[12] And the Golden Matrix speech[13] appeared in the Riga journal *Rodnik* (*Spring*) (but full of errors: those Rigans were correcting my faulty Russian—"otobranie"? . . . no such word, should be "otobrazhenie"; "vtolakivanie"? . . . no, it's "vtolkovanie"—and other, similar refinements.)[14] —But people were reading me. In my homeland. It was a joy, but annoying, too: was this how the avalanche of my work would begin its descent—skirting the *Archipelago*? —Grigori Baklanov asked for *In the First Circle* and *Cancer Ward* for his journal *Znamya* (*Banner*) (but they'd already been promised to Zalygin). —And the new glossy magazine *Nashe Nasledie* was insisting on *The Oak and the Calf*—all of them were playing deaf to the author's wish: first, *Archipelago*.

In March we were surprised to receive a tempting, and unsettling, phone call from Lenfilm:[15] "Let us film *Cancer Ward*!" It was tempting because we weren't talking about print here—this was cinema. So—maybe let them? . . . No, we'd made a vow. And I refused the director: "It's not the right time."

There really was movement in the USSR surrounding my name; was it now inexorable?

And, on top of all that, the Moscow Aviation Institute then found a reason for an evening event: the fifteenth anniversary of my expulsion from the USSR. —And, seeing the leak reach such threatening proportions, the prescient Roy Medvedev warned, in *Moskovsky Komsomolets* (*Moscow Young Communist*), that, yes, perhaps we ought to publish Solzhenitsyn—only not *Archipelago*. And if it did come to that, it would have to be with serious clarifications and commentaries—that is, we must tip the balance and extinguish the author's point of view. Tell the story our way. The Party way.[16]

As for Zalygin, he stood firm, publicly affirming that, yes, it was certainly *Archipelago* that he would be publishing.

In February '89 Dima and I by chance wrote each other letters—which crossed in the post—with the same idea. What I wrote to him was: I would like to know your opinion. Anticipating a possible boom in the future, when my books are allowed for publication, should I, and could I, give someone official authorization to represent my publishing rights in the USSR? And who would it be? And Dima, almost on the same day, wrote that as a result of "my efforts regarding *Archipelago*, 'tidings of me have spread throughout the Russian realm';[17] and it is to me that people come with their inquiries anyway . . . as if to your publishing representative." And he suggested that I should write to him, saying that I entrust him with allowing or refusing publication. —And as soon as his letter reached me, that same month of March, I sent him a power of attorney, notarized by the local Vermont administration, and: "I am sincerely grateful to you for taking on this enormous, complicated work. . . . I put my trust in your literary and societal taste, and in our shared way of thinking." (Later, at Dima's request, I sent him an even more official power of attorney, now validated by the US State Department.)

All these breakthroughs and fluctuations brought us a good few extra worries. And with such a quantity of these flooding in from the Soviet Union, they must have contributed to the return after two years, in spring 1989, of my angina. The attacks were now frequent, almost every other day, and two bad ones lasted a whole day each. They were probably microinfarcts, but I hadn't looked into it sufficiently. They'd gotten worse because I hadn't delved into all the direct effects of angina on the heart—I'd never doubted the health of mine. Which is why I never stayed the course when it came to taking medications or even, ignoramus that I was, taking nitroglycerin: in accordance with my overall, long-held attitude to illnesses, I considered that you have to "sit out" the pain, just wait and take as few medications as possible. I began to move carefully, delicately. I could have made the round trip to a good hospital in about four hours, but with my long-standing, stay-at-home way of life I was not amenable to that.

Anyway, I'd already got a lot done in my life. Perhaps I was at the final reach, and the river would not be offering me another bend ahead. I finished *April 1917*, the Node of *The Red Wheel* that I'd decided would be the last, in early May. This work had taken exactly twenty years, in all. And two days later I said to Alya: "You know, even though I have a grave waiting for me near Paris,[18] there'd be no point in making that my temporary resting place, now that such changes are underway in Russia. Bury me right here for the time being," and I pointed out a good location on our plot, by the giant pines and birches. "From here you can take me straight on to Russia."

But my heart would not surrender to that final reach.

And as for the *Wheel*, yes, I had finished it now. But—was it truly finished? Over the half century (since 1936) of my searching, collecting, and reflecting, abundant materials, incidents, plotlines had come together for all the Nodes I'd envisaged, and an integral plan—conveying the five-year transition into the Soviet world from 1917 to 1922, by way of the Civil War and War Communism—had been constructed in my mind. To describe that in detail, as I had always anticipated, was impossible now due to the limitations of both my lifespan and people's available reading time. But—maybe a Summary volume? The basic structure could be conveyed by leaving out all the fictional characters and retaining only the historical figures, and the most important true events. They would not just be enumerated but examined in depth and given the color of the successive, changeable, momentary opinions that had accompanied each of the chosen Nodes. Starting from a survey of just the events, leading into a survey of opinions on them.

And I threw myself into this new work with great enthusiasm: summer 1917, autumn 1917, the October coup, and then the weeks immediately following it—which had been eclipsed, shrouded in darkness: a lot had been covered up and was hard to find. And each month chilled me again to the core, as I sensed the striking psychological similarity of that time to our own, when in the joy of liberation, but in its frivolity too, days that would prove decisive to the future of Russia were racing past.

The work turned out to be even more voluminous than I had expected, and would take me much longer. I had to read even more newspapers of the time in my search for details and for people's attitudes. Of course, normal readers would not read it in such a condensed form—but those curious about history would. And I would feel I had completed the Construction.

As for Alya, collaborating with me on the *Wheel*, she sometimes worked for twelve hours a day, sometimes as long as sixteen, perceiving all our laboring as "magicking away the evil spells" in our history—and now she could see the finishing line as clearly as I did. Her first contact with the *Wheel* dated back to the very start of my work, which coincided with the beginning of our relationship. For twenty years the book, with its powerful magnetic field, had permeated our life together. (Acquaintances would ask: "But how can you endure such solitude in the middle of a forest?" And she would reply: "When you're this isolated—that's when work gets done. You have the feeling of a constantly spouting geyser.")

But no, for Alya that was not the end of *The Red Wheel*: now she must, without delay, prepare to publish my many-years-long *Diary R-17*[19]

(Revolution of '17), which had accompanied my work for the previous twenty years. And, once I finished the Summary volume—that would also need preparing. And then *Invisible Allies* as well: that wasn't ready yet, and how many things we needed to ask the protagonists—across oceans and borders—and how many agreements about who could be mentioned in print and who couldn't, and all this correspondence having to go through clandestine mail. And I pitched in too, sending Lyusha question after question.

In addition to Alya's backbreaking everyday work, now she also had to satisfy demands coming through the newly freed-up communication channels with the USSR. Desperate requests for medications made their way through to us—they had to be bought, and ways found to send them over. Or someone in Moscow would be in urgent need of a heart valve that was impossible to get: Alya must have it bought in Zurich and, from a distance, arrange for it to be sent to Paris, and from Paris to the patient. For a neglected cancer she must send Swiss ampoules. Or there was a hearing aid to be manufactured—in accordance with an earmold impression sent from Leningrad—and shipped. —And the Chernobyl League in Belorussia found us and asked for help—we had to help them, of course. —And hardly had the Catacomb Church[20] resurfaced when it too needed our help. But so did the radio station Voice of Orthodoxy. And a nursing home in Brazil for émigrés nearing the end of life. Well-known dissidents, having suffered in the USSR, were now turning up in the West, one after the other in rapid succession—we had to support them too. —And now that friends and acquaintances were flying to Moscow, it was no longer suitcases but crates, baggage of a hundred kilos or more, that Alya was packing full of medicaments, stationery, and food, food, and more food. And all the car journeys over our hills that that meant, the frequent snowstorms, with the snow not cleared off the road, sometimes thaws, rains, or sheet ice, and—for three weeks in spring—muddy sludge. —And the more connections we forged, the more accompanying letters there were to write as well. (Alya managed to write these, phrase by phrase, sitting next to the typesetting machine as it steadily tapped out her most important work: our final, edited text.)

But Alya's constant joy, which communicated itself to me, was our close bond with our sons who—despite our living in foreign lands, scattered across the world—were all growing into fine men. One of them would send frequent, substantial letters, the others might just visit or phone. —In 1989 Yermolai left Eton with top grades for everything and was urged to apply to Oxford or Cambridge—but he was longing to get back to America, and decided on Harvard. (Where he immediately jumped a year, thus freeing himself to spend a whole year in Taiwan in the future, to perfect his Chinese.) After his first year at Harvard, he stayed in Boston for the summer, working for a freight transport company and driving forty-foot trucks through Boston's narrow streets. —Ignat had now spent two years in England and was homesick there. He had already had occasion to play at London's Queen Elizabeth Hall and at Rostropovich's festival in Évian. Rudolf Serkin's celebrated summertime Marlboro Festival also attracted him, and now Rostropovich started nudging him onto a different track: "Splendid as your lessons with Maria Curcio are, it's time for you to go further afield. I myself cut my musical teeth spending time with Prokofiev, Shostakovich, and Britten." In the summer of 1990 Ignat returned to America, was introduced to the eighty-four-year-old Claudio Arrau, played some Schubert and Beethoven for him, and was honored with an invitation to accompany Arrau on his forthcoming international tours. But before long, that very autumn, the great Chilean fell ill and soon died. Deciding not to return to Europe, Ignat applied to the top American conservatoires, Curtis and Juilliard, was accepted at both, and chose Curtis. —Stepan, meanwhile, had long since surpassed the curriculum of the local school but had been steadfastly resisting his parents' efforts to move him to a very good private school for his last two years ("I don't want to be in some elite club"). Nevertheless, once he'd been to look at St. Paul's, a New Hampshire preparatory school, he was captivated by its friendly, cheerful atmosphere and agreed to change schools in autumn '89. There he could take both the Latin he so loved and French, and he ran the school's radio broadcasts. —As for Dimitri, for the 1990 New Year he was the first of the family to go to Moscow, to his homeland, never forgotten, to his unforgotten family and friends. (And we too welcomed that '90 New Year with high hopes. . . .)

The accounts of Moscow that we heard from the now-frequent leavers painted a disturbing picture: a maelstrom of discussions, mutual misunderstandings, skewed comparisons, head-on clashes. Alya was now phoning friends in Moscow—each time with great emotion, and concentrating hard—and then relaying to me what she'd heard. Muscovites were by now under a somber cloud of despair at what felt like the final stage of collapse. But now the letters arriving from the provinces, which had begun to get through to us at a rate of ten or so a week (and how many more had been swept aside by the censors?), were usually genial, and sometimes really touched our hearts. Alternating with appeals for me to defend them against the authorities, there were also bold intellectual, cultural, and economic projects. And in the provinces people were completely untouched by the flurries of pseudo-intellectual battles going on in the capitals.

And somewhere there, seen through the undulating Moscow prism, stood Zalygin, unwavering in his unbelievable, impossible decision to publish *Archipelago*. And the public's support had not weakened the slightest bit. And something seemed to be changing in the corridors of the Central Committee. Now, having sniffed out the whole situation, the crafty Korotich (who had, in Brezhnev's time, so often defamed me in *Sovetskaya Rossiya*) shrewdly abandoned the ranks of my persecutors to join, unbidden, my benefactors and—without Dima Borisov's permission or even knowledge—published "Matryona's Home" in *Ogonyok* in June of '89. (With a barbed foreword by Ben Sarnov, to the effect that by starting to publish Solzhenitsyn we are finally, at long last, "opening him up to criticism"—as if they'd been doing anything other than that in the West for the last fifteen years.) Which is how Korotich did, despite everything, rob *Archipelago* of its place first in line. I felt despondent—although, of course, "Matryona" had now, in three million copies, begun her journey towards a mass readership.[21]

As for Zalygin, he was doing as much as he could, little by little, to move things forward: the July issue with the Nobel Lecture, banned the previous December, was now about to be printed and was already in Glavlit,[22] awaiting the signal to start. (In the editorial office they were already checking the page proofs of the first chapters of *Archipelago* for the following issues.) Suddenly, on the morning of 28 June there was a call from the Central Committee, summoning Zalygin to an urgent meeting with the Ideology secretary, Vadim Medvedev. Clearly, this did not bode well. Zalygin went, in a state of high tension. And Medvedev did indeed tell him that publication of *Archipelago* in the country's leading journal, with a print run of 1.5 million, was impossible. Stop the typesetting! (But, as a concession, he gave the CC's agreement to allow the book to be brought in from abroad and even to be published, in a limited print run, in some of the Soviet republics—only not in *Novy Mir*!) But the steadfast Zalygin said: "In that case, I and all the editorial staff will hold up the entire issue, and by tomorrow the whole world will know about it." Medvedev spent an hour trying to break Zalygin, to keep him quiet, and then let him go with the threat that he would, tomorrow morning, put the matter before the Politburo.

Dima recounts: an extremely gloomy Sergei Pavlovich had returned to an equally gloomy editorial staff. From the early morning of the 29th, the *Novy Mir* offices were full of friends who had heard the news, all in a solemn, cheerless state of mind. Suddenly, around midday, having received a phone call, an excited and now younger-looking Zalygin emerged from his office and announced that the Politburo had refused to consider the question of publication because it was "outside their sphere of competence"! And they had entrusted the secretariat of the Writers' Union with "examining the question as a matter of urgency."*

It was an absolutely incredible decision!—not that the constitution of the secretariat seemed to promise a favorable outcome, though. But then an idea emerged: the *Novy Mir* team set to phoning round the journals and publishing companies, urging them to cable the Writers' Union, or turn up in person, to make their own position clear. And many of them did, with no backsliding. And first thing the following morning, the 30th, there was already a bundle of these appeals delivered to the secretariat, and the more

* Now (in *Nezavisimaya Gazeta* [*Independent Gazette*], 12 February 2000, 8) Vadim Andreevich Medvedev has told his side of the story. In October 1988 he had conferred with some top KGB people and other government officials. The head of the Fifth Directorate of the KGB, Abramov, and the subsequently notorious party patriarch, Anatoli Lukyanov, had declared themselves "in favor of continuing the work of unmasking Solzhenitsyn." Others convinced Medvedev to insulate the Politburo from the "juridical aspects of the deportation," which, they said, had no legal basis. It was during those weeks that Medvedev had got down to reading my books. Yes, he said, he'd given his opinion in public, but had "not placed any vetos on publication."

At the top, they'd felt "the pressure of public opinion" at the end of 1988, and again in spring 1989. In April, Zalygin had again pressed his cause, and Medvedev suggested that he reissue the old works already published in *Novy Mir*, plus *Cancer Ward* and *In the First Circle* (which by that time had already been taken out of the "restricted access" section of libraries), but not *Archipelago*. "Why must you comply with his conditions? You should try to convince the author." However, during their last conversation, on 28 June, "Sergei Pavlovich's stance turned out to be even firmer" and "it was impossible to put the publication of the *Gulag*, which was already being prepared, into reverse." (Why, what truly desperate courage! Head-on war with the Central Committee!) The pressure from readers was mounting, and on 29 June 1989 the matter was discussed in the Politburo. "It was clear, from certain rejoinders and the expression on people's faces, what a dim view many of my Politburo colleagues took of the situation." No resolution was adopted: "It was felt that the writers themselves should take the decision." And the following day, the writers (some of their own free will, others feeling compelled, according to what Dima Borisov wrote to us) did take one. And, at the same time, agreed "not to make too much of this and turn it into a sensation." (Author's note, 2000.)

impatient types who'd sniffed out the news were thronging the Directorate entrance and the little park adjoining Povarskaya Street. The *Novy Mir* people, who'd been invited, went inside.

It was a scorching-hot day. The chairman (Vladimir Karpov) took his jacket off, put it over the back of his chair, and told his colleagues, openly, that "it would be pointless for us to stick to the old tactic of banning Solzhenitsyn's work. Why, actually, is *The Gulag Archipelago* not suitable for us? Everything in it is honest, its facts truthfully reported. We support this initiative." —And after that, they all—some quite sincerely (such as Afanasi Salynsky, supportive since 1966), some through gritted teeth—agreed, with no objections. And the chairman wound up the meeting with: "It's a long time since we've had such unanimity in the secretariat." And the resolution was passed: publish *Archipelago*; reverse Solzhenitsyn's exclusion from the Soviet Writers' Union; and request that the Supreme Soviet revoke its stripping him of his citizenship.[23]

The meeting had taken less than two hours. (An hour later exuberant merrymaking broke out in the editorial offices of the much-loved journal.)

And just a few days later my Nobel Lecture appeared in *Novy Mir*, and a month after that the first, very substantial chunk of *Archipelago*, with a print run of 1.6 million.[24] We'd been thirsting for that, fighting for it, and now, to an extent that was almost impossible to take in, this closely-guarded, brutal truth was finally bursting out across the whole country!

Several Soviet publishers immediately sent requests to publish *Archipelago* after *Novy Mir* had done so—and all agreed between them to publish simultaneously. —On the other hand, the TV channel that was to air a program about *Archipelago*—which included the story of my arrest and expulsion and my call, back in '69, for glasnost—pushed it back to half past one in the morning. Despite everything, the *powers that be* hadn't nodded off. —But a month later, an excerpt from *The Red Wheel* appeared in *Literaturnaya Gazeta*.[25]

Nothing is lost to one who knows how to wait.

I just hoped that I'd be read broadly throughout my homeland, not only in Moscow and Leningrad.

So would the settled trade winds of constant curses be replaced by a fickle monsoon of glory? Ah, but now, careful: how was I to use this brief surge of glory to serve Russia, unerringly and fittingly?

And I did, of course, still have those "treason" and "stripped of his citizenship" labels hanging round my neck. . . .

However, after the appearance of *Archipelago*, the Sinyavskys, husband and wife, were seized with a worry that gnawed at them. With renewed vigor the essayist threw himself into an international tour to oppose me, and neglected no opportunity. At a conference in Bergamo it was: Solzhenitsyn is the standard-bearer of Russian nationalism! Any moment now he'll return in triumph and take the lead in a clerical fascist movement! (He gave his audience the impression that he was obsessed, going on and on in such a frenzy that the Italians argued back forcefully.) —At the Kennan Institute of Washington's Wilson Center: "Solzhenitsyn is a racist and monarchist, and in five years he'll be running Russia!" (And the Kennan Institute distributed Sinyavsky's speech in leaflet form.) And he went even further—surely, the rusty trumpet of his failsafe "anti-Semitism" line wouldn't let him down! and the gullible American Slavists meekly took it all in.

And there was Radio Liberty—that crew were always on the lookout for a chance to attack me. And it was that same Sarnov, who now had "the right to criticize" me, and Boris Khazanov, and others of that ilk, speaking on the undoubted anti-Semitism of *The Red Wheel*—which was the principal danger now about to sweep the country. And what could you use to launch the speediest assault on Soviet ears? They cranked up their usual refrain—a third broadcast of the whole of Voinovich's fantasy, *Moscow 2042*.[26]

Each did what he could. In Moscow, *Sovetskaya Rossiya* reprinted an old (1971) pack of lies about me from *Stern*.[27] *Znamya* published Sakharov's harsh 1974 response[28] to my *Letter to the Soviet Leaders*, which had still not been published in the USSR. (So as to keep the peace, I hadn't wanted to publish my social and political writing for the time being, and inflame people's passions—but no, I got dragged into it.) And what could *Pravda* manage? They launched a series of articles attacking *Archipelago* and there, brandishing his hunting spear, was Roy Medvedev.[29]

And what should we do? As Goethe once wrote in reply to Schiller: "Let us proceed with our labors, and leave to them the torment of negation."[30]

And what did we get? Reactions to *Archipelago*, from shocked readers. That was enough for us.

During that happy year it appeared that my screenplay *The Tanks Know the Truth* would also force its way through to reality. Back in July of 1988, Irina Ilovaiskaya had informed me from Paris, where the celebrated Polish film director Andrzej Wajda was living, that he wanted to film my *Tanks*: before this he had feared being stripped of his citizenship, but now, apparently, he could take that risk. So he was asking whether I would agree. —Would I?

And how! with great pleasure. —In January 1989 Irina told me that Wajda had phoned her: things were moving with regard to the film; they had decided to film in Poland and were awaiting permission from the authorities. When they had received that, then we must meet. —In summer 1989 Wajda sent me a letter saying he was ready to make the film: "The fact that you have been willing to entrust me with directing a film written by you is the greatest honor and joy that could have befallen me in my life." He was, in truth, still somewhat inhibited by the "fear of problems when returning to Poland after taking such a step." But "I think the time has come when . . . it is possible to shoot the film in Poland, and with Russian-speaking actors, in the original language. I am working on this solution and I humbly beg you for a little more patience."

A splendid proposal! At one time a California group had been intending to do it—that would certainly have been a failure.[31] But Poles—yes, Poles could produce this film; the white heat of the Gulag was accessible to them, within their reach—and the Slavic features seen in crowd scenes would not be fake.

Joyfully, I replied: "I have no doubt that you would manage it brilliantly, with absolute understanding of the spirit of those events." But I suggested that it would be more natural for him to shoot in Polish and then dub into Russian. And I alerted him to the fact that my screenplay would be published in the USSR by December, in one of the journals.

Towards the end of the year, Wajda wrote that he was, for the time being, busy shooting a film about Korczak, but the idea had not been abandoned: he wanted "to shoot in Poland, where we can easily find the right natural exteriors," but "it would be ideal if the film could be shot in Russian. We would invite Russian actors to come from the USSR in the context of a co-production," and he even said this setup would be, for him, "the only acceptable way."

But time was passing, the project was losing momentum and then, for some reason I didn't totally understand, it was shelved and the production never happened.*

---

* Eleven years later I read, unexpectedly, an interview with Wajda in *Moskovskie Novosti* (*Moscow News*) (6–12 March 2001, 16: "Andrzej Wajda, the Exorcist"):[32] "Once in my life I had the opportunity to make a Russian film, but I did not take it. And, to this day, I am tortured by remorse. . . . The producers made me a tempting offer . . . to make a film based on [Solzhenitsyn's] screenplay *The Tanks Know the Truth*. It was about the suppression of a Soviet labor camp rebellion. The screenplay was magnificent: memorable male and female characters, explosive plot dynamics. In a word, a director's dream. Moreover, I was flattered that it was me the great writer

My screenplay had lain motionless for thirty years—was it to lie for another twenty or thirty?

In September 1989 Dima Borisov came to see us in Vermont, on a mission from *Novy Mir*, and stayed with us for three weeks. When we met, it was with the same great warmth as before, quite undiminished. It seemed he had not changed, even after fifteen hard years. Despite that long separation, he still thought almost exactly as we did. Amidst the bitter literary-political wrangling in Moscow he had, in all his answers to the press, pursued our *line* impeccably. Now we were discussing our future steps in the USSR.

For many months now, people had been jumping the gun and sending both of us demands for Nodes of *The Red Wheel*—now the time had come when we could start publishing it in journals. But *Novy Mir* would be publishing so many of my works now, one after the other, that we decided to give the *Wheel* to other journals, one Node, or even one part of a Node, at a time. (This was rather unhelpful in practice: how was the reader to follow the parts, scattered over such a vast range of destinations, if he wanted to read the *Wheel* in order? But publishing it in *one* journal—that would take five years.)

The main thing Dima was concerned about was the book printing, which had already begun. He took, for reprinting, the paste-ups of *Circle*, *Cancer Ward*, and *Archipelago* that Alya had prepared, and also my *Dictionary*,[33] which had been typeset in New York. He did not like having to hand all that over to state-owned publishers ("they're all tainted"), imparted to us his plans to create his own publishing company attached to *Novy Mir*, and told us what he would start publishing there. (During the time he was away, the Soviet Writer publishing house issued the first volume of *Archipelago*: the printers had, *of their own accord*, sped up the release and printed the book in two weeks!)

---

had chosen. Of course, I understood that Solzhenitsyn, being in emigration, as a free man, saw in me another free man. But I was not free of my country, for whose viewers I was accustomed to work. After such a film there could be no more thought of returning to Poland. I couldn't take the decision to emigrate, just as I couldn't imagine myself outside Poland. How could I possibly have supposed that the entire system would collapse during my lifetime? Later, I often thought: maybe I should have dropped everything and made this film? I keep thinking that it would have played an important role in my life." (Author's note, 2001.)

In Moscow, Dima would face a hail of editors' inquiries, reporters' questions, and readers' letters, which would last for a good while. (But it never even occurred to us to formalize every jot and tittle of our business relationship—it remained just as warm as before, in our underground days.)

Dima left—and disappeared from view. . . . Two months later, I could not wait any longer and wrote to him: "To be honest, I am worried: you have already taken on so many commitments, besides representing me, that it will be hard for you to cover everything equably. May God give you strength and focus." And again I asked him to give the green light, with no restrictions, to all the *regional* publishers for *Archipelago*, and then also for the books that were to follow. "The publishing house you are planning, attached to *Novy Mir*, will be a long-term, complicated endeavor, and you will encounter more problems and more botheration than you can even imagine now. I beg you most earnestly not to let those future plans put any obstacles in the way of publishing houses wanting to print something of mine. My prose must go to *anyone who asks for it*, and without delay."

. . . Now that writing to me was no longer dangerous, the direct flow of letters to Vermont from the Soviet Union increased—now there were two or three dozen a week. But we would wait in vain for the majority of missives now flooding in to express any ideas, any feelings. Or rather, feelings there were, but they were pleas, exhortations, cries from the most varied and distant localities: Send money! money! send me regular parcels! help get my narrative poem published in the West! my novel! get my invention patented in the States! help my whole family get into America, here are all our passport details!

These letters revealed, without a shadow of doubt, a vast process that had already begun: Russia was fleeing from Russia. The first to flee were the scholars, the actors, the talkers—but now the same hunger for flight was also erupting from deep within our masses. The picture was terrifying.

Later, Nadya Levitskaya and Lyusha would send on to me the letters arriving at *Novy Mir*, great bundles of them. These were from real readers, and through them we could take a deep breath of just what had accumulated in Russia, layer by layer, over these many years.

As 1989 spilled over into 1990, our homeland made itself known to us, firstly by a frenzied ringing at our gate: the rock group Mashina Vremeni (Time Machine) was proposing to organize my tour across the Soviet Union! And then by a more measured phone call from Washington, from Soviet television: it was time for me to appear on their screens, and in the press generally.

But people there had only just started reading my works. And what could I say before they had read them? What could I say that was more important than my books, which had been piling up unpublished?

But now there were my books. Let those words pour out.

But as to how the publishing was progressing, I was left in the dark regarding both journals and books, which exasperated me. Dima was, unfortunately, not coping very well with the pace of work now flooding in, which he'd never experienced before.

He was getting slower and slower with the information we wanted: how were things progressing? what decisions was he taking? Many of the questions that we had asked two or three times remained unanswered. He didn't explain the misunderstandings and muddles that were arising—and there would be two or three months between his letters: the long silences were torture. Even over the phone Alya couldn't get any clarity—and carried away a troubling impression, an ominous foreboding.

Could he not find the opportunity for a clandestine letter? In January 1990 I wrote: "I would have thought you could sometimes take ten or fifteen minutes to write me even an ordinary letter. It would still get here in two or three weeks, and bring us a bit of information. As it is, we know nothing for months on end." —And in March: "Why do you stay silent for so long, leaving us in the dark?" It had now been three months and "there has been no letter from you, not so much as a scribbled note . . . and you haven't phoned, either, for more than a month. . . . Dima dear, I can well understand the burden you have on your shoulders and how harassed you are by phone calls, letters, requests, visits, and stupid proposals; and I know that to crown it all you were ill this winter. . . . But it's just that, compared with this great load, one substantial, informative letter a month to me would not add any great burden, but it would do a lot to clarify things for me. Please do not neglect to do this."

At the same time my published works, which filtered through to us months late, were sometimes shocking—negligently produced and manifesting an indifference to quality and even simple literacy. (As he left us, Dima had been ready and keen to look after the proofreading of texts, even taking it on personally—fat chance! Gross oversights appeared. They had printed *Tanks* taking no heed of my screenplay format, but Dima only learned from us that the screenplay had already been printed, when it was too late to do anything. They'd bashed out *Prisoners* with extra spaces between lines, rhythm and rhyme lost, and with quantities of misprints—it was clear that no one at all had been correcting proofs. And in one Moscow journal they had published individual chapters from the *Wheel*, linking them together in a way that made no sense at all.)

But what could we do? was it simply his Russian nature, to work in this disorganized fashion?

To speed up communications, we sent a fax machine to his home, and a photocopier to *Novy Mir*. This, together with phone calls, made things easier, but not by much.

He complained that he'd had no time to conclude contracts with regional publishers, and difficulties had arisen getting paper for the journal. This was why issues were late, and they were at war with the *Izvestia* printers. And it was hard to find deliverymen outside of the Ministry of Communications. And paper was costing so much now, and cardboard . . .

But in the summer of 1990, Dima sent a long letter enumerating everything now published and the plan he'd worked out for further publications. By that time the publishing cooperative—which had taken the name "*Novy Mir* Center," though it was independent of the journal—had received from Dima exclusive publishing rights ("we don't need anyone else's publishing brand now")—and from now on, he said, Dima would conclude all contracts in my name with the Center only, and the Center would start publishing books with partners who had paper, ceding publishing rights to them in return for a specified percentage of the revenue. Dima was pressing me to "agree to this arrangement."

Although the Center shared the *Novy Mir* name, I was still shocked by his insistence. Did this mean that anyone who wanted to publish Solzhenitsyn first had to *buy* that right from the Center? Why did we need this kind of monopolistic middleman? And I wrote to Dima (10 July 1990): "Your proposal to transfer all my books to your publishing Center is *absolutely* unacceptable to me: it would mean stopping everything and holding back. And no—those rights must be given to *all* the publishers who want them: *that* is the whole point of your activities on my behalf, and *that* is what I am insisting on. And this applies above all to regional publishers. The provinces are, to me, most important of all. Your Center is only in its infancy—let's see how it gets on, and talk about it then." —And a month later: "I beg you to avoid applying the brakes in any way, even inadvertently, to requests from publishers, making them wait until all the details are clarified. You must satisfy *all of them* straightaway, *not put them on hold* 'for a future date': the future will be nourished by its own publications. . . . *Every* regional and central publishing house wanting to publish must be allowed to publish. Don't slow them down: it could happen that, in a year or two, thanks to Russia's situation, people won't feel like reading anymore."

Dima was very unhappy about my refusal to transfer exclusive rights to the Center. To him it seemed to be a "simple, clear solution to all the problems," especially that of the publishing *quality*, which the Center would have been able to guarantee: our Center will issue beautiful books! —No, I countered, that is not how a good enterprise is set up: "It's quite impossible for me to accept the idea of a center such as you have proposed, holding a monopoly. I cannot accept the control your Center would have over other publishers (and publishers that have already existed for many years, while the Center has not yet made a name for itself). The fact that regional publishing houses can allow misprints and howlers—well we can't help that, it just shows the standard the country has sunk to now. . . . No one is preventing the Center from acting independently, *along with* the others—not taking their place, not reining them in to its own advantage."

With that, I considered the subject closed. But during that transitional period many more problems were in fact still seeping out and swirling about. Dima wrote of paper supplies to the journal being blocked, of the complicated fortunes of the seven-volume edition he had planned, and of the whole system of book publishing breaking down in our homeland.

And in our Homeland!—in our homeland everything, whether redoubtable or ephemeral, was ready to boil over. The year 1989 had been dense with catastrophes. In many border areas of the Union (though nowhere in Russia itself) blood had been spilled—due to both ethnic disputes and military crackdowns. And on top of that, that spring was electrified by the first grandiose imitation of free popular elections since the end of the Communist regime. An imitation, partly because it had departed from the generally accepted form of "fair equality," universal suffrage. *Assignments* were allocated to organizations (first in line being the Communist Party Central Committee), academies, and unions representing the creative arts, all being guaranteed quotas of seats. It is true that, for the other seats, elections from several candidates were allowed, which caused a sensation, but they were filtered through sham "district assemblies." All this took on the appearance of "free" elections, but the guiding hand of the Communist Party was manipulating every bit of it.

After that came the two-week Congress of "People's Deputies," which was broadcast on televisions everywhere, commanding the full attention of millions. What a joy it was, how overwhelming to see and hear something that had, all their lives, been unimaginable, unthinkable. But they weren't sitting in front of their screens to learn the truth of their situation—that they knew only too well—but hoping desperately that perhaps, after this Congress, their life might change for the better.

Academician Sakharov, driven, inspired as much by personal as collective fervor, was battling passionately for the right to be elected deputy to the Congress, speaking out at the electoral assemblies of several districts, and, of course, running for the Academy of Sciences. There he did win a seat, despite many obstacles and machinations: for the Gorbachev authorities were, not without reason, wary of Sakharov.

Throughout the Congress (and for all the rest of 1989), Sakharov continued to manifest exceptional energy (surprising, considering his physical condition at the time), along with constancy in his principles. He also spoke at mass rallies at Luzhniki Stadium. He was becoming a dangerous opponent to Gorbachev.

Sakharov had, it's true, said of him quite audibly and more than once, including at the Congress, that he couldn't see anyone else who could run the country. (But why, actually? What was so outstanding about Gorbachev? It was not perspicacity in affairs of state, or strength of will, and neither was he loved by the people. He had nothing—just the inertia of Communist Party succession.) And there was no one to challenge him that year anyway. But Sakharov, judging by the efforts he made, seemed to want to *elevate* Gorbachev, get him to adopt the highest principles. From his first step at the Congress—trying to organize a discussion on programs and principles before the election of a chairman (in which he was not, of course, successful)—he went on to have a personal conversation with the leader during the dramatic days of the Congress, and to try desperately, again and again, to be given the floor, be given a chance to speak from the platform—where Gorbachev simply, rudely, turned off his microphone. During the course of the Congress, Sakharov won for himself the role of *de facto* leader of the opposition: no important issue escaped his notice; and he had to shout loudly enough to top the noise in the hall, and be subjected to a constant angry hubbub and obstructive behavior. And, as he correctly concluded: "This scene made a great impression on everyone watching it on television. . . . In one hour I acquired massive support from millions of people, popularity such as I've never had in our country." And that popularity was maintained throughout the final months of his life, right up to his funeral: the people had clearly seen in him their persecuted defender.

Once more, on the final day of the Congress, thanks to his persistence, Sakharov managed to get a fifteen-minute slot to speak. As part of this address he read out a "Decree on Power" (he explained that "perestroika is a revolution, and 'decree' is the most appropriate word"), in which he demanded that the Communist Party's right to lead be revoked; and he finished with the Leninist slogan of '17, "All power to the Soviets!"

Thus the year 1989 marked the finest hour of Sakharov's life.

Then the striking Vorkuta miners called for him to come, but he could not: he was exhausted from his Supreme Soviet battles.

The situation in the country was changing rapidly and constantly taking on new aspects: to appraise it properly, to get one's bearings reliably and make the correct, statesman-like moves at the right moment demanded great, almost superhuman qualities, of a kind no one in our homeland had manifested in recent years.

Who at that time would have predicted that the liberating reforms so hungrily awaited (and they wanted them faster, faster!) would lead to even more extreme, large-scale demolition and pillaging of Russia?

During the months following the Congress, Sakharov became the moving spirit of the short-lived "Inter-Regional Group," and appealed, in its name, for the whole population of the USSR to initiate political strikes. And just before he died, he noted with satisfaction that there had been "sufficient strikes," including the Donets Basin, Vorkuta, and "in many localities"; that "this has been a significant politicization of the country"; and that "the people have finally found the right form in which to express their will." (And who was it that benefited from their expressing it? . . .)

No, the *people* couldn't be persuaded to abandon their everyday common sense—they charitably agreed not to notice the weakness of Sakharov's projects. They came to love Sakharov not for what those projects actually were, but for his capacious heart.

The project for a Constitution of the USSR that Sakharov proposed at the end of 1989 would have been even more disastrous: from then on, the Union was to consist of *republics*, equal in all respects (autonomous oblasts and even national districts would also be raised to that status, so there would have been far more than fifty in all—with no other structural unit apart from the *republic*). The creation of a new national Union was supposed to begin with its total dismantling: after being proclaimed *independent*, each of these large or tiny republics (sovereign states!) could express, or decide not to express, its wish to join the Union. Each republic would have had its own citizenship; its own monetary system; its own armed forces; its own law-enforcement bodies, independent of central government; its constitution would have taken priority over the laws of the Union (but all of them would, on the other hand, have been subject to the laws of a World Government[34]); the *republic* would have owned all its land, mineral resources, and water; and its language would have been the official language there. —In this draft, there was just one lonely mention of the "republic of Russia," without any explanation of exactly which leftover scraps it would be made up of, and what geographical construct might be used for this, and would its rights at least equal those of, say, the Taymyr district?[35] Which meant that Russia would have been fatally splintered and weakened—the fondest hope of all the diplomats of countries hostile to us. Where, in all that, was even a scintilla of consciousness of Russia's history and its spiritual experience?

Having begun so precipitately, what would he have proposed next, what would Sakharov have called for in the following months and years? It was frightening even to think of.

But, to be fair, no one did as much as Sakharov to fortify our disintegrating country: his nuclear legacy would support its power for a good while, even as it collapsed. Now the West, wary of nuclear chaos in Russia, *feared* the sudden collapse that it had, by and large, been wishing for.

Brought low by a few months of crippling stresses and conflicts, Sakharov died in his sixty-ninth year.

In his Christian smile and his sad eyes, something fatal, unavoidable, had always been reflected.

The coffin bearing Sakharov's body was accompanied along Leninsky Prospect by an unending flow of people, in the hundreds of thousands. Moscow could not remember such a vast throng—and impelled there by their hearts. It was a mild December day, and people were walking ankle-deep in slush. Starting the day before, and continuing that day, mass meetings paid their last respects in many Soviet cities.

My wreath was also there, at the funeral: "To dear Andrei Dmitrievich with love Solzhenitsyn."

But surely my fellow countrymen must, sometime, form a clear idea of themselves?

At the beginning of February 1990 I made a note: "every day, every evening, and every morning I take a fresh look at things, rearrange my thoughts, and make some guesses as to what I should do and what I can do vis-à-vis the events unfolding in Russia. Clearly, my explanation of February 1917 has, in practice, arrived too late: that experience would not instruct anyone in relation to this current *February*. (But at least something will have been written about 1917! Who *today* would take it on himself to spend twenty years doing that?) On the other hand, am I myself late arriving at those events? But what could I do now to change them? Did Blok or Bunin accomplish much in 1917? Even Lev Tolstoy, if he'd still been alive in '17—would anyone have listened to him, in that pandemonium? After all, they didn't listen to Korolenko. My job is to finish my works. Earlier in my life, in various prisons, I imagined the end of Communism as a great commotion and, immediately afterwards, a new heaven and a new earth. But this was, intrinsically, impossible, and had become entirely impossible since the Communist system allowed the whole body of our country, its whole population, to become rotten. And now, the abandonment of Communism is manifesting itself in distorted forms: there is no less crookedness, or even scum, amongst those running the country or those making themselves heard. . . . But I must, all the same, look for ways."

But—*how*? . . .

For over a year already, I'd been distracted from my immersion into 1917 by a growing sense of self-reproach: I had not rendered any useful assistance against the tumult and confusion of minds in the Soviet Union, either in untangling the mess of ideas or giving practical advice. The warnings, meanwhile, were thronging inside me.

And I imagined it not in the form of a routine commentary article, but one that would be a most heartfelt, open, direct appeal to the great unreachable mass of my countrymen. At that time my name had become (for a short while) respected in Russia. Immediately after the *Archipelago* breakthrough, surely my voice would be listened to? *Exactly how* this might take place I could not yet tell; and that was not my starting point; rather, the pages poured out, of their own accord, as a mixture of the feelings I had amassed and our country's national experience in the decades before 1917. My knowledge of Russian political history in the twentieth century was certainly more than adequate.

Ideas for this work—how should Russia be rebuilt after Communism? in which direction should it move, and how?—had been piling up for nine years or so, but had roots even in my post-war prison cells, in our discussions there in 1945–46. (In camps there's never as much time or freedom for thinking and discussing as in prisons.) What was coming into focus was not a comprehensive government program—that was beyond me from this distance, especially without economics in it, because I was not well-versed in that area—but, all the same, it would be advice I was competent to give, based on my long years of historical investigations.

A true rebirth of Russia was not, of course, a matter of speed; it was one of quality. But everything was boiling over now: it would not wait. And it was getting harder and harder to know which direction to take.

And with such tumultuous changes going on, by the time you've written it, published it—and *where*?—it'll be out of date, too.

From early in 1990, fragments of text, phrases, were already coming together, unbidden, in my mind. Now I was spurred on by the idea that I might be too late—had I delayed too long?

As well as that, I was impelled by appeals from the capital announcing the impending, total, and definitive collapse of the material necessities of life (in the capital, which knew nothing of life in the provinces). And we too, across the ocean, could not help but fall under the influence of this feeling that was setting in thick and fast: that Russia was already at the very brink of imminent destruction. (Actually, the greater part of our slide into ruin was still, at that time, ahead of us.)

But I was, all the same, starting to think this way: surely it wasn't sensible to chase down and capture this instant only? Shouldn't I offer a calmer, more farsighted analysis—looking a long way ahead? It was impossible to produce any kind of "definitive" plan, but it should at least call attention to some ideas that might calm passions and challenge assumptions.

And for several summer months in 1990, in my forest isolation in Vermont, I was consumed by this alone. That "nationalities question," whose white-hot acrimony the myopic Gorbachev clique had failed to notice, was fearsomely memorable to me, already from my camp years; and wasn't that the question with which one should begin a frank discussion? Not by insisting categorically on the principle of *indivisibility*, but by listening attentively to the expectations of national groups, yet with ominous warning against the chaos that accompanies division. Indeed, this "nationalities question" had been seething, menacingly, for decades, even beyond the wide expanses of the Soviet Union. —And then, what about the warped Soviet legacy in matters of agriculture and land ownership? Wasn't this an even more acute and painful problem, crying out for our attention? What about the ossified inequality between the capitals and provinces (that is, all of Russia!)? And what about our schools? (As a schoolteacher, I felt their problems with my every fiber.)

But then, shouldn't one begin with the central ailment afflicting the entire state system?—while taking stock of all the previous Russian (pre-Soviet) thought and deliberation on the topic of government. So much of this had accumulated during my years of work on the Russian epic, and back home people are not versed in these topics, are uninformed. So that is what I now tried to convey to my countrymen, from the basic principles to the details—both the different forms in which the people might be represented, and the important choice between election methods. And then, all the glorious traditions of the Russian *zemstvo*[36] and, separately—the importance of *consultative* bodies and their interaction with governmental power.

These two ideas formed the basis of, respectively, the first and second parts of my booklet *Rebuilding Russia*.[37]

I wrote without any strict, preconceived plan; it came together of its own accord, section by section—there was no stopping it. I'd finished in a month. Then I worked on it together with Alya. Our sons were also beginning to understand such things, and by now I was conferring with them as well. And, to test the water, I sent the text to some émigrés, asking their advice. (And received important suggestions from Yuri Orlov, Mikhail Bernshtam, and Aleksandr Serebrennikov.)

I was writing this booklet for an ostensibly open period, that of "glasnost," but it wasn't yet that of free thought—far from it. There were still many problems that I couldn't raise and discuss in the detail and to the extent that I'd have liked, since they were beyond the scope of perestroika, and I couldn't speak out candidly: not only were millions of readers unprepared for such a conversation, but neither would the authorities—it was still the same nomenklatura in charge—publish it, and that would be that. (Judging from the publications that came our way, I could see clearly just how very, very frightened people were of touching on Lenin or Bolshevism *as a whole*. From the letters in *Knizhnoye Obozrenie* I could see ossified fragments and even massive chunks of people's Communist upbringing.) So here I'd had to dwell on the continuity of a *state* identity, without which a peaceful evolution would be impossible—but diverting that "continuity" away from Leninist Party power. And, before it was too late, I'd needed to warn readers of the irresponsible traits of parliamentary democracies—but I wouldn't be able to frighten our pining, hungry people with the possible flaws of a democratic society, would I? As far as they were concerned, it was: just give us democracy!—once we've got it, we'll eat our fill, doll ourselves up, and have some fun!

And, lastly, there was the actual *language* of the booklet. I could not sink to the hackneyed newspaper style to which the Soviet reader of political literature was now so solidly attached. My language is richer, more colorful, imbued with that emotion without which I could not speak of the current Soviet situation—and I allowed myself to go overboard with the expressiveness of my vocabulary. "At the End of Our Endurance"—by now the state of the country seemed this calamitous to me, as it did to many others. I had no idea, as yet, what great reserves of destruction still awaited us.

One of the main destructive tendencies was, it seemed to me, the breakup of the Soviet Union, which was now fully matured, ready to go. Much pointed that way: the acute ethnic conflicts, which had, in everyday Soviet life, been drowned out by the trumpeting of "friendship of peoples," as well as the reckless destruction of the economy and society that had begun under the shortsighted Gorbachev. That impending breakup of the country was clearly visible to me—but how did it seem from inside? could they see it? The collapse of the Soviet Union was irreversible. But how could we prevent historical Russia also being destroyed in its wake?—and I wanted to give that warning in a tone sounding almost like an alarm. But just try warning them, both the authorities and the public, and particularly those of a "great power" orientation, who pride themselves on the imagined might of their vast land. The breakup of the state would be a devastating blow to millions of lives, millions of families. In a discrete chapter, "The Process of Separation," I called for the timely creation of a commission of experts from all sides, to anticipate the likely ravages to people's everyday lives; to facilitate solutions for the many people displaced; to do a meticulous analysis of personal preferences in choosing new places to live and receiving dwellings, assistance, and jobs; and to guarantee the rights of people remaining in their old locations, and to handle the painful splitting apart of national economies while preserving all lines of trade and cooperation.

And I revealed how fruitlessly, how senselessly as far as the people were concerned (and very profitably for the Party nomenklatura) the six perestroika years had been wasted, and how we were *already* strutting round in the "gaudy circus attire of February"—at a time when a society of unlimited rights could not stand its ground if tested.

And, on top of all that, I suggested that political life is not life's most important aspect (but that was what people were babbling about so animatedly, all over the country), and that a pure atmosphere in society cannot be created by any juridical legislation, but by moral cleansing (and by the repentance of countless major and minor transgressors); and that true stability in society cannot be achieved by any struggle, and not even by balancing party interests—only by people rising to the principle of *self-limitation*. And by each of us working skillfully in the position he has.

In separate chapters I analyzed the fundamental issues: local life, the provinces, land ownership, and school and family. And it was the discussion of nationhood that presented the most acute difficulty, especially in the case of the Ukrainian nationalists, who were for the most part from Galicia and had, therefore, lived for centuries outside Russian history—but now were actively trying to swing public opinion in all Ukraine round to their side. I knew they hated the *moskals*,[38] but I appealed to them as to *brothers*: it was my last hope of making them see reason. I was challenging them on their weakest point: ostensibly anti-Communist, they had happily grasped the poisoned chalice of *Lenin's borders*;[39] ostensibly democrats, they feared, more than anything else, allowing parents free choice of the language in which their children would be taught. —My proposal was that eleven republics of the Union be given, immediately and unconditionally, the freedom to separate, and that only the friendliest of efforts be made to preserve the union of four of them—the three Slavic republics and Kazakhstan.

This was only the first part of the booklet, dealing with the *present*. (I recognize that in my emotional exposition—but a calm tone regarding people's troubles could have been taken as indifference on the part of someone speaking from afar—I allowed myself to use the word "we" without defining, absolutely precisely, its triple function: "we" as *everyone*, the human race; "we" as inhabitants of the USSR; and "we" as Russians.)

And then came the second part, unemotional, methodical, condensing everything that I'd managed to assemble from historical experience, over many years studying history. —Views on state structures in general. —Democracy as a means of escaping tyranny—and how democracy in its parliamentary form is always doomed to be shaped by the money men. —How the way out of that deformity is a "democracy of small areas," a *zemstvo* with a four-stage election system developing out of it. —"A Combined System of Government," consisting of a rigid vertical to run the state from the top down and a creative *zemstvo* vertical, working from the bottom up. —Various electoral systems (proportional, plurality, and absolute majority)—and how to avoid the nation becoming exhausted, their lives in turmoil from these elections.

And I offered all that, not as a surefire recipe but as *Reflections and Tentative Proposals*—and with a question mark in the title of the booklet.

And then? Things began promisingly, moving ahead by leaps and bounds. No sooner had Alya phoned *Komsomolskaya Pravda* (*Young Communist Truth*) to tell them of my article's existence and its scope, than the editorial office boldly accepted it, immediately, without even reading it! (We chose *Komsomolskaya Pravda* because of its massive print run, and also because it had just published "Live Not by Lies.") Hearing of this, *Literaturnaya Gazeta* immediately undertook to publish it as well, not too proud to accept second place, coming out a day later. And all this on the basis of my name alone—no one had read it or gained an understanding of it. And so, in September 1990, in a matter of days, my booklet was published in the pages of newspapers with the unimaginable print run of twenty-seven million copies. (*Komsomolskaya Pravda*, however, dropped my question mark from the title, which changed the tone significantly, giving it a categorical quality absent from my booklet—I was explicitly not foisting my ideas on my countrymen, but *asking questions*.)[40]

This was a success we had certainly not expected.

So—were all the basic elements in place for a broad, truly nationwide discussion?

Not a bit of it.

It began, probably, with Gorbachev. He was so furious, so outraged by my forecast of the inevitable breakup of the USSR that he even spoke about it in the Supreme Soviet, for the whole world to see.[41] He had, allegedly, read the booklet "attentively, twice, pencil in hand"—yet, in leveling a mighty blow, he missed the actual issue: Solzhenitsyn, he said, is "living entirely in the past" and has shown himself to be a *monarchist*. (??—but there was not a whisper of monarchism here: this was still the same label stuck on me from time to time, a particle of grime that would waft in from here and there. Who came out with it first? Kissinger, I suppose.) Which is why this booklet, and all its ideas, are totally unsuitable *for us*. —Two Ukrainian deputies made speeches in support of the leader, expressing the anger of "the whole Ukrainian people" over my implying that we were brothers, and so did one Kazakh deputy.[42] In Kazakhstan itself the reaction was more violent: in Alma-Ata they defiantly burned the *Komsomolskaya Pravda* issue with my article in it, on a city square.[43] Publicly, all "discussion" ended there.

But, out of the public eye, there was no doubt that the *Komsomolskaya Pravda*, *Literaturnaya Gazeta,* and all the press generally, had been ordered not to print reactions to my booklet, not to discuss it at all, and to remain silent. Editorial offices had had time to tell us that "hundreds of letters have come flooding in, and we'll be printing them issue by issue." But only in the first couple of issues did readers' letters, meaty, passionate, with a wide range of opinions, slip through the net—then suddenly stopped. (Two months later, at the end of November, comments suddenly reemerged—the policing had become careless—and died away again.) The Party's heavy hand still made itself felt on Glasnost, just as before.

In the West, my booklet was appraised no more accurately than it had been by Gorbachev. The BBC judged it an "unrealistic plan for a return to the *past* (?)," Solzhenitsyn "cannot rid himself of his *imperial mentality*" (and this after I'd proposed that eleven of the fifteen republics be given immediate freedom, and that the remaining three should also have no obstacles put in their way). The *New Republic* depicted me on their cover in a Lenin-style cloth cap arriving, they said, at Finland Station.[44] And, in keeping with the depressing uniformity of the "pluralist" Western political press, others joined in on a similar level. (Scammell could not refrain from adding his own tawdry comment—how could he, the "top specialist on Solzhenitsyn," hold his tongue when everyone was asking for a response?—and so: Solzhenitsyn has "nothing to say on glasnost . . . if anything, he felt that glasnost had gone too far."[45] My *biographer* had forgotten that I'd been the one shouting for that "glasnost" in 1969, when no one else could even articulate the word.[46] And now, he said, Solzhenitsyn has been revealed as a "patriarchal populist [with a] Slavophile passion for consensus"—which, of course, is harmful.[47]) —In Germany and France my ideas were conveyed hastily and in distorted form. —And Voinovich, ever at the ready, responded with another four broadcasts on Radio Liberty.

It was clear that my booklet had angered the nationalist separatists of Ukraine and Kazakhstan. As for Russian nationalists and the "great power" Bolsheviks—they didn't want to hear talk of the looming disintegration of their Empire. And those superficial parliamentary democrats couldn't stand even the thought of taking a close look at the essence of democracy, still less, heaven forbid, that of genuine rule of the people. Those getting overheated on the political carousel were asking why we needed these detailed ideas for a possible configuration of the state when, on this public square or that one, political rallies were humming with discussion of current issues?

But there were, of course, also millions of "simple folk," ordinary readers, and my article, at three kopecks, begged to be bought. Even if no route lay open for those millions to have their say in print—they did *read* it, didn't they? and what did they think? how did they feel about it?

The months passed, and occasional letters from them reached me in Vermont (in those years many letters would go missing in the Soviet mail). Some readers wrote very perceptively, others in utter bewilderment.

But publicly there was almost total silence, even from high-profile political commentators, journalists to whom the ban on speaking out didn't apply. There were, on the other hand, several long, angry, detailed articles attacking my *Rebuilding*—one of them, for some reason, from the prominent Estonian writer Arvo Valton (I hadn't laid a finger on the Estonians): no, Russia can't get off scot-free! It'll have to pay everyone for everything, every single thing![48] And there was a verbose, caustic article, almost overflowing with rage, by the political commentator Leonid Batkin, which appeared in several publications at once and, what's more, based its case on dishonest misrepresentation when quoting me.[49]

And the rest of *Society*?

People were surprised by the alarm bells I'd been ringing—what had got into me?—and by my painstaking analysis of state structures—what use was that to anyone now? (We'd soon learn the hard way. . . .)

That indifference of the masses, in their many millions, was palpable, and it gave me my answer. Was it because, having crossed the ocean, I'd lost my connection with the realities of Soviet life? because I was not there, going round the public meetings? Or was it because, with the great concentration of historical experience that I had accumulated and the eloquence I'd gained, I had arrived too early with my *Rebuilding*?

Yes, I was not too late—I was too early.

In 1973, from within the heart of my homeland I had proposed (in *Letter to the Soviet Leaders*) a timely and, I dare say, clear-sighted reform. And the leaders had not lifted a finger. The pseudo-intellectuals had responded with a furious attack; the West—with derision.

Seventeen years of exile had now passed, and from across the ocean I was proposing a program that could save the nation and was worked up in minute detail regarding state structures. The government had no trouble stifling all debate; nationalists in the republics and the pseudo-intellectual circles in Russia pitched into it furiously. And as for the people—they said nothing.

Oh, there was still a long way to go. And our path—in the far distance.

For a good few years now, I'd lived with a melancholy, lonely feeling that I was ahead of my fellow-countrymen in the painful knowledge I'd acquired—and there were no rapid routes to mutual understanding.

So that's Banishment, then!—a measure of spiritual execution mindfully devised already in antiquity.

And yet *this* was, in effect, my attempt to *return* to my homeland. And, at the same time, a way of testing: was I needed over there now? would they understand me? should I hurry over, to develop what I'd said, put it into practice? —And the answer was: no, I was not needed. No, they hadn't understood me. Reflections on the state—for us, that would be premature.

As early as December 1989, the Gorbachev government had graciously announced, through gritted teeth, that "persons stripped of their Soviet citizenship may apply for it to be restored" (and the *New York Times* had immediately made a beeline for us: would I be applying?[50]—would I, in other words, be kneeling guiltily, asking the Soviet government for forgiveness? . . .). —In January 1990 they reinstated Rostropovich's and Vishnevskaya's Soviet citizenship. (They were not inclined to return home: "We won't come back until Solzhenitsyn does"—so it all came down to me again.) — In April 1990 *Literaturnaya Gazeta*, which had once called me a "literary Vlasovite," was, now with a belated fearlessness (and, most likely, even now under orders from above), demanding that "Solzhenitsyn's citizenship must be restored!"[51] As far as one expelled with such a hue and cry was concerned, this would have made sense and signified that the government was admitting it had made a "mistake," at least. But Gorbachev, always equivocal, indecisive, could not summon the courage to take that step. In June 1990—perhaps in response to applications, perhaps not, I don't know—they restored citizenship to Aleksandr Zinoviev, Vladimir Maximov, and Zhores Medvedev. But then, in August 1990, they came up with this: a list of two dozen émigrés, almost all of whom had left of their own free will, having applied to the Visa Department for an exit visa, and they put both Alya and me on the list, announcing that people on the list could have their citizenship back.[52] After which the head of the pardons department of the Supreme Soviet (Gennadi Cheremnykh) leapt into action with a lie, saying publicly that I'd had high-level contact with the Soviet authorities and already agreed in advance.[53] —Why such lies? There'd been no contact whatsoever! —But all the news agencies were phoning us. Alya refuted the claim.[54] —Even so, that Cheremnykh stuck to his story. And the reporters started phoning again—this was a sensation! Alya responded with a strong statement via the news agencies and in the *New York Times*: stripping Solzhenitsyn of Soviet citizenship was *one of three* illegal acts. More serious than this one were the charge of *treason* and the decree ordering his forcible *expulsion*, depriving him of his homeland and friends—and condemning his sons to grow up in a foreign land. So they should start with those two.[55]

But Gorbachev did not want to take *that* on, and didn't.

Soon after this, also in August 1990, the Prime Minister of the RSFSR Ivan Silaev showed himself to be evidently at variance with the Gorbachev brand of indecision (but endowed with a Yeltsinian decisiveness, Yeltsin at that time seeming to be an independent Russian voice amidst the Soviet hubbub). Silaev (with his boss Yeltsin at his back . . .) publicly announced in *Sovetskaya Rossiya* (which had for years been one of the most malicious slanderers of me and our Fund) an invitation for me to come to Russia *as his personal guest*: "Now, when the contradictions [of Russian life] have reached such heights as to threaten a new split . . . you would not, in coming here, be bound by any conditions relating to the subsequent course of your life. As for the program for your journey, you would specify it, and my mission would be to render assistance."[56]

An important moment. My "program for the journey"?—was he a mind-reader? did this mean I could realize my long-cherished dream of returning through Siberia?

But it was clearly a political game. Yeltsin's side was playing the Solzhenitsyn card in his contest with Gorbachev. Did I have to get involved in this now? What had changed in the System? Nothing, as yet.

Were I to devote myself entirely to politics—then of course I'd have to go, immediately!

And hang around those Moscow rallies? Speak on those little platforms, between Telman Gdlyan and Gavriil Popov? (1917-style—so familiar to me . . .) I had played a political role at a time when vociferous types were few and far between. But now that there were so many? . . .

I had just finished *Rebuilding*. That was the biggest and most profound contribution I could make to the current situation. That was where my hope lay.

My reply to Silaev was: "It is impossible for me to be a guest or tourist in my native country. . . . When I return home, it will be to live and to die there."[57] . . .

After that, Gorbachev's secretariat roused themselves, now jealous, and the editor-in-chief of *Komsomolskaya Pravda*, Fronin, phoned us in Vermont on their behalf. The secretariat felt it was "important that the president and the great writer should maintain good relations!" But how could we *maintain* them, when we'd never had them?

Two days later there was a phone call from Silaev himself with a proposal to collaborate. And straight after that, a live courier came to Vermont on his behalf, with the pamphlet "500 Days."[58] . . . (Alya immediately, to test out this collaboration, asked him to start the process of legalizing on the territory of the RSFSR our Fund for aiding former Gulag prisoners.)

In December 1990 it was announced that I had been awarded the RSFSR literature prize for *Archipelago*.[59] I did not accept: in our country, the Gulag disease has not yet been overcome—either legally or morally; "this book is about the suffering of millions, and I cannot reap an honor from it."[60]

Meanwhile, in the autumn months of 1990, one of the last strongholds of the Bolshevik diehards, the *Voenno-Istoricheskii Zhurnal* (*Military-Historical Journal*), published[61] some mendacious "recollections" about me, purportedly written by the ex-Vlasovite journalist Leonid Samutin[62]—from whom *Archipelago* had been impounded in 1973—but dictated by the KGB. And they carried on publishing these until Samutin's widow exposed their fabrications publicly[63] and later took them to court. Then the journal started hammering in the same old rusty nail,[64] the "denunciation" that had been disproved fourteen years earlier.[65] Their scrappy little document was old—so they should cook up a new one!—but no, it was still the same, still the same. How they seethed with rage against me! And how obtuse they were.

For a short while—a year, two years?—it had seemed that the public's will, the demands at public rallies, might change the course of events. But no, not yet.

In Russia—even before, but especially in today's maelstrom—it is only the one holding the reins of power who can influence and lead events. And for every one of us—including me, if I were now suddenly to plunge back in there—the only way to exert any influence would be to fight a way through to the center of power. But for me this would not suit my character, my inclination, or my age.

And so—I did not go at the moment when there were the greatest expectations of me, politically, in my homeland. And I'm sure I was not wrong then. It was the decision of a writer, not a politician. I have never, not for a moment, run after political popularity.

If *Rebuilding* had shown any promise of changing the country, then I'd have gone like a shot! gone for that very rebuilding.

But it had been spurned, unwanted.

What my pen hadn't achieved, my voice wouldn't, either.

CHAPTER 16

Nearing the Return

In the weeks leading up to the 1991 New Year, things in the USSR felt very unsettled. In December the wily Shevardnadze—after everything he'd bungled in his foreign-affairs role, things he'd given way on—suddenly (and with menacing overtones) announced that he was stepping down, and warned grimly of some kind of *dark powers* plotting something terrible. (Had he already, privately, decided to shift into Georgian politics?) The public immediately started worrying, and appeals were published: don't let a dictatorship gain hold. But Gorbachev was the wrong man to address with such appeals. Although over the previous six years he had managed, using equivocal maneuvers, to give people's lives in the country a terrible jolt and throw them into chaos, he would not have found the courage either to set up his own dictatorship or oppose someone else's. With the public mood in steep decline, Gorbachev's next ineffectual step was to call a March referendum as to whether the USSR should be preserved—a fevered quest for the people's support.

But with the whole country in such an unstable condition, what weight could a referendum carry—what kind of backing could it provide? It was carried out in such a superficial way that in six months its result vanished into thin air.

Year after year it was ever more apparent to me that the current happenings were not even a repeat of February 1917, but a kind of parody, so much more petty, uncouth, and disreputable were those pontificating today than the franchised classes[1] of earlier days. (In February 1991 David Remnick, who had, more than other American observers, penetrated the essence of what was going on, wrote in the *New York Review of Books*: When Solzhenitsyn wrote, in *Rebuilding Russia*, that perestroika had not borne fruit, those words appeared harsh. But now it seems he was right.[2])

Anyway, I had, in 1990, divested myself of the *Red Wheel* armor I'd had on for half a century—I'd finished!!

What next?

I looked around, took a peek—and how much unfinished work there was! I hadn't even sorted through it all.

First off, the mass of materials I had collected in Tambov (and how I'd journeyed round the oblast to get it . . .). It had all been intended for *The Red Wheel*, but by now it was clear—it had been cut out and would not go into the book. Kuzmina Gat, the peasants' unparalleled march on Tambov, carrying pitchforks and greeted by the ringing of bells in villages along the way. The uprising in Pakhotny Ugol. The insurgency center in Kamenka—which I'd so carefully prepared in *October 1916*. The rebellion at Tugolukovo (I'd already broadly dealt with that in *August 1914*) and partisan combat, both trench warfare and lightning guerrilla strikes. Partisan activity along the Sukhaya and Mokraya branches of the Panda, and in the bushland along the Vorona. And Tambov itself—I'd already started on that in *October*, with Father Aloni and Zinaida. And the rebellious Karavainovo. And how Arseni Blagodarev became the commander of the partisan regiment. And Tukhachevsky's HQ in Tambov. The families of the insurgents—sent to concentration camps; anyone failing to denounce the insurgents—shot! And Georgi Zhukov in the detachment that crushed the rebellion. And Kotovsky's men pulling Father Mikhail Molchanov out of church in the middle of the liturgy and hacking him to death on the parvis. And the whole, highly charged story of Ego. Ah, what use was it now. . . .

And what about the spread of the Liberation movement that had started way back in 1901? The nesting period for the liberal parties and subgroups, with expanding ambitions and pretensions. A roaring, ever-increasing torrent. And how the rampant liberalism of *society* squeezed out the capable, modest, creative *zemstvo*. And there was this, too: the history of the late stages of Russian liberalism was bound up with the struggle for equal rights for Jews in Russia, which had continued to escalate. And, starting in the early 1900s, Socialist Revolutionary terrorism. Over years and years, a mountain of all these materials had piled up.

How very much had been stored up—and then left beyond the outer edge of *The Red Wheel*. I had compressed and cut, so that the rim would hold and not burst open. But where could I put all that now? just abandon it throw it away?—that would be a pity.

Perhaps I could rescue something, even from that same Tambov, in the form of separate short stories. A long time ago I'd conceived the idea of *bi-*

nary tales—a genre I was longing to try. A genre that just cried out to be brought to life. I could imagine several types and forms of such tales. The simplest: one character, or two or three of them, the same in both halves of the tale but separated by a span of time—it could be a short time, or years. (This is, of course, frequently seen in literary narratives, even where the author has not done it deliberately.) The second type: the two halves are connected by a common theme or idea, while the characters are completely different. Third type: the link between the two halves can be some object or event that has touched both of them. The fourth type: with different variations. There is a single tale up to a certain point, after which it splits into two: after this fork, things could go this way (and we see what happens) or that (and we see what happens). This is, actually, more of a three-part tale.[3]

And I wanted to try those kinds of short stories. Because you cannot live without having your *next* task in mind—it's an inescapable law: it installs itself in you even before the previous one is completed. It also interferes badly with the completion of each book—it steals your time, it distracts you. But this same process also offers the prospect of unabated motion.

In late May 1991 a request reached us by telephone, from the newly created, as yet tenuous, uncertain, Ministry of Foreign Affairs of the RSFSR: Yeltsin (who at that time had not yet been elected Russian president, but would be in a few days) was to visit the United States for the first time in late June. And he wanted, while hurrying to introduce himself to the president, to come and see me in Vermont for two hours or so. Was I prepared to receive him?

This was very unexpected for us. And, given the tight schedule for Yeltsin's American visit, it didn't even seem serious: where could he cut out the time for it? To get from Washington to the airport nearest us would take two hours, if they were lucky, and from there to us almost an hour. Which meant he'd need seven hours in all—where would he find them? But they were waiting for my reply.

It was with such directness—physically direct, from across the ocean, and with a directness imposing considerable responsibility on me, given the visitor's high office—that this living and demanding hand was suddenly reaching out to me, from Russia to Vermont. Yeltsin couldn't be undertaking such a complicated exercise out of just a warmhearted impulse—it was clearly based on a political calculation, and it was clear what that was: he wanted to present me as his ally against Gorbachev.

I had already suggested something of this in *The Oak and the Calf*: what if they invite me to meet the leaders?[4] Western reviewers had explained these lines in the shallow fashion that was all they could manage: as ambition, as megalomania. They had understood nothing: I'd declined to meet the king of Spain and two American presidents,[5] and I considered Soviet leaders the lowest of the low—so what kind of honor would I derive from meeting them? But what if it were possible to exert some influence on my country's progression towards a healthier state? And now the Russian president himself was coming to see me?

Alya phoned Andrei Kozyrev in New York and gave him my agreement regarding the proposed date: we would meet him at the airport nearest us and then take him, without a great entourage, to our home and talk there for an hour.

What would I say to Yeltsin tête-à-tête? Oh, what a lot there was. Starting with that reckless caper: "Russia's sovereignty," "Russia's independence day"—independence *from whom*? And what about the millions of Russians in the other republics? what would we do with them—abandon them? How on earth did that make sense to him? And what kind of mirage was that "confederation of states," consisting of the republics of the Union? And that law, then brand-new (announced in May), giving State Security unlimited rights—what was that all about? And then? . . . And then? . . .

I understood that none of the figures who had emerged during Perestroika had any sense of the great duration of historical Russia, any consciousness of their responsibility for the continuity of History—and where could they have acquired that sense, that consciousness, in their Party-dominated past? And they certainly weren't going to acquire it in that political bear garden. But perhaps, in a one-on-one conversation, I could convey to him something worthwhile. From a distance, Yeltsin had struck me as likable, and I believed I could support him in some important matters. He needed, he really needed to raise the level of his ideas and actions; this was very obvious from his blunders.

At the beginning of June it was confirmed to us that Yeltsin had accepted the conditions for our meeting and was looking forward to it. He was expected in the States by 20 June. He would be accompanied on his visit to us by security guards from the State Department.

However, the rush of his whirlwind visit and the need to make instant political statements were—for me, after so many years in the same routine—a severe shock to the system. Must I now, immediately, dive into the thick of Russian politics? The fact is that days, weeks, months, and years had passed with me working, at a measured pace, on manuscripts, on books, moving from one writing table to another; and, although my heart had sometimes pounded in passionate response to political events, urging me to take up arms, now that the call for political action had reached me at Five Brooks in such a direct manner, I felt I was not ready for it, or certainly not at this speed. And what if this was only the beginning? What if, following Yeltsin, others started arriving, now that the path had been opened up? And what would become of my work?

But on the 15th there was a call from Moscow, from an official at the Foreign Ministry of the RSFSR who was favorably disposed towards us: "I can't tell you everything by phone, but in Moscow they're having some doubts. There's opposition—both to the American trip in general and, especially, the visit to Cavendish." (Alya had been expecting it—that the moment Yeltsin's plan to visit me got out beyond his circle of close advisers, the doubters would immediately start arguing against it and trying to prevent the trip.)

And we felt some relief.

A few days later the tension lifted entirely. Yeltsin had arrived in Washington—and for the first twenty-four hours there was no phone call. Then, toward midnight, Kozyrev called: he wasn't coming, it couldn't fit into the schedule. Alya asked, cheekily: "Why, wouldn't they let him? Did they pressure him?" Kozyrev hemmed and hawed: "Yes, they did. And Boris Nikolaevich was very upset." Alya: "Tell him he shouldn't be upset." And she hurried to get this in: "Only, however much they press him, he shouldn't agree to the 'Harvard group' or the International Monetary Fund programs[6]—they'll make slaves of us." Kozyrev's tone sounded more interested now: "Why? Everyone here is really insisting." Alya, well enough armed with the facts, laid out for him all the harm in this plan, which would doom Russia to founder in the debt trap. But it was in vain. . . . No one foresaw the great morass in which that Kozyrev, who was then totally unknown, would bury us.

As to how much I could have helped Yeltsin then with my advice—probably not at all.

And, freed of that duty, I plunged back into my work.

At that same period, grateful to our neighbor, Dartmouth College, for help over many years with all my orders from libraries all over America, I accepted an honorary degree from them. Every year I was invited to take an honorary degree somewhere—and I invariably refused. But this time I couldn't—how could I have done my work all these years without Dartmouth's library?

I was also in great pain during those weeks. Because of gallstones passing into the bile duct, I needed surgery, which had complications.

And then things erupted in Moscow on 19 August and, in our excitement, we all, our sons included, erupted.

The creation of the State Committee on the State of Emergency was characterized, by lightweights, as a "putsch," which was absolutely unjustified. A "putsch" is always a coup d'état, with some gang or the other overturning the existing government and taking its place. On 19 August 1991 a gang that was already running the country tried to strengthen its weakened position. (And they even had total power, because Gorbachev's crafty escape to Foros didn't fool anyone:[7] he was, given his constant indecision, simply covering himself in case the "putsch" failed.) It was by fits and starts like this that the screws had been tightened throughout the whole history of the USSR, with dozens of similar episodes, never meeting opposition from the people and never being called "putsches." This was the only new thing, the fact that strong public opposition was seen, and Yeltsin took charge of it in time. The Communist government—and this was the sign that times were changing—now lost the readiness it had always had for a crackdown and froze, at a loss. Glasnost had stirred up society to such an extent that thousands and thousands assembled, of their own free will, to defend the White House[8]—unarmed, but animated by a determination not to yield to Communism again. All age groups had come together there, right down to young boys, and women pensioners, and girl students trying to persuade tank crews not to crush the demonstrators. And the soldiers themselves had changed during the glasnost years: they now had doubts as to whether it was acceptable to go into action against a crowd. (I hesitate to write something here that I don't know for sure, but it seems that the Americans were at that period both feeding Yeltsin information about the actions of his opponents and taking some kind of measures to support him.) The Muscovites' fervor in front of the White House was utterly revolutionary. They stayed there, fewer in number, at night, lighting fires and leaping to their feet at every suspicious sound.

When we saw, on television, a crane pulling down the "bottle," that accursed Dzerzhinsky[9]—how could a *zek*'s heart not skip a beat?! In *Archipelago* I had already acknowledged that, being against Great Revolutions in principle, I'd been a wholehearted supporter of the *zeks*' spontaneous uprisings. And it was the same on 21 August—I waited, my heart calling for the same rebellious impulse now, for the crowd to storm the Lubyanka![10] The crowd, now supplemented by ordinary folk, was sufficiently worked up for that, and could easily have stormed it, and with such major consequences—the whole course of that "revolution" would have been different and could have led to a rapid cleansing. But our weak-willed democrats dissuaded the crowd—and saved, to their own detriment, both the old KGB and the CPSU, and lots more of that type.

Epoch-making events! It seemed to me (for twenty-four short hours) that I had never, in all my life, experienced a day as great as this. Our lofty emotion, Alya's and mine, was, by now, shared by our sons. (Their ages ranged from sixteen to nineteen and they were, as it happened, still with us, Yermolai about to leave for Taiwan, Stepan having finished school and soon to go to Harvard, and Ignat, after three years in London, about to leave for the Curtis Institute in Philadelphia. They were discussing it all ardently, and Dimitri phoned excitedly from New York; and as for Yermolai, politics was a lifelong passion, from his earliest youth.)

But I, thanks to my experience of history, knew well the *rapidly changing moods of revolutions*: the directions later taken by whole eras are defined by the short hours and half hours when the participants take their decisions and actions. And I was anxiously counting off those half hours and awaiting defining deeds from the victors.

Minutes slipped by, and then hours: the legal validity of the October coup d'état of 1917 should have been revoked, which would immediately have cleared a site for building a renewed Russia, with the right to inherit all that was best in historical Russia.

But no! It turned out that the main action they took was a petty grabbing of prestigious accommodation in the Kremlin and on Staraya Square, not forgetting government cars.

A crucial moment, on the brink of great change!—but Yeltsin could not discern any overarching sense of history, or any of the splendid prospects opened up by this successful coup; it seemed that the only significance he saw in it was his victory over the man he hated, Gorbachev. And when the whole future of Russia was like wax in his hands and would have submitted to creative sculpting hour by hour, minute by minute, and he could have, rapidly and without the slightest opposition, cleared Russia's path—they were grabbing offices and property. . . . That was their level.

But the forty-eight-hour coup had not simply deliquesced into a wordy froth—it was immediately solidifying and was, with new, sharp ribs, slicing up the body of Russia. Having lived through the Moscow events from a safe distance, and satisfied themselves as to their final outcome, the Communist masters of the "Union republics"—Kravchuk, Nazarbaev, Karimov, and others—had, in those forty-eight hours, turned into fervent nationalists and, one after the other, proclaimed "sovereignty and separation" following the false Lenin-Stalin borders.[11]

My impulse was to write, immediately, a short open letter to Yeltsin saying he must not recognize the administrative borders between republics as state borders! reserve the right to review them! and don't rashly accept assistance from the International Monetary Fund!

But I came up against a brick wall in the person of Alya. She persuaded me not to do it: it would not help Yeltsin, and I could be interfering ineptly and to no avail. And my public trumpeting of advice across the ocean would seem tactless. Her argument was wrong: it was not Yeltsin that I had to help, but the nation's understanding—and at the right moment. But I gave in to her. And I deeply regret having missed my chance: I could, in fact, have bolstered the statement that the president's press secretary, Pavel Voshchanov, was to put out two days later. Of Yeltsin's entourage, it was only Voshchanov who dared voice the sensible proviso that "Russia reserves the right to review our borders with certain republics" (i.e., the right to political memory, to jog that memory in discussions, to exert political pressure). —My goodness, what an uproar then! what fury over this "Russian imperialism," not only in the United States, with their own keenest interests in mind, but even more so among Moscow radical-democrats of the Sakharov school (Elena Bonner, Leonid Batkin, and others of that ilk). And Yeltsin immediately took fright at the idea that he could be considered "imperialist" and thirsting for dictatorship—and retracted what his aide had said. And he sent Rutskoy on an urgent mission to Kiev, and Stankevich to Alma-Ata, to capitulate immediately, which they did.* Russian nerves had proved weak when faced with Ukrainian nationalists and insistent Asian demands. (And what about the Crimea?—which had, of course, never been Ukrainian; what about Sevastopol? And, as for the Black Sea fleet—they hadn't even thought about that.)

And now this very crowd was indeed waiting at that time for a thundering declaration from me—or rather, not thundering: they wanted some

---

* Recently, Pavel Voshchanov (*Novaya Gazeta* [*New Gazette*], 23–26 October 2003, 7) recalled and explained the story behind that statement of his: Yeltsin had given those orders without actually intending to rescue any Russian territories separated when administrative boundaries became borders. This was just his *pro forma* way of reminding the leaders of other republics that Moscow remained powerful, that "Yeltsin is no Gorbachev." (Another adviser to Yeltsin said: "You don't really think we need these territories?! What we need is for Nazarbaev and Kravchuk to know their place.") But when Kiev and Alma-Ata expressed their anger, Yeltsin got scared, disavowed the very words he had dictated to his press secretary, and sent emissaries to ferry his apologies to Kiev and Alma-Ata.

In this incident—just as in everything, always—Yeltsin acted not out of state interests, but his own. (Author's note, 2003.)

kind of joyful telegram saluting the "victory over the putsch." They were already astounded, already wrathful: how had I *dared* not to express, publicly, my delight? That I had, a year before, proposed my program for *Rebuilding Russia*—so what? That wouldn't be of use to anyone—it would take too long to read. But right now, that short expression of my fervent support—where was it??

This was an exact repeat of the previous situation—how had I dared remain silent about Perestroika? I should have been in raptures over it.

Well, for one thing, unbridled joy is not in my nature—I immediately step over the joyous moment, as something that's already accomplished beyond doubt, and look around: what's next? And, what's more, I was now anxiously counting, counting—with a sinking heart—the hours lost by Yeltsin and his confidants. (Even in America they were so dissatisfied by the lack of a joyful declaration on my part that the magazine that was most favorably disposed towards me, the *National Review*, suddenly published extracts from *Rebuilding Russia*, changing the tenses of verbs where necessary, as if I'd written it not a year ago but right now, in response to the August events.[12])

I had not guessed the reason for Yeltsin's holiday in Sochi—that he simply wanted two or three weeks of drunken festivities on the Black Sea shore; partying, in other words, on the little remaining scrap of Russian coastline— while all the rest of that sea, access to which had caused Russia to wage eight wars over two centuries, he had cheerfully handed over to Ukraine, with the Azov Sea thrown in, along with half a dozen Russian oblasts and 11–12 million Russian people.

As for me, I felt that since he had, not long before, been intending to meet me, I was within my rights to raise a hue and cry about the main dangers of the moment. And I wrote him a worried, and not now "open," letter. A letter saying that "some decisions cannot be corrected later." [32]

Alya sent the text by fax to Moscow on 30 August—straight into Kozyrev's hands. (And again—we'd backed the wrong horse. . . .)

Almost a month passed with no response. At the end of September a letter, somewhat bombastic in tone, arrived from Yeltsin, with complacent assurances that Russia was on the right track. (Yes, mother Russia will "endure anything."[13] Endure anything—but for how long?) And not a word in response to the basic point of my letter. [33]

In that reply, I encountered a totally different Yeltsin—not the one who had appeared, not long before, to be a fighter for justice, and not the one I'd recently been awaiting, with my naïve, futile advice, in Vermont.

But before Yeltsin's response, during that same September, we were treated to a bit of unexpected fun: the state of Vermont was celebrating its bicentennial, on different days in various towns. A date was also announced for our Cavendish, and I was invited to attend. Since my trip to England, I'd not gone anywhere, either to remote destinations, such as Korea, or even around the States—but how could we not honor our hospitable neighbors at their unassuming festivities? Alya, Katya, Stepan, and I went. And it was a really delightful celebration, with an enchanting parade of diverse elements along Main Street. And Vermont's Senator Leahy came (and brought me a personal letter from President Bush)—but that meant the press was there as well, and NBC television. Which meant I had to answer questions from the TV people.

And what profundity in those questions! (Which will come as no surprise to anyone familiar with twentieth-century broadcast and print media, especially in America.) "Do you agree with Russia's move to a market economy?"

My goodness! I'd had to spend a half century cogitating *The Red Wheel* and sit, permanently hunched over it, for twenty years. I'd had to allow the whole mass of Russian history and Russian problems since the end of the nineteenth century to flow through me. To read our twentieth-century thinkers. To publish my two volumes of political writing. To compose, earlier, *Letter to the Soviet Leaders*, one program; and now *Rebuilding Russia*, a second program. And, powerless in my distant abode, I'd had to eat my heart out over the troubled convulsions of Russia's situation. But who needed that? who was interested? Here was the famous businesslike American approach: did I or didn't I agree with the market economy?

Americans are genuinely unaware of the existence in Russia, even before the great October Revolution, of the *Market* they were now hoping for. And it had been a healthy market (even when not based on legal documents but on the word of honest merchants), and the people's attitude to it had been healthy. There may have been other problems, but there was a Market. And what kind of market would there be *now*? Whose inexperienced hands would set that top spinning—what topsy-turvy progress could we expect? And there was another little doubt in my mind: to Americans, did there exist, apart from the Market, any other characteristic, any trait, any aspect of a nation's life? And now they wanted me to express all of that, its whole volume and full extent, briefly—preferably with a "yes" or "no."

Yes—I did agree. But, I said (according to the text quoted in the newspapers), after seventy years of Communism and six years gambled away on perestroika, the approaching winter, with its possible food shortages, would test the new state order.[14]

And with that the question was settled.

Three days later, in Moscow, the new Prosecutor General announced that the charge of treason had been revoked: "In the absence of elements constituting a crime, the Aleksandr Solzhenitsyn case is dismissed."[15]

So now, for the first time, I really could return home.

So let's go! —When? —But you can't move into a total vacuum, with nothing prepared. Now, having savored the experience of working in profound seclusion, I would be even less able to survive in the cramped bustle of a city. And where ever could I find space for the enormous archives collected over my seventeen years abroad, and for my library?

And so, Alya dear, you'll need to do some reconnaissance there. But not heading into late autumn—shall we make it the coming spring? To find a plot somewhere out of town. To buy or build a house. (This would be our third major move since being exiled. And they say just two moves equal a house fire.)

Where to? There were many places across Russia that attracted us, places where we'd feel at home. I had lived my whole life far from the capitals. After *Ivan Denisovich*, when they'd kept calling me to Moscow, I didn't move there. But now, for the last part of my life, I felt I could live in the environs of Moscow. All our contacts, all practical matters would be simpler. (As for Alya, she was Moscow-born and -bred, and loved it with a passion, everything about it, even with today's urban developments.)

And our return absolutely had to be in the spring, so that we could travel through Siberia and the North in the summer and manage, by the autumn, to visit the Northern Caucasus too, my native land. So that meant spring '93, then?

For the time being, then, I would work, just as before. With the constant whirl of events in Russia and the explosion of demands, I could not complete very much. (Even here, where we'd been for fifteen years, we hadn't managed to sort the archives we'd brought with us from Zurich.)

Then, unexpectedly, a proposal arrived—and this was the first such—from the new director of Ostankino Television, Egor Yakovlev: they wanted me to give them, here in Vermont, a wide-ranging interview.

To address my fellow-countrymen directly? Face to face? My ideas would start crowding each other out: what to say first? what was most important?

But—who's that fellow that's going to talk on TV? Why should we listen to him all of a sudden? Seventeen years banned at home was no trifle.

Whole generations had grown up having read nothing of mine. I'd always imagined that my books would precede me, that they would pave the way for readers to understand me. Now—yes, it had been two years since they'd started publishing me, but, with the current state of disarray, books were getting stuck, not advancing deep into the country. Outside the capitals, Russia had read little of my work. Now, following the books, my political writing was getting published—but that, too, had either come too late to fire up people's passions or had outstripped their understanding. And was I to set it all out now orally? Start all the way back, from the very beginning?

I postponed the interview until spring '92. To give the books some more time.

But—just you try staying silent! October '91 gave cause—glaring, screaming cause—to speak out: a referendum on Ukrainian independence was announced, for 1 December. And how shameless, the wording of the question (no more shameless, though, than Gorbachev's question of six months earlier): do you want a Ukraine that is independent, democratic, prosperous, where human rights are protected—*or not*? (i.e., a Ukraine that does *not* thrive, is *not* democratic, where human rights are flouted, etc.). I had to intervene! For the Russian part of Ukraine, splitting off would be a tragedy of historic proportions and would break my own heart as well! But how to make my voice heard? What megaphone could I use? My appeal[16] was published in *Trud* (*Labor*), the most widely distributed paper among ordinary people—both the Donetsk miners and the Crimeans would read it. (I proposed that the vote-counting should be done oblast by oblast—perhaps at least a section of the Russian-speaking ones would gravitate back to Russia?) But no—they voted for separation.

I had made my appeal. . . . In vain. (It turned out that, for the whole month before the referendum, all the Ukrainian newspapers and TV channels had been closed to voices speaking for unity with Russia. And Bush hadn't restrained himself, before the referendum, from intervening publicly: he, you see, was *in favor* of separation for Ukraine.[17])

Our people had been duped. In this way we lost twelve million Russians, and another twenty-three million who considered Russian their mother tongue. What a horrifying, shattering rift—for centuries to come? . . . (Two months later Alya had occasion to be in New York and happened to meet a delegation of Donetsk miners there. "How could you vote for separation?" "Because you're eating us out of house and home," they replied. "Your lot turn up by the busload to snap up our food. When we separate, we'll get more to eat." —"And what if they stop your children speaking Russian and force them to attend Ukrainian schools?" —"Well, we'll see about that when it happens—if it happens . . .")

How very, very many people in Russia had lost everything under the Communists, even down to their sense of nationhood, and almost every ambition above mere survival.

But Yeltsin and his government didn't even bat an eyelid over the skewed Ukrainian referendum. Ukrainian independence was opening up like a gaping maw—but Yeltsin, trusting, was letting Kravchuk lead him by the nose, while homing in on his only goal: to crush Gorbachev totally, to yank his throne from under him. So they agreed on Belovezh[18]—and did not tell Nazarbaev their plan (did they fear a sudden recalcitrance on his part?). Having, in so doing, given up on another six or seven million Russians in Kazakhstan, Yeltsin went off to a boisterous dinner at Belovezh and signed the declaration, having received from Kravchuk *no guarantee whatsoever* of any concrete federative union with Ukraine in the future. Kravchuk, victorious in the referendum, had, to put it bluntly, hoodwinked Yeltsin (as he would hoodwink him at *all* their subsequent meetings): Ukraine would immediately, and belligerently, push back from all its links with Russia (except its cheap gas).

And so it was that within a few short months, from August to December, Russia had launched its whole unwieldy hulk into what can only be described as a Third Time of Troubles, following the First (1605–1613) and Second (1917–1922).[19] The scale of events was beginning to seem immense.

Belovezh caused the other republics' leaders to get worried—so the trio of Slav leaders cobbled together the feeble, illusory CIS, the Commonwealth of Independent States, to replace the fragmented Soviet Union. For Russia, it was a temporary delusion, a yoke, and a cover for the abandonment of twenty-five million defenseless fellow-countrymen. —In this way, step by step, Yeltsin progressed blindly, impulsively—and every step he took was the worst possible choice for Russia.

At the same time, he couldn't summon the courage to admit the unavoidable consequences of Belovezh: that it was impossible to glue together any kind of "CIS" in place of the USSR—for the Party people who had been running the republics before had now, of course, become national potentates with all the arms stocks, airports, bases, and even military units that had been located there. —Then (28 February 1993) this grandiose announcement: "Russia must be the guarantor of security within the confines of the CIS"[20]—*what for*? what kind of power itch was this? Shevardnadze immediately started complaining that we wanted to destroy Georgia; and, from Ukrainian voices, "we don't need an older brother, or any brother!" (you couldn't imagine a more heavy-handed way to scare them), and the Ukrainian government instantly complained to the UN about Russia's "great power" ambitions. —The reason for this was (according to Yeltsin's profound words in his New Year 1994 address) that "we [the CIS] simply do not have the right to live separately: *our peoples would not permit it*."[21] If their "peoples would not permit it," they should have thought about that before, at Belovezh. (On one occasion, later, Yeltsin bragged of having "effectively protected the Russian population in the CIS states"—only they hadn't actually lifted a finger to help.)

And within Russia? Elected president in June 1991, Yeltsin now issued his first decree, "On Education"—what a high-minded start!—only not a line of it was put into action in the following three years. —Following the example of his rival, Gorbachev, Yeltsin let his own head, too, be turned by the praise he received for being a democrat, "dedicated to humanist values"—and, unique among leaders of the "Union republics," chose not the national interests of his own people but an undefined "universal democracy."

And now that fourteen republics had peeled off, did he still feel responsible for the integrity of the Russia that remained? No! "Help yourself to some sovereignty—as much as you can swallow!"[22] Believing, perversely, that he needed to shower charitable handouts on all the autonomous republics threatening to separate from Russia, he unleashed in them an appetite for the right to pay no taxes to the Center—let the purely Russian oblasts provide for the whole of Russia. Then Yeltsin set to work concluding individual agreements with the oblasts. (Agreements between the whole and its parts?—what other state in the world would do that??) And the sting of Siberian separatism was even more painful: if he didn't watch out, the whole lot might separate off (there'd been several such attempts in 1917). Broadcast after broadcast, the American station Radio Liberty was gloatingly, basely inciting the Siberians: separate! separate!

No sooner had Yeltsin finished celebrating the Belovezh dismemberment than he blindly, insanely pushed sick Russia into taking another new *leap*, plunging it even further into the Troubles by unbridled plundering, and dubbing this ruination of millions of people the long-awaited economic "reforms"—at the same time also delivering Russia into the hands of random young upstarts.

And this was when the Supreme Calamity came crashing down on Russia! As for me, I had, from a distance and in utter despair, described in *Rebuilding Russia* the stage of destruction already reached. But that turned out to be only a foretaste of what was still to come. Then, before this Time of Troubles, it had still been possible to live. But it turned out that everything up to then in Russia, while Gorbachev was in charge, was only the eve of the supreme calamity, of Gaidar's reckless, pitiless "reform"[23]—and the resulting avalanche of destitution that fell upon the people.

With a theoretical scheme ready in their heads, though with no understanding of the crux of the issue, they launched into a frantic slashing and surgical dissection of Russia's defenseless body. (They were going to "abolish price controls," when the producers had a monopoly!—could they have set up any more wayward system? And what kind of penetrating, powerful foresight led Gaidar to predict a fall in prices "in two or three months"?)

To me, having lived fifty-five years on Soviet kopecks, that gigantic, unchecked price rise seemed inconceivable—and it was far more inconceivable to my fellow-countrymen as they fell into the abyss. (People brought me the new, tinny Soviet "ruble," the 1992 coin—it was the size of the previous two-kopeck piece, but there were no kopecks at all now!—and I almost cried. Between this pathetic, feather-light little coin and the previous, heavy silver Nikolai ruble lay the whole depth of our downfall. . . . But no, not the whole depth, not all: even now the fall was just beginning, and not causing the powers above the slightest concern. . . .)

In 1992, the gigantic, historic Russian Catastrophe began to unfurl: the nation's life, morality, and social awareness unraveled, unstoppable; in culture and science rational activity ceased; school education and childcare descended into a fatal state of disorder. I felt the rapid collapse taking place in Russia as my own personal catastrophe: I had dedicated my life to overcoming Bolshevism and now it had been dumped—and what was the result?? I'd feared this, and begun my *Rebuilding Russia* with the warning that "we must take care not to be crushed beneath its rubble instead of gaining liberty."[24]

Had I foreseen all this? Not *this* particular form of collapse—no. But I did see that the situation could go astray and become another February—that had for a long time been my greatest fear. And the whole *Red Wheel*—which reached Russia too late—was about that. Yes, Gorbachev had unleashed exactly that, a new February. And Yeltsin had set it rolling at full pelt, smashing everything in its way.

What kind of man was Yeltsin? Inside, I was even now harboring my initial liking for him. (Was it because I hoped he would make up for Gorbachev's missed opportunities?) In his appearance, his speeches, his behavior, I could now see much that was awkward, clumsy, slow-footed—but I did not sense in him any self-interest save a bit of pretty basic ambition and naïveté; but no guile, no duplicity. And because of this presumed honesty I was, to all intents and purposes, a supporter, despite the growing list of his monstrous blunders, disastrous errors, his illogical decisions, for all of which there was a price to pay. Who by? Certainly not him, but Russia—in the form of its territory, its inhabitants, its riches, and its moral state. The damage from these losses was almost indescribable, ungraspable—but no damage, I hoped, had been caused by evil design on Yeltsin's part, only thoughtlessness. I wanted to believe there was no shameless self-seeking there. (My reply to the frequent letters I received, angry at Yeltsin, blaming him, was: what can we do? This is our Russian character: the arm's ready for action but the brain's lazy, hard to get started, a blockhead's in charge. So that's how we'll have to disentangle it all, just as we are.)

Because Russia began—this unexpectedly??—such a rapid decline into banditry and poverty, I experienced, from 1992, a breakdown of my worldview that would be hard to withstand at over seventy years of age. I'd have to take a sharp turn away from the whole of my previous life, away from the epoch I'd lived in up to then, away from the efforts I'd made—apparently wasted?—to be able to join the new life of the country. (Yes and, after eighteen years immobile and immersed in your work, how do you so rapidly exchange that for a cracking pace? From a forest lair straight into the hustle and bustle? My inner world would also somehow have to change inside me.)

But just where in Russia were the Russian patriots? Alas!—the patriotic movement these days had become hopelessly entangled with Communism and, evidently, they could not be untangled. The "National Salvation Front" announced in October 1992 a "historic reconciliation between the Whites and the Reds": "let's draw a line under the Civil War." *On whose behalf* were they announcing this reconciliation? And where were the *Whites* among them? And as for "drawing a line," the Cheka had already done that by 1921.

A healing, salutary, moderate patriotism must—if ever given the chance—build on an absolutely clear site and on new foundations. But how? I myself don't understand it yet, but it would obviously: (1) come from the provinces; and (2) be based on the inescapable fact that our national character is woolly, will not hold its ground, is not good at acknowledging responsibility, and is not amenable to organizing itself.

By spring 1991 it had been two years since I'd entrusted Dima Borisov with the publication rights to my works in the USSR. Meanwhile, every spring Alya was supposed to send the Fund's annual accounts to Switzerland, showing how much *Archipelago* had earned for the Fund worldwide and how much of that the Fund had spent—and on what. By 1990 *Archipelago* was already being published in the USSR, and by more than one publisher, and those figures had to go into the global accounts—Alya had been pestering Dima for these since the autumn. But even so, until now Dima had not sent a single copy of either the contracts on any of the books or any statements of income or expenditure—only listings of the journal publications currently under way and the books being prepared for publication. (And then, on top of all that, a scandal blew up over the seven-volume subscription edition including *Archipelago*, which everyone had been waiting for; Dima had entrusted it to some commercial organization called INKOM-NV, which had resulted in an explosion of irate letters: the publishing quality was abysmal and the price including delivery was three times higher than originally quoted!) Alya was insisting that he must immediately send us the contracts and records on *Archipelago* editions or, by now, relating to all editions in general. Even before this, Dima had taken every concrete question from us as an insult. Now we wrote him a letter: Dima dear, our absolute trust in you cannot automatically extend to your co-publishers and partners, especially in times such as these. —Dima dragged his feet, kept putting it off but finally, in April 1991, the picture started to get clearer.

Much later we learned that Dima had already, between March and May '90, signed two dozen or so contracts with his Center without my knowledge, and given it *exclusive* rights to my books for three years. (Upon which the Center had immediately ceded the rights for a fee to various partners, for it did not itself have the wherewithal to publish.) But it wasn't until June that he suggested I should *consider* that scheme, as though it were just a *plan*. And when I immediately, decisively, rejected the idea, Dima did not admit that it had already been activated, and didn't say a word about those contracts—and not for another whole year. And in August '90, when he had already had a firm refusal from me, Dima signed a contract under that same scheme with these unsavory INKOM publishers, who were now fleecing subscribers and driving even Dima to despair. The terms were an injustice for the Fund, an injustice for the *zeks*. Alya launched a grueling effort to untangle things and start renegotiating in the Fund's favor—in the course of which all the rest was revealed. (And even then we were still being duped, and the Fund received almost nothing from the millions of copies of *Archipelago* published in Russia.)

Things went from bad to worse. In letters from readers, first one of my books published under the Center's brand name would happen to pop up, then another, now in Petropavlovsk-Kamchatsky, now in Kherson—but there was no trace of these books either in Dima's previous listings or in the folder he'd finally sent with the assurance that all the contracts were now here. (And the Center had not, in a single one of these contracts, included a single clause protecting the quality of the publishing or protecting the author from abuses. But there was in every contract, without fail, a clause about the author's financial obligations to the publisher. It was exactly like Carlisle in her time. . . .[25]) And that wasn't all! That summer, while Dima was abroad, ten contracts for my books, which had not been mentioned to us, were discovered at the same time in the editorial office. (And never, not even at a meeting with Alya, was Dima able to explain that.)

It was beyond belief. At home the mood was mournful—as if we'd lost a loved one. A mistake could be forgiven, even a massive one. But fraud was intolerable.

The last straw was a letter from Novosibirsk. In November 1990 a new publisher, Germes, had approached Dima's Center with a proposal to publish *Archipelago* for Siberia. They had "contacted Vadim Borisov personally" and told him that they had paper stocks for a print run of three hundred thousand, in hard covers. They'd "had a series of telephone conversations with him, during which [they] felt that agreement had been reached" on the form of the edition, the deadlines, and the percentage payable to the Center for the rights. Then "Vadim Borisov referred [them] to the commercial director" of his Center, who told them that their "publishing *Archipelago* is unnecessary, since *Novy Mir* [Center] is bringing it out in a print run of three million." But, he added, it would be possible for them to publish it if they paid the Center a three-times-greater percentage. —This put the Siberians "in an awkward position."

But how did this happen? Had I not begged that everyone, anyone be allowed to publish *Archipelago*, immediately—especially in the provinces? Were *my representative* and his companions suppressing *Archipelago*? Because their self-styled "Center," that usurper, was not being paid enough??

We were beside ourselves with frustration at our inability to snatch Dima from the grasp of his enterprising colleagues. In the brisk, freewheeling Gorbachev years, artful fixers thrived under most favorable circumstances: they just took the mask of "cooperatives." That was the designation used as a shield by Dima's advisers, who cooked up that *Novy Mir* Center publishing cooperative. Some well-aimed positioning here: taking the name of a venerable and much-loved journal while at the same time appropriating the personal authorization that Vadim Borisov had received from me. Thus they resourcefully captured the fate of my first books in Russia.

We began to learn about these books—that they were being published on trashy grey paper in cramped, smeary type, barely readable, with a cover like a school exercise book—first through letters from angry readers, but soon enough directly, since furious readers provided us with samples of that abomination. From the very first print run, ten thousand subscribers refused to pay for this horribly produced volume. And where did they send their letters with so many signatures?—to INKOM, but also to the blameless publishers of the journal whose brand name had been adopted by the Center, to the flabbergasted Zalygin, and direct to me in Vermont.

"We have received the first book of *The Gulag Archipelago* and we are simply outraged—it looks as if that subscription was designed to make someone a tidy profit" (eighteen signatures). —"If the subscribers to A. Solzhenitsyn had known that . . . you had decided to line your pockets from such a book, such an author . . . Your business practice knows no bounds of conscience" (Smolensk). —"We have always subscribed to your journal and, having absolute trust in you, we were happy to subscribe to this collection of works by Aleksandr I. Solzhenitsyn. Our joy was premature. We have encountered an absolute racket" (nine signatures, Perm). —"We have been deceived: the paper is of bad quality, the cover is soft, and we were not made aware in advance that the price was being doubled; and it was the same for the delivery charge. That's 'live not by lies' for you." —"*Novy Mir* subscribers are the victims of a confidence trick. Your organization is like a small-time trader, palming off trash at exorbitant prices" (Student). —"What joy, what expectations we had when the subscription was announced. . . . I well remember the times when Solzhenitsyn was being dragged through the mud wherever you turned and in every publication. And now they've decided to make themselves a hefty profit from his name" (Leningrad). —"Deceit and treachery . . . Paying for this wretched publication out of a pension feels insulting and painful" (Oryol). —"I never expected this kind of 'sharp practice' from such a reputable journal. Please give us Solzhenitsyn's address so that we can let him know how his name and his popularity are being used to cheat people" (Yaroslavl). —[To Solzhenitsyn and Zalygin:] "Do you really 'know not what you do,'[26] you who so passionately want to rebuild Russia and are telling us how to do it?" (Ryazan).

What shame, what pain, to see *just what* my books' return to their homeland had come to. . . .

My heart ached. I had written my books too early. And they had reached their readers too late. And I could do nothing about it.

And what an unexpected symmetry. Just as my books, when flowing from East to West, had fallen victim to distortions and abuses, so now the same was happening on their way from West to East, only in a different form.

What about Alya and me? . . . After a dozen battles on the newspaper and public-debate fronts, after two decades away from our homeland, after the distressing publishing travails we'd already experienced, we were just tired. And busy with other things. For a quarter century already we'd been so immersed, wholly and wholeheartedly, into the boundless epic of the Russian Revolution that we hadn't expected this calculating, artful scurrying amidst the gathered sheaves of our literary harvest. We didn't notice it in time. Indeed, we couldn't even have suspected such devilry emanating from the Homeland being restored to us. We couldn't change, just like that, the angle and scope of our vision.

Both *there* and *here* we were paying the Price of Banishment.

And now we experienced bitterness and pain for our close friend and confidant. No one, of course, at the time when I'd vested Dima with power of attorney, could have imagined the cruel, ruthless times that were about to descend on Russia. And how very many people would get knocked off course and lose their head in the temptations of the "Market" that was now running wild.

And our longtime friend had also been carried off in that surge. Reluctantly? Couldn't he help himself? He had been best man at our wedding, the godfather of two of our sons, and Alya and I of his daughters. Then, Dima and Tatiana took in my poor aunt Irina from Georgievsk—where she was at death's door and in miserable penury at the age of ninety—so that she could live out her final months in their Moscow apartment; and then buried her at an Orthodox cemetery near the shores of the Klyazma.

What pain, both for the loss of a friend and for everything else—for everything now going on in our homeland.

At the beginning of 1992, Zalygin came to the States, visiting one of the universities. We invited him to come and see us in Vermont and welcomed him with open arms, his visit happening to coincide with the start of Shrovetide.

His breakthrough with *Archipelago*, albeit in another form, had nevertheless echoed Tvardovsky's with *Ivan Denisovich.*

Sergei Pavlovich had barely changed—he was as openhearted as before and our conversation was warm, as he told us of his ecology struggle, a taxing enterprise and a risky one. He gave a colorful account of current Russian life generally. And we discussed publishing issues, too. There were many things in the affairs of the Center—which bore the *Novy Mir* name—that Zalygin had not even suspected.

But his visit to me was also put to good use by Gorbachev's people. We had already had reports from Moscow that "the wartime diaries of the writer have been found and will be returned to him." There'd been a lot in the press about it. I'd have been very happy if I could have believed it, if I'd thought they hadn't been burned. (And for a moment I did believe it.) And now Zalygin was "charged by Gorbachev" to hand over to me some things taken from my Lubyanka file. And what were they? They turned out, of course, not to be the promised diaries: there was one notepad containing my political notes written at the front, and some letters and photos from my correspondence while there. There was only one find that was dear to me: among the notes was the actual original of the "Resolution No. 1" that Nikolai Vitkevich and I had foolishly drawn up in January 1944, and each traced out in his own hand so that we both had a copy—which had, when added to our correspondence, destined us to a spell behind bars.[27]

At the end of April a film crew from Ostankino, headed up by Stanislav Govorukhin, arrived and shot a film-interview. I managed to say a few things, but some important things were later cut out, to keep to the allotted running time. The most sobering part of it was Govorukhin's objection when I came out with my crazy dream that *at least some* of the butchers, the oppressors, the nomenklatura would repent of *something* at least. And he was right, of course. But this meant Russia's path was to be impure, unexpiated, and slow and tortuous. (The film was not shown in Russia until four months later.)[28]

When the film crew arrived, I was immediately struck by the quick thinking, humor, and warm geniality of the cameraman, Yuri Prokofiev. For three days they worked in our home, and at our final dinner together he offered "to help in any way I can." My reply: "Well, I'll need it." (It had suddenly come to me that I might enlist his services for our journey through Siberia.) With no more detailed discussion, we made that a firm agreement.

Then in May my old friend, the writer Boris Mozhaev, came to visit us in Vermont (Yermolai had whisked him up to us from New York, Boris having extricated himself from his delegation). It was a joyous, companionable reunion. He and I had become close not only through our Ryazan connection but also, especially, thanks to our trips together to the places where he grew up around Ryazan—and then the Tambov oblast, where he was extremely helpful to me in collecting materials about the peasant rebellion of 1920–21. He radiated directness, openness, a constant readiness to do a good turn. We had not seen each other for eighteen years, since he came with Yuri Lyubimov to visit me, when I was under siege at Peredelkino before being exiled. Eighteen years—but it felt like a day: everything was as before, as if we hadn't changed.

Now it was with him that I first discussed my plan to return via the Russian Far East[29]—which would, I thought, be in the spring of '93—so that he could help me in Vladivostok and Khabarovsk, which he knew well, as he'd served there as a naval engineer. Having learned of the existence of an Oceanology Institute in Vladivostok, I asked him to arrange, as a priority, a meeting for me with the people running that very unusual establishment.

And Boris suggested, in passing, that I should publish a newspaper in Russia! I didn't pay much attention—if anything, I was surprised. —But a month later the idea came back to me, as if it had been my own, an inspiration: why not a paper, indeed? And that idea immediately gave me a boost, gave my return to Russia more force. (My considerable experience of reading the Russian prerevolutionary press, from the era before things went out of control, would also stand me in good stead.) Ideas flashed through my mind. I'd want to run it as a "people's paper," a "paper of the Russian backwoods"—that was who it was for, the *backwoods*, and it would express *their* aspirations. It would be a small, four-page paper, but substantial in terms of content, appearing twice a week. No advertisements. But—who would pay for it? We'd need an enormous amount of money, especially to get it distributed across the broken country—where would we find such donors? and staff? —No, we did not have the strength for this.

That same month, June 1992, I had a letter from the Russian ambassador in Washington, Vladimir Petrovich Lukin (whom I already knew personally: he had visited us at home, was very enlightened in his actions, and a warmhearted person). He told me that Yeltsin would be coming to the States again for a short visit: he would have liked to come and see me, but again there would not be enough time. Could I perhaps come to Washington for the evening of 15 June? if not, could a phone conversation be arranged?

I wouldn't even have entertained the idea of that journey to meet him—especially as it would have cost me three working days. But I couldn't avoid the phone conversation, even though I had, over the past year, become deeply disillusioned with Yeltsin thanks to the general, ever-increasing devastation he'd tolerated. That spring Yeltsin had promised his dumbfounded nation: "If things are not better by September, I'll lie down on a railway track" (which the people would always hold against him). You had to wonder if he believed it himself. What ever did the whole Gaidar team expect to happen?

Our phone conversation lasted forty minutes, Yeltsin taking up the time ladling out fancy words of welcome, inviting me to Moscow. As for me, I'd have liked, in the course of the conversation, to hammer home a good few points, but how plausible was that? (And indeed, our conversation resembled the forceful Vorotyntsev talking to the ponderous General Samsonov at Ostrolenka.[30])

Points about the ruinous progress of the Gaidar reforms, for example. (But Yeltsin would, of course, in a few hours be having talks with the highest levels of American power—why cut the ground from under him?) I did say that Gaidar was out of touch with everyday life; that what he was doing wasn't right. Yeltsin: "He's growing into the job; but the main thing is that he's bold."—And about the borders with Ukraine and Kazakhstan—again. (It was useless: here Yeltsin said he felt he wanted to be *friends* with Kravchuk. And just look where that got him. . . .) —And that the way for Russia to defend itself against terrorism by the Caucasians in the South was not to keep hold of Chechnya but partition it off instead, keep it isolated from Russia. They want to leave us—so let them leave, as long as they don't take any of the Terek Cossack lands with them. —And how to avoid a larcenous privatization, and stop dainty morsels getting snapped up. (Even then I still couldn't imagine the scale of the Pillaging!) And how necessary a strong government was, and how severely those selling off Russia's riches must be punished. —Yeltsin, in turn, asked me whether it was all right to give up those four Kuril Islands[31] (it was being hotly disputed at the time) and was very surprised that I raised no objections. (If it was *all right* to give Ukraine and Kazakhstan ten or so provinces that really were Russian, why should we hang on so tenaciously to those little islands—that didn't actually belong to us—and their negligible populations? it was a local matter, and Japan would repay us handsomely.)

I didn't convince him of anything. Without a face-to-face meeting, of course we wouldn't understand each other. But even if we had met face-to-face, would my words have lodged in his mind for very long? or only till his conversation with the next person?

In early July, in Moscow, he gave Alya a warm welcome and she gave him, on my behalf, some recently published materials, about how Russia might be protected from uncontrolled import-export trading and the leakage abroad of Russian capital—and he promised to read them without fail—but it was all, of course, in vain. He gave the Kremlin Commandant the job of finding me a dacha to buy, near Moscow—this wouldn't go smoothly, either. Alya had already spent a month crisscrossing the Moscow environs with our friend Valeri Kurdyumov; they'd looked everywhere. Now something hopeful had appeared, and she returned home with a plot promised but not finalized, and without the necessary paperwork. And, on that land, should we build another house? who'd do the job? how? It seemed it was beyond us. (And it certainly couldn't be done by the following spring.)

In Moscow, Alya also had to take care of her greatest concern: completing the legalization of our Fund in Russia, a process already begun in 1990, in Silaev's time. During this 1992 trip she was going back and forth between various institutions, moving things along—the officials had no experience of this kind of thing—but by the time 1993 dawned the Fund was operating legally in Russia.

For all those years since Gorbachev had wound up the political Gulag, Alya had been looking for new forms for the work of our Fund. Now a new possibility had appeared, to help earlier *zeks* as well, from the Stalin times, from "my" Archipelago; and now those who'd been dispossessed as kulaks began appealing to the Fund, as well as children of victims of repression and even those who'd served in the labor armies[32]—for there was no end to our country's woes. There were not enough willing carriers to take medications now, and the normal postal service offered no guarantee that a parcel would arrive safely, or indeed that it would arrive at all. It was the responsive and tireless Lyusia Thorne who came to our aid again: first she found a safe outbound route via the US Health Department, and then tracked down a reliable addressee—the Socio-Juridical Board of the RSFSR, which would receive our boxes and pass them on to the Fund. And throughout '91 and '92, Alya sent out an enormous number of parcels to elderly *zeks* living out their days in poverty: medicines, vitamins, soup cubes, and tea. She also gave their addresses to charitable organizations in America that were keen to send help to Russia. She bought a little motorboat for the Solovetsky Monastery—they had no means of reaching the mainland. —And in '93 our whole parish, that of Father Andrew Tregubov, joined in, collecting warm clothes and shoes; the Fund was buying canned food, vegetable oil, dried fruit, and underwear, and the parishioners, led by Father Tregubov's wife, Galina, packed it all up. And now we were sending whole containers out from America, filled with hundreds of heavy boxes—to Moscow, Tomsk, Vladimir.

In the summer of 1992, Alya, Yermolai, and Stepan spent several weeks in Russia (and the boys took a trip to the South, where I come from, and were warmly welcomed). Alya herself spent those six weeks in Moscow, seeing many old friends and new acquaintances. She also met Yuri Prokofiev there and revealed to him what was behind our provisional agreement: my planned return through Siberia and my hope that he might play a part. He set to work on it with great enthusiasm; we had not been wrong about that man.

Alya came back—but her mind was already ensconced in Russia; here she looked at everything with unseeing eyes.

In all my thoughts I, too, was in Russia—I hadn't been away for so much as a day. Over the last two years my concern with the course of Russian events had been so painfully acute that it sometimes brought on my angina.

I was receiving a good few letters coming direct to me from Russia (and even more were getting lost on the way). In them people I didn't know were discussing whether or not I should return. Those advising against far outweighed the rest: "We hope you won't be hurrying back to Russia"; "don't rush your move back!"; "Russia is now ridden with all the vices ever invented; the young people don't know you"; "you'll do more good *there* than you will if you come back"; "we still feel the clutches of the old government—wait a bit before you come back!" And one ex-*zek*—criminal, not political—in a friendly tone: "Watch out they don't bash your head in over here, those well-wishers of yours."

But others felt differently: "Come over, don't waste any time!"; "everyone striving for a better future for Russia must live here"; "someone must rally the voiceless millions, form the Russian people into rescue forces"; "our Homeland needs—we can feel it—your presence here, in person, needs to hear the sound of your voice; come over!"

Yes, of course I'm needed by *those* people! And, yes, there could be knife-wielding, pistol-toting fanatics as well—but the Lord will be there, too. He's all the protection I need. And that's exactly it—I must go back while I still have the strength to travel through the oblasts, strength to give to Russian life all the experience I have accumulated. Oh, if only my return could become some kind of lever to launch improvements in Russia. (And be, at the same time, a life lesson for my sons and the many, many people in Russia who have not yet run off to the West or are doomed to stay put.)

Ever since 1987, alarmed political commentators among the Third Wave had been issuing warnings that I was "already packing [my] bags," "secretly preparing to hop over to the USSR." Now their chums back home were changing their tune: why's he sitting there in Vermont? why doesn't he come over? but he's too late—he's already missed everything, hasn't he? and he'd be no use to anyone here—"put him into mothballs!"

Where did it come from, that extraordinary irritation with me that the pseudo-intellectuals have harbored for so many years? It wouldn't be because my behavior towards the Soviet government was, in practice, a reproach to them, would it? because it had been possible not to give in, because I had dared act when they, in their hidey-holes, had not. And there was, of course, my national orientation: "being Russian," "Russianness"—these were to be kept hidden inside, washed clean as if shameful, and no staunch Russian feelings expressed, no matter what.

After the surge of accolades of not so long ago, the Russian press, fearless now they were free, rushed to start mudslinging—as if the Soviet press hadn't savaged me enough when they weren't free. It's always the way, an invariable principle in psychology. Newspaper headlines, ever more derisive, started appearing ("Solzhenitsyn? which one?," "Three beards in a bowl,"[33] and more in that vein). They can mock all they want but meanwhile, over the course of the glasnost years, the pseudo-intellectuals gradually, unnoticed, had to acknowledge what a great statesman Stolypin had been and how degrading that February. In essence, they conceded that I'd been right.

And, on top of that, Communist fanatics were also growing hoarse from all the hatred they'd been leveling at me. At lectures about my books, there was always someone shouting threats. Russian nationalists, meanwhile, hadn't forgiven me for not expressing steadfast determination to defend "Great Russia" in her imperial incarnation. (Surely hatred from such *different* sides at once was sufficient demonstration that my line was sound?)

And as for the masses—what they wanted, and desperately needed, was something, someone to believe in. After all the changes they'd seen, how could the country not be waiting for a miracle, without fail and without delay? My potential intervention had looked like one such possible miracle: let's hope this fellow will come over and get things moving, and it might all change.

But what are the active Russian brains occupied with today? With economics and more economics, "reform," "vouchers," commercial banks—all the subjects in which I'm least knowledgeable. (The only thing I do understand, and you'd have to be blind to miss it, is that the people are being shamelessly and ingeniously robbed.) And it was unimaginable that I would be able, the minute I arrived, to get the new crooks and new civil servants to repent and stop preying on the people.

Russia was also calling out to me in a different way: in dozens, if not hundreds, of requests. The most frequent was to help a family emigrate to America. And another good few letters wanted me to get a sick person, plus companion, to Europe or America for treatment, but they had no idea how much that would cost—tens, if not hundreds, of thousands of dollars—and how much work would be needed to organize it. And who could do that? did they think I had the staff for it? —And, from the republics that had now split off: "Please, I beg of you, help our family move to Russia! . . ." Some were heartrending: "In Christ's name I implore you, please help us!" Opening my heart to all this was painful. —Then there were a good number of requests to get a manuscript printed in the West, get a book published—and this was while Russian publishers here were suffering a total meltdown—and of course they didn't understand that either. —And vast quantities of manuscripts, poetry collections, just turned up, and would I read them please, give an opinion—but how could I read them all? . . . I wouldn't be too wide of the mark in saying that nine out of every ten letters from home contained only requests, and just one might have had ideas of any substance regarding Russia and today's woes.

A writer's mailbag . . . (And how will it be in Russia? The same but a hundred times worse.)

I started taking an occasional look at the latest literature, some by Third Wave emigrants and some emerging into the West from the Soviet underground. Yes, a rupture had evidently occurred in Russian literature; a sharp borderline now ran across it. Its techniques and criteria were outrageously alien. Reading it was of absolutely no interest—repugnant, even. Was it a sign of the changing times, and irreversible? Or was it just *Debased Literature*? Well, that was what I named it, to myself.

Meanwhile the political mêlée in the new Russia was getting more and more heated—and entirely fruitless. Twenty-five million Russians were left to fend for themselves in ex-Soviet republics (and no one had lifted a finger to get them out, not even from a burning Tajikistan, or Chechnya where people were harassing, robbing, and killing Russians with impunity). And as to the abyss the country was falling into thanks to those disastrous Gaidar reforms—no one cared. And all that aggression, as with the two goats confronting each other across a narrow bridge,[34] went into the struggle between the Yeltsin and the Khasbulatov camps. Just as, a year before, Yeltsin had seen only one enemy, Gorbachev, and apparently considered the dismembering of Russia to be of secondary importance, so now the crucial thing was to crush Khasbulatov and the traitor Rutskoy.[35] As a result of all that, by the end of 1992 a tension had developed that threatened total chaos in the country.

(But the paradox, the irony of history, unnoticed by the participants in that battle, was that the "democrats"—for the sake of supporting the one seen as their great hope, Yeltsin—were defending the draft constitution of an authoritarian Russia. And the Supreme Soviet—most of whom were Communists and absolutely devoted totalitarians—were obliged, for no other reason than to undermine Yeltsin, to champion democracy. So that both sides were acting not according to their principles but their political tactics.)

For Yeltsin the idea of appearing before the people regularly, and *explaining* his actions and plans, as Reagan and other Western leaders did, would have been unimaginable—he had neither the ability nor any inclination to do so (and his advisers were also incapable of drafting *what* he should say in the midst of such fiascos, such glaring discrepancies between words and actions). But it had clearly been impressed on him that, when it came to the Moscow intelligentsia, he did have to explain himself sometimes. And he would assemble select groups, usually in the ceremonial setting of the Kremlin. And at a "congress of intelligentsia" in November 1992, two months after he did not "lie down on a railway track," reading from a text prepared for him, he voiced these wise words: "We underestimated the inertia of the previous system. And the pace of the reforms has turned out to be governed to a lesser extent by the radical actions of the government and far more by the rhythm of Russian life, by people's stereotypical behavior."[36] (Shame on you! If you didn't even foresee *inertia*, whatever were you thinking about when you cooked up this mess? —With you, it's that incorrigible *people* that's to blame again; don't they appreciate your generosity?) —Two months later another explanation, at the Council of Ministers: Yeltsin did "not agree that 1992 was a wasted year for Russia. We would have faced a catastrophe had we not launched our reforms. They accorded with our only [already!] possible option. There was a great shortage of courageous people ready to take on all the burden of that responsibility. In those circumstances, discussions [even discussions?] about what model of reforms to introduce would have been inappropriate, and we had no choice regarding the team. . . . [And they found Gaidar and Chubais. . . .] No one had any experience of solving these kinds of problems. . . ." —They had the nerve to take it on, though, even without the experience. Was it just to thumb his nose at the timid Gorbachev? And to that end Yeltsin had demanded, and seized, from the Supreme Soviet "emergency powers" for a year and a half.

But when he could think of no actual policy steps, or sensible changes to the course the government had taken, Yeltsin acquiesced to a plan smacking of hysteria: to vanquish his enemies by all the kerfuffle of a universal referendum (in April 1993)—"a political lever for reform." All those appeals, all that propaganda—what a waste of the people's moral resources and state funds. And, of course, they were openly buying votes (by tripling the money supply, which appeared to increase salaries and pensions, and deceiving the public by not raising energy prices before the referendum—they did so immediately afterwards). To placate his opponents, Yeltsin even gave an interview to *Pravda* (2 March 1993): "we must respect the Communists and all other parties except those with fascist tendencies."[37] All the "best of the democratic forces" rushed to support Yeltsin, and there was Elena Bonner's manifesto as well: every effort must be made to support Yeltsin! "Every soldier knows his role."

Among the referendum questions was one offering the possibility of a straight *condemnation* of the Gaidar-Chubais reforms. (The unbelievable response of the plundered nation was that it *approved* of them—clear evidence that the ballot had been rigged.) But as for supporting a strong presidential power, even I could see no alternative.

Here I had an exchange of open letters with Ambassador Vladimir Lukin. A peace accord had to be sought, which would keep some kind of balance between opposing sides of the dispute. I wrote: "In the space of fourteen months the people have been plunged into utter destitution and desperation"; "mass pillaging is taking place, on a scale never before seen, and Russia's property is being sold off at bargain prices. In this chaos, the country is being pilfered, irretrievably"; "the president and his ministers must not, cannot make light of the people's wails over the last year that the reform is going *off track*." And yet, looking into Russia's long-term future, it was clear that the very principle of presidential power required support, now, for that impulsive Yeltsin, who'd already made so many gross errors.[38]

Alas, from the very moment that power fell into Yeltsin's hands, it became ever more obvious that he was not up to the job of running Russia. He thought he could consolidate his position by creating a state apparatus that was broad in reach and a hive of activity—and within a short time under Yeltsin the excessively ponderous apparatus of the Soviet state was *tripled*(!) and became even more unwieldy and pointless. If we try to observe it in its entirety, it looks like either a monster or a joke. There is the Presidential Administration (massive in volume). The Administration of Affairs. The Presidential Council. The Security Council. The Council for Personnel Policy (made up of three commissions, for judiciary, foreign, and military personnel). The Analytical Service. The Expert Council. The Center for Special Presidential Programs. The Office of Advisers—some close, some less so. And another, separate body for cooperation between the president and parliament. Also the official government (in which some ministers are apathetic, others impotent, and others on the make), with a varying number of vice-presidents, sometimes five, even seven, or it might be just two—and a few days later it increases again. And, on top of that, a murky circle of the closest advisers—chief of security, main tennis coach—it was even worse than Rasputinshchina![39]

Reports began to reach Yeltsin that democratic civil servants, who had proliferated into the thousands, had for some reason started taking mind-boggling bribes and selling off the nation's property. And in April 1992 he issued a draconian decree: "On the battle against corruption among government employees"—and not a single line of it was ever put into practice, no check conducted on any of its provisions—and not a single major predator ever put to public trial. The president had, of course, once let this slip: "I don't betray *my people*." (A television camera captured the response of a woman in the street: "Aren't we *his people*?" . . .)

For the moment, the job of setting us up in Russia was on Alya's shoulders. An architect, Tatiana Mikhailovna Chaldymova, had been recommended, and she (visiting us in Vermont) and Alya had started discussing the layout of our future home. There needed to be room for those massive archives—which had accumulated over twenty years (and might it be dangerous to take them into our troubled homeland straightaway?) and which would further increase in Russia. And room, too, for the library. It wouldn't be so easy to squeeze the two buildings we'd occupied in Vermont—one to live in, one for work—into one, which meant it had to be substantial. To insulate me from the noises of family life and housekeeping, Chaldymova had come up with two wings forming an angle, which worked very well. She was artistic, inventive, and tasteful in all respects. In early spring 1993 she started the actual construction, at—to everyone's delight—a blistering pace from the word go. (By that time we had completed the purchase of a house on this unoccupied plot in Troitse-Lykovo, but the house, given its dilapidated condition and its size, had been unsuitable.) In late spring 1993 Alya, in Moscow again, saw the plot and was captivated by its woodland greenery, its tranquillity, and the proximity to Moscow. The construction proceeded at whirlwind speed all summer and autumn but then, as so often happens, hit a rash of problems—and that winter, at the very first thaw, the whole roof leaked. In January 1994 it became clear there would be no home in time for our arrival, and we might not be able to take up residence until the end of the year. (The Kurdyumovs, husband and wife, who had agreed to share our future life, had to deal with the endless complications.) But we could not defer our return to Russia any longer—we'd have to set up home temporarily in town.

But even the journey itself, after twenty years of exile, would be no hop back to town from the dacha. For two years already, anticipating my return to Russia, several TV companies, some American, some British, one Japanese, and one French, had been sending me constant requests for the exclusive rights to shoot a film about my return to my homeland. And we had to give that right—it was actually unavoidable—to someone, if only to prevent a distasteful and embarrassing scuffle, a free-for-all between competing film crews. But all these companies were, of course, assuming that I would fly direct into Sheremetyevo (an option Alya and I had never even discussed) and, well, just drive home, across Moscow. No one could even have imagined a long, circuitous route through the Far East.

But *how* were we going to cross Siberia? Boarding twenty trains, alighting from the same twenty, sitting at stations at various times of the day and night, dependent on being able to get enough tickets all together in the same carriage? And the number of hotel rooms we needed? And then, after those ordeals and not enough sleep—and waking with a thick head—meeting locals? making speeches? taking trips around the region?

It was only Boris Mozhaev and Yuri Prokofiev who knew of our definite plan not to arrive via Sheremetyevo. And it was Yuri who'd explained to Alya in Moscow that none of the Russian TV companies, given their current state of organizational and financial disarray, would be able to arrange such a journey and shoot such a film. Which meant we had to choose from the Western companies. Out of all those who'd expressed an interest, we preferred the BBC, a company with an excellent reputation over a great many years. And the indefatigable Prokofiev set out to procure a railway carriage for the whole trip—of the kind he had used with the *Vremya* on-location broadcast team, which had crisscrossed the country in one for an entire year.

In the April referendum Yeltsin had "won the day"—and then what? What was the result of that victory? Well—nothing. Yeltsin was out of his depth. As usual, he was not able to propose or actually do anything *of practical use*. At the top level the same dual-power stalemate was still seething (or was it simmering down now?). Production was still falling catastrophically, and the ruble was falling (to Liliputian levels, which was advantageous to the crooks in finance). Looters in both the public and private sectors were hijacking our rich mineral resources and sending them abroad, with the hard-currency proceeds staying over there; Russia had already stopped feeding itself, and in the second year of the great reforms the food sold in cities was from the West, and prices were climbing by the week. *But*—to hell with the prices! the Supreme Soviet couldn't be defeated with all that going on! . . . And a brilliant new idea was conceived (May 1993) in the president's entourage: conduct *another referendum*—to ratify the Constitution! But they did, after all, come to feel ashamed, and held instead a totally absurd Constitutional Conference—composed of arbitrarily selected and unrepresentative delegates—which had no right to ratify the Constitution and could only make recommendations.

And it was *that* dispiriting period, when the inept dual-power contest was dragging on longer and longer, those months from May to September 1993 that were, I sensed, the most dangerous for Russia—months when the question was being decided: would the country fall to pieces or remain intact? (And for me these months were made even more distressing by my new medical problems and the two operations that awaited me. I told Alya that my chest felt constricted the whole time: "If I die on our way across Siberia—it could happen at any time—don't take me any further: bury me in a suitable spot nearby. I'll be happy if I'm laid to rest in Siberia.")

The Supreme Soviet, of course, took advantage of the nation's strong antagonism towards the pseudo-reforms and moved to become, vis-à-vis Yeltsin and his government, the opposition. But with its largely Communist origin, and given the ambition of Khasbulatov (chosen by Yeltsin himself!—an expert judge of men . . .), that opposition took on the most destructive forms. Khasbulatov's Supreme Soviet, now even stronger thanks to the desertion of Rutskoy (chosen by Yeltsin himself!—an expert judge of men . . .), did not collapse, but was, as before, raring to go into battle with the president. And the Communists organized, for May Day of that same year, 1993, a partially armed street event, with some scuffles.

Both the Khasbulatov and the Yeltsin sides were working feverishly to haul in new allies by bribing them, both men rushing to hand out ruinous inducements in the form of promises to the autonomous national republics—and the significance and the demands of those republics were escalating by the week. And Yeltsin conceded some real rights and privileges, which he would never manage to take back later—and wouldn't even try. (During those months of crisis for Russia, a "Council of Leaders of the Republics" became ever more active, depriving the Russian people of its historical leading position: Russia had one voice there, alongside the twenty-one from autonomous republics.[40]) In May 1993 Yeltsin indulged them yet again: a "foreign affairs and defense policy of the autonomous republics"—he was allowing that too! (Tatarstan immediately started sending its international representatives abroad; the Yakut constitution proclaimed that it would have its own army.) There were numerous rounds of negotiations with Tatarstan—and new concessions each time from Yeltsin. And then the abandoned, orphaned Russian oblasts and krais became desperate for equal status and proclaimed themselves, too, "republics"—the Far East, the Urals, the Perm republics, and goodness knows which others. . . . The total collapse of Russia was imminent—perhaps weeks away.

My heart was breaking at the sight of it all. That pernicious dual-power contest was torture to me. To those in the midst of the events, the twists and turns of party conflicts probably seemed more important, but from a distance you were more likely to notice the fissures across Russia's body, to see how deep they were by now—already a geological phenomenon. And now—Russia would not pull through without strong presidential power, for we'd had no experience of parliamentary governance. I was forced to stay on Yeltsin's side, despite his clumsiness, and despite so many failures already (it was Russia's destiny: no farsighted leader, concerned for the people, would come to the fore). If only, if only Russia survives!

The spring and summer of 1993 were my last in Vermont, the last chance to work in the setting I was used to. Here I wrote my two forthcoming speeches, one to be given in Liechtenstein and one in the Vendée, and generally, and assiduously, readied myself for the European trip that Alya and I had planned for September–October time, as our "farewell to Europe." (We had spent very little time there in these twenty years laboring away, and now I was beginning to doubt that I'd ever manage to get back to Europe again after this; indeed, even on this trip, I was setting off with my strength already diminished.) In my Liechtenstein address I was, basically, repeating my earlier criticism of Western society, but more gently, and now associating the new Russia with that same destiny—for it had started down the same course, without even questioning it.[41]

But before that, in June 1993, I went for the second time to Harvard Yard, which I remembered well from the occasion fifteen years before when I gave my address there[42]—but this time it was for Yermolai's graduation ceremony. That summer (with Alya in Moscow and Ignat at the Marlboro Festival), Yermolai and Stepan worked harder now, on two computers, to help me wrap up my work before our move.

. . . In Liechtenstein, at the International Academy of Philosophy, I delivered my speech in Russian, in short, separate phrases, and Yermolai, having translated the speech in advance, stood next to me giving the English version of what I'd just said.

Our old acquaintance, Prince Franz Josef II, had by now passed away.[43] It was his oldest son and successor, Hans-Adam II, who gave a banquet in our honor. He was, however, extremely preoccupied with the government crisis in his principality that had blown up that very day. The following morning he would face a parliamentary battle in defense of his trusted prime minister. Which is why we would be looking round the castle and its many collections without our hosts in attendance.

We stayed for a couple of days with the Bankouls in the little village of Unterehrendingen. —And it was there that our unforgettable "invisible ally"

Stig Fredrikson joined us with a Swedish TV crew. We greeted each other warmly—and I gave Swedish television the interview that I'd promised them so very long ago.[44]

We took a farewell walk around Zurich—which is, after all, a delightful town, combining in a very natural way a centuries-old, but durable, antiquity with the most fashionable (and not always durable) modernity. (And what riches it had provided for my Lenin chapters!)

After that we took off by train for Paris.

In France, as always for me, the atmosphere was particularly friendly. A great number of Parisians recognized me in the street, greeted me, and stopped to express their gratitude; for twenty years now I had felt, when in France, as if in a second, quite unexpected, motherland. There was a meeting with Paris intellectuals. Two or three interviews.[45] A big "roundtable" event for television, still, as before, with Bernard Pivot.[46] We talked a lot about today's Russia, and they asked what I'd do when I got back to my homeland. I assured them that I would not be taking any government appointment or launching any electoral campaigns, but that as I was going to speak out, heedless of the political authorities, I wouldn't be surprised if my access to television and to the press were restricted.[47]

Prime Minister Balladur received Alya and me, while Mayor Chirac came to visit me at the hotel. I used these two final meetings for an impassioned attempt to inspire them with some ideas that could benefit suffering Russia (what difference would it make to them, if they let us off our tsarist-era debts? . . .). I also said my farewell to the team at YMCA-Press, to Claude Durand, and to my translators of many years' standing, tireless, talented, and, what's more, supremely conscientious in checking details, the nuances of words (they would send me lists of questions needing clarification)—José and Geneviève Johannet, husband and wife. (The whole of *The Red Wheel* had fallen on their shoulders, as well as some of the other works I'd published along the way over those years.)

As for the trip to the Vendée, it had been agreed about a year before with Philippe de Villiers, the president of the General Council of the province, via the good offices of Nikita Struve. When thinking of this trip I'd kept it under wraps—and now I was realizing the plan, to the irritation of left-wing circles in France (so blindly did they admire, to this day, their cruel revolution.[48]) De Villiers entertained us with a visit to his inimitable folk extravaganza, based on local tradition (but availing itself of the most up-to-date technical means), telling the story of the Vendée Uprising. The show was in the open air, in an enormous arena, when night had already fallen, but with quantities of lighting effects.[49] Alya and I had never seen anything like it and could not even have imagined it. Over the following days we visited a historical village where all the everyday life and crafts of the eighteenth century were preserved, and went round an underground museum with very striking re-creations of the insurgents' hiding-places.

What a bittersweet impression it made—never to be forgotten. Would anyone in Russia ever reproduce such images of the people's opposition to Bolshevism, from cadets and students in the Volunteer Army to the despairing peasants with their beards and pitchforks?

Now we were to visit Germany. I very much wanted to go, for I'd only seen it from its Prussian edge, during the war. We traveled (by train from Paris toward the Rhine) to the welcoming home of the Schönfelds, who had once brought the *Wheel* archive, mercifully preserved, to us in Zurich.[50] Peter Schönfeld had arranged a meeting in Bonn with the German President Weizsäcker. Over lunch and afterwards I spoke, probably too forcefully, in defense of Russian interests; Weizsäcker became politely guarded—and somehow managed to get the very many photos reporters had taken around the residence suppressed, with only one accidentally slipping through into print.[51] —Apart from that, we stayed out of the German capital. Thanks to the quiet sojourn we'd chosen at the Schönfelds, my time in Germany was low-profile—but, on the other hand, gave us a unique chance to take a calm look at life in the small towns of the Middle Rhine and to visit the "Great Germania" statue—the Watch on the Rhine[52]—on a steep slope on the right bank, facing France. No longer a favored tourist attraction, it is impressive, though. We also had the opportunity to see, and receive highly detailed explanations about, the cathedrals of Mainz and Worms. We viewed with great respect these somber Gothic monuments and delighted in the cozy little streets of small, well-appointed German towns. We were making our acquaintance with the ancient stones of Europe and at the same time taking our leave of them—but the images forming before our eyes were the half-devastated fields of Russia that awaited us, the secluded copses of Central Russia, with rough planks bridging streams, and log cabins still standing long past their allotted span.

But my interview with the German First Channel had been fixed in advance, for 4 October—what a coincidence!—to be conducted in the Schönfelds' tranquil home. That afternoon we heard the unexpected news of cannon fire in Moscow; it was as yet vague, impossible to make judgments—but this was the main thing on which I was questioned.[53] The dissolution of the Supreme Soviet*—which, though it was not yet clear and we had no details, was the consequence of the whole conflict preceding it—I saw as difficult, but as a way out of the agonizing impasse of dual power in Russia. It seemed to me that the current conflict between the two powers was an inevitable and natural stage in the years-long journey awaiting us, of emancipation from Communism. I understood it this way: it was *inevitable*, if the Russian state was destined to survive into the future—it could have no real existence under dual power; and *natural*, because the losing side must be the one waving the Communist banners.** (And a week later I expressed similar views in an interview for Russian television.[55])

The Bankouls came by car to pick us up in Germany—and take us across Austria into Italy. By now we had no time left for a visit to Vienna; but we passed through Salzburg and western Austria, which we found extraordinarily beautiful. Once a great empire, Austria had now contracted into a small country, but preserving in abundance the distilled essence of its centuries-old traditions. May God protect it from the ravages of the Future.

Italy was not new to me, after our trip there with Viktor Bankoul in 1975.[56] Then we had not made it as far as Rome, but now we did, and even spent four days there, and did a lot of walking. The Forum Romanum, the Coliseum, and the Catacombs made a truly deep impression. All the rest was actually disappointing, after greater expectations. Perhaps it was a symptom of my worsening sickness.

---

* My enduring aversion to Communism had blinded me at that time to the fact that this Supreme Soviet was actually voicing opposition to the Gaidar-Chubais "reforms." And the figure of Khasbulatov as the father of Russia was very disturbing to me. (Author's note, 1995.)

** Only when back in Russia did I understand that it was absolutely not statesmanship that had motivated Yeltsin, but just a thirst for personal power. The punishment inflicted in the streets was gratuitously violent and even pointless—intended, rather, to cause general fear by the use of terrorism. The number of dead on 4 October was greater than that of the victims of Nikolai II's never-forgiven "Bloody Sunday" in 1905.[54]

But the patriotic wing would not forget what I had said about an *inevitable* and *natural* stage. (And Vladimir Maximov, issuing, in his later years, more extreme press comments about everyone within range, made things worse by misrepresenting me, saying I had called the dissolution not "inevitable" but *indispensable*. Just look at him, he said, our great humanist writer; how low he's sunk.) (Author's note, 1996.)

In Rome there was an audience with Pope John Paul II. (I went with Alya and Viktor Bankoul, who speaks Italian, but the whole conversation was translated by Irina Ilovaiskaya, a devoted Catholic since time immemorial, who was now giving active assistance to the pope.) The pope had fixed our meeting on an important day for him: the fifteenth anniversary of his accession to the Vatican throne.

In the magnificent enfilade of the Vatican Palace, I walked towards the pope full of respect and well disposed towards him. In previous years there had been, via verbal communications through third parties, signs that seemed to indicate a solid alliance between us against Communism, and I had mentioned this in some of my public appearances. He also saw an important ally in me—but that would, perhaps, be further than I could go. I expressed this clearly in our conversation, recalling that in 1922–27, when the Russian Orthodox Church was being crushed, Catholic hierarchs were trying to establish collaboration with the Communists, calculating openly (if shortsightedly) that they would help the Catholic Church gain a firm foothold in the USSR, on the ashes of Orthodoxy. My observations were clearly not news to the pope, but they cast a gloom over him. He countered that that had been the initiative only of some isolated church leaders (which it was hard to believe, knowing the Catholics' discipline). —In the course of the conversation, I mentioned Pope Leo XIII's encyclical *Rerum Novarum*, and from John Paul's reaction I gathered that questions of social justice were certainly not alien to him—which is easy to understand, and natural for the hierarch of a Christian church.*

Unexpectedly, I received a telegram from Yeltsin in December, wishing me a happy seventy-fifth birthday.[57] (Didn't he know I'd been criticizing him so fiercely in Europe?) I had to respond—it was unavoidable. I replied with a rigorous list of the ills of today's Russia (of which he was the main culprit). [34]

My jubilee was also noticed by several Western newspapers—but with the same old judgments and criteria: "Solzhenitsyn is dangerously close to

* That Slav pope would see a near-doubling of his time on the Vatican throne—and so very much travel around the world, preaching the gospel with his last ounce of strength. But the tensions with the Orthodox Church haven't disappeared, and the pope's visit to Russia, which he had so hoped for, has still not happened. (Author's note, 2002.)

the nationalists and chauvinists: will he, on his return to Russia, fall into the embrace of the wrong side?" (What a bad conscience they must have had for all these years, to make them literally invoke the Heavens to have me appear as a ferocious "ayatollah," enter Moscow on horseback, and immediately take power. Without this, their final jigsaw piece is lacking, somehow. And how very disappointed they'll be when nothing of the kind materializes. But they'll get over that very easily, as if they hadn't been droning on in that vein for more than a decade now.)[58]

And there was another constant motif: "Who needs Solzhenitsyn in today's Russia? who'll follow his Orthodox moral precepts?"—especially since "the era of such authorities in Russia is past." (That thesis is another that they've been whipping up for a long time—they just need, desperately need to be sure no moral authorities ever appear in Russia in future: how much easier it will be for everyone without them.) "No one will take any notice of his fiery speeches to the people."[59]

But on this point I must disagree: despite my twenty-year absence, I am sure people will take notice—and how! only it won't be the Moscow "elite," but those in the provinces, the ordinary people—and that is why I'm taking that route.

But there is also, in the skeptical predictions of the Western press, an element of clear-sightedness. During my twenty years of banishment the Communist government has never tired of sullying my name either—indefatigably, in every way, and at every opportunity. Even in the democratic press a good few pens were showing wariness on my account. I'm under no illusion, as I set out for home, that I can overcome that deep-seated hostility the minute I arrive—or even by the end of my life.

The current situation is that neither *Rebuilding Russia*, nor my appeal about the Ukrainian referendum, nor the interview with Govorukhin have been of any use and have not moved anything forward. And my books have barely penetrated into the heart of the country; and *The Red Wheel*, scattered around different journals,[60] has not had a chance to start working.

But never mind that! Even the demand for *Archipelago* is not satisfied yet—complaints are still rolling in: "I was an officer on the front line, now retired, the same age as Solzhenitsyn. His book *The Gulag Archipelago* is not available in Kazakhstan" (Tole Bi district, Kazakhstan); "*The Gulag Archipelago* is not on sale in the bookshops, and on my pension I can't afford black-market prices" (Nizhni Tagil); "I've been wanting to read *The Gulag Archipelago* for a long time now, but it's still not possible. It is not on sale, and in the library it's always out on loan" (village of Shushenskoye, Krasnoyarsk krai); "The mother of four children, I am appealing to you on a question that's tormenting me. I cannot buy Aleksandr Solzhenitsyn's book *The Gulag Archipelago*. I need the book for my children to read, so they won't grow up to be idiots" (Ust-Ilimsk).

So I would, after all, arrive before my books. I'd be doing the legwork myself.

Legwork . . . During my European travels with Alya I'd had some trouble walking—the gait of an old man. On our return to Vermont I'd had, in addition, those two operations, without which I would not have risked the journey ahead. I was wondering, apprehensively, where I'd find the strength for this long transit across Russia starting in the spring, and how I could be free of the angina I'd suffered for five years—if only for a while. I can confidently say that it was my months of daily prayers and my belief that they would be answered. And now, as that spring, so crucial to me, approached, I suddenly acquired new strength—I was unrecognizable; and that spring I began to walk the steep Vermont roads, feeling not a trace of angina! A miracle.

During the final winter in Vermont, while devoting myself to my binary tales, I also set about bringing together what I had digested and retained on the subject of seventeenth-to-nineteenth-century Russian history ("*The Russian Question*" . . .). It will upset many fervent patriots—but it was like that. That was how it happened. And it must be published immediately and in our homeland, in *Novy Mir*. The end of the essay comes all the way up to the latest current affairs (. . . *At the End of the Twentieth Century*).[61] And now I've also lived through it, held on right up to the changes taking place in Russia. But we never dreamed they would be like this. . . . There are times when I'm overcome with gloom: I can barely see any way for Russia to get out of this abyss. How might it be pulled out, and by whom?

. . . The spring of '94 was, in our house, the "packing epoch": archives and books were stowed away into hundreds and hundreds of cardboard boxes, sealed with a tape gun, and the sides of the boxes were marked with identification signs and numbers (we didn't know when we'd be in a position to unpack them all, but at least we'd know where to look for what we needed). —That year Yermolai was working in Taiwan and, living in a solely Taiwanese milieu, had begun to speak fluent Chinese. By May he was getting ready to fly straight to Vladivostok to meet us, without returning to the States. —Ignat was studying at the conservatoire—two majors at once, piano and conducting. It was intense but he was happy, and the previous autumn he had been on tour in Moscow, St. Petersburg, and the Baltics for the first time. —Stepan was in his third year at Harvard, studying city planning, and with a parallel course at the Massachusetts Institute of Technology. They still had to finish their studies. —And our oldest, Dimitri, was eagerly awaiting the return to our homeland: he had lived in Russia until the age of twelve, and now his memories and attachments were exerting a strong pull.

Now there was another job to do: we had said our farewell to Europe—perhaps we should say farewell to America?

With our local Vermonters the farewells were very warm: at the end of February we went to the annual Town Meeting and I thanked everyone sincerely for being such tolerant and friendly neighbors. [35] I gave them, for their library, a dozen of my books in English, and they unexpectedly gave us a marble plaque with a cordial engraved inscription, saying that they extended their hands in a gesture of farewell to our family, but that, if we ever came back, they would again extend a heartfelt welcome.[62] We were touched—but no, we wouldn't be back. We wouldn't.

And suddenly, on 18 March, we were stunned by a savage blow—Dimitri's death, instantaneous, at the age of thirty-two. As untimely a death as that of his great-grandfather, grandfather, and uncles on his father's side. Clean-limbed, handsome, in the full flush of youth. And that is how he is forever frozen—on the threshold of a return to his homeland, and leaving a widow and five-month-old daughter, Tatiana. We were distraught with grief—and not only the family and his dozens of friends far and wide, but our whole parish, too. We buried him in the Orthodox corner of the evergreen Claremont cemetery.

And so we left a tomb in America. Such was our farewell. . . .

Again—the Price of Banishment . . .

But what about the American "elite," that reading, writing, high-and-mighty clan, who for all these years had never given ground, never wanted to be reconciled with me?—must I bid farewell to them, too?

I was persuaded to give an interview to CBS ("you can't leave America without doing that"). I really did not want to do that interview—and I was right. Mike Wallace asked dull and then vile questions—still the same well-oiled refrain that had been running for decades;[63] nothing of any interest came of it, and no *farewell* to the States came out of it.

But *Forbes*, an influential magazine for businessmen and financiers, proposed an interview (with Paul Klebnikov), and there I did speak out, from the bottom of my heart.[64] And here, finally, was my *farewell.*

But it was the Vermont one that spread around the world and requests, and more requests, for interviews rained down on me from here, there, and everywhere.

But not now; it was too late. No more, not to anyone. I was inclined to talk now—but with Russians and in Russia.

Ambassador Lukin suggested that I should, despite everything, notify Yeltsin in advance of my unusual itinerary. He convinced me that courtesy required this. And I sent a letter via the embassy. [**36**]

I had also received a fair number of private letters from Russia urging me to run for president.[65] And there were newspaper articles saying the same.

But no, I have no plans of this kind. It would not be appropriate to my age or my line of work. The ability to run a bureaucracy is a different skill from that of a writer.

Farewell, blessed Vermont, so gentle with us! But to stay here, to live out my days here would rob my destiny of its thrust, its spirit. I had in fact been worried that I might live in Vermont till I die, or until the final stages of physical infirmity. I had to get to Russia in time to die there.

But I must get there even earlier—return to Russia while I still have vitality. While I still feel some resilience in me. I'm thirsting to get involved in Russian events—I have the energy to get things done. My shoulders have not yet sagged from all the fighting and I actually feel a surge of strength—even if that does fly in the face of the saying, "Youth is for battles, old age for thought."

I am going—perhaps to be ridiculed, given today's total lack of restraint in the press, among journalists, and any "commentators" who want to spit in my face. But I don't care about that now, after the long years of hounding from two sides—between two millstones.

But I count as friends the vastnesses of Russia. The Russian provinces. The small and medium-sized towns.

Perhaps I'll still manage to say something and get something done.

And if people come to understand Russia's interests rightly, my books could also be needed much later, when there has been a more profound analysis of the historical process. The deep furrows that History has plowed across Russia are unswerving, and that unfailing purpose will eventually appear.

Appear later, some kind of long-term effect, after I am gone.

And, whatever it may be, I keep Lomonosov's words in mind: "I do not worry about death: I have lived, and I have suffered, and I know the children of our Fatherland will mourn me."[66]

Vermont
March–April 1994

APPENDICES

LIST OF APPENDICES

(Page numbers in parentheses designate the location of appendix number references in the text.)

Chapter 12. Alarm in the Senate

[none]

Chapter 13. A Warm Breeze

[none]

PART FOUR (1987–1994)

Chapter 14. Through the Brambles

Chapter 15. Ideas Spurned

[none]

Chapter 16. Nearing the Return

[25]

SHAME!
LETTER TO SAMIZDAT

April 1979

That maelstrom of discontent, suspicions, accusations, threats, and extortion that has begun whirling around the Russian Social Fund—and mostly in our capital city, less penurious than the rest of the country—is our shame. Never before, in old Russia, had charitable works—widely practiced then—been subjected to anything remotely like today's attacks of envy, greed, and distrust. I do not mean either real extortioners or those sent by the KGB. Nor do I have in mind Roy Medvedev, who from time to time complaisantly steps forward in order to please the authorities. I mean the aspersions that are disseminated by real people but garner no worthy response even from those who have themselves received aid from the Fund. Many of them likely remain oppressed from being habitually passed over or duped during the Soviet decades; and it is by now easier for them to yield than to believe that, this time, they are not being deceived.

But the work of the Fund is unique—almost miraculous, given Soviet conditions—and is carried out under unbearable oppression and hounding by the government; its first selfless fearless organizer has already been jailed. Must we really now add "dissident" slandering to the KGB's own efforts? If this is who we are ourselves—then why keep blaming the regime? And what, then, is in store for our future?

I am well acquainted with the principles used by the Fund in distributing its aid, and I approve of them. The process is conducted impartially. When conditions in our Homeland permit it, all the facts and figures will be made public. I implore us not to disgrace, by these dark dust clouds, our awakening, or that Archipelago—made extinct many times over—from whose burial-ground sprang the first shoots of the Fund.

Aleksandr Solzhenitsyn

[26]

LETTER TO PRESIDENT CARTER

Cavendish, Vermont
4 June 1979

Dear Mr. President:

An outstanding son of the Russian people, Igor Ogurtsov, who had sought Christian paths of development for Russia, has, for thirteen continuous years now, been cruelly confined under pitiless conditions; the threat of eight more years, which he would not survive, hangs over him. His liver and stomach have dropped, and, at forty-two, he is losing his hair and teeth.

The current situation presents you with a rare opportunity to free at least a few people from such hopeless long confinement. From myself, and on behalf of the Russian people, I implore you to help rescue Mr. Ogurtsov for treatment and recovery.

Aleksandr Solzhenitsyn

[27]

FOOTNOTE ABOUT OLGA CARLISLE IN THE US EDITION OF *THE OAK AND THE CALF*[1]

1979

I did not expect to divulge any names, but Olga Carlisle has hastened to do this herself. That's the way it always happens: those who perform the main task are not the ones who seek glory. The selfless Western people who aided me in substantial ways in my struggle, who assured the steady flow of my publications in the West, and who secretly brought out my large archive after my expulsion from the country—they are all modestly silent to this day. A large and completed section of this book is dedicated to them, but the time has not yet come for it to appear in print.[2] I see Olga Carlisle's role in the fate of my works as consistently negative. Due to a combination of circumstances—owing to my confidence in the Andreev family from which she stems, rather than to any close knowledge of Olga Carlisle or the kind of person she is—she was entrusted with the manuscript texts of *The First Circle* and *The Gulag Archipelago*, both of which had already been brought out of the USSR. At no point did she herself risk anything whatever. The American translation of *The First Circle* was peremptorily edited by her husband Henry Carlisle, who knows no Russian, with the result that considerable further editorial work was necessary. The translation was rejected by the British publisher. She permitted other translations of *The First Circle* to be produced in perfunctory ways: many are inferior in quality, the French especially so. This was the extent of Olga Carlisle's labors, labors that she now claims took six years of her life, involved "huge risks," disrupted her journalistic career, the life of a free painter. On these grounds, probably, she appraised her own services, expenses, sacrifices, losses, sleepless nights, and those of her husband and their lawyer to be worth about half the royalties from the worldwide sale of the novel during the time that she directed it. The struggle described in these pages she characterizes as "Italian opera" and a world of petty intrigue. Her attitude and manner of dealing with people were sharply at odds with all our conceptions during these years of struggle. In the spring of 1970 a message was delivered to me in the USSR from Olga Carlisle through an intermediary that the American translation of *Gulag* was finished and ready for the press. This gave me the false assurance that at a critical moment *Gulag* could quickly be published in the most widely read language in the world. But in fact, this translation was not ready even in 1973, when the blow fell on the Russian manuscript. The result was that the English-language edition appeared later than all the other translations.

[28]

LETTER TO PRESIDENT REAGAN[3]

Cavendish, 3 May 1982

Dear Mr. President:

I admire many aspects of your activity, rejoice because the United States at last has a president such as you, and unceasingly thank God that you were not killed by the villainous bullets.

But I never sought to obtain the honor of being received at the White House—either under President Ford (the issue arose on their side without my being involved) or later. During the past months, indirect inquiries reached me through different channels concerning the circumstances under which I would accept an invitation to the White House. I always answered that I would be prepared to go for a substantive conversation with you, in a setting that would make an effective, in-depth exchange of views possible—but not for a merely formal ceremony. The lifespan at my disposal does not leave any time for symbolic encounters.

It was not, however, a personal meeting with you that was announced to me (by telephone call from an adviser, Mr. Richard Pipes), but a luncheon including émigré politicians. From the same sources the press publicized that it is to be a luncheon for "Soviet dissidents." But a writer and an artist belongs neither to the first group nor to the second, in the Russian mind. I cannot allow myself to be placed in a category that is not mine. Moreover, the fact, the form, and the date of the reception were established and transmitted to the press before I was informed of them. Even up to this very day I have not received any clarification, nor even the names of those among whom I have been invited for 11 May.

It is even worse that the White House's variations and hesitations were publicized by the press in advance, as also the reason why a personal meeting with me was considered undesirable, in terms that have not been denied or corrected by the White House: allegedly, I "have become a symbol of an extreme Russian nationalist position." Such a wording is offensive for my fellow countrymen, to whose suffering I have dedicated my entire life as a writer.

I am not at all a "nationalist": I am a patriot. This means that I love my country—and therefore well understand other people's love for theirs. I have declared publicly on many occasions that the vital interests of the peoples of the USSR demand an immediate termination of all Soviet attempts to conquer the globe. If individuals thinking as I do would come to power in the USSR, their first action would be to withdraw from Central America, from Africa, from Asia, from Eastern Europe, leaving all these peoples to their own untrammeled fate. Their second step would be to cease the deadly arms race, and to direct all the nation's forces toward healing the internal, almost century-long wounds of a nearly dying population. And, beyond any doubt, they would throw wide open the exit gates for those who wish to emigrate from our hapless country.

But how surprising: all this does not suit some of your close advisers! They want something different. They define such a program as "extreme Russian nationalism," while some US generals suggest selectively destroying the Russian population by an atomic assault.[4] It is strange how Russian national consciousness inspires the greatest fear in the world today for the rulers of the USSR—and for your entourage. It is the revelation of a hostility to Russia as such, to her people and to the country, as distinct from the state structure, which is characteristic of a significant part of the American educated community, American financial circles, and, alas, even some of your advisers. Such a frame of mind is pernicious for the future of both our nations.

Mr. President, it is hard for me to write this letter. But I think that if, anywhere, a meeting with you were deemed undesirable because you are an American patriot, you would also feel insulted.

When you are no longer president, if you ever happen to be in Vermont, I cordially invite you to come and visit me.

Since this entire episode has already received wide and distorting publicity, and it is highly probable that the reasons for my nonparticipation will likewise be distorted, I fear that I shall be compelled to publish this letter. Please forgive me.

Respectfully and sincerely yours,

A. Solzhenitsyn

[29]

LETTER TO ELIZABETH II, QUEEN OF GREAT BRITAIN AND NORTHERN IRELAND

Cavendish, Vermont
3 January 1991

Your Majesty!

In the years 1945 and 1946, the British Government and its military command, which up to that time, it seems, had led a war for universal freedom, conspired with Stalin's administration and betrayed to him tens, even hundreds of thousands of refugees from the USSR, who helplessly resisted that treacherous act. I met some of those who were not immediately executed in the camps of the Gulag, where many of them then perished. Not all the officials of the British administration of that time knew about the Yalta conspiracy, but all those actually carrying out the operation saw with their own eyes the boundless despair of those being turned over, and even their suicides. And all of those officials (even Brigadier Toby Low) must have understood the horrible meaning of what was being done.

This massive handing over of people to ruin placed a dark stain on the British conscience, one that will poison, for a century or longer, a future Anglo-Russian understanding. After all, peoples live in segments of time different from us separate individuals. The heavy weight of the committed treachery was even further magnified by the fact that the free all-knowing British press did not once utter a sound about this grave crime for thirty years, and only spoke out when revelations had been made outside Britain.

And so a kinsman of Lev Tolstoy, as if having adopted the agonising searches of the great writer's conscience—Nikolai Tolstoy, in whom come together Russian descent and English affiliation—investigated these events as thoroughly as it was possible, and published the book *Victims of Yalta* where, quite naturally, he named the acting participants. By this he accomplished a spiritual feat in clarifying and loosening the grim knot that was cruelly tied between our peoples in 1945.

Then, in connection with one of the collateral, private consequences of the revelations made in Tolstoy's book, he placed himself under legal responsibility voluntarily, without any practical necessity, only in order to confirm the truth. And an English court, which is called, as I understand it, always to correspond to the truth in its full volume?—amazingly, sentenced the courageous lover of truth to an unprecedented fine of £1.5 million!—by this action condemning Tolstoy to bankruptcy, and his family to calamity. That court also dealt what amounts to a final blow from the British side to those who perished in the Gulag. This same action must have intimidated anyone who might dare in the future to stir up the ashes of this postwar crime. Thus, this case turned out to be directly contrary in its implication to the Nuremberg trials, and its significance stretches beyond the personal efforts of this blameless plaintiff to receive his desired purse before he sets off to face the Highest Judgment.

But it now becomes apparent that never, at no time in the future, will the guilt of even one of the participants of this mass crime be determined. Thus, in England, no one will ever be accused officially of this crime, no one will ever be punished, and, in the meantime, some may have even received awards and honours. Masses of defenceless people are turned over to disaster—and no one is to blame. For a long time in the USSR the annihilation of millions of people was called only a "mistake" of the Communist Party. Can it be that in England, too, all of this will pass under the modest aspect of a "postwar mistake"?

Your Majesty! In my understanding, a monarch cannot be indifferent to anything that takes place in his or her fatherland and, in the highest sense, carries a share of responsibility for everything that transpires therein, even when not vested with the right to direct events. Clearly, you do not have the power to influence decisions of the court. But you are able to take some moral step that would put the whole matter into a new light. What step exactly—I do not know, your intuition will advise you better. If you give to understand wherein lies the Truth—such a gesture by you shall not remain unnoticed in history. . . .

Please accept my highest respect.

I would like to express my most sincere best wishes to Prince Philip and Prince Charles.

Yours very sincerely,

Aleksandr Solzhenitsyn

[30]

LETTER TO SERGEI ZALYGIN

2 August 1988

Most esteemed Sergei Pavlovich!

On 1 August I received your telegram of 27 July. I thank you for the efforts you have undertaken to print my novels in your journal.

I would, of course, gladly have given both *Cancer Ward* and *In the First Circle* to *Novy Mir*, to which I offered them twenty years ago.

However, it was for *The Gulag Archipelago* that I was charged with "treason to the homeland" (Article 64). It was for that book that I was forcibly exiled, a banishment now in its fifteenth year. It was for that book that people were sent to prison camps. There can be no pretending that *Archipelago* never happened, to gloss over it. Our debt before those who perished does not permit this. Our living countrymen, too, have by their suffering earned the right to read this book. Doing so now would be a contribution to the shifts that have begun. If it is still not allowed, then what are the limits of glasnost?

My reentry into the literature permitted in our homeland can only begin with *The Gulag Archipelago*—moreover, without abridgments and not as a limited showcase (for the bookshops on Kuznetsky Most and for the West), but in an authentic mass print run, such that the three volumes could be freely available for purchase at least in every regional city of the USSR at least for one year.

I understand that this does not depend on you. I write to you, however, as you are the only person who has addressed me. Perhaps you will find it possible to so inform those on whom it does depend. I thank you in advance.

After publication of *Archipelago* there would be no difficulties whatsoever with publishing both *Ward* and *Circle* in *Novy Mir*.

My very best wishes to you personally and to the journal.
With understanding,

Aleksandr Solzhenitsyn

[31]

EXCHANGE OF TELEGRAMS WITH "MEMORIAL"

Moscow, 5 September 1988

Most esteemed Aleksandr Isaevich!

We ask for your agreement to join a Civic Council to oversee the creation of and work on a memorial complex to the victims of lawlessness and repression.

Based on a poll of citizens, the following were elected to the Council: Adamovich, Yuri Afanasiev, Baklanov, Bykov, Evtushenko, Yeltsin, Karyakin, Korotich, Likhachyov, Roy Medvedev, Okudzhava, Razgon, Rybakov, Sakharov, Solzhenitsyn, Ulyanov, Shatrov.

Executive Committee of "Memorial"

Cavendish, 6 September 1988

To the Organizing Committee of "Memorial"

I thank those who elected me—I am honored.

To the memory of those who perished in 1918–1956 I have already dedicated *The Gulag Archipelago*, for which I was rewarded with the charge of treason. It is not possible to pass over this.

Moreover, being located outside the country, it is impossible to actually participate in its civic life.

Heartfelt regards.

Aleksandr Solzhenitsyn

[31a][5]

SOVIET PROPAGANDA HAS NO ANSWER FOR *ARCHIPELAGO*[6]

Stanford, California
18 May 1976

During the past fourteen years, the entire bungling propaganda apparatus of the Soviets and all of their hired historians have been unable to answer my publications with any facts or logical arguments. Since they have nothing on hand—no evidence, no ideas of their own—the KGB, in accordance with its fraudulent ways, recently produced a falsified document dated 1952 which suggests that I had informed them about the revolutionary movement in forced-labor camps. This piece of bunk has begun to be fed to foreign correspondents, one of whom has sent me a "photocopy."

Two years ago the KGB had already been caught once, falsifying my handwriting on my purported correspondence with Vasili Orekhov (a Russian émigré leader), whom I have *never* written. Even though *Time* magazine had in May 1974 presented portions of my own handwriting, comparing it with the KGB fabrication, they have again shamelessly chosen the same path. With the help of my ex-wife, they used some letters that I had written her during my labor camp days and, as well as they could, diligently copied my handwriting of that time. (The KGB had already secretly tried to plant these letters in the West, and copies of these forgeries are in my hands.) However, remaining trapped on their own level, lowered from men to apes, they could not forge my imagery and indeed my own self. This distinction can be seen by any decent person who has read *Ivan Denisovich* or *First Circle*, or who would lay *Archipelago* side by side with the KGB's pitiful slander. Furthermore, the fabricators miscalculated in their portrayal of labor-camp realities. The third volume of *Archipelago* conveys the fiery spirit of those days of the Ekibastuz camp rebellion to which the KGB's latest forgery dares to attach itself. The time will come when my Ukrainian fellow inmates too will gain their free voice; they will openly mock these concoctions and will tell of our true friendship. KGB lies are prepared just in such a way as to provoke discord and disrupt harmony in Eastern Europe, for it is precisely the consolidation of our forces that the Communists fear most of all.

Over the course of sixty years, the Communist authorities in our country have acquired the taste of slandering everyone whom they persecuted as agents of the Okhrana or the Siguranţa, the Gestapo, or of Polish, French, British, Japanese or American intelligence. This same fool's cap was fitted on everyone without exception. But never before have our authorities displayed such laughable weakness and insecurity as to accuse their enemy of collaborating . . . with themselves! . . . with the Soviet system and its blood-brood secret police! Given all its military and police might—what a frank manifestation of mental confusion.

A. Solzhenitsyn

[32]

LETTER TO PRESIDENT YELTSIN

30 August 1991

Dear Boris Nikolaevich!

I am taking advantage of an opportunity to securely transmit this letter directly into your hands.

I am filled with admiration for the bravery you and all those around you showed during those days and nights.

I am proud that Russian people found in themselves the strength to shake off the longest-lasting, tightest-gripping totalitarian regime on Earth. Only now, and not six years ago, begins the true liberation, both of our people and, quickly spreading, the republics along our rim.

Right now you are in the whirlwind of events, which call for immediate decisions, every one of them important. But that is why I dare intervene with this letter to you: because there are some decisions that cannot be corrected later. Thankfully, while I was writing these lines, you let it be known that Russia reserves the right to review its borders with some of the now-separating republics. This is especially critical for our boundaries with Ukraine and Kazakhstan, which the Bolsheviks drew arbitrarily. The expansive South of today's Ukrainian SSR—Novorossiya—and many parts of the Left Bank were never part of historical Ukraine, to say nothing of Khrushchev's outrageous whim about Crimea. And if they are finally felling monuments to Lenin in Lvov and Kiev, why do they hold sacred Lenin's false boundaries, drawn after the Civil War for tactical reasons that suited the moment? Likewise, in revenge for Southern Siberia's uprising in 1921, and for the Ural and Siberian Cossacks' resistance to the Bolsheviks, all these territories were forcibly transferred from Russia to Kazakhstan.

And so, that is why I hurry to ask you to protect the interests of those many millions who have no wish to separate from us. Please use your great influence to take all measures to ensure that the Ukraine referendum, on 1 December, be conducted absolutely freely, without any pressure (very much a risk!), without distortions in the voting—and that its result be tallied separately in every oblast, to see where each leans. There will immediately be screams, and threats, that "This is war!" No, it is merely the freedom of the vote, which we all must obey.

Why, Lenin's nefarious Sovnarkom, in exchange for peace and recognition of its own regime, hurriedly gave Estonia on 2 February 1920 a piece of Pskov's ancient lands, with the sacred sites of Pechory and Izborsk, as well as heavily Russian-populated Narva. And now, while accepting without any conditions Estonia's separation, we nevertheless must not set the loss of these places in stone.

I wrote a year ago in *Rebuilding Russia* that I am not an opponent of the separation of the Soviet Union's republics, and even think it desirable for the healthy development of Russia. However, a federation is the real, actual cooperation of peoples in a whole state. Meanwhile, the recently floated political "Confederation of Independent States" is an artificial construct, an oxymoron, and in practice will turn into a burden for Russia (like the Commonwealth of Nations has for Britain).

And another urgent thing, Boris Nikolaevich! It is very dangerous right now to hastily accept any economic project whose consequences have not been clearly thought through, whereby in exchange for tempting rapid foreign subsidies we would be required to strictly adhere to the givers' program, giving up our independence in economic decisions, then shackling ourselves with innumerable debts for many years. I fear that such is the program of the International Monetary Fund and the World Bank for Reconstruction (known as the "Yavlinsky Plan"). Latin America and Poland have been caught in the inescapable vice grip of debt, but those debts will have to be forgiven, for they have no collateral to give. But Russia's debts will not be forgiven, and instead the resources beneath our long-suffering soil will be extracted. And then, having fallen into foreign economic dependency, Russia will inevitably lose political independence, as well. I fear such a future for our country. And I fervently ask you: do not permit that we give ourselves over to one aggressively touted project; require that alternatives be studied, as well. For example, a plan that activates our country's inner reserves, letting us manage without foreign loans—a plan supported by Milton Friedman, a leading authority in Western economics.

With a firm handshake,

A. Solzhenitsyn

[33]

REPLY FROM PRESIDENT YELTSIN

Moscow
24 September 1991

Most esteemed Aleksandr Isaevich!

I am grateful for your letter. I understand and identify with your pain for the state of our Fatherland, your fears for its future.

Over the past decades, Russia has lost much of what had been its vital essence. Yet we have been able to preserve what is surely most important—the great resiliency of our people, their moral qualities, their deep faith in the power of justice and good. The fear that shackled the will of millions upon millions of our citizens turned out to be weaker, after all, than the indefatigable desire for freedom; and the regime, which had seemed eternal, collapsed. But it did not take with it the problems that it created.

We have already started the reform of our national economy, although of course there are more questions before us than answers.

I am convinced that no one except the people of Russia themselves can lead our economy out of its crisis. But we do not want to restore an economic "iron curtain." That is why we are stimulating the attraction of foreign capital for the revival of various sectors of Russia's national economy.

The events of August 1991 struck the heaviest of blows against the Communist empire. The USSR as we knew it no longer exists, but peoples who for centuries lived next to each other remain. Today it has become especially apparent that in the heart of a disintegrating empire new approaches have been developing, ones based on equal rights, the freedom to choose, and mutual interest in cooperation.

I think that is a more reliable, healthy foundation for a Union than violence and coercion. Of course, there is the risk that a newly created Union will end in failure.

If that happens, Russia will act just as other governments do, in accordance with international law. We are already starting to learn how to live in the new way, and I hope we will learn it.

Esteemed Aleksandr Isaevich, my congratulations that, at long last, the unjust charges against you have been lifted.

I wish you and your family health and well-being. I do not doubt that in the future you will continue to respond, with your heart, to the events that occur in Russia.

B. Yeltsin

[34]

REPLY TO SEVENTY-FIFTH-BIRTHDAY CONGRATULATIONS

Cavendish, 13 December 1993

Esteemed Boris Nikolaevich!

I thank you for your congratulations on my seventy-fifth birthday. Perhaps, returning to Russian soil, I might be able to be useful, somehow, to our tormented homeland.

I, too, hold out hope in our people's strength of spirit. But it pains me to see the terrible fall into poverty of the majority of our populace, a privatization that benefits the chosen few, the continuing shameless pilfering of the national wealth, the thorough venality of the government apparatus, and the impunity of criminal gangs. In no way does it appear that any break in this circle of misfortunes is forthcoming—unless we fearlessly and selflessly start to tackle these festering wounds, which are getting the better of us.

With good wishes,

A. Solzhenitsyn

[35]

FAREWELL TO PEOPLE OF CAVENDISH[7]

28 February 1994

Citizens of Cavendish, our dear neighbors!

At the town meeting seventeen years ago I told you about my exile and explained the steps that I took to ensure a peaceful working environment, without the burden of constant visitors.

You were very understanding; you forgave me my unusual way of life, and even took it upon yourselves to protect my privacy. For this, I have been truly grateful throughout all these years; and now, as my stay here comes to an end, I thank you. Your kindness and cooperation helped to create the best possible conditions for my work.

I have worked here for almost eighteen years. It has been the most productive period in my life. I have done all that I wanted to do. Today, I offer those of my books that have been translated well into English to the town library.

Our children grew up and went to school here, alongside your children. For them, Vermont is home. Indeed, our whole family has felt at home among you. Exile is always difficult, and yet I could not imagine a better place to live, and wait, and wait for my return home, than Cavendish, Vermont.

Now, at the end of May, my wife and I will go back to Russia, which is going through one of the most difficult periods in its history—a period in which the majority of the population lives in poverty, and standards of human decency have fallen, a period of lawlessness and economic chaos. That is the painful price we have had to pay to rid ourselves of Communism, during whose seventy-year reign of terror we lost up to sixty million people, just from the regime's war on its own nation. I hope that I can be of at least some help to my tortured nation, although it is impossible to predict how successful my efforts will be. Besides, I am not young.

Here in Cavendish, and in the surrounding towns, I have observed the sensible and sure process of grassroots democracy, in which the local population solves most of its problems on its own, not waiting for the decisions of higher authorities. Unfortunately, we do not have this in Russia, and that is still our greatest shortcoming.

My sons will complete their education in America, and the house in Cavendish will remain their home.

Lately, while walking on the nearby roads, taking in the surroundings with a farewell glance, I have found every meeting with any neighbor to be warm and friendly.

And so today, both to those of you whom I have met over these years, and to those whom I haven't met, I say: Thank you and farewell. I wish all the best to Cavendish. God bless you all.

[36]

INFORMING PRESIDENT YELTSIN ABOUT RETURNING TO RUSSIA VIA THE FAR EAST

Cavendish, Vermont
26 April 1994

Esteemed Boris Nikolaevich!

As you perhaps know, I am returning to Russia with my family at the end of May, in about a month's time. I always believed that this return would become possible during my lifetime, and twenty years ago already I planned the route along which I would come back. Now I believe it my duty to inform you in advance—absolutely confidentially, and only, personally you.

I will be returning via the Far East, traveling unhurriedly across the country. Now, when the country is changing so cardinally and so swiftly, I must acquaint myself with how people live, before making any public steps. And I especially want to start with Siberia, which I knew very little—and from the windows of a prison car, at that.

I write this to you first of all for your personal knowledge, but also with a request: please do not send anyone from Moscow to Vladivostok to meet me. While I ride across the countryside, my goal will be to meet local people (including your local representatives). Hence, by the time I arrive in Moscow, before our potential meeting, I hope to receive a good many new, personal impressions of the situation of our country and people.

All best to you!

Aleksandr Solzhenitsyn

NOTES TO THE ENGLISH TRANSLATION

Chapter 6. Russian Pain

1. "In solitude you're happy—you're a poet!": from Pushkin's 1817 poem "Дельвигу" ("To Delvig"), not to be confused with his homonymous poem of 1821.

2. "Exiled to Kok-Terek": Solzhenitsyn is referring to his "internal exile" in Kok-Terek, Kazakhstan, on the edge of the desert, which began in 1953, immediately upon the conclusion of his eight-year camp sentence, and was to continue in perpetuity (but was cut short by Stalin's death and the subsequent changes under Khrushchev). See especially Aleksandr Solzhenitsyn, *The Gulag Archipelago, 1918–1956: An Experiment in Literary Investigation*, trans. Thomas P. Whitney and Harry Willetts (New York: HarperCollins, 2007), vol. 3, pt. VI, chaps. 5–6: 415–43.

3. "The freely chosen solitude I desired, this time in Vermont": Solzhenitsyn and his family had moved from Zurich, Switzerland, to Cavendish, Vermont, in 1976.

4. "Stolypin volume of *August 1914*": the expanded version of *August 1914*, specifically the substantial chapters on Prime Minister Pyotr Stolypin. See Aleksandr Solzhenitsyn, *August 1914: The Red Wheel, Node I* (New York: Farrar, Straus and Giroux, 2014). For more on the genesis of this version, see Aleksandr Solzhenitsyn, *Between Two Millstones, Book 1: Sketches of Exile, 1974–1978* (Notre Dame, IN: University of Notre Dame Press, 2018), chap. 4: 250.

5. "Except for my Harvard speech": Solzhenitsyn's famous Harvard commencement address of 8 June 1978. See *Between Two Millstones, Book 1*, chap. 4: 283–93.

6. "During the first hustle and bustle in Zurich": after his expulsion from the USSR on 13 February 1974, Solzhenitsyn and his family had initially settled in Zurich, Switzerland. See *Between Two Millstones, Book 1*, especially chap. 1: 40–45.

7. "Hoover Institution": located in Palo Alto, California, under the umbrella of Stanford University, the Hoover houses the preeminent Western archives on the Russian Revolution. For Solzhenitsyn's time there, see *Between Two Millstones, Book 1*, especially chap. 3: 174–75 and chap. 4: 229–34.

8. "The whole enormous edifice of *March*": *March 1917*, whose four volumes make up Node III of *The Red Wheel*. See Aleksandr Solzhenitsyn, *March 1917: The Red Wheel, Node III, Book 1* (Notre Dame, IN: University of Notre Dame Press, 2017) and Aleksandr Solzhenitsyn, *March 1917: The Red Wheel, Node III, Book 2* (Notre Dame, IN: University of Notre Dame Press, 2019).

9. "Alya": Solzhenitsyn's second wife, Natalia Dmitrievna Solzhenitsyna.

10. "Father Andrew": Fr. Andrew Tregubov, the parish priest in Claremont, New Hampshire, where Solzhenitsyn and his family attended services throughout their stay in Vermont. See *Between Two Millstones, Book 1*, chap. 4: 248–49.

11. "Old New Year's Eve": 13 January, which is New Year's Eve according to the old Julian calendar.

12. "Those days when inspiration descends on you like an *avalanche*": for Solzhenitsyn's more detailed description of his "avalanche days," see *Between Two Millstones, Book 1*, chap. 3: 198.

13. "Old Russian lady from Zurich": Ekaterina Pavlovna Bakhareva, "Granny Katya." See *Between Two Millstones, Book 1*, chap. 1: 43.

14. "Algol, the 'demon star'": a multiple "variable" star in the Perseus constellation, traditionally associated with blood and violence.

15. "The abbot, Father Laurence": Fr. Laurence Mancuso (1934–2007), founding abbot of the New Skete Monastery in Cambridge, New York.

16. "Our new friend and neighbor Sheree": Sheree Vaughn-Tucker.

17. Richard "Dick" Bliss was the founder (mid-1960s) and headmaster (until its closure in 1989) of East Hill Farm and School in Andover, Vermont.

18. "Flew the school flag at half-staff in mourning": this episode is also recounted in John Tierney, "A Cold Morning in Vermont," *New York Times,* 13 June 2004, 38; nytimes.com/2004/06/13/us/political-points.html.

19. "Such Russian boys"; Nikolai Volkov-Muromtsev's extraordinary memoir recalls how he and other teenage boys enlisted with the Volunteer Army during the Russian Civil War (1917–22) in a doomed attempt to save Russia from the Bolsheviks.

20. "No, thank you": one of the great monologues (Act II, Scene 8) from *Cyrano de Bergerac* by Edmond Rostand (1868–1918).

21. "Stolypin volume of *August 1914*": see 459, note 4 in this volume.

22. "Five Brooks": the name the Solzhenitsyns gave to their Cavendish property. See *Between Two Millstones, Book 1*, chap. 4: 222.

23. "The heavenly cipher": Solzhenitsyn credits the linguist Vyacheslav Vsevolodovich Ivanov (1929–2017) with formulating this idea of a mystical cipher, available for each person to decode. See Aleksandr Solzhenitsyn, *The Oak and the Calf: Sketches of Literary Life in the Soviet Union*, trans. Harry Willetts (New York: Harper & Row, 1979), chap. 4, "The Wounded Beast": 111, 115, 146.

24. "The Third Wave": frequently throughout this book Solzhenitsyn alludes to the three waves of Russian emigration. The First Wave refers to those who fled Russia after the Revolution; the Second Wave, to persons displaced in the cataclysm of World War II; and the Third Wave, to an emigration made up mostly of Soviet Jews in the 1970s. At times, Solzhenitsyn refers to these waves as the First Emigration, Second Emigration, and Third Emigration.

25. "Malyshki": Solzhenitsyn's own affectionate term (literally, "little ones," normally used in reference to small children) for the high-quality, small-format volumes of his twenty-volume Собрание сочинений (Collected Works), published in Paris by YMCA-Press from 1978 until 1991. These were published in parallel with the standard large-format hardbacks, but were far easier to smuggle into the USSR.

26. "Fund": the Russian Social Fund for Persecuted Persons and Their Families, Solzhenitsyn's charitable foundation. See *Between Two Millstones, Book 1*, chap. 1: 49, 67, and chap. 2: 161.

27. "*October*": *October 1916*, whose two volumes make up Node II of *The Red Wheel*, covering 14 October to 4 November (per the Julian calendar in use at the time in Russia), i.e., 27 October to 17 November by the Gregorian calendar. For that reason, it was first published in English under the title *November 1916*. See Aleksandr Solzhenitsyn, *November 1916: The Red Wheel, Node II* (New York: Farrar, Straus and Giroux, 2014). Future editions will seek to restore the title *October 1916*, according to the author's wish that each Node's title be uniform across languages.

28. "*Publitsistika*": publicistic works, i.e., speeches, essays, statements, interviews, forewords, etc.

29. "The interrogations of Bogrov": for Dmitri Bogrov's assassination of Prime Minister Stolypin and its aftermath, see *August 1914*, chaps. 60–73.

30. "*The Tanks Know the Truth*": Solzhenitsyn's screenplay about the labor-camp uprising in Kengir in 1954. Published in English (trans. Michael Nicholson) in *Studies in Russian & Soviet Cinema* 7, no. 1 (March 2013): 73–157.

31. "Menacing wartime song": Solzhenitsyn is referring to "Священная война" ("Sacred War"), a universally known Soviet patriotic song of World War II, but one that he uses to accompany the literal crushing of the prisoners' uprising in the climactic scene of *The Tanks Know the Truth*.

32. "The *zeks*": *zek* (="зэк," derived from "заключённый")—a prisoner in the Gulag labor-camp system.

33. "That Czech émigré Vojtěch Jasný": see *Between Two Millstones, Book 1*, chap. 1: 28.

34. "The Ukrainians at Ekibastuz even turned their back on the uprising": Solzhenitsyn was himself both eyewitness to, and participant in, the Ekibastuz camp uprising of 1952.

35. *Den første kreds* (*The First Circle*), directed by Aleksander Ford, cinematography by Wladyslaw Forbert (1973), 98 min; *One Day in the Life of Ivan Denisovich*, directed by Caspar Wrede (1970), 100 min; *One Word of Truth*, directed by Peter J. Sisam (1981), 27 min.

36. "The tale of Georgi Tenno's escape": see *The Gulag Archipelago*, vol. 3, pt. V, chap. 7, "The White Kitten," 154–92.

37. "Studies in Modern Russian History": this historical series (Исследования Новейшей Русской Истории, Russian acronym ИНРИ, i.e., I. N. R. I.) brought forth twelve volumes from YMCA-Press in Paris between 1980 and 1995. It was then taken over by Moscow publisher Русский путь, which issued another nine volumes between 1995 and 2005. See also *Between Two Millstones, Book 1*, chap. 4: 246.

38. "Raznochintsy": in prerevolutionary Russia, ideologically progressive intellectuals from mixed social ranks. Some noted *raznochintsy* were Vissarion Belinsky, Nikolai Dobrolyubov and Nikolai Chernyshevsky.

39. "Liberation movement": in prerevolutionary Russia, ideologically progressive intellectuals (like Pyotr Struve, Ivan Petrunkevich, and Dmitri Shakhovskoy) associated with the founding of the unsanctioned fortnightly *Osvobozhdenie* (*Liberation*), which, in turn, gave rise to the Soyuz Osvobozhdeniya (Union of Liberation), advocating for constitutional monarchy.

40. Georgi Katkov, Февральская революция (*The February Revolution*), Studies in Modern Russian History 4 (Paris: YMCA-Press, 1984). Viktor Leontovich, История либерализма в России, 1762–1914 (*A History of Liberalism in Russia, 1762–1914*), Studies in Modern Russian History 1 (Paris: YMCA-Press, 1980).

41. Независимое рабочее движение в 1918 году (*The Independent Workers' Movement in 1918*), ed. Mikhail Bernshtam, Studies in Modern Russian History 2 (Paris: YMCA-Press, 1981); and Урал и Прикамье: ноябрь 1917–январь 1919 (*The Urals and the Prikamye: November 1917–January 1919*), ed. Mikhail Bernshtam, Studies in Modern Russian History 3 (Paris: YMCA-Press, 1982).

42. For more on Lenin and Ganetsky (Hanecki) in Poronino, Austria (today Poronin, Poland), see *August 1914*, chap. 22.

43. "To *Posev* and to YMCA-Press": *Посев* (*Posev* or *Possev*, meaning *Sowing*) was a journal published since 1945 in Frankfurt by the NTS (Narodno-Trudovoi Soyuz rossiyskikh solidaristov, or National Labor Alliance of Russian Solidarists); YMCA-Press, a Parisian publishing house initially funded by the (American Protestant) Young Men's Christian Association, became the foremost champion and publisher of Russian-language theological, philosophical, and sociological literature from the mid-1920s onward.

44. "My appeal to émigrés": see *Between Two Millstones, Book 1*, chap. 4: 249.

45. For more on the Bakhmeteff Archive, and its precursor in Prague, see *Between Two Millstones, Book 1*, chap. 4: 260–61.

46. "Okhrana": the secret police in prerevolutionary Russia.

47. "GPU": one of the multiple incarnations of the Soviet secret police (Cheka, GPU, OGPU, NKVD, KGB, etc.).

48. "All-Russian Memoir Library": this memoir series (Всероссийская мемуарная библиотека, Russian acronym ВМБ, i.e., V. M. B.) brought forth twelve volumes from YMCA-Press in Paris between 1983 and 1995. It was then taken over by Moscow publisher Русский путь, which issued another fourteen volumes between 1997 and 2009. See also *Between Two Millstones, Book 1*, chap. 4: 248–49.

49. "Samizdat": derived from the Russian sam=сам=self and izdat=издат=publish, this was the unofficial underground press, a way to copy and distribute essays and literature that could not otherwise see the light of day.

50. Aleksandr Solzhenitsyn, "A Wave of Repression," *Baltimore Sun*, 26 January 1981, A13. For Russian text, see Aleksandr Solzhenitsyn, *Publitsistika v triokh tomakh* (Yaroslavl: Верхне-волжское книжное издательство, 1995–97), vol. 2, 547 [hereafter *Publitsistika*].

51. "The anniversary of Sakharov's exile": the famed physicist and dissident Andrei Sakharov had been sent in January 1980 to internal exile in the city of Gorki (today Nizhni Novgorod).

52. Louis Berney, "Solzhenitsyn Says Soviets Crippling His Fund to Aid Political Dissidents," *Burlington Free Press*, 8 December 1981, 1. For Russian text, see *Publitsistika*, vol. 2, 590.

53. The Lubyanka, on Moscow's Lubyanka Square, was both the headquarters of the KGB and the site of one of its most infamous prisons.

54. "Soviet Scholar Arrested," *Guardian*, 21 May 1980, 14. For full text, see *Publitsistika*, vol. 2, 540.

55. "Here again Ludmilla Thorne helped enormously": Thorne had a few years earlier been instrumental in the defense of Aleksandr Ginzburg; see *Between Two Millstones, Book 1*, chap. 4: 258–59.

56. Iosif G. Dyadkin, *Unnatural Deaths in the USSR, 1928–1954* (New Brunswick, NJ: Transaction Books, 1983).

57. "Those same cadets": students of Russia's military academies who did not accept the Revolution and formed an important element of the anti-Bolshevik White armies during the Civil War of 1917–22. Not to be confused with the political party of Kadets (see 464, note 80 in this volume).

58. "NTS": see 462, note 43 in this volume.

59. "CPSU": Communist Party of the Soviet Union.

60. "Silver Age": the exceptional flowering of Russian poetry from about 1890 to 1920 (following the "Golden Age" of Pushkin and Lermontov, from about 1810 to 1840).

61. "Even our Church is split into three": Russian Orthodox parishes in the West would typically belong to the Moscow Patriarchate (MP), the Russian Orthodox Church Outside Russia (ROCOR; also known as the Russian Orthodox Church Abroad), or the Orthodox Church in America (OCA).

62. "Russian University": see *Between Two Millstones, Book 1*, chap. 1: 60–61.

63. "To travel from Zurich to Oxford": see *Between Two Millstones, Book 1*, chap. 1: 80.

64. "Solzhenitsyn Praises Strikers," *Boston Globe*, 21 August 1980, 4. For Russian text, see *Publitsistika*, vol. 2, 544.

65. *Honolulu Advertiser*, 5 December 1980, 76. For Russian text, see *Publitsistika*, vol. 2, 546.

66. Alexandre Soljénitsyne, "Pologne: la leçon principale," *L'Express*, 15 January 1982, 90–91. For a partial English text, see A. Solzhenitsyn, "The Real Lesson of Poland," *Calgary Herald*, 26 January 1982, A7. For full Russian text, see *Publitsistika*, vol. 3, 7–10.

67. This third and final Sapiets-Solzhenitsyn interview (after the ones in 1974 and 1975) was recorded in Vermont on 2–3 February 1979 and broadcast on the BBC Russian Service on 13 and 18 February. It was first published in the *Listener*, 15 and 22 February 1979, then in the *Kenyon Review* (Summer and Autumn 1979 issues), and then reprinted in Aleksandr Solzhenitsyn, *East and West*, trans. Alexis Klimoff and Hillary Sternberg (New York: Harper & Row, 1980), 145–82. For Russian text, see *Publitsistika*, vol. 2, 483–504.

68. "Lethe": In Greek mythology, one of the five rivers of the underworld; also the name of the Greek spirit of forgetfulness and oblivion, with whom the river was often identified.

69. "February fever": to better understand what Solzhenitsyn implies by this term, see this description in chap. 14: 330 of this volume: "And how very familiar all this was to Alya and me, from February 1917: the boundless enthusiasm of the population; and the drunken fogginess of their hopes; and that recklessness in the way they expressed themselves. So much happy intoxication after such a long wait!—but in that state, all sense of proportion was getting lost, deformed. And there was a negligence towards the historic paths Russia had taken, an indifference to her singularities, a heedlessness of any duty to preserve them." And for more on Solzhenitsyn's sense of the special mindset prevailing during the February Revolution, see *Between Two Millstones, Book 1*, chap. 4: 225–27.

70. "When the October victory was celebrated": Solzhenitsyn is referring to the Bolshevik takeover in the October Revolution (1917) and the sympathetic reaction it elicited in Western progressive circles.

71. "General Dourakine": the unflattering title character of the Comtesse de Ségur's 1863 novel about a Russian general.

72. "Shame Berdyaev's no longer with us!": Solzhenitsyn is implying that Third Wave émigrés are out of their depth in discussions of grand historical-philosophical themes such as the Third Rome, a concept more suited for the likes of the philosopher Nikolai Aleksandrovich Berdyaev (1874–1948), who wrote extensively on the fate of Russia and her place in the world.

73. Olga Carlisle, *Solzhenitsyn and the Secret Circle* (New York: Holt, Rinehart and Winston, 1978).

74. Olga Carlisle, "Reviving Myths of Holy Russia," *New York Times Magazine*, 16 September 1979, 48–65. See also *Between Two Millstones, Book 1*, chap. 2: 156.

75. "*Lenin in Zurich*": Solzhenitsyn took what would become the first fourteen Lenin chapters of *The Red Wheel* and brought them out as a separate book under the title *Lenin in Zurich* (New York: Farrar, Straus and Giroux, 1976).

76. See, e.g., David K. Shipler, "A Russian Nationalism Is on Rise," *New York Times*, 12 November 1978, 1.

77. Abraham Brumberg, "The Changing Party Line," *Washington Post*, 14 December 1980, sec. Book World, BW4.

78. Aleksandr Solzhenitsyn, "The Persian Ruse," *Jerusalem Post*, 20 December 1979, 8. For Russian text, see *Publitsistika*, vol. 2, 511–12.

79. "Solzhenitsyn and Russian Nationalism: An Interview with Andrei Sinyavsky," *New York Review of Books*, 22 November 1979, 3.

80. "Kadet": from the abbreviation ("K-D") of the party name in Russian for members of the moderate-left Constitutional-Democratic party, also known as Constitutional Democrats. Not to be confused with cadets (see 463, note 57 in this volume).

81. "A striking and *exact* match with Sakharov's formulation!": see *Between Two Millstones, Book 1*, chap. 1: 35–36.

82. For Solzhenitsyn's essay "Repentance and Self-Limitation in the Life of Nations," see Aleksandr Solzhenitsyn, *The Solzhenitsyn Reader: New and Essential Writings, 1947–2005*, ed. Edward E. Ericson Jr. and Daniel J. Mahoney (Wilmington: ISI Books, 2006), 527–55. For Russian text, see *Publitsistika*, vol. 1, 49–86.

83. Aleksandr Solzhenitsyn, "Solzhenitsyn on Communism," *Time* 115, no. 7 (18 February 1980): 48–49. For Russian text, see *Publitsistika*, vol. 1, 329–35.

84. Aleksandr Solzhenitsyn, "Misconceptions about Russia Are a Threat to America," *Foreign Affairs* 58, no. 4 (Spring 1980): 797–834. For Russian text, see *Publitsistika*, vol. 1, 336–81.

85. Boris Souvarine, "Soljénitsyne et Lenine," *Est et Ouest*, no. 570 (1–15 April 1976), 145 (abridged English translation in *Dissent*, Summer 1977, 324–36). See also *Between Two Millstones, Book 1*, chap. 4: 240.

86. Boris Souvarine, Солженицын и Ленин ("Solzhenitsyn and Lenin"), *Vremya i My*, no. 22 (October 1977), 128–46, and no. 23 (November 1977), 153–165.

87. Alexandre Soljénitsyne, "Lenine et l'argent allemande," *L'Histoire*, no. 22 (April 1980), 69–71. For Russian text, see *Publitsistika*, vol. 2, 513–18.

88. Letters to the editor from Robert C. Tucker, Silvio J. Treves, Robert W. Thurston, Eugen Loebl, John R. Dunlap, and Alexander Dallin, in response to Solzhenitsyn, appeared in *Foreign Affairs* 58, no. 5 (Summer 1980): 1178–84 and 59, no. 1 (Fall 1980): 187–96.

89. Aleksandr Solzhenitsyn, "The Courage to See," *Foreign Affairs* 59, no. 1 (Fall 1980): 196–210. For Russian text, see *Publitsistika*, vol. 1, 382–405.

90. Aleksandr Solzhenitsyn, *The Mortal Danger* (New York: Harper Colophon, 1981).

91. Boris Souvarine, "Soljénitsyne: le roman et l'histoire," *L'Histoire*, no. 25 (July–August 1980), 110–11.

92. Alexandre Soljénitsyne, "La réponse de Soljénitsyne: Les 'fragments de M. Souvarine,'" *L'Histoire*, no. 26 (September 1980). For Russian text, see *Publitsistika*, vol. 2, 541–43.

93. *Publitsistika*, vol. 2, 505.

94. The Sakharov Hearings were organized by the International Sakharov Committee to expose human-rights violations in the Soviet Union and Eastern Europe. The first such hearings took place in Copenhagen in 1975, the second in Rome in 1977, the third in Washington in 1979.

95. Aleksandr Solzhenitsyn, "A Plea for Igor Ogurtsov," *Spectator*, 3 November 1979, 8. For Russian text, see *Publitsistika*, vol. 2, 508–10.

96. "My ninety-year-old aunt Irina": Irina Ivanovna Shcherbak.

97. "Solzhenitsyn Aunt Denied Apartment," *Washington Post*, 19 November 1977, A15.

98. The final version of *The Oak and the Calf*, including, e.g., this Appendix 46, has not, as of 2020, appeared in English. However, the same document by KGB major Boris Ivanov appears as Appendix B to Aleksandr Solzhenitsyn, *Invisible Allies*, trans. Alexis Klimoff and Michael Nicholson (Washington, D.C.: Counterpoint, 1995), 306–18. See also David Remnick, "KGB Plot to Assassinate Solzhenitsyn Reported," *Washington Post*, 21 April 1992, D1. For more of Solzhenitsyn's perspective, see author's note in *Between Two Millstones, Book 1*, chap. 5: 301–2.

99. E.g., *Kontinent*, no. 23 (1980): 200–201.

100. "All four State Dumas": the prerevolutionary Russian parliament that met, over four distinct sessions, from 1906 until 1917.

101. Andrei Sakharov, *My Country and the World* (New York: Vintage Books, 1975); see earlier mention in *Between Two Millstones, Book 1*, chap. 3: 204–5.

102. The Jackson-Vanik amendment was passed by the US Congress in 1974 to deny normal trade relations to Communist countries that restricted freedom of emigration.

103. "Red Brigades": ultra-left terrorist organization active in Europe in the 1970s and '80s.

104. "When the fate of Poland was being decided before Jaruzelski": it was on 13 December 1981 that Gen. Wojciech Jaruzelski declared martial law in Communist

Poland in an attempt to crush the pro-democracy Solidarność (Solidarity) workers' movement.

105. "Vashchenko family": Pyotr, Avgustina, Lidia, Lyubov, and Lilia Vashchenko, together with Timofei and Maria Chmykhalov, together sometimes referred to as the "Siberian seven," were Pentecostalists who took refuge in the US Embassy in Moscow from June 1978 until April 1983, when they were finally allowed to emigrate.

106. "Right down to Nizhni": Solzhenitsyn is playing on the word нижний=nizhni=lower, the lower strata of society, and also the city named lower—or, Nizhni—Novgorod.

107. "Februarist": a participant in, or supporter of, the February Revolution (1917) or its ideas.

108. "*Ubi bene, ibi patria*": "Where I am happy, there is my homeland."

109. E.g., *Kontinent*, no. 23 (1980): 200–201.

110. Andrei D. Sakharov, "In Answer to Solzhenitsyn," trans. Guy Daniels, *New York Review of Books*, 13 June 1974. See *Between Two Millstones, Book 1*, chap. 1: 33–39.

111. "Great-Russian"=великорусский=velikorusski: of "Greater Russia" or "Outer Russia" (the lands extending north and east of "Core Russia" or "Inner Russia"). The territory of "Greater Russia" broadly corresponds to today's Russian Federation, while "Core Russia" corresponds to Ukraine. Sakharov's pejorative moniker "Great-Russian nationalist" implied that Solzhenitsyn held Russian-supremacist views.

Chapter 7. A Creeping Host

1. Tomáš Řezáč, Спираль измены Солженицына (*The Spiral of Solzhenitsyn's Treason*) (Moscow: Progress, 1978). See *Between Two Millstones, Book 1*, chap. 5.

2. Aleksei (1904–1918): only son and youngest child of Emperor Nikolai II and Empress Aleksandra Fyodorovna; hemophiliac; murdered, together with his parents and sisters, by the Bolsheviks.

3. "GHQ": General Headquarters (in Russian: Ставка=Stavka) of the high command of the Russian Imperial Army during World War I. The GHQ was located in what is today Belarus.

4. George Feifer, "The Dark Side of Solzhenitsyn," *Harper's Magazine*, May 1980, 49–58.

5. "*Novy Mir* after Tvardovsky": after Tvardovsky's ouster as editor-in-chief in 1970.

6. Vladimir Lakshin, *Solzhenitsyn, Tvardovsky and "Novy Mir,"* trans. Michael Glenny (Cambridge, MA: MIT Press, 1980). For Solzhenitsyn's discussion of Lakshin's article (book), see *Between Two Millstones, Book 1*, chap. 4: 272–77.

7. "Literary Vlasovite and renegade": Soviet propaganda terms of denunciation. *Literary Vlasovite*, in particular, was coined specifically to demonize Solzhenitsyn, who'd made an attempt to understand the emergence of Gen. Andrei Vlasov and his movement in *The Gulag Archipelago* (see especially vol. 1, pt. I, chap. 6, "That Spring," 251–62).

8. Judy Stone, "Olga Carlisle: A Controversial Footnote on Solzhenitsyn," *Los Angeles Times*, 13 April 1980, K3.

9. Stephen F. Cohen, "Voices from the Gulag," *New York Times*, 4 May 1980, sec. 7 (Book Review), 1, 36–38.

10. Tomas Venclova, *New Leader* 63, no. 9 (5 May 1980): 15.

11. Max Geltman, "Solzhenitsyn's Sketchy Memoirs," *Midstream* 26, no. 10 (1980): 53–54.

12. *The Oak and the Calf*, Third Supplement, "Encounter Battle," 378.

13. According to Kaiser himself, his review of *The Oak and the Calf* appeared in "an obscure magazine published in Dallas." See Robert G. Kaiser, "The Giant of Russian Literature," *Washington Post*, 5 August 2008, C1.

14. *The Oak and the Calf*, Third Supplement, "Nobeliana," 331.

15. "Invisible allies": the individuals who had secretly helped Solzhenitsyn, frequently at great personal risk. They are described in his book *Invisible Allies* [=Fifth Supplement to *The Oak and the Calf*].

16. "I was too late to see Aleksandr Yashin": in the final version of *The Oak and the Calf* (forthcoming from University of Notre Dame Press), Solzhenitsyn expresses regret at being half an hour late to visit the writer and poet Aleksandr Yakovlevich Yashin (1913–1968) on his deathbed.

17. Harlow Robinson, "Solzhenitsyn: Shrill," *Christian Science Monitor*, 14 July 1980, 13.

18. Hilton Kramer, "A Talk with Solzhenitsyn," *New York Times*, 11 May 1980, sec. 7 (Book Review), 3, 30–32.

19. "If Solzhenitsyn Went Home . . . ," *Christian Science Monitor*, 8 September 1980, 27.

20. "The loss of my archive on 11 September 1965": see *The Oak and the Calf*, chap. 4, "The Wounded Beast."

21. "Pages from his mother": see *Between Two Millstones, Book 1*, chap. 4: 282.

22. B. Danilov, Без царя в голове ("Harebrained"), *Literaturnaya Gazeta*, 17 March 1976, 15. Russian state archives show that this "feuilleton" was commissioned directly by KGB Chairman Yuri Andropov. See Российский государственный архив новейшей истории (Russian State Archive of Modern History), fund 5, section 69, file 2897, page 2; http://ргани.рф/fond-5-opis-69-otdely-ck-kpss.

23. Nikolai Yakovlev, ЦРУ против СССР (*The CIA versus the USSR*) (Moscow: Молодая гвардия, 1979). Later appeared in English as *CIA Target—The USSR* (Moscow: Progress, 1982).

24. Nikolai Yakovlev, *Living in Lie* (Moscow: Novosti Press Agency Publishing House, 1976).

25. Pavel Fyodorovich Smerdyakov: the murderous servant in Dostoevsky's *Brothers Karamazov*.

26. "Literally the indoctrination given at the US State Department too, as I've already mentioned": see *Between Two Millstones, Book 1*, chap. 4: 231.

27. For these various incidents with *Stern* magazine, see *Between Two Millstones, Book 1*, 65, 137, 200–203.

28. "The whole Creeping Host": for Solzhenitsyn's description of his term for this subset of Third Wave "pen-wielding" émigrés, see 105–6 later in this chapter. See also *Between Two Millstones, Book 1*, chap. 4: 279–80.

29. UPI report (25 October 1980) of Carlisle news conference available at upi .com/4578904.

30. Betta Markstein, Fritz Heeb, and Nikita Struve were Solzhenitsyn's "Three Pillars of Support": see, e.g., *Invisible Allies*, Sketch 12.

31. "The Swiss scandal over the Fund": see *Between Two Millstones, Book 1*, chap. 4: 262–70.

32. "Libel Suit against Solzhenitsyn Is Dismissed," *Jerusalem Post*, 26 July 1981, 4.

33. "He had included a hand-drawn map": for this footnote to the English edition, see *The Oak and the Calf*, Third Supplement, "Encounter Battle," 369. (This map is also described in Western press accounts at the time, e.g., Charlotte Saikowski, "Solzhenitsyn's Nobel Plans in Ashes," *Christian Science Monitor*, 8 April 1972, 1.) It is noteworthy that Harry Willetts mistranslated what should have read "a hand-drawn map . . . of how to get to my Moscow apartment" as "the floor plan of my . . . Moscow apartment," perhaps unwittingly emboldening Zhores Medvedev to threaten a lawsuit on a technicality.

34. For the YMCA-Press lawsuit against Flegon, see *Between Two Millstones, Book 1*, chap. 1: 47.

35. Alec Flegon, Вокруг Солженицына (*Around Solzhenitsyn*) (London: Flegon Press, 1981).

36. "Luka Mudishchev": a notorious lewd poem long attributed to Lomonosov's student Ivan Semyonovich Barkov (1732–1768).

37. "Piracy": for Flegon's pirated editions of *First Circle*, *August 1914*, and *The Gulag Archipelago*, see *Between Two Millstones, Book 1*, chap 1: 47–48, and chap 2: 141–42.

38. "Writer Sues Solzhenitsyn," *Sunday Telegraph*, 15 November 1981, 3.

39. Aleksandr Solzhenitsyn, Бодался телёнок с дубом (*The Oak and the Calf*) (Paris: YMCA-Press, 1975), 568–69.

40. *Between Two Millstones, Book 1*, chap. 2: 138–42.

41. "Smith and Kaiser omitted that part of the interview, and so it didn't appear in English": see Hedrick Smith, "Solzhenitsyn Tells of Struggle to Write Despite Soviet Pressures," *New York Times*, 3 April 1972, 1, 10; and Robert G. Kaiser, "Solzhenitsyn Speaks Out in Russia," *Washington Post*, 3 April 1972, A1, A17.

42. "The interview with the Americans was included as an appendix": Бодался телёнок с дубом, Appendix 22: 560–78.

43. "Chekist": agent of the Cheka (ChK) secret police, or its multiple incarnations (GPU, OGPU, NKVD, KGB, etc.).

44. Aleksandr Solzhenitsyn, "Our Pluralists," *Survey: A Journal of East and West Studies* 29, no. 2 (Summer 1985): 1–28. For Russian text, see *Publitsistika*, vol. 1, 406–44.

Chapter 8. More Headaches

1. "The same relationship as a sick man and his disease": see, e.g., *Solzhenitsyn Speaks at the Hoover Institution on War, Revolution and Peace, Stanford University, California, May–June 1976* (Stanford: Hoover Institution, 1976); or Aleksandr Solzhenitsyn, "Remarks at the Hoover Institution, May 24, 1976," *Russian Review* 36, no. 2 (1977): 184–89, available at jstor.org/stable/128896; or Solzhenitsyn's "Speech at the

Town Meeting of the Residents of Cavendish, 28 February 1977," *Between Two Millstones, Book 1*, Appendix 20: 384.

2. "Moskals": Ukrainian pejorative for "Muscovites," i.e., Russians.

3. Public Law 86-90 was signed into law by President Eisenhower on 17 July 1959. Available at legislink.org/us/pl-86-90. See *Between Two Millstones, Book 1*, chap. 3: 186.

4. "In Winnipeg I had talked to the heads of the Ukrainian Congress": see *Between Two Millstones, Book 1*, chap. 3: 180–81.

5. "To the Conference on Russian-Ukrainian Relations," *Publitsistika*, vol. 2, 548–52.

6. "Captive Nations Week": as of 2020, every third week of July continues to be designated as "Captive Nations Week" in the United States by presidents of either party. See *Between Two Millstones, Book 1*, chap. 3: 186.

7. US-funded, Munich-based Radio Liberty came to be a leading source of independent news for millions inside the Soviet Union during the Cold War, despite heavy jamming of its signal by the Soviet government. In 1976 it merged with Radio Free Europe (which broadcast to the Communist countries of Eastern Europe) to form Radio Free Europe/Radio Liberty (RFE/RL).

8. The Solzhenitsyn-LeBoutillier interview was recorded on 12 October 1981, then broadcast in two parts (on 27 and 28 October 1981) on NBC's *Tomorrow Coast to Coast*.

9. See, e.g., Arthur Unger, "Solzhenitsyn Warns US Not to Aid, Arm China—TV Interview," *Christian Science Monitor*, 26 October 1981.

10. Aleksandr Solzhenitsyn, "The Soft Voice of America," *National Review*, 30 April 1982, 477–81. For full Russian text, see *Publitsistika*, vol. 2, 554–77.

11. For Reagan and Solzhenitsyn in 1976, see *Between Two Millstones, Book 1*, chap. 4: 230–31.

12. On Erich Gayler, see *Between Two Millstones, Book 1*, chap. 4: 267–69.

13. For Solzhenitsyn's earlier interactions with Richard Pipes, see *Between Two Millstones, Book 1*, chap. 4: 229, 283–84.

14. Robert G. Kaiser, "Reagan, Solzhenitsyn to Dine," *Washington Post*, 8 April 1982, A13.

15. "He could not forgive my criticizing his distorted history of Russia": for Solzhenitsyn's Hoover speech that included critical remarks about Pipes's *Russia under the Old Regime*, see *Between Two Millstones, Book 1*, chap. 4: 229, and *Solzhenitsyn Speaks at the Hoover*; or Aleksandr Solzhenitsyn, "Remarks at the Hoover Institution, May 24, 1976," *Russian Review* 36, no. 2 (1977): 184–89, available at jstor.org/stable/128896.

16. Aleksandr Solzhenitsyn, "Misconceptions about Russia Are a Threat to America," *Foreign Affairs* 58, no. 4 (Spring 1980): 802.

17. Robert G. Kaiser, "Solzhenitsyn Refuses Invitation to White House," *Washington Post*, 11 May 1982, A6.

18. "Solzhenitsyn Explains 'No' to Reagan Invite," *Rutland Herald*, 13 May 1982, 1, 6.

19. "No Use for Formal Gestures, Solzhenitsyn Tells President," *Washington Post*, 14 May 1982, A10; and "Solzhenitsyn to Reagan: Spasibo, Nyet," *Washington Post*, 16 May 1982, C2.

20. Kronid Lyubarsky, О письме А. Солженицына Президенту Р. Рейгану ("About A. Solzhenitsyn's Letter to President R. Reagan"), *Forum*, no. 1 (1982): 226–31.

21. "Were they already reaching for the reins of Gogol's Troika": according to Gogol's famous image from *Dead Souls*, for the reins of Russia itself.

22. "The American generals who were aiming, in the event of an atomic war, to destroy Russians selectively": Solzhenitsyn is referring to Gen. Maxwell D. Taylor (Army Chief of Staff from 1955 until 1959; Chairman of the Joint Chiefs of Staff from 1962 until 1964); see, e.g., his "A New Measure for Defense," *Washington Post*, 14 January 1982, A29. Taylor himself credits the "ethnic factor" to Professor Gary L. Guertner, "Strategic Vulnerability of a Multinational State: Deterring the Soviet Union," *Political Science Quarterly* 96, no. 2 (Summer 1981): 209–23.

23. Vitali Korotich, Свет и надежда планеты ("The Light and Hope of the Planet"), *Sovetskaya Rossiya*, 2 May 1982, 1.

24. *The Gulag Archipelago*, vol. 3, pt. V, chap. 2, "The First Whiff of Revolution," 49.

25. Solzhenitsyn is referring to Innokenti Volodin, one of the principal characters in his *In the First Circle*, in its true uncensored ninety-six-chapter version—with a plotline dealing with Soviet stealing of nuclear secrets from America—in contrast with his "lightened" eighty-seven-chapter version, where an experimental-drug plotline is substituted. While the latter version had appeared in the US as early as 1968 (Aleksandr Solzhenitsyn, *The First Circle* [New York: Harper & Row, 1968]), the former would not appear there until after the author's death (Aleksandr Solzhenitsyn, *In the First Circle* [New York: HarperCollins, 2009]).

26. Solzhenitsyn's interview with Barry Holland, then-head of the BBC's Russian Service, was recorded in Cavendish, Vermont, on 8 June 1982, and broadcast on the Russian Service in November 1982, twenty years after the first publication of *One Day in the Life of Ivan Denisovich*. For Russian text, see *Publitsistika*, vol. 3, 21–30.

27. South Sakhalin, known in Japan as Karafuto Prefecture, was contested between Russia and Japan in the 1800s, and was the site of fierce Soviet-Japanese fighting in August 1945, after which it passed into Soviet hands.

28. "It's what Wrangel's Crimea could have been for us": Solzhenitsyn is referring here to the Russian Civil War (1917–1922). The White anti-Bolshevik forces of the Russian South were by March 1920 defeated in the whole region except the Crimean peninsula. General Pyotr Wrangel not only defended Crimea but sought to create there a viable economy based on private land ownership by the peasantry. (Wrangel's Crimea was recognized by France as the *de facto* Russian government, but was overrun by the Red Army in November 1920, after which Wrangel led the orderly evacuation of 120,000 people from the Crimea to Constantinople.) In his Taipei speech of 23 October 1982, Solzhenitsyn would expand on this theme, imagining how a prosperous free Crimea might have compared advantageously with Bolshevik Russia, as indeed a free Taiwan showed how Red China could have developed absent the Communist yoke.

Chapter 9. Around Three Islands

1. Ivan Goncharov (*The Frigate "Pallada,"* 1858) and Boris Pilnyak (*Roots of the Japanese Sun*, 1927) were Russian novelists who had traveled in Japan and written notable books based on their experiences.

2. "Manchukuo" (Manchuria): a puppet state of the Japanese Empire from 1932 until 1945.

3. "Herostratus": a Greek who achieved the infamy he desired by burning down the magnificent Temple of Artemis in Ephesus in 356 BC.

4. "Cross the ill-omened Tsushima Strait": site of the Battle of Tsushima, a devastating defeat for Russia in the Russo-Japanese War of 1904–5.

5. Solzhenitsyn's interview with Japan's Nippon TV (Gosuke Utimura and Shinsaku Hōgen, moderators) was broadcast on 5 October 1982. For full text, see *Publitsistika*, vol. 3, 46–59.

6. Solzhenitsyn's Tokyo speech of 9 October 1982 was translated into English by Michael Nicholson and Alexis Klimoff and published as Aleksandr Solzhenitsyn, "Three Key Moments in Modern Japanese History," *National Review*, 9 December 1983, 1536–46. For Russian text, see *Publitsistika*, vol. 3, 60–73.

7. "Beauty will save the world": the famous, enigmatic maxim from Dostoevsky's great novel *The Idiot*.

8. This roundtable discussion took place in Tokyo on 13 October 1982, and was published in *Yomiuri Shimbun* the next day. For Russian text, see *Publitsistika*, vol. 3, 74–95.

9. For Solzhenitsyn's 5 October 1983 statement "On Lech Wałęsa Being Awarded the Nobel Prize," see *Publitsistika*, vol. 3, 168.

10. As Solzhenitsyn mentions earlier in this chapter, *Yomiuri Shimbun* had specifically requested from him an article about the current situation in the USSR, which it published on 23 October 1982. The French translation was published in *L'Express* on 10 December 1982, and the English in *National Review*, 21 January 1983, 28–34 (Aleksandr Solzhenitsyn, "Communism at the End of the Brezhnev Era"). For Russian text, see *Publitsistika*, vol. 3, 31–44.

11. See, e.g., "Solzhenitsyn Angry Trip Is Disclosed," *Rutland Herald*, 18 October 1982, 11.

12. "Solzhenitsyn Assails U.S. For Treatment of Taiwan," *New York Times*, 24 October 1982, 5.

13. Joan Hanauer, "Over-Attention," UPI, 20 October 1982, available at upi.com /4803046.

14. "Written Gaosiun but it is far closer to Kao-Shyon": and the standard English spelling is Kaohsiung.

15. "The poor Taiwanese, spurned by the world": Solzhenitsyn is referring to the growing isolation of Taiwan (=ROC=Republic of China=Free China), as country after country, in the 1960s and especially '70s, switched diplomatic recognition from the ROC to the PRC (People's Republic of China=Red China=Communist China). The crucial blow was Taiwan's 1971 ouster from not only the Security Council but also the UN General Assembly itself.

16. This is the Sun Moon Lake Wen Wu Temple in Yuchi.

17. "Vlasov movement": the Russian Liberation Movement, headed by Gen. Andrei Vlasov (1901–1946), sought to overthrow Stalin and the Communist regime in Russia via armed alliance with the Nazis. The Prague meeting of November 1944, to which Solzhenitsyn refers in the same paragraph, issued the Prague Manifesto and

formally established the ill-fated Russian Liberation Army. Solzhenitsyn took great interest in this tragic and controversial movement since first learning about it through leaflets dropped among his Red Army unit's front lines. For his attempt to understand its origins and aims, see esp. *The Gulag Archipelago*, vol. 1, pt. I, chap. 6, "That Spring," 251–62, and vol. 3, pt. V, chap. 1, "The Doomed," 27–33 ("I will go so far as to say that our folk would have been worth nothing at all, a nation of abject slaves, if it had gone through that war without brandishing a rifle at Stalin's government even from afar, if it had missed its chance to shake its fist and fling a ripe oath at the *Father of the Peoples*" [31]).

18. In 1959 Radio Liberty began transmitting from Taiwan to the eastern oblasts of the USSR.

19. An excerpted version of the speech was published as Aleksandr Solzhenitsyn, "Taiwan's Betrayal Shows Weakness of the West," *Philadelphia Inquirer*, 3 November 1982, 3. The full English translation appeared in Taiwan, alongside an excerpted version of Solzhenitsyn's Tokyo speech, as *Solzhenitsyn Speaks: "To Free China" and "Choices for Modern Japan"* (Taipei: Kuang Lu, 1982). For full Russian text, see *Publitsistika*, vol. 3, 96–102.

20. "The liberal press didn't even mention it": it seems likely that Solzhenitsyn was not aware that the *Philadelphia Inquirer* had published an excerpted version of the speech; in any case, it appears to have been the only major US newspaper to do so.

21. "*Vestnik*" (*Messenger*): the premier émigré journal of Russian intellectual and Orthodox thought, edited by Nikita Struve and published in Paris by YMCA-Press. See chap. 6: 30 in this volume.

22. "The Smatterers": one of three essays by Solzhenitsyn to appear in Aleksandr Solzhenitsyn et al., *From Under the Rubble*, translated by A. M. Brock et al., under the direction of Michael Scammell; with an introduction by Max Hayward (Boston: Little, Brown, 1975). Throughout this English translation of *Between Two Millstones*, this neologism of Solzhenitsyn's (образованщина=*obrazovanshchina*) is translated as "pseudo-intellectuals," which one hopes brings the reader within range of the inimitable sense of the Russian original.

23. "They were right to pick out both my poem in *Archipelago* and the separate 'A Prayer'": The poem first appeared, untitled, in *The Gulag Archipelago*, vol. 2, pt. IV, chap. 1, "The Ascent," 614–15, trans. Thomas Whitney, and later, under its restored title, "Acathistus," in the *Solzhenitsyn Reader*, 21, trans. Ignat Solzhenitsyn. Meanwhile, "A Prayer" is the eighteenth and final "miniature" from the first set of 1958–63. It has been translated into English several times; the authorized translation is by Ignat Solzhenitsyn in *Solzhenitsyn Reader*, 624–25.

24. "She protected *Archipelago* until the KGB turned up": For the tragic and providential story of Elizaveta Voronyanskaya, keeper of *Archipelago*, see *The Oak and the Calf*, 345–48, and *Invisible Allies*, Sketch 5.

25. "One of his speeches on the subject": the speech sent to Solzhenitsyn by Sikorsky's son was "The Evolution of the Soul," delivered by Sikorsky in Lansing, Michigan, on 15 November 1949. Available at sikorskyarchives.com/evolution.php. Russian text in *Vestnik RSKhD*, no. 141 (1984): 91–113.

26. "Northern river reversal project": the epitome of utopian central planning, this project aimed to reverse the flow of the great northern rivers of Russia and Siberia—Pechora, Irtysh, Ob, and others—away from the Arctic Ocean and into the arid lands of Central Asia. After years of preparations, it was eventually abandoned in the mid-1980s due to what even the Soviets saw would be unmanageable economic and environmental cost.

27. "Professor Guertner's scientific proposals for the selective annihilation of ethnic Russians": see 470, note 22 in this volume.

28. 11 May 1983 London press conference: its "shreds and tatters" indeed appeared in a multitude of Western newspapers, e.g., David Millward, "Solzhenitsyn Accuses Disarmers," *Daily Telegraph*, 12 May 1983, 1; Jeff Bradley, "Solzhenitsyn: Being Red Is Slow Death," *Philadelphia Inquirer*, 12 May 1983, 23A; "N-Protesters Called Blind," *Vancouver Sun*, 12 May 1983, 9. For full text, see *Publitsistika*, vol. 3, 104–19.

29. "That scorpion, Flegon": see chap. 7: 100–105 in this volume.

30. Martin Walker, "Writers Brew Up Storm in Samovar," *Guardian*, 1 August 1981, 3.

31. David Burg: see *Between Two Millstones, Book 1*, chap. 2: 122–23.

32. Oleg Lenchevsky, letter to the editor, "Russian Dirt," *Guardian*, 5 August 1981, 10.

33. "The ashes of Claes beat upon my heart too": in Charles de Coster, *The Legend of Thyl Ulenspiegel and Lamme Goedzak* (an 1867 adaptation of the 1515 German folk book *Till Eulenspiegel*), Ulenspiegel carries, in a locket around his neck, the ashes of his father, as a reminder of his unjust death.

34. "The sentence in *The Oak and the Calf* was hard to defend": see 468, note 39 in this volume.

35. For example, "Russians Meet a Solzhenitsyn," *Rutland Herald*, 6 May 1983, 1; "Soviet Visitors in Vermont Encounter the Echo of a Dissenter," *New York Times*, 7 May 1983, 9.

36. The Russian Orthodox Church Abroad (or Russian Orthodox Church Outside Russia) separated from the Moscow Patriarchate in 1927, in response to the latter's pledging allegiance to the Bolshevik regime. The churches reunited in 2007.

37. "Holding the icon and a cloth": *Times*, 9 May 1983, 1.

38. Aleksandr Solzhenitsyn, "Response on Receipt of the Templeton Prize," Buckingham Palace, 10 May 1983. Full English text (trans. Alexis Klimoff) in *National Review*, 22 July 1983, 872–73. Available at nationalreview.com/2018/12/aleksandr-solzhenitsyn-men-have-forgotten-god-speech/. For Russian text, see *Publitsistika*, vol. 1, 445–46.

39. The *Times*'s abridged version appeared as: Aleksandr Solzhenitsyn, "Godlessness, the First Step to the Gulag," *Times*, 11 May 1983, 10. The complete Aleksandr Solzhenitsyn, "Templeton Lecture," Guildhall, 10 May 1983, appeared in full in English (trans. Alexis Klimoff) as "Men Have Forgotten God," *National Review*, 22 July 1983, 872–76. Available at nationalreview.com/2018/12/aleksandr-solzhenitsyn-men-have-forgotten-god-speech/. For Russian text, see *Publitsistika*, vol. 1, 447–56.

40. Editorial, "Ultimate Things," *Times*, 11 May 1983, 15.

41. Letters to the editor, *Times*, 14, 17, 24, 25, 27 May 1983.

42. 11 May 1983 Solzhenitsyn meeting with Margaret Thatcher: *Daily Telegraph*, 12 May 1983, 1; *Times*, 12 May 1983, 4.

43. "Plead on behalf of the arrested Aleksandr Ginzburg": for the campaign to rescue Aleksandr Ginzburg, see *Between Two Millstones, Book 1*, chap. 4: 258–59.

44. "Alya's inimitable work in Vermont": for the details of how Natalia (Alya) produced these collected works, see chap. 6: 14–17 in this volume, and also *Between Two Millstones, Book 1*, chap. 4: 248.

45. Zoya Krakhmalnikova: samizdat publisher of Christian texts, for which she was arrested in August 1982 and charged under Article 70, potentially carrying a sentence of seven years in prison plus five in exile. After Solzhenitsyn had brought up her case in Japan (in his article for *Yomiuri Shimbun*, as well as at his Tokyo roundtable), and after Alya's intervention in New York City, the US delegation to the UN raised the matter publicly, which may have contributed to Krakhmalnikova's eventual "soft" prison sentence of one year plus five in exile ("Writer's Sentence," *Guardian*, 5 April 1983, 5).

46. *One Word of Truth*, directed by Peter J. Sisam (1981), 27 min.

47. "Birnam Wood": readers will recall Birnam Wood's role in the witches' prophecy in Shakespeare's "Scottish play," *Macbeth*, and its "march" in Act V, Scene 5, associated ever since with the seemingly impossible coming true. For Solzhenitsyn, it had especially strong meaning, as he had more than once linked Russia's eventual awakening from the spell of Communism to this very metaphor—e.g., while awaiting the imminent publication of *The Gulag Archipelago*: "In my life, this is the great moment, this struggle, perhaps the reason why I have lived at all. . . . But what does it mean to them? Is the time, perhaps, at hand when Russia will at last begin to wake up? Is this the moment foretold by the foul midnight hags, when Birnam Wood shall walk?" (*The Oak and the Calf*, Third Supplement, "Encounter Battle," 378–79.)

48. "BBC *Panorama* interview with Michael Charlton": Solzhenitsyn's interview with Michael Charlton of BBC One's flagship news program *Panorama* was recorded on 22 February 1976 and broadcast on 1 March 1976; it was rebroadcast in America on PBS's *Firing Line* on 27 March 1976. For text, see Aleksandr Solzhenitsyn, *Warning to the West* (London: Vintage Classics, 2019), 91–111. For Russian text, see *Publitsistika*, vol. 2, 330–45. See also *Between Two Millstones, Book 1*, chap. 3: 209–11.

49. 16 May 1983 Bernard Levin interview with Aleksandr Solzhenitsyn, "Time to Stand up for Britain," *Times*, 23 May 1983, 11. For Russian text, see *Publitsistika*, vol. 3, 120–36.

50. Bernard Levin, "Prisoners' Friend Who Now Needs Help Himself," *Times*, 13 May 1983, 14.

51. Solzhenitsyn's 16 May 1983 television interview with Malcolm Muggeridge was first broadcast on 4 July 1983 on BBC Two, and subsequently rebroadcast several times. A partial transcript appeared in *Human Life Review* 38, no. 4 (Autumn 2012). Available at questia.com/read/1P3-2902512721/socialism-is-absolutely-opposed-to-christianity. For full Russian text, see *Publitsistika*, vol. 3, 137–44.

52. 17 May 1983 speech at Eton College: contemporaneous press reports and photos in, e.g., John Izbicki, "Solzhenitsyn Warns Eton to Keep Faith," *Daily Telegraph*,

18 May 1983, 3, and Jon Ryan, "The Laughing Pessimist," *Daily Mail*, 18 May 1983, 3. Incidentally, both these pieces remark how unusual it was to hear applause, let alone an ovation, at Eton. For full Russian text, see *Publitsistika*, vol. 3, 145–55.

53. "Russians had been handed over to Stalin in 1945": For more on forcible repatriation by the British of Russian Cossacks into Stalin's hands, see chap. 10: 202–3 in this volume, and also *Between Two Millstones, Book 1*, chap. 2: 123.

54. Prince Philip, *A Question of Balance* (Wilton: M. Russell, 1982).

55. "Kornilov affair": Unsuccessful attempt in September 1917 by Lavr Kornilov, supreme commander of Russia's armed forces, to assert authority in Petrograd following months of revolutionary violence. Kornilov's defeat paved the way for the Bolshevik coup of November 1917 and the ensuing Russian Civil War.

56. For example, "Solzhenitsyn Accepts Religion Prize, Blasts Council of Churches, Graham," *Arizona Daily Star*, 12 May 1983, 9.

57. "Return to God: Solzhenitsyn Speaks Out," *Time* 121, no. 21 (23 May 1983): 57.

58. *New Yorker*, 30 May 1983, 30–31.

59. "Lobsters in boiling water": for example, "Solzhenitsyn Calls Demonstrators Blind," *Chicago Tribune*, 12 May 1983, 5.

60. Roy Medvedev, "Maclean, a Dissident Abroad," *Times*, 31 May 1983, 12.

61. Jack Moron, "Put a Sock in It!," *Daily Telegraph*, 13 May 1983, 16. "Jack Moron" was one of the pen names used by British satirist Michael Wharton.

Chapter 10. Drawing Inward

1. "The Challenge of Democracy," *York County Coast Star*, 1 June 1983.

2. "Correction," *York County Coast Star*, 22 June 1983.

3. Evidently, John Train's account appeared not in *Reader's Digest* but in the *Wall Street Journal*: John Train, "The Lonely Voice of Alexander Solzhenitsyn," *Wall Street Journal*, 23 June 1983, 30.

4. Aleksandr Solzhenitsyn, "Men Have Forgotten God," *National Review*, 22 July 1983, 872–76. Available at nationalreview.com/2018/12/aleksandr-solzhenitsyn-men-have-forgotten-god-speech/.

5. "That major interview in Zurich": for Walter Cronkite's interview with Solzhenitsyn for CBS, see *Between Two Millstones, Book 1*, chap. 1: 51.

6. This, Solzhenitsyn's second of four major interviews with Bernard Pivot, was recorded on 31 October 1983, and first broadcast on France 2 on 12 December 1983. For full Russian text, see *Publitsistika*, vol. 3, 173–93. Video (1h 18m) available atyoutu.be/G2ikGWwTyvs or ina.fr//video/CPB86008810. (For the first Pivot interview, of 11 April 1975, see *Between Two Millstones, Book 1*, chap. 1: 102–3.) French press reactions were very positive; see, e.g., Jean-Paul Iommi-Amunategui, *Le Matin de Paris*, 9 December 1983, 37; Pierre Daix, *Le Quotidien de Paris*, 10–11 December 1983, 15; Renaud Matignon, "Soljénitsyne ermite," *Le Figaro*, 10–11 December 1983, 30; Pierre Emmanuel, "La Hache de Soljénitsyne," *France catholique*, 11 December 1983, 20, 16; Nicole Zand, "Quand Soljénitsyne s'adresse à l'Occident," *Le Monde*, 12 December 1983, 20.

7. For Solzhenitsyn's essay "Our Pluralists," see chap. 9: 167–68 in this volume.

8. Efrem Yankelevich, letter to the editor, *Vestnik RKhD*, no. 140 (1983): 311–15.

9. "Yomiuri roundtable": see chap. 9: 147–48 in this volume.

10. Aleksandr Solzhenitsyn, letter to the editor, *Vestnik RKhD*, no. 140 (1983): 316–18. Also in *Publitsistika*, vol. 3, 169–72.

11. Andrei Sakharov, "The Danger of Thermonuclear War: An Open Letter to Dr. Sidney Drell," *Foreign Affairs* 61, no. 5 (Summer 1983): 1001–16.

12. Stephen S. Rosenfeld, "Sakharov's Call to Arm," *Washington Post*, 8 July 1983, A21.

13. "*In the First Circle* with its real-life 'atomic' plot": see 470, note 25 in this volume.

14. "Honorary citizen of the United States": In the very first days of Solzhenitsyn's exile to the West, Senator Jesse Helms had introduced a Senate bill to name Solzhenitsyn an honorary citizen of the United States, an honor previously granted only to Lafayette and Churchill. The bill passed the Senate, but later stalled in the House of Representatives, for fear of upsetting détente with the Soviets. See *Between Two Millstones, Book 1*, chap. 1: 22, 77, and Appendices 2, 3, and 4.

15. "Save Alik Ginzburg and win the case against the Carlisles": See, respectively, *Between Two Millstones, Book 1*, chap. 4: 258; and chap. 7: 97–99 in this volume.

16. "Britain's betrayal of the Russian Cossacks in Austria in the spring of 1945": Building upon Julius Epstein in the *Sunday Oklahoman*, 21 January 1973, 18, and Nicholas Bethell, *The Last Secret: Forcible Repatriation to Russia, 1944–47* (London: André Deutsch, 1974), Count Nikolai Tolstoy published two books detailing the forcible repatriation by the British of Russian Cossacks into Stalin's hands in 1945, and its sequel, Operation Keelhaul, in 1946–47: *Victims of Yalta* (London: Hodder and Staughton, 1977) and *The Minister and the Massacres* (London: Century Hutchinson, 1986). See also *Between Two Millstones, Book 1*, chap. 2: 123.

17. "The funeral service they held for themselves in anticipation of their death": For a partial description, see *The Gulag Archipelago*, vol. 1, pt. I, chap. 6, "That Spring," 259–60; but the full description of this episode was part of the author's additions for the 1980 YMCA-Press *Sobranie sochineni* edition of *Archipelago*, which are to be reflected in a future definitive English-language edition.

18. "The role of Warden": at Winchester College, the equivalent of Chairman of the Governing Body.

19. "How many defenseless Cossacks were later handed over across all of Europe!": another passage from the 1980 YMCA-Press *Sobranie sochineni* edition of *Archipelago*, which is to be reflected in a future definitive English-language edition.

20. St. Vladimir Memorial Church in Jackson, New Jersey.

21. "*September 1917*": For the conclusion of Solzhenitsyn's thoughts on how to present this and other subsequent Nodes in a Summary volume, see chap. 15: 361 in this volume.

22. "February fever": see 463, note 69 in this volume.

23. "The way Wrangel ran the Crimea": see 470, note 28 in this volume.

24. "Chronicle of Russian Emigration": See chap. 6: 23–24 in this volume.

25. Aleksandr Gerasimov, На лезвии с террористами (*On the Knife's Edge with Terrorists*), All-Russian Memoir Library 4 (Paris: YMCA-Press, 1985).

26. "Ten plus five": ten years in prison plus five in exile.

27. "Erich Gayler, the benefactor who saved our Fund from those false allegations": see *Between Two Millstones, Book 1*, chap. 4: 267–69.

28. Edward E. Ericson Jr., *Solzhenitsyn: The Moral Vision* (Grand Rapids, MI: Eerdmans, 1980).

29. Aleksandr Solzhenitsyn, *The Gulag Archipelago, 1918-1956: An Experiment in Literary Investigation*, trans. Thomas P. Whitney and Harry Willetts, abridged by Edward E. Ericson Jr. (New York: Harper & Row, 1985).

30. "Such bombs have to go off at the right time, not wait. And wait for what?": Soloukhin did not publish his book, Последняя ступень (*The Final Step*), until as late as 1995, when, ten years into *perestroika*, it had minimal effect.

31. "They're cobbling together a 'Russian party'": for Third Wave attacks on Solzhenitsyn, excitedly claiming that he was preparing to start up some kind of Russian nationalist movement or party, see, e.g., chap. 6: 42–51, chap. 11: 251, and chap. 12: 275–77.

32. "Pierre Pascal's Russianist group": see *Between Two Millstones, Book 1*, chap. 1: 101–2.

33. "Ezekiel's chariot": Ezek. 1:15–21.

34. Georges Nivat, *Soljénitsyne* (Paris: Seuil, 1980).

35. "The celebrated Trubetskoys": an aristocratic Russian family prominent in politics, science, and the arts.

36. Luke 12:20.

37. "Sharashka": research laboratory where prisoners were held in improved conditions compared to regular prisons or, especially, labor camps. (*In the First Circle*, e.g., is set at the Marfino *sharashka*, near Moscow, where Solzhenitsyn was himself interned from 1947 until 1950.) The *sharashka* at Sergiev Posad (Soviet name: Zagorsk) was Solzhenitsyn's place of incarceration for only four months, from March to July 1947, but it was there that he began his decades-long work on Dahl's dictionary.

38. Vladimir Ivanovich Dahl (1801–1872) was a leading linguist, lexicographer, and collector of folklore, who distilled his decades of work with the spoken Russian language and its regional dialects in his 200,000-word *Explanatory Dictionary of the Living Russian Language*, first published in the 1860s.

39. "Literary Collection": Solzhenitsyn would go on to publish parts of it in *Novy Mir* and other journals after his return to Russia. Most recently, the first five issues of the *Studying Solzhenitsyn* almanac have contained his reflections on Leskov, Astafiev, Bulgakov, Goncharov, Ostrovsky, and Akhmatova.

40. Anna Vasilievna Isaeva (1924–1991) was a free worker at the Marfino *sharashka* who saved several of Solzhenitsyn's manuscripts despite the threat of severe repercussions. She was an "invisible ally" who could not yet be named in the 1995 English-language edition of *Invisible Allies*, but will take her rightful place in Sketch 10 in the forthcoming definitive English-language edition of *The Oak and the Calf*.

41. Ps. 4:1.

Chapter 11. Ordeal by Tawdriness

1. Harry Thürk, *Der Gaukler: Roman* (*The Street Clown: A Novel*) (Berlin: Verlag Das Neue Berlin, 1978).

2. "Ostap Bender": a famous con-man character in Stalin-era novels by Ilf-Petrov.

3. "That his scar was from anti-Semitism": for the story of Solzhenitsyn's childhood scar, see *Between Two Millstones, Book 1*, chap. 5: 311–13.

4. "Losing the literary flavor and allusion": Flegon changed Solzhenitsyn's В круге первом to В первом кругу—different suffix, adulterated word order, utter loss of allusion to Dante.

5. "Fund": see 460, note 26. See also *Between Two Millstones, Book 1*, chap. 1: 49, 67, and chap. 2: 161.

6. "The trial, occasioned by that half a sentence": see chap. 7: 103 in this volume.

7. A. Flegon v. O. Lenchevsky, Royal Courts of Justice, Queen's Bench Division. Judgment, 8 June 1987. Before Mr. Justice Phillips. No. 84/NJ/3264; see also "Solzhenitsyn Critic Falls in Letters Libel Action," *Guardian*, 9 June 1987, 2.

8. "*Letter to the Soviet Leaders*": for the circumstances of its publication in English, see *Between Two Millstones, Book 1*, chap. 1: 32.

9. Michael Scammell to Aleksandr Solzhenitsyn, 18 April 1974, from the personal materials of Aleksandr Solzhenitsyn (hereafter referred to as "Solzhenitsyn archives").

10. "Reshetovskaya's memoirs": see *Between Two Millstones, Book 1*, Appendix 23.

11. Michael Scammell, "A Glimpse of the Giant," *Times*, 23 February 1985, 8.

12. Michael Scammell to Aleksandr Solzhenitsyn, 21 September 1974, Solzhenitsyn archives.

13. Aleksandr Solzhenitsyn to Michael Scammell, 1 October 1974, Solzhenitsyn archives.

14. Michael Scammell to Aleksandr Solzhenitsyn, 18 October 1974, Solzhenitsyn archives.

15. Aleksandr Solzhenitsyn to Michael Scammell, 8 November 1974, Solzhenitsyn archives.

16. Michael Scammell to Aleksandr Solzhenitsyn, 28 December 1974, Solzhenitsyn archives.

17. Michael Scammell to Aleksandr Solzhenitsyn, 28 December 1974, Solzhenitsyn archives.

18. Michael Scammell to Aleksandr Solzhenitsyn, 6 February 1975, Solzhenitsyn archives.

19. Michael Scammell to Aleksandr Solzhenitsyn, 12 July 1976, Solzhenitsyn archives.

20. "Refute the KGB lies forwarded by a Swiss journalist": See *Between Two Millstones, Book 1*, chap. 4: 231–33; and Appendix 31a in this volume.

21. *The Trail*, along with other early works, has since been re-issued by Vremya (2016) as volume 18 of their ongoing publication of a thirty-volume collected works of Solzhenitsyn.

22. "GPU": see 462, note 47 in this volume.

23. "Second Five-Year Plan": the period from 1933 through 1937.

24. Michael Scammell to Natalia Solzhenitsyn, 1 July 1977, Solzhenitsyn archives.

25. Aleksandr Solzhenitsyn to Michael Scammell, December 1977, four pages of answers to eighteen Scammell questions, Solzhenitsyn archives.

26. Michael Scammell to Natalia Solzhenitsyn, 29 January 1979, Solzhenitsyn archives.

27. Aleksandr Solzhenitsyn to Michael Scammell, 20 February 1979, Solzhenitsyn archives.

28. Michael Scammell to Aleksandr Solzhenitsyn, 23 March 1979, Solzhenitsyn archives.

29. Aleksandr Solzhenitsyn to Michael Scammell, 6 June 1979, Solzhenitsyn archives.

30. Michael Scammell to Aleksandr Solzhenitsyn, 24 October 1980, Solzhenitsyn archives.

31. Natalia Solzhenitsyn to Michael Scammell, 12 January 1981, Solzhenitsyn archives.

32. Michael Scammell to Natalia Solzhenitsyn, 2 April 1981, Solzhenitsyn archives.

33. "*Index on Censorship*": London quarterly journal whose founding editor was Michael Scammell.

34. Michael Scammell to Aleksandr Solzhenitsyn, 27 July 1984, Solzhenitsyn archives.

35. Natalia Reshetovskaya, В споре со временем (*At Odds with the Age*) (Moscow: Novosti, 1975). This book soon appeared in English under the title *Sanya: My Life with Alexander Solzhenitsyn*, trans. Elena Ivanoff (Indianapolis: Bobbs-Merrill, 1975).

36. Michael Scammell, *Solzhenitsyn: A Biography* (New York: Norton, 1984), 15–19, 924–25, 997, 1009.

37. Paul Johnson, "Solzhenitsyn: A Hero of Our Time," *Washington Post*, 2 September 1984, sec. Book World, 1, 11.

38. Scammell, *Solzhenitsyn: A Biography*, 389–90.

39. "Sacred Baikal": a famous Russian folk song dating to the mid-1800s.

40. Scammell, *Solzhenitsyn: A Biography*, 231–32, 324, 346, 428.

41. *The Oak and the Calf*, chap. 3, "On the Surface," 55.

42. *The Oak and the Calf*, chap. 4, "Wounded Beast," 119.

43. Andrei Sakharov, "Reflections on Progress, Peaceful Coexistence, and Intellectual Freedom," *New York Times*, 22 July 1968, 13–16.

44. Aleksandr Solzhenitsyn, "As Breathing and Consciousness Return," in *From Under the Rubble*, 3–25.

45. "Hiding Place": Arnold Susi's farm near Tartu, Estonia, where Solzhenitsyn secretly completed *The Gulag Archipelago* in the mid-1960s. See *Invisible Allies*, Sketch 4, "The Estonians."

46. *The Oak and the Calf*, Third Supplement, "Encounter Battle," 342.

47. Scammell, *Solzhenitsyn: A Biography*, 446, 539, 557–58, 639–40, 803.

48. *The Oak and the Calf*, Appendix 2: 462.

49. Scammell, *Solzhenitsyn: A Biography*, 589.

50. *The Oak and the Calf*, chap. 3, "On the Surface," 101–2; *Invisible Allies*, Sketch 3.

51. Scammell, *Solzhenitsyn: A Biography*, 537.

52. *The Oak and the Calf*, Second Supplement, "Asphyxiation," 281–83.

53. Scammell, *Solzhenitsyn: A Biography*, 540, 687–89.

54. For Reshetovskaya's attempt to negotiate between the KGB and Solzhenitsyn regarding publication of *Cancer Ward*, see *The Oak and the Calf*, Third Supplement, "Encounter Battle," 361–67.

55. Scammell, *Solzhenitsyn: A Biography*, 818, 825.

56. Scammell, *Solzhenitsyn: A Biography*, 377.

57. *The Oak and the Calf*, Fourth Supplement, "End of the Road," 446.

58. *The Oak and the Calf*, Fourth Supplement, "End of the Road," 448.

59. Scammell, *Solzhenitsyn: A Biography*, 843–45.

60. Speech on 30 June 1975 to the AFL-CIO in Washington, D.C., published in *Warning to the West*, 3–46.

61. Solzhenitsyn's radio address was recorded on 26 February 1976 and broadcast on BBC's Radio 3 on 24 March 1976. For text, see *Warning to the West*, 112–32.

62. Scammell, *Solzhenitsyn: A Biography*, 913, 936, 938, 982, 986.

63. Scammell, *Solzhenitsyn: A Biography*, 978.

64. Scammell, *Solzhenitsyn: A Biography*, 850.

65. Edmund Fuller, "A Prickly Prophet," *Wall Street Journal*, 2 October 1984, 28; Michael Futrell, "Solzhenitsyn: Heroic Life of a Stern Titan," *Chicago Sun-Times*, 30 September 1984, 27; Michael J. Bonafield, "Solzhenitsyn: Getting to Know the Enigmatic Figure," *Washington Times*, 11 December 1984, C1; Jaroslaw Anders, "A Prophet of Gloom," *Newsweek*, 17 December 1984, 95–96.

66. Norman Stone, "A Writer 'Pitched Headfirst into Hell,'" *New York Times*, 28 October 1984, sec. Book Review, 1, 34.

67. D.M. Thomas, "The Artist as Oracle," *Observer*, 24 February 1985, 26; Christopher Booker, "Years in the Life of Solzhenitsyn," *Sunday Telegraph*, 24 February 1985, 14.

68. "In Peredelkino, during my darkest days": with no other place to go in the winter of 1973–74, Solzhenitsyn had accepted the Chukovskayas' invitation to take refuge in their dacha in Peredelkino, a complex of writers' dachas southwest of Moscow. After volume 1 of *The Gulag Archipelago* appeared in Paris (on 28 December 1973, about ten days earlier than anticipated), there followed a massive Soviet propaganda campaign against Solzhenitsyn and his "slanderous" new work: TASS pieces for Western consumption began appearing from 4 January 1974, and then, from 14 January, a massive hate campaign, begun by *Pravda* and continued for weeks in every possible outlet, culminating in Solzhenitsyn's arrest on 12 February and expulsion from the USSR on 13 February. See *The Oak and the Calf*, Fourth Supplement, "End of the Road," 383–85, 390. This episode is also described in *Invisible Allies*, Sketch 10, "The Column in the Shadows," 189.

69. Carl R. Proffer, "Russia in Prussia," *New York Times*, 7 August 1977, sec. Book Review, 10.

70. Carl R. Proffer, "Russian Odyssey," *New Republic*, 15 October 1984, 35–39.

71. "He initially contemplated turning professional": see Sasha Sokolov, *Vremya i My*, no. 79 (1984): 244.

72. Carl R. Proffer, "Russian Odyssey," *New Republic*, 15 October 1984, 36.

73. Scammell, *Solzhenitsyn: A Biography*, 231–32, 262.

74. *In the First Circle*, chap. 12, "Number Seven," 63.

75. "I recoiled from Lev's first telling of this secret case": for Solzhenitsyn's (Nerzhin's) reaction to Kopelev's (Rubin's) proposal to "catch the rascal" who had placed the admonitory phone call, see *In the First Circle*, chap. 47, "Top-Secret Conversation," 335–42.

76. "After all, there's nothing of the kind in your published memoirs": there's the rub—Solzhenitsyn had never seen Kopelev's book of memoirs, but only the excerpt published in *Vremya i My*, no. 40 (1979): 178–205.

77. Aleksandr Solzhenitsyn, "Peace and Violence," *New York Times*, 15 September 1973, 31. This was the essay in which Solzhenitsyn nominated Andrei Sakharov for the Nobel Peace Prize.

78. "Black Hundreds": the name of an ultra-Russian-nationalist movement in the early 1900s; soon became a pejorative for anyone accused of right-wing views.

79. "Suggesting that Suslov and I were kindred spirits": in one and the same breath, Kopelev identifies Solzhenitsyn as an anti-Communist and sees a kinship with Mikhail Suslov, longtime chief ideologue of the CPSU.

80. "He was the one doing the catching, not me": see *In the First Circle*, chap. 36, "Phonoscopy"; chap. 47, "Top-Secret Conversation"; chap. 87, "At the Fount of Science."

81. Sinyavsky's journal *Syntaxis* published Kopelev's entire 30 January 1985 letter in its no. 37 (2001): 87–102.

82. Lev Kopelev, Утоли моя печали (*Assuage My Sorrows*) (Ann Arbor, MI: Ardis, 1981). Subsequently in English: Lev Kopelev, *Ease My Sorrows*, trans. Antonina W. Bouis (New York: Random House, 1983).

83. "There was none of that calumny there": because Kopelev had only sent Solzhenitsyn the aforementioned four xeroxed pages, but omitted pages 101–2 (corresponding to 77–78 in the English edition), which is where he'd claimed that "Solzhenitsyn himself participated happily in this game [of trying to catch the diplomat]."

84. "It was different from what had appeared in the wretched little magazine": see 481, note 76 in this volume.

85. Kopelev, Утоли моя печали, 78–79; in English: Kopelev, *Ease My Sorrows*, 60.

86. "Mother Russia, You Bitch": article by Abram Tertz [pen name of Andrei Sinyavsky], Литературный процесс в России ("The Literary Process in Russia", *Kontinent*, no. 1 (1974): 183. For Solzhenitsyn's reply ("for samizdat"), see *Between Two Millstones, Book 1*, chap. 1: 71–72.

87. Alexandre Soljénitsyne, *Nos pluralistes* (Paris: Fayard, 1983).

88. Andreï Siniavski, "Camarade prophète!," *Le Nouvel Observateur*, 9 December 1983, 76–77, and Andreï Siniavski, "Un chêne intransigeant et un prophète," *Le Monde*, 12 December 1983, 20. Expanded version of the *Nouvel Observateur* appeared later in

Russian as A. Sinyavsky, Солженицын как устроитель нового единомыслия ("Solzhenitsyn as Organizer of a New Unanimity"), *Syntaxis*, no. 14 (1985): 16–32.

89. "Cheka": see 462, note 47 in this volume.

90. "Our Pluralists," 21.

91. "Kum": a multi-pronged term claiming relation and endearment, not unlike the old English "kith"; it can mean anything from "godfather of my child" to "father of my godchild" to "fellow godparent of a third party's child," etc.

92. Sinyavsky, *Syntaxis*, no. 14 (1985): 17, 21.

93. Michael Davie, "The Dissidents Who Are at War with Solzhenitsyn," *Observer*, 26 February 1984, 56.

94. "Our Pluralists," 19–20.

95. I. Shelkovsky, *Tribuna*, no. 5 (January 1984): 22.

96. "Our Pluralists," 15.

97. For Boris Shragin's original text, see the New York weekly *Novy Amerikanets* (*New American*), no. 105 (1982): 10.

98. I. Shelkovsky, *Tribuna*, no. 5 (January 1984): 21.

99. I. Shelkovsky, *Tribuna*, no. 5 (January 1984): 21.

100. Natalia Solzhenitsyn, *Vestnik RKhD*, no. 142 (1984): 298–99.

101. Sinyavsky, *Syntaxis*, no. 14 (1985): 17, 21, 31.

102. Sinyavsky, *Syntaxis*, no. 14 (1985): 19, 21.

103. Israel Shamir, *Syntaxis*, no. 15 (1985): 158–59.

104. Pyotr Vail and Aleksandr Genis, *Syntaxis*, no. 16 (1986): 74.

105. Abram Tertz [pen name of Andrei Sinyavsky], Очки ("Spectacles"), *Syntaxis*, no. 5 (1979): 40.

106. "Parvus": for Aleksandr Parvus's role in *The Red Wheel*, see *Between Two Millstones, Book 1*, chap. 1: 98.

107. Sergei Khmelnitsky, Из чрева китова ("From the Belly of the Whale"), *22: A Social, Political, and Literary Magazine for Jewish Intellectuals from the USSR in Israel*, no. 48 (1986): 151–81.

108. Lyudmila Alekseeva, *Soviet Dissent: Contemporary Movements for National, Religious, and Human Rights* (Middletown, CT: Wesleyan University Press, 1985).

109. "Sinyavsky's interview with Olga Carlisle": see 464, note 79 in this volume.

110. Pyotr Abovin-Egides, Андрей Сахаров: трагедия великого гуманиста (*Andrei Sakharov: Tragedy of a Great Humanist*) (Paris: Poiski, 1985), 184.

111. Vadim Belotserkovsky, Открытое письмо Солженицыну ("Open Letter to Solzhenitsyn"), 1 October 1984, Solzhenitsyn archives. Published at the time in *Sem Dnei* (*Seven Days*), a small New York weekly. Available in Russian at biography.wikireading.ru/194458.

112. In December 1986, Soviet authorities at last allowed Sakharov to return from his internal exile in Gorki and resume both his work and his membership in the Academy of Sciences.

113. "His book about the future of the Soviet Union": Vladimir Voinovich, *Moscow 2042*, trans. Richard Lourie (San Diego: Harcourt, Brace, Jovanovich, 1986).

114. From a humorous duo of Aleksei Konstantinovich Tolstoy's 1869 poems entitled Послания к Ф.М. Толстому ("Missives to F. M. Tolstoy").

Chapter 12. Alarm in the Senate

1. "Talk of the Town," *New Yorker*, 24 February 1986, 23–24.

2. Chapter 74 (on Nikolai II) and chapter 22 (on Lenin) in *August 1914*.

3. Lev Loseff, Великолепное будущее России: Заметки при чтении "Августа Четырнадцатого" А. Солженицына ("Russia's Splendid Future: Notes Upon Reading A. Solzhenitsyn's *August 1914*"), *Kontinent*, no. 42 (1984): 289–320.

4. Lev Roitman to James Buckley, 27 August 1984, Solzhenitsyn archives.

5. Vadim Belotserkovsky to James Buckley, [undated], ca. 25 August 1984, memo, Solzhenitsyn archives.

6. Lev Loseff to Yuri Olkhovsky, 4 September 1984, Solzhenitsyn archives.

7. Editorial, "Taking Radio Liberties," *New Republic*, 4 February 1985, 8–9.

8. Lars-Erik Nelson, "Radio Liberty: Tax-Paid Anti-Semitism," *Daily News* (New York), 23 January 1985, 36.

9. James L. Buckley, "James L. Buckley's Response to Nelson," *Daily News* (New York), 27 January 1985, 33.

10. Lars-Erik Nelson, "Radio Liberty, Point by Anti-Semitic Point," *Daily News* (New York), 27 January 1985, 89.

11. Frank Shakespeare and Ben Wattenberg, "Radio Liberty's Reply," *New Republic*, 18 February 1985, 2.

12. "The Editors Reply," *New Republic*, 18 February 1985, 2.

13. Editorial, "International Bloopers," *Los Angeles Times*, 28 January 1985, sec. "Metro," 4.

14. "Great-Russian": see 466, note 111 in this volume.

15. Joanne Omang, "Version of Solzhenitsyn Novel, Broadcast by VOA, Causes Flap," *Washington Post*, 4 February 1985, A18.

16. Joanne Omang, "New 'August 1914' is Alleged to Have Anti-Semitic Tone," *Boston Globe*, 5 February 1985, 6.

17. Roger Straus to Claude Durand, 11 February 1985, Solzhenitsyn archives.

18. Aleksandr Solzhenitsyn to Roger Straus, 22 February 1985, Solzhenitsyn archives.

19. John Train to Aleksandr Solzhenitsyn, 5 March 1985, Solzhenitsyn archives.

20. Natalia Solzhenitsyn to John Train, 12 March 1985, Solzhenitsyn archives.

21. "Заговор против Страны Советов" (*The Plot against the USSR*), directed by Ekaterina Vermisheva (1984), 59 min. Available at youtu.be/qJpnYnYArq8 and net-film .ru/film-9006.

22. Norman Podhoretz, "The Terrible Question of Aleksandr Solzhenitsyn," *Commentary*, February 1985, 17–24.

23. "Oleg Kostoglotov": the protagonist of *Cancer Ward*.

24. Kurt R. Sax, Alexander Rosenberg, Bertram Lippman, Michael Scammell, Kinsley F. Nyce, Mikhail Bernshtam, William F. Rickenbacker, Henry Regnery, letters to the editor, *Commentary*, June 1985, 4–6, 9, 13.

25. Arthur Lyons, Kurt R. Sax, Bertram Lippman, Elias M. Schwarzbart, letters to the editor, *Commentary*, June 1985, 5, 6, 13, 14.

26. Norman Podhoretz, response to readers, *Commentary*, June 1985, 15–16.

27. Press release by the *Nation*, "Unveiling Solzhenitsyn's Anti-American Message," 8 March 1985; Vadim Belotserkovsky, "Solzhenitsyn Speaks: Undoing the West in the Soviet Union," *Nation*, 16 March 1985, 289, 306.

28. Herbert Aptheker, "Solzhenitsyn and Reagan," *Daily World*, 22 March 1985, 7D.

29. Editorial, "Trouble in the Air," *Washington Post*, 26 February 1985, A16.

30. Michael Kenney, "A War of Words Heats Up," *Boston Globe*, 10 March 1985, A17–A18.

31. Jeremy Campbell, "The Liberty Taker," *[London] Evening Standard*, ca. 11–16 March 1985.

32. U.S. Congress, Senate, Hearings before the Committee on Foreign Relations, 99th Congress, 1st Session, 29 March 1985, as published in *Foreign Relations Authorization, Fiscal Years 1986 and 1987: Hearings Before the Committee on Foreign Relations, United States Senate, Ninety-Ninth Congress, First Session on S. 496 . . . S. 659 . . . S. 684 . . . S. 732 . . . S. 785 . . . March 28, 29, and April 1, 1985, United States. Congress. Senate. Committee on Foreign Relations* (US Government Printing Office: 1985), 103–4, 134, 240–45. Available at play.google.com/books/reader?id=FoOB-KA0klAC.

33. Editorial, "Free Radio Free Europe," *Wall Street Journal*, 26 March 1985, 30; William F. Buckley Jr., "Anti-Semitism: Where It Isn't," *Washington Post*, 27 March 1985, A23; Lawrence J. Smith, "Anti-Semitism: It's More Than the Broadcast," *Washington Post*, 30 March 1985, A21.

34. "They are dignifying him by using his first name and patronymic": addressing a person by first name and patronymic (e.g., Aleksandr Isaevich) is the standard form of polite address in Russian, approximately equivalent to "Mr. [last name]" in English.

35. *Almanac Panorama* [Los Angeles weekly], no. 217 (7 June 1985): 12, 14.

36. *Almanac Panorama* [Los Angeles weekly], no. 219 (21 June 1985), no. 235 (11 October 1985), no. 263 (25 April 1986).

37. Lev Navrozov, *New York City Tribune*, 18 February 1985.

38. Lev Navrozov, "Aloof American-Born Officials Fail to Understand Émigrés from Soviet Union," *New York City Tribune*, 8 April 1985, 1B; Albert L. Weeks and Evans Johnson, "Solzhenitsyn Seen Aiding Soviets by Anti-West Stand," *New York City Tribune*, 17 June 1985, 1A; Editorial, "The Limits of Solzhenitsynism," *New York City Tribune*, 1 July 1985, 11A; "Magazine Articles Generate Controversy over Solzhenitsyn, Writings," *New York City Tribune*, 1 July 1985, 10A.

39. Lev Navrozov, "Solzhenitsyn: A Double-Faced Totalitarian of Stalin's Vintage," *New York City Tribune*, 1 July 1985, 2B.

40. "Magazine Articles Generate Controversy over Solzhenitsyn, Writings," *New York City Tribune*, 1 July 1985, 10A.

41. Mark Perakh, "Solzhenitsyn and the Jews," *Midstream* 22, no. 6 (June–July 1977): 3–17.

42. "Smelled of manure": see 467, note 11 in this volume.

43. Lev Navrozov, "Solzhenitsyn: A Double-Faced Totalitarian of Stalin's Vintage," *New York City Tribune*, 1 July 1985, 2B.

44. Lev Navrozov, "Solzhenitsyn's World History: *August 1914* as a New *Protocols of the Elders of Zion*," *Midstream* 31, no. 6 (June–July 1985): 46–53.

45. "Why does Tsezar receive parcels? and why does Ivan Denisovich look after him?": In *One Day in the Life of Ivan Denisovich*, Tsezar Markovich frequently receives parcels from home, while Ivan Denisovich, who has not received one in a long while, performs sundry favors for Tsezar in exchange for bread or tobacco, etc.

46. Richard Grenier to Aleksandr Solzhenitsyn, 10 July 1985, Solzhenitsyn archives.

47. Aleksandr Solzhenitsyn to Richard Grenier, 17 July 1985, Solzhenitsyn archives.

48. Richard Grenier to Aleksandr Solzhenitsyn, 30 July 1985, Solzhenitsyn archives.

49. Aleksandr Solzhenitsyn to Richard Grenier, 6 August 1985, Solzhenitsyn archives.

50. Richard Grenier to Aleksandr Solzhenitsyn, 1 September 1985, Solzhenitsyn archives.

51. Richard Grenier, "Solzhenitsyn and Anti-Semitism: A New Debate," *New York Times*, 13 November 1985, C21.

52. "In that same newspaper in 1974 it had been anathematized": for the *New York Times* reaction to Solzhenitsyn's *Letter to the Soviet Leaders*, see *Between Two Millstones, Book 1*, chap. 1: 32.

53. "Solzhenitsyn Refutes Charge of Anti-Semitism," *Rutland Herald*, 14 November 1985, 9, 20.

54. Tony Allen-Mills, "Solzhenitsyn Denies He Is Anti-Semitic," *Daily Telegraph*, 15 November 1985, 5; Lev Loseff, letter to the editor, "Loseff on Liberty," *Spectator*, 12 April 1986, 26.

55. Letters to the editor, *New York Times*, 4 December 1985, A30.

56. Si Frumkin, "Station's 'Coup' Fosters Anti-Jewish Stereotypes," *Israel Today*, 11 October 1985, 1, 6, 7.

57. "My words about Wallenberg at the 1974 Stockholm press conference": see *Between Two Millstones, Book 1*, chap. 1: 85–86. For a partial transcript/translation of this press conference, including discussion of the mysterious story of the Swedish diplomat and humanitarian Raoul Gustaf Wallenberg (1912–?), see "Solzhenitsyn Speaks Out," *Congressional Record (Extensions of Remarks)* for 4 June 1975, vol. 121 (1975, 94th Congress, 1st Session), 17137–39; or *National Review*, 6 June 1975, 603–9. The full text (in Russian) is in *Publitsistika*, vol. 2, 167–201.

58. Philip Slomovitz, "Solzhenitsyn Cleared of Anti-Semitic Charge, Commentary Recalled," *Detroit Jewish News*, 29 November 1985, 2.

59. Philip Averbuck to Aleksandr Solzhenitsyn, 23 January 1986, Solzhenitsyn archives.

60. Third World Congress for Soviet and East European Studies, Washington, D.C., 30 October to 4 November 1985. The Congress was sponsored by the International Committee for Soviet and East European Studies (ICSEES).

61. Lev Navrozov to Roger Straus, 18 November 1985, Solzhenitsyn archives.

62. "Dukhobors": a pacifist religious sect that moved from Russia to Canada in 1900 and eventually settled in British Columbia.

63. Lev Navrozov, "Solzhenitsyn—Stalin's Victim: A Study in Totalitarianism," *Midstream* 32, no. 1 (January 1986): 26, 29, 30.

64. Alexis Klimoff, "Solzhenitsyn and the Jews: A Reply to Lev Navrozov," *Midstream* 32, no. 6 (June–July 1986): 38–41.

65. Lev Navrozov, "Lev Navrozov Responds," *Midstream* 32, no. 6 (June–July 1986): 42, 46.

66. *Alef* [Russian-language Israeli weekly], no. 137 (12 August 1986), no. 138 (19 August 1986), no. 141 (9 September 1986), no. 154 (9 December 1986), no. 157 (6 January 1987).

67. Aleksandr Serebrennikov, Убийство Столыпина: Свидетельства и документы (*The Assassination of Stolypin: Eyewitness Accounts and Documents*) (New York: Telex, 1989).

68. Vadim Belotserkovsky, *Almanac Panorama* [Los Angeles weekly], no. 297 (12 December 1986). For Solzhenitsyn's 23 October 1982 Taiwan speech, see chap. 9: 161 in this volume.

69. Lars-Erik Nelson, "Dateline Washington: Antisemitism and the Airwaves," *Foreign Policy*, 1 December 1985, 181–97.

Chapter 13. A Warm Breeze

1. "February fever": see 463, note 69 in this volume.

2. "Returning from exile": see 459, note 2 in this volume.

3. A. Solzhenitsyn, . . . Колеблет твой треножник (". . . Shakes Thy Tripod"), *Publitsistika*, vol. 3, 226–50. The essay's title is taken from the final line of Pushkin's 1830 poem Поэту ("To the Poet").

4. A. Solzhenitsyn, Фильм о Рублёве ("A Film about Rublyov"), *Publitsistika*, vol. 3, 157–67.

5. A. Solzhenitsyn, По донскому разбору ("The Don Debate"), *Publitsistika*, vol. 3, 210–24. In this essay Solzhenitsyn analyzes the language and context of *Virgin Soil Upturned*, and proposes that Mikhail Sholokhov could not have authored at least Part One of this novel, just as he perhaps did not author *And Quiet Flows the Don*.

6. Nikolai Tolstoy, Жертвы Ялты (*Victims of Yalta*), Studies in Modern Russian History 7 (Paris: YMCA-Press, 1988).

7. Joachim Hoffmann, *Geschichte der Wlassow-Armee* (*A History of the Vlasov Army*) (Freiburg im Breisgau: Rombach, 1984). Later brought out in Russian translation as История власовской армии (*A History of the Vlasov Army*), Studies in Modern Russian History 8 (Paris: YMCA-Press, 1990).

8. Fyodor Cheron, Немецкий плен и советское освобождение (*German Captivity and Soviet Liberation*); Ivan Lugin, Полглотка свободы (*A Small Sip of Freedom*), All-Russian Memoir Library 6 (Paris: YMCA-Press, 1987). Pyotr Pali, В немецком плену (*In German Captivity*); Nikolai Vashchenko, Из жизни военнопленного (*From the Life of a POW*), All-Russian Memoir Library 7 (Paris: YMCA-Press, 1987).

9. "Unpleasant memories of clashing with *Der Spiegel* in 1974": see *Between Two Millstones, Book 1*, chap. 1: 65–66, and Appendix 14: 376.

10. "Solzhenitsyn's Wife Naturalized," *Washington Post*, 25 June 1985, C3; Lev Navrozov, "Solzhenitsyn: A Double-Faced Totalitarian of Stalin's Vintage," *New York City Tribune*, 1 July 1985, 2B; "Thinking It Over," *Boston Globe*, 5 December 1986, 2.

11. *Reforme*, 27 July 1985.

12. *Le Point*, 7 April 1985.

13. Lois Webby and Vyto Starinskas, "Pittsfield Woman Slain by Rochester Man, 29," *Rutland Herald*, 25 October 1983, 1; Albert Parry, "We Shouldn't Blame Russians for Doings of Soviets," *St. Petersburg Times*, 4 November 1984, sec. D, 1.

14. "Gift of the Bering Shelf": Solzhenitsyn is referring to the USSR–USA Maritime Boundary Agreement.

15. "Six plus five": six years in prison plus five in exile.

16. "Author's Wife Says Soviet Extends Dissident's Prison Term," UPI, 19 May 1986. Available at upi.com/5009827.

17. K. Yuriev, Операция "Фонд" ("Operation 'Fund'"), *Sovetskaya Rossiya*, 18 July 1986.

18. "NEP": New Economic Policy (1921–28), a period of slightly relaxed economic controls, reluctantly introduced by Lenin to assuage the very crises his confiscatory Bolshevik regime had precipitated.

19. "US space shield": Ronald Reagan's Strategic Defense Initiative.

20. K. Yuriev, Доноры мошенников ("Swindlers' Donors"), *Sovetskaya Rossiya*, 15 March 1987.

21. *Kontinent*, no. 51 (1987), 240–41.

22. "NTS": see 462, note 43 in this volume.

23. "Sabra and Shatila": September 1982 massacre in Beirut, in the aftermath of which Israel drew intense condemnation.

24. "Be it the designers of a monument in Israel or Simon Markish": *Kontinent*, no. 45 (1985): 393–94, 419–23; no. 46 (1985): 372–80.

25. On Solzhenitsyn's press conference of 20 March 1976 in Madrid, see *Informaciones*, 22 March 1976, 20–21, or *Publitsistika*, vol. 2, 460–68.

26. *Vremya i My*, no. 88 (1986): 168–87.

27. *Publitsistika*, vol. 2, 117–18.

28. "From some malign turning-point when Kirov was assassinated": a standard feature of "progressive" Communist groupthink in the late Soviet period was the notion that the 1934 assassination of Leningrad party boss Sergei Kirov—widely believed to have been ordered by Stalin—turned the USSR away from the purportedly salubrious path of the Lenin, and early Stalin, years.

29. "Soviets Said to Lift Ban on Novel," *Boston Globe*, 4 March 1987, 3; "Soviets to Print Solzhenitsyn's 'Gulag' Novel," *Los Angeles Times*, 4 March 1987, 2; Editorial, "A Test for Soviet Openness," *Omaha World-Herald*, 5 March 1987, 1; Charles Trueheart, "Soviets to Publish Solzhenitsyn?," *Washington Post*, 5 March 1987, B4.

30. Charles Trueheart, "Soviets to Publish Solzhenitsyn?," *Washington Post*, 5 March 1987, B4.

31. An example is an anonymous private letter to Solzhenitsyn, 16 March 1987, Solzhenitsyn archives.

32. Basile Karlinsky, "Soljénitsyne en v.o. à Moscou," *Libération*, 5 March 1987, 15–16.

33. "No Plans to Publish Solzhenitsyn Work, Soviet Official Says," *New York Times*, 6 March 1987, A10.

34. Irina Ilovaiskaya to Aleksandr Solzhenitsyn, 31 March 1987, from Solzhenitsyn archives.

35. Susan Potter Thiel, "Solzhenitsyns Say Book Will Not Be Published," *Rutland Herald*, 7 March 1987, 1, 5, 10, 16.

36. Celestine Bohlen, "Moscow: No Solzhenitsyn Publication," *Washington Post*, 6 March 1987, B1, B9.

37. Editorial, "Siberian Rainbow," *Wall Street Journal*, 6 March 1987, 30.

38. C.-M. V., "Bataille autour de Soljénitsyne," *Le Matin de Paris*, 6 March 1987.

39. "Then the notorious Astafiev-Eidelman debate erupted": In 1986, the private correspondence between historian Natan Eidelman (1930–1989) and "village prose" writer Viktor Astafiev (1924–2001), consisting of but three letters, was disseminated in samizdat and turned into a milestone of Russian social thought. It was first published in the journal *Daugava* (Riga), 6 (1990): 62–67, and has been republished many times since.

40. Lev Navrozov, letter to the editor, *Policy Review*, no. 38 (Fall 1986): 93.

41. "Lyubers": a youth subculture originating in Lyubertsy (near Moscow) in the 1970s.

42. Ilya Suslov, Почему Вы молчите, мастер? ("Why Do You Keep Silent, Master?"), *Novoye Russkoye Slovo*, 24 July 1987, 3.

43. "Solzhenitsyn, who had called for honest and total *glasnost* eighteen years ago": for Solzhenitsyn's original call for *glasnost* in the USSR, see Aleksandr Solzhenitsyn, "Open Letter to the Secretariat of the RSFSR Writers' Union," 12 November 1969, *Solzhenitsyn Reader*, 509–11; also as "Letter of Soviet Writer," *New York Times*, 15 November 1969, 11.

44. Aleksandr Podrabinek, Открытое письмо правительству Советского Союза ("Open Letter to the Government of the Soviet Union"), *Russkaya Mysl*, 10 April 1987, 5.

45. Felicity Barringer, "Moscow Magazine Is Leader in New Openness," *New York Times*, 22 March 1987, 18.

46. *East and West*, 157.

47. Anatoli Kalinin, Ответ учителю словесности ("A Reply to a Language Teacher"), *Pravda*, 16 May 1987, 3, 6.

48. After decades-old whispers disputing Mikhail Sholokhov's authorship of *And Quiet Flows the Don* (for which he was awarded the 1965 Nobel Prize in Literature), the first serious academic work to tackle the subject and launch this accusation dispassionately and substantively was Irina Medvedeva-Tomashevskaya's (publishing anonymously as "D–") Стремя "Тихого Дона" (*Troubled Waters of the "Quiet Don"*) (Paris: YMCA-Press, 1974). See *Invisible Allies*, Sketch 14, "Troubled Waters of the Quiet Don."

49. Aleksandr Solzhenitsyn, "The Courage to See," *Foreign Affairs* 59, no. 1 (Fall 1980): 210; or *The Mortal Danger*, 129.

50. For the full text of the 29 June 1987 radio interview about *March 1917* for the BBC Russian Service, see *Publitsistika*, vol. 3, 273–84.

Chapter 14. Through the Brambles

1. “Head torturer of the Georgian KGB”: Solzhenitsyn is referring to Eduard Shevardnadze (1928–2014), who had earned a reputation for cruelty and torture while head of the Georgian KGB. See, e.g., his obituary, *New York Times*, 7 July 2014, B15.

2. “Excerpts from the NBC News Interview with Gorbachev,” *Washington Post*, 1 December 1987, A16.

3. “Socially friendly”: the preferred euphemism of Soviet ideology for common crooks, thieves, murderers. See *The Gulag Archipelago*, vol. 2, pt. III, chap. 16, “The Socially Friendly,” especially 434.

4. Charles Trueheart, “Solzhenitsyn and His Message of Silence,” *Washington Post*, 24 November 1987, D1, D4.

5. “*Glasnost*, which I myself had called for twenty years ago”: see 488, note 43 in this volume.

6. “February fever”: see 463, note 69 in this volume.

7. “Those *particular bars* convey the force of revolution amazingly well”: the passage Solzhenitsyn chose from Tchaikovsky’s Second Symphony in C minor, Op. 17 was the closing theme of the exposition of its first movement, i.e., bars 138–57 (or from Figure G until Figure H).

8. Voice of America has posted one of those broadcasts at golos-ameriki.ru/a/2034224.html. In this one, Solzhenitsyn reads chapters 408, 415, 417, and 418 of *March 1917*, culminating with the killing of Admiral Nepenin.

9. “London music school”: Ignat Solzhenitsyn completed Sixth Form at the Purcell School, which was located, in those days, in Harrow.

10. “Man lügt über mich wie über einen Toten,” *Der Spiegel*, no. 44 (26 October 1987): 218–51. Available at spiegel.de/spiegel/print/d-13526566.html. For full Russian text, see *Publitsistika*, vol. 3, 285–320.

11. “Pamyat” (Memory): a short-lived political movement that arose during the late 1980s with an initial aim of restoring long-trampled Russian national memory and traditions, but soon began verbally attacking Jews and other ethnicities living in the USSR. Pamyat quickly petered out in the 1990s.

12. “Transcripts of New Year’s Greetings from Reagan and Gorbachev on TV,” *New York Times*, 2 January 1988, 6.

13. “Soviets Urged to Cut Barriers to West’s Ideas,” *New York Times*, 11 April 1988, A3.

14. “Excerpts from Reagan Talks to Dissidents and at Monastery,” *New York Times*, 31 May 1988, A13; Bill Keller, “For Soviet Journalists, Finding the Right Angle Was Never This Rough,” *New York Times*, 31 May 1988, A12.

15. Bill Keller, “Moscow Summit: Gorbachev Voices Irritation at Slow Pace of Missile Talks; Reagan Impresses Soviet Elite,” *New York Times*, 1 June 1988, A1, A13.

16. Eduard Krieger-Voinovsky, Записки инженера: Воспоминания, впечатления, мысли о революции (*Notes of an Engineer: Recollections, Impressions, Thoughts about Revolution*), All-Russian Memoir Library 4 (Moscow: Русский путь, 1997).

17. Sergei Trubetskoy, Минувшее (*Days Gone By*), All-Russian Memoir Library 10 (Paris: YMCA-Press, 1989).

18. Nikita Okunev, Дневник москвича, 1917–1924 (*Diary of a Muscovite, 1917–1924*), All-Russian Memoir Library 11 (Paris: YMCA-Press, 1990).

19. Ivan Schitz, Дневник "Великого перелома": март 1928–август 1931 (*Diary of the "Great Turning": March 1928–August 1931*) (Paris: YMCA-Press, 1991).

20. "Malyshki": see 460, note 25 in this volume.

21. "Still greenlit by personnel departments": Soviet citizens, in 1988, could still not travel abroad without being authorized to do so by KGB-monitored personnel departments.

22. Efim Etkind, О единстве русской литературы ("About the Unity of Russian Literature"), *Strana i Mir*, no. 2 (1988): 102.

23. "*Ivan Denisovich*, 'Matryona,' and 'Krechetovka' had been burned in the Soviet Union": all three of these Solzhenitsyn stories had been published in *Novy Mir* between November 1962 and January 1963 but, soon after, withdrawn from circulation and destroyed.

24. "The KGB proposal of September 1973": see 480, note 54 in this volume.

25. "Solzhenitsyn Plans Visit to Moscow," *Guardian*, 16 July 1988, 6.

26. "Prophet's Return," *Economist*, 23 July 1988, 43.

27. "An Apology," *Economist*, 13 August 1988, 36.

28. Lev Voskresensky, "Hello, Ivan Denisovich!," *Moscow News*, no. 32 (14 August 1988): 11.

29. Elena Chukovskaya, Вернуть Солженицыну гражданство СССР ("Restore Solzhenitsyn's Soviet Citizenship"), *Knizhnoye Obozrenie*, 5 August 1988, 15.

30. For example, "Soviet Citizenship Urged for Exiled Writer," *Globe and Mail* (Toronto), 6 August 1988, C4.

31. Letters to the editor, *Knizhnoye Obozrenie*, 12 August 1988, 6–7; and 2 September 1988, 4–5.

32. "Власть Соловецкая" (*Solovki Power*), directed by Marina Goldovskaya (1988), 93 min. Available at ivi.tv/watch/52949.

33. Paul Quinn-Judge, "The Decensoring of Solzhenitsyn," *Christian Science Monitor*, 5 April 1989, 6.

34. "Memorial": an organization that arose in 1987 (and continues to this day), with a mission to research and memorialize totalitarian repression and its victims in the USSR.

35. Bill Keller, "Solzhenitsyn, in Exile, Is Asked to Join Soviet Panel," *New York Times*, 1 September 1988, A8.

36. Andrew Rosenthal, "Solzhenitsyn Bars Offer by Soviets," *New York Times*, 8 September 1988, A13.

37. Andrei Smirnov to the Chairman of the Presidium of the Supreme Soviet of the USSR, October 1988, *Referendum* [samizdat journal], no. 21 (16–30 November 1988): 9. And see "Moscow Asked to Review Solzhenitsyn Exile," *New York Times*, 5 October 1988, A3.

38. Civic Council of "Memorial" to Mikhail Gorbachev, *Referendum* [samizdat journal], no. 21 (16–30 November 1988): 11.

39. From twenty-seven writers [signatures] to the Secretariat of the Union of Soviet Writers, *Referendum* [samizdat journal], no. 21 (16–30 November 1988): 10.

40. Aleksandr Solzhenitsyn, Жить не по лжи! ("Live Not by Lies"), *Rabochee Slovo*, 18 October 1988, 1.

41. As reported, e.g., in *Kontinent*, no. 58 (1988): 359.

42. For example, Stephens Broening, "Soviets Said To Have Misgivings about Publishing Solzhenitsyn," *Baltimore Sun*, 19 October 1988, 17; David Remnick, "Soviet Journal Switches Plans," *Washington Post*, 22 October 1988, C1.

43. Sixteen writers [signatures] to Mikhail Gorbachev, 21 October 1988, *Referendum* [samizdat journal], no. 21 (16–30 November 1988): 12; eighteen writers [signatures] to Mikhail Gorbachev, ca. 23 October 1988, *Referendum* [samizdat journal], no. 21 (16–30 November 1988): 13; 291 citizens [signatures] to the Presidium of the Supreme Soviet, 24 October 1988, *Referendum* [samizdat journal], no. 21 (16–30 November 1988): 13.

44. "Soviet Authorities Censor Solzhenitsyn Announcement," Agence France Presse, 20 October 1988; N. E., Истина и ритуал ("Truth and Ritual"), *Referendum* [samizdat journal], no. 21 (16–30 November 1988): 18; David Remnick, "Solzhenitsyn—A New Day in the Life," *Washington Post*, 7 January 1990, B3.

45. Felicity Barringer, "Kremlin Keeping Solzhenitsyn on Blacklist," *New York Times*, 30 November 1988, A1.

46. Felicity Barringer, "Stalin Victims Are Mourned by Throngs," *New York Times*, 28 November 1988, A7; Michael Dobbs, "Moscow Affirms Ban on Works of Solzhenitsyn," *Washington Post*, 30 November 1988, C1.

47. Aleksandr Solzhenitsyn to Sergei Zalygin, 1 December 1988, Solzhenitsyn archives.

48. "The liberation of Karabakh": Solzhenitsyn is referring to the Armenia-Azerbaijan conflict over the territory of Nagorno-Karabakh—especially acute in the late 1980s, and still unresolved as of 2020.

49. Yuri Afanasiev, ed., Иного не дано (*There Is No Other Way*) (Moscow: Progress, 1988).

50. Felicity Barringer, "Sakharov, in New Forum, Still Dissents," *New York Times*, 4 June 1988, 1.

51. "When Alya and the children had not yet landed in Zurich": see *Between Two Millstones, Book 1*, chap. 1: 33–37.

52. Felicity Barringer, "Soviets Allow Solzhenitsyn To Be Praised," *New York Times*, 13 December 1988, A7.

Chapter 15. Ideas Spurned

1. "Two passenger trains colliding head-on, catching fire, and killing six hundred people": the infamous Ufa train disaster of 4 June 1989. See, e.g., Bill Keller, "500 on 2 Trains Reported Killed by Soviet Gas Pipeline Explosion," *New York Times*, 5 June 1989, A1.

2. "Patriots": As radical arguments grew ever more heated, during the period Solzhenitsyn describes, the very terms "patriot" and "democrat" became pejorative. As Solzhenitsyn would say in 1992: "Woe to that country where the word 'democrat' has

become a curse word. But a country where 'patriot' has become a curse word will equally perish" (28 April 1992 television interview with Stanislav Govorukhin, broadcast on 2 and 3 September 1992 on Channel One in Russia; for full text, see *Publitsistika*, vol. 3, 361–82).

3. "His co-defendant, Yuli Daniel": Sinyavsky and Daniel were co-defendants in a 1966 trial that came to be seen as a defining moment for the dissident movement.

4. Bill Keller, "In the Russian Motherland, Fascination Now with Those Who Chose Exile," *New York Times*, 8 January 1989, 3.

5. "That whole Host": see 467, note 28 in this volume.

6. "*Praise like that will cost him dear*": Не поздоровится от этаких похвал—a famous line said by Chatsky in Griboyedov's 1823 comedy *Woe From Wit* (Act III, Scene 10).

7. For example, Celestine Bohlen, "A Double Coup for Solzhenitsyn," *New York Times*, 1 July 1989, 11; Edward J. Brown, "Solzhenitsyn Collides with History," *Boston Globe*, 9 July 1989, A15–A16.

8. Roger Rosenblatt, "He Saw the Past and It Did Not Work," *US News & World Report*, 19 December 1988, 8.

9. Irving Howe, "The Great War and Russian Memory," *New York Times*, 2 July 1989, sec. Book Review, 1.

10. Michael Scammell, "Rewriting the Russian Revolution," *Washington Post*, 13 August 1989, sec. Book World, M4.

11. Viktor Konetsky, Париж без праздника: Непутевые заметки, письма ("Paris Not on Holiday: Notes and Letters Not along the Way"), *Neva*, no. 1 (1989): 109–11.

12. Bill Keller, "Obscure Soviet Magazine Breaks the Ban on Solzhenitsyn's Work," *New York Times*, 20 March 1989, A1; Aleksandr Solzhenitsyn, Жить не по лжи! ("Live Not by Lies"), *Vek XX i Mir*, no. 2 (1989): 24–25.

13. "The Golden Matrix speech": see *Between Two Millstones, Book 1*, chap. 1: 56–58. Full English text available at nationalreview.com/2019/01/aleksandr-solzhenitsyn-decries-materialism-modern-society/.

14. *Rodnik* (Riga), no. 3 (1989): 40–41.

15. "Lenfilm": after Moscow-based Mosfilm, Leningrad-based Lenfilm was the second-largest film studio in the USSR.

16. Roy Medvedev, "Смотреть правде в глаза" ("Looking Truth In the Eye"), *Moskovsky Komsomolets*, 1 January 1989, 2; "Historian Disputes Solzhenitsyn," *Rutland Herald*, 3 January 1989, 12.

17. "Tidings of me have spread throughout the Russian realm": from Pushkin's famous 1836 poem "Я памятник себе воздвиг нерукотворный" ("I've raised a monument built not by human hands").

18. "I have a grave waiting for me near Paris": see chap. 12: 293 in this volume.

19. "*Diary R-17*": Дневник Романа (*Diary of a Novel*), sometimes referred to as *Diary R-17*, is a detailed journal kept by Solzhenitsyn, over decades of writing and thinking about *The Red Wheel*, about how best to present that novel's overwhelming variety and volume of historical material. While not yet published in Russian or English

(as of 2020), the diary is out in French: Alexandre Soljénitsyne, *Journal de La Roue Rouge* (Paris: Fayard, 2018).

20. "Catacomb Church": echoing the secret catacombs during Roman persecution of early Christianity, this was the unofficial term for a loose network of Orthodox believers who worshipped in secret from 1927 (when Patriarch Sergius professed the official Church's allegiance to the Soviet government) until resurfacing in the early 1990s.

21. *Ogonyok*, no. 23 (3–10 June 1989): 12–16; no. 24 (10–17 June 1989): 20–23.

22. "Glavlit": Main Administration for Literary and Publishing Affairs (=Главное управление по делам литературы и издательств=Главлит). This was the central agency responsible for censorship in the USSR from 1922 until its dissolution in 1991. Although, like so many Soviet agencies, it frequently changed names, it was widely referred to by its original abbreviated name, Glavlit.

23. "Solzhenitsyn Is Readmitted to Soviet Writers' Union," *New York Times*, 5 July 1989, C20.

24. *Novy Mir*, no. 7 (1989): 135–144; no. 8 (1989): 7–94.

25. *Literaturnaya Gazeta*, 20 September 1989, 6.

26. "*Moscow 2042*": see chap. 11: 260–61 in this volume.

27. "An old (1971) pack of lies about me from *Stern*": see *The Oak and the Calf*, 321–24 and 508–11.

28. Andrei Sakharov, О письме Александра Солженицына "Вождям Советского Союза" ("About Aleksandr Solzhenitsyn's *Letter to the Soviet Leaders*"), *Znamya*, no. 2 (1990): 14–21.

29. *Pravda*, 18 December 1989, 7; and 29 December 1989, 4.

30. Johann Wolfgang von Goethe to Friedrich Schiller, 7 December 1796, no. 247 from *Correspondence between Schiller and Goethe, from 1794 to 1805*, trans. George H. Calvert (New York: Wiley and Putnam, 1845), 208.

31. "A California group had been intending to do it—that would certainly have been a failure": see chap. 6: 17–18 in this volume.

32. "Andrzej Wajda, the Exorcist": an abridged version of the article (without this vignette) appeared in the English-language version of *Moscow News*, no. 11 (14–20 March 2001): 11.

33. "*Dictionary*": see chap. 10: 217–18 in this volume. The dictionary was first published in 1990: Aleksandr Solzhenitsyn, Русский словарь языкового расширения (*Russian Dictionary of Language Expansion*) (Moscow: Nauka, 1990)—and has been republished several times since.

34. "World Government": an idea that persisted with Sakharov since at least as far back as his 1968 essay "Reflections on Progress, Peaceful Coexistence, and Intellectual Freedom," and one that he wrote into his constitution project in 1989 (see, e.g., Sergei Kovalev in *Sakharov Remembered: A Tribute by Friends and Colleagues*, ed. Sidney D. Drell and Sergei P. Kapitza [New York: American Institute of Physics, 1991], 271).

35. "Taymyr district": the USSR's northernmost and least-densely populated district.

36. "Zemstvo": an institution of local self-government first established in the Russian Empire in 1864.

37. Aleksandr Solzhenitsyn, *Rebuilding Russia: Reflections and Tentative Proposals*, trans. Alexis Klimoff (New York: Farrar, Straus and Giroux, 1991). For Russian text, see *Publitsistika*, vol. 1, 538–98.

38. "Moskals": Ukrainian pejorative for "Muscovites," i.e., Russians.

39. "Lenin's borders": To punish the Cossacks for their resistance in the Russian Civil War (1917–1922), and to ensure the loyalty of the neighboring Ukrainian authorities, Lenin carved off a part of Cossack lands—a region known as the Donets Basin, or Donbass—in favor of Ukraine.

40. Aleksandr Solzhenitsyn, Как нам обустроить Россию?—Посильные соображения ("How Might We Organize Russia?—Possible Considerations" [later translated into English under the title *Rebuilding Russia: Reflections and Tentative Proposals*]), *Komsomolskaya Pravda*, 18 September 1990 (printed without the question mark); and *Literaturnaya Gazeta*, 18 September 1990 (*Literaturnaya Gazeta* is a weekly paper that has always come out on Wednesdays, including on the Wednesday of that particular week, i.e., on 19 September 1990—but, to the widespread amusement of the Moscow intelligentsia, it printed "18 September 1990" on the folio, in order not to be "late" to *Komsomolskaya Pravda* even though it had assured Solzhenitsyn that it was willing to come out second); "Excerpts from Solzhenitsyn Article," *New York Times*, 19 September 1990, A8.

41. Celestine Bohlen, "Gorbachev Rebuke for Solzhenitsyn," *New York Times*, 26 September 1990, A6.

42. *Izvestia*, 26 September 1990 (evening Moscow edition).

43. For example, David Remnick, "Native Son," *New York Review of Books*, 14 September 1991.

44. *New Republic*, 19 November 1990, front cover.

45. Michael Scammell, "To the Finland Station?," *New Republic*, 19 November 1990, 18.

46. "I'd been the one shouting for that 'glasnost' in 1969, when no one else could even articulate the word": see 488, note 43 in this volume.

47. Michael Scammell, "To the Finland Station?," 20.

48. Arvo Valton, Об империализме: открытое письмо А. Солженицыну ("On Imperialism: An Open Letter to A. Solzhenitsyn"), *Strana i Mir*, no. 5 (1990): 94–97.

49. Leonid Batkin, Как не повредить обустройству России ("How Not to Rebuild Russia"), *Oktyabr* (*October*), no. 4 (1991): 146–65; also in *Strana i Mir*, no. 5 (1990): 74–93. For Solzhenitsyn's brief response, see Aleksandr Solzhenitsyn, Рецензировать, но не передёргивать ("Review, but Don't Falsify"), *Oktyabr*, no. 10 (1991): 193; or *Publitsistika*, vol. 3, 352.

50. Felicity Barringer, "Solzhenitsyns Criticize Soviet Offer of Return," *New York Times*, 9 December 1989, 10.

51. *Literaturnaya Gazeta*, 11 April 1990, 1.

52. "Solzhenitsyn, 22 Others Get Citizenship Back," *Pittsburgh Press*, 16 August 1990, 8.

53. Gennadi Cheremnykh, В советском гражданстве восстановлены ("Restored to Soviet Citizenship"), *Izvestia*, 16 August 1990 (afternoon Moscow edition); Celes-

tine Bohlen, "Solzhenitsyn's Citizenship Likely to Be Restored," *New York Times*, 16 August 1990, A12; "Solzhenitsyn Cool as Moscow Confirms Offer," *New York Times*, 17 August 1990, A5.

54. "Writer's Wife Denies an Accord," *New York Times*, 17 August 1990, A5.

55. "Solzhenitsyn Cool as Moscow Confirms Offer," *New York Times*, 17 August 1990, A5; Mary Dejevsky, "Dissidents Restored to Favour," *Times*, 17 August 1990, 9; Ann Carrns, "Solzhenitsyn Denies Soviet 'Lie' on Citizenship," *Rutland Herald*, 17 August 1990, 7; Gloria Negri, "Citizenship Offer for Solzhenitsyn Is a Lie, Wife Says," *Boston Globe*, 18 August 1990, 27.

56. Ivan Silaev, *Sovetskaya Rossiya*, 18 August 1990; "Prime Minister Invites Solzhenitsyn to Russia," *New York Times*, 19 August 1990, 3; "Russian Premier Invites Solzhenitsyn Back to Visit," *Newark Advocate*, 19 August 1990, 7A.

57. Aleksandr Solzhenitsyn, Ответ Солженицына ("Solzhenitsyn's Reply"), *Sovetskaya Rossiya*, 25 August 1990; "TASS Says Solzhenitsyn Rejects Soviet Citizenship," *Rutland Herald*, 24 August 1990, 7; *Publitsistika*, vol. 3, 345–46.

58. "500 Days": an unofficial program of economic reform, developed in 1990 by a group of influential Soviet economists, that gained strong public support from Boris Yeltsin upon its release.

59. *Sovetskaya Rossiya*, 11 December 1990; "Solzhenitsyn Gets Russian State Prize," *Los Angeles Times*, 11 December 1990, P10.

60. *Izvestia*, 12 December 1990; Roger Cohen, "Award Is Spurned by Solzhenitsyn," *New York Times*, 12 December 1990, A10; *Publitsistika*, vol. 3, 350.

61. Leonid Samutin, Не сотвори кумира ("Thou Shalt Not Make Unto Thee Any Graven Image"), *Voenno-Istoricheski Zhurnal*, no. 9 (1990): 19–27; no. 10 (1990): 46–55; no. 11 (1990): 67–77.

62. "Ex-Vlasovite journalist Leonid Samutin": see *Invisible Allies*, Sketch 5.

63. Tatiana Samutina, "Мой муж написал эту книгу по заданию КГБ . . ." ("My Husband Wrote This Book on Assignment from the KGB . . ."), *Knizhnoye Obozrenie*, 19 October 1990.

64. Frank Arnau, Ветров, он же—Солженицын ("Vetrov—AKA Solzhenitsyn"), *Voenno-Istoricheski Zhurnal*, no. 12 (1990): 72–77.

65. "The 'denunciation' that had been disproved fourteen years earlier": see Appendix 31a in this volume.

Chapter 16. Nearing the Return

1. "Franchised classes": the property-holding (and hence enfranchised, empowered) segments of prerevolutionary Russian society, who alone were permitted to hold legislative, judicial, and administrative positions.

2. David Remnick, "Native Son," *New York Review of Books*, 14 September 1991.

3. Solzhenitsyn ended up writing eight binary tales between 1993 and 1998. They can be roughly categorized according to the three types outlined above. First type: "Ego," "Times of Crisis," "The New Generation," "Zhelyabuga Village." Second type:

"Nastenka," "No Matter What." Third type: "Apricot Jam," "Fracture Points." These eight tales appear, together with the war story "Adlig Schwenkitten," in Aleksandr Solzhenitsyn, *Apricot Jam and Other Stories*, trans. Kenneth Lantz and Stephan Solzhenitsyn (Berkeley, CA: Counterpoint, 2011).

4. "What if they invite me to meet the leaders?": see *The Oak and the Calf*, Fourth Supplement, "End of the Road," 437.

5. "I'd declined to meet the king of Spain and two American presidents": regarding King Juan Carlos I, see *Between Two Millstones, Book 1*, chap. 3: 219–21; regarding President Gerald Ford, see *Between Two Millstones, Book 1*, chap. 3: 191–93; regarding President Ronald Reagan, see chap. 8: 110–16 in this volume.

6. "The 'Harvard group' or the International Monetary Fund programs": in the early 1990s, the Harvard Institute for International Development (frequently referred to as the "Harvard group") and the International Monetary Fund were given largely free rein by Yeltsin's government to implement, in Russia, policies like "shock therapy," "voucher privatization," and "loans for shares" that came to be viewed by most Russians as grossly unfair and a direct cause of large-scale criminal activity.

7. "Gorbachev's crafty escape to Foros didn't fool anyone": many observers have noted that several of the purported facts concerning Gorbachev's stay at his dacha in Foros, Crimea, during the days of the "putsch" may not entirely add up. See, e.g., Charles Clover, "Last Days of the USSR," *Financial Times*, 19 August 2011, 15. Available at ft.com/content/c778192e-c94a-11e0-bc80-00144feabdc0.

8. "White House": administrative building in Moscow, on Krasnopresnenskaya embankment, that housed the Supreme Soviet of the RSFRSR from 1981 until 1993. Twice, it served as the focal point of opposition: as gathering-place for pro-Yeltsin forces against the August 1991 "putsch," and again during the constitutional crisis of 1993—but this time as the stronghold of the anti-Yeltsin parliament. In 1994, the parliament (by then known as the State Duma) moved to Okhotny Ryad, while the White House became the seat of the Russian prime minister and government.

9. "A crane pulling down the 'bottle,' that accursed Dzerzhinsky": The famous, intimidating monument to Felix Dzerzhinsky, the father of the Soviet secret police, was memorably pulled down from its commanding place at the heart of Lubyanka Square on 22 August 1991, immediately following the historic events of 18–21 August that Solzhenitsyn is describing in these pages. The "bottle" refers to the long, cylindrical shape of the statue and its pedestal.

10. "Lubyanka": see 462, note 53 in this volume.

11. "False Lenin-Stalin borders": the internal borders between the Russian Republic (RSFSR) and many of its fellow republics within the USSR had been drawn, by Lenin or Stalin, and later Khrushchev, without regard for historical, cultural, or geographic sense; oftentimes, these newfangled borders were intended to punish Russia or reward other republics; specifically regarding the border with Ukraine, see 494, note 39.

12. Aleksandr Solzhenitsyn, "Our Own Democracy," *National Review*, 23 September 1991, 43–44, 59.

13. "Mother Russia will 'endure anything'": Solzhenitsyn is referencing the line "Вынесет всё, что Господь ни пошлёт!" ("Will endure anything that God sends!") from Nikolai Nekrasov's iconic 1864 poem "Железная дорога" ("The Railway").

14. Susan Smallheer, "Solzhenitsyns to Go Home," *Rutland Herald*, 15 September 1991, 1, 6.

15. TASS report, 17 September 1991; see also Andrew Rosenthal, "Soviets Drop Solzhenitsyn Treason Charges," *New York Times*, 18 September 1991, A8.

16. Aleksandr Solzhenitsyn, Обращение к референдуму 1 декабря 1991 ("Appeal Regarding the 1 December 1991 Referendum"), *Trud*, 8 October 1991, 1; or *Publitsistika*, vol. 3, 357–58.

17. Andrew Rosenthal, "U.S., Turning from Moscow, Would Grant Recognition to an Independent Ukraine," *New York Times*, 28 November 1991, A1; Francis X. Clines, "Kremlin Indicates Irritation at Bush on Ukraine Stand," *New York Times*, 29 November 1991, A1; Editorial, "Chicken Kiev, the Sequel," *New York Times*, 30 November 1991, 18.

18. "So they agreed on Belovezh": the Belovezh Accords (= Minsk Agreement), dissolving the USSR, were signed on 8 December 1991, after a secret meeting in Belovezhskaya Pushcha National Park in Belorussia, by Boris Yeltsin, Stanislav Shushkevich, and Leonid Kravchuk—leaders of the three Slav republics (Russia, Belorussia, Ukraine) that originally "founded" the USSR in 1922.

19. "Time of Troubles": a violent interregnum (1598–1613) between the Rurikid and Romanov dynasties when Russia was besieged by Polish-Lithuanian armies and its very survival hung in the balance. Solzhenitsyn here suggests that the Russian Civil War was a "Second" Time of Troubles, and the chaotic collapse under Gorbachev and Yeltsin a "Third"—a comparison he also makes in *Diary R-17* and "'The Russian Question' at the End of the Twentieth Century" (on the latter, see later in this chapter, 428).

20. "Yeltsin Calls for Powers to Stop Ethnic Conflicts," *Boston Globe*, 1 March 1993, 2.

21. Deborah Seward, "Yeltsin Asks Russians for Help in Keeping Peace in New Year," *Indianapolis Star*, 1 January 1994, A3; video of Yeltsin's address available at youtu.be/_1EV-MFTnnQ?t=117.

22. "Help yourself to some sovereignty—as much as you can swallow!": Yeltsin's notorious declaration, on 6 August 1993 in Kazan, and later that month in Ufa; see yeltsin.ru/news/boris-elcin-berite-stolko-suverineteta-skolko-smozhete-proglotit/.

23. "Gaidar's reckless, pitiless 'reform'": as Yeltsin's finance minister, then prime minister, Egor Gaidar promulgated a self-described "shock therapy" scheme that remains hugely unpopular amongst ordinary Russians to this day; also see 496, note 6 in this volume.

24. *Rebuilding Russia*, 3.

25. "It was exactly like Carlisle in her time": see *Between Two Millstones, Book 1*, chap. 2: 128–29.

26. Luke 23:34.

27. For Solzhenitsyn's and Vitkevich's joint "Resolution No. l," as they naïvely called it, see *Between Two Millstones, Book 1*, chap. 5: 332–33; and "Statement by A. Solzhenitsyn, 2 February 1974," *The Oak and the Calf*, Appendix 34: 535–37; excerpts in *New York Times*, 4 February 1974, 1, 14. See also *The Gulag Archipelago*, vol. 1, pt. I, chap. 3, "The Interrogation," 134–35.

28. Interview on 28 April 1992 with Stanislav Govorukhin, broadcast by Russia's Channel One on 2 and 3 September 1992. For full text, see *Publitsistika*, vol. 3, 361–82. Available at youtu.be/8lKEyIi1Vvs (part 1) and youtu.be/QjZ2Te_yMyU (part 2).

29. "My plan to return via the Russian Far East": Solzhenitsyn had imagined returning via this unusual route as far back as 1975: see *Between Two Millstones, Book 1*, chap. 3: 180.

30. "The forceful Vorotyntsev talking to the ponderous General Samsonov at Ostrolenka": see *August 1914*, chap. 11.

31. "Those four Kuril Islands": as early as 1982, in preparation for his Japan trip, Solzhenitsyn had studied the issue and concluded that the Kuril Islands should properly belong to Japan, not Russia: see chap. 8: 118–19 in this volume.

32. "Labor armies": Red Army troops who were redeployed by Trotsky and Lenin, during 1920–21, to perform forced labor; also, the 1941–46 NKVD labor columns—Soviet citizens, often ethnically German, conscripted into forced labor—became colloquially known as labor armies.

33. "Three beards in a bowl": mocking reference to three wise men who "went to sea in a bowl" from the old English nursery rhyme "Wise Men of Gotham," famously translated into Russian by Samuil Marshak as "Три мудреца в одному тазу."

34. "The two goats confronting each other across a narrow bridge": see Aesop's fable "The Two Goats" or its many modern incarnations, such as Sergei Mikhalkov's children's poem "Бараны" ("Rams"); the moral is that excessive stubbornness can lead to disaster.

35. "The crucial thing was to crush Khasbulatov and the traitor Rutskoy": both Ruslan Khasbulatov, chairman of the Supreme Soviet, and Aleksandr Rutskoy, vice-president of Russia, were increasingly setting themselves against Yeltsin throughout 1992 and into 1993.

36. Yeltsin's 28 November 1992 speech at the "Congress of Intelligentsia," Moscow. Available in Russian at yeltsin.ru/archive/paperwork/10657/.

37. Борис Ельцин ищет согласия с оппозицией ("Boris Yeltsin Seeks Accord with Opposition"), *Pravda*, 2 March 1993, 1.

38. Solzhenitsyn's 4 March 1993 open reply to Ambassador Lukin was read out on the weekly TV news program "Итоги" (*Summing Up*) on 7 March, then published, together with Lukin's original 2 March letter, on 10 March in *Komsomolskaya Pravda* and 14 March in *Moskovskie Novosti*; also see *Publitsistika*, vol. 3, 390–92.

39. "Rasputinshchina": the time, from about 1906 until 1916, when a previously obscure provincial mystic, Grigori Rasputin (1869–1916), exercised extraordinary and compromising influence over Russia's imperial court.

40. This "Council of Leaders of the Republics" was created by Yeltsin's presidential order no. 603, of 23 October 1992, and met three times in the spring and summer of 1993. See docs.cntd.ru/document/901607882 and pravo.gov.ru/proxy/ips//?docbody=&prevDoc=102113309&backlink=1&&nd=102019191 and yeltsin.ru/day-by-day/1993/03/10/38067/.

41. 14 September 1993 speech in Liechtenstein: "We Have Ceased to See the Purpose: Address to the International Academy of Philosophy," trans. Yermolai Solzhenitsyn, available in *Solzhenitsyn Reader*, 591–601; for Russian text, see *Publitsistika*, vol. 1, 599–612.

42. "Harvard Yard, which I remembered well from the occasion fifteen years before when I gave my address there": for Solzhenitsyn's 8 June 1978 Harvard commencement address, see *Between Two Millstones, Book 1*, chap. 4: 283–93.

43. "Our old acquaintance, Prince Franz Josef II, had by now passed away": for Solzhenitsyn's earlier visits to the principality of Liechtenstein, and meeting with Franz Josef II, see *Between Two Millstones, Book 1*, chap. 3: 194–95.

44. "And I gave Swedish television the interview that I'd promised them so very long ago": 16 September 1993 interview with Stig Fredrikson for Swedish television (aired in the first days of October 1993); for Russian text, see *Publitsistika*, vol. 3, 405–15.

45. "Two or three interviews": see especially "Alexandre Soljenitsyne: réponse aux perroquets" ("Aleksandr Solzhenitsyn: A Response to the Parrots"), *Le Figaro*, 22 September 1993, 26; available in French at lefigaro.fr/histoire/archives/2018/12/10/26010-20181210artfig00243-soljenitsyne-en-1993-le-communisme-etait-historiquement-condamne-des-le-jour-de-sa-naissance.php; for Russian text, see *Publitsistika*, vol. 3, 436–43.

46. This, Solzhenitsyn's third of four major interviews with Bernard Pivot, was broadcast live on France 2 on 17 September 1993 as an installment of Pivot's renowned *Bouillon de culture* program. For full Russian text, see *Publitsistika*, vol. 3, 416–35. (For the first Pivot interview, of 11 April 1975, see *Between Two Millstones, Book 1*, chap. 1: 102–3. For the second Pivot interview, of 31 October 1983, see chap. 10: 198 in this volume.)

47. "I wouldn't be surprised if my access to television and to the press were restricted": this is exactly what happened when Solzhenitsyn's TV program "По минуте в день" (*A Minute Per Day*: fifteen-minute-long conversations broadcast every fourteen days—hence the title) was suddenly taken off air, without explanation, after the first twelve programs ran on Russia's Channel One from April to September 1995. A compilation of those broadcasts is available, with English subtitles, at youtu.be/VjUVlrRdVOo.

48. On 25 September 1993, as part of the 200th-anniversary commemorations of the Vendée Uprising (brutally suppressed by the "infernal columns" of the Terror), Solzhenitsyn gave a notable address at the dedication of a memorial in Lucs-sur-Boulogne. See "French Revolution Erred, Solzhenitsyn Says," *New York Times*, 27 September 1993, A10. For full text, see *Solzhenitsyn Reader*, 602–5; for Russian text, see *Publitsistika*, vol. 1, 613–15.

49. "The show was in the open air, in an enormous arena, when night had already fallen, but with quantities of lighting effects.": Solzhenitsyn is referring to the Cinéscénie night show ("le spectacle"), performed nightly by three thousand volunteers at the Puy du Fou historical theme park in Les Epesses, Vendée.

50. "The Schönfelds, who had once brought the *Wheel* archive, mercifully preserved, to us in Zurich": see *Between Two Millstones, Book 1*, chap. 1: 56.

51. "Only one accidentally slipping through into print": the photo appeared, for example, in "Solzhenitsyn Abroad," *Rutland Herald*, 6 October 1993, 11.

52. "The 'Great Germania' statue—the Watch on the Rhine": the Niederwalddenkmal (Niederwald Monument) near Rüdesheim am Rhein in Hessia, dedicated in 1883 after the Franco-Prussian War and the unification of Germany. The words to the German patriotic anthem "Die Wacht am Rhein" ("The Watch on the Rhine") are engraved beneath the statue.

53. For a brief report on Solzhenitsyn's 4 October 1993 interview with the German channel Das Erste, see "Nobelist: 'Decommunization' Was Needed," *Boston Globe*, 5 October 1993, 13.

54. "Nikolai II's never-forgiven 'Bloody Sunday' in 1905": Solzhenitsyn is referring to 9 January 1905, when unarmed demonstrators were shot at by the tsar's guards, resulting in many casualties and ushering in the Revolution of 1905.

55. Interview of 21 October 1993 with Vladimir Kondratiev, broadcast by Russia's Channel One on 24 and 26 October 1993. For full text, see *Publitsistika*, vol. 3, 463–70.

56. "Italy was not new to me, after our trip there with Viktor Bankoul in 1975": see *Between Two Millstones, Book 1*, chap. 1: 103–6.

57. "Yeltsin Sends Greetings to Solzhenitsyn in Vermont," *Burlington Free Press*, 12 December 1993, 2A.

58. Alex Beam, "Shut Up, Solzhenitsyn," *Boston Globe*, 10 February 1993, 11; Richard Balmforth, "Solzhenitsyn Going Home to Mother Russia; Red Carpet for Ex-Gulag Con," *Daily News* (New York), 1 June 1993, 4; Margaret Shapiro, "A Dacha in the Life of Alexander Solzhenitsyn," *Washington Post*, 29 June 1993, D1, D2; Elisabeth Rich, "Letter from Moscow: The Exile's Return," *Washington Post*, 1 May 1994, sec. Book World, 15.

59. David Remnick, "The Exile Returns," *New Yorker*, 14 February 1994, 64–83; Elisabeth Rich, "Letter from Moscow: The Exile's Return," *Washington Post*, 1 May 1994, sec. Book World, 15.

60. "*The Red Wheel*, scattered around different journals": see chap. 15: 369 in this volume.

61. Aleksandr Solzhenitsyn, "Русский вопрос" к концу XX века ("'The Russian Question' at the End of the Twentieth Century"), *Novy Mir*, no. 7 (1994): 135–77; appeared in English as Aleksandr Solzhenitsyn, *"The Russian Question" at the End of the Twentieth Century*, trans. Yermolai Solzhenitsyn (New York: Farrar, Straus & Giroux, 1995).

62. Susan Smallheer, "'Thank You and Farewell': Solzhenitsyn Bids Goodbye to Town," *Rutland Herald*, 1 March 1994, 1, 10; Sara Rimer, "Cavendish Journal: Shielding Solzhenitsyn, Respectfully," *New York Times*, 3 March 1994, A14. The full text on the plaque reads:

> This plaque is presented to Aleksandr Solzhenitsyn as a token of esteem from the Town of Cavendish, Vermont upon the occasion of his address to the people of Cavendish as he prepares to return to his beloved homeland of Russia.
>
> Be it known to all who may read this that Aleksandr Solzhenitsyn and his family resided in this town for seventeen years. The Solzhenitsyn family will be remembered as good neighbors and respected, productive members of this community. We understand the need to return to one's native land and extend our hands as we say farewell to those members of the Solzhenitsyn family who now leave us. We were pleased to have had them as our neighbors and, should they ever decide to return to us, our hands will be extended again to welcome them back.
>
> It is our hope that the Solzhenitsyns and the people of Russia find peace, happiness and prosperity in their reborn nation.
>
> *Cavendish Town Meeting—February 28, 1994*

63. Solzhenitsyn's 1 March 1994 interview with Mike Wallace was broadcast on CBS's long-running *60 Minutes* newsmagazine on 24 April 1994.

64. Paul Klebnikov, "An Interview with Aleksandr Solzhenitsyn," *Forbes*, 9 May 1994, 118–22; available at forbes.com/2008/08/05/solzhenitsyn-forbes-interview-oped-cx_pm_0804russia.html#2cf333ce5f53. For Russian text, see *Publitsistika*, vol. 3, 474–82.

65. "I had also received a fair number of private letters from Russia urging me to run for president": Political polling, too, indicated a groundswell of support. For example, the *New Yorker* wrote at the time: "A political poll taken in St. Petersburg [in November 1993] showed that forty-eight per cent of the respondents would like to see Solzhenitsyn as President of Russia, despite his stated refusal ever to hold office. Only seventeen per cent picked Boris Yeltsin" (David Remnick, "The Exile Returns," *New Yorker*, 14 February 1994, 64–83).

66. Mikhail Lomonosov, early March 1765, draft points for conversation with Empress Catherine II, paragraph 10.

Notes to the Appendices

1. *The Oak and the Calf*, Third Supplement, "Nobeliana," 320.

2. "A large and completed section of this book is dedicated to them, but the time has not yet come for it to appear in print": Solzhenitsyn was referring, in 1979, to the Fifth Supplement to *The Oak and the Calf*, which could not yet be published for fear of bringing harm to his "invisible allies" in both East and West. *Invisible Allies* eventually appeared in English in 1995 as a separate book, but in the forthcoming definitive English-language edition of *The Oak and the Calf* it will take its proper place as the Fifth Supplement.

3. This letter appeared in the *Rutland Herald*, 13 May 1982, and the *Washington Post*, 16 May 1982. It is rendered here in that translation, with a few corrections for style and accuracy.

4. "Some US generals suggest selectively destroying the Russian population by an atomic assault": see 470, note 22 in this volume.

5. This Appendix 31a is identical to Appendix 18 in *Between Two Millstones, Book 1*, 380–81. It has been renumbered in this volume as 31a for the convenience of the reader: to avoid disrupting either the consecutive numeric sequence of the appendices or their ensuing numeration.

6. This statement, together with a sample forgery, was published in the *Los Angeles Times*, 24 May 1976, D7, under the headline "Solzhenitsyn Claims KGB Agents Forged Letter Defaming Him." It is rendered here in that translation, with a few corrections for accuracy.

7. Solzhenitsyn's farewell speech to the people of Cavendish appeared in the *Rutland Herald*, 1 March 1994, 1, 10, and later in the *Solzhenitsyn Reader*, 607. It is rendered here in that translation by Stepan Solzhenitsyn.

INDEX OF SELECTED NAMES

A. B. *See* Polivanov, Mikhail Konstantinovich.

Akhmatova [born Gorenko], Anna Andreevna (1889–1966): one of the preeminent Russian poets of the twentieth century, wife of the poet Nikolai Gumilyov, mother of the scholar Lev Gumilyov.

Alberti. *See* Ilovaiskaya [married name Alberti], Irina Alekseevna.

Aldington, Toby Austin Richard William Low, 1st Baron Aldington [Brigadier Toby Low] (1914–2000): British politician, businessman, key figure in the forcible repatriation of the Lienz Cossacks to Stalin in 1945.

Aleksandr I (1777–1825): emperor (tsar) of Russia, reigned from 1801 until his death in 1825; succeeded by his brother, Nikolai I.

Aleksandr II (1818–1881): emperor (tsar) of Russia, reigned from 1855 until his death by assassination in 1881; succeeded by his son, Aleksandr III.

Alekseev, Gen. Mikhail Vasilievich (1857–1918): infantry general, Nikolai II's chief of staff, after the October Revolution organized the first White Army on the Don.

Alekseev, Georgi Aleksandrovich (n.d.): Russian engineer, active in the Vlasov movement, emigrated to Australia in 1954.

Alekseeva, Elizaveta Konstantinovna, "Liza" (b. 1955): mathematician, stepdaughter-in-law of Andrei Sakharov, whose hunger strike in November 1981 garnered worldwide attention and forced the Soviets to allow Alekseeva to emigrate to the United States and rejoin her husband, Aleksei Semyonov.

Alekseeva, Lyudmila Mikhailovna (1927–2018): human-rights activist, founding member (and later chair) of the Moscow Helsinki Watch Group, emigrated 1977, returned to Russia in 1993.

Alexeeva, Liza. *See* Alekseeva, Elizaveta Konstantinovna, "Liza."

Alexeeva, Lyudmila. *See* Alekseeva, Lyudmila Mikhailovna.

Alliluyeva [born Stalina], Svetlana Iosifovna (1926–2011): philologist, daughter of Stalin, lived in the West from 1966 until 1984 and again from 1986 until 2011.

Alya. *See* Solzhenitsyna [née Svetlova], Natalia Dmitrievna.

Anderson, Sir William Eric Kinloch (1936–2020): British educator, headmaster of Eton College from 1980 until 1994, and provost there from 2000 until 2009.

Andreev, Leonid Nikolaevich (1871–1919): Russian Silver-Age playwright and novelist.

Andreev, Nikolai Efremovich (1908–1982): emigrated 1919, literary critic and historian, influential Slavist, professor at University of Cambridge from 1948.

Andropov, Yuri Vladimirovich (1914–1984): chairman of the KGB from 1967 until 1982, then leader of the USSR from 1982 until 1984.

Arrau, Claudio (1903–1991): great Chilean pianist, mentor to Ignat Solzhenitsyn.

Astafiev, Viktor Petrovich (1924–2001): prominent Russian writer, posthumous laureate of the Solzhenitsyn Prize for 2009.

Augstein, Rudolf Karl (1923–2002): German journalist, founder and publisher of the weekly journal *Der Spiegel* from 1947 until his death in 2002.

Azbel, Mark Yakovlevich (1932–2020): Soviet-Israeli physicist, emigrated 1977, professor at University of Tel-Aviv. (NB: not to be confused with chemist David Azbel.)

Bailey, George (1920–2001): American journalist, director of Radio Liberty from 1982 until 1985, author of *Germans: Autobiography of an Obsession.*

Bakhtin, Mikhail Mikhailovich (1895–1975): Russian-Soviet philosopher and literary theorist. (NB: not to be confused with Leonid Batkin.)

Balladur, Édouard (b. 1929): French politician, prime minister of France from 1993 until 1995.

Bankoul [née Kirpichyova], Maria Aleksandrovna (b. 1929): professor of Russian language and literature at the University of Zurich, wife of Viktor Bankoul.

Bankoul, Viktor Sergeevich (1931–2003): Russian-Swiss engineer, close friend of Solzhenitsyn, husband of Maria Bankoul.

Batkin, Leonid Mikhailovich (1932–2016): Soviet historian and culturologist. (NB: not to be confused with Mikhail Bakhtin.)

Batlle Ibáñez, César Luis (1930–2016): Uruguayan pianist and teacher, friend and assistant of Rudolf Serkin, teacher of Ignat Solzhenitsyn, longtime participant at Marlboro Festival, son of Uruguayan president Luis Conrado Batlle Berres, brother of Uruguayan president Jorge Luis Batlle Ibáñez.

Belotserkovsky, Vadim Vladimirovich (1928–2017): journalist and human-rights activist, emigrated 1972, returned 1993.

Belov, Vasili Ivanovich (1932–2012): prominent Russian writer, exponent of the "village prose" movement.

Bely, Andrei [pen name of Boris Nikolaevich Bugaev] (1880–1934): Russian Silver-Age poet, novelist, literary critic.

Bernshtam [Bernstam], Mikhail [Michael] Semyonovich (b. 1940): historian, economic demographer, human-rights activist, founding member of the Moscow Helsinki Watch Group, emigrated 1976, research fellow at the Hoover Institution, Stanford University.

Bernstam. *See* Bernshtam [Bernstam], Mikhail [Michael] Semyonovich.

Bethell, Nicholas William, 4th Baron Bethell (1938–2007): English politician, historian, supporter of Soviet dissidents, co-translator (with David Burg) of *Cancer Ward,* author of *The Last Secret: Forcible Repatriation to Russia, 1944–47.*

Betta. *See* Markstein [née Koplenig], Elisabeth.

Billington, James Hadley (1929–2018): prominent American historian and academic, Librarian of Congress from 1987 until 2015.

Bloch, Lionel Herbert (1928–1998): Romanian-British journalist and solicitor.

Blok, Aleksandr Aleksandrovich (1880–1921): great Russian poet of the Silver Age.

Bogrov, Dmitri Grigorievich [born Mordko Gershkovich Bogrov] (1887–1911): anarchist, double agent, assassin of Prime Minister Pyotr Stolypin. See *August 1914.*

DiLisio, Leonard (b. 1936): translator and personal secretary to Aleksandr Solzhenitsyn in Vermont from 1979 until Solzhenitsyn's return to Russia in 1994.

Dima. *See* Borisov, Vadim Mikhailovich.

Dimitri. *See* Turin, Dimitri Andreevich.

Dobroshtan, Igor Mikhailovich (1923–2003): Soviet engineer, incarcerated from 1948 until 1956, legendary leader of the Vorkuta camp uprising in 1953.

Dorman [née Shtein], Elena Yurievna (b. 1955): editor, translator, emigrated 1972, returned to Russia 1992, daughter of Yuri and Veronika Shtein.

Dostoevsky, Fyodor Mikhailovich (1821–1881): one of the greatest Russian writers, author of *Crime and Punishment, The Idiot, Demons, The Brothers Karamazov.*

Douglas-Home, Charles Cospatrick (1937–1985): Scottish journalist, editor-in-chief of the *Times* from 1982 until his death in 1985, nephew of British Prime Minister Alec Douglas-Home.

Dudko, Fr. Dmitri [Sergeevich] (1922–2004): Russian Orthodox priest, writer, preacher.

Durand, Claude (1938–2015): French writer, publisher, longtime worldwide literary agent of Solzhenitsyn.

Dyadkin, Iosif Getselevich (1928–2015): geophysicist, human-rights activist, member of the Moscow Helsinki Watch Group, incarcerated from 1980 until 1983, author of *Unnatural Deaths in the USSR, 1928–1954,* which calculated the Communist death toll in the Soviet Union to be far higher than Western experts had previously imagined.

Dzerzhinsky, Felix Edmundovich, "Iron Felix" (1877–1926): founder and director of the Soviet secret police.

Dzhemilev, Mustafa Abduldzhemil (b. 1943): human-rights activist, dissident, arrested six times in the late Soviet period, longtime leader of the Crimean Tatars.

Eagleburger, Lawrence Sidney (1930–2011): American diplomat, served in five administrations, US secretary of state from 1992 until 1993.

Efros, Anatoli Vasilievich (1925–1987): Soviet film and television director.

Ehrenburg, Ilya Grigorievich (1891–1967): Bolshevik revolutionary, Soviet writer, translator, memoirist.

Elagin [born Matveev], Ivan Venediktovich (1918–1987): Russian émigré poet, professor of Russian literature at University of Pittsburgh.

Elchaninova. *See* Struve [née Elchaninova], Maria Aleksandrovna.

Elizabeth II [Elizabeth Alexandra Mary] (b. 1926): queen of the United Kingdom since 1952.

Elizarova [née Ulyanova], Anna Ilyinichna (1864–1935): Bolshevik revolutionary, Soviet functionary, older sister of Vladimir Lenin.

Ericson, Edward E., Jr. (1939–2017): professor of English literature at Calvin College, Grand Rapids, Michigan, author of several books on Solzhenitsyn, authorized abridger of *The Gulag Archipelago.*

Etkind, Efim Grigorievich (1918–1999): philologist, historian, translator, emigrated 1974.

Eva. *See* Stolyarova, Natalia Ivanovna.

Evtushenko [born Gangnus], Evgeni Aleksandrovich (1932–2017): prominent Soviet-Russian poet.

Feifer, George (1934–2019): American writer and journalist, co-author (with David Burg) of *Solzhenitsyn: A Biography.*

Felshtinsky, Yuri Georgievich (b. 1956): historian, emigrated to United States in 1978, author of Большевики и левые эсеры: октябрь 1917–июль 1918 (*Bolsheviks and Hard-Left Social Revolutionaries: October 1917–July 1918*), Studies in Modern Russian History 5 (Paris: YMCA-Press, 1985).

Finkelstein [pseudonym Vladimirov], Leonid Vladimirovich (1924–2015): journalist, writer, translator, incarcerated from 1947 until 1953, defected in 1966, worked at Radio Liberty from 1966 until 1979 and BBC Russian Service from 1979 until 2006.

Flegon, Alec [born Oleg Vasilievich Flegont] (1924–2003): London-based publisher.

Ford, Gerald Rudolph, Jr. (1913–2006): American politician, fortieth vice-president of the United States from 1973 until 1974, then thirty-eighth president of the United States from 1974 until 1977.

Foyle, Christina Agnes Lilian Foyle (1911–1999): English bookseller and owner of Foyles bookshop.

Franco Bahamonde, Gen. Francisco (1892–1975): Spanish general who ruled over Spain as "Caudillo" from 1939, after the Nationalist victory in the Spanish Civil War, until his death in 1975.

Franz Joseph II (1906–1989): prince of Liechtenstein from 1938 until his death in 1989, father of Hans-Adam II.

Fredrikson, Stig (b. 1945): Swedish correspondent in Moscow, acted as courier for Solzhenitsyn, smuggling out books and documents to the West. See *Invisible Allies*, Sketch 13, "The Foreigners."

Friedberg, Maurice (1929–2014): American Slavist, professor of Russian literature at University of Illinois at Urbana-Champaign from 1975 until 2000.

Friendly, Alfred, Jr. (b. 1938): American journalist for the *New York Times*, later *Newsweek* Moscow bureau chief.

Gaidar, Egor Timurovich (1956–2009): Russian economist, politician, finance minister from 1991 until 1992, prime minister (1992), promulgated a self-described "shock therapy" scheme that has remained hugely unpopular amongst ordinary Russians.

Ganetsky [Hanecki], Yakov Stanislavovich [born Jakub Fürstenberg] (1879–1937): prominent Polish revolutionary, close associate of Lenin, instrumental in arranging secret German funding for the Bolsheviks, notable Soviet functionary, shot in 1937.

Gayler, Erich (1916–1989): Swiss lawyer.

Gdlyan, Telman Khorenovich (b. 1940): Soviet politician.

George V [George Frederick Ernest Albert] (1865–1936): king of the United Kingdom from 1910 until his death in 1936, first cousin of Nikolai II.

Ginzburg, Aleksandr Ilyich, "Alik" (1936–2002): journalist, poet, dissident, compiler of the "White Book" on Sinyavsky-Daniel trial, founding member of the Moscow Helsinki Watch Group, first administrator of the Russian Social Fund, arrested three times, deported to the United States in 1979.

Gippius, Zinaida Nikolaevna (1869–1945): Russian Silver-Age poet, writer, critic, emigrated 1920, wife of Dmitri Merezhkovsky.

Glad, John (1941–2015): American Slavist, critic, translator, professor of Russian studies at the University of Maryland.

Glazunov, Ilya Sergeevich (1930–2017): renowned Soviet painter.

Glenny, Michael Valentine Guybon (1927–1990): British translator of Russian literature, including Solzhenitsyn.

Gogol, Nikolai Vasilievich (1809–1852): one of the greatest Russian writers and playwrights.

Goldman, Marshall Irwin (1930–2017): American scholar, professor of economics at Wellesley College, associate director of the Davis Center for Russian Studies at Harvard University from 1975 until 2006.

Goodpaster, Gen. Andrew Jackson (1915–2005): American general, Supreme Allied Commander of NATO from 1969 until 1974, superintendent of the US Military Academy at West Point from 1977 until 1981.

Gorbachev, Mikhail Sergeevich (b. 1931): Soviet politician, leader of the USSR from 1985 until its dissolution in 1991.

Gorlov, Aleksandr [Alexander] Moiseevich (1931–2016): Soviet-American mechanical engineer, forced to emigrate in 1975, professor at Northeastern University from 1976 until his death in 2016, inventor of the Gorlov helical turbine, husband of Ella Gorlova.

Gorlova, Ella (b. 1934): Soviet-American engineer, forced to emigrate in 1975, translator, author of books on Boston and Massachusetts history, translator, wife of Aleksandr Gorlov.

Govorukhin, Stanislav Sergeevich (1936–2018): renowned Soviet actor, director, screenwriter, activist.

Graham, Rev. William Franklin, Jr., KBE, "Billy" (1918–2018): prominent American evangelical preacher, infamously claimed to have noticed no persecution of Christians on his visit to the USSR in 1983, laureate of the Templeton Prize for 1982, father of Rev. Franklin Graham.

Granin, Daniil Aleksandrovich (1919–2017): Soviet writer.

Grenier, Richard (1933–2002): American journalist, columnist for the *Washington Times* from 1985 to 1999, film critic for *Commentary* and the *New York Times*.

Griboyedov, Aleksandr Sergeevich (1795–1829): Russian playwright, poet, diplomat, author of the classic verse play *Woe from Wit*, ambassador to Persia, where he was murdered by an angry mob in 1829.

Grigorenko, Gen. Pyotr Grigorievich (1907–1987): Soviet general, forsook a top military career to protest numerous Soviet injustices, founding member of the Moscow Helsinki Watch Group, condemned to prisons and notorious psychiatric wards until his eventual release to the West in 1977.

Gromyko, Andrei Andreevich (1909–1989): Soviet politician, foreign minister of the USSR from 1957 until 1985.

Grossman, Vasili Semyonovich [born Iosif Solomonovich Grossman] (1905–1964): prominent Soviet writer and journalist, author of *Life and Fate*.

Gruzenberg [pseudonym Borodin], Mikhail Markovich (1884–1951): Bolshevik revolutionary, Comintern agent, instrumental in spreading Communism in China in the 1920s, incarcerated in 1949, died in prison camp.

Guchkov, Aleksandr Ivanovich (1862–1936): founder of the Octobrist Party, president of the Third Duma from 1910 until 1911, minister of war in the first Provisional Government (February–May 1917), emigrated 1918.

Guertner, Gary Lee (b. 1940): American defense and foreign-policy expert, professor at California State University, Fullerton, US Army War College, University of Arizona.

Gul, Roman Borisovich (1896–1986): Russian writer, participated in the famed Ice March during the Russian Civil War, emigrated 1919, editor-in-chief of the literary quarterly *Novy Zhurnal* (*New Review*) from 1959 until his death in 1986.

Gumilyov, Nikolai Stepanovich (1886–1921): prominent Russian poet, executed by the Cheka in 1921, husband of the poet Anna Akhmatova, father of the scholar Lev Gumilyov.

Gvozdev, Kozma Antonovich (1883–1956): blue-collar worker, Menshevik leader, member of the Central Committee of the Petrograd Soviet, minister of labor in the Fourth Provisional Government, incarcerated from 1930 until his death in 1956.

Hanecki. *See* Ganetsky [Hanecki], Yakov Stanislavovich.

Hans-Adam II (b. 1945): prince of Liechtenstein since 1989, son of Franz Joseph II.

Harriman, William Averell (1891–1986): American businessman, politician, diplomat, ambassador to the Soviet Union from 1943 until 1946.

Hayward, Harry Maxwell, "Max" (1924–1979): British translator of Russian prose, including Solzhenitsyn.

Heeb, Fritz (1911–1994): Swiss lawyer charged with oversight of Solzhenitsyn's publications and translations in the West and one of Solzhenitsyn's "Three Pillars of Support" there (together with Elisabeth Markstein and Nikita Struve) in the years before the author's expulsion from the USSR. See *Invisible Allies*, Sketch 12.

Heifets, Mikhail Ruvimovich (1934–2019): Russian-Israeli writer, journalist, historian, incarcerated from 1974 until 1980, emigrated to Israel in 1980.

Herschensohn, Bruce (b. 1932): author, screenwriter, commentator, worked in Nixon and Reagan administrations, ran for Senate from California in 1986 and 1992, senior fellow at Pepperdine University.

Hōgen, Shinsaku (1910–1999): Japanese diplomat.

Holland, Barry (1937–1996): longtime head of the BBC Russian Service.

Ilovaiskaya [married name Alberti], Irina Alekseevna (1924–2000): Russian émigré journalist and activist, editor-in-chief of *Russkaya Mysl* (*Russian Thought*)—the premier Russian newspaper in the West—from 1979 until her death in 2000, assistant, translator, personal secretary to Aleksandr Solzhenitsyn in Vermont from 1976 until 1979.

Ivan Ivanovich. *See* Sapiets, Janis.

Izyumov, Yuri Petrovich (b. 1932): Soviet journalist, deputy editor of *Literaturnaya Gazeta* from 1980 until 1990.

Jackson, Sen. Henry Martin, "Scoop" (1912–1983): American politician, served as Democratic senator from Washington from 1941 until 1983.

Jaruzelski, Gen. Wojciech Witold (1923–2014): Polish military officer, politician, Communist leader of Poland from 1981 until 1989.

Jasný, Vojtěch (1925–2019): Czech film director, screenwriter, professor, emigrated 1968, returned 1990.

John Paul II, Pope Saint [born Karol Józef Wojtyła] (1920–2005): Polish bishop, cardinal, pope from 1978 until his death in 2005, canonized in 2014.

Kaiser, Robert G. (b. 1943): American journalist, *Washington Post* correspondent from 1964 until 2014, its Moscow bureau chief from 1971 until 1974.

Karimov, Islam Abduganievich (1938–2016): leader of Uzbekistan from 1989 until his death in 2016.

Karpov, Vladimir Vasilievich (1922–2010): writer, commentator, editor-in-chief of *Novy Mir* from 1981 until 1986, first secretary of the USSR Writers' Union from 1986 until 1991.

Karyakin, Yuri Fyodorovich (1930–2011): Russian literary critic and writer.

Kasanzew. *See* Kazantsev, Nikolai Leonidovich.

Katkov, Georgi [George] Mikhailovich (1903–1985): Russian-British historian, philosopher, emigrated 1921, professor of Russian history at University of Oxford from 1947 until 1950, author of *The February Revolution* and *The Kornilov Affair*, great-nephew of Mikhail Katkov.

Katkov, Mikhail Nikiforovich (1817–1887): prominent writer on current affairs, critic, editor-in-chief of *Moskovskie Vedomosti* (*Moscow Gazette*) from 1863 until 1887, founding father of Russian political journalism, great-uncle of Georgi Katkov.

Katsuda, Kichitarō (b. 1928): Japanese political scientist, professor at Kyoto University.

Katya. *See* Svetlova, Ekaterina Ferdinandovna.

Kazantsev, Nikolai Leonidovich [Nicolas Kasanzew] (b. 1948): Russian-Argentine journalist, commentator, war correspondent, editor-in-chief of Buenos Aires–based *Nasha Strana* (*Our Country*) since 1967.

Kelly, Laurence (b. 1933): English writer, biographer of Griboyedov and Lermontov, son of British Ambassador to the USSR Sir David Kelly.

Kemp, Rep. Jack French (1935–2009): American football player, politician, served as a Republican congressman from New York from 1971 until 1989.

Kennan, George Frost (1904–2005): American diplomat, historian, author of the policy of "containment" vis-à-vis the USSR.

Kerensky, Aleksandr Fyodorovich (1881–1970): Russian lawyer, revolutionary, prime minister of Russia in 1917, emigrated 1918, father of Oleg Kerensky.

Kerensky, Oleg Aleksandrovich, CBE (1905–1984): Russian civil engineer, notable bridge designer, emigrated 1920, son of Aleksandr Kerensky.

Khasbulatov, Ruslan Imranovich (b. 1942): Chechen-Russian economist and politician, chairman of the RSFSR Supreme Soviet from 1991 until 1993, central figure in the Russian constitutional crisis of 1993.

Khlebnikov. *See* Klebnikov, Paul.

Khodorovich [Khodorovitch], Sergei [Serge] Dmitrievich (b. 1940): engineer, computer programmer, administrator of the Russian Social Fund from 1977 until 1983, incarcerated from 1983 until 1987, emigrated 1987.

Klimoff, Evgeni Evgenievich (1901–1990): notable Russian painter, father of Alexis Klimoff.

Knowlton, Winthrop (b. 1930): American publisher, head of Harper & Row from 1970 until 1987.

Kolchak, Adm. Aleksandr Vasilievich (1874–1920): Russian polar explorer, naval admiral, commander of the Black Sea Fleet, recognized by White forces as Supreme Ruler of Russia from 1918 until 1920, captured by the Reds, executed.

Kopelev, Lev Zinovievich [Zalmanovich] (1912–1997): writer and historian of literature, incarcerated from 1945 until 1954, including at the Marfino *sharashka* together with Solzhenitsyn, emigrated 1980, prototype of Lev Grigorievich Rubin in Solzhenitsyn's novel *In the First Circle*.

Koppel, Edward James Martin, "Ted" (b. 1940): highly influential American TV journalist, host of ABC's *Nightline* from its inception in 1980 until 2005.

Korczak, Janusz [pen name of Henryk Goldszmit] (1878/79?—1942): Polish-Jewish educator, children's author, pedagogue, director of orphanage in Warsaw, sent by Nazis to Treblinka death camp.

Kornilov, Gen. Lavr Georgievich (1870–1918): tsarist general, Supreme Commander from July 1917; his attempt to forestall the Bolshevik coup was frustrated by Kerensky; organized the White armies after the death of Alekseev; killed in battle in the Civil War.

Korolenko, Vladimir Galaktionovich (1853–1921): prominent Russian journalist and writer.

Korotich, Vitali Alekseevich (b. 1936): Soviet Communist poet, journalist, editor-in-chief of *Ogonyok* (*Little Flame*) from 1986 until 1991.

Korsakov, F. *See* Svetov, Feliks Grigorievich.

Kosolapov, Valeri Alekseevich (1910–1982): Soviet critic, editor-in-chief of *Literaturnaya Gazeta* from 1960 until 1962, then of *Novy Mir* (replacing Tvardovsky) from 1970 until 1974.

Kotovsky, Grigori Ivanovich (1881–1925): leader of criminal gang, notable Red commander during Russian Civil War (1917–22); appears in two of Solzhenitsyn's binary tales, "Ego" and "Times of Crisis."

Koverda [Kowerda], Boris Sofronovich (1907–1987): Russian exile, editor, author of sensational 1927 assassination, in Warsaw, of Soviet ambassador Pyotr Voikov, in retaliation for the latter's personal direction of the 1918 murders of Nikolai II and his family.

Kowerda. See Koverda [Kowerda], Boris Sofronovich.

Kozyrev, Andrei Vladimirovich (b. 1951): Russian politician, minister of foreign affairs under Yeltsin from 1990 until 1996.

Kramer, Hilton (1928–2012): American art critic, essayist, co-founder of *New Criterion*.

Kravchuk, Leonid Makarovich (b. 1934): Soviet-Ukrainian politician, president of Ukraine from 1991 until 1994.

Krymov, Gen. Aleksandr Mikhailovich (1871–1917): tsarist general, associate of Guchkov and the Octobrists, committed suicide in September 1917 after the failure of Kornilov's attempt to forestall the Bolshevik coup.

Lomonosov, Mikhail Vasilievich (1711–1765): great Russian polymath, founder of Moscow University.

Loseff [Losev, born Lifschitz], Lev Vladimirovich (1937–2009): Russian poet, essayist, critic, emigrated 1976, professor of Russian at Dartmouth College from 1979 until his death in 2009.

Louis, Victor [born Vitali Evgenievich Louis] (1928–1992): British-Soviet journalist with longtime direct ties to the KGB. See *The Oak and the Calf*, 205–9, 483, 508.

Low, Toby. *See* Aldington, Toby Austin Richard William Low, 1st Baron Aldington.

Lukin, Vladimir Petrovich (b. 1937): historian, political scientist, Russian ambassador to the United States from 1992 until 1994, founding member of Yabloko party, Russian Federation ombudsman for human rights from 2004 until 2014.

Lukyanov, Anatoli Ivanovich (1930–2019): Soviet-Russian politician, last chairman of the USSR Supreme Soviet from 1990 until 1991.

Lyubarsky, Kronid Arkadievich (1934–1996): astrophysicist, human-rights activist, incarcerated from 1972 until 1977, emigrated 1977, returned 1992, chairman of the Moscow Helsinki Watch Group from 1994 until 1996.

Lyubimov, Yuri Petrovich (1917–2014): Russian theater director and actor, director of the Taganka Theater from 1964 until 1983 and again from 1989 until 2012, emigrated 1984, returned 1988.

Lyusha. *See* Chukovskaya, Elena Tsezarevna.

MacArthur, Gen. Douglas (1880–1964): renowned American general, viceroy of Japan from 1945 until 1951.

Macmillan, Maurice Harold, 1st Earl of Stockton (1894–1986): British politician, closely linked to the forcible repatriation of thousands of Russian Cossacks to the USSR in 1945, prime minister of the United Kingdom from 1957 until 1963.

Maklakov, Vasili Alekseevich (1879–1957): lawyer, one of the founders and leaders of the Kadet party, *de facto* ambassador to France from 1917 until 1924, brother of politician Nikolai Maklakov.

Maksimov. *See* Maximov, Vladimir Emelianovich.

Maltsev, Yuri Vladimirovich (b. 1932): Soviet-born critic, journalist, translator, emigrated 1974.

Mao, Tse-tung [Zedong] (1893–1976): Chinese Communist revolutionary, leader of Red China from 1949 until his death in 1976.

Markov, Georgi Mokeevich (1911–1991): Soviet Communist writer and playwright. (NB: not to be confused with the renowned Bulgarian writer Georgi Ivanov Markov.)

Markstein [née Koplenig], Elisabeth, "Liza," "Betta" (1929–2013): Solzhenitsyn's friend and translator, Austrian professor and translator of Russian literature, translated the first German edition of *The Gulag Archipelago* under the pseudonym "Anna Peturnig," one of Solzhenitsyn's "Three Pillars of Support" in the West (together with Fritz Heeb and Nikita Struve) in the years before the author's expulsion from the USSR. See *Invisible Allies*, Sketch 12.

Marx, Karl Heinrich (1818–1883): German philosopher, founding father of Communism.

Osipov, Vladimir Nikolaevich (b. 1938): right-wing publicist, founder of the samizdat journal *Veche* (*Assembly*), longtime political prisoner.

Palchinsky, Pyotr Akimovich [Ioakimovich] (1875–1929): engineer, economist, politician, executed on a trumped-up charge of вредительство (sabotage). See *The Red Wheel*, where he appears as Pyotr Akimovich Obodovsky.

Panin, Dmitri Mikhailovich (1911–1987): thinker and author, friend of Solzhenitsyn from the camps, including from the Marfino *sharashka*, emigrated 1972, the prototype of Dmitri Aleksandrovich Sologdin in Solzhenitsyn's novel *In the First Circle*.

Paramonov, Boris Mikhailovich (b. 1937): Soviet-born philosopher, essayist, radio presenter, emigrated 1977.

Parvus, Aleksandr Lvovich [born Israel Lazarevich Helfand] (1867–1924): revolutionary, played prominent part in the Revolution of 1905, invented theory of "permanent revolution," successful businessman, funded revolutionaries (especially Bolsheviks).

Pascal, Pierre (1890–1983): renowned French historian and Slavist.

Pashina, Elena Anatolievna (1923–2007): librarian at the Hoover Institution, wife of Nicholas Pashin.

Pasternak, Boris Leonidovich (1890–1960): renowned Russian poet, laureate of the Nobel Prize in Literature for 1958.

Pearson, Malcolm Everard MacLaren, Baron Pearson of Rannoch (b. 1942): British entrepreneur, politician, leading Eurosceptic in the House of Lords, son-in-law of Martin Charteris.

Pell, Sen. Claiborne deBorda (1918–2009): American politician, served as Democratic senator from Rhode Island from 1961 until 1997.

Perakh, Mark [born Mark Yakovlevich Popereka] (1924–2013): Soviet-American mathematician.

Philip, Prince, Duke of Edinburgh (b. 1921): prince consort, husband of Queen Elizabeth II.

Piper, Klaus (1911–2000): German publisher, head of Munich publisher Piper Verlag from 1953 until 1994.

Pipes, Richard Edgar (1923–2018): Polish-American academic, professor of Russian history at Harvard, author, director of East European and Soviet Affairs under Ronald Reagan from 1981 until 1983, father of Middle-East expert Daniel Pipes.

Pirozhkova, Vera Aleksandrovna (b. 1921): Russian-born journalist, fled the USSR in 1944, professor of political science at University of Munich, publisher of the journal *Golos Zarubezhiya* (*Voice of the Abroad*) from 1976 until 1998, returned in the mid-1990s.

Pivot, Bernard (b. 1935): French journalist, longtime host of cultural television programs such as *Apostrophes* (1975–1986) and *Bouillon de culture* (1991–2001).

Platonov, Andrei [pen name of Andrei Platonovich Klimentov] (1899–1951): Russian writer and playwright.

Plekhanov, Georgi Valentinovich (1856–1918): leading Menshevik revolutionary and theoretician.

Plyushch, Leonid Ivanovich (1938–2015): mathematician, human-rights activist, incarcerated from 1972 until 1975, emigrated 1976.

Templeton, Sir John Marks (1912–2008): American-British investor, philanthropist, founder in 1972 of the Templeton Prize for progress in religion.

Teresa, Mother Mary, Saint Teresa of Calcutta [born Anjezë Gonxhe Bojaxhiu] (1910–1997): Albanian-Indian Catholic nun and missionary, laureate of the Templeton Prize for 1973, laureate of the Nobel Peace Prize for 1979, canonized in 2016.

Teush, Veniamin Lvovich (1898–1973): engineer, anthroposophist, secret keeper of Solzhenitsyn archives, "invisible ally." See *Invisible Allies*, Sketch 3.

Thatcher, Margaret Hilda, Baroness Thatcher (1925–2013): British politician, served as prime minister of the United Kingdom from 1979 until 1990.

Thorne [née Zemlis], Ludmilla [Lyudmila] Karlisovna, "Lyusia" (1938–2009): emigrated as a child in the Second Wave, public figure and human-rights campaigner, actively defended dissidents in the USSR, including Aleksandr Ginzburg, worked at New York's Freedom House from the mid-1970s until 1997.

Thürk, Harry (1927–2005): East-German Communist writer, author of the anti-Solzhenitsyn hatchet job, *Der Gaukler*.

Timofeev, Lev Mikhailovich (b. 1936): writer, journalist, economist, incarcerated from 1985 until 1987. (NB: not to be confused with the critic and translator Leonid Timofeev.)

Tolstoy, Aleksei Konstantinovich (1817–1875): renowned Russian lyric poet, writer, playwright, translator. (NB: not to be confused with the Soviet author Aleksei Nikolaevich Tolstoy, the "Red Count.")

Tolstoy, Lev [Leo] Nikolaevich (1828–1910): one of the greatest Russian writers, author of *War and Peace* and *Anna Karenina*.

Tolstoy-Miloslavsky, Count Nikolai Dmitrievich (b. 1935): Russian-British historian, writer, politician, author of books (*Victims of Yalta, The Minister and the Massacres*) exposing the forcible repatriation by the British of Russian Cossacks and others into Stalin's hands after World War II.

Toyama, Kagehisa (b. 1919/20?): Japanese owner and director of Nippon Radio.

Train, John (b. 1928): American investor, author, co-founder of the *Paris Review*, father-in-law of journalist Paul Klebnikov.

Trakhtman, Avraam Mendelevich (1918–2003): Soviet radio engineer, chief engineer at the Marfino *sharashka* from 1940 until 1950, prototype of Adam Veniaminovich Roitman in Solzhenitsyn's novel *In the First Circle*.

Tregubov, Fr. Andrew [Semyonovich] (b. 1951): Russian-American archpriest, lecturer, iconographer, artist, emigrated 1976, rector since 1979 of Holy Resurrection Orthodox Church in Claremont, New Hampshire, where Solzhenitsyn and his family attended services, husband of Galina Tregubova.

Tregubova [Tregubov, née Vasilieva], Galina Borisovna (b. 1950): Russian-American artist, emigrated 1976, specialist in ancient Russian art of church embroidery, wife of Fr. Andrew Tregubov.

Trotsky [born Bronshtein], Lev [Leon] Davidovich (1879–1940): Social Democrat Revolutionary, chairman of the Petersburg Soviet during the 1905 Revolution, returned to Russia after the February Revolution and engineered the Bolshevik coup

GENERAL INDEX

Page numbers in *italics* indicate entries found in the Index of Selected Names.

ABOUT THE AUTHOR

Aleksandr Solzhenitsyn (1918–2008), Nobel Prize laureate, was a Soviet political prisoner from 1945 to 1953. His story *One Day in the Life of Ivan Denisovich* (1962) made him famous, and *The Gulag Archipelago* (1973) further unmasked Communism and played a critical role in its eventual defeat. Solzhenitsyn was exiled to the West in 1974. He ultimately published dozens of plays, poems, novels, and works of history, nonfiction, and memoir, including *In the First Circle, Cancer Ward, The Oak and the Calf,* and *Between Two Millstones, Book 1: Sketches of Exile, 1974–1978* (University of Notre Dame Press, 2018).